COUNSELING AROUND the WORLD

An International Handbook

Editors
Thomas H. Hohenshil
Norman E. Amundson
Spencer G. Niles

• • •

AMERICAN COUNSELING
ASSOCIATION
5999 Stevenson Avenue
Alexandria, VA 22304
www.counseling.org

An International Handbook

10 9 8 7 6 5 4 3 2 1

American Counseling Association
5999 Stevenson Avenue
Alexandria, VA 22304

Director of Publications • Carolyn C. Baker

Production Manager • Bonny E. Gaston

Editorial Assistant • Catherine A. Brumley

Copy Editor • Beth Ciha

Cover and text design by Bonny E. Gaston

Library of Congress Cataloging-in-Publication Data

Counseling around the world : an international handbook / editors, Thomas H. Hohenshil, Norman E. Amundson, Spencer G. Niles.
p. cm.
Includes index.
ISBN 978-1-55620-316-9 (alk. paper)
1. Counseling. 2. Cross-cultural counseling. I. Hohenshil, Thomas H. II. Amundson, Norman E. III. Niles, Spencer G.
BF636.6.C674 2013
158.3—dc23 2012023713

Table of Contents

Section 3 Counseling in Asian Countries

Counseling in European Countries

Counseling in Middle Eastern Countries

Section 6 Counseling in North American Countries

Section 7 Counseling in Oceania Countries

Section 8 Counseling in South and Central American Countries

Foreword

In their comprehensive text *Counseling Around the World,* Thomas H. Hohenshil, Norman E. Amundson, and Spencer G. Niles provide something that never has been attempted: a snapshot of the counseling profession from a global perspective. The scope of the book is impressive in that countries from all continents are included and the range of knowledgeable authors spans a diverse scope of educators, professional counselors, and scholars worldwide. The chapters are uniformly engaging, thought provoking, and informative.

Early in the book issues of diversity are defined and contribute to a clearer understanding of the need for global literacy. Readers of this book will experience an enormous increase in their own global literacy. Thus, we highly recommend the book as required reading for all who aspire to become or who already have become professional counselors. The subtle influences of culture in the development and implementation of counseling services requires that one have a full awareness of these issues prior to reading the other chapters in the book.

The editors' introductory and concluding chapters are not to be missed, as they provide an overview of the challenges to the globalization of counseling and a succinct yet comprehensive and in-depth analysis of similarities and differences across nations. The scope of similarities is at once surprising in its simplicity and complex in its implications. Whereas counselors in the United States might imagine that their challenges to forming a clear professional identity are unique to their culture, the authors note that counselors in other countries face similar challenges. These include educating various publics about the counselor's wellness, preventive, developmental approach to helping; establishing educational standards and recognition for those who call themselves counselors; and overcoming professional competitiveness and jealousies. Though counselors in many countries face similar challenges to the development of the profession, issues of language, culture, and diversity combine to make these challenges unique in each setting. The editors extend their analysis to a discussion of future challenges, defining both the state of counseling globally and directions for the future.

Credence is given to the valuable leadership of NBCC International and the Council for Accreditation of Counseling and Related Educational Programs (the International Registry of Counsellor Education Programs) in the global development of the counseling profession. Chi Sigma Iota within its mission and practice also seeks to support the goals identified in the final chapter, especially networking and sharing between and among countries and practicing professional counselors, counselor educators, and counseling researchers and scholars. This book provides a strong foundation for such networking and allows readers to grasp the nuances of the counseling profession as it has evolved and continues to evolve within varying cultural contexts.

This book is destined to be a classic cited for generations to come, as it establishes the evolution of the counseling perspective to this point in time, identifies challenges and barriers to its advancement, and proposes needs to be addressed as counselors move into the future. *Counseling Around the World* merits integration into core counseling programs and courses that deal with all aspects of diversity and professional practice. East meets West in very basic, practical ways when theories of counseling are challenged as to their applicability in more collectivist cultures or when spirituality and counseling are thought of as one in the same for helping. Continuing education programs for professional counselors will also find this book to be an important resource for planning continuing education. In the coming years, counselors in settings from schools to private practice will find more children, family members, and persons of other countries of origin coming to them for assistance. The editors of this book are to be commended for providing a resource that is global in scope, in depth in content, and at once both realistic and aspirational in terms of defining both the challenges and potential for the globalization of the counseling profession. *This is essential reading for all counselors!*

—Jane E. Myers
Executive Director, Chi Sigma Iota
Professor, University of North Carolina at Greensboro

—Thomas J. Sweeney
Executive Director Emeritus, Chi Sigma Iota
Professor Emeritus, Ohio University

Acknowledgments

Thomas H. Hohenshil

It has been an exciting and extraordinary learning experience working with my excellent coeditors and the contributing authors of this book. Both coeditors have contributed significant editorial assistance and many excellent suggestions. The 100+ contributing authors collectively contributed international knowledge about the counseling profession that is not available anywhere else. To the contributing authors I extend a hearty *thank you* for helping transform me into a more globally literate counselor. Thanks to Carolyn Baker and the other members of the American Counseling Association publications staff, whose expertise was quite helpful throughout the publication process. And finally, a special thanks to my wife Sue for her encouragement and assistance throughout the development of this book. Sue was a professional counselor for more than 20 years and, thanks to her undergraduate major in English, is an excellent editor in her own right.

• • •

Norman E. Amundson

The breadth of this project is truly quite remarkable and much needed in a time of increasing globalization. Pulling all of this together has required ongoing support from the American Counseling Association as well as a team of editors and international writers who have committed themselves fully to the task. I am thankful to be part of such a team, and I look forward to continued collaboration. Like Tom, I also must acknowledge the help of my wife Jeanette, who works as a spiritual director and is someone I can turn to on an ongoing basis for editorial and technological support. The creation of any new product is truly the result of many minds and hands, and I am very thankful to be part of the process.

• • •

Spencer G. Niles

I am grateful to my coeditors for their excellent work and leadership on this project. I am also especially grateful to the international colleagues with whom I have had the honor of working (many are contributors to this book). They have taught me much about the international perspective on counseling in the 21st century. We are fortunate to have such leaders in our global profession.

• • •

About the Editors

Thomas H. Hohenshil

Dr. Thomas Hohenshil is a Professor Emeritus of Counselor Education at Virginia Tech (the Virginia Polytechnic Institute and State University, Blacksburg) and a licensed professional counselor in Virginia. He is the author or coauthor of 125 publications; has served on the editorial boards of eight national and international counseling and psychology journals; and is currently the associate editor of the *Journal of Counseling & Development*, with major responsibilities for international counseling. Dr. Hohenshil has also delivered approximately 125 presentations on a variety of mental health topics at state, national, and international conferences and workshops. He has received the Distinguished Alumni Award from Kent State University, the Arthur A. Hitchcock Distinguished Professional Service Award from the American Counseling Association (ACA), the William H. Van Hoose Career Service Award from the Virginia Counselors Association, and the ACA Fellow Award and was elected to the Academy of Teaching Excellence at Virginia Tech. His professional interests are broad and include international counseling, the use of technology in counseling and counselor education, the use of diagnosis based on the *Diagnostic and Statistical Manual of Mental Disorders* in counseling, and counseling persons with special needs.

• • •

Norman E. Amundson

Dr. Norman Amundson is a professor of counseling psychology at the Faculty of Education, University of British Columbia, Canada. His professional interests center on career and cross-cultural counseling with a more dynamic and metaphoric experiential approach (active engagement). He is currently an associate editor of the *Journal of Counseling & Development* and was previously the editor of the *Journal of Employment Counseling*. Dr. Amundson is the author of many professional articles and has also written a number of books. His books have been translated into 14 different languages. He has received awards from many associations, including the National Career Development Association, the National Employment Counseling Association, the Canadian Counselling and Psychotherapy Association, the British Columbia Career Management Association, the Canadian Education and Research Institute for Counselling, and the Swedish Career Development Association. He has also received an honorary doctorate from Umea University in Sweden.

• • •

Spencer G. Niles

Dr. Spencer Niles is a Distinguished Professor and Department Head for Educational Psychology, Counseling, and Special Education at The Pennsylvania State University. He is also the director of the Center for the Study of Career Development and Public Policy at Penn State and serves as the director of research for Kuder, Inc. (a Web-based career planning service). Dr. Niles is a National Career Development Association (NCDA) Fellow and an American Counseling Association (ACA) Fellow and is the recipient of the NCDA Eminent Career Award, ACA's David Brooks Distinguished Mentor Award, the ACA Extended Research Award, and the University of British Columbia Noted Scholar Award. He has served as president of the NCDA and editor of *The Career Development Quarterly*. He is currently the editor of the *Journal of Counseling & Development* and serves on the editorial boards of an additional six national and international journals. He has authored or coauthored approximately 120 publications and delivered more than 125 presentations on career development theory and practice. He has lectured in more than 15 countries and is an honorary member of the Japanese Career Development Association, an honorary member of the Italian Association for Educational and Vocational Guidance, and a lifetime honorary member of the Ohio Career Development Association.

• • •

About the Contributors

Norman E. Amundson, PhD, is a professor of counseling psychology, University of British Columbia, Canada (Book coeditor, Coauthor Introductory and Summary chapters).

Ma. Lourdes Arellano-Carandang, PhD, is a professorial lecturer in psychology, University of the Philippines, and founder of the Ma. Lourdes Arellano-Carandang Institute for Children and Families, Quezon City, Philippines (Coauthor, Philippines chapter).

Krista E. Benes, MA, is a consultant for the Canadian Career Development Foundation, Ottawa, Ontario, Canada (Coauthor, Canada chapter).

Lucrecia Sánchez Berneman is a licensed psychologist and an assistant professor at Holos San Isidro Institute, Buenos Aires, Argentina (Coauthor, Argentina chapter).

Jenny Bimrose, PhD, is a professor and deputy director, Institute for Employment Research, University of Warwick, England (Coauthor, England chapter).

Andres Sánchez Bodas is a licensed psychologist and university professor, founder and director of the first counseling program (Primera Escuela Argentina De Counseling and Holos San Isidro Institute) in Buenos Aires, and chief executive officer of NBCC Argentina (Coauthor, Argentina chapter).

McLytton Nkonde Clever, DClinPsych, is a mental health clinician, Ballarat Psychiatric Services, regional Victoria, Australia (Coauthor, Zimbabwe chapter).

Don C. Combs, EdD, is an associate professor and department chair, Department of Educational Psychology & Special Services, University of Texas at El Paso, United States (Coauthor, Taiwan chapter).

Kayte Conroy, PhD, LMHC, CRC, is an assistant program director and clinical coordinator, Rehabilitation Counseling Program, University of Buffalo, United States (Coauthor, Ireland chapter).

Andrés J. Consoli, PhD, is a professor and associate chair, Department of Counseling, College of Health & Human Services, San Francisco State University, United States (Coauthor, Guatemala chapter).

Christine L. Currie, PhD, LPC, NCC, is a professor, director of the Center for Counseling and Soul Care, and Coordinator of International Relations, School of Social Work and Counseling, Russian-American Institute, Moscow, Russia (Coauthor, Russia chapter).

Thelma Duffey, PhD, is a professor and chair, Department of Counseling, University of Texas at San Antonio, United States (Coauthor, United States chapter).

Alexandra Durcikova, PhD, is an assistant professor, Eller College of Management, University of Arizona, United States (Coauthor, Czech Republic chapter).

Bradley T. Erford, PhD, is a professor of education specialties, Loyola University Maryland, United States (Coauthor, United States chapter).

Marcheta Evans, PhD, LPC-S, NCC, is associate dean (Downtown Campus) and an associate professor, University of Texas at San Antonio, United States (Coauthor, United States chapter).

Dale S. Furbish, EdD, is a senior lecturer and program leader, Graduate Diploma and Master of Career Development, School of Education, Auckland University of Technology, Auckland, New Zealand (Coauthor, New Zealand chapter).

Antoinette Ginés-Rivera, PhD, is an assistant professor and Director of Internship & Field Placement, Alliance Graduate School of Counseling, Nyack College, New York City, United States (Coauthor, Honduras chapter).

Theodoros Giovazolias, PsyD, is an assistant professor of counseling psychology, University of Crete, Greece (Coauthor, Greece chapter).

Samuel T. Gladding, PhD, is a professor and chair, Department of Counseling, Wake Forest University, United States (Coauthor, United States chapter).

Tomoko Kudo Grabosky, PhD, is an associate professor/counselor, Department of Counseling Services, Shippensburg University of Pennsylvania, United States (Coauthor, Japan chapter).

María del Pilar Grazioso, PhD, is director of the Master's Program in Counseling Psychology and Mental Health, Universidad del Valle de Guatemala (Coauthor, Guatemala chapter).

Jean Guichard, PhD, is a professor of vocational psychology and career counseling, Institut National d'Etude du Travail et d'Orientation Professionnelle—Conservatoire National des Arts et Métiers, Paris, France (Coauthor, France chapter).

Oya Yerin Güneri, PhD, is an associate professor, Guidance and Psychological Counseling Program, Middle East Technical University, Ankara, Turkey (Coauthor, Turkey chapter).

Yuh-Jen Guo, PhD, LPC-S, NCC, is an assistant professor of counselor education, Department of Educational Psychology & Special Services, University of Texas at El Paso, United States (Coauthor, Taiwan chapter).

Stacy Henning, PhD, LPC, ACS, is an assistant professor and Worldwide Director of Counseling, Webster University, United States (Coauthor, Switzerland chapter).

J. Scott Hinkle, PhD, is Director of Professional Development, National Board for Certified Counselors, United States (Coauthor, Mexico chapter).

Thomas H. Hohenshil, PhD, LPC, is Professor Emeritus of Counselor Education, Virginia Polytechnic Institute and State University, United States (Book coeditor, Coauthor Introductory and Summary chapters).

Sareena Hopkins, MEd, CCC, GCDFi, is the coexecutive director of the Canadian Career Development Foundation, Ottawa, Ontario, Canada (Coauthor, Canada chapter).

Sharon G. Horne, PhD, is an associate professor, Department of Counseling and School Psychology, University of Massachusetts, Boston, United States (Coauthor, Kyrgyz Republic chapter).

Deirdre Hughes, PhD, OBE, is an Associate Fellow, Institute for Employment Research, Warwick University, United Kingdom, and an associate at the Centre for Educational Sociology, Edinburgh University, United Kingdom (Coauthor, England chapter).

Claudio Simon Hutz, PhD, is a professor of psychology, Federal University of Rio Grande do Sul, Brazil (Coauthor, Brazil chapter).

Aida Hutz-Midgett, EdD, is an associate professor of counselor education, Boise State University, United States (Coauthor, Brazil chapter).

Harue Ishii, PhD, is a counselor, Office of International Affairs, Hokkaido University, Sapporo, Japan (Coauthor, Japan chapter).

Moshe Israelashvili, PhD, is an associate professor, Department of Special Education & School Counseling, Tel Aviv University, Israel (Author, Israel chapter).

Sachin Jain, PhD, is an assistant professor, Department of Counseling, Oakland University, United States (Coauthor, India chapter).

Jennifer Johnson, MA, is a doctoral candidate, Counselor Education Department, University of Central Florida, Orlando, United States (Coauthor, Ireland chapter).

Jennifer Keller, MA, is a graduate of the master's program in counseling psychology and mental health, Universidad del Valle de Guatemala (Coauthor, Guatemala chapter).

Elena Kim, MA, is a doctoral candidate and assistant professor, Psychology Program, American University of Central Asia, Bishkek, Kyrgyz Republic (Coauthor, Kyrgyz Republic chapter).

Muthoni Kimemia, PhD, is an assistant professor, Department of Educational Psychology and Special Education, Southern Illinois University, Carbondale, United States (Coauthor, Kenya chapter).

Eitan Kleinberg, MS, NCC, is a counseling trainer at Universidad Iberoamericana in Mexico City and coordinator of NBCC Mexico and its certification affiliate, the Asociación Mexicana de Orientación Psicológica y Psicoterapia A.C., Mexico (Coauthor, Mexico chapter).

Patrick Marius Koga, MD, MPH, is an associate clinical professor of international health, Department of Public Health Sciences, University of California–Davis School of Medicine, United States (Coauthor, Kyrgyz Republic chapter).

Elena Kosterina, MA, is chair, Psychology Program, American University of Central Asia, Bishkek, Kyrgyz Republic (Coauthor, Kyrgyz Republic chapter).

Marina V. Kuzmina, MA, is a clinician at Compass Youth and Family Services, LLC, Norfolk, Virginia (Coauthor, Russia chapter).

Kanykei Latipova, MSW, is an instructor, Psychology Program, American University of Central Asia, Bishkek, Kyrgyz Republic (Coauthor, Kyrgyz Republic chapter).

Sang Min Lee, PhD, is an associate professor, Department of Education, Korea University, Korea (Coauthor, South Korea chapter).

Ben K. Lim, PhD, LMFT, is a professor of marriage and family therapy, Bethel University, San Diego, California, United States (Coauthor, China chapter).

Soh-Leong Lim, PhD, LMFT, is an associate professor of marriage and family therapy, San Diego State University, California, United States (Coauthor, China chapter).

Messiah R. Makuane, MSc, is a rehabilitation counseling graduate, Faculty of Health Sciences, University of Sydney, Australia (Coauthor, Zimbabwe chapter).

Maria Malikiosi-Loizos, EdD, is a professor of counseling psychology, University of Athens, Greece (Coauthor, Greece chapter).

Davide Mariotti, Diploma di Laurea (DL), is director, Associazione Culturale Komidé—Studio e Scuola di Counseling, Pesaro, Italy (Coauthor, Italy chapter).

Shizuno Mase, MS, is a part-time college counselor, Temple University Japan and Musashi University, Tokyo, Japan (Coauthor, Japan chapter).

Renae D. Mayes, MEd, is a doctoral student, The Ohio State University, United States (Coauthor, Global Diversity chapter).

Garrett J. McAuliffe, EdD, is a university professor of counseling, Old Dominion University, Norfolk, Virginia, United States (Coauthor, Ireland chapter).

Magen M. Mhaka-Mutepfa, MEd, is Student Counseling Services Director, the University of Zimbabwe (Coauthor, Zimbabwe chapter).

Sehar Mikhemar, MEd, is an assistant lecturer, Faculty of Education, Ain Shams University, Egypt (Author, Egypt chapter).

Judi H. Miller, PhD, is an associate professor and Coordinator of Counsellor Education, Health Sciences Centre, College of Education, University of Canterbury, Christchurch, New Zealand (Coauthor, New Zealand chapter).

Elena Molchanova, MD, PhD, is an associate professor of psychology, American University in Central Asia, Bishkek, Kyrgyz Republic (Coauthor, Kyrgyz Republic chapter).

R. Esteban Montilla, PhD, is an assistant professor and Coordinator of Latin American Program Development, St. Mary's University, San Antonio, Texas, United States (Author, Venezuela chapter).

James L. Moore III, PhD, is an associate provost, Office of Diversity and Inclusion, professor of counselor education, and director of the Todd Anthony Bell National Resource Center on the African American Male, The Ohio State University, United States (Coauthor, Global Diversity chapter).

Elias Mpofu, PhD, DEd, is a professor and head of rehabilitation counseling, Faculty of Health Sciences, University of Sydney, Australia (Coauthor, Zimbabwe chapter).

Jabulani Mpofu, MEd, is a lecturer in psychology and special needs education, Zimbabwe Open University (Coauthor, Zimbabwe chapter).

Ruslan I. Nadyuk, PhD, is the dean of the School of Social Work and Counseling, Russian-American Institute, Moscow, Russia (Coauthor, Russia chapter).

Sylvia C. Nassar-McMillan, PhD, LPC, NCC, ACS, is a professor and Program Coordinator of Counselor Education, North Carolina State University, United States (Coauthor, Global Diversity chapter).

Patricia Ncube, MSN/PGDE, is deputy director, Affiliated Institutions, and a doctoral candidate, Counselling and Human Services, University of Botswana (Coauthor, Botswana chapter).

Roberta A. Neault, PhD, is president of Life Strategies Ltd., Aldergrove, British Columbia, Canada (Coauthor, Canada chapter).

Cristina Nedelcu, PhD, is executive assistant, NBCC Romania (Coauthor, Romania chapter).

Maureen Neihart, PsyD, is an associate professor and head of psychological studies, National Institute of Education, Nanyang Technological University, Singapore (Coauthor, Singapore chapter).

Spencer G. Niles, EdD, is Distinguished Professor and Department Head, The Pennsylvania State University, United States (Book coeditor, Coauthor Introductory and Summary chapters).

Amy Nitza, PhD, is an associate professor and Coordinator of School Counselor Education, Indiana University–Purdue University, Fort Wayne, United States (Coauthor, Botswana chapter).

Kannikar Nolrajsuwat, EdD, is an assistant professor, Counseling Program, Chulalongkorn University, Bangkok, Thailand (Coauthor, Thailand chapter).

Kayi Ntinda, MSW, is a doctoral candidate, Counselling and Human Services, University of Botswana (Coauthor, Botswana chapter).

Lois Achieng Ochieng, MA, is a counseling psychologist and director, Healing Talk Counseling Services, Uganda (Coauthor, Uganda chapter).

Jane E. Atieno Okech, PhD, is an associate professor, Counseling Program, University of Vermont, United States (Coauthor of Kenya chapter).

Aneneosa A. G. Okocha, PhD, is a full professor (2000–2003 chairperson), Counselor Education Department, University of Wisconsin–Whitewater, United States (Author, Nigeria chapter).

Padraig O'Morain, MA, MIACP, is a core tutor, Institute of Integrative Counselling and Psychotherapy, Dublin, Ireland (Coauthor, Ireland chapter).

Fidan Korkut Owen, PhD, is a retired full professor, Counseling and Guidance Program, Hacettepe University, Ankara, Turkey (Coauthor, Turkey chapter).

Georgina Panting-Sierra, EdD, is a clinician in private practice and adjunct professor, Asbury Theological Seminary, Orlando, Florida, United States (Coauthor, Honduras chapter).

Yegan Pillay, PhD, is an associate professor in the Department of Counseling and Higher Education, Patton College of Education, Ohio University, Athens, United States (Coauthor, South Africa chapter).

Peter Plant, PhD, is a professor in the Career Counseling Program, Faculty of Arts, Aarhus University, Copenhagen, Denmark (Coauthor, Denmark chapter).

Jacques Pouyaud, PhD, is a senior lecturer in work psychology, vocational psychology, and career counseling, University of Bordeaux Segalen, France (Coauthor, France chapter).

Theodore P. Remley Jr., JD, PhD, is a professor and the Batten Endowed Chair, Department of Counseling and Human Services, Old Dominion University, Norfolk, Virginia, United States (Coauthor, Italy chapter).

Kimberly A. M. Richards, PhD, NCC, SACC, is a faculty researcher, Department of Public Health, Oregon State University, Corvallis, United States, and a consultant with the Harare Research Group, Zimbabwe (Coauthor, Zimbabwe chapter).

Daya Singh Sandhu, EdD, NCC, NCCC, NCSC, LPCC, ACA Fellow, is a Distinguished Professor of Research and former chairperson (1996–2004), Department of Educational and Counseling Psychology, University of Louisville, Kentucky, United States. He twice received the Senior Fulbright Research award for India (Coauthor, India chapter).

Varunee Faii Sangganjanavanich, PhD, is an assistant professor, Department of Counseling, The University of Akron, Ohio, United States (Coauthor, Thailand chapter).

Margot J. Schofield, PhD, is a professor of counseling and psychotherapy and head, Department of Counselling and Psychological Health, La Trobe University, Melbourne, Australia (Author, Australia chapter).

Ruth M. Senyonyi, PhD, is a counseling psychologist, Bank of Uganda, Kampala (Coauthor, Uganda chapter).

Blythe C. Shepard, PhD, is an associate professor, Faculty of Education (Counselling), University of Lethbridge, Alberta, Canada (Coauthor, Canada chapter).

Jack D. Simons, MEd, is a doctoral student, Division of Counseling and Family Therapy, University of Missouri–St. Louis, United States (Coauthor, Czech Republic chapter).

Robert L. Smith, PhD, is a professor and chair, Department of Counseling & Educational Psychology, Texas A&M University at Corpus Christi, United States (Coauthor, Ecuador chapter).

Shannon D. Smith, PhD, is an associate professor in the Department of Educational and Clinical Studies, College of Education, University of Nevada, Las Vegas, United States (Coauthor, South Africa chapter).

Rex Stockton, EdD, is Chancellor's Professor and Counseling Psychology Program Training Director, Indiana University, United States (Coauthor, Botswana chapter).

Josef Strasser, PhD, is an associate professor of education, University of Augsburg, Germany (Author, Germany chapter).

Antonio Tena Suck, PhD, is director of the Psychology Department, Universidad Iberoamericana in Mexico City, and director of NBCC Mexico (Coauthor, Mexico chapter).

Roberto Swazo, PhD, is an associate professor and Coordinator of the Counseling Program, College of Education, Florida A&M University, Tallahassee, United States (Coauthor, Guatemala chapter).

Andreea Szilagyi, PhD, is director of NBCC Romania, vice-president of the European Board for Certified Counselors, and an associate professor, Petroleum-Gas University of Ploiesti, Romania (Coauthor, Romania chapter).

Soo Yin Tan, PhD, is a senior lecturer in psychological studies, National Institute of Education, Nanyang Technological University, Singapore (Coauthor, Singapore chapter).

Marco Antônio Pereira Teixeira, PhD, is an associate professor of psychology, Federal University of Rio Grande do Sul, Brazil (Coauthor, Brazil chapter).

Mercedes Ballbé ter Maat, PhD, is an associate professor, Counselor Education Program, Nova Southeastern University, Ft. Lauderdale, Florida, United States (Coauthor, Argentina chapter).

Roslyn Thomas, DPhil, is a professor and head of psychology, sociology, and counseling, Webster University, Geneva, Switzerland (Coauthor, Switzerland chapter).

Rie Thomsen, PhD, is an assistant professor in the Faculty of Arts, Aarhus University, Copenhagen, Denmark (Coauthor, Denmark chapter).

Ma. Teresa G. Tuason, PhD, is an associate professor in the Clinical Mental Health Counseling Program, University of North Florida, Jacksonville, United States (Coauthor, Philippines chapter).

Maria Alexandra Valarezo, MS, is a graduate student, Department of Counseling & Educational Psychology, Texas A&M University–Corpus Christi; and a research assistant, Antonio E. Garcia Art & Education Center, Corpus Christi (Coauthor, Ecuador chapter).

Tommaso Valleri, Diploma di Laurea (DL), is the secretary general, AssoCounseling Associazione Professionale di Categoria, Milan, Italy (Coauthor, Italy chapter).

Shu-Ching Wang, PhD, CSC, is an adjunct professor of counselor education, Department of Educational Psychology & Special Services, University of Texas at El Paso, United States (Coauthor, Taiwan chapter).

Heather A. Warfield, MA, NCC, is a doctoral candidate in counselor education, North Carolina State University, United States (Coauthor, Global Diversity chapter).

Eunjoo Yang, PhD, is an associate professor, Department of Psychology, Korea University, Korea (Coauthor, South Korea chapter).

Lay See Yeo, PhD, is an associate professor of psychological studies, National Institute of Education, Nanyang Technological University, Singapore (Coauthor, Singapore chapter).

Sergei V. Yevdoschenko, MA, MDiv, NCC, is a Gestalt therapist and a professionally practicing psychotherapist, Krasnodar, Russia (Coauthor, Russia chapter).

Shupikai Zebron, MEd, is a lecturer in counseling, Zimbabwe Open University, Zimbabwe (Coauthor, Zimbabwe chapter).

• • •

Setting the Stage for Global Counseling

1 Introduction to Global Counseling

Thomas H. Hohenshil, Norman E. Amundson, and Spencer G. Niles

Leaders of many nations understand that the positive mental health of their citizens is a valuable economic and social asset. They also recognize that professional counseling is one of the tools that can help advance the mental health of their people. Counseling has a strong tradition in many Western countries, and there is ample evidence that other countries on almost every continent are now developing similar programs. Although the profession is at varying developmental stages in different countries, significant advancements in counseling are progressing with increasing momentum. It is clear that the globalization of communication technology, transportation systems, medicine, religion, and business has stimulated the growth of mental health programs, and this is resulting in significant global expansion of professional counseling as well (Erford, as cited in Shallcross, 2012; Hohenshil, 2010).

Counseling theory and practice over the next several decades must focus on understanding human development and relationships in a broad global context. Counselors in all countries will need to become globally literate. Global literacy is the basic information people need to maneuver through life in the highly interconnected world of the 21st century. Thanks to today's sophisticated technology, the world is becoming a place in which people from diverse cultural backgrounds interact in ways that would have been unimaginable even 50 years ago. Although dealing with diversity is an important goal for all professional counselors, acquiring global literacy must now be a new goal for counselors who wish to practice in a culturally competent manner (Lee, as cited in Shallcross, 2012).

World Demographics

The world is composed of nations and peoples that are highly diverse in terms of economic opportunity, social policies, religious practices, and political organization. The planet's population exploded from 1 billion in 1820, to 3 billion in 1960, to 5 billion in 1987, to 7 billion in 2011. The addition of 80 million people each year is exacerbating problems of employment, pollution, poverty, and the depletion of natural resources. In terms of literacy, approximately 84% of the world's population can read and write. But of all of the illiterate adults in the world, about two thirds are women. The lowest literacy rates are concentrated in three regions: the Arab states, South and West Asia, and sub-Saharan Africa, where around one third of men and half of all women are illiterate. At the same time, communication technology is expanding exponentially throughout the world. In 2010, for example, there were approximately 5.3 billion cell phone users in the world and 2.1 billion users of the Internet. It is not unusual in some countries to see a person riding down the road on a donkey while talking on a cell phone (Central Intelligence Agency, 2012; David Sanger Photography, 2012; Mundi Index, 2012).

The 20th century was marked by two major world wars, the end of colonial empires, advances in science and technology, the end of the Cold War, the advent of space travel, and increased concern about the environment. In the 21st century, continued growth in science and technology raises both hopes and fears. Hopes revolve around advances in medicine, advances in agriculture, and improved methods of achieving peaceful conflict resolution. Fears for the 21st century revolve around the development of more lethal weapons of war, pollution, climate change, and poverty (Central Intelligence Agency, 2012). It is in this global environment that professional counseling services are being initiated and developed.

The Global Development of Counseling

A number of organizations and individuals, mostly from the West, are helping other countries expand their counseling programs. For example, the American Counseling Association (ACA), NBCC International (NBCC-I), the Chi Sigma Iota Counseling Academic and Professional Honor Society International (CSI), the Council for Accreditation of Counseling and Related Educational Programs (CACREP), and various universities are all reaching out globally.

CACREP introduced the International Registry of Counsellor Education Programs, which encourages high professional standards sensitive to the realities of global counseling. NBCC-I is providing support and expertise to more than 35 countries while helping them develop credentialing processes and training (J. S. Hinkle, personal communication, February 18, 2012). ACA is finding ways to encourage international membership and is developing an interest network to represent international counseling (Erford, as cited in Shallcross, 2012; Sandhu, 2012). CSI is becoming more involved internationally as well as through the frequently used global section of its website (http://www.csi-net.org/displaycommon.cfm?an=1&subarticlenbr=768) and several other international activities (Sweeney, 2012). Although the West has some of the world's most advanced counseling systems, most other countries do not want to simply adopt those practices out of hand. In fact, they warn against the wholesale application of Western counseling theories and techniques to their cultures. The vast majority of countries advocate the development of their own counseling programs to meet their own unique mental health needs or the tailoring of Western practices to meet the needs of their cultures (Hohenshil & Amundson, 2011).

From an international and historical perspective, the International Association for Counselling (IAC), which was established in 1966, has long been an advocate for global counseling. IAC's mission is to promote the well-being of people worldwide through the advancement of counseling practice, research, and policy. Among other activities, IAC sponsors yearly conferences that involve representatives of the United Nations, various counseling associations, and counseling leaders throughout the world (Lee, 2012). Another international counseling organization, the International Association for Educational and Vocational Guidance (IAEVG), has been in existence for more than 50 years and has several thousand members on six continents. Its general mission is to advocate that all people who need and want educational and vocational guidance and counseling are able to receive these services from competent professionals. IAEVG also sponsors annual conferences and other professional activities (IAEVG, 2012). Both associations have provided assistance to numerous countries wishing to implement and further develop their counseling programs. In addition to these two organizations, there are a number of other highly respected international and regional counseling associations that are listed in the Appendix.

Counseling, Professional Counseling, and Professional Counselors

Basic counseling functions are practiced in every culture in the world, sometimes by professional counselors and sometimes by others. They are provided by families, friends, tribal leaders, indigenous healers, spiritual leaders, medical personnel, and credentialed mental health professionals. Each culture has unique characteristics and needs, and counseling skills are unusually adaptable to meeting those needs, regardless of who uses them (NBCC-I, 2011). The need to expand the counseling profession is gaining considerable global support because of the increased industrialization that is resulting in changing family structures, new political alliances, and advances in communication technology. All of these developments have worldwide repercussions that produce significant stressors for individuals and groups.

Definitions of Counseling

There are as many definitions of counseling as there are groups defining it. NBCC-I contends that the specific definition of professional counseling varies because counseling practice must adapt to local cultural conditions. However, NBCC-I generally describes counseling as a process in which specially trained people provide academic and career guidance, problem-solving expertise, expertise related to specific biological threats, and other support and expertise to people and communities as they work toward maximum wellness (NBCC-I, 2011). In 2010, ACA adopted a definition that described counseling as a professional relationship that empowers diverse individuals, families, and groups to accomplish mental health, wellness, education, and career goals (ACA, 2012). CSI endorsed the ACA definition of counseling in the following statement:

> Professional counselors hold their highest graduate degree in counselor education from a nationally accredited preparation program, are credentialed by authorized state and/or national agencies, and adhere to its competency standards on matters of ethics, diversity and behavior in order to contribute to the realization of a healthy society by fostering wellness and human dignity. As a consequence, *counseling is a professional relationship that empowers diverse individuals, families, and groups to accomplish mental health, wellness, education, and career goals.* (CSI, 2011, emphasis in the original)

Professional Counselors

Professional counselors undergo an educational program that is usually prescribed by some type of governmental agency, university, or mental health group (such as a professional association) and must successfully pass an examination to demonstrate that they possess the required knowledge and skills endorsed by the particular credentialing group. Professional counselors differ from other helping individuals because they have received formal training and supervision in counseling and they follow an approved code of ethics or standards of practice. Although counseling codes of ethics differ from country to country, each provides an approved path to follow when questions of ethical practice arise (NBCC-I, 2011).

The Purpose of the Book

This book is designed to provide information about the global status of professional counseling as well as counseling provided by those without extensive professional training. The countries represented herein are highly divergent in many ways and represent every continent except Antarctica. Some countries in the book are relatively new on the world stage, whereas others have been in existence for centuries. There are also significant differences in the countries' social orientations (individualist vs. collectivist) and in their political and economic systems. Although there is a significant lack of research regarding the global status of the counseling profession, it is expected that counseling services have developed in different ways in different countries. It is also expected that counselor education programs vary widely, from virtually none in some countries to those that offer graduate degrees and use the CACREP Standards in others (CACREP, 2012). Finally, some countries may have drawn heavily from counseling professionals and organizations in the West to develop their programs, whereas others may have received help from other regions of the world. This book was designed to collect this kind of information.

The authors writing about the 40 countries in this book were asked to follow a similar format for their chapters. The intent was to develop a common structure for reporting information that would facilitate a comparison of counseling from country to country. Authors from each country were responsible for collecting the necessary information from a review of published and unpublished documents, personal experience, and communication with colleagues. As expected, the chapters differ in the extent to which all topics are addressed because there is a lack of organized information about counseling in some countries.

Historical Development

One of the topics included for each country is the historical development of counseling in that country. This usually includes such things as historical information about the country itself as well as information about the development of mental health services in general and counseling in particular. This section sets the stage for the rest of the chapter, because the historical development of a country often shapes the way counseling develops. It gives the reader a feel for the country; its people; and its political, economic, and social systems.

Current Status

The historical development section is followed by a description of the current status of counseling in each country. This includes such things as the number of counselors and where they are employed (e.g., schools, agencies, private practice, industry). Other topics in this section include descriptions of professional associations; credentialing procedures; and the relationship between counselors, psychologists, social workers, and other mental health professionals. The types of services provided by counselors in the country are also described.

Best Counseling Practices

Each chapter has a section that describes the counseling practices that work best in that particular country. For example, how do counselors handle assessment and diagnosis, the counseling process, and follow-up? Is a particular theory predominant in the country, or are a certain set of counseling techniques particularly effective? Other topics involve the use of the Internet and additional forms of technology in counselor practice and counselor education. Authors were also asked to indicate whether counselors use mostly talk therapy or whether they use other techniques, such as art, play, and drama.

Diversity

How counselors in other countries deal with diversity is an important and consistent theme in the book; a separate chapter is devoted to the topic, and there is a diversity section in each individual country chapter. The diversity theme touches on topics of ethnic and gender diversity, immigration, identity, age, special needs, sexual orientation, and socioeconomic issues that may influence the counseling process. Of special interest is how such issues are identified and how they are handled by counselors and other mental health professionals in the country.

Counselor Education

Authors were asked to include a description of the way in which counselors are prepared. This section normally involves a description of how and where counselor education is offered as well as the curriculum and standards involved. For example, if a country does not have a well-developed counselor education program, where are counselors trained, and by whom? Of particular interest is whether there are national curricula similar to the CACREP Standards and, if not, whether procedures are in place to develop similar standards.

The Future

Authors were also asked to project 5–10 years into the future and indicate how they saw counseling developing in their countries. This section might include a discussion of the servicing of different client groups; new kinds of services; innovation in counseling techniques; advances in counselor education and credentialing; research; or coordination of services with other mental health providers, such as psychiatrists, social workers, psychologists, and indigenous healers.

Influential People and Counseling Approaches

Authors from each country were asked to include the most relevant and important references in the reference sections of their chapters. Thus, it is possible to review those sections to identify the most influential people, theories, and techniques in the global development of the counseling profession. These sections also provide information about counseling theories and techniques that have been developed by professionals in non-Western parts of the world that may be applicable to other regions and cultures.

The Selection of Authors and Countries

Because it was obviously not possible to include chapters for all of the nearly 200 countries in the world, it was decided to include representative countries from each of the continents except Antarctica. A listing of those countries appears in the Table of Contents. The chapter authors were solicited through a number of sources. The most effective method was the posting of several announcements on the counselor education listserv CESNET-L. Other authors were identified through a review of the international counseling literature and recommendations by counselor educators who had considerable international experience. Every attempt was made to select at least one author who was a native of that country, and this goal was met for almost all of the 40 country chapters. Because several of the chapters have multiple coauthors, a total of 109 authors participated in the writing of this book. See "About the Contributors" for a listing of the authors.

Summary

In this introductory chapter the stage has been set for a global analysis of the counseling profession. The remainder of the book includes chapters about counseling in 40 different countries representing virtually every continent. Each chapter follows a common format intended to facilitate the comparison of counseling among the countries. As noted previously, the chapters include a discussion of (a) the historical development of counseling services in the country, (b) the current status of the profession, (c) the kinds of counseling theories and techniques that seem to work best in the country, (d) how diversity issues are handled, (e) how counselors are educated, (f) how the authors see the future development of counseling in the country, and (g) influential people and publications in the country. The last chapter in the book is an analysis and synthesis of the information in the 40 country chapters. Readers will find the Appendix helpful because it includes a listing of English-language international counseling journals, references to international counseling articles, and a list of international and regional counseling associations.

Given the sweeping scope of this book, it was necessary to restrict the amount of information that could be provided for each country. The intent was to provide an overview of counseling in the various countries as well as some useful references. It is hoped that those who are interested in particular countries will use this information as a foundation upon which to conduct further research. It is also our hope that readers of the book will become increasingly globally literate and will come to appreciate the contributions to the counseling profession of professionals from around the world.

References

American Counseling Association. (2012). *Counseling today.* Retrieved from http://ct.counseling.org/

Central Intelligence Agency. (2012). *The world factbook.* Retrieved from https://www.cia.gov/library/publications/the-world-factbook/geos/xx.html

Chi Sigma Iota Counseling Academic and Professional Honor Society International. (2011). *What is a professional counselor?* Retrieved from http://www.csi-net.org/displaycommon.cfm?an=1&subarticlenbr=679#Counselor

Council for Accreditation of Counseling and Related Educational Programs. (2012). *International program approval.* Retrieved from http://www.cacrep.org/template/page.cfm?id=103

David Sanger Photography. (2012). *Greece, Hydra, Man on donkey with cell phone.* Retrieved from http://www.davidsanger.com/stockimages/3-701-39.manwithphone

Hohenshil, T. H. (2010). International counseling introduction. *Journal of Counseling & Development, 88,* 3. doi:10.1002/j.1556-6678.2010.tb00140.x

Hohenshil, T. H., & Amundson, N. E. (2011). Publishing international counseling articles. *Journal of Counseling & Development, 89,* 313–317. doi:10.1002/j.1556-6678.2011.tb00095.x

International Association for Educational and Vocational Guidance (2012). *About IAEVG.* Retrieved from http://www.iaevg.org/iaevg/nav.cfm?lang=2&menu=1&submenu=1

Lee, C. C. (2012, September). The promise of counsel(l)ing's globalization. *Counseling Today, 55(3),* 14–15.

Mundi Index. (2012). *World demographic profile, 2012.* Retrieved from http://www.indexmundi.com/world/demographics_profile.html

NBCC International. (2011). *Thinking and acting globally.* Retrieved from http://www.nbccinternational.org/

Sandhu, D. S. (2012, August). The internationalization of counseling. *Counseling Today.* Retreived from http://ct.counseling.org/2012/08/the-internationalization-of-couneling/

Shallcross, L. (2012, March). What the future holds for the counseling profession. *Counseling Today.* Retrieved from http://ct.counseling.org/2012/03/what-the-future-holds-for-the-counseling-profession/

Sweeney, T. (2012). CSI: International. *Chi Sigma Iota Exemplar, 27*(1). Retrieved from http://www.csi-net.org/associations/2151/files/81000.pdf

• • •

Global Diversity Issues in Counseling

2

Sylvia C. Nassar-McMillan, James L. Moore III, Heather A. Warfield, and Renae D. Mayes

With the increased focus on globalization in counseling training programs and the counseling profession, strong consideration should be given to general factors that affect nations throughout the world. Scholars spanning the helping professions have begun to recognize the roots and current status of counseling movements across virtually every region of the planet as well as identify guidelines for developing regulations for moving forward in counseling research, training, and practice (Gerstein, Heppner, Ægisdóttir, Leung, & Norsworthy, 2009; Heppner et al., 2009; McFadden & Moore, 2002). Concurrently, attention has also been focused on domestic issues of cultural diversity and their impact on mental health needs and effective counseling interventions (e.g., Hoshmand, 2006).

A contemporary view of mental health practice illustrates the dichotomous influences culture can have on the psychological functioning of individuals, groups, and families. It is widely understood that culture and its effects can include resilience and positive coping strategies while at the same time bringing about a variety of psychological stressors (P. T. P. Wong & Wong, 2006). This dynamic can occur both inter- and intraculturally.

Worldwide immigration numbers are on the rise. These statistics include scenarios ranging from individuals and families seeking basic needs (e.g., food, shelter, and employment) to individuals seeking physical safety and freedom from religious or political persecution (U.S. Committee for Refugees and Immigrants, 2009). In the United States and elsewhere, counselors are not always prepared for the transcultural attitudes, interactions, and dispositions that clients often bring to counseling (D'Ardenne & Mahtani, 1999; Nassar-McMillan & Lee, 2011). Thus, it behooves mental health professionals to identify commonalities in cultural competencies to apply both within and outside their professional context.

As the world becomes increasingly interconnected, counselors must learn how to work across, through, and beyond cultural and continental differences (McFadden & Moore, 2002). McFadden (1999) suggested that "confusion and shifts in political, social, and economic problems that have never been greater than at this time present themselves in every aspect of our lives" (p. xviii). It is reasonable to believe that individuals throughout the world are likely to need assistance from professionals such as mental health counselors. The general consensus among counseling professionals who are consistently being exposed to diverse cultures is that there is a need to learn how to create a caring counseling environment that "transcends cultural, ethnic, racial, and national boundaries" (McFadden, 1999, p. xvi).

In support of a global paradigmatic framework for counseling, Gerstein and Ægisdóttir (2007) suggested that counselor training should have an expanded focus on popular and scientific literature outside of the counseling field in such disciplines as political science, cultural anthropology, and linguistics. They also recommended that more attention be given to international topics, including human rights on a global scale and the role of counselors within this human rights framework.

In congruence with the Universal Declaration of Human Rights, Alladin (2009) developed a nine-dimensional model for use in a client-centered approach to counseling and health care. This framework considers biological, psychological, social, and spiritual elements of functioning within the context of cultural and ethnic identity. Moreover, the model considers factors such as the sociopolitical climate, health concepts, religion, the scope and practice of various types of counselors, and ethnic issues. Of specific significance to the counseling profession is the direct impact of factors related to psychological well-being (Arredondo, Tovar-Blank, & Parham, 2008). In order for counselors to appropriately address the diverse global needs, beliefs, and circumstances of their clientele, they first need to be cognizant of social and cultural factors that often shape their clients' psychological experiences. Without this knowledge base, counselors will likely be ineffective at facilitating the counseling process with their clients. Therefore, it is critical that counselors become culturally competent in order to successfully understand and work with globally diverse populations.

With this in mind, in this chapter we present pertinent content that can be used to empower counselors who are working with globally diverse clients. An overview of counseling and its global status is provided, as are implications for counseling practice. Globalization has created a need for this kind of information.

Sociopolitical Issues and Diversity

Counselors should have a general understanding about the sociopolitical climate of a given country or region and its history as well as a firm grasp of their role as change agents within a global system. This was reflected by Katz (1985), who observed that counselors become integrated into culture, and, through this integration, counseling becomes "a sociopolitical act" (p. 615). One element of culture is geographical location and the history of the people in the area. Although geographic boundaries delineate one country from another, these boundaries do not necessarily represent a cohesive group or national identity.

Within the boundaries of any particular country are diverse groups of people who identify themselves in a myriad of ways. This dynamic, among other factors, interfaces with the larger social and political systems. For example, in Sudan, the existence of hundreds of tribal subdivisions and ethnic and religious subcultures has resulted in decades of war, intraethnic conflict, and genocide and ultimately resulted in the establishment of the Republic of South Sudan as a separate country in July 2011. In addition, events in North Africa and the Middle East, typically referred to as the *Arab Spring,* are signals of the role of sociopolitical factors in the lives of individuals and communities. Changes within these systems are impactful in several ways, such as through a vacillation in levels of freedom, access to health care, exposure to trauma, and role adjustment within the society. These types of changes have wide-reaching implications for counselors' own identity as well as for the counseling relationship.

Ethnic Diversity

In addition to sociopolitical factors, counselors seeking a global paradigmatic framework need to consider ethnic issues. These issues can be categorized as both inter- and intraethnic in nature and often emerge as notable because of conflict. As mentioned previously, the Republic of South Sudan was established as the result of such ethnic conflict. According to the U.S. Department of State (2011), Sudan's population is one of the most diverse on the African continent. Within two distinct major cultures there are hundreds of ethnic and tribal subdivisions and language groups, which makes effective collaboration among them a major challenge. In the decades leading up to the establishment of the Republic of South Sudan, violence in that region resulted in major destruction and displacement; for the period 1983 to 2005, the number dead stood at 2 million and the number displaced at 4 million.

Ethnic conflict also influences countries that were once part of the Soviet Union. An article about interethnic conflict in Russia found that study participants reported (a) the need to regularly address unfriendly statements about groups other than their own, (b) the persistence of prejudices that prevented the establishment of amicable relations between representatives of different peoples, (c) hostile attitudes toward people of other nationalities coming to work or to live permanently in their locality, (d) the use of religion to arouse interethnic hostility, (e) the appointment of people to leadership or prestigious posts on the basis of ethnic status, and (f) the absence of representatives in government agencies of certain nationalities living in their locality (Ivanov, 1993). This type of unfriendly and often hostile living environment creates barriers for people living within these types of systems. Therefore, counselors need to become aware of the realities experienced by people in these environments to establish meaningful client relationships and to implement societal change. Additional considerations regarding ethnic issues include varying perspectives and definitions of what a counselor is. For some indigenous populations, seeking help from a licensed professional is not an option, but seeking the counsel of a respected tribal elder or religious shaman is sometimes appropriate (Vontress, 1991). As the counseling profession expands on a global level, an awareness of these considerations is needed for effective practice.

Religious Diversity

Another area for contemplation with regard to global counseling is the impact of religion and spirituality on individuals and societies. Max Weber (1922/1963), in his classic work *The Sociology of Religion,* addressed the far-reaching influence of religion in societies around the world. Specifically, he categorized multiple dimensions of religion that include beliefs, practices, and the influence on social strata. These dimensions have a direct impact on the perspectives of counseling from both an individualist and collectivist framework. One's religious framework often dictates a worldview that influences nearly every domain of life, from beliefs about the origin of the world and humanity, to one's identity within the community, to moral and ethical decision making, to perspectives on relationships within family and community structures, to rites of passage.

Individuals' religious worldviews can also directly influence the type of help they seek for mental health, development, and career-related issues. The 21st century has brought with it an increased recognition of the importance of spirituality within mental health practice. Alladin (2009) asserted that "the role of spirituality has been increasingly recognized in a holistic approach to psychology, counselling and human rights" within a global context (p. 19). Furthermore, counseling within a global perspective requires a deeper understanding of the diversity of spiritual and religious beliefs and practices. Vontress (2001) suggested that "people in traditional societies submit to, and depend on, the direction of a supreme entity in their daily lives, whereas individuals in modern counterparts tend to place more importance on science and rationality" (p. 86). Thus, there are additional considerations regarding the role of religion when one views counseling in the contextual framework of societies that embrace modernization and those that do not.

Gender Issues

Counselors should be sensitive to how gender and gender role expectations affect individuals and societies. Gender expectations can be influenced by societal, familial, religious, and philosophical beliefs of what an ideal man, woman, and family should encompass. Across cultures and continents, these expectations are taught early in life and provide the framework for an individual's self-concept, self-esteem, and goals in life (Novi & Meinster, 2000). Although gender roles have been changing, women still take a more passive role by focusing on being the main family caregiver and are ultimately responsible for the emotional and psychological well-being of the family (Chung, 2001). Men have traditionally been the breadwinners and have provided for the physical well-being of the household. Patriarchal societies often privilege men and view stereotypical male attributes (e.g., logic, rationality, assertiveness) as the norm and desirable (Black & Stone, 2005). Because men are often privileged by the power structures, women are often silenced and overlooked.

Because of these different expectations, the counseling concerns that people may have could differ based on their gender. For those who subscribe to traditional gender roles, concerns may be related to their perceived position in society. Individuals who do not subscribe to traditional gender roles may still be influenced because of living in a society with traditional values and expectations. It is important for counselors working from a global perspective to be fully aware of their own self-perceptions relative to gender so as to mindfully avoid imposing these perceptions and corresponding expectations on their clients. Moreover, it is important to use counseling modalities and interventions that are sensitive to individuals' needs.

Other Sexual Issues and Diversity

Counselors working in a global context must understand not only sexuality but also how heteronormativity in a given society can affect clients. In some societies, identifying as lesbian, gay, bisexual, or transgender (LGBT) has a negative connotation and may be seen as abnormal, perverted, and even mentally ill. Identification as LGBT or even suspicion of being LGBT could lead to a variety of negative consequences in both the family and society, including discrimination and aggression from family, friends, and institutions such as school or work (Sangganjanavanich & Cavazos, 2010; Vella, Nowottnick, Selun, & van Roozendaal, 2009). In some societies, being LGBT is undesirable and can lead to banishment (Peña, 2007). Some countries have legislation that makes same-sex relationships illegal and punishable by law. The consequences for those caught or suspected of being in a same-sex relationship can involve harassment, humiliation, arrest, or even life in prison (Mujuzi, 2009).

Given that societal and familial values around people who are LGBT can vary greatly from country to country, the lived experience of the coming out process may also vary. For example, individuals who come out may face physical isolation, stigmatism, and even a lack of positive role models; however, types of support and resources may vary greatly depending on the country in which the client lives (Roberts, 2007). Counselors can serve as such a resource. In order for counselors to be effective in working with LGBT clients, they should have an understanding of societal and familial realities as well as use appropriate techniques and interventions that respect clients' dignity.

Age Diversity

In many cultures, there are distinguishing characteristics between groups based on age. For example, children, adults, and older populations are viewed differently from one another and maintain a specific status. Treatment of children often changes with the age of the child. For example, parents may indulge their infants but then shift their focus to socializing them after they have reached a certain age. Children are often silenced in that they are not engaged in a dialogue but rather told to complete a task and punished if they fail to complete it (Bowes, Chen, San, & Li, 2004). Moreover, this socialization continues in the types of opportunities afforded to children. In some countries, education is readily accessible for all children, whereas in other countries access to education is dependent on other factors, such as socioeconomic status, gender, and the needs of the country (e.g., the need to form a militia; Branyon, 2005).

The status of adults and older people is much different than that of children. Expectations of adulthood may include added responsibility, financial stability, marriage, and children, all of which are heavily influenced by the cultural background, values, and definitions of adulthood. For example, individualist cultures may place more of an emphasis on self-reliance and self-sufficiency, whereas collectivist cultures may focus on duties toward others (Nelson, Badger, & Wu, 2004). The older adult population continues to increase, likely because of greater access to health care and the baby boom after World War II. Older adults' role depends heavily on the norms and values of the culture and society in which they live. For example, older adults may have caregiving responsibilities, may be more susceptible to illness, may be living or cared for by daughters and sons-in-law, or may fall victim to abuse or violence (Malley-Morrison, Nolido, & Chawla, 2006). Given the impact of culture on age expectations and experiences, counselors should make themselves aware of the potential strengths and challenges associated with age in order to better help their clients.

Physical Health Issues and Diversity

Countries around the world are faced with issues related to disease and death. Leading causes of death internationally include heart disease, stroke and other cerebrovascular disease, lower respiratory infections, pulmonary diseases, diarrheal diseases, and HIV/AIDS (World Health Organization, 2011b). However, a comparison of leading causes of death for high-income and low-income countries yields striking results. In high-income countries, heart disease, cerebrovascular disease, lung cancers, dementia, and lower respiratory infections lead the list of the top 10 causes of death, with HIV/AIDS not represented. In low-income countries, lower respiratory infections, diarrheal diseases, HIV/AIDS, heart disease, and malaria make up the top 5 killers. Thus, economic and environmental conditions, with their corresponding challenges to sanitation, contribute heavily to the two leading causes of death in countries in which poverty is ever present.

Next in line is HIV, one of the world's leading infectious killers, which has claimed 25 million lives over the past 30 years (World Health Organization, 2011a). HIV weakens the immune systems of its victims, leading to increased susceptibility to cancer and infection. In 2010, 34 million people worldwide were living with HIV. Also in 2010, 6.6 million persons with HIV in low- and middle-income countries were receiving medical treatment, whereas more than 7 million others were not (World Health Organization, 2011a). More than 60% of HIV victims reside in sub-Saharan Africa (World Health Organization, 2011a). According to the Joint United Nations Programme on HIV/AIDS (1997), despite empirical evidence that good counseling has provided critical support to those living with and otherwise affected by HIV and AIDS, obstacles and inadequacies found worldwide include a lack of established counseling services; barriers to accessing services; and a lack of follow-up support for individuals, spouses, partners, and families.

Another global health concern cited by the World Health Organization (2011c) is disability. Physical and mental disabilities, including impairments, blindness, loss of limbs, chronic pain, and intellectual disability, directly affect about 15% of the world's population, or 785 million people. Poverty does not necessarily cause disability but appears to be correlated with a higher prevalence of it. Moreover, like with all health issues, barriers such as stigma, financial issues and other accessibility issues, and a lack of appropriate medical and treatment knowledge and services impede access to appropriate counseling services for clients with disabilities and their families.

Indigenous Populations

How indigenous groups are treated varies widely from country to country and affects the nature of counseling services and how these services are delivered. It is important to note that within any particular country, indigenous populations are not homogenous. Thus, it is imprudent and unethical for counselors to generalize particular knowledge about one indigenous group to another. However, it is likely that mainstream counseling services may not meet the needs of most indigenous populations or that existing services may not be the initial point of contact for those seeking help. For example, the Aboriginal people of Australia, who have strong kinship ties, usually seek help for familial survival needs prior to seeking outside welfare or social service assistance (Fan, 2007). Thus, counselors need to develop an increased knowledge base about the indigenous populations they serve. In addition, Yeh, Hunter, Madan-Bahel, Chiang, and Arora (2004) suggested that counselors be open to the idea of indigenous healing, initiate relationships with indigenous healers, and invite indigenous healers into the counselor–client relationship, if appropriate. Resources for increasing knowledge include the Indigenous Ways of Knowing program at Lewis & Clark College (http://graduate.lclark.edu/community_engagement/native_communities/indigenous_ways_of_knowing/).

Immigration

Culture can serve as a resilience variable or as a stressor. This stressor can be referred to as *acculturative stress* (Berry, 2006; Matsumoto, Hirayama, & LeRoux, 2006; Takano, 2006; L. C. J. Wong, 2006). Compared to their later generation counterparts, first-generation immigrants represent a unique array of issues. Although the reasons for immigrating can greatly affect one's adjustment to the new culture, direct immigrants in all cases are in a culture that is different to some degree from their home culture. For example, those who immigrate voluntarily may be in search of improved economic conditions, whereas others may immigrate to escape oppressive regimes in their countries of origin. Yet both groups are faced with needing to learn new cultural systems, including systems of education and employment. This adaptation process is referred to as *acculturation.*

Although there are vast differences in acculturation processes among individuals and families from varying cultures, these are mediated by issues such as the reason for immigration and the person's age at the time of immigration. Additional layers of trauma may compound acculturative stress levels among immigrants who leave their countries of origin and enter another as refugees, in either temporary or permanent asylum resettlement. Those who experience trauma (e.g., torture or other persecution) either prior to or during an intermittent stay in a refugee camp or after their immigration (e.g., through profiling or discrimination in their new host culture) may experience elevated levels of posttraumatic stress disorder, anxiety, and depression along with elevated levels of other mental health diagnoses (Jamil, Nassar-McMillan, & Lambert, 2007; Kira, Amer, & Wrobel, in press). The issue of immigration requires heightened sensitivity to the potential traumas clients have undergone throughout the immigration process and cultural knowledge about clients' culture of origin as well as their experience in the new culture. Effective diagnoses and treatment must take these immigration circumstances into account, and counseling interventions need to focus on helping clients develop appropriate coping and other psychological skills (Matsumoto et al., 2006).

Socioeconomic Status

The socioeconomic status of an individual can also be influenced by outside factors. For example, a nation's history can privilege or disadvantage specific groups through access to educational, social, and economic opportunities (Black & Stone, 2005). Individuals from higher socioeconomic backgrounds tend to have greater access to these opportunities; therefore, they have more stability than individuals from lower socioeconomic backgrounds. Individuals from socioeconomically disadvantaged backgrounds experience many challenges in various areas, including education, occupation, and health.

Children from rural areas of less developed countries often suffer a socioeconomic disadvantage that translates to even greater challenges in school and society at large. These children may lag behind academically compared to students in urban areas. In addition, children in rural areas often attend schools with poor conditions and have less support at home for their studies (Zhang, 2006). These educational challenges also contribute to increased unemployment and lower paying jobs. In addition to creating educational and vocational challenges, socioeconomic status is related to physical health. Because of a lack of access to health care and resources, individuals from lower socioeconomic backgrounds have increased exposure to disease and poor health conditions (Blas & Kurup, 2010). Counselors working within a global context need to understand how issues related to socioeconomic status can influence the experiences and concerns of individuals.

Educational and Vocational Issues

Educational and vocational counseling can occur in both school and nonschool settings. If a community does not have a professional counselor in the school or in a community setting, students may turn to teachers, parents, peers, church organizations, and nongovernmental organizations for career exploration and decision making (Osoro, Amundson, & Borgen, 2000). Regardless of the source, educational and vocational counseling helps individuals plan the next step in their career development. In planning this next step, counselors need to be sensitive to the norms, values, beliefs, and society in which the individuals live. Political and economic factors often guide the educational and vocational opportunities available to people in a given country (Gati, Krausz, & Osipow, 1996). For example, economic stability, employment shifts, and a changing labor force affect the opportunities that are available to individuals within a given country. Moreover, global competition and national initiatives, such as Race to the Top (United States) and Free Schools (Great Britain), can also push for specific educational and vocational outcomes, such as greater interest and competence in the fields of science, technology, engineering, and mathematics.

In addition to the political and economic climate, individuals' norms, values, and beliefs influence their educational and vocational decisions. As mentioned previously, dimensions of religion can also impact individuals' view of themselves and the world around them. Although educational and vocational decisions are thought to be guided by the individual, people with a collectivist orientation may also consider their roles and family obligations within a group context. As a counselor working within a global framework, it is important to address collectivist issues for individuals with this particular worldview (Lowe, 2005).

Conclusion

With the advent of globalization and technological advancements, nations around the world are connected in ways unlike at any other time in history. This connection is interdependent with changes in how people interact with one another and how information is transmitted from culture to culture, family to family, and nation to nation. Clearly, these changes have brought about more intense social interactions with individuals and groups. Although global geography is still an issue for nations, it no longer presents the same obstacles that it once did. Individuals and groups are more able to increase their social interactions with other cultures and nations; however, as with any advancement, there are still challenges.

As the world becomes more interconnected, people are challenged with maintaining their own customs, histories, and values. Challenges of sociopolitical history, intraethnic diversity, religious diversity, gender, and immigration remain intact. Individuals and groups are faced daily with these issues, and threats of mental health problems are constant. Shifts in social, political, and economic structures throughout the world have created instability for various groups. Issues in the larger society often become clients' concerns in counseling. This often promotes feelings of psychological vulnerability, such as hopelessness and powerlessness. These emotions are common when individuals are confronted with events over which they do not have control.

A central premise of this chapter is that the world is a community of nations that are increasingly interconnected and interdependent. With this in mind, it is critical that today's counselors are equipped with the global knowledge and skills they need to work across cultural and continental divides. Thus, counselors' undergraduate and graduate study must include topics related to global diversity and cultural issues. Having adequate transcultural counseling training is a must as the world becomes increasingly interconnected. Understanding the ways in which sociopolitical history, intraethnic diversity, religious diversity, gender, immigration, and other factors influence the worldviews of clients should be a major part of this training.

References

Alladin, W. (2009). An ethno biopsychosocial human rights model for educating community counsellors globally. *Counselling Psychology Quarterly, 22,* 17–24.

Arredondo, P., Tovar-Blank, Z. G., & Parham, T. A. (2008). Challenges and promises of becoming a culturally competent counselor in a sociopolitical era of change and empowerment. *Journal of Counseling & Development, 86,* 261–268.

Berry, J. W. (2006). Acculturative stress. In P. T. P. Wong & L. C. J. Wong (Eds.), *Handbook of multicultural perspectives on stress and coping* (pp. 287–298). New York, NY: Springer.

Black, L. L., & Stone, D. (2005). Expanding the definition of privilege: The concept of social privilege. *Journal of Multicultural Counseling and Development, 33,* 243–255.

Blas, E., & Kurup, A. S. (Eds.). (2010). *Equity, social determinants and public health programmes.* Retrieved from http://whqlibdoc.who.int/publications/2010/9789241563970_eng.pdf

Bowes, J. M., Chen, M., San, L. Q., & Li, Y. (2004). Reasoning and negotiation about child responsibility in urban Chinese families: Reports from mothers, fathers and children. *International Journal of Behavioral Development, 28*(1), 48–58.

Branyon, J. B. (2005). Education for all: Gender equity in Kenya. *Delta Kappa Gamma Bulletin, 71*(2), 8–11.

Chung, R. (2001). Psychosocial adjustment of Cambodian refugee women: Implications for mental health counseling. *Journal of Mental Health Counseling, 23,* 115–126.

D'Ardenne, P., & Mahtani, A. (1999). *Transcultural counseling in action* (2nd ed.). London, England: Sage.

Fan, B. (2007). Intervention model with Indigenous Australians for non-Indigenous counsellors. *Counselling, Psychotherapy, and Health, 3*(2), 13–20.

Gati, I., Krausz, M., & Osipow, S. H. (1996). A taxonomy of difficulties in career decision making. *Journal of Counselling Psychology, 40,* 510–526.

Gerstein, L. H., & Ægisdóttir, S. (2007). Training international social change agents: Transcending a U.S. counseling paradigm. *Counselor Education and Supervision, 47,* 123–139.

Gerstein, L. H., Heppner, P. P., Ægisdóttir, S., Leung, S. A., & Norsworthy, K. L. (2009). A global vision for the future of cross-cultural counseling: Theory, collaboration, research, and training. In L. H. Gerstein, P. P. Heppner, S. Ægisdóttir, S.-M. A. Leung, & K. L. Norsworthy (Eds.), *International handbook of cross-cultural counseling: Cultural assumptions and practices worldwide* (pp. 503–522). Thousand Oaks, CA: Sage.

Heppner, P. P., Ægisdóttir, S., Leung, S. A., Duan, C., Helms, J. E., Gerstein, L. H., & Pedersen, P. B. (2009). The intersection of multicultural and cross-national movements in the United States: A complementary role to promote culturally sensitive research, training, and practice. In L. H. Gerstein, P. P. Heppner, S. Ægisdóttir, S.-M. A. Leung, & K. L. Norsworthy (Eds.), *International handbook of cross-cultural counseling: Cultural assumptions and practices worldwide* (pp. 33–52). Thousand Oaks, CA: Sage.

Hoshmand, L. T. (2006). Culture and the field of psychotherapy and counseling. In L. T. Hoshmand (Ed.), *Culture, psychotherapy, and counseling: Critical integrative perspectives* (pp. 25–46). Thousand Oaks, CA: Sage.

Ivanov, V. N. (1993). Interethnic conflicts. *Russian Social Science Review, 34,* 24–36.

Jamil, H., Nassar-McMillan, S. C., & Lambert, R. G. (2007). Immigration and attendant psychological sequelae: A comparison of three waves of Iraqi immigrants. *Journal of Orthopsychiatry, 77,* 199–205.

Joint United Nations Programme on HIV/AIDS. (1997). *Counseling and HIV/AIDS: UNAIDS technical update.* Retrieved from http://data.unaids.org/Publications/IRC-pub03/counstu_en.pdf

Katz, J. H. (1985). The sociopolitical nature of counseling. *The Counseling Psychologist, 13,* 615–624.

Kira, I., Amer, M. M., & Wrobel, N. (in press). Refugee trauma, resilience, and recovery. In S. C. Nassar-McMillan, K. Ajrouch, & J. Hakim-Larson (Eds.), *Biopsychosocial care of Arab Americans: Perspectives on culture, development, and health.* New York, NY: Springer.

Lowe, S. M. (2005). Integrating collectivist values into career counseling with Asian Americans: A test of cultural responsiveness. *Journal of Multicultural Counseling and Development, 33,* 134–145.

Malley-Morrison, K., Nolido, N. V., & Chawla, S. (2006). International perspectives on elder abuse: Five case studies. *Educational Gerontology, 32*(1), 1–11.

Matsumoto, D., Hirayama, S., & LeRoux, J. A. (2006). Psychological skills related to intercultural adjustment. In P. T. P. Wong & L. C. J. Wong (Eds.), *Handbook of multicultural perspectives on stress and coping* (pp. 387–405). New York, NY: Springer.

McFadden, J. (1999). Introduction. In J. McFadden (Ed.), *Transcultural counseling* (2nd ed., pp. xv–xxiv). Alexandria, VA: American Counseling Association.

McFadden, J., & Moore, J. L., III. (2002). Intercultural marriage and intimacy: Beyond the continental divide. *International Journal for the Advancement of Counseling, 23,* 261–268.

Mujuzi, J. D. (2009). Even lesbian youths or those presumed to be lesbians are protected by the Constitution of Uganda—but to a limited extent: Rules the High Court. *Journal of LGBT Youth, 6,* 441–445.

Nassar-McMillan, S. C., & Lee, S. (2011). Counseling with diverse clients. In S. C. Nassar-McMillan & S. G. Niles (Eds.), *Developing your identity as a professional counselor: Standards, settings, and specialties* (pp. 108–129). Independence, KY: Brooks/Cole.

Nelson, L. J., Badger, S., & Wu, B. (2004). The influence of culture in emerging adulthood: Perspectives of Chinese college students. *International Journal of Behavioral Development, 28*(1), 26–36.

Novi, M. J., & Meinster, M. (2000). Achievement in a relational context: Preferences and influences in female adolescents. *The Career Development Quarterly, 49,* 73–84.

Osoro, B. K., Amundson, N. E., & Borgen, W. A. (2000). Career decision-making of high school students in Kenya. *International Journal for the Advancement of Counselling, 22,* 289–300.

Peña, S. (2007). "Obvious gays" and the state gaze: Cuban gay visibility and U.S. immigration policy during the 1980 Mariel Boatlift. *Journal of the History of Sexuality, 16,* 482–514.

Roberts, W. H. (2007). An exploration of the issue of "coming out" and possible counseling interventions in relation to young people. *International Schools Journal, 27*(2), 29–41.

Sangganjanavanich, V., & Cavazos, J. (2010). Workplace aggression: Toward social justice and advocacy in counseling for transgender individuals. *Journal of LGBT Issues in Counseling, 4*(3/4), 187–201. doi:10.1080/15538605.2010.524844

Takano, Y. (2006). Coping with violence by Japanese Canadian women. In P. T. P. Wong & L. C. J. Wong (Eds.), *Handbook of multicultural perspectives on stress and coping* (pp. 319–360). New York, NY: Springer.

U.S. Committee for Refugees and Immigrants. (2009). *World Refugee Survey 2009.* Retrieved from http://www.refugees.org/resources/refugee-warehousing/archived-world-refugee-surveys/2009-world-refugee-survey.html

U.S. Department of State. (2011). *Sudan.* Retrieved from http://www.state.gov/p/af/ci/su/

Vella, D. R., Nowottnick, L., Selun, B., & van Roozendaal, B. (2009). Empowering LGBTQ youth in Europe: The work of IGLYO. *Journal of LGBT Youth, 6*(1), 101–105.

Vontress, C. E. (1991). Traditional healing in Africa: Implications for cross-cultural counseling. *Journal of Multicultural Counseling and Development, 70,* 242–249.

Vontress, C. E. (2001). Cross-cultural counseling in the 21st century. *International Journal for the Advancement of Counselling, 23,* 83–97.

Weber, M. (1963). *The sociology of religion* (Ephraim Fischoff, Trans.). Boston, MA: Beacon Press. (Original work published 1922)

Wong, L. C. J. (2006). How visible minority students cope with supervision stress. In P. T. P. Wong & L. C. J. Wong (Eds.), *Handbook of multicultural perspectives on stress and coping* (pp. 361–386). New York, NY: Springer.

Wong, P. T. P., & Wong, L. C. J. (Eds.). (2006). *Handbook of multicultural perspectives on stress and coping.* New York, NY: Springer.

World Health Organization. (2011a). *HIV/AIDS.* Retrieved from http://www.who.int/mediacentre/factsheets/fs360/en/index.html

World Health Organization. (2011b). *The top ten causes of death.* Retrieved from http://www.who.int/mediacentre/factsheets/fs310/en/index.html

World Health Organization. (2011c). *World report on disability.* Retrieved from http://www.who.int/disabilities/world_report/2011/report/en/index.html

Yeh, C. J., Hunter, C. D., Madan-Bahel, A., Chiang, L., & Arora, A. K. (2004). Indigenous and interdependent perspectives of healing: Implications for counseling and research. *Journal of Counseling & Development, 82,* 410–419.

Zhang, Y. (2006). Urban-rural literacy gaps in sub-Saharan Africa: The roles of socioeconomic status and school quality. *Comparative Education Review, 50,* 581–602.

• • •

Section 2

Counseling in African Countries

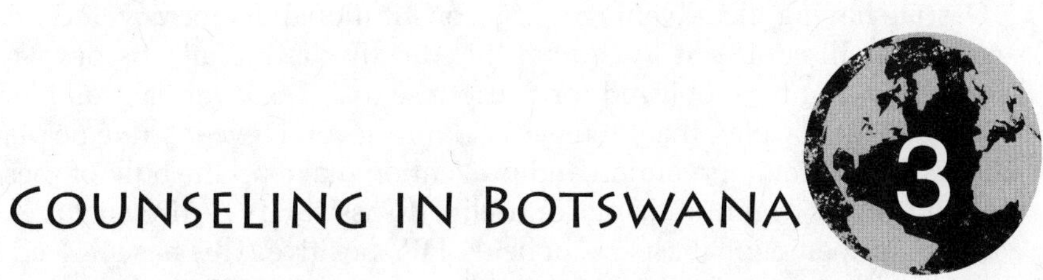

Counseling in Botswana 3

Rex Stockton, Amy Nitza, Kayi Ntinda, and Patricia Ncube

This chapter examines the development of professional counseling in Botswana. Since gaining independence in 1966, Botswana has developed into one of the most stable democratic countries in Africa. This democratic stability has been supported by economic stability and growth; what once was regarded as scrubland has, since independence, yielded three of the largest diamond mines in the world. The resulting mining industry has been lucrative and has allowed the government to reinvest heavily in the further development of the country and its resources. Thus, what once was an agricultural economy based largely on cattle has been able to develop into a strong mining and high-end tourism industry economy that provides health, educational, and infrastructure benefits to its population.

The Historical Development of Counseling

Career and School Counseling

As in many other countries, counseling in Botswana has developed alongside this process of transition from a traditional agricultural state to a more industrialized state. As a transition that included social and cultural changes, the need for career, school, and mental health professionals emerged. Shortly after Botswana's independence, initial counseling services were developed specifically to address the need for career guidance to support the demands of the rapidly growing economy. Beginning in the 1980s, these services expanded into more comprehensive guidance and counseling programs in schools and subsequently a university program to train teachers to provide these services. In the 1990s, the need for comprehensive counseling and guidance services was reflected in national government planning documents (Republic of Botswana Ministry of Education, 1994) and in this way became a part of the overall national development plan (Stockton, Nitza, & Bhusumane, 2010).

Community-Based Mental Health Counseling

In addition to the comprehensive school counseling and guidance movement, another thread in the development of counseling has been efforts to provide mental health services.

A community-based mental health care plan has been in place in Botswana since 1978; this program has been largely developed and operated by the nursing profession in the country (Seloilwe & Thupayagale-Tshweneagae, 2007). This system remains in effect today, although Seloilwe and Thupayagale-Tshweneagae (2007) have argued that the promises of this approach have not yet been fulfilled.

In a dramatic, tragic, and unforeseen manner, the HIV/AIDS epidemic contributed to the development of mental health counseling in Botswana. The prevalence rate of HIV/AIDS among adults ages 15–49 is approximately 23% (Joint United Nations Programme on HIV/AIDS & World Health Organization, 2008), making Botswana one of the countries hardest hit by the epidemic. In fact, Botswana was called the "AIDS capitol of the world" in 1997 (Heald, 2005, p. 33).

Despite having the advantages of a constitutional democracy and relative wealth, Botswana was ill equipped to combat this deadly disease and its devastating social challenges. The country mobilized for a response to AIDS as far back as 1987. It began with a 1-year emergency plan that then evolved into several 5-year strategic plans (Heald, 2005). Although medical intervention and prevention make up the bulk of these strategic plans, the country has begun utilizing counseling to assist HIV/AIDS clients in coming to terms with the socioemotional aspects of being HIV positive. This has allowed for rapid growth in the number of counselors whose primary responsibility is to work with HIV-positive clients but who also see clients with other socioemotional problems. These efforts have had the related effect of advancing the development of mental health counseling at a more rapid pace than prior to the onset of the epidemic.

Traditional and Western Health Care Systems

It is essential to note that in Botswana, two health care systems operate concurrently: the traditional system and the Western system (Seloilwe & Thupayagale-Tshweneagae, 2007). Many Batswana continue to visit traditional doctors and seek assistance from the Western system only if the traditional system does not resolve the problem satisfactorily. Particularly when it comes to mental health problems, the usual practice may be to seek traditional health care first (Seloilwe & Thupayagale-Tshweneagae, 2007). The development of an effective and culturally appropriate counseling profession in Botswana will necessitate continued attention to how the two systems can best support and learn from each other.

The Current Status of Counseling

School Counseling

Consistent with its history, a major function of counseling in Botswana remains the provision of guidance and counseling services to students in primary and secondary schools. Such services are provided in the areas of academic work, personal life, social development, and career or vocational development. The broad aim of these services is to produce graduates who are ready to join the field of work. Psychosocial support related to HIV/AIDS is also provided in schools, as many families, students, teachers, and educational officers are either affected or infected.

The Ministry of Education's School Guidance and Counseling Department plays a larger role in the daily lives of schools than is the case in the United States. The School Guidance and Counseling unit within the Curriculum and Evaluation Department is responsible for policy design and implementation of guidance and counseling programs in the schools (Scholarship Development Enterprise Africa [ASDE], 2010). This includes curriculum development and dissemination in school guidance and counseling. What is interesting is that specialized counseling services are also provided directly by Ministry staff. Students may be referred to the Ministry of Education from either the secondary or primary department (ASDE, 2010). Following counseling, staff make recommendations and coordinate any follow-ups directly with the referral source.

An innovative telephone counseling service designed for rural and underserved areas implemented by the Ministry of Education is coordinated by the School Guidance and Counseling unit. The program was funded by a grant from the World Bank and offers counseling for students at all grade levels, teachers, lecturers, and out-of-school youth. The phones are staffed by four full-time counselors, two at any one time. Counselors help students with a wide variety of issues, from study skills to love relationships, sexual harassment, HIV/AIDS stigma, and other social and emotional problems. They help teachers with problems related to the working environment, mistreatment by supervisors, dysfunctional family relationships, and retirement issues (M. Mogomotsi, personal communication, July 6, 2011).

In the schools, counselors spend time attending to the needs of individual students regarding abuse at school or at home; school performance; and, especially for students with special needs, placement in other venues, which might include hospital assistance. In addition to these duties, baccalaureate-level counselors are expected to teach two courses, one of them a counseling and guidance course. They are then available for individual or group counseling but have limited time to perform these functions (L. Mokgwathise, personal communication, August 15, 2011).

Mental Health Counseling

As noted previously, a major area of mental health counseling work is directly related to HIV/AIDS. In a process known as Voluntary Counseling and Testing, individuals meet with a counselor both before they receive an HIV test and after they receive their results. Voluntary Counseling and Testing involves providing information and resources and may also involve offering psychosocial support. Clients may be seen for several follow-up sessions and may also be offered additional referrals.

Comprehensive mental health counseling services are being offered in an increasing number of settings. The University of Botswana Careers and Counseling Center provides services to students and the university community, including individual counseling, group counseling (largely in the form of psychoeducational groups), crisis intervention, and information and education on a variety of psychosocial and wellness issues (University of Botswana, 2008). The center is staffed by a director, three deputies (careers unit, counseling unit, and placement unit), and 11 counselors. All have a minimum of a master's degree in either counseling, clinical psychology, or social work, and several hold doctorates.

Outside of the university a small but increasing number of agencies, nongovernmental organizations (NGOs), and faith-based organizations employ counselors and provide some form of mental health counseling. For example, Tebelopele Voluntary Counseling and Testing Center is Botswana's largest nongovernmental provider of voluntary HIV counseling and testing services, which are offered free to all people living in the country. This center, which first opened in 2000, uses both professional counselors and lay counselors who are trained in house. Lifeline Botswana is an NGO that offers free, confidential counseling services. The agency provides behavior modification as well as person-centered counseling in areas such as HIV/AIDS, suicide, bereavement, relationships, marriage, rape, abuse and violence, mental problems, and trauma.

In addition to public schools and higher education, counselors may also be employed by private and public hospitals and clinics, churches, government agencies (e.g., the Ministry of Health or the National AIDS Coordinating Agency), or industry (e.g., banks or mining). In many cases, the counseling is provided by social workers. In the case of industry, the counseling services are similar to employee assistance programs in the United States.

There are also a small number of private practitioners in full- or part-time practice. Most of these counselors are located in and around the capital city of Gaborone; counselors are less frequent in the rural areas of the country.

The Botswana Counseling Association (BCA) is currently being rejuvenated (S. Msimanga-Ramatebele, personal communication, July 12, 2011). One of the projects being undertaken by the BCA executive board is determining the number of counselors in the country. The BCA's plan is to register all mental health providers in the counseling field, including both professional and lay counselors, in order to improve collaborative working relationships and increase referrals. A related effort under way involves the development of a formal set of standards for counselor practice (S. Msimanga-Ramatebele, personal communication, July 12, 2011). At present, counselor training and service provision are informally guided by the standards of the American Counseling Association. However, the BCA, along with counselor educators and students in the Department of Educational Foundations at the University of Botswana and staff at the University of Botswana Careers and Counseling Center, have been working together to develop a set of locally and culturally relevant standards to guide training and service provision.

Relationships Among Mental Health Professions

In addition to counselors, psychologists, social workers, and community mental health nurses are all involved to some extent in the provision of mental health services in Botswana. Psychology is an emerging profession in Botswana. A number of psychologists are trained in the West, and the University of Botswana is currently training practitioners at the bachelor's level. Efforts to develop legal regulations and standards of practice for psychologists are currently under way. Social workers work largely with the Ministry of Local Government under the Department of Social and Welfare Services, although a few work for various NGOs. Specialized training in community mental health nursing is available at the University of Botswana, and nursing is a cornerstone of the country's mental health care policy (Seloilwe & Thupayagale-Tshweneagae, 2007).

Some challenges do exist in the relationships among these professions. Both social work and nursing are more strongly established in the country, and mental health services have largely been the purview of these two professions. As the counseling profession continues to develop, scope of practice issues is one potential challenge. Social workers, through the Social Welfare Department, have a legal mandate and the most established operational responsibility for the delivery of psychosocial services for vulnerable populations, including children. By contrast, the Ministry of Education and Skills Development (which includes the Division of Guidance and Counseling, the agency largely responsible for counseling to date) does not have a direct legal mandate to deliver psychosocial support services, except insofar as they are implied by the Education Act and related policies (e.g., the Revised National Policy on Education 1994; ASDE, 2010). Given their broad training and legal mandate, social workers often provide counseling and psychotherapy (T. Paul, personal communication, July 20, 2011). Such an overlap in scope of practice can inhibit the referral of clients to either counselors or psychologists when such referrals might be appropriate. This dilemma necessitates further exploration and provision of clear legal directives to guide each field in its scope of practice and reduce professional and occupational overlap.

Best Counseling Practices

Counseling in Botswana has been heavily influenced by Western approaches. Many counselors and other mental health professionals were trained in the West, and current practice and training in the country are informally guided by Western professional organizations, including the American Counseling Association and the Council for Accreditation of

Counseling and Related Educational Programs. However, these Western models cannot be blindly applied in cross-cultural contexts. At its core, Botswana, like other African countries, is a collectivist culture. As a Motswana colleague commented to the first author when inviting him to provide some group counselor training in Botswana, "In Africa, we solve our problems in groups" (D.-B. Bhusumane, personal communication, March 9, 2002).

A primary issue facing the profession, therefore, is that of *indigenization*, or the process of "modifying or adapting imported ideas and practice to make them appropriate to the local contexts" (Osei-Hwedie, Ntseane, & Jacques, 2006, p. 570). As described previously, Western counseling and training models exist alongside a traditional health care system that includes its own ideas about mental health. Traditional healers (*Dingaka*) have had legal status in Botswana since 1983. Counselors in Botswana are likely to be most successful when they collaborate with and learn from the traditional health care system. Doing so will allow them to promote change in a way that is consistent with the worldview of the Batswana.

Several aspects of the philosophies and practices of indigenous healers may be particularly beneficial to the work of counselors. Indeed, some of these are consistent with good Western counseling theory and practice. Sabone (2009) noted that "traditional healers derive their power from their extensive knowledge of the social networks that clients find congruent with their belief system and that western healers lack" (p. 781). A related source of strength is their knowledge of and ability to work with clients' extended family systems, which are a vital source of guidance and support in Botswana. Indigenous healers also practice within a holistic framework that recognizes the connection between "the mind and the body, the person and his or her environment, as well as the significance of human relations in the health of the body and mind" (p. 781). This framework may also expand across time to include the connection between individuals and their ancestors. Traditional healers also utilize reconciliation and forgiveness as healing interventions. Given the interconnectedness of Botswana's collective society, illness can be viewed in part as a disturbance in interpersonal relationships. Prescribing rituals or practices to promote strong interpersonal relationships is therefore an important part of a traditional healer's work (Sabone, 2009).

These traditional beliefs and practices offer several important suggestions for effective counseling in Botswana. For example, counselors must understand that their clients may also be seeing indigenous healers for assistance with the same—or different—concerns (L. Lopez-Levers, personal communication, August 8, 2011). Counselors who are disconnected from the social or familial networks of their clients may need to pay particular attention to this issue and become as familiar as possible with clients' social networks and extended family support systems and the role(s) of these networks in clients' lives. Counselors must also be able to understand and honor the holistic viewpoint of clients, including the important role of ancestors, as they conceptualize and intervene. Approaches that emphasize the strengthening of interpersonal relationships may also be particularly beneficial. However, the most important strategy counselors can use to provide culturally appropriate services may be to listen carefully to the narratives of clients and the worldviews and beliefs embedded within them (L. Lopez-Levers, personal communication, August 8, 2011).

Another important issue is the identification of counseling modalities that are likely to be most appropriate and effective for use with Batswana. Much of the current practice of counseling in Botswana is done individually. Yet in the collectivist culture of Botswana, change at the individual level is often of secondary importance to change at the group level. Likewise, group processes have traditionally been used to promote change. Similarly, the extended family plays a very important role in individuals' lives and can be a strong influence on individuals' decision making. Group and family counseling may therefore be more culturally appropriate modalities than individual counseling, although work in these areas is just beginning to emerge.

Currently some group work does take place. A few psychoeducational groups are offered at the Careers and Counseling Center at the University of Botswana. Groups are also "a popular delivery format for other services including HIV preventions education in the workplace and guidance lessons in schools. However, these services are largely didactic in nature and are frequently delivered by paraprofessionals or others lacking formal group training" (Nitza, 2011, p. 224). Efforts are currently under way to advance the use of group interventions. In 2004, the first and second authors along with several other Batswana colleagues initiated a series of group counseling training workshops.

A recent study of group processes by the second author, conducted during her year as a Fulbright Scholar at the University of Botswana, found that although group dynamics appear to operate differently than in Western group counseling models, adaptations of such models have the potential to be effective interventions. In particular, group experiences that promoted cognitive insight and self-exploration were ranked highly by participants (Nitza, 2011).

Little work has been done in the area of couples and family counseling. However, with increased awareness of issues such as domestic violence and couples with discordant HIV status (in which one partner is HIV positive and the other is not), interest in this area has been increasing. It is an area much in need of further advancement in terms of practice, research, and the indigenization of Western marriage and family therapy models.

Research into counseling effectiveness or the efficacy of specific theories and interventions has taken a back seat to practice and training development in Botswana. Currently little outcome data exist to guide practitioners. However, studies are beginning to emerge. In addition to the Nitza (2011) study described previously, a recent countrywide study conducted by Stockton, Paul, Morran, Yebei, Chang, and Voils-Levenda (in press) examined the perceptions and experiences of HIV/AIDS counselors in Botswana. Major findings indicated that the majority of the counselors were satisfied with the quality of the training that they received, perceived themselves as effective counselors, were relatively untroubled by social stigma issues, and perceived few barriers to effective counseling. However, findings also indicated that a large percentage of those counselors had received 8 weeks or less of formal training, generally received little or no in-service supervision, and in many cases experienced stress and burnout. In addition, counselors who had completed more academic work were less likely to perceive themselves as competent counselors, leading the investigators to speculate that counselors with more training understood more of what they did not know as opposed to the certitude of those with less knowledge and training. Other perceived problem areas included the need for more learning resources and additional training related to promoting safe sex practices and medication adherence among clients.

As the profession continues to develop and expand, the need for further research is essential. Such research must include the extent to which Western counseling theories and interventions are effective with clients in Botswana, how such theories can most effectively be combined with indigenous practices, and how Western and traditional models of healing can best support each other for the benefit of clients.

Diversity Issues

Like counselors in any other place in the world, counselors in Botswana need to be able to deal competently with diversity issues, including issues of ethnicity, gender, and sexual orientation. Cultural differences also exist between the urban areas around the capital city of Gaborone (which houses the University of Botswana) and the rural areas and villages that make up much of the rest of the country.

Ethnicity

Tribal affiliation is the primary ethnic distinction among the Batswana. The largest ethnic group in Botswana is the Tswana, which makes up 79% of the population. Eleven other ethnic groups as well as a small population of Whites and Asians make up the rest of the population. Among the smaller ethnic groups are the Basarwa (San), who are considered to be the only people indigenous to the country. The plight of the San is the subject of ongoing contention and debate in the country.

Although Setswana and English are the two official languages of the country and the languages of instruction, many tribes have their own languages that are the primary languages of their people. In the group counseling workshops taught in Botswana by the first and second authors, many of the participants were teachers of guidance and counseling in primary and secondary schools. These participants discussed the cultural divides they had experienced when assigned to schools in villages of tribes different from their own where they did not know the local language spoken by their students.

Gender

Despite much progress, particularly in terms of educational achievement and employment opportunities, gender inequality remains a major social challenge facing Botswana (Osei-Hwedie et al., 2006). Notions of gender discrimination and inequality are embedded in many of the country's cultural traditions, including the stories, myths, songs, and proverbs that are a cornerstone of the oral history of the country (Chilisa, Mmonadibe, & Malinga, 2011). A number of other economic, social, and cultural forces continue to reinforce these embedded notions of gender inequality. Although this gender inequality predated the arrival of HIV/AIDS in the country, the consequences are now directly life threatening: A lack of social, interpersonal, and economic power puts girls and women at greater risk of HIV infection.

A major need in the counseling profession in Botswana is the development of counseling strategies and interventions that empower girls and women to resist the oppressive messages and broader social forces that endanger them. A recent advancement in such efforts was the development of a group-based intervention titled *Mbizi* (Nitza, Chilisa, & Makwinja-Morara, 2010). Using a series of traditional practices adapted to a Western psychoeducational group context, the broad objectives of the *Mbizi* group were to heighten girls' awareness of the social contexts in which they live and how these contexts influence their behaviors and to assist them in developing efficacy, skills, and a supportive peer network for coping with challenges.

Sexual Orientation

The sexual minority population in Botswana is an at-risk yet underserved group. Not only are there strong cultural taboos against homosexuality, but homosexual activity is illegal and punishable by a prison sentence of up to 7 years (Ehlers, Zuyderduin, & Oosthuizen, 2001). What is more, Batswana continue to deny the existence of homosexuality in the country (Phaladze & Tlou, 2006). Efforts by the Botswana human rights group Ditshwanelo and the group Legabibo (Lesbians, Gays, and Bisexuals of Botswana) are increasing awareness of homosexuality. However, the sexual minority population may be at risk for social and mental health difficulties that are currently not being sufficiently addressed.

Counselor Education

Counselors in Botswana are educated in a variety of settings. Counselors are trained at the master's and doctoral levels at the University of Botswana through its counselor education program in the Department of Educational Foundations in the Faculty of Education. At the graduate level, clinical experiences are an important part of the curriculum. Students conduct practica and internships in a variety of settings. The University of Botswana Careers and Counseling Center offers placements for counseling students to conduct practica and internships supervised by professional counselors. In addition to the University Counseling Service, students are encouraged and assisted to seek placement in other institutions and agencies for diverse experiences. Graduates can become full-time school counselors or work in other settings, including hospitals and prisons.

In addition to graduate-level training, the program offers counselor training at the undergraduate level. Training at the undergraduate level is also conducted at five teacher-training institutions. Undergraduate programs educate students to become teacher-counselors. Students in such programs normally train for two teaching subjects, for instance English as their major subject and guidance and counseling as their minor subject. Graduates are normally assigned to schools based on their major subject; they then teach guidance and counseling as a secondary subject. Many also do counseling because of the large demand for these services, although they have not been specifically trained to provide this type of direct service (L. Mokgwathise, personal communication, August 2, 2011).

Training for most paraprofessional counselors usually consists of only 4 weeks of classroom training on the basics of HIV/AIDS counseling and 4 weeks of supervised clinical field experience. With such limited training, these counselors are severely challenged to successfully deal with the mental health issues of their HIV-positive clients. Currently there are no clear guidelines for the treatment of mental health conditions and disorders for individuals living with HIV (Reece, McBride, Shacham, & Williams, 2005), making the provision of effective treatment more difficult and the training of HIV/AIDS counselors challenging.

The Future

Although counseling in Botswana has become relatively well established, it lacks a formal legal identity. Thus, efforts to establish this through accreditation and the development of uniform standards, as well as public recognition, can be expected. In the United States this typically takes a major effort and occurs over a period of several years. Also, there is a need to develop culturally relevant interventions or treatment approaches in specialized areas such as sexual abuse, domestic violence, substance abuse, and HIV/AIDS. Understanding that a large number of clients will also be consulting with traditional healers should lead to greater collaboration between Western-trained counselors and traditional healers.

Botswana is increasing its bandwidth to allow for greater use of the Internet. This will make it possible for counselor educators to use the latest technology and for counselors to use technology more in their practice. The beginnings of this trend can be seen in the use of telephone counseling for those in underserved and/or remote areas.

There is increasing interest at the level of the Ministry of Education in applied research and evaluation studies that provide useful information. Therefore, more of this type of study is likely to be done in the next few years. This can include research that supports indigenization and the development of culturally relevant practices.

References

Chilisa, B., Mmonadibe, P., & Malinga, T. (2011). Indigenizing research methods: Language, texts, and stories in the construction of adolescent sexual behaviors. *Pula: Botswana Journal of African Studies, 25,* 17–32.

Ehlers, V. J., Zuyderduin, A., & Oosthuizen, M. J. (2001). The well-being of gays, lesbians and bisexuals in Botswana. *Journal of Advanced Nursing, 35,* 848–856.

Heald, S. (2005). Abstain or die: The development of HIV/AIDS policy in Botswana. *Journal of Biosocial Science, 38,* 29–41. doi:10.1017/S0021932005000933

Joint United Nations Programme on HIV/AIDS & World Health Organization. (2008). *Report on the global AIDS epidemic.* Geneva, Switzerland: United Nations.

Nitza, A. (2011). Group processes in experiential training groups in Botswana. *Journal for Specialists in Group Work, 36*, 222–242.

Nitza, A., Chilisa, B., & Makwinja-Morara, V. (2010). *Mbizi:* Empowerment and HIV/AIDS prevention for adolescent girls in Botswana. *Journal for Specialists in Group Work, 35*, 105–114. doi:10.1080/01933921003705990

Osei-Hwedie, K., Ntseane, D., & Jacques, G. (2006). Searching for appropriateness in social work education on Botswana: The process of developing a Master in Social Work (MSW) programme in a "developing" country. *Social Work Education, 4*, 569–590.

Phaladze, N., & Tlou, S. (2006). Gender and HIV/AIDS in Botswana: A focus on inequalities and discrimination. *Gender & Development, 14*, 23–35.

Reece, M., McBride, K., Shacham, E., & Williams, B. (2005). Therapist's expectations of psychotherapy duration for individuals living with HIV. *Journal of HIV/AIDS and Social Services, 4*(1), 71–89.

Republic of Botswana Ministry of Education. (1994). *Revised national policy on education.* Gaborone, Botswana: Botswana Government Printers.

Sabone, M. B. (2009). The promotion of mental health through cultural values, institutions, and practices: A reflection on some aspects of Botswana culture. *Issues in Mental Health Nursing, 30*, 777–787. doi:10.3109/01612840903263579

Scholarship Development Enterprise Africa. (2010). *Psychosocial support services and mechanisms for delivery in the Ministry of Education and Skills Development.* Gaborone, Botswana: Author.

Seloilwe, E. S., & Thupayagale-Tshweneagae, G. (2007). Community mental health care in Botswana: Approaches and opportunities. *International Nursing Review, 54*, 173–178.

Stockton, R., Nitza, A., & Bhusumane, D.-B. (2010). The development of professional counseling in Botswana. *Journal of Counseling & Development, 88*, 9–12.

Stockton, R., Paul, T., Morran, K., Yebei, P., Chang, S., & Voils-Levenda, A. (in press). A survey of HIV/AIDS counselors in Botswana: Satisfaction with training and supervision, self-perceived effectiveness and reactions to counseling HIV positive clients. *Journal of HIV/AIDS & Social Services.*

Stockton, R., Terry, L., & Nitza, A. (2007, January). *Group counselor trainings in Africa.* Presentation at the Hawaii International Conference on Education, Honolulu.

• • •

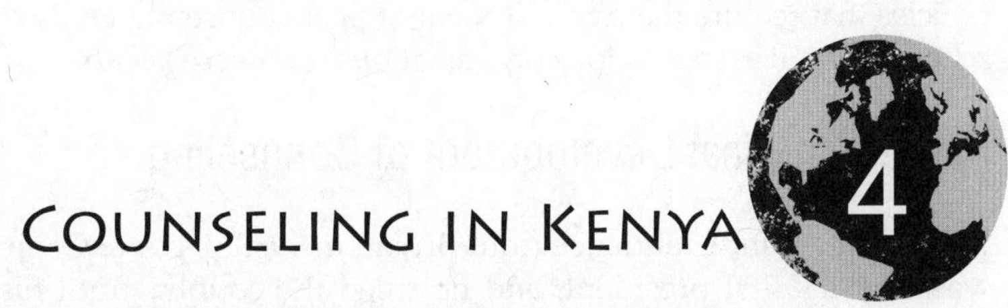

Counseling in Kenya

Jane E. Atieno Okech and Muthoni Kimemia

The counseling profession in Kenya has experienced exponential growth in the past 20 years. Much of this growth has been in direct response to multiple social and economic changes during this period. The concept of counseling, however, is hardly new in Kenya. Indeed, as the majority of African societies have very strong oral traditions, the talking cure has been around for a long time. In traditional African communities, interpersonal and social problems were addressed through well-established social structures that consisted of relatives, clan elders, and traditional healers. There was also an informal but well-established order in which these parties were consulted, beginning with close family members and extending outward to include clan elders or traditional healers if the issues were not resolved at the nuclear and extended family levels. Personal and family matters were not to be discussed outside of the family or clan unless all previous interventions proved unsuccessful. The practice of discussing personal or family problems with a stranger was unusual and was generally frowned on. As a result, Kenyans were initially slow to embrace the formal process of counseling and the counseling profession. The growth of counseling in Kenya can be attributed to several factors: (a) the onset of the HIV/AIDS epidemic and the establishment of Voluntary Counseling and Testing (VCT) centers to address the epidemic, (b) an increase in incidents of student unrest and violence in schools, and (c) governmental policies that emphasized the need for the provision of guidance and counseling services to Kenya's youth in both social and academic settings (Ministry of Home Affairs, Heritage, and Sports, 2002).

Since Kenya gained independence from Britain in 1963, numerous reports from commissions set up by the government have highlighted the need for professional counseling services, particularly in the school system. The Ominde Report of 1964 (Republic of Kenya, 1964) was the first of several postindependence reports that placed emphasis on the provision of counseling services in schools and to the general public. Earlier reports were more concerned with career guidance in efforts to prepare a workforce to take over jobs that were occupied by colonialists. Later reports broadened in scope with regard to the need for counseling services, especially among the youth (Ministry of Home Affairs, Heritage, and Sports, 2002).

The development of the counseling profession was also fueled by the emergence of HIV/AIDS. In response to the crisis, the government, in conjunction with many nongovernmental organizations, set up VCT centers around the country. A "Know Your Status" campaign that urged people to get tested for HIV helped to popularize counseling among the general population. However, counseling at the VCT centers was limited to brief pretest and posttest sessions and was provided by individuals who lacked adequate counselor training. In addition, the introduction of counseling to the majority of Kenyans was in the highly stigmatized context of HIV/AIDS, resulting in a similar stigmatization of counseling. More recently, student unrests in schools, which have been accompanied by unprecedented violence, have highlighted the need for counseling services in schools. The Ministry of Education and the Teachers Service Commission have taken note of these issues and have responded with policies that require the establishment of peer counseling clubs and guidance counselors in schools as well as in religious organizations that serve youth.

The Historical Development of Counseling

Kenya gained independence from Britain in 1963 (Ogot & Ochieng, 1995). Jomo Kenyatta was Kenya's first president, and he ruled the country until his death in 1978. His vice-president, Daniel arap Moi, took over the leadership of the country and ruled Kenya for 24 years until he was replaced by Mwai Kibaki in 2002. Although Kenya has enjoyed relative peace and stability since its independence, there have been incidents of national unrest, such as one following a failed military coup in 1982 and civil unrest following a disputed general election outcome in 2008. During the latter episode, more than 1,500 people were killed and more than 300,000 individuals were forced to flee their homes. According to the Humanitarian Policy Group (2008), approximately 100,000 children were internally displaced, with as many as 75,000 children scattered across more than 200 camps for displaced people. The displacement of people and the trauma of the civil unrest created a tremendous need for professional counseling services and qualified personnel to provide these services.

Kenya is also an economic leader in the East and Central African region. Its key sources of foreign income include tourism, tea and coffee farming, and, more recently, horticultural farming. However, the country continues to struggle with a high rate of unemployment, 40% in 2009 (World Bank, 2010). Most jobs are concentrated in urban areas, creating a high rate of rural–urban migration in which people move to major urban areas in search of employment. This movement has caused significant disruption for communities and families, and this has contributed to the disintegration of the traditional support systems that served as a safety net for mental and emotional problems. As a result, there is a growing need for counseling services in both rural and urban areas (Okech & Kimemia, 2012).

The education system in Kenya has also undergone several changes since independence. From 1963 to 1985, Kenya continued the British system of education that was in place during the colonial era. This system consisted of 7 years of primary school education, 4 years of high school at the Ordinary Level, 2 years of higher learning at the Advanced Level, and 3 years of university education. In 1985, Kenya changed to a system similar to the American system of education that became known as the 8-4-4 system (Amutabi, 2003). In this system, students have 8 years of primary school education, 4 years of high school education, and 4 years of university education. At the end of both primary and high school, students take national examinations that serve as entrance exams for the next level. A government policy offering free primary education was introduced in 2002. This policy resulted in a substantial increase in the number of students seeking primary education. Unfortunately, the increase in the number of students was not matched with an increase in resources, and many public schools were overwhelmed with an influx of students in the face of limited infrastructure. At the same time, students continue to compete for limited places in high schools. A growing trend is for middle-class families to take their children to the many private schools and academies that have mushroomed all over the country as people seek education of better quality than that offered in the overpopulated, understaffed, and underresourced public schools (Mukudi, 2004).

There are also a limited number of places at the university level. Admission into public universities is highly competitive and includes a complex qualifying process based on performance on the national exam taken at the end of high school (Amutabi, 2003). For a long time there were only four public universities (University of Nairobi, Kenyatta, Moi, and Egerton University) and three private universities (United States International University, Baraton, and Daystar University). However, from 2002 to 2012, the number of public universities has risen to seven, with 15 constituent colleges together serving more than 160,000 students (Mugenda, 2011). There are a total of 27 private universities with a combined enrollment of more than 200,000 students. A decade ago only two private universities had counselor training programs (United States International University and Daystar). These offerings have now increased, with each of the public universities and other private universities also offering a counseling or guidance program.

The Current Status of Counseling

The practice of mental health counseling is expanding greatly in Kenya in response to educational, economic, and social factors. Mental health counselors, both professionally trained and untrained, can now be found practicing in private settings, institutions of higher learning, and community-based agencies. The practice of mental health counseling has evolved from the early 1980s, when the Catholic Church predominantly engaged in counseling to encourage the use of natural family planning methods; to the 1990s, when the focus was predominantly on pre– and post–HIV testing counseling in VCT centers; to the current period, in which the government has developed policies that recognize the value of counseling and now requires the provision of counseling opportunities to youth in both academic and social settings (Ministry of Home Affairs, Heritage, and Sports, 2002). In a recent study on the practice of counseling in Kenya, participating counselors identified counseling as necessary to address the challenges of "HIV/AIDS, drug usage, addictions, marital difficulties, adolescent sexuality, culturally based gender inequalities, child abuse, female gender mutilation, and the empowerment of women" (McGuiness, Alred, Cohen, Hunt, & Robson, 2001, p. 297).

The development of school counseling as a practice has been influenced by the same factors that have boosted the growth of the practice of mental health counseling. Public schools in Kenya have traditionally placed a great deal of emphasis on academic achievement. This achievement-based approach to education has placed students under a great deal of pressure, a situation further compounded by the shortage of resources, the toll of HIV/AIDS on students and their family structures, behavioral issues attributed to access to recreational drugs, and limited postsecondary training and employment opportunities for students in the country. These factors, along with authoritarian school administration styles, have been blamed for the increased incidences of student unrest in schools and the escalating school violence (Okech & Kimemia, 2012). The recent violence in schools has extended beyond the boycotting of classes to the destruction of school and public property and to physical violence against fellow students (East African Standard Team, 2001). The 2008 parliamentary and presidential elections, which saw widespread community-based violence and interethnic conflict that extended into schools, has highlighted the need for counseling services within schools.

The need for counseling services in schools has been recognized by the government of Kenya through the development of the Kenya National Youth Policy by the Ministry of Home Affairs, Heritage, and Sports (2002). Although Section 8.2 of this policy contains key directives about the establishment of guidance counseling units and peer counseling programs in all public schools and other academic and religious institutions, it does not address the minimum qualifications and training requirements of the counselors who would implement such policies. As a result, although guidance counseling units and peers counseling programs are now widespread in public schools, postsecondary academic institutions, and religious institutions, they are mostly run by teachers and instructors with minimal, if any, training in the practice of counseling. This is in contrast to private and international schools and universities, in which counseling units have traditionally been run by trained professional counselors and psychologists.

As the practice of mental health and school counseling expands in Kenya, the profession's greatest challenge remains the lack of regulatory bodies to oversee the training, practice, and credentialing of counselors. The absence of a regulatory body makes it difficult to obtain an accurate count of the number of professional counselors and their specific areas of practice. However, from the number of HIV/AIDS VCT centers that are staffed by counselors of varying qualifications, it follows that the largest numbers of counselors work in VCT centers, schools (primary and secondary), hospitals, and child protection agencies. The emergence of several professional counselor associations may be seen as a response to the vacuum created by the lack of regulatory bodies to monitor the practice, training, and credentialing of counselors.

The two main national professional associations in Kenya are the Kenya Association of Professional Counsellors (KAPC) and the Kenya Counselling Association (KCA). Each of these associations holds independent professional national conferences and offers training and supervision services. The KAPC offers professional training programs in counseling (Diploma, BA, MA, and PhD in collaboration with the University of Manchester, England) through its School of Counseling Studies; professional counseling services to individuals, groups, and corporate bodies; and chartered counselor designations to qualifying members (KAPC, 2009). The KCA has focused its efforts on advocacy for supervision credentials and more recently has begun to offer "institutional accreditation in addition to seven different accreditation levels for its members based on the members' professional training which ranges from level 1, ordinary membership to level 7, senior supervisor" (KCA, 2011). The existence of two independent competing professional associations that are actively involved in the advocacy, training, and credentialing process raises unique challenges in a country where professional counseling is just beginning to receive formal recognition. Because it is still in its formative years, counseling remains less recognized and impactful than psychology. The profession of psychology is well established, with a single national professional association, namely the Kenya Psychological Association. It also has fairly consistent training requirements and standards in addition to a clear professional function that counseling has yet to establish. In many ways the profession of social work is facing the same formative challenges as the counseling profession. There are multiple social work associations and institutions of training, with varied standards of training; this creates a multitude of challenges for the emerging profession. Among the three helping professions—counseling, psychology, and social work—psychology enjoys the greatest recognition and has the most established training programs in Kenya's institutions of higher learning.

Best Counseling Practices

Formal counseling as a practice is an emerging profession in Kenya. As a result, the manner in which counseling is viewed and practiced is greatly influenced by the culture and beliefs held by the founders of the profession in Kenya. The same is also largely true about the curriculum used in training emerging counselors in the country. In the early years of the profession, the evolving curriculum was based on that of the country of origin of the trainers and the perception of these trainers of what was relevant to Kenyan counselors.

Depending on the Kenyan institution in which they were trained, counselors were likely to be grounded in a curriculum based on British or U.S. requirements for training counselors. This pattern is now changing, with institutions moving toward the development of more culturally relevant curricula. As indicated earlier, the lack of regulatory bodies to oversee the training curriculum and the practice and credentialing of counselors renders the practice of counseling as diverse in nature as the training institutions in the country.

The counseling process, assessment, and action planning depend on the kind of counseling services sought by clients. For example, if clients are seeking counseling related to HIV testing, then the protocol is determined by the manual at the specific VCT center. If clients are seeking family planning counseling, then the information and services offered may be determined by the needs of particular clients, their gender, or their marital status (Kim, Kols, Mwarogo, & Aswasum, 2000). In schools, counseling services tend to be based on a talk therapy format. The nature of the counseling interaction is determined by the gender and age of the student and the kind of school (secular or religious). Referrals may be made to peer counselors but are only made beyond the school in cases of serious mental health concerns. In both school and mental health settings, assessments are informal, with minimal documentation of the counseling process. In all settings the initial step usually involves a history taking, in which clients (and their family members) get the opportunity to tell their story. The exception tends to be in VCT centers, in which clients have the option to provide a history or not. The history taking is followed by an informal conceptualization of the clients' concerns and the development of a treatment plan, which is also shared with clients.

Because the introduction of the counseling profession was based on Western practices and ethical standards, the concept of confidentiality in the Western mode was also introduced in Kenya. The most challenging aspect of navigating confidentiality stems from the fact that (a) sharing personal challenges with a professional stranger was until recently an alien concept, (b) sharing personal struggles that are kept private from family members is also alien, and (c) developing an intimate relationship with a professional stranger who does not become an honorary member of the family is also unusual. Therefore, unlike in the traditional approach in which the entire family, community elders, and close relatives were often drawn in or notified of a challenging interpersonal or intrapersonal issue, the new form of counseling is unusual in that it does not necessarily involve relatives in the process except if the client is a minor. School counselors typically notify and engage significant family members or guardians when there are concerns with the academic performance or behavioral patterns of a particular student.

Counseling of all kinds is predominantly done face to face in either an office, a church, or the home of the client. The use of informal settings such as the client's home is typical when a family intervention is deemed necessary. In all of these settings counseling predominantly utilizes the talk therapy format, which may also incorporate the use of metaphors in interventions with clients. The utilization of art and play therapy is more common in private school settings and community-based agencies that offer counseling services to minors. There has also been minimal incorporation of the Internet or technology in the practice of counseling. With the rapid increase in the number of Internet users—which stood at 7.8 million in 2010, or 19.9% of the population (Communications Commission of Kenya, 2010)—the Internet is the next frontier for counselor training and practice in Kenya. Although current and specific labor market information related to the counseling profession is not available, the growth of the profession and the expansion of Internet service are sure to change this in the future.

Diversity Issues

There are more than 54 tribes in Kenya, each with its own language and set of cultural practices. This diversity in cultural background requires special considerations in the design and delivery of counseling services. More than half of Kenya's high schools are also boarding schools in which students reside for 3 months at a time, the length of a school term. It is at this stage that mental and emotional problems reach their peak and the need for counseling services is greatest (Nyutu & Gysbers, 2008). Boarding schools also tend to have a mix of students and teachers from various tribes and varying socioeconomic backgrounds. Teacher-counselors must bear in mind the social and cultural differences among their students and tailor their services in order to meet the needs of individual students. An emerging challenge has been the acknowledgment of same-sex relationships, particularly in boarding schools. In a country whose constitution contains a clause banning homosexual behavior, this may present unique challenges for both students as well as teacher-counselors.

In most traditional African communities, there are very clear gender roles as well as rules that govern relationships between the sexes. However, given the influence of colonization, exposure to Western education and media, and general social evolution, the extent to which an individual or community adheres to the established social norms regarding relationships and gender roles may vary. Youth as well as individuals who have received a Western education might hold views that differ greatly from those of their parents. People in rural areas may also have views that are vastly different from those of individuals who live in urban areas. As a result, there are conflicting understandings of roles and responsibilities in relationships. By the same token, when duties and responsibilities are shared in a manner that contravenes tradition, the extended family may find this to be an objectionable arrangement. Counselors therefore need to be familiar with varying orientations and work with clients to equip them with skills to navigate traditional expectations and emerging redefinitions of gender roles. This calls for counselors who are well informed and flexible enough to work within the framework of varying levels of cultural identification.

The majority of Kenyans are not able to access counseling services, as the cost is often prohibitive. The typical rate of 1,000 Kenya Shillings ($1.12) for a counseling session (Amani Counseling Center and Training Institute, 2011) is beyond the reach of the average Kenyan. Most private practitioners charge even higher rates, thereby perpetuating the notion that counseling is for the elite. It is important for counselors to come up with innovative ways to reach the masses of Kenyans who need counseling services but who are unable to access them because of the exorbitant cost.

Counselor Education

The increased need for counseling services has resulted in a corresponding increase in interest in counseling as a career. This has led to a need for counselor training, and institutions have responded by creating programmatic offerings in counseling and/or guidance at various educational levels. Currently all seven public universities in Kenya and some of their constituent colleges offer either a bachelor's or master's degree in counseling and/or guidance. In addition, many of Kenya's private universities and independent institutions offer counseling programs that award certificates or degrees at the bachelor's, master's, or doctoral level.

A review of available course offerings for the various counseling programs indicates a variety of approaches and curriculum among them. Kenyatta University, for example, houses various counseling degrees in different departments. The School of Humanities and Social Sciences offers a BA in counseling, whereas the School of Applied Human Sciences has a BA in counseling psychology. In addition, the School of Education has a master of education degree in guidance and counseling and a diploma in the same. Egerton University has a diploma in guidance and counseling, a postgraduate diploma in guidance and counseling, and a master of education in guidance and counseling and science education. The University of Nairobi offers a bachelor's degree in counseling psychology, whereas Moi University has a bachelor of education degree in guidance and counseling.

Core courses in these programs include many of the courses found in counseling programs in other parts of the world. These include theories of counseling, techniques, tests and measurements, group dynamics, human development, career counseling, and research methods. There are experiential components in the form of practica and attachments. More recently, the public universities have made clear efforts to offer courses that relate to topical concerns in Kenya. Egerton University, for example, has courses such as Biology of HIV/AIDS and Society, Policy and Welfare Administration, Psychology of Refugees and Displaced Persons, Food Security and Development in Africa, and Culture and Human Behavior. Courses such as Project Planning and Evaluation, Conflict Resolution and Management, Society and International Humanitarian Law, and Disaster Management are also well placed to prepare counselors for the realities of working with nongovernmental organizations.

The BEd degree in guidance and counseling at Moi University is clearly geared toward the preparation of teacher-counselors. The course work for this degree includes two courses in a teaching subject in each semester and a semester of student teaching. The implication is that individuals with a degree in guidance and counseling will also be teachers who are charged with teaching academic subjects in addition to performing their counseling duties. This degree also includes course work in pastoral counseling, counseling delinquents, and terminal illness and bereavement counseling.

Counselor education is clearly quite varied in terms of curriculum, the nature of institutions that offer training, and the duration of training programs. The result is that counselors vary greatly in their professional training and level of expertise.

The Future

The Kenyan government has instituted many policy changes in an effort to provide counseling services across the country. For example, in 2002, the Ministry of Home Affairs, Heritage, and Sports released a National Youth Policy, in which they stressed the importance of counseling and guidance services for Kenya's youth. Similarly, in 2005, the Ministry of Education, Science, and Technology instituted the Kenya Education Support Program, which included guidance and counseling services. The Ministry of Health (2006) continues to expand its mental health services beyond the initial programs that targeted persons living with HIV/AIDS. All of these initiatives indicate significant progress in recognizing the value of counseling services as well as the growing need for consolidated efforts to address the need for trained counselors.

The entry of major public universities into the counselor training arena is a welcome addition that will hopefully move the profession forward. For example, the bachelors of guidance and counseling programs at Kenyatta and Egerton Universities seek to train teacher-counselors. The curricula indicate that these programs seek to train teachers who will have the skills to double as counselors in schools. However, this raises questions about the professional identity of students graduating from these programs. Yet it may be that this is the way of the future for professional school counselors. In the face of limited resources, public schools may not have sufficient funds to hire full-time counselors. Having teachers who are trained counselors, or vice versa, who can serve the dual roles of teacher and counselor might be one way to provide counseling services to students in an environment with limited resources. Although the appointment of teacher-counselors by the Teachers Service Commission has helped in this regard, the selection process for these teacher-counselors is currently based on a loose set of criteria that head teachers subjectively interpret and that do not include professional training. The offering of the guidance and counseling degree is an innovative step in the creation of a formal training process for this category of teacher-counselors.

Although the increased number of public and private universities that offer counselor training programs should augur well for the growth of the counseling profession in Kenya, there are concerns about the quality of these programs. The majority of private universities are for-profit institutions, and the major public universities have also adopted an entrepreneurial approach. With the influx of counselor training programs, care should be taken to ensure that the quality of training is not compromised. Furthermore, there is need for the Kenya Institute of Education (KIE), the body charged with the development of curriculum, to partner with the public universities and other counselor training entities to develop a core curriculum for counselor training in the country. This will ensure that all graduates of these programs meet a certain level of basic competency, thereby lending credence to any emergent certification or licensure process that may follow.

It is worth noting that the key professional organizations for counselors in Kenya are all engaged in counselor training and supervision. Professional organizations in most professions seek to provide leadership as well as professional development opportunities for their members. In order to do this, they often adopt a role that is complementary to that of training institutions rather than competitive. The multiple functions served by the professional organizations for counselors in Kenya create a conflict of interest that needs to be addressed if these institutions are to become key players in the regulation of professional practice and training (Okech & Kimemia, 2012).

We recommend the formation of an independent body under the oversight of the KIE that would be charged with identifying core competencies that are to be required of all counselors in Kenya and a curriculum that will address these competencies. The affiliation of this entity with the KIE would give it the necessary governmental mandate so that all key players in the counseling field recognize it. This body should have representatives from public and private universities and government ministries in areas such as health, education, and youth that have counseling and guidance as a major focus.

Furthermore, we recommend the formation of another body whose main charge would be to regulate the postgraduate practice of professional counseling and supervision. This body would develop a nationally recognized counselor certification and/or licensure process and ensure that only those individuals who have had adequate training can brand themselves professional counselors. Given the various levels of counselor training, it is particularly important to have several levels of certification that would recognize this variation; for example, those graduating from a 1-year diploma program may not qualify for the same level of certification as those graduating from a 4-year degree program or a graduate program. This organization would also develop a culturally congruent code of ethics for the profession in Kenya, enforce ethical practice among counseling agencies as well as individual practitioners, and address any ethical violations that are raised by the public against individual practitioners or agencies. This body may also develop a separate set of competencies for the retroactive certification of individuals who have already completed their training and are already in practice.

In conclusion, current developments indicate a trajectory of growth for the counseling profession in Kenya. The challenges discussed here are not unique to Kenya, and an examination of the history of the counseling profession in countries in which it is more established indicates that many of the same challenges were faced in the formative years. In order to sustain the growth of the counseling profession in Kenya, it is imperative that counselor training programs continue to respond to the current needs of the population. Counselor training programs must collaborate with other stakeholders in the development of a curriculum that is culturally congruent. If practicing counselors are deemed to be culturally relevant, Kenyans are more likely to see value in the counseling process and to seek professional help when needed, thereby ensuring the continued growth of the profession.

References

Amani Counseling Center and Training Institute. (2011). *Counselling services.* Retrieved from http://www.amanicentre.org/counselling.php

Amutabi, M. N. (2003). Political interference in the running of education in post-independence Kenya: A critical retrospection. *International Journal of Educational Development, 23*(2), 127–144. doi:10.1016/S0738-0593(01)00055-4

Communications Commission of Kenya. (2010). *Quarterly sector statistics report.* Retrieved from www.cck.go.ke

East African Standard Team. (2001, April 23). School tragedies related to indiscipline. *The East African Standard Media Group,* p. 8.

Humanitarian Policy Group. (2008). *Crisis in Kenya: Land displacement and the search for "durable" solutions.* Retrieved from http://www.odi.org.uk/resources/download/1522.pdf

Kenya Association of Professional Counsellors. (2009). *Counsellor training courses.* Retrieved from http://www.kapc.or.ke/

Kenya Counselling Association. (2011). *Our objectives?* Retrieved from http://www.kenyacounsellingassociation.org/

Kim, M. Y., Kols, A., Mwarogo, P., & Aswasum, D. (2000). Differences in counseling men and women: Family planning in Kenya. *Patient Education & Counseling, 39,* 37–47.

McGuiness, J., Alred, G., Cohen, N., Hunt, K., & Robson, M. (2001). Globalizing counselling: Humanistic counseling in Kenya. *British Journal of Guidance & Counselling, 29*(3), 293–300. doi:10.1080/03069880120073012

Ministry of Education, Science, and Technology. (2005, July 25). *Kenya Education Sector Support Programme 2005-2010.* Retrieved from http://planipolis.iiep.unesco.org/upload/Kenya/Kenya%20KESSP%20FINAL%202005.pdf

Ministry of Health. (2006, October). *Trainer's manual for rape trauma counselors in Kenya.* Retrieved from http://www.svconference2008.org/publications/Rape%20trauma%20counsellors%20training%20manual.pdf

Ministry of Home Affairs, Heritage, and Sports. (2002). *Kenya National Youth Policy.* Nairobi, Kenya: Government of Kenya.

Mugenda, O. (2011, November). *Introduction to Kenyatta University.* Presentation at the International Association of Universities International Conference, Nairobi, Kenya.

Mukudi, E. (2004). Education for all: A framework for addressing the persisting illusion for the Kenyan context. *International Journal of Educational Development, 24*(3), 231–240. doi:10.1016/j.ijedudev.2003.10.009

Nyutu, P. N., & Gysbers, N. C. (2008). Assessing the counselling needs of high school students in Kenya. *International Journal for Educational and Vocational Guidance, 8*(2), 83–94. doi:10.1007/s10775-008-9140-1

Ogot, B. A., & Ochieng, W. R. (1995). *Decolonization and independence in Kenya—1940-1993.* London, England: James Currey.

Okech, J. E. A., & Kimemia, M. (2012). Professional counseling in Kenya: History, current status, and future trends. *Journal of Counseling & Development, 90,* 107–118.

Republic of Kenya. (1964). *Kenya Education Commission Report Part 1.* Nairobi, Kenya: Government Printer.

World Bank. (2010). *Kenya at the tipping point? With a special focus on the ICT revolution and mobile money.* Retrieved from http://siteresources.worldbank.org/KENYAEXTN/Resources/KEU-Dec_2010_powerpoint.pdf

• • •

Counseling in Nigeria

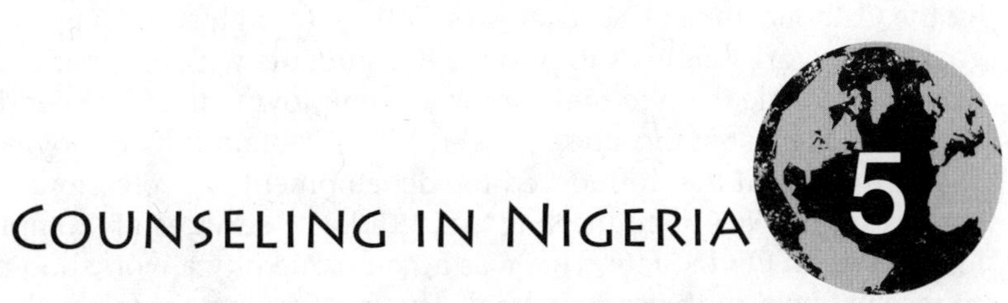

Aneneosa A. G. Okocha

Nigeria is often described as the "giant of Africa" because, with more than 152 million inhabitants, it is the most populous country on the continent (Central Intelligence Agency, 2011). It is located on the western coast of the continent, has a presidential system of democratic government, and is about one third larger than the state of Texas. English is the official language, but the indigenous population speaks more than 50 languages spread across 250 distinct ethnic groups. The largest ethnic groups are the Hausa-Fulani and Kanuri, who are mostly in the north; the Igbo, mainly in the southeast; and the Yoruba, predominantly in the southwest. Other ethnic groups, such as the Efik, Annang, Ibibio, Urhobo, Edo, Ishan, Ijaw, Tiv, and Itsekiri, are sometimes regarded as minorities in the country.

Nigeria gained its political independence in October 1960. Today it consists of 36 states and Abuja, the Federal Capitol Territory located in the center of the country. Religious practice is diverse and reflects primarily Christian and Moslem influences. Islam is embraced by the Hausa-Fulani and Yoruba, whereas Christianity is practiced by the Igbo, the Yoruba, and the ethnic minorities. Indigenous religious traditions are also important among some Nigerian ethnic groups.

Although they are religiously diverse, Nigerians are generally characterized by a collectivist worldview in which the group or community takes precedence over the individual (Akande, 1999). Thus, families and extended family members are very important in the Nigerian culture. Nigeria is also a patriarchal country; the man is often recognized as the head of the family, and significant gender role differences exist (Okocha & Perrone, 1992).

The Historical Development of Counseling

Traditional or indigenous methods of counseling and healing were always used by Nigerians prior to the emergence of professional counseling (Alao, 2004; Gesinde, 2008; Makinde, 1980; Pelter, 1995). In fact, the World Health Organization (2002) reported that up to 80% of Africa's population utilizes traditional healing methods for their health care needs, including mental disorders. Traditional counseling is a service rendered by native or traditional practitioners to facilitate their clients' ability to solve their problems and attend to their mental well-being. Adekson (2005) elaborated on this view by indicating that for the Yoruba ethnic group "traditional counseling is inherently embedded in Yoruba tradition because people seek help for different problems from traditional healers as a way of living a holistic lifestyle and finding meaning for their lives" (pp. 8–9). Traditional or indigenous counseling practitioners are referred to as *babalawos* among the Yorubas, *dibias* among the Igbo people, and *duba* in the Hausa culture.

The Development of Professional Counseling

A number of key events led to the development of professional counseling in Nigeria. One of them was a 1959 workshop on career guidance organized for the graduating students by the Catholic nuns at St. Theresa's College (a high school) in Ibadan (Okon, 1983). The goal of the workshop was to provide the students with occupational and job search information to enable them to make informed employment and career decisions. The goal was achieved, as most of the students were able to obtain full employment after graduation.

Another event that influenced the development of professional counseling was the introduction in 1963 of counseling and guidance services at Comprehensive High School in Aiyetoro in Ogun State. This was accompanied by a workshop on the role of guidance counselors held in the same school. The next prominent factor that influenced the emergence of counseling in Nigeria was the active role played by the Nigerian federal government when it intentionally introduced guidance and counseling services at the secondary school level via the 1977 National Policy on Education, which has since been revised a number of times (Federal Ministry of Education, 2004). One of the main goals of this policy was to help Nigerian students understand how to navigate the newly restructured secondary education system that evolved from 5 to 6 years of secondary education. This new system was subsequently further split into two levels—3 years of junior secondary education and another 3 years of senior secondary education.

Another milestone in the development of counseling was the formation of the Counselling Association of Nigeria (CASSON; 2011) in 1976. The primary mission of the association is to improve members' counseling competence through professional conferences and research as well as advance the status of counseling as a profession in Nigeria. Consequently, CASSON holds an annual professional development conference and has established a professional journal, *The Counsellor.* The journal offers an outlet for CASSON's members and other counseling professionals to publish their research as well as learn about effective counseling strategies for working with clients and counselor training (CASSON, 2011).

The Current Status of Counseling

Counseling in Nigeria is practiced mainly in educational institutions, primarily at the secondary school level. There are no counselors in the primary schools because the federal government made no provision for counseling services at that level of education. Furthermore, counseling services are not provided in all Nigerian secondary schools because of financial constraints. Such services are usually limited to federal and state-owned secondary institutions (Aluede, Afen-Akpaida, & Adomeh, 2004). In addition, in some schools counseling services are delivered by career masters and mistresses who are not professionally trained counselors. These are trained teachers with very limited experience in counseling, having perhaps taken only the introductory course in guidance and counseling during their teacher education preparatory program. It is also important to note that career masters and mistresses are usually saddled with teaching responsibilities, which often results in their counselor functions being relegated to the background.

Professional counselors in Nigerian schools perform a number of other functions as well. For example, they offer orientation programs for students. This is crucial for students who come from elementary schools to junior secondary schools and for those who transition from the junior to the senior secondary level or directly into the world of work. Thus, Nigerian counselors provide students with career guidance in an effort to help them make informed career decisions based on their interests, values, and abilities. Given the fact that Nigeria is a collectivist culture, counselors usually collaborate with students' family members in order to achieve the best outcome for the students (Otti, 2010). Other functions that counselors perform include the following:

1. Addressing students' personal concerns, such as drug abuse, friendship issues, and relationship issues.
2. Offering sex education.
3. Helping students explore and formulate their postsecondary school plans.
4. Providing academic counseling for course load, time management, study skills, and retention issues.
5. Working as consultants to classroom teachers as well as parents.

Counseling in the tertiary institutions exists at a very minimal level. Some universities have counseling centers in which counselors provide counseling on academic and personal issues. Counseling in noneducational settings exists at a skeletal level in a few Nigerian cities. For example, counseling is provided in work settings, such as in government ministries and banks, to help workers address interpersonal problems, manage stress on the job, as well as shape career development plans for promotion or retention (Otti, 2010).

Another rarity in Nigerian counseling is private practice. This is because the demand for counseling is very low, partly because of a lack of public awareness regarding the benefits of counseling and partly because of the high rate of poverty in the country. The law requires that the few Nigerian counselors involved in private practice register their business (just like any other private practice) with the Nigerian Corporate Affairs. However, private counseling practices are not regulated by any professional body.

Apart from the lack of professional regulation of counseling in Nigeria, there is a very limited relationship between counselors, psychologists, and social workers. Whatever minimal contact does exist usually occurs in the areas of consultation and referral. For instance, when working with families or juveniles, social workers may consult with counselors regarding the best options for their clients. In addition, counselors may refer clients with severe mental illness to psychologists and psychiatrists.

Best Counseling Practices

There is a strong Western, especially U.S., influence on counseling in Nigeria. Nigerian pioneer counselor educators were mostly trained in the United States, and their philosophy of practice tended to mirror that of the United States (Aluede, McEachern, & Kenny, 2005). Thus, just like in the United States, Nigerians believe that counseling practice should be guided by a counseling theory (e.g., person-centered or cognitive behavior). Furthermore, the choice of theory by the counselor depends on the client's needs or concerns and the counselor's comfort with the theory.

Counseling itself usually takes place in the counselor's office. The process entails (a) building a relationship or developing a rapport with the client; (b) implementing the working phase, which involves identifying goals and using specific strategies and interventions to attain these goals; (c) evaluating the counseling outcome; and (d) terminating the relationship. Counselors can refer clients to a psychiatrist or a social worker if they deem it necessary. Also, after termination, counselors do a follow-up with clients to see whether they are maintaining the gains derived from their counseling sessions. Specific strategies utilized during the counseling process generally include interviews facilitated by active attending and listening skills, autobiography, bibliotherapy, and role plays. Counselors use assessment tools such as personality, intelligence, aptitude, and achievement tests. In addition, secondary school counselors often invite professionals from various fields to share ideas about their professions with students during orientation programs. This is very helpful in terms of making the students aware of role models in different occupational fields.

In Nigeria, counselors rely primarily on local labor market information available in print and electronic media. These media contain brief descriptions of different careers and their entry-level qualifications. Counselors, particularly those at the secondary school level, also use admission brochures from postsecondary institutions as a guide to providing occupational information to their clients.

The use of technology in training and in the practice of counseling is more limited than in the United States. Ogunsanmi (2004) advocated for the integration of technology competency into counselor education and counseling practice. Currently technology is primarily used to promote occupational awareness among Nigerians. For example, employers advertise position vacancies on their websites, via radio, and on television. These advertisements usually contain a description of the position, qualifications, job functions, salary, and fringe benefits (Akume, 2010). Counselors use these websites as sources of occupational information when working with clients. In addition, counselors sometimes use the telephone for brief counseling sessions, especially in crisis situations (Gesinde, 2008). The Internet is also utilized for research and consultation by counselors and counselor educators regarding best strategies for working with clients.

Counselor Education

Bachelor's Programs

The training of counselors in Nigeria is mainly undertaken by local universities. The minimum level of training in order to practice as a professional counselor is a bachelor of education degree in guidance and counseling (Aluede et al., 2005). Most counseling programs are housed or cohoused in teacher education departments because school counselors are usually teachers who specialize in counseling. Thus, school counselors-in-training take both teacher education and counseling courses. Undergraduate counseling programs are accredited by the Nigerian National Universities Commission. This body stipulates the required courses that counseling programs must offer. These include

> a) a basic foundation in psychology with emphasis in sociology; b) techniques of appraisal for educational and vocational adjustments; c) group guidance methods; d) placement; e) counseling in special settings; f) counseling follow-up techniques; g) abnormal psychology; h) developmental psychology; i) educational psychology; j) research and educational statistics. (Aluede et al., 2005, p. 376)

There is also an expectation of clinical experience via practicum or internship. This is usually for a period of 6 weeks (Aluede et al., 2004).

Graduate Programs

In addition to undergraduate counseling programs, there are graduate programs that offer master's and doctoral degrees in guidance and counseling. A few graduate counseling programs are just beginning to venture into preparing students for community mental health practice. Graduate programs are not regulated by any external professional body. Rather, each program is approved by its university faculty senate. Furthermore, counselors in Nigeria currently do not have to be certified or licensed in order to practice. But CASSON has begun working with the National Board for Certified Counselors (NBCC) regarding credentialing (Kolo, 2010).

Diversity Training

In the United States, one of the eight core curricular areas required for the accreditation of graduate counseling programs by the Council for the Accreditation of Counseling and Related Educational Programs (CACREP; 2009) is social and cultural diversity. This area is absent in the Nigerian counseling curriculum. This is a critical concern because Nigeria is a multicultural country. Consequently, integrating multiculturalism into the Nigerian counseling curriculum is strongly encouraged. Fortunately, CASSON is already beginning to pay attention to this issue, as a couple of subthemes of its September 2011 conference in Kano were related to multicultural issues in counseling (CASSON, 2011).

The Future

Counseling in Nigeria is a relatively young and promising profession that is confronting a number of challenges. Nevertheless, its future is bright, especially given the powerful efforts by CASSON to professionalize counselor training and counseling practice in the country. An example of CASSON's effort is its work with NBCC International, a division of NBCC, and affiliates regarding the credentialing of counselors in Nigeria. Furthermore, CASSON is consulting and collaborating with CACREP on the accreditation of counseling programs in Nigeria. The process is being done via the International Registry of Counsellor Education Programs.

With CASSON's strong advocacy with the Nigerian National Council of Education on behalf of its members regarding the lack of counselors in the schools (CASSON, 2011), there is hope that the number of high schools in Nigeria that have professional counselors will increase. Also, counseling services could be extended to elementary schools.

Although mental health concerns loom large in Nigeria, the future of community mental health counseling looks good. It is likely that the number of graduate programs offering community mental health counseling will increase.

Thus, the future of counseling in Nigeria calls for increased and purposeful collaboration as well as cooperation between counselors and other human service professionals such as social workers, psychologists, and psychiatrists for the benefit of the client. Moreover, given the multicultural and collectivist nature of Nigeria, I anticipate an increase in the number of counselors using postmodern perspectives, such as solution-focused and narrative approaches. Furthermore, it is expected that going forward, mental health counseling will entail the exploration of the possible integration of traditional or indigenous methods of counseling with contemporary or professional approaches aimed at fostering effective, holistic care for Nigerians.

Finally, I envision a promising future for the counseling profession in Nigeria. I anticipate an intensification of the ongoing promotion of the counseling profession spearheaded by CASSON. This promotional effort will involve educating the Nigerian public about the benefits of counseling as well as advocating for CASSON members. The probable corollary to this effort is an increased demand for counseling services that could positively impact private practice in counseling.

Conclusion

Counseling as a profession is steadily and surely emerging in Nigeria. CASSON is playing a very crucial role in this regard, especially in trying to address the challenges facing the profession. Given ongoing efforts at the globalization and standardization of counseling by NBCC International and CACREP, it is important that CASSON continue to strengthen the status of the counseling profession in Nigeria via the accreditation of counseling programs and the credentialing of CASSON members.

References

Adekson, M. (2005). *The Yoruba traditional healers of Nigeria.* Newark, NJ: Routledge.

Akande, A. (1999). Intercultural and cross-cultural assessment of self-esteem among youth in twenty-first century South Africa. *International Journal for the Advancement of Counselling,* 2(3), 171–187.

Akume, G. T. (2010). *Personality development and vocational guidance.* Makurdi, Nigeria: Destiny Ventures.

Alao, K. (2004). Silver and gold we have none but what we have, we give unto thee: Indigenous African healing and the rest of the world. *International Journal for the Advancement of Counselling, 26*(3), 249–256.

Aluede, O., Afen-Akpaida, J. E., & Adomeh, I. O. C. (2004). Some thoughts about the future of guidance and counselling in Nigeria. *Education, 125,* 296–305.

Aluede, O., McEachern, A. G., & Kenny, M. C. (2005). Counseling in Nigeria and the United States of America: Contrasts and similarities. *International Journal for the Advancement of Counselling, 27,* 371–382.

Central Intelligence Agency. (2011). *Background note: Nigeria.* Retrieved from http://www.state.gove/pa/ei/bgn/2836.htm

Council for the Accreditation of Counseling and Related Educational Programs. (2009). *2009 CACREP accreditation manual.* Alexandria, VA: Author.

Counselling Association of Nigeria. (2011). Promoting the ongoing development and recognition of the counselling profession globally: Presentation of IRCEP 2010 CASSON International conference. *Counselling Association of Nigeria News Bulletin, 32.* Retrieved from http://2011casson.org

Federal Ministry of Education. (2004). *National policy on education* (4th ed.). Lagos, Nigeria: Federal Ministry of Information Press.

Gesinde, A. M. (2008). *Guidance and counselling in institutions of learning.* Ibadan, Nigeria: Foludex Press.

Kolo, I. (2010). The consolidated transformation agenda. *Counselling Association of Nigeria Bulletin, 31,* 9–10.

Makinde, O. (1980). Indigenous counselling techniques among the Yoruba and Igala people of Nigeria. *International Journal for the Advancement of Counselling, 3,* 1–84.

Ogunsanmi, J. O. (2004). Incorporating computer education into guidance and counselling practice in schools. *Nigerian Journal of Guidance & Counselling, 9,* 25–36.

Okocha, A. G. A., & Perrone, P. (1992). Career salience among Nigerian dual-career women. *The Career Development Quarterly, 41,* 84–93.

Okon, S. E. (1983). Guidance and counseling services in Nigeria. *Personnel and Guidance Journal, 61,* 457–458.

Otti, S. (2010). *Everybody needs counselling: A report of an interview with a Nigerian counseling psychologist, Dr. Celene Njoku.* Retrieved from http://www.nigerianbestforum.com

Pelter, P. (1995). *Psychology and health in African cultures.* Frankfurt, Germany: IkO-Verlag fur Interkulturelle Kommunikation.

World Health Organization. (2002). *WHO traditional health care strategy, 2002-2005.* Geneva, Switzerland: Author.

• • •

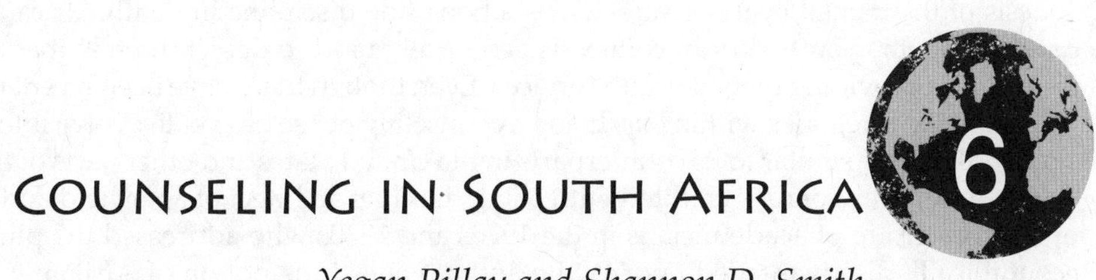

Counseling in South Africa 6

Yegan Pillay and Shannon D. Smith

The Historical Development of Counseling

All facets of the contemporary South African social fabric have been and continue to be significantly impacted by the legacy of *apartheid.* South African society, including the evolution of the mental health profession, has to be reviewed in the context of an institutionalized ideology of racial supremacy. The industrial revolution that occurred as a result of the discovery of diamonds in 1867 and gold in 1869 can be identified as the defining period in the history of South Africa. The shift from an agrarian to an industrialized mode of production set the stage for a rapid transformation of society and heralded the race-based social engineering that continued to be dominant until the birth of democracy in 1994 (Louw & Foster, 2004).

In the wake of rapid industrialization, Africans migrated from the rural to the urban areas. This resulted in the promulgation of various draconian laws, such as the Glen Grey Act of 1894, the 1913 Native Land Act, and the 1923 Native Urban Areas Act, to segregate and restrict the movement of Africans in the urban areas (Louw & Foster, 2004; Nicholas, 2010). Nested within the race-based legislation was the passage of the Mental Disorders Act of 1916, which was a significant development for the field of psychology because it required that people with mental illness be tested, identified, and registered (Louw & Foster, 2004). Although this legislation was of benefit only to mentally ill patients who were classified as White, it set the stage for the use of testing to legitimize racial segregation. Louw and Foster (2004) reported that during the 1920s and the 1930s poverty impacted a significant number of Whites and resulted in their position in society becoming indistinguishable from that of Africans. The "poor White problem," as this became known, raised concerns about interracial fraternization and the racial and moral degradation of the White race. The poor White problem was investigated by a commission funded by the Carnegie Corporation of New York at a time when growth in vocational guidance and psychometric testing was burgeoning in the United States (Maree & van der Westhuizen, 2011). Nicholas (2010) asserted that "this commission . . . laid the groundwork for apartheid legislation that would lay waste to black families" (p. 44). The ascendance of the testing movement in the United States was linked to the evolution of the mental health profession in South

Africa, particularly through providing empirical measurement instruments to support the perceived intellectual differences between the races (Naidoo & Kagee, 2009).

Louw and Foster (2004) reported that South African psychologists who trained at leading academic institutions in the United States, such as Harvard and Columbia, supported the status quo and the advancement of the mental health discipline in two unique ways. First, they used IQ test results to confirm the perception that African children were inferior to White children—supporting the need for segregation to prevent the degeneration of the White race. Second, by focusing on the poor White problem and making recommendations based on what appeared to be valid psychometric evidence, these researchers were able to convince the state of the relevancy and the role of mental health professionals (specifically psychologists) in addressing the social issues that had emerged. This can be considered the genesis of the mental health profession as a bona fide discipline in South Africa. The term *counseling* in the South African context is generically used to depict the role that psychologists play in providing mental health services. Even though there have been recent initiatives to expand the categories within psychology, counseling per se has yet to evolve into a profession or discipline similar to its counterparts in the United States and other parts of the world.

Hendrik F. Verwoerd is credited with being the chief architect of apartheid and was part of the core group of academicians in the 1920s and 1930s who addressed the plight of the economically disadvantaged poor White and advanced the notion of Afrikaner nationalism and racial supremacy. Verwoerd completed his MA and PhD in psychology at Stellenbosch University and was appointed as professor of applied psychology at the same institution in 1927 (Naidoo & Kagee, 2009). He then chaired the continuation committee of the Carnegie Commission on the Poor White, which is purported to have resulted in the birth of social work as a bona fide discipline in South Africa (Nicholas, 2010).

Several authors (Cooper, Nicholas, Seedat, & Statman, 1990; Leach, Akhurst, & Basson, 2003; Naidoo & Kagee, 2009) have contended that Verwoerd's ascendency to prime minister in 1958 facilitated the creation of a separate discipline, namely counseling psychology, that focused on career issues, job opportunities, health development, the prevention of psychological disorders, and economic empowerment. Because the already established discipline of clinical psychology was embedded in the more liberal English-speaking departments, Verwoerd used his political muscle to influence the creation of counseling psychology, which targeted Afrikaner students with the intent of aligning psychology with and perpetuating Afrikaner nationalism and racist ideologies (Cooper et al., 1990; Leach et al., 2003; Naidoo & Kagee, 2009). In 1974, counseling psychology was awarded the status of being one of five registration categories for psychologists (the others were clinical, educational, industrial, and research psychology). Following this 1974 legislation and consistent with the vision of Verwoerd, counseling programs began at primarily Afrikaans universities (Naidoo & Kagee, 2009).

It is evident from this historical vantage point that the mental health profession was steeped in and inextricably linked to the racial social engineering by Afrikaner academics during the period of industrialization, with the focus of perpetuating racist ideology and maintaining minority White dominance (Maree & van der Westhuizen, 2011; Watson & Fouche, 2007). It was only during the late 1980s when the dismantling of apartheid was gaining momentum that counseling psychology programs at the University of the Western Cape and other progressive White institutions provided the catalyst for the discipline to "shift toward greater social relevance and [address] the needs of the disenfranchised groups" (Naidoo & Kagee, 2009, p. 424).

The Current Status of Professional Counseling Associations

To understand the current professional subdisciplines and credentialing agencies, one has to see the professionalization of counseling through the lens of its historical antecedents. Although psychology was not formally recognized until 1974, the first professional association, the South African Psychological Association (SAPA), was formed in July 1948 with 34 members (Maree & van der Westhuizen, 2011). This year also marked the beginning of institutionalized apartheid when the Nationalist Party assumed power. The formation of SAPA was driven by the medical profession, which wanted to set standards for the training and the qualifications of clinical psychologists, who became more active in the mental health field after World War II (Louw & Foster, 2004). SAPA's Whites-only professional membership policy was challenged in 1956 when Josephine Naidoo, a woman classified as Indian according to the South African Population Registration Act, applied to become a member. The organization was in a quandary as to how to respond to an application for membership by a psychologist who was not classified as White. Naidoo was asked to withdraw her application to allow the SAPA council to discuss the possibility of having non-White members. It was only 5 years later—which suggests just how contentious this issue was among the SAPA membership—that the council resolved to admit those who were not codified in the population register as White (see Louw & Foster, 2004).

This decision resulted in approximately 200 dissenting conservative members in the now multiracial SAPA to break ranks in 1962 and form a splinter group. This group, which became known as the Psychological Institute of the Republic of South Africa (PIRSA), was composed exclusively of Afrikaans-speaking White psychologists (Louw & Foster, 2004; Naidoo & Kagee, 2009; Stead, 2004). For more than 20 years (from 1962 to 1983) mental health professionals were represented by two professional bodies, SAPA and PIRSA, whose ideologies were sharply divided along racial lines. This was not an anomaly because it mirrored a racially divided society and marked a tumultuous watershed period in South Africa's sociopolitical history. Naidoo and Kagee (2009) asserted that despite their divergent ideologies, SAPA and PIRSA were forced to engage in dialogue in 1974 to establish the standards for the registration of psychologists and to collaborate on forming the Professional Board of Psychology (PBP). They hosted a joint conference in 1977 and launched the *South African Journal of Psychology.* In 1978, a third association, the Society for Student Counseling in Southern Africa, was formed by White male delegates from 15 universities (Maree & van der Westhuizen, 2011). Growing internal resistance and international pressure following the Soweto student revolt in 1976 rendered the existence of PIRSA untenable and resulted in the amalgamation of PIRSA and SAPA in 1983 to form the Psychological Association of South Africa (PASA).

The formation of PASA was not a panacea for unity in the mental health profession, and many Black psychologists dissociated themselves from the organization, citing the fact that there was not enough acknowledgment of the racism inherent in the formation of PIRSA. Moreover, it was argued that the organization was complicit in supporting apartheid by not challenging apartheid policies and by adopting a pseudopolitical stance with regard to torture, detentions without trial, and discrimination (Louw & Foster, 2004; Naidoo & Kagee, 2009; Nicholas, 1993; Stead, 2004). From 1983 until the first democratic elections in 1994, many progressive psychologists aligned with three antiapartheid organizations (the Organization for Alternative Social Services in South Africa, the Psychology and Apartheid Group, and the South African Health and Social Services Organization) that were "engaged in challenging the apartheid system, locating mental health within a political context, and engaging with emerging mental health challenges the country was facing" (Naidoo & Kagee, 2009, p. 425). PASA dissolved in 1992, which resulted in the formation in 1994 of the single inclusive Psychological Society of South Africa (PsySSA).

According to the PsySSA website (www.psyssa.com), the society is a voice of the discipline on matters concerning the mental health and psychosocial well-being of all South Africans and is dedicated to the reconstruction and development of postapartheid South African society. PsySSA describes itself as a trade union for the discipline and negotiates with relevant bodies to set tariffs and to represent its members. PsySSA is nationally accredited to provide training and continuing education courses and provides a forum for mental health professionals to network. The 2010 Annual Report of the PsySSA indicated that as of June 30, 2010, there were 2,726 members in the various subcategories of registration (PsySSA, 2010).

Categories of Mental Health Professionals

Mental health professionals in South Africa have until recently specialized in one of six areas in psychology: psychometry, clinical psychology, counseling psychology, industrial psychology, educational psychology, and research psychology. The categories of registered counselor, neuropsychologist, and forensic psychologist have been added to the areas of specialization to address the mental health needs of a constantly evolving society. Each area of specialization is strictly governed by a scope of practice and educational requirements as delineated by the PBP under the auspices of the state regulatory authority, the Health Professions Council of South Africa (HPCSA). Minister of Health Dr. Aaron Motsoaledi published an intent to amend the scope of practice of mental health practitioners in Government Notice No. R263 of April 6, 2010. A detailed description of the scope of practice of each category can be viewed at http://www.psychologyafrica.com/wp-content/uploads/2010/05/scope-of-practice.pdf.

Current Trends

A current snapshot of the mental health profession in South Africa portrays a discipline that is in a state of flux as it wrestles with issues of identity and relevance in the provision of psychological services to a society in the throes of transformation. The postapartheid era has seen revisions to scopes of practice and categories of licensure given that the societal landscape is still marked by inequitable access to psychological services among the majority of South Africans. Such services are provided by first-tier registered psychologists. Moreover, the register of psychologists in 2000 revealed that 90% of psychologists were English- or Afrikaans-speaking White psychologists who were unable to provide psychological services to previously disenfranchised clients in their native language (Louw, 2002).

To confront these challenges, a second tier of registration called "registered counselor" was created in 2003 to make basic primary psychological counseling services available to previously disadvantaged populations and to increase the number of mental health professionals who qualify each year. Although the category of registered counselor is in its infancy, recent studies have suggested that its viability is in serious jeopardy (Abel & Louw, 2009; Elkonin & Sandison, 2006, 2010). These authors have found that the number of registered counselors is growing at a slow pace, even though the time frame for qualifying as a registered counselor is less than that for qualifying as a psychologist (4.5 years vs. 7 years, respectively). They have also found that employment opportunities for registered counselors in the public sector (in hospitals, the police, the army, community mental health, or education) are very limited, with the result that less than half of registered counselors are working as registered counselors. Because of the lack of employment opportunities, the training to become a registered counselor is being used as a stepping-stone to licensure as a psychologist rather than to increase the number of mental health professionals to serve the previously disenfranchised. The tenuous future of the category of registered counselor within the discipline of psychology is encapsulated in the following assertion by Abel and Louw (2009):

> It is clear that the category "registered counsellor" has not been able to make inroads into this "market." The chances of turning this situation around seem slim, as universities generally appear to be disillusioned with the BPsych degree. In an informal survey, conducted among 12 heads of department of psychology, it emerged that only four departments were admitting students to B. Psych. degrees in 2008, the degree aimed specifically at training registered counsellors. (p. 106)

Recent studies have suggested that in the practical sense the category of registered counselor is falling short of its intended objective to increase the number of mental health professionals to serve the previously disadvantaged and that its future appears bleak. Elkonin and Sandison (2010) were critical of the role of the PBP, specifically that the board "dictates that universities should train the registration categories as decreed, but does not see its role in supporting the need for job creation" (p. 95). They noted that the issue of job creation was not carefully thought through in the creation of this tier of mental health professional.

The continuous change within the discipline is evident in a recent notice published in the Government Gazette (No. R.263, April 2010) by the Department of Health that delineated the revised regulations regarding the scope of practice of mental health practitioners. The revisions reflect the omission of the mental health assistant as a previously envisaged category of specialization but the addition of two new categories—neuropsychologist and forensic psychologist. The revised scope of practice recently came under attack by counseling and educational psychologists after the psychology liaison to the HPCSA, Emmanuel Chanza, sent a letter via the Board of Health Care Funders (which represents more than 100 medical insurance companies) to its members stating that clients who have depression or anxiety disorders can only be treated by a psychiatrist or a clinical psychologist. This can be attributed directly to language that clearly delineates the scope of practice of a counseling psychologist as diagnosing and treating individuals with *developmental* and *adjustment* issues, whereas terms such as *psychological distress, psychopathology,* and *psychiatric disorders* are used to describe the scope of practice of clinical psychologists. This limitation in the scope of practice has created an unprecedented furor among psychologists who are not registered as clinical psychologists but who are trained to and have previously diagnosed and treated depression and anxiety in addition to other *Diagnostic and Statistical Manual of Mental Disorders* (*DSM*) disorders.

The Board of Health Care Funders uses International Classification of Diseases–10 codes for reimbursement. This significantly restricts the number of mental health conditions that nonclinical psychologists can diagnose and treat because under the recently promulgated scope of practice a separate code for each category of registration defines what each psychologist is permitted to do. Botha (2011) predicted that two thirds of practicing psychologists will be faced with empty consulting rooms and that the existing number of clinical psychologists will not be able to cope with providing psychological services when counseling and other psychologists are forced to stop diagnosing and treating individuals who meet criteria for a *DSM* diagnosis.

A counseling psychologist who is in private practice and a university faculty member expressed frustration at the current status quo and the uncertainty facing counseling psychology as a bona fide category of psychology. She added that counseling psychologists will continue to diagnose and treat individuals with *DSM* diagnoses but may fraudulently provide an adjustment disorder diagnosis so that they will be reimbursed by insurance companies. Recent interviews with psychologists by the first author suggested that there is a sense of uncertainty regarding the status of counseling psychologists in South Africa (V. Goliath, personal communication, June, 24, 2011; A. Sandison, personal communication, July 5, 2011). The following larger questions that remain to be answered: Why would students want to specialize in counseling psychology if they will only be able to facilitate the adjustment of individuals and not treat conditions in the *DSM,* such as depression, anxiety, and posttraumatic stress disorder (which are commonly manifested in societies in transition)? What are the job opportunities in the public sector? Are counseling psychologists destined for the same fate as registered counselors?

Best Counseling Practices

Counseling in South Africa is still steeped in Western models and interventions. As noted earlier, psychology as a discipline evolved out of the testing movement in the United States in the 1920s. A perusal of the current list of psychometric tests published in the *Handbook for Intern Psychologists and Accredited Institutions* (HPCSA, 2010) reveals that the majority of tests were developed overseas and continue to be used in their original format (e.g., the Minnesota Multiphasic Personality Inventory, the California Psychological Inventory, the Spielberger Trait/State Anxiety Scale, and the Hamburg Neuroticism and Extroversion Scale–Vienna Test System), whereas some have been adapted or developed specifically for the South African context (e.g., the South African Wechsler Adult Intelligence Scale, the South African Vocational Interest Inventory, and the Individual Scale for Zulu Speaking Pupils). The area of psychological assessment can best be described as a work in progress, as stakeholders are working to identify psychometric measures that serve all citizens in a culturally fair manner as opposed to in the apartheid era, when psychological testing was used to subjugate the indigenous people.

Best practices regarding counseling interventions are nebulous and untapped because they are limited to the narrow slice of the privileged minority who have access to and utilize psychological services. Leach and colleagues (2003) asserted that although the majority of South Africans need psychological services, they do not trust the Western-based interventions used by the predominantly White cadre of therapists to address psychosocial problems. Naidoo and Kagee (2009) added that the widespread acceptance and use of indigenous healers, especially in rural areas, may explain the reluctance to support mental health professionals. Person-centered therapy gained popularity among mental health professionals in the 1980s, especially after a visit to South Africa by Carl Rogers. Like in the West, other mainstream theoretical models have developed. Viljoen, Beukes, and Louw (1999) asserted that almost half of the therapists who participated in a study reported being eclectic in their theoretical preference. Grief and loss therapy was the most frequently used technique, followed by cognitive therapy, person-centered therapy, rational emotive behavior therapy, reality therapy, play therapy, behavior therapy, and short-term psychodynamic therapy. Given the popularity of these Western-influenced theoretical models, it can be inferred that the counseling environment and the practice of counseling in South Africa is indistinguishable in many respects from the practice of psychotherapy in other parts of the Western world (see Painter & Terre Blanche, 2004).

Diversity Issues

South Africa's transition to a democratic society in 1994 has been heralded as one of the great success stories of the modern political era. The bloodbath and civil unrest that was predicted by some commentators did not come to fruition and the constitutional democracy remains intact. However, the fledgling democracy is faced with multiple and complex challenges that have stretched providers of mental health services to unprecedented levels. These include, but are not limited to, the rampant HIV/AIDS pandemic, poverty, unemployment, crime, alcohol and drug addiction, homelessness, acquaintance and stranger violence, and partner and child abuse.

According to the World Health Organization, UNAIDS, and UNICEF (2011), South Africa's HIV epidemic is the most severe in the world, affecting approximately 5.6 million (17.8% of people worldwide living with HIV/AIDS). This corresponds to the number of people living with AIDS in all of Asia. Moreover, at the end of 2009 there were 330,000 AIDS-related deaths and approximately 2 million AIDS-related orphans (UNAIDS, 2009). The statistics illuminate two issues relevant to counseling. First, as the trajectory of the virus continues, most people will be affected by the death of a friend or family member. Ruane (2010) found that grief associated with HIV/AIDS was one of the primary reasons individuals sought professional mental health counseling. It is evident from the statistics that scores of people will continue to require psychological services as they experience the trauma associated with family members and friends becoming terminally ill as a result of the virus. The challenge is that the number of trained mental health professionals is disproportionately low relative to the current need, and the majority of possible consumers of mental health services are distrustful of a predominantly White mental health profession that operates primarily from a Western-influenced paradigm.

Second, it is evident that an alarming number of children have become AIDS-related orphans, and this has affected South Africa's family structure in significant ways. Grandparents take on the responsibility of caring for grandchildren whose parents have died. When grandparents are unable to care for their grandchildren because of limited financial resources, siblings have to be separated and sent to live with distant relatives or friends. In worst case scenarios children themselves head households when no family members or friends are willing to adopt them. The consequences are dire because these children drop out of school and become prime targets for being drawn into prostitution and other nefarious activities as they try to eke out a living on the streets. Another concern of significance is that many orphans may experience alienation from their peers, or if they have been separated from their siblings and a familiar environment they may be challenged with issues of identity and belonging. This may be another reason why they drop out of school. This is a major concern because it is through awareness initiatives in the schools that children become knowledgeable about HIV and other health-related matters. By not attending school to avoid victimization and alienation, they are less informed than their peers and the cycle of HIV is perpetuated. Accompanying HIV/AIDS is the scourge of poverty, which, similar to the virus, impacts every facet of South African society in a significant way.

The Medium Term Strategic Framework (2009–2014) by the South African government outlines a strategy to reduce poverty and unemployment by half by 2014. Although some progress is being made, in 2011 unemployment was at 25% and 34.8% of the population earned below the $2.50 per day poverty line for a medium-size economy (Millennium Development Goals Report, 2010). Racial inequity with regard to poverty continues to prevail. For example, in 2006 Blacks, who constituted 79% of the population, earned 41.2% of the total income compared to Whites, who made up 9% of the population but earned 45.3% of the total income. Although there is no conclusive evidence of the causal link between poverty, crime, violence, addictions, and sexual abuse, Black communities are disproportionately subjected to the stressors of poor living conditions, homelessness, hunger, and limited access to health care services compared to their White counterparts. The irony from a socioeconomic perspective, which has implications for counseling, is that White communities who are more affluent and may have relatively less of a need for psychological services have greater access to a predominantly White pool of counselors.

Counselor Education

Two levels of accreditation govern education and training in South Africa. The South African Qualifications Authority is a statutory body that was formed in 1995 to develop and implement a National Qualifications Framework (NQF). The primary role of the NQF is to integrate education and training into a unified, nationally recognized structure. Integral to the NQF is the Higher Education Quality Committee of the Council on Higher Education, which has the responsibility for quality assurance in higher education as defined in the Higher Education Act of 1997 (Act No. 101 of 1997). The Council on Higher Education is responsible for generating and setting standards for all higher education qualifications and for ensuring that such qualifications meet South African Qualifications Authority criteria for registration on the NQF.

The other level of accreditation is provided by professional bodies that determine whether a qualification offered by a higher education institution meets the requirements for the registration, membership, or licensing of graduates in a specific profession. In the case of psychology, academic institutions have to be accredited and meet the standards set by the PBP, which operates under the auspices of the HPCSA. There are three primary registration categories, namely psychometrist, registered counselor, and psychologist. The psychologist category is further divided into seven areas of specialization: counseling, clinical psychology, educational psychology, organizational psychology, research psychology, forensic psychology, and neuropsychology.

Psychometrists and registered counselors are required to complete a 4-year BPsych degree that is accredited by the PBP. In addition, a practicum of 6 months under the guidance and supervision of a psychologist is required. The supervising psychologist has to have been registered with the PBP for at least 3 years. The practicum forms part of the 4-year BPsych degree, and universities are responsible for developing the curriculum and supervising the practicum. The curriculum for psychometry emphasizes psychological testing and assessment; the curriculum for registered counseling focuses on training counselors in career, trauma, community mental health, family, school sports, HIV/AIDS, human resources, pastoral, and employee well-being counseling. Once the course work and practical training are completed the candidate must complete the National Examination of the Board to be licensed as a psychometrist or a registered counselor with the HPCSA. In 2010, there were 7,740 psychometrists and 1,209 registered counselors registered with the HPCSA.

The traditional route to qualifying as a psychologist begins with a 3-year BA degree with psychology as one of the majors, followed by a 1-year Honours degree in psychology. The 4-year BPsych degree also qualifies for entry into the professional training. Thereafter, a master's degree in psychology must be completed.

Admission into the master's degree program is very competitive because there are currently only 18 accredited institutions in South Africa, and each institution admits only 15 students. Students can specialize as clinical, counseling, educational, industrial, research, or forensic psychologists or neuropsychologists. With the exception of the research category, course work is followed by a 1-year internship and, in the case of clinical psychologists, one additional year of community service. A student has to successfully complete the National Board exams to qualify for registration as a psychologist with the HPCSA. In 2010, there were 9,742 psychologists registered with the HPCSA. In an effort to ensure that the public interest is protected and that psychologists maintain and update their competence, continuing professional development is required of everyone registered with the HPCSA and is endorsed by the Health Professions Act of 1974 (Act No. 56 of 1974). Since 2007, psychometrists, registered counselors, and psychologists have been required to complete 30 hours of professional development per year, of which 6 hours must be related to ethics.

The Future

Counseling in South Africa has to be seen as a thread within a very complex sociopolitical tapestry. A concern expressed by Painter and Terre Blanche (2004) that "as South Africa reaches the end of the first decade of democracy, there are worrying signs that organized psychology in South Africa may be becoming virtually indistinguishable from its counterparts in the UK and US" (p. 537). This observation begs the question: Is organized psychology relevant in postapartheid South Africa, and for whom?

In the past two decades there has been evidence of progress and transformation at the structural level of the PBP and the HPCSA, particularly from the perspective of representation and policy formulation. However, modeling the profession on the Western paradigm to which that Painter and Terre Blanche (2004) referred runs the risk of maintaining the status quo of serving the privileged. Recent revisions by the PBP to restrict the scope of diagnosis and treatment by counseling psychologists to issues of adjustment while simultaneously expanding specialist categories such as neuropsychology and forensic psychology suggest a movement in the direction of pathologizing and medicalizing everyday phenomenological experiences and natural reactions to confronting poverty, crime, HIV/AIDS, and violence.

Based on its current form, it is evident that psychology continues to be classified as an elitist profession in South Africa because the vast majority of individuals who require psychological service do not have access to such services. Empirical data indicate that the category of registered counselor, which was conceived to serve the disadvantaged population, has not been successful. Elkonin and Sandison (2010) asserted that this lack of success could be attributed in part to a lack of support from the HPCSA. At a conceptual level the training of registered counselors is relevant given the contextual variables and the track record of success in other parts of the world. It appears that being embedded within the discipline of psychology constrains its efficacy. It seems that at this juncture it may behoove relevant stakeholders to examine the viability of developing counseling as an independent discipline with a focus on the strengths and resilience of individuals rather than a basis on deficit and pathology.

It is evident that psychology in its current iteration is not serving the majority of South Africans. Given current developments there are no firm indicators that the status quo is changing or going to change in the near future. Although they were steeped in a racist ideological paradigm that served a small segment of the population, it was the academic visionaries of the 1920s and 1930s who advanced the mental health profession in South Africa. It is going to take a similar type of initiative and vision to transform the mental health system to include indigenous healing, language that does not require translation, and intervention modalities that are culturally relevant to all strata of contemporary South African society. There is still a long way to go!

References

Abel, A., & Louw, J. (2009). Registered counsellors and professional work in South African psychology. *South African Journal of Psychology, 39,* 99–108.

Botha, E. (2011). *Psychologists on the war path.* Retrieved from http://www.timeslive.co.za/lifestyle/health/2011/06/13/psychologists-on-war-path

Cooper, S., Nicholas, L. J., Seedat, M., & Statman, J. M. (1990). Psychology and apartheid: The struggle for psychology in South Africa. In L. J. Nicholas & S. Cooper (Eds.), *Psychology and apartheid: Essays on the struggle for psychology and the mind in South Africa* (pp. 1–21). Johannesburg, South Africa: Vision/Madiba.

Elkonin, D. S., & Sandison, A. (2006). Mind the gap: Have the registered counsellors fallen through? *South African Journal of Psychology, 36,* 598–612.

Elkonin, D. S., & Sandison, A. (2010). Perceptions of registered counsellor efficacy. *South African Journal of Psychology, 40,* 90–96.

Health Professions Council of South Africa. (2010). *Handbook for intern psychologists and accredited institutions.* Retrieved from http://www.hpcsa.co.za/downloads/psychology/intern_psychology_hand_book.pdf

Leach, M. M., Akhurst, J., & Basson, C. (2003). Counseling psychology in South Africa: Current political and professional challenges and future promise. *The Counseling Psychologist, 31,* 619–640. doi:10.1177/0011000003256787

Louw, J. (2002). Psychology history and society. *South African Journal of Psychology, 32,* 1–8.

Louw, J., & Foster, D. (2004). Race and psychology in South Africa. In A. S. Winston (Ed.), *Defining difference: Race and racism in the history of psychology* (pp. 171–197). Washington, DC: American Psychological Association. doi:10.1037/10625-007

Maree, J. G., & van der Westhuizen, C. N. (2011). Professional counseling in South Africa: A landscape under construction. *Journal of Counseling & Development, 89,* 105–111.

Millennium Development Goals Report 2010. (2010). Retrieved from http://www.statssa.gov.za/news_archive/Docs/MDGR_2010.pdf

Naidoo, A. V., & Kagee, A. (2009). The quest for relevance: Counseling psychology in South Africa. In L. H. Gerstein, P. P. Heppner, S. Ægisdóttir, S.-M. A. Leung, & K. L. Norsworthy (Eds.), *International handbook of cross-cultural counseling: Cultural assumptions and practices worldwide* (pp. 421–433). Thousand Oaks, CA: Sage.

Nicholas, L. J. (1993). The response of counsellors to apartheid: A reply to Dryden (1990) and de Jager (1992). *British Journal of Guidance and Counselling, 21,* 331–334. doi:10.1080/03069889308258688

Nicholas, L. (2010). The history of South African social work. In L. Nicholas, J. Rautenbach, & M. Maistry (Eds.), *Introduction to social work* (pp. 40–47). Claremont, South Africa: Juta.

Painter, D., & Terre Blanche, M. (2004). Critical psychology in South Africa: Looking back and looking ahead. *South African Journal of Psychology, 34,* 520–543.

Psychological Society of South Africa. (2010). *Annual report.* Retrieved from http://www.psyssa.com/documents/Annual%20Report.pdf

Ruane, I. (2010). Obstacles to the utilization of psychological resources in a South African township community. *South African Journal of Psychology, 40,* 214–225.

Stead, G. B. (2004). Psychology in South Africa. In D. Wedding & M. J. Stevens (Eds.), *The handbook of international psychology* (pp. 59–74). New York, NY: Brunner-Routledge.

UNAIDS. (2009). *AIDS epidemic update.* Retrieved from http://data.unaids.org/pub/Report/2009/JC1700_Epi_Update_2009_en.pdf

Viljoen, D. J., Beukes, R. B. I., & Louw, D. A. (1999). An evaluation of the training of psychologists at the University of the Free State. *South African Journal of Psychology, 29,* 201–209.

Watson, M. B., & Fouche, P. (2007). Transforming a past into a future: Counseling psychology in South Africa. *Applied Psychology, 56,* 152–164. doi:10.1111/j.1464-0597.2007.00282.x

World Health Organization, UNAIDS, and UNICEF. (2011). *Global HIV/AIDS response: Epidemic update and health sector progress toward universal access.* Retrieved from http://www.who.int/hiv/pub/progress_report2011/hiv_full_report_2011.pdf

• • •

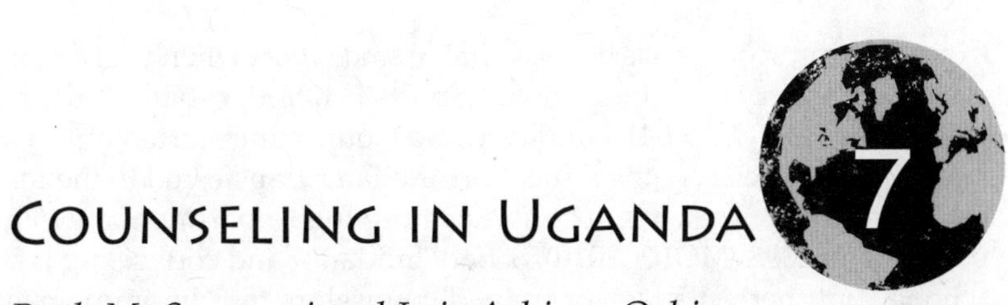

Counseling in Uganda

Ruth M. Senyonyi and Lois Achieng Ochieng

The Republic of Uganda is a landlocked country in East Africa that covers 241,038 square kilometers and has a population of 31.7 million (UNdata, 2009). It is bordered on the east by Kenya, on the north by South Sudan, on the west by the Democratic Republic of Congo, on the southwest by Rwanda, and on the south by Tanzania. The British Protectorate Administration took control of the region from 1894 until 1962, when Uganda gained independence and was granted self-rule. Uganda was later proclaimed a republic with Milton Obote as its Executive President in 1967. Uganda became notorious for its human rights abuses during the military dictatorship of Idi Amin (1971–1979), when thousands of Ugandans were killed. These abuses continued after the return to power of Milton Obote (1980–1985). The National Resistance Army took over in 1986 under President Yoweri Kaguta Museveni, who brought relative stability when he introduced democratic reforms and improved human rights. However, Museveni's government was riddled with civil war for more than two decades, with the Lord's Resistance Army waging guerrilla wars from bases in northern Uganda and southern Sudan.

Uganda has been through political and civil strife, with two thirds of the country exposed to civil war from 1987 to 2011. In addition, corruption, poverty, instability, and disease (especially HIV/AIDS) have led to poor mental and psychosocial health, which has been exacerbated by inefficient health services. These factors have led to an increase in the number of crisis counselors without sufficient counselor training.

The Historical Development of Counseling in Uganda

Counseling in Uganda can trace its foundation to three areas: the support system offered in the traditional culture, guidance in schools for choosing subjects and careers, and counseling offered to curb the 30-year epidemic of HIV/AIDS.

Traditional Culture Guidance and Counseling

The traditional culture in Uganda upheld its legacies by passing on what was important through the nuclear family, extended families, and the community. This included providing traditional support for community members experiencing such fundamental life events as pregnancy, birth, adolescence, marriage, and death. Parents, aunties, uncles, grandparents, elders, and other members of the community had clear roles and responsibilities in maintaining the well-being of community members. Traditional religions played their part by counseling in accordance with culture and religious beliefs. Traditional counseling is more objective and situational than Western counseling, which tends to be more subjective and personal. However, the responsibility of the community has been continuously eroded with the breakdown of communities and families due to modernization, individualism, and urbanization.

Guidance and Counseling in Schools

Counseling in schools has been available since 1968, when the Ministry of Education (MOE; now the Ministry of Education and Sports [MOES]) established a policy on guidance and counseling (MOES, 2004). Guidance and Counseling started out as an office under the Department of Special Needs Education and later transferred to the Inspectorate Department under the MOE. The Guidance and Counseling Department grew into an autonomous department in 2008 (MOES, 2010). School guidance and counseling is still supported in many schools, but there is a lack of trained counselors to fully implement it. Student guidance and counseling, mainly dealing with academic services, is performed by deans and senior teachers with little or no counseling skills. These counselors are ill equipped to deal with the challenges that children face at school and home.

Counseling for HIV/AIDS

Approximately 1.5 million people in Uganda are infected with HIV, and up to 350,000 people are believed to have AIDS (Katabira, 2009). There has been a shift in the concentration of the HIV/AIDS epidemic from younger to older individuals, with the highest prevalence for men (9.9%) among 35- to 39-year-olds and the highest prevalence for women (12.1%) among 30- to 34-year-olds (Government of Uganda, 2010). People in that age group occupy a critical position in families, communities, and workplaces and are responsible for the next generation. The psychosocial consequences of HIV/AIDS on Ugandans are immense and include a lack of basic needs, family dissipation, emotional distress, and educational breakdown. Studies in Rakai and Masaka established symptoms such as sadness, loneliness, worry, low energy, crying easily, lack of interest, worthlessness, and suicidal thoughts among the local communities affected by HIV/AIDS. Counseling has been very key in these situations and a major factor in the fight against HIV/AIDS (Uganda Counselling Association [UCA], 2008).

Counseling centers and agencies sponsored by nongovernmental organizations (NGOs) provide counseling services to help clients cope with issues associated with HIV/AIDS. Agencies such as The AIDS Support Organization (TASO) and Mildmay Uganda train their own counselors to deal with the overwhelming impact of HIV/AIDS. TASO, an indigenous NGO, provides counseling, social support, and medical care for opportunistic infections at seven centers affiliated with district hospitals in Uganda (Kaleeba & Kalibbala, 1997). Mildmay Uganda provides comprehensive services to HIV-infected and AIDS-affected adults and children (Government of Uganda, 2008). Services provided by the HIV centers since 1990 were initially pre- and posttest counseling or Voluntary Counseling and Testing, although many centers are moving to a more community-based counseling approach (Balmer, Seeley, & Bachengana, 1996). An evaluation of TASO services indicated that counseling assisted people with AIDS in coping with their situation and helped families accept and provide care, but TASO realized the need to improve its counseling services in order to deal with the progression of AIDS (Kaleeba & Kalibbala, 1997).

The Current Status of Counseling

Professional counseling requires an advanced level of training and regulated practice. It is a new field in Uganda, especially compared to the traditional community support system, career guidance in schools, and counseling provided in response to the HIV/AIDS epidemic. The extended family support system has disintegrated because of the increased urbanization in many parts of Africa, and this has necessitated another form of organized support (Stockton, Nitza, & Bhusumane, 2010). This breakdown of the traditional family support system and the increased stress related to jobs, schools, and homes in the urban areas has led to the need for a more professionalized approach to counseling. Ugandans are increasingly turning to professional counseling to attain psychosocial well-being. Guidance and counseling on student subject selection remains important, but a recent emphasis has shifted to meeting the emotional needs of pupils (MOES, 2004). The 30-year HIV/AIDS epidemic is now more complicated, and Voluntary Counseling and Testing alone cannot address the many psychosocial problems, such as loss, grief, depression, and anxiety, associated with HIV/AIDS. This fact too has led to the need for professional counseling to support HIV/AIDS clients at various levels.

An important step in the development of professional counseling has been the establishment of UCA, an NGO that was formed in March 2002 to bring together all professional counselors in Uganda. UCA was formed to ensure a high level of competence, holistic services, ethical standards, and regulation of the counseling practice countrywide. UCA provides an avenue for learning, recognition, acquisition of professional qualifications, and professional visibility (UCA, 2010). Membership in UCA is open to all professionally trained counselors; paracounselors; students enrolled in counselor training programs; and those who provide counseling at their places of work, such as human resources managers, teachers, social workers, counselor educators, and service workers. By March 2010, UCA had more than 800 members and 15 corporate associates, including institutions of higher learning, HIV/AIDS service organizations, and government departments.

The word *counselor* in Uganda has been loosely used to mean anyone who has undergone counselor training ranging from 3 days to 3 years. This makes it difficult to differentiate between a professional counselor and one who is trained in a few basic counseling skills. For this reason, UCA designated various counselor titles to be used in Uganda. Individuals who assist with the psychosocial needs of people within society are called "paracounselors" and include HIV/AIDS counselors trained by HIV/AIDS service providers such as TASO, Mildmay Uganda, and the AIDS Information Centre. Individuals who have completed a formal diploma and undergraduate degree program, with case supervision, personal counseling hours, and a practicum of a minimum of 180 hours, are called "counselors." Individuals who have completed a master's or doctoral degree, including case supervision, personal counseling, and a practicum of a minimum of 360 hours, can use the title "counseling psychologist."

Counseling in Uganda is fast evolving into a profession, and UCA is pursuing the legal authority to regulate practice and training. Counseling services are provided by professional counselors (counseling psychologists) and by many other trained and untrained paracounselors in diverse settings throughout the country. Services are available in primary and secondary schools, universities, hospitals, medical and/or counseling clinics, churches, workplaces, police stations, and prisons. Counselors provide services to individuals, couples and families, students, patients with terminal illnesses, substance abusers, displaced persons, refugees, prisoners, and employees in corporate settings. Counseling psychologists are mainly employed in colleges and universities as teachers, supervisors, researchers, and services providers. Others are employed in independent practice, mental health centers, rehabilitation agencies, business and industrial organizations, and consulting firms.

In the educational setting, counselors who provide guidance and counseling tend to concentrate on helping learners develop life skills relevant for the world of work. Their services include guiding students in career and vocational placement, personal and social life, and psychosocial care and providing counseling to those with learning problems. In primary and secondary schools, the head teacher appoints counselors and guidance teachers, also known as "senior men/women" or "career masters/mistresses," to play the dual roles of teacher and counselor without any additional remuneration or decrease in their teaching load. These schools do not employ full-time counselors, although a government white paper (Government of Uganda, 1992) accepted the recommendation of the Kajubi Educational Review Commission of 1989 to place two counselors in each school. Especially since the advent of free education in primary school under the Universal Primary Education scheme, MOES has taken on the roles of training senior teachers in basic counseling skills and training peer counselors to carry on the important guidance role.

Universities, in contrast, employ professional counselors to deal with the increasing number of problems faced by college students. The current status of professional counseling in educational institutions is seen in its focus on counselor training offered at universities. Many government and private universities now offer postgraduate diplomas and bachelor's degrees in guidance and counseling and master's degrees in counseling and clinical psychology.

Counseling is most accessible in social settings, where NGOs concentrate on community and social issues such as refugee resettlement, youth challenges, substance abuse, sexual abuse, prostitution resettlement, crisis pregnancy, trauma, war-related problems, job–work balance, family dysfunction, and crisis management. HIV/AIDS counseling remains an integral part of services provided in hospitals, clinics, and other types of health care facilities. Many privately owned hospitals now employ full- or part-time counselors to provide counseling.

A number of counseling psychologists are in private practice providing services for a fee. By 2011, there were 16 registered private practice firms located mainly in the capital city of Kampala and in the major towns of Uganda. The services provided by private firms are mainly accessed by the middle and upper working class and deal with work issues and family and individual challenges, including HIV/AIDS. Each counselor who operates a practice is required to register with UCA and to renew his or her registration on a yearly basis. UCA is in the process of seeking a legal mandate to regulate counseling firms to ensure quality control.

In line with its obligation to regulate counselor training and practice in Uganda, UCA developed and published the first edition of *Accreditation and Certification Guidelines for Counselling in Uganda* in March 2010. It is stipulated that accreditation shall regulate the various counselor degree preparation programs and that certification will allow the individual counselor to practice counseling in Uganda. *The Counsellors' Code of Ethics* (UCA, 2009) provides basic guidelines for counselors in providing professional services.

The relationship among the practice of counseling, psychology, and social work is not clearly defined in Uganda. The three groups work separately but occasionally refer clients to one another. No procedure has been set by institutions or the government for how the three professions could or should work with one another for the benefit of clients.

Best Counseling Practices

The Rogerian theory of counseling has for many years been the model used to train professional counselors in Uganda, and emphasis is placed on a directional, situational, client-centered, and culturally sensitive approach. More recently, other models have been introduced in the country, such as solution-focused brief therapy, eye-movement desensitization and reprocessing, cognitive behavior therapy, and experiential therapy.

Many Western-style assessment tools are not yet contextualized to fit the different African cultures, and little is known about their reliability and validity in Uganda. In addition, assessment tools are often outdated, expensive, or simply unavailable to Ugandan counselors. Given clients' poor reading and writing skills and the need to translate most instruments, written assessments can be tedious for both clients and counselors.

UCA offers training in crisis and trauma counseling that has enabled counselors to respond to disaster emergencies and provide psychosocial support in partnership with communities and response teams. UCA counselors have responded to such disasters as a fire that killed 20 schoolchildren at Budo Junior School (April 2008), a landslide in Bududa District after torrential rain that killed more than 700 people (March 2010), and a terrorist bombing at a famous rugby club (July 2010). These responses to national tragedies have given professional counselors much-needed recognition for their mental health services.

Diversity Issues

Uganda is a country of cultural diversity. It has approximately 32 tribes that speak different dialects and take pride in preserving tradition and keeping face. A great deal of emphasis is placed on hierarchy, and value is placed on status, education, role, age, and power. Feelings are often not openly expressed, and there are no vernacular words for feelings in most of the languages. Therefore, counselors have to be aware of these cultural issues and work around them appropriately. Parents and extended family are often consulted well before the client seeks professional counseling. Some clients must consult with their relatives even after seeking counseling and are not expected to make individual decisions.

Although counselors in Uganda are trained to be sensitive to the cultural heritages of various tribes and races, having to deal with these can be very challenging. Language differences often become a stumbling block to effective multicultural counseling (Romero, 1985) and hinder the counseling process when clients cannot express their thoughts and feelings. Counselor training in Uganda is conducted in English, the official language used in schools, but most clients are able to express themselves more fluently in their mother tongue. Counselors often need to translate counseling words or phrases into the local language; sometimes two or three sentences are required to explain just one word in English. At times, counseling has to be done using an interpreter, and this may require significantly more time per session. All of this can easily lead to counselor frustration, misdiagnosis, and/or inappropriate placement and treatment.

Counseling has not been fully embraced by many Ugandans because they do not yet see its importance, especially because guidance and counseling is still viewed as a family responsibility more than a paid-for service. Thus, the professional profile of the counselor, and defining roles and responsibilities, must always be emphasized. Witchcraft, superstition, and myths contribute to negative attitudes toward counseling because it often does not provide a quick magical solution to problems.

Multiple losses and trauma in children are major challenges for the Ugandan counselor. During the 20-year civil war in northern Uganda that ended in 2006, an estimated 35,000 Ugandan children were abducted by the Lord's Resistance Army; trained as soldiers; and forced to kill people, who in some cases included their own parents, siblings, and relatives. Rehabilitation centers that offer counseling have been established to assist escapees and rescued children. Many other children in other parts of the country have been orphaned by HIV/AIDS and have experienced the pain of losing a parent or sibling. A study in Uganda by Rujumba, Mbasaalaki-Mwaka, and Ndeezi (2010) identified a lack of counseling skills to assist children with issues such as sexual abuse, identity crisis, addressing an uncertain future, and death. Counselors in Uganda need to use child therapy techniques that address the concerns of children in crisis.

Refugees and asylum seekers who are displaced because of wars, famine, or tribal conflict also need counseling support. Interventions aim at addressing the psychosocial consequences of the traumatic experiences that refugees, internally displaced persons, and asylum seekers encounter. Often the biggest challenge for the counselor is the language barrier.

Counselor Education

Counseling as a growing practice in Uganda has attracted many training institutions and practitioners. In 2011, at least 20 institutions of higher learning offered counselor training programs at different levels. Without standardized counselor training and practice, the profession risks having practitioners who do not meet professional standards. In line with the obligation to regulate the training and practice of counseling, UCA has developed guidelines and procedures for accrediting counselor training programs. UCA recognizes the following levels of counselor training: certificate, diploma, bachelor's degree, postgraduate diploma, master's degree, and doctorate. The curriculum framework for counseling programs was developed by UCA and approved by the National Council for Higher Education, the body responsible for setting the standards that govern the establishment and operation of higher education in Uganda. The approved curriculum details the course units that have to be completed for each level. Presently, all institutions of higher learning that offer training in counseling are required to adhere to the approved curriculum.

HIV/AIDS counselor training is taking a new direction under the Strengthening HIV Counselor Training (SCOT) project in collaboration with TASO, the Centre for Disease Control, and UCA. SCOT's main role is to strengthen and standardize the training and practice of HIV/AIDS counseling and to enhance collaboration among stakeholders involved in this training. In 2010, SCOT developed and launched standardized training curricula for national use and established the minimum standards for HIV counselor training. SCOT also updated the list of trainers and service providers in the country. Some of the organizations that use this curriculum include TASO, Mildmay Uganda, the AIDS Information Centre, and the Joint Clinical Research Center. In a period of 3 years (2006–2008), TASO trained 7,022 paracounselors.

The Future

It is anticipated that professional counseling in Uganda will continue to grow to maturity. According to the 2008–2012 strategic plan, UCA wants to have all professional counselors available, recognized, registered, and licensed by 2012. UCA is therefore in the process of obtaining a mandate, through a parliament bill, to take charge of all accreditation and certification of counselor training and practice in Uganda. This will be a great step forward in building the counseling profession in Uganda. UCA as a professional body needs support to develop an appropriate coordinating mechanism with the ministries of health, gender, education, and other stakeholders on issues of quality assurance in training, curriculum coordination, certification, standards, and professional ethics.

Systematic, quality counselor education directed toward building professionalism is an important area that needs urgent attention. A number of counselors have gone to other countries to obtain their PhDs in counseling, and their return to the country in a few years will help transform the profession. To accommodate the multicultural aspects and diversities of the Ugandan culture, counselor training needs to incorporate both traditional and modern methods. Clinical supervision of student counselors in practica and internships, as well as supervision of counselors in practice, needs to be streamlined to ensure ethical and professional responsibility. There is a need for continuous local research conducted and published by Ugandan counselors. The writing of culturally appropriate books should also be encouraged. In addition, Ugandan counselors need to develop standardized assessment tools that are culturally appropriate and sensitive to the needs of their clients.

The field of professional counseling will also need to embrace developing technology to introduce and strengthen e-services, such as telephone counseling, online counseling, and online counselor training. Counselors will need to keep abreast of areas that are new to Uganda but not necessarily the rest of the world, such as counseling for personality disorders, homosexuality, sexual addictions, and critical stress management.

Significant effort has been made to reduce the number of new HIV infections, but the burden of HIV/AIDS remains overwhelming. Corporations and workplaces need to be more involved by investing in the care and treatment of staff (Kironde & Lukwago, 2002). HIV counselor training needs to evolve with the disease. New curricula needs to be developed to cover relatively new but rapidly changing issues such as antiretroviral therapy, the prevention of mother-to-child transmission, home-based counseling and testing, basic preventive care, routine counseling and testing in clinical settings, and prevention with positives counseling. Curriculum content, skill levels, and training duration need to be introduced in accordance with the level and intensity of counseling provided by trainees. Certification, licensure, and accreditation of training providers are all key to improving quality. Finally, major NGO training providers need institutional development support to increase their training capacity in order to meet the demands of growing programs under the HIV/AIDS national strategy.

References

Balmer, D. H., Seeley, J., & Bachengana, C. (1996). The role of counselling in community support for HIV/AIDS in Uganda. *Counselling Psychology Quarterly, 9*(2), 177–190.

Government of Uganda. (1992). *Government white paper on the education policy review commission report.* Kampala, Uganda: Author.

Government of Uganda. (2008). *UNGASS country progress report: Uganda.* Retrieved from http://data.unaids.org/pub/Report/2008/uganda_2008_country_progress_report_en.pdf

Government of Uganda. (2010). *UNGASS country progress report: Uganda.* Retrieved from http://data.unaids.org/pub/Report/2010/uganda_2010_country_progress_report_en.pdf

Kaleeba, N., & Kalibbala, S. (1997). Participatory evaluation of counseling, medical and social services of The AIDS Support Organization (TASO) in Uganda. *AIDS Care, 9*(1), 13–26.

Katabira, E. (2009). Facts and figures about HIV/AIDS in Africa. In S. Musisi & E. Kinyanda (Eds.), *Psychiatric problems of HIV/AIDS and their management in Africa* (pp. 2–13). Kampala, Uganda: Fountain.

Kironde, S., & Lukwago, B. (2002). Practice points: Corporate response to HIV/AIDS epidemic in Uganda. *African Health Sciences, 2*(3), 127–135.

Ministry of Education and Sports. (2004, August). *The national report on the development of education in Uganda at the beginning of the 21st century.* Retrieved from http://www.ibe.unesco.org/International/ICE47/English/Natreps/reports/uganda_rev.pdf

Ministry of Education and Sports. (2010). About the department of guidance and counseling. *Journal of Guidance and Counseling, 1*(1), 1–2.

Romero, D. (1985). Brief reactions for the practitioner. *The Counseling Psychologist, 13,* 665–671. doi:10.1177/0011000085134010

Rujumba, J., Mbasaalaki-Mwaka, C. L., & Ndeezi, G. (2010). Challenges faced by health workers in providing counselling services to HIV-positive children in Uganda: A descriptive study. *Journal of the International AIDS Society, 13,* 1–9. doi:10.1186/1758-2652-13-9

Stockton, R., Nitza, A., & Bhusumane, D.-B. (2010). The development of professional counseling in Botswana. *Journal of Counseling & Development, 88,* 9–12.

Uganda Counselling Association. (2008). [Strategic development plan (2008-2012)]. Unpublished raw data.

Uganda Counselling Association. (2009). *The counsellors' code of ethics.* Kampala, Uganda: Author.

Uganda Counselling Association. (2010). *Accreditation and certification guidelines for counselling in Uganda.* Kampala, Uganda: Author.

UNdata. (2009). *Uganda.* Retrieved from http://data.un.org/CountryProfile.aspx?crname=Uganda

• • •

Counseling in Zimbabwe 8

Elias Mpofu, Messiah R. Makuane, Kimberly A. M. Richards, Magen M. Mhaka-Mutepfa, Jabulani Mpofu, Shupikai Zebron, and McLytton Nkonde Clever

Zimbabwe is a country rich in history and culture. Its cultural roots date back to at least the early 10th century. The major cultural-linguistic communities are the Shona (80% of the population), the Ndebele (about 15% of the population), and other smaller groups (English, Indians, Kalanga, Shangaani, Tonga, and Venda). Over the past 200 years, Zimbabwe has experienced significant sociocultural transformation. Major gains resulted in the provision of education and social services dating from the colonial period (1890–1980) and the two decades after. However, the country saw significant reversals in social services from 2000 to 2009, mostly the result of political and economic mismanagement (International Commission of Jurists, 2006). For instance, the United Nations Development Programme (2010) ranked Zimbabwe last of 169 countries in the area of human development. Despite being known as the Jewel of Africa in the 1980s, Zimbabwe has been ranked as one of the top six most failed states of the first decade of the millennium (The Slate Group, 2011). The average Zimbabwean has been exposed to significant risk for poor mental health because of the traumatic collapse of social services and policy institutions in a once thriving country.

The country appears to be on the path to recovery from a transitional political dispensation, allowing for national, regional, and international confidence in its future. This political and economic recovery has been accompanied by a resuscitation of basic social services, including education and health services. Full and sustained recovery may take up to a decade of development work involving partnerships between the government and civil society.

As a society in transition, the country has a complex profile of counseling services: traditional (indigenous) kin affiliation-oriented services, translational hybrid services (or those that combine indigenous and modern counseling services), and modern counseling services. Clients present with counseling needs consistent with their evolving social identities (Mpofu, 2006a). They may have transitional or emergent counseling and human service systems consistent with their rapidly changing needs. Livelihoods counseling is a common vehicle for community counseling (Mpofu, Bakker, & Levers, 2011).

The Zimbabwean indigenous cultural worldview is built on the foundation of *hunhuism/ ubuntu/buthu* (beingness; Mpofu, 1994b). The underlying concept of *hunhuism* is social connectedness. *Hunhu* manifests itself in a number of ways, including as selfless mutual caring and love of the other as the self. *Hunhuism* serves as both an ethical standard and a philosophy in the practice of indigenous counseling (Mpofu, Peltzer, & Bojuwoye, 2011). It subsumes a belief in the inherent human worth, personal and collective integrity, genuineness in interpersonal relationships, the unconditional acceptance of others, a forgiving attitude, and social responsibility. Behaviors that take away from the dignity of collective others do happen in tradition-led communities in Zimbabwe, and these are regarded as anti-*hunhu,* or reason for counseling (Mangena, 2009). Some segments of Zimbabwean become quite adept at counselor service selection, although many would benefit from formal education on the available options (Mpofu & Harley, 2002; Piachaud, 1994).

This chapter considers counseling in Zimbabwe, which is a developing country with a recent history of major sociopolitical transition. It begins with a discussion of school and other types of counseling. Next we present counseling approaches and techniques, highlighting the importance of livelihoods counseling. Counselor education and training for professional and indigenous counselors is also considered. Finally, diversity issues and the future prospects for counseling in Zimbabwe are discussed.

School Counseling

School counseling is a readily available service to learners because it is provided for as part of the national education policy. It is provided mostly by the Ministry of Education, Sport, and Culture. Counseling service provision is decentralized across the country, so each of the country's 10 regions has a Guidance and Counseling Officer. The Guidance and Counseling Officer coordinates a team of school counselors and may also provide direct counseling services. Every school has a designated counselor who is a regular class teacher, often with no professional counselor training (Mpofu, Maree, Kasayira, & Van der Wethuizen, 2011).

School counselors provide education in preventive health and life skills to students (Mpofu, Mutepfa, Chireshe, & Kasayira, 2007). Some schools offer career counseling, which may focus on basic employment skills, such as résumé preparation and interviewing techniques. In career counseling, counselor-teachers and learners engage in open-ended conversations about postschool occupational prospects. Students may pursue vocational training with government departments, in the private sector, or in colleges of further education. Students are likely to acquire more skills in vocational self-development from these in-school conversations than from any other source.

Psychoeducational assessment, counseling, and referral is also provided, mostly to students with special learning needs (Mpofu et al., 2007). The use of psychoeducational tools to identify gifted learners is the exception. Most psychoeducational tests are imported from the United Kingdom or United States, and they have no local norms. Users of these tests, usually school psychologists, consider the findings as a basis for discussion rather than for prescribing any educational programming. Curriculum-based tests have greater utility for learner–teacher advising than do standardized tests (Mpofu & Nyanungo, 1998). In selecting curriculum materials to determine a learner's needs for support, a counselor uses the school materials to establish the student's current learning potential and, on the basis of the findings, to map the learning progression likely to be most productive. Because counselors use materials already used in the schools, suggestions for remediation are transparent to both teachers and learners and are likely to be implemented.

Parents or caregivers are involved at the outset in the counseling of children with special educational needs. For instance, they provide background information on opportunities and constraints that influence the child's learning from having a disability. Depending on their literacy level, parents or guardians may help with assigned homework to further reinforce learning gains. Teachers also provide educational assessments to students using mostly curriculum materials to identify students who need remedial or extension teaching. Remedial learner support is available to students who are experiencing difficulties from gaps in their previous learning or from lacking prerequisite or assumed knowledge for current or expected learning. Extension learning is enrichment learning that enables students to excel in a certain aspect of the curriculum to achieve higher learning outcomes than would be the case otherwise. Most school curriculum materials, particularly at the primary and elementary school levels, include remedial and extension learning activities, which increases the chances that teachers will provide such instruction.

A school-based remedial education program has been in use since 1983 (Mpofu et al., 2007). To access the program, students attending Grade 4 take a curriculum-based assessment with remedial learning support officers from the Ministry of Education, Sport, and Culture and school-based remedial teachers. The assessment tasks are in English and mathematics and cover mostly basic concepts. Based on their performance on the learning tasks, students may be assigned to an hour of group instruction in English or mathematics each school week. School norms are used to select students for additional instruction such that students who score below the 50th percentile among their peers in the same grade are selected for supplemental or remedial instruction.

Students in tertiary-level studies access counseling through student support services. College students may present with a variety of counseling needs, including examination anxiety, depression, suicidal ideation, relationship issues, sexuality, family problems, self-harm, or, to a lesser extent, eating disorders. International students may have cultural adjustment needs. Financial problems pose the greatest challenge for the majority of students because of the increasing inability of the state to provide tuition support. In most universities or colleges in Zimbabwe, counseling is provided by a professional counselor or psychologist. Counselors with teaching assignments may work part time with reduced teaching loads.

Nonschool Counseling

Public social services provide mostly health counseling, whereas the civic community (i.e., nongovernmental organizations [NGOs]) provide broad-based community counseling, including livelihoods counseling. Health counseling broadly construed is more developed than other types of counseling provided by the Zimbabwean civil service. Primary health care counseling in particular is relatively well established.

Health Counseling

Despite strong beliefs in indigenous heath care, residents of urban Zimbabwe are 8 times more likely to consult modern health care counseling services (Winston & Patel, 1995). The proportion may be lower for residents in rural areas, where clinics are very widely dispersed or inaccessible because of distance. The average resident of rural Zimbabwe is also likely to self-treat with herbs or consult a traditional healer or prophet (charismatic church leader) as a first line of treatment prior to seeking health counseling at a hospital or clinic. This is likely unless a health-threatening condition is commonly known by the villagers to require hospital treatment.

As a measure of the success of formal health care counseling services in Zimbabwe, by the mid-1980s the country had one of the best primary health care systems on the African continent. The child and maternal health care counseling services available were in many ways exemplary. For instance, child and maternal mortality was at a low 5% during this period as a result of effective primary health care counseling and education. The high levels of literacy among the population, which were in excess of 87% among the general population by the mid-1990s, facilitated the phenomenal success of primary health care counseling. However, both the quality of and access to primary health care counseling decreased significantly with the socioeconomic meltdown of 2000 to 2009. Consequently, child and maternal mortality increased a phenomenal fourfold (to about 20%) and has remained at an elevated level since (Munjanja, 2007).

With the advent of the HIV/AIDS pandemic in the 1980s, health counseling in Zimbabwe has generally focused on HIV/AIDS prevention and healthy living for those affected and infected. Specific issues for counseling include voluntary HIV testing, stigma reduction for HIV/AIDS, work participation counseling, prevention of mother-to-child transmission, and medical referral support services.

The public health and social welfare sector has historically been involved in the care and treatment of people with psychiatric disabilities. Resources have mostly been committed to the treatment and care of people with severe psychotic disorders. Treatments by public health services typically involve psychotropic drugs, and the patient becomes an outpatient once the psychosis shows signs of remission. Nicotine is also provided to patients with psychotic disorders because of its significant effects on symptom reduction and its wide availability.

Rehabilitative Care Counseling

Counseling for care and risk prevention includes the home-based care of patients and other vulnerable groups in the community (e.g., orphans). Home-based care is provided by community volunteers to assist people and families living with HIV/AIDS. This includes support to orphans living with relatives and to child-headed households. Generally this type of counseling support is provided on site or through community outreach by clinics or hospitals. Multilateral organizations such as Population Services International and New Start are major players in providing counseling for community support. For example, New Start, which is funded by the U.S. government, provides HIV Voluntary Counseling and Testing services. Trauma counseling is mostly provided by civic bodies or associations. Some organizations may also focus on specific problems of living, such as suicide prevention, bereavement, domestic violence, and human rights abuses. For example, the Samaritans provide suicide prevention counseling, and Island Hospice provides bereavement counseling. The Musasa Projects are a national leader in supportive counseling of survivors of domestic abuse, whereas the Counselling Services Unit provides counseling to victims of political violence.

Best Counseling Practices

Counseling in Zimbabwean communities is traditionally provided through elders, family, peers, and community leaders (Charema & Shizha, 2008; Gelfand, 1978). This counseling covers all aspects of life-span/life-space issues: personal growth and development, community living, marriage, work, spirituality, and leisure. However, in the practice of traditional counseling aspects of social participation with a bearing on the presenting issue are also addressed. The counseling typically combines both individual- and group-focused facilitative counseling for effective and responsive social participation within the kinship, family, and community. Livelihoods counseling is a major technique for structural or community-level interventions in the country.

Facilitative Counseling

In facilitative counseling, the potential for growth in self and others is assumed by social others, and counseling intervention interactions are aimed at drawing out or exploiting this potential. In the social practices of indigenous cultures, the counseling role is embedded in all life activities. Facilitative counseling skills are acquired as part of the growth process, and evidence of their appropriate use a major indicator of cultural maturity. For instance, an important if not critical yardstick of personal maturity is effective and socially responsible participation (i.e., *kuva nemusoro,* or "of constructive disposition" in the Shona language; Mpofu, 1994b) in family and the community and the capacity to assist in the full inclusion of others in the community. This entails recognizing and responding empathically to the needs of others in the collective and supporting them to achieve a collective sense of humanity. There is an assumption in indigenous counseling that individuals with the facilitative support of kin, family, and community groups are capable to successfully resolve issues of social participation.

Facilitative counseling in the context of Zimbabwean indigenous cultures is essentially about resolving problems of living in the context of a collectivist culture. In a collectivist culture, the values of the collective are joined with those of the individual. Within the broad sub-Saharan worldview of *ubuntu/hunhu/buthu* (beingness; Mpofu, 1994b), the individual is because of the community, which is part of him or her, and the collective community defines the individual. Counseling efforts are keyed toward social facilitation to nurture in the self and the collective others the very best of beingness, and the quality of beingness is expected in all. Family and kin (*vobgo* in the Shona language) are primary counselors, and tradition-led Zimbabweans consider their role unmatched by that of outsiders such as professional counselors (Mpofu, 1994a).

Narrative therapy is a preferred counseling approach in the indigenous cultural communities of Zimbabwe. It is achieved through storytelling, with key counseling lessons emphasized by repetition of lyric (Maree & du Toit, 2011). Narrative counselors consider the contextual and cultural locations of issues and encourage clients to actively reconstruct and adopt enabling behaviors for the environments in which they live. Among tradition-led Zimbabweans, issues of counseling are embedded in narratives about social participation (as with family, kin) and stories are told by the person to others and also of the person by knowing others (or *vokuziva,* or "those in the know" in the Shona language).

Providers of facilitative counseling for livelihoods are mostly NGOs. These may be regional, national, or multilateral agencies. Next we consider the type and scope of livelihoods counseling offered by NGOs or civil society.

Livelihoods Counseling

Livelihoods refers to the assets and activities required for people to help themselves and their families out of poverty (Toner, 2003). Such assets include natural resources, community participation, vocational skills, and social support and networks (Allison & Ellis, 2001). The need for livelihoods counseling interventions is particularly acute in developing countries that have fragile socioeconomic support systems and marginal welfare services (United Nations Development Programme, 2010). Livelihoods counseling programs seek to promote self-reliance and sufficiency through self-employment for income generation or active community participation to improve the social and economic quality of life. They are intended to generate income, create employment, improve food security, and increase the resource base at the household level. Livelihoods systems encompass a diverse set of economic, social, and physical approaches, enabling access to activities and assets for living. Therefore, livelihoods counseling is participatory in nature. Livelihoods are enabled when individuals can access opportunities and resources for a meaningful living.

In livelihoods counseling, a facilitator agency (which could be an NGO) provides counseling support for sustainable development. Often it is provided in the context of community development to alleviate poverty and to protect vulnerable segments of the community (i.e., those underserved by social services). For instance, in their social justice–oriented counseling, NGOs in Zimbabwe engage in social and political lobbying to equalize access to social services among the marginalized. NGOs usually work in consultation with public services departments in the areas in which they are providing development assistance. During the Zimbabwean sociopolitical meltdown of 2000 to 2009, NGOs alone provided livelihoods support and counseling.

Some NGOs provide facilitative livelihoods counseling to specific segments of the community (e.g., women, people with disabilities, senior citizens). Examples of NGO services for particular community segments include the Women's Action Group for women's rights and HelpAge for the health of senior citizens. Community support and building groups may assist in the development of vegetable and herb gardens for community health and microfinanced community income-generating projects.

Faith-based organizations are major providers of livelihoods counseling to individuals, families, and communities across the country. In addition to addressing the spiritual needs of communities, many faith-based organizations take care of functions typically associated with public services, such as education, health care, and community development. Their pastoral counseling focuses on the application of spiritual content and processes to the alleviation of human distress (Louw, 2011). Some faith-based organizations in Zimbabwe have distinguished themselves in providing a variety of social services, including refugee services (e.g., the Jesuit Refugee Service Zimbabwe), youth counseling (e.g., the Simukai Street Youth Project), and spiritual counseling (e.g., the International Scripture Union Movement).

In the Zimbabwean context, churches with significant involvement in supporting health and well-being with community development tend to be those set up by missionaries from Western countries. Those founded by charismatic indigenous leaders tend to provide supportive counseling only to members of the specific church organization (Daneel, 1987).

Diversity Issues

In any counseling situation, counselors need to be aware of local contextual factors in order to understand the world and experience of the client (Mpofu, 2006b). Counselors should strive to become culturally sensitive and gain skills that will enable them to be competent counselors.

As previously noted, Zimbabwe is a multicultural country with at least three major cultural-linguistic communities (i.e., Kalanga, Ndebele, Shangani, Shona, Venda) and a number of other minor cultural groupings (e.g., White, Indian). The indigenous groups, such as the Shona, Ndebele, Venda-Shangaan, and Tonga, share a worldview rooted in *ubuntu/hunhu*-ism (beingness) and perceive counseling issues and best practices similarly. However, they also have differences in the emphasis or salience they ascribe to aspects of social participation. For example, whereas in the Shona culture persons would expect younger people to ask after the health and well-being of older others, this would not be the case in the Ndebele culture. The Ndebeles believe that a younger person, being less experienced about health issues overall, would not be able to provide assistance to an older person should he or she report being unwell, which would cause social embarrassment to both parties. Similarly, counselors who are younger and/or of a different sex or language group than their clients may be perceived as less credible. Counselor–client matching ideally takes into account age, gender, and language differences.

Given the belief in spiritual mediation in the health and well-being by Zimbabweans, it is important for counselors to know how to work with clients who believe that their psychological problems are connected to their ancestral spirits. Competencies in spirituality counseling are important for effective counseling with Zimbabweans.

Counselor Education

Counselors in Zimbabwe mostly train within provider organizations, and this is especially true of paraprofessionals. Some are formally trained by counseling departments in an institution's universities. Here we distinguish between the training of professional and indigenous counselors. Professional counselors hold these roles in formal, paid employment. Indigenous counselors are mostly lay counselors, some of whom have training in traditional healing. They provide counseling services as needed and within the social groups with which they are involved.

Professional Counselors

Providers of formal counselor education and training include government departments and civic bodies (or NGOs). Each government ministry with human or social service functions runs in-house counseling workshops. For instance, HIV/AIDS counselor training is provided by the Ministry of Health and Child Welfare and the Ministry of Education, Sport, and Culture. Government agencies, such as the National AIDS Council, also provide HIV/AIDS counselor training. The training tends to be workshop style and graduates paraprofessionals (also called "primary care counselors") with the minimum skills to work relatively independently in the community. The purpose of the training is to equip lay counselors to assist community members in reducing their risk for contracting HIV and to address the psychological issues of those infected or affected.

CONNECT and CONTACT are two private education institutions that also provide counseling and counselor training. Graduates receive certificates in a variety of counseling roles, such as HIV counseling, child counseling, and family counseling. These programs are generally 2 to 4 weeks long spread out over a period of 6 months to a year. Community-based organizations such as the Batsirai Group also provide training in basic counseling skills, including training in herbal therapy treatment for the care of those living with HIV.

The Zimbabwe Open University offers certificate, bachelor's, and master's degree courses in counseling. The majority of Zimbabwe Open University counseling students work in the civil service, such as in schools and hospitals, and thus are not community counselors. The University of Zimbabwe provides education and training in clinical psychology and in personnel and human resources counseling. This same university also trains educational psychologists who provide counseling in school settings.

Indigenous Counselors

With informal family- or kin-oriented counseling, education and training occurs through participation in counseling in everyday settings and around specific life areas. Counselor educator–student roles interchange frequently and are dictated by the specific perceived personal counseling needs in the context of the values of the collective. The counselor educator–student roles may also be influenced by seniority or social position in the kin network. Senior people or those with designated counselor roles within kin networks (nephews, aunties, and uncles) normally provide appropriate counselor education around naturally occurring opportunities for personal or group development. A participatory rather than didactic approach is preferred, and individuals can choose from the usually large kinship network those on whom they desire to model their own learning. Counselor education in the context of the family or kinship also occurs from observing others who are providing or receiving counseling from appropriate others. Some opportunities for acquiring counseling skills occur within gender groupings and in culturally scripted roles.

Traditional healers undergo counselor training by shadowing experienced healers in an informal apprenticeship system. Trainee healers work with those providing services in the practice areas in which they seek specialization. However, the average traditional healer performs numerous functions in his or her community, including veterinary consultant, herbalist, weatherperson, ancestral spirit priest, goblin terminator, and crop and soil scientist. Thus, the trainee healer has opportunities to learn situated counseling skill applications. The training is also largely participatory, with focused demonstration and practice tailored to the learner's perceived needs.

The Future

The professionalization of counseling in Zimbabwe is still in its infancy, and most counseling is performed in community settings by family and socially networked others. Indigenous counseling networks operate alongside and often complementary to formal counseling services. It is likely that counselors in Zimbabwe in the foreseeable future will continue to adopt and use methods respectful of their clients' personal and cultural worldviews. In this regard, they will need to develop culturally responsive interventions for health and well-being.

The majority of counselors in Zimbabwe are paraprofessionals with minimal training. Professional counselor supervision is lacking (Chireshe, 2009). If supervision occurs, it is often agency based and is likely to emphasize and support the agency's mission, goals, and activities. Counselor supervision training is an area of great need in Zimbabwe. Counseling services in Zimbabwe need to be based more on evidence for the theories and techniques used than on cultural traditions alone. The evidence base for counseling practices in the country is very limited. For instance, most of the works on counseling in Zimbabwe are activity and policy reports by service providers with very limited circulation.

Studies are needed on replicable approaches for translating aspects of core Zimbabwean culture (e.g., *unhuism,* ancestral consciousness) into the counseling process or specific counseling techniques. Research could focus on identifying general practice and specific techniques that are useful in working with clients who are located in traditional or blended cultures.

Conclusion

Counseling is an indelible part of diverse Zimbabwean communities. The way it is conceptualized continues to evolve and be influenced by both historical cultural traditions and modernity. Counseling practices in Zimbabwe bridge indigenous, transitional, and modern worldviews to empower the health and well-being of citizens in the context of a collectivist cultural worldview. The country is undergoing social and economic transition as a result of both local and global influences, allowing counselors to experiment with a variety of ways of delivering counseling services.

Despite the near collapse of social services since 2000, counseling services in Zimbabwe appear to be on a trajectory toward recovery. Both professional and paraprofessional counseling are open to development and research. Blended counseling services that combine indigenous and modern counseling are likely to continue to be the treatment of choice among Zimbabweans.

References

Allison, E. H., & Ellis, F. (2001). The livelihoods approach and management of small-scale fisheries. *Marine Policy, 25*(5), 377–388.

Charema, J., & Shizha, E. (2008). Counselling indigenous Shona people in Zimbabwe: Traditional practices vs. Western Eurocentric perspectives. *AlterNative, 4,* 123–140.

Chireshe, R. (2009). *An assessment of the effectiveness of school guidance and counselling services in Zimbabwean secondary schools.* Unpublished doctoral dissertation, University of South Africa, Pretoria.

Daneel, M. L. (1987). *Quest for belonging: Introduction to a study of African independent churches.* Gweru, Zimbabwe: Mambo Press.

Gelfand, M. (1978). *The genuine Shona.* Gweru, Zimbabwe: Mambo Press.

International Commission of Jurists. (2006). *Findings on the human rights situation in Zimbabwe by United Nations and regional human rights bodies.* Geneva, Switzerland: Author.

Louw, D. J. (2011). Pastoral care and counseling. In E. Mpofu (Ed.), *Counseling people of African ancestry* (pp. 155–165). New York, NY: Cambridge University Press.

Mangena, F. (2009). The search for an African feminist ethic: A Zimbabwean perspective. *Journal of International Woman's Study, 11*(2), 18–30.

Maree, J. G., & du Toit, C. M. (2011). The role of oral tradition in counseling people of African ancestry. In E. Mpofu (Ed.), *Counseling people of African ancestry* (pp. 22–40). New York, NY: Cambridge University Press.

Mpofu, E. (1994a). Counsellor role perceptions and preferences of Zimbabwe teachers of a Shona cultural background. *Counselling Psychology Quarterly, 7,* 311–326.

Mpofu, E. (1994b). Exploring the self-concept in an African culture. *Journal of Genetic Psychology, 155,* 341–354.

Mpofu, E. (2006a). Majority world health care traditions intersect indigenous and complementary and alternative medicine. *International Journal of Disability, Development and Education, 53,* 375–379.

Mpofu, E. (2006b). *Theories and techniques for counsellors applied to African settings.* Harare, Zimbabwe: College Press.

Mpofu, E., Bakker, T., & Levers, L. L. (2011). Counseling in African cultural heritage settings: The challenges and opportunities. In E. Mpofu (Ed.), *Counseling people of African ancestry* (pp. 313–316). New York, NY: Cambridge University Press.

Mpofu, E., & Harley, D. (2002). Disability and rehabilitation in Zimbabwe. *Journal of Rehabilitation, 68,* 26–33.

Mpofu, E., Maree, J. G., Kasayira, J. M., & Van der Wethuizen, C. N. (2011). School counseling. In E. Mpofu (Ed.), *Counseling people of African ancestry* (pp. 111–125). New York, NY: Cambridge University Press.

Mpofu, E., Mutepfa, M. M., Chireshe, R., & Kasayira, J. M. (2007). School psychology in Zimbabwe. In S. R. Jimerson, T. Oakland, & P. Farrell (Eds.), *The handbook of international school psychology* (pp. 437–452). Thousand Oaks, CA: Sage.

Mpofu, E., & Nyanungo, K. R. L. (1998). Educational and psychological testing in Zimbabwean schools: Past, present and future. *European Journal of Psychological Assessment, 14,* 71–90.

Mpofu, E., Peltzer, K., & Bojuwoye, O. (2011). Indigenous healing practices in sub-Saharan Africa. In E. Mpofu (Ed.), *Counseling people of African ancestry* (pp. 3–21). New York, NY: Cambridge University Press.

Munjanja, S. P. (2007). *Maternal and perinatal mortality study.* Harare, Zimbabwe: Ministry of Child Welfare and Health.

Piachaud, J. (1994). Strengths and difficulties in developing countries: The case of Zimbabwe. In N. Bouras (Ed.), *Mental health in mental retardation* (pp. 382–392). Cambridge, England: Cambridge University Press.

The Slate Group. (2011). *Foreign policy.* Washington, DC: Author.

Toner, A. (2003). Exploring sustainable livelihoods approaches in relation to two interventions in Tanzania. *Journal of International Development, 15,* 771–781.

United Nations Development Programme. (2010). *Human development report 2010—The real wealth of nations: Pathways to human development.* New York, NY: Author.

Winston, C. M., & Patel, V. (1995). Use of traditional and orthodox health services in urban Zimbabwe. *International Journal of Epidemiology, 24,* 1006–1012.

• • •

Section 3

Counseling in Asian Countries

Counseling in China

Ben K. Lim and Soh-Leong Lim

China, currently the second largest economy in the world, is expected to top the chart as the world's largest economy in the next decade or so. With its hefty defense budget, China is likely to emerge as the next superpower in the world as well. Its phenomenal growth economically and militarily, however, does not seem to match its growth in mental health services and resources. During the May 12, 2008, Wenchuan earthquake, buildings were leveled and an estimated 80,000 people died, leaving 5,500 orphans behind and 5 million homeless. At the third anniversary of the 7.9-magnitude earthquake, Premier Wen Jiabao proudly announced that China had been able to rebuild the cities in 2 years, a year ahead of the 3-year goal set by the government. Although this is admirable, progress lagged in meeting the mental health needs of the people. Zhang Jianxin of the Institute of Psychology, who was commissioned to help in the psychological reconstruction of the victims, reported that there were not enough resources to help the survivors. Reports of posttraumatic stress disorder left largely untreated point to the vast need for more mental health and psychotherapeutic services in China. And there is increasing awareness of the need for such services. Both the 5th World Congress for Psychotherapy (October 2008) and the International Psychiatry Congress (September 2010), both held in Beijing, had the support of the Chinese leadership. This support augurs well for the development of mental health services in China.

Different authors over the past decade have chronicled the historical development of counseling in China. Qian, Smith, Chen, and Xia (2002) identified four developmental stages of counseling. After the early Soviet influence of Pavlov's behavioral psychology (1949–1965), China subsequently went through a period of politicization and demonization of mental health services during Mao's Cultural Revolution (1966–1976). After this period, China experienced the emergence and popular embrace of Freudian and psychoanalytic psychology (1978–1986). Finally, from 1987 to the present, there has been an influx of Western literature and practices, especially in hospitals and mental health clinics. This period diversified mental health practice in China because of its increasing openness to Western modalities of therapeutic practice.

Yip (2005) provided a snapshot of mental health services before and after the formation of the People's Republic of China in 1949. He pointed out the contribution of Western missionary doctors who formed mental asylums in psychiatric hospitals in different cities in China. Yip (2005) explained that with the formation of the People's Republic of China, efforts to indigenize mental health services became the foundation for the development of future psychiatric and psychological services. The use of methods other than medical treatment, such as traditional Chinese medicine (TCM), physical therapy, occupational therapy, and psychoeducation, to treat mental illnesses was stipulated. He attributed the more favorable attitude toward mental health services in China to the open door policy of Deng Xiaoping in 1987. Along with this milestone came an emerging interest in psychotherapeutic publications, with the market being supplied by both the translation of foreign literature and the production of indigenous Chinese works.

Using the Cultural Revolution (1966–1976) as a benchmark, Lim, Lim, Michael, Cai, and Schock (2010) identified the three broad generations of Chinese currently living, who would likely present with different mental health issues because of the differing sociocultural and political contexts within which each generation was embedded. First, those who were born before the Cultural Revolution directly experienced the events of this painful period in Chinese history; they are likely to present with trauma. Second, those who were born during the revolution were impacted by the revolution in their early childhood years; they are likely to present with issues of secondary trauma. Third, those who were born after the Cultural Revolution were spared the immense sufferings of this sociopolitical era of Chinese history. They may know little of what happened in the country, as this is still a sensitive topic in China. They may also be unaware of the effects of intergenerational trauma, which they may have experienced. What is apparent, however, is that the sociocultural context of this generation is fraught with stressors brought about by rapid urbanization, industrialization, economic prosperity, and a competitive marketplace.

Lim et al. (2010) pointed out that with 100 million people suffering from various psychological problems, mental illness is the most widespread disease in China. They also cited a high suicide rate of around 20–30 per 10,000 compared to the worldwide of 14 per 10,000. The highly competitive educational system has created immense psychological stress for students to perform well on entrance examinations. All of this, together with the rapid urbanization of the rural population, makes counseling and psychological well-being a significant venture worthy of both local and global attention.

The Current Status of Counseling

Mental health counseling in China encompasses both psychological counseling/consultation (*xinli zixun* 心理咨询) and psychotherapy (*xinli zhiliao* 心理治疗). Generally speaking, *xinli zixun* is used in reference to various counseling activities, including psychoeducation, informal supportive advice, and drop-in psychological consultation (Chang, Tong, Shi, & Zeng, 2005; Hou & Zhang, 2007). *Xinli zhiliao* is sometimes used interchangeably with *xinli zixun*, but officially the designation *xinli zhiliao shi* (心理治疗师) or certified psychotherapist is used for those with a medical degree (Qian, Gao, Yao, & Rodriguez, 2009).

Hou and Zhang (2007) explained that there are three broad groups of counselors in China. The first group serves the severely mentally ill in hospital settings. Because of the medical context, severe mental illness is the focus; counseling tends to follow the medical reductionist model, with prescriptions of drugs by doctors.

The second group works within the educational system of the country. Under the auspices of the Ministry of Education, school counselors are mainly involved in mandatory mental health education. Many of these counselors are homeroom teachers who are responsible for the administrative aspects of students' education and development. Included in their responsibilities is psychological counseling. The number of mental health educators employed is very low, with only 10% employed in urban schools and less than 1% employed in the rural provinces (Jiang, 2007, as cited by Cook, Lei, & Chiang, 2010). Universities have a similar need for more counselors. Professor Bingjie Zhao, the director of the Fujian Association for Mental Health and the director of HuaQiao University's Mental Health Education and Counseling Center, stated that the law mandates that there must be a psychological counselor for every 3,000–5,000 students. However, Zhao lamented the fact that the ratio tends to be higher because of the lack of trained counselors. The role of the university counselor is that of a full-time faculty member. He or she is involved not only in counseling but also in teaching and research (B. Zhao, personal communication, June 24, 2011). From a national perspective, all counseling and mental health education includes political and thought education as directed by the Ministry of Education. There has been criticism of this inconvenient union (Leung, Guo, & Lam, 2000; Yip, 2006). According to X. Gao et al. (2010), in the early days of the formation of the People's Republic of China, "mental illness and other forms of deviance were cast as problems of misdirected political thinking to be addressed through re-education, rather than mental health care" (p. 80).

The third group of counselors consists of those working with commercial companies and those practicing in the private sector. Most of these counselors are found in the larger cities on the eastern coast. The development of independent centers in which locally certified counselors provide counseling to the Chinese is in its infancy. However, some counseling groups have well-credentialed counselors. These include the Harmony Counseling Center, which serves local Chinese in Shenyang, and the Shanghai International Mental Health Association, which provides services to the growing international community in China.

There are three important aspects of the development of counseling as a profession in China. The first aspect relates to the training of counselors: More counselors need to be trained by the universities. China has 2,429 institutes of higher learning, but only about 60 universities offer counseling as a discipline of study (Lim et al., 2010). A nationwide survey of 1,391 mental health professionals showed that approximately 70% had a bachelor's-level education or less, only 36.4% had majored in psychology, and about 60% were employed part time (X. Gao et al., 2010). Whereas some counselors are locally trained, others are trained abroad in the United States, Hong Kong, Japan, Russia, or Germany.

The second aspect of note concerns the existence of professional associations for counseling in China. There are currently two important counseling associations: the Chinese Psychological Society (CPS) and the Chinese Association of Mental Health (CAMH). Both are registered with the Chinese Science and Technology Association and therefore have legal governmental sanction. The CPS was the first of the two professional psychological bodies to be established. It became defunct soon after its formation in 1921 but was reactivated in 1975. The aim of the CPS is to foster academic exchange as well as research and clinical development among psychologists with graduate degrees. The CPS also seeks to advance developmental psychology as a discipline in China and to contribute to China's societal development and transformation. Two scientific journals, *Acta Psychologica Sinica* and *Psychological Science*, are published under the auspices of the CPS. The CAMH, first established in 1936, was suspended during the Cultural Revolution but reinstituted in 1985. The CAMH is a multidisciplinary psychological organization whose membership includes people with varied educational and career backgrounds. The CAMH seeks to promote the development of mental health science and improve the mental health status of the Chinese people through psychoeducation and conferences. The CAMH is also organized at certain provincial levels. The CAMH publishes three journals and one magazine: the *Chinese Mental Health Journal*, the *Chinese Journal of Clinical Psychology*, the *Chinese Journal of Health Psychology*, and *Psychology and Health Magazine*.

The third aspect of note in the professionalization of counseling relates to the certification of Chinese counselors. There are three types of certificates. The first two, the Certificate of Psychological Counseling and the Certificate of Marriage and Family Therapy, are issued by the National Labor Bureau, Chinese Ministry of Labor and Social Security. The Certificate of Marriage and Family Therapy is not popular yet, as the discipline is still in its infancy in China and most counseling is done individually. The third certificate, the Certificate of Psychological Psychotherapy, is provided by the Chinese Ministry of Health and Ministry of Personnel. This certificate is for those who work in a medical setting (Qian et al., 2009). In addition to these three types of certificate, a coveted recognition for those who aspire to be master counselors is to be a Registered Psychologist (注册心理师) with the CPS. Since the introduction of the Registered Psychologist designation in 2009, about 200 counselors have been given this recognition.

Obviously, China realizes the need for counseling training. It has a centralized societal structure for a network of psychological and counseling platforms, ranging from the school to university systems and from public to private settings. However, in reporting the quandary of the present counseling field, Hou and Zhang (2007) lamented the fact that universities that have counseling programs seem to emphasize book learning and theoretical knowledge while deemphasizing the practical application of this knowledge. Counselors, therefore, lack the necessary skills to counsel effectively. Moreover, workshops offered on an ad hoc basis tend to focus on experiential hands-on practice at the expense of a strong theoretical foundation. The felt need in China is for strong practice based on empirical research and theory. Another area of critical need in the country is ongoing supervision for counselors (X. Gao et al., 2010). Currently there is little opportunity for supervised practicum or internship experiences for counseling graduates in China.

Best Counseling Practices

Although traditional Chinese philosophy is rich in holistic ideas and concepts that can form the foundation for the development of Chinese psychology, there is currently no well-articulated indigenous theory of counseling in China (Hou & Zhang, 2007). Psychoanalytic theory and Freudian understanding of the ego still forms the basis of most Chinese understanding of counseling and therapy. In practice, however, most counselors draw from a variety of Western theoretical models (e.g., cognitive behavior therapy, gestalt therapy, object relations, solution-focused brief therapy, person-centered therapy, Satir conjoint family therapy). At the same time there are efforts at integrating traditional Chinese ideas of holistic health such as TCM (中医) with Western psychotherapy. An example is the work of Shu (2003), who integrates TCM, psychodrama, and the creative arts. TCM views all internal or chronic diseases as being caused by seven major emotions. These are anger, shock, joy, fear, brooding, anxiety, and sorrow (Chen, 2006).

Confucianism and Taoism form an important part of conservative morality and philosophical ideas that continue to influence Chinese sensibilities about the practice of counseling in China. Zhang et al. (2002) developed Chinese Taoist cognitive psychotherapy and found that it effectively regulates general anxiety and disordered negative affect. In the same vein, therapists can tap into many other aspects of China's rich cultural tradition and integrate them with Western counseling theories and practice. Some aspects of Chinese cultural practice that contribute to holistic health include Chinese music and calligraphy, mindfulness practice, Zen ideas, mind–body holism in TCM, acupuncture, and self-soothing techniques such as *taiji* (太极) and qigong (气功). In counseling, the Confucian doctrine of the Mean (*zhong yong* 中庸) can guide the Chinese counselor toward an integrated balanced practice that incorporates the best of Eastern and Western traditions.

Currently counseling in China is done both formally and informally, with different degrees of integration of Eastern and Western practices. On the formal end, Western-style talk therapy is available in offices in the larger cities, such as Beijing and Shanghai. Y. Gao (2001) noted that the Chinese style of counseling tends to be more directive; this is consistent with Chinese cultural tradition. However, he also argued that with China's transition from a planned economy to a market economy, Chinese clients are beginning to appreciate a nondirective style in which they are empowered to generate their own solutions to problems. Most counselors see only individuals, usually female clients, who are more amenable to asking for help. Culturally speaking this is understandable, as most people prefer to solve their problems within the family rather than involve outsiders. However, with the family under increasing stress, there is an urgent need for family counseling in China. For such work, an understanding of Chinese thinking and Chinese contextual variables is useful. Filial piety (*xiao* 孝), benevolence (*ren* 仁), propriety (*li* 礼), and harmony (*he* 和) form the bedrock of any counseling involving more than one person in the counseling room. The counselor's ability to reframe and depathologize family dysfunctions helps couples and families to continue in counseling. For instance, in couples therapy, the counselor does not seek to fix either the husband or wife; instead, he or she treats the relationship. Similarly, when men are reluctant to come for therapy, asking them to become consultants in the family session will encourage them to participate in the counseling process.

Overall, there is still a strong social stigma attached to counseling in China. It is often associated with mental illnesses, which in China are usually treated in hospitals and in the criminal justice system. However, some informal paraprofessional counseling approaches may not be as stigmatizing and are used to mitigate psychological problems and promote psychological well-being. An important example is peer counseling in schools. Another is voluntary mediation in the community. In August 2010, China passed a law on community mediation for the resolution of family or community disputes. Since then, more than 820,000 mediation committees have been formed in both urban neighborhoods and rural villages (Xin, 2011).

Another important form of paraprofessional counseling is telephone counseling. Telephone hotlines in China are largely directive, staffed by volunteers who have undergone some short-term training in basic listening skills and crisis intervention. It is a well-accepted counseling modality in China. It saves face, is anonymous, and offers a quick solution to a practical problem (Y. Gao, 2001). Online suicide telephone counseling has been in existence since the 1980s; in 1989, the first suicide prevention organization, the Pei'ai Suicide Prevention Center, was established in Guangzhou. Since then, some newspapers, television programs, and radio programs have set up psychological counseling hotlines and columns (S. Huang, He, & He, 2008). Disaster relief, another important form of psychological service in the country, is in need of further development in China. He Dan, the program director of the Red Cross Society of China, spoke of setting up a national database of emergency response teams and compiling training manuals and other resources in order to address people's mental health needs whenever there are disasters, such as the 2008 Wenchuan earthquake (Dan, 2011).

In addition to these practices, Chinese counselors utilize the Internet for therapy and, where available, for supervision. There are no laws governing the use of technology in counseling. Given the lack of trained counselors and supervisors, technology can be gainfully used to advance the field of counseling in China. A collaborative effort is under way between the Department of Labor and Hua-Xia PsychCn, an innovative Web-based organization, to train lay counselors to listen to people in distress (W.-J. Huang, 2005).

Because counseling is on its ascendency and is slowly gaining acceptance, it is important that counseling be done in an ethical manner. In the Chinese context, relationships (*guanxi* 关系), favors (*renqing* 人情), and face-saving (*mianzi* 面子) can present ethical dilemmas as they relate to dual relationships, boundaries, and confidentiality. The CPS, together with support from the CAMH, realizes the challenges facing the counseling profession and has formulated a code of ethics covering all areas of training, research, and professional practice (CPS, 2007; Qian et al., 2009). However, these standards will need to be given teeth by necessary legislation and enforcement from the central government.

Diversity Issues

The 6th National Population Census, which took place in 2010, confirmed that China, with its 1.37 billion people, is still the world's most populous country. China has seen an increase of 73.89 million people since 2000. China is not a homogeneous country. Although the majority of its population (92%) is Han Chinese, there are 54 nationally recognized ethnic minorities, each with a distinct culture, history, and language. The one-child family policy in China does not apply to ethnic minority families (who are allowed two children) or rural families (who are allowed two children if the firstborn is a girl). A culturally competent counselor will not assume that minority families are the same as majority Han families.

China's population growth and the current rate of rural–west to urban–east migration create great psychological stress on individuals, families, and communities. In 2010, more than 261 million Chinese, 40% of whom were younger than age 18, moved from their rural hometowns to the highly populated eastern seaboard in search of better living (Jing, 2011). Migrant families face great challenges in the cities. They lack access to basic public amenities, including education, housing, transportation, and natural resources. Psychologically speaking, they grapple with problems such as identity issues, depression, and anxiety. Migrants' inability to obtain permanent residential permits (*hukou* 户口) and to become part of the urban social security system contribute to the widening social gap between the rich and poor. Tobin (2011) reported that inequality in China has now surpassed that in the United States.

Also challenging for China, as for many other countries, is population aging. The gerontological care of senior citizens (those older than 65) is a pressing issue.

Traditional family support in China is deeply rooted in the Confucian value of filial piety. Although there is an indication that filial piety remains an important value among the young in China, there is concern that the traditional moral foundation of family support is breaking down. In a society that depends on the Confucian value of filial piety for the support and welfare of aging parents and people with disabilities, the increasing mobility of Chinese families and changing values in a competitive market economy are threatening the family system. Thomason and Qiong (2008) reported that generational differences result in breakdown of filial piety and a failure in communication; they suggested that this contributes to greater computer and video game addictions among adolescents.

Another demographic issue is the gender ratio. According to the National Population and Planning Commission (2011), there is a birth sex ratio imbalance of 120 males to 100 females; in comparison, the global ratio is 103–107 males to 100 females. Because of Confucian influences, there is still a preference for males (to bring good fortune 多字多福). This imbalance has resulted in an excess 20 million males in the country. Themes that surface in counseling because of China's one-child policy and society's preference for males include females who present with problems associated with being the less preferred gender (rejection, preferential treatment accorded to a brother), only children on whose shoulders lie the filial responsibilities of caring for their aging parents, and unreasonable expectations of parents for their only children. Only children often carry high levels of stress as they strive for success in school and university entrance examinations and contemplate job prospects in a highly competitive social environment.

An important diversity issue is the psychological and medical significance of homosexuality in China. Professor Zhang Beichuan of Qingdao University, the country's leading expert on homosexuality and AIDS, estimated that there are 30 million homosexuals in China—of these, 20 million are gay and 10 million are lesbians (Zhiling & Ao, 2010). The central government does not officially forbid homosexuality. It is significant that the word *comrade* (同志), which traditionally refers to a Communist Party loyalist, is widely used to refer to fellow gays and lesbians. Although Confucius is silent on homosexuality, his much-embraced definition of unfiliality includes disobeying one's parents, not supporting one's parents, and not continuing the family line (Sun, 2008). Because of this Confucian tradition, homosexual couples in China face unique difficulties, especially in families with one child. Professor Zhang estimated that 90% of gays have fake marriages to display a public façade of traditionality as a way to cope with the expectation to continue the family line. Some even have children to appear "normal" and to be accepted in their family and society (Werff, 2010). Many rural gay men cope by working in urban areas; they are open about their sexual orientation in the cities but return home a few times a year to be traditional family men.

These unique diversity issues are part of the counseling context in China. Although each family is unique, the family is also culturally embedded and contextually influenced by diversity issues such as gender, religion, ethnicity, generational differences, social class, poverty, sexuality, and disability. A culturally competent counselor will take all of these factors into consideration for effective work in counseling Chinese families.

Counselor Education

The Confucian-based entrance examination (*ke ju* 科举) permeates the entire education system in China. This includes the field of counseling. Centers have sprung up in China that coach potential counselors to take the licensing examinations. Licensing in China does not take into account one's aptitude, clinical skills, counseling experience, or supervision hours. The consequence of focusing on book knowledge to the exclusion of skills is that licensed counselors find it hard to convert their knowledge to contextualized individual or familial presenting problems. In practice, counselors tend to focus on intellectual psychoeducation or advice giving rather than emotional support (Cook et al., 2010). Counselors also tend to adopt a medical model that is more content based. Overall, they may be able to talk about assessment but have limited ideas about how to engage in the counseling process and do treatment planning because of a lack of theoretical integration. In their nationwide survey of 1,391 counselors, X. Gao et al. (2010) noted an absence of peer-based counseling case reviews. They also noted that "only 41.6% reported having professional certificates approved by the Mental Health Counseling Training Program (MHCTP) and substantial percentages reported no affiliation or membership in organizations related to mental health practice (36.7%)" (p. 81).

Most counseling programs are found in university medical departments as part of medical students' training. However, other universities, such as the Normal University System (which includes Beijing Normal University, Capital Normal University, Tianjin Normal University, Northeast Normal University, East China Normal University, Nanjing Normal University, and Shandong Normal University), are well known for training teachers to do psychological counseling. Other comprehensive first-tier urban universities, such as Fudan University, Beijing University, Hangzhou University, and Tsinghua University, have undergraduate- and graduate-level counseling programs. These programs provide very strong foundations in psychology and counseling theories. However, they are lacking in teaching counseling skills within the context of a firm theoretical foundation (Leung et al., 2000).

The certification of counselors by the National Counseling Licensing Board is based on a well-defined mental health counseling training plan. Level 3 counselors are those with a bachelor's degree who successfully complete the government-approved courses and examination (covering such areas as basic counseling skills, developmental and social psychology, personality disorders, and psychological assessments). Those who pass Level 3 can proceed to study Level 2 courses and take the Level 2 examination, which covers such areas as advanced counseling skills, diagnosis, the assessment of mental disorders, and the use of various psychometric inventories. Level 1 is still on the drawing board. It is reserved primarily for those who have qualifying doctoral degrees in the fields of education, medicine, or counseling and have worked as therapists for at least 3 years. However, Level 1 has not been implemented yet (X. Gao et al., 2010). Since the implementation of these levels of certification, Chinese nationals have shown a high level of interest in being certified. In July 2006, there were 112 locations preparing candidates for Level 3 and Level 2 Certificate of Psychological Counseling examinations; by September 2007, there were 120,000 certified psychology counselors in China (Kong & Xu, 2008).

Lim et al. (2010) reported that there are freestanding certification programs, such as the German–Chinese Psychotherapy Training Program, the International Psychosomatic

Medicine Training Program (in Wuhan), the Training Program of Psychoanalysis (in Nanjing), and the Harmony Counseling Training Program in Marriage and Family Therapy (in Shenyang). Since the 1980s, many other programs have come from abroad. They tend to emphasize workshops and hands-on experience with either specific theories of therapy such as gestalt therapy or Satir conjoint family therapy or experiential modalities, such as psychodrama, art therapy, music therapy, and sand therapy.

A significant part of any counselor's training is the use of psychological psychometrics. Many inventories, such as the Minnesota Multiphasic Personality Inventory, the Wechsler Intelligence Scales, and the Sixteen Personality Factor Questionnaire, have been translated from the West. Thus, there are questions of psychometric validity, even though these instruments have been modified to the Chinese context. The Psychological Testing Commission of the CPS was formed in 1984 to regulate the use of measurements in counseling with the Chinese (Higgins & Sun, 2002).

The Future

The CPS (2004) reported that the ratio of counselors to members of the general population is 2.4 per 1 million. This is a poor ratio compared to the United States, where there are 3,000 counselors per 1 million people. The need for counselors in China is urgent. Obviously, there is a lot of work to be done for the future of mental health in China. A recent census indicated that illiteracy was down from 6.72% in 2000 to 4.08% in 2010 (National Bureau of Statistics in China, 2011). This corresponds with the more than 100% increase in university education enrollment since 2000. These statistics are an indication of the increased sophistication of the Chinese populace, which likely points to an increased awareness of psychological needs and counseling.

With the millions of young men and women graduating each year from universities in China (7.3 million in 2011 alone), career counseling and interpersonal social skills in schools and universities will need to be given priority; however, career counseling is only offered in Beijing University and Beijing Normal University (Hou & Zhang, 2007). Although China has a governance and school system in place to provide psychological help for her people, there is a need for training that is integrated in theory and practice. At the same time, more work needs to be done to incorporate both Eastern and Western philosophies and research. A systematic training program that emphasizes a research-practitioner model is needed. Counselors need to know not just what they are doing but also why they are doing it. Because the scientist-practitioner model is better developed in the West, Chinese institutions could cooperate with Western universities or training institutes to include a program of study that includes practica. The two leading psychological associations, the CAMH and the CPS, can harness their resources so that a higher level of counseling and psychotherapy education, training, and research can be achieved. The fruits of their conferences, trainings, and integrative activities need to be documented in the journals they publish.

In addition to the state-run Red Cross Society of China, private nongovernmental organizations that specialize in treating people's mental and psychological needs should be encouraged. The announcement by Minister of Civil Affairs Li Liguo to allow social welfare nongovernmental organizations to cut through the red tape and register directly with civil affairs bureaus is a welcome step toward addressing the many mental health issues affecting the country (Le, 2011).

While China is marching forward on the global economic and military fronts, it can prove its leadership by progressing in a holistic and harmonious way through an investment in psychological and mental wellness. China can show the world that progress does not need to come at the expense of social problems and psychological health. According to Xin Chunying, vice director of the Commission for Legislative Affairs of the Standing Committee of the National People's Congress, the first priority of the National People's Congress 12th Five-Year

Plan (2011–2015) is to enact laws to promote not just the material well-being of the citizenry but also their mental health (Xinhua, 2011). This is certainly a step in the right direction.

References

Chang, D., Tong, H., Shi, Q., & Zeng, Q. (2005). Letting a hundred flowers bloom: Counseling and psychotherapy in the People's Republic of China. *Journal of Mental Health Counseling, 27*(2), 104–116.

Chen, Z. (2006, June 28). TCM doctors take on emotions. *China Daily.* Retrieved from http://china.org.cn/english/Life/173064.htm

Chinese Psychological Society. (2004). *Psychology in China.* Retrieved from http://www.icp2004.psych.ac.cn/inchina.htm

Chinese Psychological Society. (2007). *Code of ethics for counseling and clinical practice.* Beijing, China: Author.

Cook, A. L., Lei, A., & Chiang, D. (2010). Counseling in China: Implications for counselor education preparation and distance learning instruction. *Journal for International Counseling Education, 2,* 60–73.

Dan, H. (2011, May 13). Counselors to help the helpers after disasters hit. *China Daily.* Retrieved from http://www.cdeclips.com/en/nation/Counselors_to_help_the%20helpers_after_disasters_hit/fullstory_65637.html

Gao, X., Jackson, T., Chen, H., Liu, Y., Wang, R., Qian, M., & Huang, X. (2010). There is a long way to go: A nationwide survey of professional training for mental health practitioners in China. *Health Policy, 95,* 74–81.

Gao, Y. (2001). Directive approach to telephone counseling in the People's Republic of China: Underlying cultural traditions and transitions. *The Counseling Psychologist, 29,* 435–453 doi:10.1177/0011000001293007

Higgins, L. T., & Sun, C. H. (2002). The development of psychological testing in China. *International Journal of Psychology, 77*(4), 246–254.

Hou, Z., & Zhang, N. (2007). Counseling psychology in China. *Applied Psychology, 56*(1), 33–50.

Huang, S., He, Y., & He, X. (2008). Development of psychological counseling: Professionalization in China. *Research in Medical Education, 7*(1), 45–47.

Huang, W.-J. (2005). An Asian perspective on relationship and marriage education. *Family Process, 44*(2), 161–173.

Jing, X. (2011). Population turning point. *Beijing Review, 54*(21), 18–23.

Kong, Q., & Xu, D. (2008). Research on the problems and counter-measures of psychological consultant's specialization in China. *Journal of Tianjin University of Technology and Education, 18*(4), 121–133.

Le, Z. (2011, May 25). *NGO registration rules to be relaxed nationwide: Civil affairs minister.* Retrieved from http://china.globaltimes.cn/society/2011-05/658729.html

Leung, S. A., Guo, L., & Lam, M. P. (2000). The development of counseling psychology in higher educational institutions in China: Present conditions and needs, future challenges. *The Counseling Psychologist, 28*(1), 81–99.

Lim, S., Lim, B., Michael, R., Cai, R., & Schock, C. K. (2010). The trajectory of counseling in China: Past, present, and future trends. *Journal of Counseling & Development, 88,* 4–8.

National Bureau of Statistics in China (2011). Communiqué of the National Bureau of Statistics of People's Republic of China on major figures of the 2010 population census. Retrieved from http://www.stats.gov.cn/english/newsandcomingevents/t20110428_402722244.htm

National Population and Planning Commission. (2011). *China world population day.* Retrieved from http://www.npfpc.gov.cn/en/detail.aspx?articleid=110714134647640846

Qian, M., Gao, J., Yao, P., & Rodriguez, M. A. (2009). Professional ethical issues and the development of professional ethical standards in counseling and clinical psychology in China. *Ethics & Behavior, 19*(4), 290–309. doi:10.1080/10508420903035273

Qian, M:., Smith, C. W., Chen, Z., & Xia, G. (2002). Psychotherapy in China: A review of its history and contemporary directions. *International Journal of Mental Health, 30*(4), 49–68.
Shu, G. (2003). *Yi Shu: The art of living with change: Integrating traditional Chinese medicine, psychodrama and the creative arts.* St. Louis, MO: F. R. Robbins.
Sun, C. T.-L. (2008). *Themes in Chinese psychology.* Singapore: Cengage Learning Asia.
Thomason, T. C., & Qiong, X. (2008). School counseling in China today. *Journal of School Counseling, 6*(11), 1–14.
Tobin, D. (2011, June 29). Inequality in China: Rural poverty persists as urban wealth balloons. *BBC News.* Retrieved from http://www.bbc.co.uk/news/business-13945072
Werff, T. V. D. (2010). The struggle of the tongzhi homosexuality in China and the position of Chinese "comrades." In I. Dubel & A. Hielkema (Eds.), *Urgency required: Gay and lesbian rights are human rights* (pp. 172–180). Hague, The Netherlands: Hivos.
Xin, L. (2011, June 27). Playing peacemaker. *China Daily.* Retrieved from http://www.cdeclips.com/en/arts_n_life/Playing_peacemaker/fullstory_67857.html
Xinhua. (2011). *China to enact mental health law in 2011.* Retrieved from http://www.chinadaily.com.cn/china/2011npc/2011-03/10/content_12152078.htm
Yip, K. (2005). An historical review of the mental health services in the People's Republic of China. *International Journal Social Psychiatry, 51*(2), 106–118.
Yip, K. (2006). Community mental health in the People's Republic of China: A critical analysis. *Community Mental Health Journal, 42*(1), 41–51.
Zhang, Y., Young, D., Lee, S., Zhang, H., Xiao, Z., Hao, W., . . . Chang, D. F. (2002). Chinese Taoist cognitive psychotherapy in the treatment of generalized anxiety disorder in contemporary China. *Transcultural Psychiatry, 39*(1), 115–129.
Zhiling, H., & Ao, Z. (2010). In a "first," gay couple tie the knot in China. *China Daily.* Retrieved from http://www.chinadaily.com.cn/china/2010-01/13/content_9310315.htm

• • •

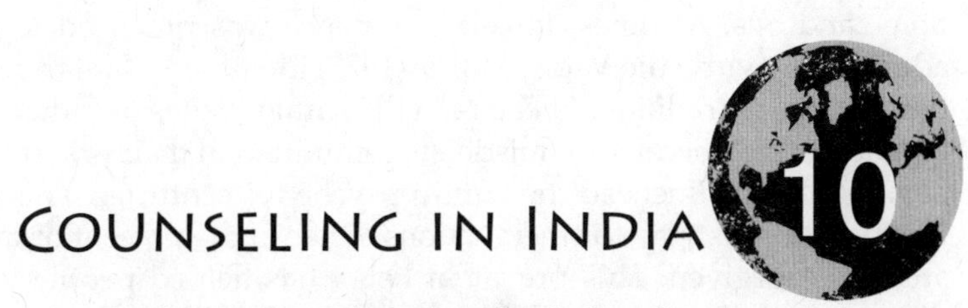

Counseling in India

Sachin Jain and Daya Singh Sandhu

India has one of the oldest civilizations and a rich cultural heritage. Thus, it also has many ancient healing traditions. With more than 1.3 billion people, it is the second most populous country in the world, next only to China. Although Hindi and English are the official languages, there are an additional 22 major languages and more than 7,000 dialects. All children are required to master at least three languages: their mother tongue, Hindi, and English. India is a land of contradictions. There is a large gap between the rich and the poor. Although there are mud huts like those highlighted in the movie *Slumdog Millionaire,* there are many skyscrapers as well. There is also a new awakening with respect to communication. It is quite common to see a person sitting on a donkey or pulling a rickshaw and talking on their mobile phone.

No civilization can remain resilient or even survive without good guidance, mental health, and spiritual help. The Indian culture is no exception. As one of the most ancient civilizations, India has a long history of help-seeking behaviors. The very essence of counseling and psychotherapy as they are known in modern times dates back to the age of the Vedas, written about as far back as 2500 BCE. What has changed over time, however, is the nature of the purposes, sources, and relationships of the help seekers and help providers.

In this chapter, the development of professional counseling in India is discussed over three major eras: ancient India, called Bharata after the name of the legendry king; medieval India, known as Hindustan; and modern India. The healing traditions of India can be viewed in three broad streams or forces, namely shamanism, spirituality, and science. These three major healing traditions can be viewed as independent approaches to mental health that sometimes work simultaneously with one another. They have also been described as local and folk traditions, mystical traditions, and medical traditions (Kakar, 1991).

Ayurveda is one of the most ancient medicines practiced in India; it was practiced as early as the 6th century BC. In Sanskrit, *Ayurveda* means "a science of life." It is a system of medicine that classifies most human problems into three major categories: the psychic, the exogenous, and the endogenous. Its psychic branch is called Bhuta Vidya, and it deals directly with mental health and psychiatric problems.

Since ancient times, Indian *rishi* and *munis* (saints) have sought to develop methods to conquer the mind. This process is a form of self-realization that integrates the personality with the spiritual. The Atharva Veda described good mental health as the restoration of equilibrium among three components of the human personality called *gunnas.* These *gunnas* are Vatta, Pitta, and Shelshma or Kaph. Practitioners of Ayurveda are called Vaids, and they believe that an imbalance of *gunnas* is the main cause of a variety of illnesses and mental health problems. For instance, the wrong food, uninhibited sexual indulgence, and environmental factors such as excessive cold or hot weather, can cause physical and mental disturbances. Similarly, excessive cold can cause depression, excessive heat can cause excitement, and excessive bile can cause hostility (Kapur, 1975). It is interesting that this very early system integrates nutrition, the environment, and psychological well-being, making it a holistic approach to mental health.

Treatment in Ayurvedic medicine includes a variety of herbs, food restrictions, decoctions, and oils. At times, forced continence was practiced to regain the equilibrium. In addition to Ayurvedic Vaids, Kapur (1975) identified Mantarwadis and Patris as two additional types of traditional healers in the rural villages of India. These healers believed that people suffered because of misdeeds committed in their present or previous lives. The Law of Karma has influenced the Hindu psyche for centuries. This deterministic belief asserts that people must pay for their actions either in the present or in their next lives. Misdeeds are never forgiven. This prevalent belief has helped people to accept their misfortunes, diseases and illnesses, as well as poverty and destitution as the consequences of personal conduct (Laungani, 2005).

Lord Shiva, the Lord of Destruction, punishes a person for misdeeds through his army of spirits or by bringing about a malign conjunction of unlucky stars. Generally speaking, Mantarwadis use their knowledge of the zodiac to treat their patients for mental problems and psychological distress through some potent mystical verses from Vedas by blowing their breath on the holy threads or by giving patients a talisman to wear (Kapur, 1975). Vedas are replete with hymns, poems, and verses that consist of secret mantras, prayers, and absolutions that are offered to Vedic gods for appeasement and forgiveness through penance and repentance.

In contrast, a Patri acts as a medium for a spirit who actually conducts the therapeutic act. Generally speaking, a Patri may induce a state of self-possession for the master spirit through incense, dance, or music and becomes his or her master's voice. According to the Patri, mental afflictions are caused by evil spirits. Animal sacrifices or ritual feasts are offered to the possessing spirits, who are asked to leave the body of the patient. Patri healers often chant sacred verses, sprinkle holy water, or give their patients a talisman to wear at all times to keep the evil spirits away. On occasions some psalms from the holy books are assigned and patients are asked to recite them several times a day and before bedtime. Patris are considered a conduit between the patient and the spirit and can negotiate an exorcism.

Beliefs in Vedic astrology have been strongly ingrained in the minds of the Indian people since Vedic times. A large number of astrologers, horoscope specialists, and palmists in India profess to understand the benevolent or malevolent influences of planets on individual lives. Beliefs in astrology and in the influences of planets are strongly ingrained in the Indian psyche.

The Current Status of Counseling

As a result of economic and social changes in India due to rapid industrialization and urbanization, people are experiencing significant multiple stressors in their lives. Some of these stressors are causing some very serious mental health concerns, including clinical depression, anxiety, mental stress, marital discords, domestic violence, and serious alcoholism and substance abuse problems. Naturally, several psychosomatic and physical health problems can develop as well, such as hypertension, cirrhosis of the liver, heart problems, and psychosocial phobias (Sandhu, 2011).

The National Mental Health Programme estimates that at least 30 million people in India are in dire need of mental health services (Barua, 2009). Older adults, women, migrants, refugees, street children, and newly emerging gay and lesbian populations are particularly vulnerable.

> In India, at a given point of time, nearly 15 million people suffer from serious psychiatric illness, and another 30 million from mild/moderate psychiatric problems . . . According to [National Institute of Mental Health and Neuro Sciences] estimates, we have a burden of nearly 100 million people with neuropsychiatric and substance abuse problems. (K. Sinha, 2010)

Of course, these figures are limited to severe psychiatric problems relating to psychosis. The number of mental health problems relating to neurosis is also very high. We believe that every tenth person in India faces a mental health challenge of some sort. Thus, the number of Indian people suffering from psychological problems could be more than 100 million.

Furthermore, it is interesting to note that most of India's problems start with the letter *p:* population, prejudice, pollution, and poverty (Sandhu, 2007). These problems are perpetuating and permanent in nature. In addition, some nonpermanent or temporary problems include police, politicians, and preachers. Most of these problems are at the societal level, but they do have the real potential to add to the mental health afflictions of individuals on a personal level. For instance, all of the *p* problems could create, aggravate, or exacerbate mental depression, stress, anxiety, fear, and suicidal ideation.

Without a doubt, there is truly a mental health crisis in India. Lack of availability and access to trained professionals is making things worse. To cope with their mental health challenges, a large number of people visit priests, spiritual healers, mystics, and indigenous practitioners, as the field of mental health counseling is still at a very early stage. The District Mental Health Program (DMHP) is a flagship initiative of the Indian government to help people cope with their mental health problems. The DMHP is designed to integrate mental health services into primary health care and is presently implemented in 125 districts. A budgetary allocation of Rs. 28 crore (approximately $280 million) was made during the Ninth Plan for the National Mental Health Program.

It is commendable that in response to the growing number of psychological problems in the country, the Government of India drafted the Mental Health Act 1987, which came into effect in all states, including the union territories, in April 1993. Although we applaud the Government of India's efforts, the Mental Health Act 1987 is limited to the treatment and care of mentally ill persons who suffer from specific diseases such as schizophrenia, bipolar disorder, and obsessive-compulsive disorder. Most of these problems are psychiatric problems generally caused by psychosis. The Mental Health Act 1987 is beneficial only in laying down guidelines for the establishment and maintenance of psychiatric hospitals and nursing homes.

The Mental Health Act 1987 is limited in scope and does not apply to persons who suffer from numerous other mental health problems, such as suicidal ideation, alcoholism and substance abuse, family and community violence, and anxiety and stress disorders, to name a few. Unfortunately, all of these unresolved psychological problems become the underlying reasons for an untold number of suicides, homicides, family and marital difficulties, school-related problems, and workplace incompetence and violence. Although the Mental Health Act 1987 and the DMHP are to be applauded for their focus on psychiatric services in hospitals and institutions, it is regrettable that they do not address issues relating to the psychological mental health of most of the population.

There is an acute shortage of trained mental health professionals in India (Barua, 2009). There are only 37 mental health institutions, 3,500 psychiatrists, and 1,000 clinical psychologists to serve a population of 1.3 billion people. It was recently reported by the Indian government that there is only 1 psychiatrist for every 400,000 persons (Kennedy, 2010). This is one of the lowest ratios anywhere in the world. In contrast, the United States has 64 psychiatrists for every 400,000 persons (Barua, 2009). Thus, there is an urgent and immediate need for trained mental health care professionals and for counseling facilities, such as university and community mental health counseling centers, to help the people of India meet their guidance and counseling needs. It is important to note that all of the problems of India (population, poverty, prejudice, etc.) are amenable to professional counseling services.

Best Counseling Practices

Traditional Mental Health Practices

Given the lack of trained professionals, families often rely on alternative healers to resolve psychiatric issues. The therapeutic approaches of these healers include reading individual horoscopes, prescribing mantras and prayers from Vedic scriptures, and making special offerings to deities at a Hindu temple. Vedic astrology considers the *nakshtra,* or the astrological sign, to be of utmost significance. It is a particular *nakshtra* that determines one's destiny at birth and charts the course of life with regard to pleasure and pain. However, planetary effects can be changed by wearing clothes of special colors or by using different types of stones as suggested by the astrologer, or *joytishi,* who has knowledge of the heavenly bodies.

In addition, a variety of other people, such as diviners, shamans, *sadhus,* swamis, *matas* (spiritual ladies), *bhagwans,* and *babas* (spiritual men), claim to possess mystical and spiritual powers to remove their clients' psychic distress through prayers and mantras. Overall, these healing traditions are quite popular, as they do not require much responsibility on the part of the afflicted persons, except to pay for the services. For this reason, most family members of a mentally ill person usually seek help from a traditional healer or a religious shrine before consulting modern-day psychiatric services.

Generally speaking, the relationship between a traditional healer and the mentally ill can be described as a relationship between a guru (teacher) and a *shishya* (disciple). In this highly epitomized relationship, the guru is considered to be similar to a spiritual guide. Because the guru and *shishya* have a deep reverence and concern for each other, their relationship is considered sacred and complete, much wider and deeper than that of the therapist and patient in Western psychotherapy.

Current Counseling Development and Practices

Professional counseling is just beginning in India. The awakening and significance of this new profession is getting wide publicity in Indian newspapers and on various websites. Chopra (2011) described counselors as confidants, advisers, and teachers who help people with family problems, mental health concerns, drug and alcohol addiction, and career decisions in different settings, including schools, clinics, nongovernmental organizations, and AIDS counseling centers. Modern-day living with its increasing pressures is driving people in India to seek more professional help for their vocational, social, and emotional problems. According to Chopra, a well-trained professional counselor will never be without a job in India.

There are some sporadic attempts by professionals trained in the United States, the United Kingdom, or Canada to provide professional counseling through private practice. For instance, one Internet advertisement referred to counseling as "life coaching" and promised to help clients deal with insurmountable problems such as handling problem children, balancing work and home, managing issues of repatriation, resolving study-related problems, meeting parental expectations, and finding meaning in life. This particular professional psychotherapist claimed to be trained in cognitive therapy and to have Indian clients from all around the world.

Association of Mental Health Counselors–India

Sandhu (2011) established the Association of Mental Health Counselors–India (AMHC-India) on May 4, 2010, basing it on the model of the American Counseling Association. As executive director of AMHC-India, Dr. Sandhu signed a memorandum of understanding with the American Mental Health Counselors Association (AMHCA) in July 2011 to develop collaborative relationships between AMHCA and AMHC-India. AMHC-India has also developed a collaborative relationship with the Counseling Association of India, which was established in 2005. The first author, Dr. Sachin Jain, played a leading role in starting and registering the Counseling Association of India as a nongovernmental organization under the Bombay Public Trust Act of 1950.

Career Counseling

Personal counseling, mental health counseling, and academic and career counseling are increasingly gaining in acceptance and popularity in India. It is important not to overlook Delhi-based Pervin Malhotra, India's top career counselor. She has become an icon in the field of career and academic counseling. Malhotra has been hailed by the media as a Career Encyclopedia and Career Queen (Sharma, 2010). Her daily columns on www.careerguidanceindia.com reach an audience of more than 50 million people, and her career guidance through her CARING (Career Information and Guidance) institute has already impacted millions of lives.

School Counseling

A survey on the importance of counseling conducted in 1993 revealed that only 5% of school heads believed that counseling in schools was important (Arulmani, 2007). Seven years later, the same survey reported that 95% of school heads agreed that school counseling was not only important but an urgently required service (Arulmani, 2007). There has been a significant economic and cultural change in India since 1991. There is a great opportunity now for professional counseling in India if it incorporates the contextual realities of Indian life. Also, the Government of India has started policy actions to support the provision of counseling services to address the needs of adolescents in a Five-Year Plan. This seems to be a golden time for school counseling in India.

Diversity Issues

The most recent census survey of India indicated that out of the total population of a little more than 1 billion, 80.5% of Indians are Hindus, 13.4% are Muslims, 2.3% are Christians, 1.9% are Sikhs, 0.8% are Buddhists, 0.4% are Jains, and 0.6% belong to other religions ("Census," 2001). The census survey also highlighted the linguistic diversity in the country: 6,600 mother tongues grouped into 122 major languages, which include the 22 official languages listed in the Constitution of India (Mohanty, 2010). The population is not homogeneous, and subgroups retain their own cultural and religious practices (Durvasula & Mylvaganam, 1994). Hierarchical differences also exist in the ethnic identity of people based on their caste (Kohli & Faul, 2005). There are four major castes followed by three sections of socially disadvantaged groups—Scheduled Caste (SC), Scheduled Tribes (ST), and Other Backward Classes (OBC), composing 16.2%, 8.2%, and 54.4% of the country's population, respectively (Bayly, 1999; "Census," 2001). Living standards in SC, ST, and OBC households are much lower than in the mainstream population, which is composed of the Hindu forward castes and members of other religions, including those belonging to the Christian, Muslim, and Sikh faiths (Gang, Sen, & Yun, 2008). Individuals from SC, ST, and OBC groups are underrepresented in high-status positions in business, government, and society (Weisskopf, 2004). The lack of role models, the lack of support, and the stigma attached to individuals belonging to socially disadvantaged groups (Naudet, 2008) may be some of the reasons for their high dropout rates at elite educational institutions such as the Indian Institute of Technology (Banerji, 2011). Neighborhoods are segregated based on religion and caste. Such segregation, coupled with a lack of education about diversity (Kohli & Faul, 2005), has led to critical biases (Sowell, 2004).

Although India is one of the fastest developing countries in the world, poverty remains widespread. Approximately 70% of the population still lives in rural settings, and more than 40% of the population lives below the international poverty line. The combination of poverty and gender disparities has put females in the poorest stratum of society and at a great disadvantage (Balatchandirane, 2003). Gender differences are reflected in educational attainment, access to nutritious food, and so on. For example, around 80% of girls from the top 20% of households on the asset index complete Grade 8 compared with only 9.5% of girls from the poorest 40% of households on the asset index (Filmer & Pritchett, 1999). To improve the condition of females, the constitution was amended in 1993 to ensure that a third of all seats in locally elected councils (in the *panchayati raj* system) were reserved for women (Mehrotra & Kapoor, 2009).

Another important diversity issue that impacts counselors is physical disability. A report by the World Bank (2007) estimated that 40–90 million individuals in India have a disability. The report also listed the statewise percentage of out-of-school children with disabilities. The percentage varied from 55% in the northeast state of Assam to 27% in the southern state of Kerala. Children with disabilities very rarely progress beyond primary school in India (Singal, 2009). Factors such as low educational attainment, poor employment prospects, and stigma (from disability being the result of the sins of the people with the disability or their parents) result in poor living conditions for families affected by disability. Previous research showed that approximately 70% of disabling conditions in India are preventable (Alkazi, as cited in Kuruvilla & Joseph, 1999). Counselors can play a major role as part of multidisciplinary teams in preventing such disabling conditions.

The other important population with whom counselors in India work is members of the lesbian, gay, bisexual, and transgender community. In July 2009, the Delhi High Court decriminalized homosexual intercourse between consenting adults throughout India. Before this legal verdict, more than 1 million members belonging to this community were often ostracized socially and persecuted by the police (Prakash, 2011).

Indian culture values the wisdom of elderly people and has always been very supportive of their needs. The traditional joint family system has reduced the prevalence of abuse against elderly people. With an increase in migration to cities there has been an increase in the number of nuclear families. Competent counselor trainees need to know how to serve this population as "younger clinicians may find that the acceptance of their role and function in counseling middle-aged and older adults takes time" (Carson, Jain, & Ramirez, 2009, p. 50).

Counselor Education

Dr. N. N. Sengupta, who worked under Professor Hugo Munsterberg, a former student of Wilhelm Wundt, established the very first Department of Psychology in 1915 at Calcutta University. It was the first time that Western-style psychological teaching and research was introduced in India. In the beginning, Western psychology was a ready-made package, and it became quite popular for replacing the intellectual and indigenous systems that had been in vogue for several thousand years (Nandy, 1974). Until the 1960s Western psychology, with its emphasis on scientific inquiry, was a very attractive field of study in many Indian universities and colleges. However, after the 1960s, a number of signs of growing crisis and dissatisfaction with Western psychology started to appear. Because of a lack of cultural relevance, Western psychology lost much of its early momentum (Pareek, 1980). Indian researchers added very little to Western psychological knowledge, and there was minimal demonstration of originality (D. Sinha, 1993). Western psychology in India was quite encapsulated, an academic subject confined to the classroom but rarely practiced in the field. However, some significant efforts are being made by the Government of India to revive the field and promote psychological research throughout the country. For this purpose the Indian Council of Social Science Research was established in 1968.

Many clinical and counseling psychology programs in India are unaccredited (Raney & Cinarbas, 2005). The University Grant Commission is authorized by the Government of India to coordinate, determine, and maintain standards of university education in India. Amity University, Bharathiar University, Delhi University, and Veer Bahadur Singh Purvanchal University are accredited by the University Grant Commission to offer a master's program (2 years) in applied psychology (with a focus on clinical and counseling skills). Guru Nanak Dev University Amritsar and the National Council of Educational Research and Training offer postgraduate diploma programs (1 year) in counseling. Annamalai University offers 1-year hybrid (distance and face-to-face components) postgraduate diploma programs in counseling. The curriculum mainly revolves around abnormal psychology, theories, research, and assessment. None of the programs have on-campus counseling centers for students' practica or internship hours. Most students complete their internships at mental health settings under the supervision of a clinical psychologist or a psychiatrist. Other settings, such as K–12 schools and special education institutions, lack qualified professionals for supervision, particularly in rural settings. A World Health Organization report showed that for every 100,000 people in India, there are 0.02 psychiatrists, 0.05 psychiatric nurses, 0.03 psychologists, and 0.03 social workers (World Health Organization and Ministry of Health, 2006). Because of this lack of qualified mental health professionals, the average caseload at psychiatric centers is 70–80 clients per day.

Preparing Professional Counselors

There is a dire need for counselor educators in India. As noted in the previous section, only a handful of universities offer training in counseling. Some of these universities include Annamalai University, Punjab University, the Tata Institute of Social Sciences, National Council of Educational Research and Training (in New Delhi), University of Delhi, and Karnataka University. Most recently, with the help of the United States India Education Foundation and Vice Chancellor, the second author, Dr. Daya Singh Sandhu, developed a postgraduate diploma in mental health counseling at the Guru Nanak Dev University Amritsar. This diploma program is for 1 year with an additional 4 months of internship experience under licensed psychiatrists practicing in the city of Amritsar. This diploma program is unique and ambitious because its course requirements are designed to meet all the Council for Accreditation of Counseling and Related Educational Programs Standards.

Regulation of Practice

The profession of clinical psychology is regulated by the Rehabilitation Council of India, but the field of counseling is not regulated by any government agency (Juvva, Redij, & Koshy, 2006). The Counseling Association of India is in the process of drafting a code of practice for counselors. Recently, AMHC-India adopted the ethical codes of the AMHCA and developed a mutually collaborative relationship with this organization (Sandhu, 2011). Despite the diversity in Indian culture, very little attention is being placed on tackling diversity issues in training. In their research on graduate students' attitudes about diversity issues, Kohli and Faul (2005) found that raising volatile diversity issues in the classroom is considered inappropriate and insensitive in India.

The Future

A number of challenges face the mental health services field in India:

1. Raising awareness levels in the general public about mental health issues and services. The complexity in terms of educational, religious, and socioeconomic backgrounds of such a diverse population needs to be considered.
2. Using support from the World Health Organization and USAID to ensure an equitable availability of mental health professionals. Presently each district hospital (serving approximately 600,000 patients) hires one counselor for HIV/AIDS prevention counseling. Additional resources are needed to ensure an even geographical distribution of mental health professionals, particularly in remote and rural settings.
3. Reducing the brain drain and attracting the Indian diaspora to help increase the number of professionals.
4. Establishing licensing/certification boards and defining the scope of practice for professionals.
5. Evaluating and expanding professional and educational training needs to continue to meet the needs of the profession in the country.
6. Improving clinical and applied research by establishing on-campus counselor training clinics.

Conclusion

India today is a rich and fertile ground for the growth of professional counseling. The cultural milieu and the zeitgeist of this rapidly developing country is such that counseling is desperately needed to address the personal and social problems of its more than 1.3 billion people. We believe that the next 30 years will be a renaissance period for counseling in India. There will be a plethora of opportunities for the field to develop because of the large population and social, economic, scientific, and technical advances. However, it must be noted that professional counseling will only supplement, not supplant, traditional healing methods because of the strong and deeply rooted historical heritage of these traditional methods in India. Spiritual healing and other healing traditions, such as Ayurveda, palmistry, *joytish vidya*, and black magic, will continue to coexist with counseling. The role of the sacred has always been salient in the past and will continue to have significance in this spiritually rich land.

References

Arulmani, G. (2007). Counseling psychology in India: At the confluence of two traditions. *Applied Psychology, 56*, 69–82.

Balatchandirane, G. (2003). Gender discrimination in education and economic development: A study of South Korea, China and India. *International Studies, 40*, 349–378.

Banerji, A. (2011). *Are Indian institutes casting a negative light on minority groups?* Retrieved from http://blogs.reuters.com/india/2011/06/30/are-indian-institutes-casting-a-negative-light-on-minority-groups

Barua, A. (2009). Need for a realistic mental health program in India. *Indian Journal of Psychological Medicine, 31*, 48–49.

Bayly, S. (1999). *Caste, society and politics in India.* Cambridge, England: Cambridge University Press.

Carson, D., Jain, S., & Ramirez, S. (2009). Counseling and family therapy in India: Evolving professions in a rapidly developing nation. *International Journal for the Advancement of Counselling, 31*(1), 45–56.

Census. (2001). Retrieved from http://www.censusindia.gov.in

Chopra, A. (2011). *A career in counseling.* Retrieved from http://www.Successcds.net/Articles/Career-in-Counselling.php

Durvasula, R. S., & Mylvaganam, G. A. (1994). Mental health of Asian Indians: Relevant issues and community implications. *Journal of Community Psychology, 22,* 97–108.

Filmer, D., & Pritchett, L. (1999). The effect of household wealth on educational attainment: Evidence from 35 countries. *Population and Development Review, 25*(1), 85–120.

Gang, I. N., Sen, K., & Yun, M. (2008). *Caste, affirmative action and discrimination in India.* Retrieved from http://www.chronicpoverty.org/uploads/publication_files/gang_sen_yun.pdf

Juvva, S., Redij, S., & Koshy, M. (2006). Family therapy study group: The Mumbai experience. *Contemporary Family Therapy, 28*(1), 73–86.

Kakar, S. (1991). *Shamans, mystics, and doctors.* Chicago, IL: University of Chicago Press.

Kapur, R. L. (1975). Mental health care in rural India: A study of existing patterns and their implications for future policy. *British Journal of Psychiatry, 127,* 286–293.

Kennedy, M. (2010). *India's mentally ill turn to faith, not medicine.* Retrieved from http://www.npr.org/templates/story/story.php?storyId=126143778

Kohli, H. K., & Faul, A. C (2005). Cross-cultural differences towards diversity issues in attitudes of graduating social work students in India and the United States. *International Social Work, 48,* 809–822.

Kuruvilla, S., & Joseph, A. (1999). Identifying disability: Comparing house-to-house survey and rapid rural appraisal. *Health Policy and Planning, 14*(2), 182–190.

Laungani, P. (2005). Hindu spirituality and healing practices. In R. Moodley & W. West (Eds.), *Integrating traditional healing practices into counseling and psychotherapy* (pp. 138–147). Thousand Oaks, CA: Sage.

Mehrotra, S., & Kapoor, S. (2009). Gender discrimination in Asia: A regional perspective. *Global Social Policy, 9,* 197–205.

Mohanty, A. K. (2010). Languages, inequality and marginalization: Implications of the double divide in Indian multilingualism. *International Journal of the Sociology of Language, 205,* 131–154.

Nandy, A. (1974). The non-paradigmatic crisis in Indian psychology: Reflections on a recipient culture science. *Indian Journal of Psychology, 49,* 1–20.

Naudet, J. (2008). Paying back to society: Upward social mobility among Dalits. *Contributions to Indian Sociology, 42,* 413–441.

Pareek, U. (1980). *A survey of research in psychology, 1971–1976.* Bombay, India: Popular Prakashen.

Prakash, S. (2011). *Time to walk the talk.* Retrieved from http://www.hindustantimes.com/StoryPage/Print/661669.aspx

Raney, S., & Cinarbas, D. C. (2005). Counseling in developing countries: Turkey and India as examples. *Journal of Mental Health Counseling, 27*(2), 149–160.

Sandhu, D. S. (2007). An ecstatic visit to a land of contrasts and contradictions. In Z. Usmani & N. K. Ghosh (Eds.), *Beyond boundaries: Reflections of Indian and U.S. scholars* (pp. 547–560). New York, NY: iUniverse.

Sandhu, D. S. (2011). Mental health problems in India: A call for urgent action. *Re-Markings, 10*(2), 49–57.

Sharma, U. (2010, April 21). *Career guidance: An interview with Pervin Malhotra.* Retrieved from http://indiaedunews.net/conversation/Pervin-Malhotra.asp

Singal, N. (2009). *Education of children with disabilities in India.* Retrieved from http://ddp-ext.worldbank.org/EdStats/INDgmrpap09a.pdf

Sinha, D. (1993). Indigenization of psychology in India and its relevance. In U. Kim & J. W. Berry (Eds.), *Indigenous psychologies: Research and experience in cultural context* (pp. 30–43). Newbury Park, CA: Sage.

Sinha, K. (2010, April 10). *Imbalanced equation: One shrink for 4-lakh Indians.* Retrieved from http://articles.timesofindia.indiatimes.com/2010-04-10/india/28123900_1_pg-seats-mental-illness-psychiatric-nursing

Sowell, T. (2004). *Affirmative action around the world: An empirical study.* New Haven, CT: Yale University Press.

Weisskopf, T. E. (2004). *Affirmative action in the United States and India: A comparative perspective.* New York, NY: Routledge.

World Bank. (2007). *People with disabilities in India: From commitments to outcomes.* Retrieved from http://www.worldbank.org.in

World Health Organization and Ministry of Health. (2006). *WHO-AIMS report on mental health system in Uttarkhand, India.* Retrieved from http://www.searo.who.int/LinkFiles/Mental_Health_Resources_WHO-AIMS_Report_MHS_Ind.pdf

• • •

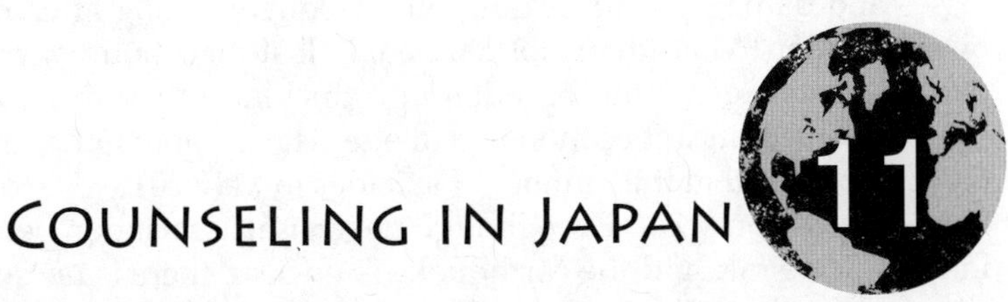

Counseling in Japan 11

Tomoko Kudo Grabosky, Harue Ishii, and Shizuno Mase

Japan experienced a rapid societal and cultural transformation beginning in the 1970s that has resulted in an ever-increasing need for quality counseling and mental health services. Japan saw substantial economic growth in the 1970s and 1980s followed by a recession beginning in the 1990s. In addition, significant changes in Japan's cultural values took place in the form of a consistent decrease in collectivist values and a corresponding increase in individualist values (Ishi-Kuntz, 1989). With the rise in individualism, the traditional social order and interdependent relationships lost their solidity, leading many people to experience significant uncertainty and isolation (Iwasaki, 2005; Watanabe-Muraoka, 2007). In tandem with these changes, the incidence of mental health problems in Japan increased dramatically. Because of the increase in mental health problems, there has been a sharp increase in the number of psychiatric patients receiving treatment. Given this situation, Japan's Ministry of Health, Labor, and Welfare (MHLW) recently identified mental illness as one of five priority diseases under the national health care plan.

In particular, a prolonged economic slump since the 1990s has resulted in economic disparities, high unemployment rates, and homelessness. It has also brought disruptions to Japanese homes, schools, and workplaces and the society at large. At home, the rise of the nuclear family structure has resulted in a weaker connection to extended families. While losing traditional networks of kinship support, Japanese families are simultaneously faced with more stress due to demands for economic and social fulfillment. In this context, many Japanese families have begun to break down. Increasing numbers of elderly people live alone and die in isolation. Divorce rates as well as reports of child abuse, domestic violence, and juvenile crimes have increased significantly (Iwasaki, 2005). In schools, bullying, school refusal, and violence among teenagers have become more severe (Iwakabe, 2008). In the workplace, Japanese employment systems have moved away from stable lifetime employment and the seniority system, resulting in increased layoffs, unstable employment contracts, and more competition to obtain positions and promotions (Iwasaki, 2005; Watanabe-Muraoka, 2007). Today more workers experience severe stress, anxiety, depression, work refusal, and some form of harassment. At the societal level, various psychosocial problems, such as social withdrawal syndrome, as well as the newer phenomena of apathy syndrome, job hopping, and NEET (not in education, employment, or training) among the youth are growing social concerns (Iwasaki, 2005). Most critically, the suicide rate in Japan has increased significantly since 1998. There have been more than 30,000 suicides every year since the recession began to take its toll in the late 1990s (National Police Agency, 2009).

On March 11, 2011, a major disaster hit Japan. The Tohoku Region Pacific Coast Earthquake struck off the northeastern coast of Japan and caused the most devastating damage the country has faced since World War II. Approximately 20,000 were reported missing or dead from the earthquake and the resulting tsunami. In addition, the disaster was followed by a nuclear meltdown, which forced hundreds of thousands of people to evacuate. Japan is currently in the process of rebuilding the country, recovering from the devastating losses and damages, and dealing with frequent strong aftershocks and ongoing anxiety over radiation. More than 200,000 people lost their houses, and many lost their jobs. Japan's agriculture, marine, and dairy product industries were severely hurt by radioactivity, causing significant economic damage. The Cabinet Office and National Police Agency (2012) reported that the number of suicides in May 2011 rose to 3,375, an increase of 21.3% from the previous year. Even though the causal association between this considerable rise in the suicide rate and the earthquake is unclear, there is no question that this is a critical situation for the nation.

Because of the devastation from the Tohoku disaster and mounting social and mental health issues, the need for counseling has increased among the Japanese public. In light of this, here we present the current status of the counseling field in the country, identify culturally relevant clinical issues, and discuss challenges for the future of the counseling profession in Japan.

The Current Status of Counseling

The counseling field in Japan is still in a state of confusion. First, the definition of counseling is unclear. There are ambiguous overlaps between *counseling, clinical psychology,* and *psychotherapy,* and these words are sometimes used synonymously without distinguishing the respective areas (Watanabe-Muraoka, 2007). Second, to date no national license or statutory regulation guides and protects the practice of professional counseling. Therefore, anyone can practice counseling in Japan. For instance, some people without any formal training claim to provide counseling when in fact they are conducting psychic readings and giving life advice. Although the field of counseling in Japan is currently underdeveloped, more and more Japanese people have begun utilizing counseling services in the following professional fields: clinical psychology, school counseling, mental health counseling, and career counseling. Next we provide an overview of counselor training in Japan as well as credentialing, scope of practice, and professional issues in each of these specialized fields.

Counselor Training

Because counseling has not yet been recognized as a distinct area of expertise within psychology, there are no formal academic programs in counselor education or counseling psychology in Japan (Watanabe-Muraoka, 2007). Individuals who aspire to become professional counselors typically pursue a master's program in clinical psychology accredited by the Japanese Board for Clinical Psychologists (JBCP). The JBCP certificate in clinical psychology is the most powerful credential enabling the practicing of counseling in Japan. In 2011, there were 165 JBCP-accredited programs consisting of a total of 26 credits (16 required and 10 electives). The required courses include professional orientation and ethics, theory, introduction to counseling/psychological services, assessment, pre-practicum, on-campus practicum, and thesis. The electives are chosen from among research and evaluation; human development; and specialization in the community, medicine, or school. The curricula appear to highlight projective testing, psychiatry, psychosomatology, gerontology, criminology, and community-based approaches in school settings (Grabosky, Ishii, & Mase, 2012). Also, the programs offer limited practicum and field experiences compared to the Council for Accreditation of Counseling and Related Educational Programs Standards in the United States (Grabosky et al., 2012).

Clinical Psychology

The professional status of clinical psychologists has increased rapidly since the founding of the JBCP in 1988. Yet the most significant development occurred in 1995 when the Ministry of Education, Science, and Culture (currently the Japan Ministry of Education, Culture, Sports, Science, and Technology [MEXT]) initiated the placement of school counselors and endorsed the JBCP certificate in clinical psychology as the requirement for school counselors. With the sponsorship of the MEXT, the JBCP certificate in clinical psychology has become the most recognized credential for practitioners of counseling in Japan. Candidates for the JBCP exam are required to complete 2 years of a master's program in clinical psychology accredited by the JBCP before taking the examination. Applicants who complete similar training programs outside of Japan are required to obtain 2 years of clinical experience in Japan prior to taking the JBCP examination.

In 2011, a total of 24,660 certified clinical psychologists (CCPs) worked in various settings, including clinics, hospitals, schools, universities, social welfare agencies, private companies, and private practices (Foundation of the Japanese Certification Board for Clinical Psychologists, n.d.). Major professional activities provided by CCPs include the following: (a) clinical interviews, including psychotherapy, counseling, psychoeducation, and rehabilitation; (b) psychological assessments; (c) community interventions; and (d) research (mostly case studies; Japanese Society of Certified Clinical Psychologists, 2007). A survey conducted by the Japanese Society of Certified Clinical Psychologists (2007) revealed that 77.4% of CCPs wanted to learn more about eclectic counseling, followed by cognitive or cognitive behavior therapy (72.8%), the psychoanalytic/analytic approach (59.6%), systems theory (52.9%), and humanistic approaches (50.3%). A strong interest in cognitive behavior therapy reflects Japan's movement toward evidence-based practice as demonstrated by the fact that cognitive behavior therapy was added to the national health insurance system for the treatment of mood disorders in April 2010.

Although clinical psychology has gained some popularity, employment conditions for CCPs are substandard. More than half of CCPs earn less than the national average, and 46.1% work only part time (Japanese Society of Certified Clinical Psychologists, 2007). Because of this and the absence of a national licensure, Japanese counseling practitioners continue to struggle to gain legal recognition as a distinct profession.

School Counseling

As mentioned previously, since the MEXT introduced school counseling systems in 1995, the number of school counselors has steadily increased. In 2006, school counselors were employed in 10,158 schools throughout Japan, which was a dramatic increase from 154 schools in 1995. In 2007, more than 80% of school counselors were CCPs (MEXT, 2007). The responsibilities of school counselors include student counseling and advisement, psychological evaluation and referral, classroom guidance, consultation to parents and faculty, and crisis intervention (MEXT, 2007). School counselors typically work with developmental issues such as school refusal, bullying, interpersonal problems, parent–child problems, and academic issues. In recent years, however, more and more cases involving severe mental health problems have been reported by school counselors (MEXT, 2007). All school counselors work part time, staying at a school for only 8 hours per week. This employment structure makes it extremely difficult for school counselors to meet the increasing demand for counseling services. Along with full-time employment, school counselors need consistent clinical supervision to obtain professional development and support. However, clinical supervisions for school counselors have not been systematically provided.

Mental Health Counseling

Clinics and hospitals are other locations in which Japanese people receive counseling services from a variety of professionals, including physicians, social workers, and clinical psychologists. However, the practice of counseling in Japanese mental health facilities is dominated by a hierarchy that places medical doctors at the top. Currently only medical doctors can make a diagnosis, and national health insurance does not cover counseling unless it is conducted under the direction of medical doctors. In clinics and hospitals, medical doctors typically place clinical psychologists and social workers under their supervision and determine whether counseling should be provided by these professionals (Kanazawa, 2007).

This hierarchy seems to hinder efficient collaboration among mental health professionals in Japan, as it impedes clients' full access to appropriate treatment options. In fact, inadequate service delivery among psychiatric facilities is a major problem in Japan. A recent national survey revealed that less than one third of medical facilities had the capacity to adequately perform any form of psychotherapy (Ono et al., 2011). Ono et al. (2011) argued that this was partially because of the significant shortage of clinicians in psychiatric hospitals trained to conduct psychotherapy. Therefore, increasing the number of competent practitioners is one of the most pressing issues confronting the mental health care system in Japan.

Career Counseling

Career counseling has gained significant status since 2001 when the MHLW implemented a national policy to train 50,000 career consultants within 5 years. This movement was further advanced in 2009 when the MEXT initiated an educational reform to strengthen career education in secondary schools in response to growing career-related concerns among Japanese youth.

Currently there are three levels of career consultant credentials: standard, advanced, and instructor. None of these credentials requires a college degree. The standard level is a certification that requires passing one of 10 MHLW-approved training programs and examinations. The advanced and instructor levels are national credentials approved by the MHLW. Both provide legal protection of the professional title *Kyaria Konsarutanto Ginoushi* (career consultant technician) without regulating professional activity, such as service delivery. Standard-level consultants who wish to obtain the advanced or instructor credential must undergo additional training or advanced professional experience in career counseling before taking the examination.

In 2011, there were 31,186 standard-level career consultants in Japan (Career Consulting Conference, 2011). Of these career consultants, 30.3% worked in public employment assistant centers, 24.2% were employed at private companies, and 17% worked at private staffing agencies. Regular consultation topics included assistance with career changes or job search activities (46.6%), résumé building and cover letter writing (45.6%), interview skills (28.9%), career planning and career skill development (26.3%), and vocational and personality assessment (23.9%; Career Consulting Conference, 2011). Although career consultants have a national-level certificate, there are two issues to consider. First, similar to CCPs, career consultants tend to be employed part time and to have lower incomes (Career Consulting Conference, 2011). Second, compared to career counseling in the United States, career consulting in Japan places less emphasis on applying career development theories and basic counseling skills, creating an ambiguous relationship with career counseling (Watanabe-Muraoka, 2007).

Characteristics Unique to Counseling in Japan

In order to work effectively with their clients, Japanese counselors incorporate a variety of cultural considerations into their practice. In this section, culturally specific counseling approaches unique to Japan are described.

Social Stigma and the Somatization of Psychological Problems

One of the challenges for counselors in Japan is to effectively address the stigma associated with seeking psychological assistance. The most notable treatment approach is to focus on psychosomatology because of the tendency of the Japanese population to experience a somatization of psychological problems. For instance, there is a large number of *Shinryo-Naika,* clinics that specialize in psychosomatic medicine, and people typically visit this type of clinic instead of a psychiatrist or counselor. The use of *Shinryo-Naika* is less intimidating because the word *Naika* means "internal medicine" (Kanazawa, 2007). Furthermore, Japanese doctors frequently use diagnostic criteria that are distinctly different from the common classifications used in the *Diagnostic and Statistical Manual of Mental Disorders* or the International Classification of Diseases–10. In Japan, a diagnosis of *Jiritsu Shinkei Shitchosho* (imbalance in the function of the autonomic nerve) is typically given to clients who present with depressive symptoms and anxiety. This diagnosis is less threatening for Japanese clients because it implies a medical condition and conceals the psychological disorder, avoiding the potential for social stigma (Iwakabe, 2008). Clients with *Jiritsu Shinkei Shitchosho* are usually advised to rest and are prescribed psychotropic medication. In addition, autogenic training, deep breathing, and relaxation training are frequently used to alleviate stress-induced psychosomatic symptoms.

Counseling Relationships and Process

Despite the stigma, an increasing number of clients are requesting counseling as a part of their treatment (Iwakabe, 2008). In addition, many practitioners have observed that Japanese clients in pharmacologically focused treatment are frustrated with how little counseling they receive from their physicians. Japanese clients' dissatisfaction with this treatment approach seems to influence their expectations of counselors; as Kanazawa (2007) noted, "Clients may be asking for a compassionate therapist who, unlike the medical doctor, is a good listener" (p. 760). Indeed, scholars and practitioners strongly advocate that the primary role of the counselor in Japan is "being with the client in pain and [being] in tune with his or her inner experiences" (p. 759). Some practitioners argue that Japanese clients' longing for acceptance, connection, and empathy in counseling is the result of a changing Japanese society in which fewer family members are available to fulfill the role of a supportive listener.

The goals of counseling in Japan focus on increasing the client's acceptance of a situation through greater insight and understanding; less emphasis is given to symptom reduction, as this represents a medical model (Kanazawa, 2007). For example, Japanese counselors frequently use personality assessments to facilitate clients' self-awareness, and many clients seem satisfied with the new knowledge they gain from counseling. Given Japanese people's tendency to be more external in their locus of control, the goal of facilitating a client's acceptance of a circumstance through developing greater awareness and insight seems appropriate for this collectivist culture, in which self-satisfaction tends to come from successfully adjusting oneself to maintain harmony within the social context (Markus & Kitayama, 1991).

Japanese Communication Styles and Nonverbal Techniques

One of the distinct characteristics of the counseling approach in Japan is its emphasis on nonverbal communication. Consistent with a high-context communication style that relies heavily on context to establish meaning, Japanese people rely less on verbal messages and communicate more through careful attention to nonverbal expression and sensitivity to the context of what is being said. Therefore, counselors must be able to send and receive ambiguous, indirect, and contextual messages to develop a therapeutic alliance with Japanese clients. Indeed, silence, nonverbal interactions, and solitary introspection are often used by Japanese counselors to facilitate therapeutic change (Iwakabe, 2008). For instance, Japanese counselors may purposefully offer vague feedback to clients, then engage in skillful use of *Ma* (a pause or silence) to quietly support clients' introspection while using *Kuuki wo Yomu* (reading the air) to decipher unspoken meaning and experiences that the clients are having in the moment.

In Japan, where tradition dictates that it is a virtue to keep one's thoughts and feelings to oneself, many people find it uncomfortable to discuss personal problems or to otherwise verbally express their feelings in face-to-face interactions. Therefore, Japanese counselors frequently utilize nonverbal media, such as the sandbox, clay sculpture, movement, painting, and projective testing, to offer clients a window into their inner world and a vehicle for expressing their feelings. The most popular nonverbal approach in Japan is *Hakoniwa* therapy (box garden therapy). *Hakoniwa* therapy uses a miniature sandbox in which clients use a variety of figures, objects, and symbols to project their inner world. In addition, the sandbox represents the context in which the presenting problems are embedded. Therefore, it allows clients to express the self in context, which is especially suitable for Japanese clients whose sense of self is strongly defined by social or relational contexts (Enns & Kasai, 2003).

Emphasis on the Mother–Child Relationship

In Japan, where traditional gender role expectations continue to be practiced widely, many mothers are devoted to raising their children while their husbands dedicate themselves to work outside the home. Thus, the counseling field in Japan has always emphasized the importance of the mother–child relationship. For instance, like the Oedipus complex in the West, Heisaku Kozawa, a Japanese psychoanalyst, developed the Ajase complex in 1932 to illustrate the complex and ambivalent quality of mother–child relationships and associated feelings of guilt experienced by the child. This was the first attempt to integrate the Japanese cultural perspective into psychoanalysis in order to better analyze Japanese people. In 1971, Takeo Doi presented the concept of *Amae* (dependency) in the mother–infant relationship and discussed its manifestations in Japanese psychology and culture. *Amae* has been used extensively to explain communication, interpersonal relationships, emotions, and social structures, among other things. Based on these theories, Japanese counselors developed a specific counseling approach that focuses on the mother–child relationship.

Parent–child concomitant counseling is widely used among Japanese practitioners. In this approach, a parent (usually the mother) and a child are asked to participate in individual counseling sessions separately but simultaneously, even when the child is an adolescent or adult. The goal of concomitant counseling is twofold: (a) to facilitate the successful treatment of the child by assisting the mother in executing an appropriate parental role and (b) to help the mother sort out her feelings regarding the child's problems while facilitating psychological growth and cognitive change. Because this format is different from the family systems model, counselors use a variety of approaches depending on their theoretical orientation. The mother–child concomitant counseling model is used most commonly for the treatment of school refusal syndrome or social withdrawal syndrome.

The Future

As Japan continues to go through societal and cultural transformation, counselors need to prepare themselves to engage with the emerging issues that are resulting from these changes. In this section, we present challenges that will impact the future of the counseling profession in Japan.

Diversity Issues

Although Japan is generally considered a culturally homogeneous nation, it is gradually becoming more diverse. For instance, the proportion of foreign nationals to the total population has almost doubled since 1990, and it is expected to increase in the future (Japan Ministry of Justice, 2010). In addition to increasing ethnic diversity, other sociocultural factors, such as age, gender, disability, and socioeconomic status, require further attention. By 2015, about one fourth of the Japanese population is projected to be older than 65. More and more women are participating in Japan's labor force. The number of people with a disability has increased to approximately 7.24 million, including 3.66 million people with physical disabilities, 550,000 people with intellectual disabilities, and 3.03 million people with mental disabilities (Cabinet Office, 2008). Furthermore, since the 1990s, income disparities in Japan have widened, and the poverty rate reached 15.7% in 2006, similar to the poverty rate in the United States (Japanese Statistics Bureau, n.d.).

These statistics reveal the changing demographics of Japan. However, Japan has long endorsed the myth of national homogeneity, resulting in a lack of recognition of diversity as a relevant issue. Hence, multiculturalism is a novel concept for most Japanese people, including counselors. In fact, counselor training programs have not incorporated diversity issues into the curriculum. Because of a lack of training, many counselors are likely to be unaware of how diversity can impact the presenting problem and the counseling process, resulting in a weak counseling relationship and poor outcomes. Thus, we believe that counselors in Japan need to develop multicultural counseling competencies and uphold social justice to meet the needs of an increasingly diverse society.

First, as ethnic diversity increases in Japan, counselors working with clients from other countries need to reexamine their own attitudes (i.e., ethnocentricity and prejudice) and identify relevant cultural issues. In addition to being adept in cross-cultural communication, counselors must work alongside the client's worldview. When working with clients from other countries, counselors should be able to apply germane concepts such as culture shock, acculturation, ethnic identity, language anxiety, and so forth. Furthermore, discrimination against foreigners has been widely reported; for example, some apartment owners refuse to lease apartments to foreign nationals. In these circumstances, counselors need to go beyond traditional office-bound activities by educating the public about the negative effects of prejudice and advocating for clients' rights.

Second, a growing emphasis on gender equality and a prolonged economic recession in Japan have increased the number of women participating in the labor force. Yet current labor conditions for women are less than optimal for their well-being: On average, Japanese women working full time tend to have less career advancement opportunities and earn significantly less than their male counterparts. Because the number of child care facilities is insufficient, working mothers are still expected to be the primary caregivers in the household. Moreover, many women give up pursuing a career because typical full-time positions demand long working hours, which makes it difficult to balance work and family life. When working with Japanese women, it is imperative for counselors to consider how social context may affect the presenting problem.

Third, counselors need to assess the salient cumulative effects of multiple diversity factors when working with clients. Census data indicate that certain sociocultural groups, such as older adults, persons with disabilities, women, and part-time workers, are likely to experience poverty. For instance, many elderly persons have disabilities, are unemployed, and live in poverty (Japanese Statistics Bureau, n.d.). Upon retirement, some elderly people may experience a loss of social support networks and financial stability. If they acquire disabilities and experience economic hardship, they may develop depressive symptoms and become even more isolated, which will exacerbate their depression. In this case, adjustment issues related to aging and disability may be discussed as underlying issues of depression. Therefore, it is critical that counselors take into account the interactive, cumulative effects of factors related to diversity in the treatment plan. In all respects, the counseling field in Japan needs to become more attentive to multicultural issues.

Disaster Mental Health

Disaster mental health is a crucial and growing field in Japan, as the country experiences frequent natural disasters because of its geographical location and unstable weather conditions. In fact, Japanese counselors play an active role in providing psychological care to victims and survivors of disasters, including the Tohoku Region Pacific Coast Earthquake. Several months after this disaster, Japan is beginning to restore a sense of stabilization and to focus on recovery. However, the critical time for counselors to help in Japan's psychological recovery continues, as an increase in posttraumatic stress and mental health problems is anticipated. In the next few years, counselors need to take a leadership position in postdisaster mental health support by expanding their role and knowledge to provide effective and culturally appropriate psychological support to disaster victims.

First, to play an active role in disaster mental health, it is crucial for counselors to become familiar with the relevant research. For example, knowledge of disaster response models helps counselors quickly establish emergency logistics and effectively work in a disaster response team. Also, skills in identifying and treating disaster-related psychological issues, such as complicated grief and posttraumatic stress disorder, are valuable in all phases of disaster response, including planning, response, and recovery. To this end, we recommend that disaster mental health training be included as a requirement in counselor training programs in Japan as well as in continuing education credits needed for professional counselors to renew their certifications.

Second, counselors need to be able to effectively implement culturally relevant approaches by considering the sociocultural backgrounds of victims and survivors. As noted earlier, counselors must develop multicultural competencies to understand how clients' social-political-cultural issues affect their disaster and recovery experiences. For instance, previous disaster research in Japan indicated that residents of temporary shelters, women, children, older adults, people with disabilities, and people of lower socioeconomic status were at highest risk for experiencing significant stress and mental health problems (Kato, 1998). This type of information can aid counselors in assessing the vulnerability of each client while advocating for the rights of victims with less power.

The need to advance disaster mental health has become a global issue. In view of this, international collaboration and resource sharing is a critical professional activity among counselors around the world. Japanese counselors who work closely with disaster victims can contribute to the internationalization of disaster counseling through research, training, publication, as well as participation in international networks. Insights into specific cultural issues unique to Japan can have valuable implications for multicultural counseling and disaster psychology.

Professional Status and Identity

The future of professional counseling in Japan relies on the field gaining legal recognition and public acceptance. In the meantime, it is critical to expand the availability of qualified counseling practitioners who are equipped with the skills and knowledge to effectively meet the psychosocial needs of Japanese society (Grabosky et al., 2012). The lack of a national system to regulate the quality of counseling practices leaves the public vulnerable in articulating the credibility and the differences among various credentials. Indeed, the counseling field is flooded with professional associations that establish their own credentials (Grabosky et al., 2012). This overflow of credentials has led to a growing number of incidents in which spurious counseling certificates have been used or sold.

The current overflow of certifications must be confronted immediately to resolve public confusion (Grabosky et al., 2012). Ongoing advocacy for national licensure to regulate professional titles and counseling activity is vital to gaining professional status. In addition, exploration of a professional identity among the various groups of counseling practitioners is recommended to highlight the strengths of each group. This can also facilitate collaboration among the different groups of counseling practitioners.

Conclusion

The demand for counseling is increasing significantly as people in Japan experience increasing social and mental health problems. Today more practitioners are providing counseling services in various professional fields, and an active effort has been made to provide culturally appropriate counseling to Japanese clients when applying Western theories and models. However, the development of counseling as a specialized and distinguished profession needs further advocacy. Given Japan's increasing psychosocial problems and the subsequent need for counseling services, we expect that there will be numerous opportunities for growth and development in Japan's counseling field.

References

Cabinet Office. (2008). *Annual report on government measures for persons with disabilities 2008.* Retrieved from http://www8.cao.go.jp/shougai/english/annualreport/2008/pdf/p1-11.pdf

Cabinet Office: Division of Suicide Prevention and National Police Agency: Community Safety Bureau/Division of Community Safety Planning. (2012). *Heisei 23 nen chyuh ni okeru jisatsu no jyoukyou* [The facts surrounding suicides committed in 2011]. Retrieved from http://www.npa.go.jp/safetylife/seianki/H23jisatsunojokyo.pdf

Career Consulting Conference. (2011). *Kyaria konsarutingu nikansuru jittaichousa kekka houkokusho* [Report of the survey results on career consulting]. Retrieved from http://www.mhlw.go.jp/stf/houdou/2r98520000016ueo-img/2r98520000018brr.pdf

Enns, C. Z., & Kasai, M. (2003). Hakoniwa: Japanese sandplay therapy. *The Counseling Psychologist, 31,* 93–112. doi:10.1177/0011000002239403

Foundation of the Japanese Certification Board for Clinical Psychologists. (n.d.). *Rinshyou shinrishi shikakunintei no jisshi* [The implementation of the certification in clinical psychology]. Retrieved from http://www.fjcbcp.or.jp/nintei_1.html

Grabosky, T., Ishii, H., & Mase, S. (2012). The development of the counseling profession in Japan: Past, present and future. *Journal of Counseling & Development, 90,* 221–226.

Ishi-Kuntz, M. (1989). Collectivism or individualism? Changing patterns of Japanese attitudes. *Sociology and Social Research, 73,* 174–179.

Iwakabe, S. (2008). Psychotherapy integration in Japan. *Journal of Psychotherapy Integration, 18,* 103–125. doi:10.1037/1053-0479.18.1.103

Iwasaki, M. (2005). Mental health and counseling in Japan: A path toward societal transformation. *Journal of Mental Health Counseling, 27,* 129–141.

Japan Ministry of Education, Culture, Sports, Science, and Technology. (2007). *Jidou seito no kyouikusoudan no Jyuujitu ni tsuite ikiki sita kodomo wo sodateru soudan taisei tukuri: sukuhru kaunserah* [The fulfillment of educational guidance for schoolchildren—For the development of a guidance system to raise lively children: School counselors]. Retrieved from http://www.mext.go.jp/a_menu/shotou/seitoshidou/kyouiku/houkoku/07082308/002.htm

Japan Ministry of Justice. (2010). *2010 Immigration control.* Retrieved from http://www.moj.go.jp/nyuukokukanri/kouhou/nyuukokukanri01_00015.html

Japanese Society of Certified Clinical Psychologists. (2007). *Dai 5 kai Rinsho-shinrishi no doukou narabini ishiki chousa houkokusho* [Report of the fifth survey on the trend and attitude of clinical psychologists]. Tokyo, Japan: Author.

Japanese Statistics Bureau. (n.d.). *Historical statistics of Japan.* Retrieved from http://www.stat.go.jp/english/data/chouki/index.htm

Kanazawa, Y. (2007). Psychotherapy in Japan: The case of Mrs. A. *Journal of Clinical Psychology, 63,* 755–763. doi:10.1002/jclp.20390

Kato, H. (1998). Posttraumatic symptoms among victims of the great Hanshin-Awaji earthquake in Japan. *Psychiatry and Clinical Neurosciences, 52,* 59–65. doi:10.1046/j.14401819.1998.0520s5S59x

Markus, H. R., & Kitayama, S. (1991). Culture and the self: Implications for cognition, emotion, and motivation. *Psychological Review, 98,* 224–253.

National Police Agency. (2009). *Suicide statistics 2008.* Retrieved from http://www.npa.go.jp/toukei/chiiki10/h19_zisatsu.pdf

Ono, Y., Furukawa, T., Shimizu, E., Okamoto, Y., Nakagawa, A., Fujisawa, D., . . . Nakajima, S. (2011). Current status of research on cognitive therapy/cognitive behavioral therapy in Japan. *Psychiatry and Clinical Neurosciences, 65,* 121–129. doi:10.1111/j.1440-1819.2010.02182.x

Watanabe-Muraoka, A. M. (2007). A perspective on counseling psychology in Japan: Toward a lifespan approach. *Applied Psychology, 56,* 97–106.

• • •

COUNSELING IN THE KYRGYZ REPUBLIC 12

Elena Molchanova, Elena Kosterina, Elena Kim, Sharon G. Horne, Kanykei Latipova, and Patrick Marius Koga

Rapid growth in the development of counseling services in the Kyrgyz Republic seems to be an outcome of the latest transformations and violent conflicts in the country. Central Asia has often been considered to be one of the least stable places of the former Soviet Union, both politically and economically (Abashin, 2007). The totalitarian regime of the Soviet era did not allow for any open expression of interethnic conflict (Tishkov, 1991) in the "stans" (Kazakhstan, Kyrgyzstan, Tajikistan, Turkmenistan, and Uzbekistan). The situation changed dramatically after the collapse of the Soviet Union with the resurgence of ethnic identities and the repositioning of leadership in the former Soviet states, all shaped by the interests of political and economic elites of local ethnic communities and tribes. At the end of the 20th century there were several interethnic conflicts in Central Asia. The beginning of the 21st century brought further conflict: the Tulip Revolution of 2005 followed by anti-Russian actions in Bishkek, Kyrgyz Republic; the 2006–2007 anti-Caucasus movements of Kazakhs in Aktau, Kazakhstan; ongoing mass unrest in Tajikistan; and the April Revolution and the Osh massacre of 2010 in the Kyrgyz Republic.

The multidimensional consequences of interethnic tensions, violence, and mass panic have had not only political, economic, and health costs but also mental health repercussions (Molchanova, Panteleeva, Popkov, & Nelubova, 2011). High suicide rates among the most vulnerable of citizens, including children and teenagers, are also among the consequences. In addition, psychological services have had to evolve to meet mental health needs resulting from maltreatment at the hands of authorities such as law enforcement agencies, who illegally practice torture in order to extract confessions from criminal suspects (Latipova, 2009). Among those particularly impacted by torture in the country are indigent migrants and members of ethnic and/or religious groups.

The magnitude of mental health problems is not matched by the quality or the amount of mental health services in Central Asia in general or in the Kyrgyz Republic in particular. The common barriers to access to services (e.g., social stigma, a limited number of specialists found primarily in urban areas, costly transportation that limits treatment options for rural individuals, underfunding, and lack of acknowledgment of mental health problems by local governments) are further exacerbated by culturally biased attitudes toward people with mental health problems. This has led to a split in mental health services between medical and psychological services and traditional approaches to healing (Molchanova et al., 2009). The need for professional help is tremendous, yet the fear of being stigmatized, the devaluation of mental health care specialists, and overpathologizing (i.e., everything being defined as "mental" or "psychological") are increasing the gap between those who have been exposed to traumatic events and those who actually receive treatment.

Nevertheless, the gap between needs and services (World Health Organization, 2011) and misperceptions about psychology and psychiatry have also driven the growing popularity of counseling, which did not exist as a separate discipline in the Kyrgyz Republic before 2009. Prior to that time, the only counselors in the country (i.e., stress counselors) served as international staff members for such organizations as the United Nations Development Programme and UNICEF and worked primarily in Bishkek, the capital of the Kyrgyz Republic. *Counseling* as it is widely used in the common vernacular refers to psychological support and bears little stigma because of its separation from the medical establishment. Thus, the practice of counseling has come to represent short-term psychotherapy in private practice as well as in the field of social services and in the professional activities of a newly emerging class of professionals called "social pedagogues" who are employed in school systems.

Diversity Issues

Like other professional mental health fields that have a longer history in the Kyrgyz Republic, the practice of counseling has a number of challenges. Mental health professionals are challenged with the need to take into account the diversity of languages in the country. Consequently, the current lack of professionals who speak both Kyrgyz and Russian, the primary languages used in the country, poses serious challenges for both counselors and clients. Counselors must also treat people of a different socioeconomic status who are often poorly informed about counseling and may distrust such services. An additional issue of particular importance in counseling is gender inequality. Along with chronic domestic violence in the country, this inequality suggests the need for a gender-sensitive approach to dealing with the needs of counseling victims exposed to violence, bride kidnapping, and rape and points to the important role of community mental health and human rights education and advocacy.

According to the National Statistics Committee of the Kyrgyz Republic (n.d.), the Kyrgyz Republic has a population of 5,477,620 people. The nation's largest ethnic group is the Kyrgyz, a Turkic people, who make up 69% of the population. Other substantial ethnic groups include the Uzbeks (14.5%), who live primarily in the south, and the Russians (9.0%), who are concentrated in the north. There are more than 80 other distinct ethnic minority groups.

The majority of citizens strongly identify themselves with one of the ethnic groups, and individuals belonging to minority ethnic groups tend to retain their own language and traditions and resist assimilation to the Kyrgyz, the main ethnic group. One of the most relevant issues for counseling certainly has to do with the Kyrgyz language. The Kyrgyz language reflects the history of the country's migration patterns and the complexity of its people. Perhaps because of a history of manual labor and a cultural prizing of self-sufficiency and independence, the Kyrgyz people find it difficult to express emotional states verbally. This cultural behavior makes communicating with mental health professionals difficult.

Kyrgyz is the state language of the country, but Russian is spoken by a significant portion of the population and is used as the official language of education. At the state level, Kyrgyz and Russian are used simultaneously. A majority of representatives of ethnic groups speak the language of their ethnic group and also speak Russian. The majority of groups of Slavic background, as well as many other Asian and Caucasian ethnic groups, usually do not speak Kyrgyz or at best speak only some. The gap between educated speakers of Russian and/or Kyrgyz and individuals who do not speak either Russian or Kyrgyz can be vast and can fuel the distrust of educated mental health professionals.

The issue of migration is relevant for all ethnic groups in the country. There was an imbalance between emigration and immigration from 1990 to 2010. The majority of people who leave the country permanently are Russians, Ukrainians, and Uzbeks, which means there are fewer counselors represented by these groups. The emigration of many Uzbek people from the Kyrgyz Republic is heavily linked to the tragic events of June 2010, when many Uzbeks and Kyrgyz were killed in ethnic conflict in southern Kyrgyz Republic. Many Kyrgyz also leave the country to work in other countries of the region, mostly Russia and Kazakhstan.

The country is also experiencing a difficult economic situation. The official unemployment rate of 8% is probably a gross underestimation, as the majority of unemployed citizens have not been registered as such. At the same time, the process of work migration to other countries suggests that a significant portion of the population cannot find a well-paid job in the country and prefer to move elsewhere in search of a better life. Many of these people do not have the legal status of work migrants. The average monthly wage in the country is $170, but this varies greatly by region and sector of the economy. Therefore, even if they desired them, many individuals could not afford counseling services, and individuals who are trained as counselors have a difficult time securing income for their profession.

Gender Equality

Gender equality is among the most critical issues in the Kyrgyz Republic today and one that significantly influences approaches to counseling in the country. Many legal documents guarantee equal rights for men and women. For example, the Kyrgyz Republic accepted the Convention on the Elimination of All Forms of Discrimination Against Women (CEDAW) in 1996 and has developed several legal documents to guarantee gender equality at the state level, specifically "On the Basis of State Guarantees of Ensuring Gender Equality" (Secretary of the National Council on Issues of Women, Family and Gender Development, 2005). Gender equality is claimed to be one of the principles on which the civil development of the country is based. It is most often interpreted as meaning gender mainstreaming in governmental structures and the court system, but it is rarely implemented in policy development or reflected in values communicated at the local and state levels.

Similar to women in other former Soviet states, Kyrgyz women have gained educational equality with men. However, the percentage of girls attending primary school declined from more than 98% in 1998 to 95.5% in 2001; boys' enrollment during the same period also declined but at a slower rate—from more than 99% in 1998 to 98% in 2001 (Shah, 2005). Although girls outnumbered boys in universities from 2000 to 2011 and performed better, women's economic activity, including rates of employment and wages, continued to decrease (National Statistics Committee of the Kyrgyz Republic, n.d.). For example, among women who were employed, salaries declined from 73% (of men's salaries) in 2000 to 64.1% in 2003. Rural women have fared even worse. They have been more adversely affected than men by land reform and the privatization of communal farms that began in the early 1990s, when ownership went largely to men. Women now own only 4% of farms. On family farms, privatization has led to an increased workload for women, with "the return to primitive agricultural production methods based on non-automated family labor contributing to the increase in paternalistic principles and values" (Moldosheva & Asylbekova, 2005, p. 17). An unintended effect of land reform has been the strengthening of Muslim traditions and common law at the expense of women's rights.

Violence against women is also increasing in the Kyrgyz Republic, including reports of the regional practice of bride kidnapping, which is when a man, usually with the support of his family, kidnaps a young woman and forces her into marriage against her will. Women's crisis centers receive approximately 3,000 reports of domestic violence annually from individual women (Osmonalieva, 2010). Although the Kyrgyz Republic ratified the CEDAW Convention in 1996, the collection of official statistics on domestic violence began only after the country received increased international attention on the reporting of gender issues associated with the Millennium Development Goals. Prostitution rates and trafficking in women, which affect mainly young rural women who are internal migrants, are thought to be increasing in prevalence (Human Rights Watch, 2006), although no official data were collected for this report. Statistics on maternal and infant mortality (a conventional measure of women's status) only add to the portrayal of inequality and injustice for Kyrgyz women. Poor health care, including inadequate access to safe abortion services, and poor maternal nutrition are blamed for maternal mortality rates that are high for Central Asia and that appear to have increased significantly since 1996. Infant and child mortality rates in the Kyrgyz Republic are the third highest across Central Asia according to the World Health Organization (2011).

The lack of representation of women in parliament was officially addressed only in 2007, when a quota of 30% was introduced to ensure the participation of women in political life. Before this, there were no women in the Kyrgyz parliament. After the passage of the quota, the number of women in parliament increased to 26%, but it has never reached 30%. The position Special Representative on Gender Issues in Parliament (represented by a woman) was recently created within parliament to work on the promotion of gender equality. These important concerns all influence the role and development of counseling in the Kyrgyz Republic and Central Asia as well.

The Current Status of Counseling

Counseling is a term that exists in the Kyrgyz Republic alongside such terms as *psychotherapy*, *psychology*, and *psychiatry*. Although mental health professionals understand the differences among these terms, a company manager who might need assistance to solve a mental health job crisis will usually seek out a psychologist to address the issue. A female employee experiencing harassment is also more likely to turn to a psychologist working in a private psychological center than a counselor. However, psychiatrists and psychotherapists working in crisis centers with secondary or tertiary disaster survivors prefer to call themselves "counselors" to avoid stigmatization by their patients and to motivate potential clients. Because of confusion associated with terminology, it is difficult to determine an accurate number of professional counselors, even though the number of other mental health care specialists in Kyrgyz Republic is known. For instance, in 2010 there were only 13 child psychiatrists and 4 officially licensed medical psychologists in the entire Kyrgyz Republic (Musabaeva, 2010) compared with 1999, when there were 38 child psychiatrists in the country. It is also important to note that the segment of the general population represented by children grew dramatically from 2000 to 2011, and the number of children ages 0 to 17 years was reported at about 1.9 million in January 2009 (National Statistics Committee of the Kyrgyz Republic, n.d.). More than half of children live in the southern region of the country, where there are only two child psychiatrists and no child psychologists.

Social Pedagogy

A newly developed specialty, social pedagogy, is intended to provide a counseling role in schools (similar to school counseling in the United States). On February 2, 2010, the Minister of Science and Education (MSEKR) signed a decree placing social pedagogues on the staffs of schools countrywide. The job description and evaluation criteria for social pedagogues were developed with support from USAID and approved by the MSEKR on July 27, 2010. The responsibilities of social pedagogues are quite similar to those of social workers (who do not work in schools) and overlap with those of school psychologists. Social pedagogues provide services that strengthen home, school, and community partnerships and alleviate barriers to learning. The social pedagogue is expected to contribute to the development of a healthy, safe, and caring environment by advancing understanding of the emotional and social development of children and the influences of family, community, and cultural differences on student success. In response to the complex interethnic situation, and following the order of the MSEKR, 2,000 teachers from the southern region of the Kyrgyz Republic received social pedagogical training from July to November 2011.

The situation with social pedagogues in rural areas is more complicated. A 2010 study showed that these positions were usually given to teachers who did not have enough teaching courses in their load to provide a full salary, and although evaluation criteria for the social pedagogues did exist (Ministry of Science and Education of the Kyrgyz Republic, 2010), they were far too complicated to be used to measure job performance. Another set of barriers to implementation in rural areas was raised by school principals, who did not understand why they had to hire an additional employee and provide him or her with a teaching load when even teachers who had two or more teaching loads were struggling with low salaries. The situation has improved since the tragic deaths of Uzbeks and Kyrgyz in June 2010. USAID and the Quality Education Project in the Kyrgyz Republic, in collaboration with the Ministry of Science and Education of the Kyrgyz Republic and independent experts, have implemented a training program for the administrative core of schools with a special focus on social pedagogues. Three continuing education centers and four methodological centers have been established, and they organize and provide courses in continuing education for teachers who wish to be trained as social pedagogues. Included in the training are basic counseling skills and basic mental health screening.

Counseling in Crisis Centers

Another population in need of counseling services in the Kyrgyz Republic is people affected by domestic violence. The number of crisis centers for victims of violence is growing, and many graduates of psychology departments are employed in them. Every center requires a counselor with a psychological or medical background and a specialist in social work. The Association of the Crisis Centers brings together 10 centers located primarily in Bishkek and Osh. Crisis centers exist because of the financial support of international donors.

Counseling in Private Practice

Private counseling centers are concentrated in Bishkek and Osh, and 32 psychologists work in such centers. The majority are alumni of psychology departments of universities in the Kyrgyz Republic and the State Medical Academy; however, eight of them do not have psychological or medical backgrounds and received a certificate after only 2 years of secondary education. A clear distinction does not exist in the Kyrgyz Republic between psychologists and counselors, although the majority of specialists working in private centers prefer to describe themselves as counselors or psychological counselors.

Counseling in Nongovernmental Organizations

A few nongovernmental organizations that provide organizational and policy counseling were established in 2000 and 2001 from international support and mainly cater to the needs of international companies working in the Kyrgyz Republic. Their activities are focused on national blue chip companies, and they concentrate on analyzing corporate culture and providing technical advice for organizations.

Counseling Organizations

There is no consolidated psychological or counseling association in the Kyrgyz Republic, although the psychological community is making efforts to establish one. An ethical framework for teaching, practice, and research has been developed, and a draft of an ethical code for psychologists was created at the end of May 2011. However, it is too early to speak about any significant impact of these efforts on the ethical practice of research and clinical work. Kyrgyz research and practice in psychology and counseling, as well as in other social sciences, is not bound by any institutional ethical regulations. Local researchers rely on their own conscientiousness and awareness of research ethics in conducting their studies. However, social workers are mostly employed in public social service jobs that focus on the administration of social support (Rutgers University Center for International Social Work, 2008). In the Kyrgyz Republic, social workers are also engaged in nongovernmental organizations that are funded internationally. They primarily serve vulnerable populations, providing them with counseling and advocacy services on site.

Best Counseling Practices

The development of counseling in the Kyrgyz Republic is an example of how interaction between the traditional culture and the modern state has influenced contemporary mental health service in a very complex way (Adylov, 2008). A unique combination of ancient beliefs and Islamic practices is a characteristic feature of contemporary spiritual life. The Kyrgyz people usually look for a combination of traditional healing and modern practices. Balancing both approaches requires a high level of awareness of Kyrgyz views on psychopathology and cultural ways of presenting problems (Molchanova et al., 2009). Both health care provider and client cognitive schemas of a presenting problem can affect the counseling process. Kyrgyz traditional culture not only determines the content of psychopathological experiences but also plays a major role in developing culture-related behaviors. For example, Kyrgyz ancient beliefs and rituals, myths, and traditional healing practices influence the interpretation of two syndromes unique to the Kyrgyz Republic: Albarsthy and Kyrgyzchylyk. Albarsthy is a mythological hero with negative magical powers and aggressive intentions. The person with Albarsthy syndrome feels a variety of unpleasant sensations during the night. These sensations are always associated with a strong feeling of the presence of a supernatural force and are understood by the client as a result of the actions of Albarsthy. Albarsthy syndrome is manifested as a possession syndrome, and from the mental health perspective it is treated as a dissociative disorder. Kyrgyzchylyk syndrome resembles a psychotic episode of a very specific kind. In the framework of the traditional cultural context, this episode indicates to the client and his or her relatives the existence of supernatural abilities in a person and is considered to be a sign of the person's future spiritual mission (Kyrgyzchylyk). When Kyrgyzchylyk syndrome hides the onset of what would be considered schizophrenia in a modern context, it is very unlikely that the client and his or her relatives will seek professional help.

Kyrgyz traditional culture particularly influences the practice of counselors working in rural areas. One challenge is the possibility of overpathologizing those behaviors that emerge from strong cultural influences on an individual's thoughts and feelings, and another is the possibility of overnormalizing what may be a mental disorder. Traditional Kyrgyz rituals are used to treat posttraumatic anxiety (not posttraumatic stress disorder) without the help of medicine. Being part of a cultural system with strong family support might decrease a client's level of anxiety, which then strengthens his or her beliefs in the positive role of culturally based methods of providing help. The strong influence of traditional culture changes the process of counseling. In order to be effective, counselors must adjust their professional approach to match the cognitive schema of the client by avoiding unknown terminology and expressing respect for traditional beliefs.

No particular counseling theory dominates in the Kyrgyz Republic. The use of systemic, cognitive–behavioral, and problem-focused approaches has been increasing since 2000 primarily as the result of numerous trainings provided by international specialists. Alumni of the Slavic and American Universities who received their graduate education in psychological counseling often prefer cognitive behavior therapy. Cognitive processing therapy, an offshoot of cognitive behavior therapy with a clear 12-step structure, has been used successfully by counselors working with clients with posttraumatic stress disorder.

Family-oriented counseling approaches include significant others in the counseling process. The psychological club AKME, established in 2008, provides family consultations and psychological services for parents and children to enhance positive interaction between parents and children.

In urban areas of the Kyrgyz Republic, access to the Internet, including Wi-Fi, is available, and online forums have become common places for people to seek counseling. Internet counseling does not currently exist in the Kyrgyz Republic, although a multidisciplinary group of mental health specialists is in the process of establishing such a service by creating a psychological services website.

Counselor Education

The status, position, and perception of counselors in the Kyrgyz Republic are reflected in the counselor education system. The present situation suggests that this profession is in a stage of progressive development. Attitudes are becoming more positive, and counselor education is receiving more government support. At the same time, the status of counseling is worsened by the perceived low status of counselors, the low prestige of the job, low wages, and pervasive biased attitudes toward counselors. Recently the Ministry of Social Development of the Kyrgyz Republic (2011) stressed the need for a more extensive exploration of the definition of counseling and the status of counselors in the country as well as for more effort in disseminating appropriate information about counseling and the development of counseling and social work systems.

In the Kyrgyz Republic, three universities provide counselor training: Bishkek Humanitarian University, the Institute of Social Development and Enterprise, and American University in Central Asia. The Department of Social Work in Bishkek Humanitarian University collaborates with the Ministry of Social Security and the Association of Social Workers to ensure an appropriate level of education for social workers and counselors. In collaboration with Bishkek Humanitarian University, the Ministry of Social Security is engaged in attracting international specialists and developing international collaborative relationships to develop the field of counseling. The Psychology Department of American University in Central Asia provides a foundational education in counseling and psychology that allows its alumni to apply to master's programs and to continue their training in universities in Europe and the United States.

The level of education of many counselors currently working in the country is not sufficient to provide appropriate counseling for all levels of care. Within the collaborative agreement described previously, the Ministry of Social Security, Bishkek Humanitarian University, and international specialists are using regional short-term projects to train counselors. Along with existing institutional efforts in education, private initiatives also commonly provide education and materials for counselors. Such projects are implemented by supportive nongovernmental organizations and foundations and take the format of short- and long-term projects for mental health specialists in regions that often lack appropriate skills or have difficulties because of local barriers to counseling and social work.

Because of the lack of specialists in the field, the philosophy behind counselor education is based on the principle of active practice and the immediate implementation of knowledge acquired at universities and in private projects. Authorities are promoting close collaboration between academic universities, social initiatives in the field, and counselors to ensure the development and implementation of innovative methods of education aimed at active practice and intervention.

The Future

We have ambivalent feelings about the potential for future development in the area of psychological counseling in the Kyrgyz Republic because of unfavorable circumstances and limited resources needed to ensure the steady growth of professional counseling services. However, a number of well-intended initiatives to improve the standards of counseling have led to various important and high-profile discussions about the establishment of a psychological and counseling community that would institute, monitor, and evaluate the implementation of internationally recognized standards of practice. A considerable number of private centers currently operate in the country and offer, among other services, psychological counseling. However, we are concerned about the lack of funding to advance and develop innovative mental health services. Indeed, the complete dependence on external funding at the present time, even to maintain current counseling services, implies a dangerous lack of sustainability of basic mental health services. Securing external international funding becomes steadily more difficult, and state provisions remain inadequate. Thus, it is not surprising that proposed initiatives to improve psychological counseling often do not translate into action, while accessible private centers continue their dependence on unsecured external resources. In addition, the lack of awareness of international standards of practice and ethical guidelines, coupled with the total absence of regulations to ensure an appropriate quality of services, stirs up fears that current mental health services could bring more harm than benefit.

On a more positive note, the most recent trends and developments in counseling do inspire some enthusiasm and hope. Psychological counseling in the Kyrgyz Republic is developing its own traditions and methods and has been shaped by a combination of the Soviet legacy in mental health approaches, new and evolving Western expertise among younger generations of practitioners, and Kyrgyz indigenous healing practices. Such a fusion makes it possible to adapt the positive characteristics of a variety of counseling approaches to the local situation and thus contribute to better overall effectiveness. More hope is instilled by the growing interest among clients in mental health counseling and the fact that institutions of higher education and vocational training increasingly offer degrees that provide students with counseling skills. Lastly, local educators and developers are continuously looking for opportunities to increase awareness in the psychological community of current trends in counseling practice, training, and licensure. Such efforts suggest that counseling in Kyrgyz is in a dynamic state of development with its own unique direction and contributions.

References

Abashin, S. (2007). *Nacionalizmi v Centralnoi Asii: V poiskah identichnosti* [Nationalisms in Central Asia: Looking for identity]. St. Petersburg, Russia: Aleteija.

Adylov, D. (2008). Healing at mazars: Sources of healing, methods of curative impact, types of healers and criteria of effectiveness. In A. Egemberdieva & M. Toknogulova (Eds.), *Mazarworship in Kyrgyzstan: Rituals and practitioners in Talas* (pp. 377–395). Bishkek, Kyrgyzstan: Aigine Research Centre.

Human Rights Watch. (2006). *Reconciled to violence: State failure to stop domestic abuse and abduction of women in Kyrgyzstan.* Retrieved from http://www.hrw.org/reports/2006/09/26/reconciled-violence-0

Latipova, K. (2009). *Embrace torture survivors on board for better treatment.* Retrieved from http://www.vof.kg/en/publications/?publications=592

Ministry of Science and Education of the Kyrgyz Republic. (2010, February 2). *Enactment of the government of Kyrgyz Republic from February 2nd 2010. On inclusion of amendments into the Enactment of Kyrgyz Republic from September 30th 1995 #404. On approval of exemplary standard staff of education institutions.* Bishkek, Kyrgyz Republic: Kyrgyz Republic Government Publication.

Ministry of Social Development of the Kyrgyz Republic. (2011). *Trebovaniya k kachestvu okazaniya organizatsiyami i uchrezhdeniyami sotsialnogo obsluzhivaniya sotsialnykh uslug naseleniyu Kyrgyzskoi Respubliki* [Quality requirements for organizations and agencies providing social services to the people of Kyrgyz Republic]. Retrieved from http://www.mlsp.kg/uslugi/168-2011-02-18-04-50-21.html

Molchanova, E., Kim, E., Horne, S. G., Aitpaeva, G., Ashiraliev, N., & Pokhilko, D. (2009). The status of counseling and psychology in Kyrgyzstan. In L. H. Gerstein, P. P. Heppner, S. Ægisdóttir, S.-M. A. Leung, & K. L. Norsworthy (Eds.), *International handbook of cross-cultural counseling: Cultural assumptions and practices worldwide* (pp. 265–277). Thousand Oaks, CA: Sage.

Molchanova, E., Panteleeva, L., Popkov, M., & Nelubova, T. (2011). Dinamika urovnya mezhetnicheskoi napryajennosti, obrazov 'sebja' i 'drugogo' u naselenja goroda Osh Kyrgyzskoi Respubliki v period s oktyabrja 2010 po fevral 2011 goda [Comparison of levels of interethnic tension and semantic images of the "self" and the "other" in the periods of October 2010 and February 2011 among Osh citizens]. *Journal of Medical Psychology in Russia, 4*, 42–58.

Moldosheva, A., & Asylbekova, N. (2005). *Gender and millennium development goals in Kyrgyzstan.* Retrieved from www.un.org.kg/

Musabaeva, S. (2010, October). [Oral report of the Statistical Department of the Mental Health Center presented at a meeting of the Ministry of Health, Bishkek, Kyrgyz Republic].

National Statistics Committee of the Kyrgyz Republic. (n.d.). *Women and gender development. Millennium development goals: Gender aspects in national statistics.* Bishkek, Kyrgyz Republic: Author.

Osmonalieva, A. (2010). *Domestic violence in Kyrgyzstan: It is necessary to change not only laws, but also mentality.* Retrieved from www.centrasia.ru/newsA.php?st=1267690320:11:12

Rutgers University Center for International Social Work. (2008). *Social work education and the practice environment in Europe and Eurasia.* Retrieved from http://www.crin.org/docs/Best%20Practices%20in%20Social%20Work%20_final_121008.pdf

Secretary of the National Council on Issues of Women, Family and Gender Development of the Administration of the President of the Kyrgyz Republic. (2005). *Convention on the Elimination of All Forms of Discrimination Against Women: Implementation guidelines.* Bishkek, Kyrgyzstan: Administration of the President of the Kyrgyz Republic.

Shah, F. (2005). *The Kyrgyz Republic: Gender-differentiated transition period: Soviet heritage and new challenges.* Manila, Philippines: Asian Development Bank.

Tishkov, V. (1991). Don't kill me, I'm a Kyrgyz! An anthropological analysis of violence in the Osh ethnic conflict. *Journal of Peace Research, 32*, 133–149.

World Health Organization. (2011). *Progress on the health-related millennium development goals.* Retrieved from http://www.who.int/whosis/whostat/EN_WHS2011_Full.pdf

• • •

COUNSELING IN THE PHILIPPINES 13

Ma. Teresa G. Tuason and Ma. Lourdes Arellano-Carandang

The Philippines is a developing country located in Southeast Asia. It is 300,000 square kilometers in size, composed of 7,107 islands (in three island groups: Luzon, Visayas, and Mindanao), and organized into 17 regions. Patterned after the United States, it is a capitalist country with a democratic system of government with three branches: executive, legislative, and judicial. The Philippines is the 12th most populous country in the world, and it was home to 88.57 million people in 2007 (National Statistics Office, 2010). According to the World Bank's (2000) definition of poverty as "living on less than $1 a day," the poverty rate was 32.9% in 2006, with powerfully high food insecurity (National Statistics Office, 2010). If one were to include those who live on less than $2 a day as impoverished, the percentage of poor people in the Philippines would be 61%.

Thus, counseling in the Philippines has evolved to address the substantial influence of social illnesses such as poverty, increased population, unfulfilled basic needs (food, shelter, and safety), insufficient health care, mental health concerns due to socioeconomic deprivation, a high crime rate and low levels of safety, increased unemployment and underemployment, illiteracy, graft, corruption and bribery, unreliable social structures, and intense social injustice. Yet resources in Philippine society and culture play a significant part in the counseling process. These resources, which contribute to strongly healing and flourishing, include religiousness and spirituality (Dy-Liacco, Piedmont, Murray-Swank, Rodgerson, & Sherman, 2009); a strong drive for survival (Tuason, 2008); the engagement of family members and friends (Grimm, Church, Katigbak, & Reyes, 1999); human concern and interaction with others, or *pakikipag-kapwa* (Enriquez, 1977); and a wonderful sense of resilience, hopefulness, and hardiness (Tuason, 2008).

A History of the Philippines

The Philippines is a conglomeration of different cultural influences: the indigenous Indo-Malay; Chinese and Islamic from trade and immigration; and Spanish, American, and Japanese from colonization (Roces & Roces, 1985). All have contributed to the Filipino phenotype and the rich diversity in culture and tradition. Such diversity is seen in the number of dialects: There are about 80 dialects in the Philippines, of which 11 are languages; the national language is Tagalog, and both Tagalog and English are spoken. The Philippines was rediscovered by Ferdinand Magellan on March 16, 1521, which began the period of Spanish colonization and occupation of the Philippines by various imperialist powers: Spain from 1564 to 1898, the United States from 1898 to 1941, Japan from 1941 to 1944, and again the United States through its lingering stronghold of military bases until the 1990s (National Statistics Office, 2010). The Philippines officially regained its independence in 1946. This long period of colonization by various countries was followed by a long history of movements, military coups, and citizen-led revolutions as the Philippines struggled to become an independent republic. Ferdinand Marcos, who was president for two decades and declared martial law in 1972, was driven out of the country in 1986 by the People Power Revolution, which brought Corazon Aquino into power. After Fidel Ramos's presidency in 1996, his successor Joseph Estrada was in office only 2 years before he was forced to step down by another people-powered revolution. Gloria Macapagal Arroyo took leadership, despite several coup attempts, and was succeeded by the current president, Benigno Aquino III, the son of Corazon Aquino. The volatile shifts in governance have all contributed to the country's economic and sociopolitical structure, and its instability and oppression, but have also demonstrated the power of the people, as hundreds of thousands of Filipinos have taken to the streets to peacefully demonstrate and stand up for what is right and just against dictatorship, graft, and corruption.

Characteristics of Counseling in the Philippines

Precolonial Philippines showed vestiges of indigenous help seeking and counseling characterized by superstition; reliance on elders, faith healers, and fortune tellers; and beliefs in the powerful influence of ancestors, souls, and spirits (Bulatao, 1992). The long years of Hispanic colonization resulted mainly in religious conquest: About 80% of Filipinos are Roman Catholics (Roces & Roces, 1985). Religion and spirituality are of utmost importance in Filipinos' lives, and they seek counseling and guidance primarily from their religious leaders: priests and nuns. The American occupation's main influence on the country was in its educational and societal structures. Consequently, the medium of instruction is English, and more esteem is granted to anything American over anything Filipino. The years that followed the U.S. occupation allowed counselors, psychologists, and counselor educators to be trained in the United States, and thus the United States has had significant effect on the development of counseling in the Philippines (Salazar-Clemeña, 2002).

The Philippines is a collectivist society (Hofstede, 2001) that values kinship and community over the values of expressiveness and autonomy found in individualist cultures. Organized according to size, the nation is divided as follows: regions → provinces → cities → municipalities → *baranggays* → several families (National Statistics Office, 2010). The family is the main unit of Philippine society, and Filipinos value their belongingness to their families (*pagkapamilya;* Enriquez, 1977). The family orientation, the sacredness of the family, is very much part of the counseling process, as when it comes to help seeking, Filipinos would rather go to family members than trust strangers to help solve their problems. This is consistent with Smith, Peterson, and Schwartz (2002), who characterized the Philippines as high in conservatism, defined as the preference for the immediate circle over outsiders. Moreover, the Philippines is also a country with high power distance (Hofstede, 2001), which means that authority and hierarchy play a significant part in interpersonal relationships. Such regard for authority dictates not only who to go to for help but whether to seek help in the first place or even acknowledge that a problem exists. People in the Philippines seek help for their problems first from family and friends, then priests and nuns, then the Internet (where they can gather information and remain anonymous); only when there is much at stake, and when things are very bad, do they seek out a counselor, therapist, or psychologist. Such reluctance to seek help is related to cultural mistrust due to the experience of prolonged colonization: Higher levels of cultural mistrust are related to lower help seeking from professionals (David, 2010).

The Current Status of Counseling

Counseling as conceived in the United States began in the Philippines during the American occupation in 1913–1934, with two colleges in Manila providing guidance services geared toward identifying professions and opportunities for employment and with the establishment of the first psychological clinic at the University of the Philippines (Salazar-Clemeña, 2002). The ensuing growth in guidance and counseling services in high schools was then stunted by the Japanese occupation. The 1940s to the 1960s was a period of counselor training and saw the birth of professional associations (Salazar-Clemeña, 2002) as Filipinos obtained their training and degrees in the United States and established counseling/clinical master's and doctoral programs on their return. The two most significant professional associations established at this time were the Psychological Association of the Philippines (http://www.pap.org.ph) and the Philippine Guidance and Counseling Association (http://pgca.org.ph). Founded in 1962, the Psychological Association of the Philippines endeavors to promote excellence, teaching, research, and the practice of psychology. Its first annual national convention was held in January 1964. The Psychological Association of the Philippines publishes the flagship journal *Philippine Journal of Psychology,* an international refereed journal that aims to promote psychological studies in the Philippines and of the Filipino people. The Philippine Guidance and Counseling Association is a professional organization for guidance counselors, supervisors, and counselor educators conceptualized in 1964 by a group of educators, psychologists, and counselors, some of whom were trained in the United States. Its first convention was held the following year, in 1965. Other significant organizations were established later. For example, the Philippine Association for Counselor Education, Research, and Supervision (http://www.pacers.org.ph) was founded March 6, 1976, and publishes *The Philippine Journal of Counseling Psychology,* an international refereed journal of research manuscripts on issues relevant to counseling. The Career Development Association of the Philippines (http://www.cdap-philippines.com) was established in 1977 with the aim of professionalizing the practice of career guidance and counseling (Salazar-Clemeña, 2002). Finally, the Family and Pastoral Counseling Association of the Philippines (http://www.fpcap.org), one of the newer associations of counselors organized in 2008, helps both family and pastoral counselors effectively contribute to the growth and development of the nation. In the 1970s and 1980s, the movement in counseling was primarily indigenization (e.g., Bulatao, 1992; Enriquez, 1977; Jocano, 1997) in terms of assessments, constructs, and theories, particularly when it came to recognizing the difference between the counseling models learned in the United States and the realities of Philippine social issues. From then until now, counseling has evolved to respond to the needs of Philippine society, which is entrenched in economic instability, paralyzing poverty, and government graft and corruption.

The terms *counselor, therapist,* and *psychologist* are generally interchangeable to the average Filipino, as are the terms *clinical* and *counseling.* In the Philippines, counseling is intertwined with both psychology and social work, and counselors are called on to navigate societal stigmas regarding the need for mental health assistance as well as widespread ignorance of the kind of help available through counseling services. Furthermore, counseling in the Philippines goes beyond the one-on-one relationship to have impact on the country's social ills. Counselors play a powerful part in alleviating people's despair due to many oppressive forces, serving as bearers of hope and advocates for mental health and resilience in difficult life circumstances.

According to Labor and Employment Secretary Rosalinda D. Baldoz, there are 49 guidance counselor networks in the Philippines with 1,739 members (Department of Labor and

Employment, 2011). Guidance counselors may also include mental health counselors, as they are employed in a variety of settings, such as schools and universities, where they primarily do testing and assessment, career counseling, and academic counseling at the elementary and high school levels. Guidance counselors may also deal with tragedies in students' lives, such as suicide, bullying, or parental separation. Children and adolescents with behavioral issues also are referred to guidance counselors. Depending on the extent of these issues, students may be referred to nonschool counselors for more intensive or longer term treatment.

Counselors are also employed in nonschool settings such as private practice clinics, group practices, nongovernmental agencies, church-related agencies, and government mental health agencies. In these settings, some counselors integrate counseling and spirituality in pastoral counseling; some work primarily with children and their families using expressive therapies, such as play therapy for developmental delay disorders such as autism (e.g., Carandang & Liwag, 1992) and for behavioral concerns; and some provide assessment services, such as for giftedness or personality assessment.

The Guidance and Counseling Act of 2004, Republic Act 9258

The most significant development in the field of counseling in the Philippines has been the passage of the Guidance and Counseling Act of 2004, Republic Act 9258, on March 26, 2004. This law was intended to professionalize the practice of guidance and counseling and to create the Professional Regulation Commission, Republic of the Philippines, Board of Guidance and Counseling. The Board of Guidance and Counseling was created in 2007 and acts to regulate the profession. The Board is the first entity in the Philippines to have developed examination, registration, and licensure in guidance and counseling. Prior to 2007, counselors and other mental health workers did not need a license to practice, nor was there a regulatory board to ensure adequate training. The examination for licensure now consists of six areas: Philosophical, Psychological, and Sociological Foundations of Guidance; Counseling Theories, Tools, and Techniques; Psychological Testing; Organization, Administration, and Supervision of Guidance Services, and Program Development; Group Process; and Career Guidance.

Counselors pioneered the way for the field to be regulated, and psychologists are following suit through Republic Act 10029, the Philippine Psychology Act of 2009. Republic Act 10029, which President Arroyo signed into law on March 16, 2010, regulates the practice of psychology and creates a professional regulatory board for licensing psychologists (Kabiling, 2010). Although all mental health providers have the same mission, counselors or psychologists with a PhD are highest on the hierarchy and counselors with an MA are next, followed by social workers. Added levels within this hierarchy relate to where the degree is obtained: a U.S.-trained counselor has more credibility than a Philippine-trained practitioner.

Best Counseling Practices

Because of the people's lack of awareness of the counseling profession, the stigma of mental illness, and the reluctance to seek help from a stranger, a person's situation is usually at its worst by the time a counselor is finally approached. Access to a counselor and the open-mindedness to seek help and contact one is best mediated by family or friends who have experienced the benefits of the counseling process and know a counselor.

The first session is of utmost significance, as this is when education about the counseling process, structure, and outcome takes place. The rapport experienced and level of trust are gauged in this first session, as is the degree of need for assistance. The true test of whether the counselor was able to create an atmosphere in which the client could feel comfortable and thus continue in counseling is whether the client makes another appointment and shows up for it.

Depending on the individual's need and the family's support, family members cooperate with the counseling process and become engaged when asked; their participation, in fact, may be called for depending on the severity of the problem. As in the United States, only family members who will not exacerbate the problem and who are therapeutic to the process will be invited to participate. In general, because of the machismo that is ingrained in the culture, it is very likely that the male family member, the father or the husband, will refuse to cooperate in counseling. And because of the woman's caregiving role, it is most often the mother, wife, grandmother, or aunt who volunteers to participate and usually becomes an invaluable resource in the process.

Much like in the United States, the end of counseling is difficult to identify and plan. Often the client terminates the counseling process when he or she is no longer willing to come, unlike in the United States, where termination is mutually agreed on. In a successful process, the client may feel forever indebted to the counselor and try to keep in touch through gifts and thank you letters or even ask to be a friend on the counselor's Facebook page.

In the United States, a counseling session usually lasts an hour. However, the Filipino concept of time is not overly concerned with punctuality (Roces & Roces, 1985), especially in terms of communication, so it is very hard for counselors to keep sessions to an hour and for clients to stop after an hour. The cost and the luxury of time against the backdrop of difficult life circumstances and poverty means that it is usually the middle to upper class who can afford counseling. Public schools, primarily at the elementary and high school levels, which have few resources and cater to destitute students, may also offer minimal counseling services. Counseling services may be hard to come by for individuals who are very impoverished, who live in squatter areas, whose children cannot study, and whose lives are a constant struggle for survival. These individuals usually do not seek counseling services, or if they do, they may approach a religious person or a counselor who would do the work pro bono. Fortunately, funded research may also provide counseling services to those who are financially oppressed (e.g., Carandang, 1996).

Because pioneers of counseling in the Philippines were trained in the United States in the 1960s and 1970s, and also because of their fit with the Philippine culture, the predominant theories in counseling treatment are humanistic, client-centered, Rogerian therapy; family systems therapy with elements of spirituality and counseling; and some cognitive behavior therapy. What has evolved is an integrated and eclectic approach to counseling characterized by a combination of counseling models with a bit more direction and much more psychoeducation about the counseling process than in the United States. Initially, there is role induction, in which the client and the counselor discuss what counseling is, why the client is there, and how the client will get better. With deep regard for the culture, the counselor must be nonthreatening and respectful of the client's need to talk and must ensure that the client is safe in terms of engaging the family and dealing with the client's sense of shame and motivation for change. In addition, Filipino clients perceive that problems are due to events outside of their control as opposed to stemming from within and expects the counselor to solve the problems imposed on them (Schumacher & Guthrie, 1984).

Because of the essential part spirituality and religion play in Filipinos' lives, pastoral counseling is one of the most used counseling practices. Counseling that is parish based uses a psychospiritual approach. For religious and laypersons alike, spiritual healing and change in counseling are usually approached from the perspective of faith and transcendence in terms of what God is communicating and the individual's wishes and prayers. Forgiveness, grief, anger, or other difficult emotions are dealt with through reassurance of being accompanied by God and from the perspective of God as the source of strength and hope. In the counseling process, it is not unusual for the path for personal growth, healing, and meaning to include what the individual believes God wants for him or her and prayers imploring God for help vis-à-vis Filipinos' difficult lives of deprivation, tragedy, and disaster. Moreover, as the Philippines is a country with many natural and manmade disasters (Bankoff, 2003), crisis intervention and stress debriefing counseling practices are necessary.

Because communication and language is indirect among Filipinos, difficult emotions are suppressed or sugarcoated if expressed, and Filipinos are not confrontational and generally avoid conflict, successful counseling practices use metaphors (e.g., Carandang, 1996). Metaphors hold much power and can guide and motivate people to change. In addition, because of Filipinos' affinity for the supernatural and superstitious beliefs, hypnotherapy works well for issues involving others who cannot participate in the counseling process (Bulatao, 1992).

Because the family is of utmost importance in Philippine society, counseling practices that work best involve the family. For example, the Center for Family Ministries and the MLAC Institute for Children and Families successfully provide counseling using family therapy and conduct research involving children and families. Problems usually arise from conflicting expectations of children and their parents and parental control and support (Schumacher & Guthrie, 1984). Family systems therapies are predominant and are the basis for premarital and marital counseling, family counseling, and support groups. Especially with children, there is a predominant use of expressive therapies such as play therapy, art therapy, and music therapy.

Diversity Issues

The counselor as a change agent in Philippine society must have strong clinical skills, be skilled at conceptualizing client problems using indigenous models, and be a powerful client advocate. Western models of counseling that focus on changing the self fall short of what Filipinos need, which is to affect the environments and relationships around them (Schumacher & Guthrie, 1984). Many diversity issues impact counseling in the Philippines and require sensitivity and competence from the counselor. These issues create the context of the Filipino's environment but, more important, set the parameters for how change happens. They affect the extent to which individuals are able to change intrapsychic matters and represent the issues from which individuals believe change can occur. Of these, the most significant are poverty, overseas working, unstable political and economic conditions, and Catholicism.

The high Philippine poverty rate necessarily leads to a social justice agenda in counseling (Tuason, 2008). Intrinsic to counseling is assistance in working through difficult life circumstances, in which survival and struggle against hunger are foremost for many people. Career counseling requires consideration of what career choice might yield possibilities for economic mobility (Salazar-Clemeña, 2002). Counseling the poor becomes a form of advocacy, as counseling services are not readily available for those who cannot pay. Poverty coexists with high crime rates, overpopulation, and illiteracy, which all impede one's ability to move upward (Tuason, 2008). In the Philippines, there is a high prevalence of murder, homicide, rape, physical injury, robbery, and theft (National Statistics Office, 2010). Social issues, such as street children, child neglect and abandonment, prostitution, malnourishment, and unsolved crimes, become counseling issues at the individual level.

Overseas working has become the nation's response to high rates of poverty, overpopulation, unemployment (7.1% in 2009), and underemployment (19.4% in 2009; National Statistics Office, 2010). Ten million Filipino people, 11% of the country's total population, leave the Philippines and work in approximately 194 countries and territories around the globe (Go, 1998). In fact, the Philippine government has enacted an official policy for Filipino laborers, touting overseas destinations as a solution to very high levels of unemployment and underemployment. Given that the family is the most important unit in Philippine society, separation issues due to family members working overseas are central in counseling as family roles are altered and children step in to substitute for a missing parent for their younger siblings (Taylor & Tuason, 2008). The second author, Ma. Lourdes Arellano-Carandang, has provided phone counseling to overseas Filipino workers working as domestic helpers in Hong Kong. This experience has revealed that the problems of overseas Filipino workers are mostly due to their pain of having to be away from their children, the irony of taking care of the children of their employers and not being able to take care of their own, philandering husbands, fathers sexually abusing their daughters, loneliness, and maltreatment by their employers. Circumstances such as these coupled with poverty teach Filipinos to be self-effacing and to sacrifice their own needs for others. Filipinos believe that if change is to occur, it must stem from changing others' perceptions and the environment rather than themselves (Schumacher & Guthrie, 1984).

Unstable political and economic conditions and the absence of consistency and structure seep into the counseling process. Sociopolitical crises stress Filipino families (Carandang, 1989). Moreover, the sense of self becomes uncertain too, resulting in a more fatalistic attitude. As anything can happen, there is little chance to plan, and Filipinos are necessarily flexible. Because of rampant graft and corruption in government offices and dishonesty in the media, the truth is hard to come by, and the absence of consequences makes it hard for people to be accountable and realize the consequences of their actions—the core of change in counseling.

Religion is a basic part of Philippine society, and individuals' spirituality and religiosity become an important part of the counseling process. It is religion that allows people to be open to change and to be hopeful but also to continue to sacrifice and to be self-effacing. Competent counselors working with Filipinos need to be sensitive to the extent of people's religiosity and respectfully involve religion in the counseling process. For instance, given generally oppressive attitudes and religiosity, counseling lesbian, gay, bisexual, and transgender (LGBT) individuals is necessarily a form of advocacy. LGBT individuals are usually closeted for their protection, and counselors become advocates for LGBT rights, educators for tolerance and respect, and allies against loneliness and rejection.

Counselor Education

There are 23 universities and colleges in the Philippines offering graduate studies in guidance and counseling, counseling/clinical psychology, and counselor education and a handful of institutes offering degrees in pastoral counseling. Most programs offer master's degrees, and a few offer doctoral degrees. The professors who teach in these universities are mostly trained in the United States and work in both academia and counseling practice. Curricula are determined by individual programs and are often patterned after courses in the United States, though there is growing recognition of the need to apply counseling models and theories to the Philippine population. Counseling models and theories are becoming indigenized, as evidenced by applied research in theses and dissertations (e.g., Nisperos, 1994; Tuason, 1992). A typical counselor training program is similar to that in the United States: At the master's level it is 2 years full time or 4 years part time, and at the doctoral level it takes about 5 years. Because of the economy, however, studying part time while working full time is the norm.

The Future

Prior to 2007, professional standards for counseling did not exist; practically anyone who wanted to be a counselor could. Currently the counseling profession is regulated by the Board of Guidance and Counseling, and the Board of Psychology soon will oversee it as well. These boards and the laws that created them signify that the Philippine society recognizes the relevance of the counseling profession and that counselors have power, status, and responsibility in Philippine society.

The counseling field will continue to develop services for the poor as nongovernmental agencies primarily pave the way for counseling services to be provided for street children, the sexually abused, victims of unsolved crimes, victims of human and natural disasters, impoverished children who cannot go to school, and others. Although these services have been provided to date, especially in the venue of research, the future holds hope for more services to be offered to more people. In the future, counseling services will be provided in conjunction with advocacy to alleviate poverty, hopefully with participation from government agencies. New counseling techniques will revolve around prevention and getting support from outside sources such as UNICEF or other countries in addition to tapping into more affluent professionals.

Much of the future focus in counseling will need to be on healing the nation. Because of the deep conflicts perpetrated by long-standing graft and corruption, bribery and injustices toward the people, and the protracted conflict between Christians in the north and Muslims in the south, and exacerbated by poverty and the inability to escape it, counseling practices and research and the training and supervision of future counselors will need to focus on restructuring societal systems to be more reliable and just. On the individual level, the counseling process will need to focus on redefining the self in the context of the system and empowering the self to create change within one's spheres of influence. Counseling models and theories will develop that are indigenous and more applicable to the field of counseling in the Philippines as the applications of counseling become more far reaching. The indigenization of theories that started with Filipino psychology by Enriquez (1977); phenomena of religion, consciousness, and culture by Bulatao (1992); and Filipino culture and values by Jocano (1997) will continue in the future, specifically identifying, labeling, and using counseling models borne of Philippine society.

Counseling organizations will be more institutionalized, gaining recognition not just from constituents but from the public and the government, and they will be more accessible and responsive to the issues in Philippine society. Because of the existence of oversight boards, the profession will be more regulated, only licensed practitioners will provide services, and thus the professional will be more credible. Availing oneself of counseling services will be more natural and fluid rather than stigmatized. Also, the counseling field will benefit from a more structured and intentional avenue for supervision, guiding counselors' professional and personal growth, which will be included in counselor training and in the academic curriculum. Though the field of counseling began by drawing from the U.S. model as a guide, it will come into its own, respecting the depth of its context and problems, utilizing the resources that are intrinsic to the Filipino soul, and impacting the Filipinos who need counseling services the most.

References

Bankoff, G. (2003). *Cultures of disaster: Society and natural hazard in the Philippines.* London, England: Routledge Curzon Press.

Bulatao, J. C. (1992). *Phenomena and their interpretation: Landmark essays, 1957-1989.* Quezon City, Philippines: Ateneo de Manila University Press.

Carandang, M. L. A. (1989). Stresses and coping strategies of Filipino families in a sociopolitical crisis. *International Psychologist, 29*(5), 75–82.

Carandang, M. L. A. (1996). *Listen to their inner voice: Street children speak through their drawings and metaphors.* Manila, Philippines: UNICEF, Australian Agency for International Development.

Carandang, M. L. A., & Liwag, M. E. C. (1992). *Making connections: A group therapy program for Filipino autistic children and their families.* Quezon City, Philippines: Ateneo de Manila University Press.

David, E. J. R. (2010). Cultural mistrust and mental help-seeking attitudes among Filipino Americans. *Asian American Journal of Psychology, 1,* 57–66. doi:10.1037/a0018814

Department of Labor and Employment, Republic of the Philippines. (2011). *PHL has 49 networks of guidance counselors, DOLE reports.* Retrieved from http://ro12.dole.gov.ph/default.php?retsamlakygee=181&resource=b640d29e78b075527b034f11f38e36c0

Dy-Liacco, G. S., Piedmont, R. L., Murray-Swank, N. A., Rodgerson, T. E., & Sherman, M. F. (2009). Spirituality and religiosity as cross-cultural aspects of human experience. *Psychology of Religion and Spirituality, 1,* 35–52. doi:10.1037/a0014937

Enriquez, V. G. (1977). Filipino psychology in the third world. *Philippine Journal of Psychology, 10*(1), 3–18.

Go, S. P. (1998). Towards the 21st century: Whither Philippine labor migration. In B. V. Carino (Ed.), *Filipino workers on the move: Trends, dilemmas and policy options* (pp. 9–44). Manila, Philippines: Philippine Migration Research Network, UNESCO-MOST.

Grimm, S. D., Church, A. T., Katigbak, M. S., & Reyes, J. A. (1999). Self-described traits, values, and moods associated with individualism and collectivism: Testing I-C theory in an individualistic (U.S.) and a collectivistic (Philippine) culture. *Journal for Cross-Cultural Psychology, 30,* 466–500. doi:10.1177/0022022199030004005

Guidance and Counseling Act, Republic Act 9258. (2004).

Hofstede, G. (2001). *Culture's consequences: Comparing values, behaviors, institutions, and organizations across nations.* Thousand Oaks, CA: Sage.

Jocano, F. L. (1997). *Filipino value system: A cultural definition.* Metro Manila, Philippines: PUNLAD Research House.

Kabiling, G. (2010). *Arroyo signs Psychology Act.* Retrieved from http://www.mb.com.ph/node/249405/new-law-profe

National Statistics Office, Republic of the Philippines. (2010). *Philippines in figures.* Retrieved from http://www.census.gov.ph/data/publications/2010PIF.pdf.

Nisperos, M. K. B. (1994). *The world of the scavenger child: A phenomenological in-depth clinical study of scavenger children from Smokey Mountain.* Unpublished master's thesis, Ateneo de Manila University, Quezon City, Philippines.

Roces, A., & Roces, G. (1985). *Philippines: Culture shock.* Singapore: Times Books International.

Salazar-Clemeña, R. M. S. (2002). Family ties and peso signs: Challenges for career counseling in the Philippines. *The Career Development Quarterly, 50,* 246–256.

Schumacher, H. E., & Guthrie, G. M. (1984). Culture and counseling in the Philippines. *International Journal of Intercultural Relations, 8,* 241–253.

Smith, P. B., Peterson, M. F., & Schwartz, S. H. (2002). Cultural values, sources of guidance, and their relevance to managerial behavior. *Journal of Cross-Cultural Psychology, 33*(2), 188–208.

Taylor, A. R., & Tuason, M. T. (2008, March). *Parenting in Filipino transnational families.* Poster presented at the 2008 International Counseling Psychology Conference, Chicago, IL.

Tuason, M. T. (1992). *Five urban poor families of alcoholic fathers: A clinically descriptive and exploratory study.* Unpublished master's thesis, Ateneo de Manila University, Quezon City, Philippines.

Tuason, M. T. (2008). Those who were born poor: A qualitative study of Philippine poverty. *Journal of Counseling Psychology, 55,* 158–171. doi:10.1037/00220167.55.2.158

World Bank. (2000, April). *Does more international trade openness increase world poverty?* Retrieved from http://www1.worldbank.org/economicpolicy/globalization/documents/AssessingGlobalizationP2.pdf

• • •

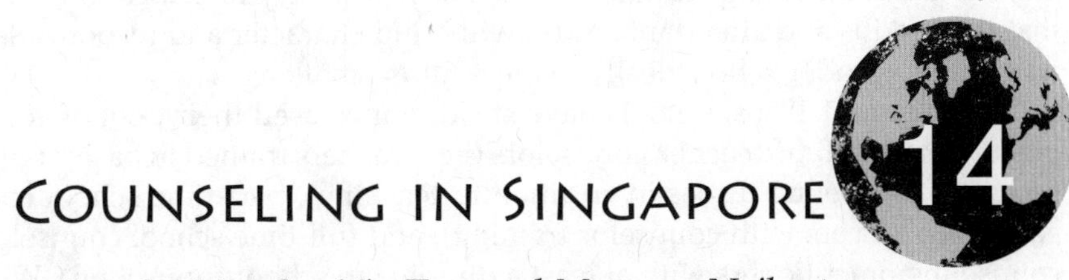

Counseling in Singapore

Lay See Yeo, Soo Yin Tan, and Maureen Neihart

Singapore is a tiny island nation tucked between the Malay Peninsula and Indonesia in Southeast Asia. Approximately 712.4 square kilometers (275 square miles) in land area, it is one of the most densely populated countries in the world. It is a multiracial and multilingual nation of 5 million people in which approximately 77% of the population is Chinese, 13% is Malay, 9% is Indian, and 1 in 3 workers is a foreigner. The name *Singapore,* which means "Lion City," was derived from the native language, Malay. There are four official languages: English, Mandarin, Malay, and Tamil. However, English is the official language of business, administration, and education. In 2011, Singapore ranked among the top 10 wealthiest nations in the world (Forbes Blogger, 2011).

A former British colony, Singapore has retained several aspects of British social and political structure, including a parliamentary government and an educational system that relies on high-stakes examinations to determine secondary and postsecondary placements. Education has always been a national priority in Singapore, which is recognized for having one of the best educational systems in the world (McKinsey & Company, 2007). The government invests heavily in technology and education with the aim of developing the nation as a regional hub for finance, education, and technology.

Counseling services in Singapore began in the 1960s when a group of Christian professionals formed the Churches Counseling Service, directed by an American Methodist pastor, Reverend Gunner Teilmann. In those early years, *counseling* was a term loosely applied to helping services provided by individuals who assumed various roles. Following the establishment of this center, counseling services were developed at social welfare agencies, religious institutions, military establishments, hospitals, schools, and other government institutions. Today counseling in Singapore is defined as a collaborative process in which a counselor or psychologist works collaboratively with people to expand their view of life and develop their abilities to cope and make choices for change in themselves, the situation, and the environment without destructive consequences to self or others (Yeo, 1993). In this chapter counseling is contextualized in terms of diverse cultural and sociopolitical challenges in this country. The chapter concludes with a discussion of future challenges and opportunities.

The Current Status of Counseling

School Counseling

School counseling in Singapore falls directly under the purview of the Guidance Branch of the Ministry of Education. A team of guidance officers, guidance specialists, and senior guidance specialists provides leadership in strengthening counseling resources in school with the aim of building a resilient citizenry for the 21st century. The key thrust of counseling in school is to promote social and emotional learning. Initiated in 2005, *social and emotional learning* refers to the acquisition of skills to recognize and manage emotions, develop care and concern for others, make responsible decisions, establish positive relationships, and handle challenging situations effectively (Ministry of Education, 2011). It is believed that these skills and attendant values will build character and responsible citizenship that will prepare students holistically to meet future challenges.

From the mid-1980s, schools have steadily increased their pool of counseling resource personnel to include teacher-counselors (i.e., teachers trained in basic counseling skills and assigned counseling duties in addition to teaching), part-time school counselors (retired education officers with counselor training), and full-time school counselors (independent counseling practitioners with at least a diploma in school counseling). Within each school, students access counseling and psychological services through a tiered systemic referral system. At Level 1, teachers are first-line advisers, provide frontline support, and consult the learning support coordinator for help with students' learning difficulties or the teacher-counselor or full-time school counselor for assistance with students' emotional difficulties. Issues addressed at Level 1 are relatively minor, such as coming late to school, skipping lessons, or being disruptive in class. At Level 2, the school's key resource personnel (e.g., the learning support coordinator and teacher-counselor) are engaged in directing interventions, encouraging parental involvement, and monitoring students' progress. Referral issues may include truancy, noncompletion of assignments, smoking, or suicidal ideation. At Level 3, students whose difficulties persist are referred, on parental consent, to the full-time school counselor, guidance officers or specialists from the Guidance Branch, educational psychologists, or professionals from external agencies. Presenting complaints are usually severe and may include gang involvement, shoplifting, abuse, or psychological disorders (e.g., depression).

In addition to counseling, career guidance programs are available in schools. In 2009, the Ministry of Education launched a Web-based education and career guidance portal for students: ecareers.sg (Ministry of Education, 2009). The portal, jointly developed by the Ministry of Education and the University of Wisconsin–Madison, provides various profiling instruments that allow students to clarify their interests and aptitudes and to explore a range of suitable career options. Also available online are training modules that students can access in their own free time to learn skills in résumé writing and job interviews. The portal was preceded by JOBS (Job Orientation Backup System) and OSCAR (Orientation System for CAReer), two computer-assisted career guidance programs developed by the National Institute of Education between 1989 and 2009 to provide vocational guidance to secondary school students.

Community Counseling

Within the community, counseling can be obtained from private counseling centers or from about 400 Voluntary Welfare Organizations (VWOs) registered with the National Council of Social Service in Singapore. Examples of VWOs are the Care Corner Counseling Center, Samaritans of Singapore, Agape Counseling and Training Center, The Hiding Place, and 37 family service centers. Family service centers, which are conveniently located across the island, seek to promote and improve the social well-being of all individuals in the family at every stage of life. Their services are accessible to everyone regardless of age, race, gender, language, or religion. In 2009, about 24,000 individuals and their families received services at the family service centers to cope with problems of daily living and to achieve stability and self-reliance. Presently community counseling services are also available from an increasing number of private counseling agencies and practitioners. However, largely because of the absence of licensure for counselors and the lack of regulation in the counseling industry, counselors struggle to establish a professional identity for themselves. In addition, it is extremely difficult for the public to discern a credible from a dubious practice in order to make an informed choice among the different service providers. This and other challenges in developing counseling as a profession in Singapore are discussed further later in this chapter.

Community counseling services currently available in Singapore include individual counseling, group counseling, online counseling, telephone counseling, and support group counseling. The exacting demands of living in a very fast-paced society and of coping with work stress and related difficulties in maintaining work and family life balance have led to an increasing need for counseling services. Counselors we interviewed while researching for this chapter reported that a generation of adults who grew up as latchkey children now experience difficulties in forming relationships. The range of referral issues encompass anxiety, depression, suicide, unemployment, marital problems, family conflicts, domestic violence, sexual dysfunction, gambling, substance abuse, chronic illness, learning-related difficulties in children and adolescents, and so on. Counselors use a variety of therapeutic counseling modalities that include but are not restricted to systemic family therapy, emotion-focused therapy, solution-focused brief therapy, cognitive behavioral therapy, and narrative therapy.

Counseling agencies tend to work independently, and collaboration is rare. However, counselors at counseling centers are increasingly acknowledging the need to collaborate with other mental health professionals, such as psychologists and psychiatrists, when they address learning-related issues (e.g., learning disabilities) or mental health issues (e.g., personality disorders). No single profession can effectively address interrelated and complex social issues across school, family, and community systems in isolation; hence, there is need for interdisciplinary collaboration and consultation among VWOs, religious groups, and political organizations.

Best Counseling Practices

Although empirical studies comparing the effectiveness of different counseling methods and techniques are still rare in Singapore, results from studies examining client and therapist beliefs, preferences, values, and perceptions suggest that certain adaptations or models may be more effective than others. Indigenous research has focused largely on the help-seeking behaviors of various client groups (Ang & Yeo, 2004; Ng & Lim, 2006; C. T. Tan, Chee, & Long, 1980), descriptive studies of counselor and client preferences for counseling practices (Foo, Merrick, & Kazantzis, 2006; Lee & Bishop, 2001; Soong, as cited in E. Tan, 2009), and the validity of Western models for the local context (E. Tan, 2009).

E. Tan (2009) has argued that the Confucian ethics of many Singaporean Chinese (e.g., emotional restraint, control, respect for elders) conflict with the emphasis in Western counseling on self-determination, independence, and self-expression. The national shared values promoted by the government stress collectivism over individualism, and the top value in Singapore is nation before community and society above self. The nation's shared values indicate that the well-being of the individual lags well behind the well-being of the group, whether it is the nation, community, or family. Hence, it might be said that there is a mismatch for many Singaporeans between the democratic ideals of individualism and self-expression reflected in the Western counseling models often used in Singapore and the Confucian ideals of harmony, obedience to authority, and self-restraint. Therefore, a counselor in the Singapore context needs to be cognizant of these existing tensions and accommodate the client's beliefs and value systems in his or her counseling approaches.

A study by Lee and Bishop (2001) provided some insight into the beliefs of Singaporean Chinese clients with respect to the etiology and treatment of psychological problems. The Chinese participants included 149 clients, 56 therapists, and 136 nonclients from 21 organizations. Most clients and nonclients were Buddhist or Taoist, whereas most therapists were Christian. Beliefs were measured with a modified Opinions About Psychological Problems questionnaire. Several relevant findings were observed. First, Buddhist and Taoist clients were more likely than nonreligious or Christian clients to endorse indigenous beliefs about the etiology and treatment of psychological problems. Chinese medicine, in particular, was the indigenous treatment most often endorsed. Second, clients and nonclients alike endorsed a Western psychological model more than indigenous models, suggesting that Chinese clients were receptive to Western beliefs about etiology and treatment. Lee and Bishop offered several explanations for their results. They proposed that Singapore's position as an international hub for finance, technology, and education means that Singaporeans experience a lot of exposure to Western views, particularly American ones. Furthermore, they noted the country's increasing emphasis on English since the 1950s, which has contributed to a breakdown in the transmission of traditional values. In addition, they mentioned Singapore's history as a British colony as a contributing factor to its greater receptiveness to Western values compared to other Chinese societies.

In addition to their belief systems, clients' preferences for counseling approaches and counselors also feature prominently in counseling practices that work best in Singapore. Studies have been conducted to explore differences in the counseling preferences of clients from different racial and language groups in Singapore (Lee & Bishop, 2001; Soong, as cited in E. Tan, 2009). Soong, for example (as cited in E. Tan, 2009), observed that whereas Hindu university clients from Indian-language-speaking homes preferred client-centered approaches, Chinese students with English-language backgrounds and Muslim students from Malay-language homes preferred cognitive approaches and behavioral approaches, respectively.

A number of studies have demonstrated that many, though not all, Singaporeans seek help from traditional healers instead of or in addition to therapists (Lee & Bishop, 2001; C. T. Tan et al., 1980). Lee and Bishop (2001) noted educational and socioeconomic differences in this regard. Their study demonstrated that among Singaporean Chinese persons from lower income families, those with less education preferred to seek help from traditional healers than professional counselors. E. Tan (2009) observed that Hindu clients may work with a counselor but also seek consultation from an astrologer. Similarly, Chinese clients may make regular offerings or pray at the temple while simultaneously working with a therapist. Taken together, these findings suggest that for many Singaporeans, an element of spirituality may be critical in the helping process.

In a multicultural society, differences in traditions, lifestyles, worldviews, values, and ways of relating all impact counseling and the effectiveness of various interventions. A counselor in Singapore needs to be familiar with the traditional norms relating to identity formation and social relationships. For example, in many Singaporean families, several generations live together communally, often with a full-time domestic helper from another country, culture, and language. Unmarried children typically live at home well into adulthood, and extended families often get together weekly. It is easy for a Western counselor to interpret this close-knit family togetherness as enmeshment. In the Singapore context, understanding the concept of family enmeshment therefore needs to be different, with due consideration for what is normal in Asian families. Similarly, whereas the goal of adolescent development in Western societies is separation and individuation, in Singapore separation is often emphasized less than *reciprocation,* or giving priority to the other over the self. Adult children continue to live at home while they are studying and may not move out, even after marrying. In the local context, not being separate from one's family of origin should not be misconstrued as maladjustment. The common practice of intergenerational communal living suggests that systems approaches will often be more relevant as a counseling modality than person-centered counseling.

In a multicultural society, within-culture differences are common as well, adding to the complexity of providing counseling services. Again, religious and language backgrounds matter a good deal, often more so than racial backgrounds. As E. Tan (2009) rightly observed, "A Christian Tamil and a Christian Chinese may have more in common than a Christian Tamil and a Hindu Tamil" (p. 210). Conversations with local practitioners reinforce this idea that the effectiveness of counseling practices is enhanced when counselors make an effort to understand and adapt to both between- and within-culture differences (Vasquez, 2007). Local community counselors indicate that clients seem to be particularly receptive to systems approaches, especially marital and family therapy, which is not surprising given the collectivist nature of Singaporean society and the shared values that emphasize the welfare of the family and community over that of the individual. Also, local counselors have related to us that technologies like Skype, chat, and e-mail are generally not used for counseling because they are not received well. This is understandable given the highly relational contexts in which most people in Singapore live.

Studies of counseling practices in Singapore suggest that it is the therapeutic alliance that is perhaps most impacted by contextual and cultural factors. It is well established in the literature that the therapeutic alliance predicts about 30% of counseling outcomes (Lambert & Barley, 2001). Studies have also suggested that similarities in worldviews are linked to the strength of the therapeutic alliance (Vasquez, 2007). It therefore seems reasonable to conclude that counselors in Singapore need to attend closely to the beliefs, values, and perceptions of their clients and understand contextual variations in mental health issues in order to be effective in treating them (Vasquez, 2007).

There is a pressing need in Singapore for research that compares the effectiveness and clinical significance of various counseling approaches for the local context. Until such studies are undertaken, clinical observation and empirical studies of help-seeking behaviors and client and counselor perceptions, worldviews, and values suggest that counseling effectiveness is improved locally when counselors adapt their approach to accommodate the beliefs, values, and preferences of their clients.

Diversity Issues

Singapore is an ethnically diverse country that possesses a variety of cultures, each vibrant in its own uniqueness. People who live in Singapore celebrate a multitude of cultural festivals and religious events annually. More important, their cultural and religious values are inextricably bound to their help-seeking behaviors; thus, counselors in Singapore need to be cognizant of and well versed in the pluralistic healing systems that exist in this community. A diverse range of indigenous psychotherapies precede and coexist alongside the wide spectrum of counseling approaches that originate from foreign cultures. Indigenous psychotherapies each have their unique cultural frame of reference for understanding the origins and etiology of emotional problems and for recommending treatment in keeping with their conception of what constitutes human well-being (Lee, 2002). In other words, culture has a huge influence on how problems and their symptoms are perceived, interpreted, and expressed. Culture also influences coping and the type of help individuals seek. The challenge, therefore, is for the counselor to establish with the client an approach to therapy that is relevant and helpful in light of the client's cultural and religious background.

Although an increasing number of individuals in Singapore are open to counseling and recognize the improved quality of counseling services available, many still seek out faith-based spiritual help (e.g., folk healers such as shamans or fortune tellers) or traditional medicine (e.g., herbal cures, massage, and tai chi). Many either remain unaware of or are skeptical about the benefits of counseling. In addition, the social stigma associated with seeing a counselor causes many people to seek support from friends and family instead of approaching professionals for aid. They tend to be more comfortable and familiar with traditional healing models that adopt holistic approaches that they believe cater to their physical, social, psychological, and spiritual needs. These models incorporate local philosophical traditions and indigenous caregiving practices that are in keeping with cultural beliefs.

In this multicultural and multireligious country, there is freedom of worship. It is common to see temples, churches, and mosques situated next to each other. Many religious institutions and nongovernmental organizations provide counseling services to believers and nonbelievers alike. For example, the Chee Hoon Kog Moral Promotion Society, a charitable home set up by the Chinese community, has incorporated other religions, including Hinduism and Islam, into their teaching. The society seeks to promote good morals, such as filial piety, compassion, and brotherliness, and it extends help to all irrespective of race or religion. A brief description of three major belief systems is warranted to provide a context for understanding the rich cultural diversity impacting counseling in Singapore.

Malays believe that evil spirits may lead to loss of *semangat,* a vital force of spiritual energy in a person. Healing practices such as *menurun* (trance), *jampi* (incantation), and *mandi bunga* (flower bath) aim to restore a person's *semangat* to its original state. Malays also practice massage therapy to reduce or remove *angin* (wind), a source of illness, from the body. The three main forms of indigenous healing in the Malay tradition are medicine, spells, and rituals (Haque, 2008). Herbal plant parts and animal sacrifices are used as part of the remedies for illnesses. The healer typically chants words during the process as a spell. The healing ritual consists of the dispensation of medicine and the casting of spells by the healer. The Islamic approach includes the reading of certain verses from the Koran, usually read over *air jampi* (drinking water). Both approaches emphasize having faith in the healer as well as Allah (God), as the healer's duty is to ask for healing, and it is Allah's prerogative to grant it.

The Chinese, however, approach the lack of well-being differently. When faced with illness, the Chinese often turn to Taoist or Buddhist approaches for healing. Taoism is oriented around the philosophy of yin and yang and the oscillation between these two forces. Various rituals and practices are deemed to bring positive change to one's physical and mental health by aligning one's spiritual forces with that of nature. Taoist healing practices such as qigong and tai chi are oriented around the concept of qi, which means "energy." These two practices refer to a wide variety of traditional exercises and movements that are therapeutic in nature. Many people perform qigong or tai chi for health purposes, such as to relieve stress, maintain fitness, and improve stamina and agility. Buddhism is similar to Taoism in its emphasis on the equilibrium between mind and body and the belief that illness arises when this equilibrium is upset by external or internal causes. Buddhists believe that all things in the universe are interrelated in an endless cause-and-effect relationship and that all things in the world are intertwined and interdependent. Likewise, the mind and body are deeply interconnected parts of the human system. Emotional problems are attributed to external causes, such as bad feng shui (i.e., an imbalance between the individual and his or her living environment) or supernatural entities (e.g., ancestral spirits, deities, or demons; Lee, 2002). Thus, the cure resides in certain rituals, such as rearranging the furniture in the house or performing a ritual (e.g., burning incense paper to appease the spirits).

Yet another approach to well-being is sought by the Indians in Singapore. Indians seek help from a healer who acts as a medium for a deity's voice. The medium, when possessed by a deity, is able to identify the cause of illness and take action in the form of rituals to cure the person. Ayurveda is a traditional Hindu science of healing, which combines *dyus* (life, vitality, health, and longevity) and *veda* (science and knowledge; Crawford, 1989). It promotes food and lifestyle as the two pillars of health and well-being. Ayurveda also stresses the relationship between mind and body (i.e., it stresses that the physical and spiritual well-being of a person is interconnected).

What is evident in the healing repertoire of Malay, Chinese, and Indian cultures is the reliance on a human spiritual figure (e.g., a medium or priest), a ritual (e.g., a chant or a prayer), and a prescribed cure (e.g., a talisman or some form of physical activity). There also appears to be an underlying belief that health or well-being consists of respecting the balance between body and mind. Although this may seem unscientific to the 21st-century way of life, it is no less rational when considered in the context of these individuals' respective cultural frames of reference.

Why is it important for the counselor to understand indigenous psychotherapies? For many counselors in Singapore who have been trained in Western modes of psychotherapy and counseling, it is easy to dismiss indigenous psychotherapies (e.g., shamanism or geomancy) as superstition and to recommend to clients an approach that seems far more rational, sensible, and salubrious. However, Lee (2002) made an excellent point when he stated, "Instead of rejecting traditional medicine and folk therapies as quack and superstitious, we should study their underlying cultural value systems to inform our counseling practice" (p. 4). A counselor working in Singapore therefore cannot hope to be effective without being sensitive to the cultural and religious frames of reference that contribute to clients' perceptions of their mental health issues. Neither can the counselor offer relevant psychotherapy without helping clients who hold strong religious beliefs to draw the connection between the benefits of counseling and the therapeutic elements present in their indigenous healing systems.

In practice, how does a multicultural counselor in Singapore factor indigenous psychotherapies into his or her counseling practice? An interesting discussion on the outworking of this delicate process with respect to the Chinese populace is available in Lee (2002). Lee suggested that combining counseling and Chinese indigenous psychotherapies is likely to be acceptable to Chinese clients in Singapore who subscribe to Buddhist or Taoist beliefs. For example, the concept of closure in managing issues surrounding bereavement may include the client burning incense papers to the deceased along with a letter expressing unresolved feelings and conflict. However, counselors in Singapore are appropriately cautious about mixing counseling with religion. In an interview with counselors at a local counseling center, we were informed that counselors do attempt to tap their clients' personal resources but will entertain religion as a part of therapy only when clients take the initiative to discuss spiritual perspectives.

Counselor Education

In the early years of counseling in Singapore, various individuals who provided social support in the community (e.g., social workers, clergy staff, and volunteers) were known as *counselors,* and few then had formal training in counseling. This, however, has changed drastically since the 1990s as counselors in Singapore have sought professional training and continuing professional development. For example, counselors we talked with at Care Corner Counseling and the Counseling and Care Center typically received their postgraduate counselor education overseas in the United Kingdom, the United States, Australia, or Taiwan. As more counselors return from overseas training and develop their expertise as practitioners, many local counseling programs have been developed to cater to aspiring counselors. For example, the Counseling and Care Center has been offering a postgraduate diploma in family and marriage therapy since 1991. In 2005, this diploma was enhanced and offered as the master of science program in family and systemic psychotherapy. Similarly, the National Institute of Education at Nanyang Technological University launched a diploma in pastoral care and career guidance, a diploma in school counseling, and master of arts in counseling and guidance program in 1988, 2005, and 2008, respectively. In addition, counselors also engage in ongoing supervision as part of their clinical practice (e.g., weekly peer supervision of taped cases, live supervision, and monthly supervision via the Internet by external clinical supervisors based overseas).

Options for counselor training are plentiful in Singapore, ranging from diplomas and short-term courses run by private enterprises to degree and postgraduate degree programs offered by local universities, off-shore universities, polytechnics, and counseling agencies. The quality of training programs varies widely, as there is presently no credentialing body to verify program credibility and ensure standards. The closest to some semblance of credentialing is presently undertaken by the Singapore Association for Counseling, which recognizes training programs that qualify its graduates for registration. In 2012, the Singapore Association for Counseling recognized 13 programs. Although the increase in the availability of counseling courses and programs is a positive development, in the absence of a central accreditation body, prospective counselors are left to make choices for training without safeguards for quality. This represents yet another challenge for the counseling profession at this stage of its development.

The Future

Counseling services are growing and improving rapidly in Singapore. With this growth and improvement, five immediate challenges confront the field.

First, like other countries in which counseling and psychology are emerging disciplines, Singapore borrowed heavily from developed nations in the early years and adopted Western theories, interventions, and research of counseling. However, it is apparent that these models do not always work well in the local context. There is an urgent need for research that tests the effectiveness of interventions for Singaporeans and that also develops theories and approaches that are culturally and contextually relevant.

Second, counseling is not regulated in Singapore and will likely not be regulated for many years to come. This means that anyone can call himself or herself a "counselor" and that services vary widely in terms of their quality and effectiveness. However, professional organizations such as the Singapore Association for Counseling and the Singapore Psychological Society do maintain training and practice requirements for counselors and psychologists in order to be members. Also, the government has begun to systematically regulate allied health professionals, and there is an indication that this regulation will eventually include psychologists and perhaps counselors. The first bill proposed to regulate physiotherapists, occupational therapists, and speech therapists is expected to pass into law in 2012. Presently professional organizations are working together to provide input into this legislation.

Third, the availability of good-quality clinical supervision is severely limited for many counselors and psychologists. Increasing numbers of individuals are entering the field with basic training, but they are often hired and expected to dive into a broad clinical practice with limited, if any, supervision. Part of the problem is a severe shortage of experienced counselors and psychologists with formal training in supervision. However, this is changing quickly, as a critical core of professionals recognize and commit themselves to the development of supervision practices that meet global standards for quality mental health care. The Counseling and Care Center offers a 9-month part-time diploma program in clinical supervision. Several professional groups and mental health agencies regularly provide quality workshops to build capacity and equip counselors with the skills needed to provide evidence-based services. For example, Shan You Counseling Center, a nonprofit organization funded by the National Council of Social Service, has been conducting workshops in motivational interviewing since 2006. Since 2010, the Psychological Studies Academic Group at the National Institute of Education has been offering an annual week-long series of skills-based workshops to counseling professionals in the community with the objective of honing clinical knowledge and skills.

Fourth, counseling in Singapore is a vocation for which there is little financial reward. Local counseling practitioners we interviewed revealed that individuals who make a mid-career switch to counseling do so at a substantial pay cut and that it is difficult to retain counselors. Indeed, a few local counselors shared that they would not be able to keep up with the cost of living in Singapore if they did not have spouses who helped to supplement the family income. Perhaps the National Council of Social Service may wish to initiate a review of remuneration for counselors in VWOs so that practitioners are not saddled with financial anxiety even as they provide an important service to the community.

Finally, a social stigma remains associated with counseling, mental health services generally, and emotional problems or mental illness in Singaporean society. Feelings of shame are strong, and the desire to save face for oneself and one's family and colleagues inhibits many individuals from seeking professional help when they or their loved ones need it. There is a great need for public education about mental health issues in general and about the usefulness of counseling in particular. However, students and people with less traditional views are more open to counseling and may pave the way for those with more traditional mindsets to consider such help.

Counseling in Singapore has come a long way from its humble beginnings in the 1960s. It is fortunate that many good counselor training programs are available and that mental health professionals are working collaboratively and creatively to address the challenges they face. It is a privilege for us to be a small part of the search for creative solutions to the ongoing challenge of how to meet growing demands for services while simultaneously building capacities.

References

Ang, R. P., & Yeo, L. S. (2004). Asian secondary school students' help-seeking behaviour and preferences for counselor characteristics. *Pastoral Care in Education, 22,* 40–48. doi:10.1111/j.0264-3944.2004.00312.x

Crawford, C. (1989). Ayurveda: The science of long life in contemporary perspective. In A. A. Sheikh & K. S. Sheikh (Eds.), *Eastern and Western approaches to healing* (pp. 3–32). New York, NY: Wiley.

Foo, K. H., Merrick, P. L., & Kazantzis, N. (2006). Counseling/psychotherapy with Chinese Singaporean clients. *Asian Journal of Counseling, 13*(2), 271–293.

Forbes Blogger. (2011, July 18). Re: *Richest countries in the world-latest list 2011* [Web log message]. Retrieved from http://www.forbesblogger.com/world-richest-country-2011-forbes/

Haque, A. (2008). Culture-bound syndromes and healing practices in Malaysia. *Mental Health, Religion & Culture, 11,* 685–696. doi:10.1080/13674670801958867

Lambert, M. J., & Barley, D. E. (2001). Research summary on the therapeutic relationship and psychotherapy outcome. *Psychotherapy, 38,* 357–361.

Lee, B. O. (2002). Chinese indigenous psychotherapies in Singapore. *Counseling and Psychotherapy Research, 2,* 2–10. doi:10.1080/14733140212331384938

Lee, B. O., & Bishop, G. D. (2001). Chinese clients' belief systems about psychological problems in Singapore. *Counseling Psychology Quarterly, 14,* 219–240. doi:10.1080/09515070110088834

McKinsey & Company. (2007). *How the world's best performing schools come out on top.* New York, NY: Author. Retrieved from http://www.mckinsey.com/App_Media/Reports/SSO/Worlds_School_Systems_Final.pdf

Ministry of Education. (2009, February 23). *MOE launches web-based education and career guidance portal for students.* Retrieved from http://www.moe.gov.sg/media/press/2009/02/moe-launches-web-based-educati.php

Ministry of Education. (2011). *Social and emotional learning*. Retrieved from http://www.moe.gov.sg/education/programmes/social-emotional-learning/

Ng, B. H., & Lim, K. M. (2006). Help-seeking behaviour of low income families in a family service centre setting. *Social Service Journal, 18*, 13–14.

Tan, C. T., Chee, K. T., & Long, F. Y. (1980). Psychiatric patients who seek traditional healers in Singapore. *Singapore Medical Journal, 21*, 643–647.

Tan, E. (2009). Counseling in a multicultural context: The Singapore perspective. In L. H. Gerstein, P. P. Heppner, S. Ægisdóttir, S.-M. A. Leung, & K. L. Norsworthy (Eds.), *International handbook of cross-cultural counseling: Cultural assumptions and practices worldwide* (pp. 209–220). Thousand Oaks, CA: Sage.

Vasquez, M. J. T. (2007). Cultural difference and the therapeutic alliance: An evidence-based analysis. *American Psychologist, 62*, 878–885. doi:10.1037/0003-066X.62.8.878

Yeo, A. (1993). *Counselling: A problem-solving approach.* Singapore: Armour.

• • •

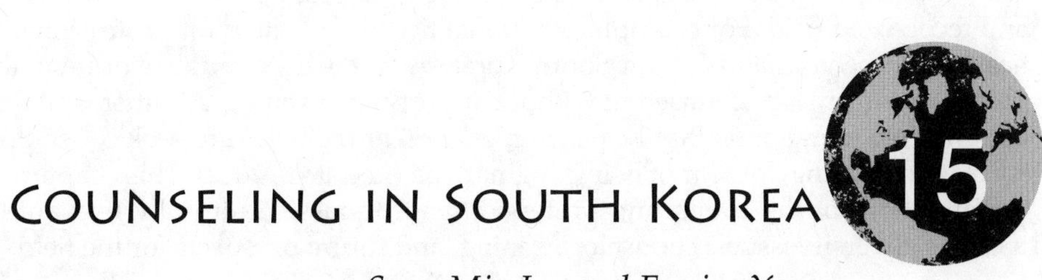

Counseling in South Korea

Sang Min Lee and Eunjoo Yang

Korea is located on the Korean Peninsula, which lies on the northeastern section of the Asian continent. The peninsula shares its northern border with China and Russia. To its east is the East Sea, beyond which neighboring Japan lies. North Korea occupies the northern half of the Korean Peninsula, and South Korea, officially the Republic of Korea, is located on the southern portion of the peninsula. South Korea has a population of almost 50 million. The capital and largest city is Seoul, with a population of 15 million. After liberation and occupation by Soviet and U.S. forces at the end of World War II, the nation was divided into North and South Korea. Korea is still referred to as the only divided nation in the world. Although military tension with North Korea is having an adverse effect on its financial markets, South Korea has one of the fastest growing economies of the 21st century. South Korea is Asia's fourth largest economy and the sixth largest exporter and tenth largest importer in the world. South Korea is a member of the United Nations, the World Trade Organization, the Organisation for Economic Co-operation and Development, and G-20 major economies.

Along with its economic growth, South Korea's counseling profession is also developing greatly. Since 1990, an increasing number of counseling programs have been established in colleges or universities, professional counseling associations have emerged and developed, professional counselors have been employed in diverse work settings, and culturally relevant counseling theories and techniques suitable for use with the Korean people have been developed (Lee, Yang, Suh, & Jang, 2012). The expansion of the counseling profession can be attributed to various societal needs, such as a rising unemployment rate among college graduates, a suicide rate among the highest in the world, exacerbated intergenerational conflict, and an extremely competitive educational environment that suffocates students early on.

Among the counseling disciplines, school counseling was first introduced to South Korea in the 1950s. Until recently, however, counseling services in the school were mainly focused on discipline or career issues; offering counseling services was secondary to teaching and performing administrative work (Lee & Yang, 2008). In contrast, college counselors have since the 1960s been the major driving force behind the growth in the counseling profession by training counselors, conducting counseling research, and creating career positions for graduates of counseling programs. The number of graduate programs in counseling within departments of psychology and education has increased greatly since the 1970s. In the 1980s, professional counseling organizations emerged. First the division of counseling psychology was established within the Korean Psychological Association. In addition, several counseling-related associations (e.g., the Korean College Counseling Association, the Korean Group Counseling Association, the Korean Career Counseling Association, and the Research Society for Children and Adolescents) emerged. Finally, in 2000, the Korean Counseling Association was established to advocate for the counseling profession by integrating the scattered counseling professional organizations.

Although it is expected that the counseling profession in South Korea will continue to grow and expand, a number of challenges face the profession as it grows into a distinct and recognized field. For example, a national licensure system for professional counselors has not yet been established in South Korea. As a result, a number of unqualified paraprofessionals practice counseling without appropriate training. Another well-documented cultural consideration is that Koreans in general are reluctant to seek psychological help, such as counseling, for fear of being stigmatized (Lee et al., 2012). This chapter reviews the current status of the counseling profession and discusses culturally relevant counseling theories, diversity issues, counselor training, and future prospects for the field.

The Current Status of Counseling

Counseling in School Settings

The development of school counseling was an important impetus for the expansion of counseling in South Korea. The earliest form of school counseling could be found in the 1950s. After the country's liberation from Japan in 1945 and the end of the Korean War in 1953, school guidance was introduced by U.S. educational delegates who came to offer support for reconstruction. Despite quite a long history of school counseling, the current form of school counseling emerged only recently. School counseling in South Korea has progressed from disciplinary guidance to career guidance to school counseling dealing with a wide range of student concerns as relevant policies have changed (Lee & Yang, 2008).

In 1963, the Ministry of Education (now the Ministry of Education, Science, and Technology) passed the Education Act mandating that disciplinary guidance teachers be placed in middle and high schools. The 1963 Education Act initiated the school counseling system in South Korea. The Ministry of Education changed teachers' title from "disciplinary guidance teachers" to "career counseling teachers" and placed a career counseling department in each local school board in 1990 to emphasize the role of career counseling. Despite such efforts, these systems had limitations, as the roles of counseling teachers were ill defined, teachers were required to have only limited training, and these individuals were burdened with teaching assignments in addition to counseling-related duties (Lee, Oh, & Suh, 2007).

The Ministry of Education reformed the school counseling system again in 1997 by renaming career counseling teachers "professional school counseling teachers." The 1997 Elementary and Secondary Education Act provided the basis for a training system for registered professional school counseling teachers, and the Ministry of Education and Human Resources Development offered the necessary training and certification. Unfortunately, most of the registered professional school counseling teachers still needed to carry a teaching load, with the exception of a few who were employed as full-time counselors (Lee et al., 2007). A more drastic change occurred in 2004, when the Ministry of Education and Human Resources Development acknowledged the problems in the existing school counseling system and reformed it to ensure the placement of full-time school counselors in each school. The revised 2004 Elementary and Secondary School Education Act ensured the provision of financial support to local school boards to develop school counseling systems. It also supported universities to offer training programs for school counselors. Subsequently, a nationwide project was initiated by the Ministry of Education and Human Resources Development in 2008 to build school counseling centers in schools and local school boards (Lee & Yang, 2008).

The progressive evolution of school counseling policies and systems had a marked impact on school counseling in South Korea. In 2011, a total of 2,045 out of 11,170 schools had full-time school counselors. In addition, many schools have begun to build their own school counseling offices called WEE (We + Education + Emotion) offices with support from the Ministry of Education, Science, and Technology. WEE offices are also being built across the country. Of 178 school boards, 124 have built student counseling centers, each with two or three registered school counselors, two youth counselors, one clinical psychologist, and one social worker. These centers provide support for school counseling services to schools within the district and function as a hub for comprehensive and intensive counseling services for students (Lee et al., 2012).

Counseling in Nonschool Settings

Counseling has shown remarkable growth outside schools as well. The development of counseling in nonschool settings was propelled by the expansion of university counseling centers. The first university counseling center was established at Seoul National University in 1962. This counseling center functioned not just as an agency to meet students' needs for psychological services but also as an institute for training in the research and practice of counseling (Cha, 2005). Although an undergraduate degree in psychology was offered as far back as the 1920s, the graduate program in counseling psychology did not exist until the 1970s (Park & Hwang, 2008). University counseling centers were subsequently established to fill the void in professional training by providing training opportunities in counseling. In 2011, university counseling centers existed in 343 out of 382 universities nationwide. University counseling centers have hired many counselors in South Korea.

Another important setting in which counselors work is youth community counseling centers. Youth community counseling centers were established by the Korea Youth Counseling Institute as part of a nationwide project in compliance with the policies for youth community counseling (Seo, Kim, & Kim, 2007). The number of youth community counseling centers has gradually increased to a total of 16 hub counseling centers in major cities and 136 local counseling centers in small cities and towns. Counseling practice has expanded to the private sector as well. The number of counselors in private practice has also grown rapidly since 2000. The Korean Counseling Psychological Association has identified approximately 170 private counseling centers nationwide. In addition, more counselors have started working in nontraditional settings such as businesses, religious organizations, court systems, and the military (Seo et al., 2007).

The increase in the number of counselors warrants the need for quality control of counseling practice or a credential system. Unfortunately, no licensure system of counselors exists as yet in South Korea. However, a national-level certification system, namely a youth counselor certification, exists to ensure professional standards. The youth counselor certification system is operated by the Ministry of Gender Equality and the Family. In 2011, a total of 4,070 individuals were certified as youth counselors. Professional organizations such as the Korean Counseling Psychological Association and the Korean Counseling Association have also developed their own counseling certification systems that require a certain number of supervised clinical hours. The first examination for certification was conducted by the Korean Counseling Psychological Association in 1973, and in 2011, a total of 749 counselors were certified by this system.

Culturally Relevant Counseling in South Korea

Korean cultural traditions and values are infused with an array of ancient myths, Confucianism, Buddhism, Taoism, and other philosophies. Recently, Korean counselors have begun to search for ways to integrate the Western counseling approaches with Korean ideologies and philosophies (Bae, Joo, & Orlinsky, 2003). Three philosophies appear to have particular relevance to this issue: Hong-Ik-In-Gan, Zen Buddhism, and Confucianism. Hong-Ik-In-Gan is the founding philosophy of Korea. Hong-Ik-In-Gan originated from the founding philosophy of the ancient Korean country, which was supposedly the first Korean country. It refers to the devotion of the welfare of man and emphasizes human dignity and interests, reflecting the integrated values of democracy and humanism. Zen Buddhism holds a phenomenological perspective. Zen Buddhists believe that psychological distress is caused by the distortion of organismic experiences and that true being can only be experienced by freeing one's mind from theories and desires that can distort one's experiences. Lastly, Confucianism is the basis for the Korean system of morals and personal virtues. Its emphases on hierarchical relationships and familism are particularly influential in current Korean culture.

These philosophies have influenced the approaches Korean counselors use to understand clients and devise therapeutic interventions. Korean counselors have tried to modify existing Western counseling approaches and even to develop new approaches to reflect the ideologies of Korean society. Among the Western counseling approaches, the humanistic approach is most preferred by Korean counselors (Joo, Bae, & Orlinsky, 2003). The humanistic approach is characterized by phenomenology, wholeness, and self-actualization (Gelso & Fretz, 2001). It proposes that human experience can be understood only from the subjective and holistic perspective, and it posits the uniqueness and dignity of individuals as well as the intrinsic need to actualize potentials (Gelso & Fretz, 2001). Person-centered theory, in particular, proposes that maladaptive problems are caused by the conditional environment creating incongruence between the ideal self and the actual self; thus, clients can achieve change when therapists manifest attitudes of empathic understanding, unconditional positive regard, and congruence (Rogers, 1961, 1980).

The tenets of the humanistic approach are in line with traditional Korean ideologies such as the founding philosophy of Hong-Ik-In-Gan, Confucianism, and Zen Buddhism. This is why the humanistic approach is used as a primary approach by many Korean counselors. Approximately 70% of Korean counselors use the humanistic approach as their primary theoretical framework (Joo et al., 2003). Korean counselors believe that the humanistic approach is compatible with Korean values, in that both emphasize empathy, relationships, and harmony (Joo, Lee, & Joo, 2007). However, some limitations to applying the humanistic approach with Korean clients exist. For example, Korean counselors find it difficult to conduct nondirective counseling with Korean clients, who tend to be accustomed to hierarchical relationships and directive guidance (Joo et al., 2007).

Alternative counseling approaches have been devised to directly reflect traditional Korean ideologies. Onmeum counseling, or whole-mind counseling, is an approach that is closely related to Zen Buddhism. Onmeum counseling proposes that psychological problems are created by the individual's imagination and reflect one's life history, ideas, knowledge, and expectations rather than one's reality. Such problems can thus be resolved only through realizing the fixation to past experience and the illusory reality. The counselor's role in this process is to empathically understand clients' subjective world, to help clients realize the illusory nature of their problems and be freed from their fixation on the past, and finally to assist clients in recreating a more adaptive subjective world by reviewing alternative perspectives (Yun, 2007). The tenets of Onmeum counseling are similar to those of Zen Buddhism, whose ultimate goal is the discovery of the true self and the dissipation of obsessions and fixations.

Another exemplary Korean counseling approach is reality dynamic counseling, which is based on the familism of Confucianism. In current Korean society there is a clash between traditional familism and the individualism introduced by Westernization. Reality dynamic counseling emphasizes the positive aspects of familism, such as a sense of community, and attempts to reconcile the differences between familism and individualism (Chang, 2007). Unlike Western counseling approaches, which focus on independence, reality dynamic counseling centers on interdependence, or an individual's roles in various interpersonal contexts. It conceptualizes psychological problems as a failure to meet role expectations. The counseling process often involves assisting clients in successfully performing their roles in different contexts, especially restoring functional parent–child relationships. Counselors using reality dynamic counseling can take on the role of not just therapist but also parent, mentor, or educator. In particular, reality dynamic counseling values the use of confrontation and strict advice, which may meet Korean clients' needs for direct guidance.

Both Onmeum counseling and reality dynamic counseling are reflective of ideologies and philosophies of the traditional Korean culture. These approaches indicate the limitations of Western counseling theories and the need for culturally relevant approaches. Although the majority of Korean counselors still rely on Western counseling approaches, and only limited empirical studies have been conducted on these culturally specific counseling approaches (Joo et al., 2007), these models serve as valuable foundations for the further development of culturally relevant counseling approaches in Korea.

Diversity Issues

According to the Ministry of Public Administration and Security (2011), 1,265,006 ethnic minorities lived in Korea in 2010, accounting for 2% of the entire population. Most of them were migrant workers, North Korean refugees, migrant spouses, and the children of biracial families. By 2020, 20% of students in South Korean schools will be racially or ethnically different (S. H. Kim, 2009). For example, the number of multicultural children increased dramatically from 6,795 in 2006 to 11,444 in 2007 to 18,769 in 2008 (Lee & Lee, 2009). The Korean Women's Development Institute (2011) forecasted that the ratio of ethnic minorities to the entire population would reach 5%–6% by 2050. This emergence of multicultural ethnic groups (e.g., foreign workers, North Korean refugees, and mixed-marriage families) means that counselors must be equipped with well-developed multicultural counseling competencies.

Song and Kang (2011) reported that ethnic minorities experienced migration-related stress and difficulty establishing a cultural identity, both of which professional counselors in South Korea are totally unfamiliar with thus far. Counselors may face communication difficulties, misunderstanding of the culture, misunderstanding of the impact of the culture on the process of counseling, misguided assumptions about cultural assimilation, different social class orientations and values, stereotypical generalizations and cultural bias, and failure to understand the worldview of the client (Baruth & Manning, 1992). Counseling professionals in South Korea need to place much energy and time into developing multicultural counseling techniques and intervention strategies that are readily applicable to these target populations because classic counseling approaches, such as psychoanalysis, the behavioral approach, the humanistic approach, and the cognitive approach, were formed from concepts and principles that echo Western values, philosophical assumptions, and language usage (Song & Kang, 2011).

Korean counselors need to be proactive in advocating for the mental health of ethnic minorities and providing needed services to help with psychological problems such as depression and anxiety caused by adjustment difficulties. Multicultural counselors will be asked to extend their traditional roles and sometimes go out of the office to meet the needs of these marginalized populations. In some cases, counselors also need to serve as advocates to secure funding for necessary counseling and social services for these underserved populations (Lee et al., 2012). In addition, multicultural counselors should consider various outreach programs such as home-based services and community-based interventions (K. S. Kim & Jung, 2010).

To date, only a few counseling programs in South Korea offer courses in multicultural counseling. Counseling programs in graduate schools need to include courses in multicultural counseling in their curricula. Through these courses, counselor trainees need to understand ethnic minorities' feelings of helplessness and powerlessness, low self-esteem, and poor self-concept and how they contribute to low motivation, frustration, ambivalence, and apathy. These courses must be designed to enhance multicultural competencies, which include multicultural awareness, attitudes, and skills.

Counselor Education

Since the 1950s, a number of counseling-related courses (e.g., school guidance, stress management, and mental hygiene) have been offered at the major Korean universities (e.g., Seoul National University). Until the 1970s, however, no master's or doctoral programs in counseling existed. In 1972, Ewha Women's University was the first to offer an official graduate program in counseling (Park & Hwang, 2008). Since then, the number of counseling programs in graduate schools has increased tremendously within various departments (e.g., psychology, education, theology).

A master's degree is usually required to become a professional counselor and provide counseling services to clients. A master's degree program typically requires 24 to 36 semester hours of graduate study, including a period of supervised clinical experience in counseling. Therefore, a master's degree generally amounts to 2 or 2.5 years of full-time graduate study culminating in a master's thesis based on original research. Fields of study in counseling have diverged over the past decade, including counselor education, counseling psychology, school counseling, marriage and family therapy, youth counseling, play therapy, art therapy, pastoral counseling, career counseling, gerontological counseling, and related fields.

Professional counselors have an obligation to develop their professional knowledge and skills, to improve their professional competence and integrity, and to make the best effort to protect their clients' welfare. Thus, professional counselors are required to achieve high levels of preservice education and training before they can call themselves professional counselors. In order to raise educational standards, the educational content of counseling-related programs needs to be standardized to provide all core counseling knowledge and skills courses. Although most counseling programs adopt a scientist-practitioner model, to date there is no nationwide standardized training model for counselors in South Korea. Because of the lack of agreed-on training models, several Korean researchers (Lee et al., 2007; Lee & Yang, 2008) have reported that the content and quality of training varies widely from program to program. In the United States, the Council for Accreditation of Counseling and Related Educational Programs created a set of training standards and evaluates the content and quality of counseling programs seeking certification. A similar model may prove useful in South Korea in order to further ensure counselor training competence across the various specialties (Lee et al., 2012).

In addition, much of the education for counselors is dependent on short-term training through workshops, seminars, and conferences. Experiential learning courses such as practica and internships are being left to individual candidates (e.g., in terms of securing sites for experiential practice). According to Seo et al. (2007), such educational and training arrangements make it difficult to control the quality of counselor education. Therefore, the development of a more systematically organized, university-based educational system needs to be discussed. Future dialogue on counselor preparation should be encouraged to result in the provision of counseling degrees at the graduate level with a standardized education curriculum in place (Lee et al., 2012).

The Future

Projecting 5–10 years into the future, it is expected that the counseling profession in South Korea will continue to develop and expand. At the same time, several challenges are in store for the counseling profession as it grows into a recognized field (Lee et al., 2012).

First, in the collectivist South Korean culture, social stigmas are attached to seeking psychological services from outside of the family. Therefore, strategies that reduce the social stigma linked to seeking psychological services should be considered. For example, replacing stereotypes with facts in various media (e.g., television, public service announcements, books, flyers, lectures, movies, videos, and other audiovisual aids) may be effective at defeating the myths surrounding receiving counseling and psychotherapy. The public needs to hear that counseling is no longer just for people with severe mental disorders. In addition, orienting the Korean public to the role of counselors and functions of counseling is critical (Lee et al., 2012).

Second, mental health professionals with different educational backgrounds will continue to compete for the same work in counseling and psychotherapy. This competition will force counseling professionals to invest their efforts in creating positions in private and public institutions. Issues of counselor identity are critical. South Korea is a country in which counselors' professional roles and boundaries are not clearly defined. Mental health services have been extended and have begun to be provided by other professionals, such as social workers. Counselor educators and counselors must make every effort to help establish professional counseling as an independent profession (Lee et al., 2012).

Third, counseling professionals need to become involved in public affairs and continue to promote policy change that supports the profession. There is no licensure system for counseling in South Korea. Because there is no legislative restriction on counseling in private practice, anyone can open a private counseling center. To avoid malpractice by paraprofessionals, it is necessary to explore the possibility of creating a national counselor licensure system. Another way to promote counseling in South Korean society is to improve medical insurance policies. Unlike several Western countries (e.g., the United States), in which counseling services are reimbursed by health insurance, South Korea does not have an insurance reimbursement policy for counseling services. Medical insurance policies on counseling and psychotherapy services will help expand the counseling profession.

In order to address these challenges, rigorous research on counseling in South Korea is needed. For example, research on culturally relevant curricula, including counseling practica and internships, can clarify concerns in the training of professional counselors. Another area of research is counselor identity development. Empirical and qualitative research on counselor identity development can help tease out a theoretical basis for intervention areas and activities and the roles of professional counselors. Finally, policy research on counseling (e.g., licensure and insurance) should be conducted to systematically expand the counseling profession.

Despite these concerns and challenges, there is unified agreement that counselors will play an important role in South Korea in the future. The rapid quantitative growth in the counseling profession may reflect this. Continuous support from stakeholders such as policy makers is critical to generating understanding about the significant positive effects of counseling. With this support, the concerns and challenges that Korean counseling is facing can become the foundations for improved counseling in the country. Having observed the passion and wisdom collected in conferences, workshops, and classrooms packed with people, we strongly believe that the counseling profession in South Korea will make giant strides forward in consolidating its position in the next decade in the highly competitive mental health market (Lee et al., 2012).

References

Bae, S. H., Joo, E., & Orlinsky, D. E. (2003). Psychotherapists in South Korea: Professional and practice characteristics. *Psychotherapy: Theory, Research, Practice, Training, 40*(4), 302–316.

Baruth, L., & Manning, M. (1992). Understanding and counseling Hispanic American children. *Elementary School Guidance and Counseling, 27*, 112–122.

Cha, J. H. (2005). Development and current status of psychology in Korea. *Korean Social Science, 27*(1/2), 167–184.

Chang, S. S. (2007). The familism and a view of integration for reality dynamic counseling. *Korean Journal of Counseling and Psychotherapy, 19,* 523–537.

Gelso, C., & Fretz, B. (2001). *Counseling psychology* (2nd ed.). Orlando, FL: Hartcourt.

Joo, E., Bae, S., & Orlinsky, D. E. (2003). The professional and practice characteristics of Korean psychotherapists: Based on the "Interpersonal Study of Development of Psychotherapists (ISDP)." *Korean Journal of Counseling and Psychotherapy, 15,* 423–439.

Joo, E., Lee, H., & Joo, E. (2007). An investigation of Korean Humanistic counseling model based on the self-report of experienced humanistic counselors in Korea. *Korean Journal of Counseling and Psychotherapy, 19,* 569–586.

Kim, K. S., & Jung, T. H. (2010). Directions and tasks of school counseling for multicultural family students [in Korean]. *Journal of Korea Elementary Education, 20,* 197–213.

Kim, S. H. (2009). *Counseling strategies for children from different cultures to improve academic competencies.* Unpublished master's thesis, Ehwa University, Seoul, Korea.

Korean Women's Development Institute. (2011). *Multicultural family in South Korea* [in Korean]. Seoul, Korea: Author.

Lee, S., & Lee, S. (2009). The effectiveness of adaptability program to school for lower grades students of elementary school in multicultural families [in Korean]. *Korean Journal of Counseling, 10,* 2273–2286.

Lee, S. M., Oh, I., & Suh, S. (2007). Comparison study of Korean and American school counseling for developing a Korean school counseling model. *Korean Journal of Counseling and Psychotherapy, 19,* 539–567.

Lee, S. M., & Yang, E. (2008). School counseling in South Korea: Historical development, current status, and prospects. *Asian Journal of Counselling, 15*(2), 157–181.

Lee, S. M., Suh, S., Yang, E., & Jang, Y. J. (2012). History, current status, and future prospects of counseling in South Korea. *Journal of Counseling & Development, 90,* 494–499.

Ministry of Public Administration and Security. (2011). *Status of foreigners in South Korea* [in Korean]. Seoul, Korea: Author.

Park, A. S., & Hwang, M. G. (2008). Issues for identification in relation to counseling in Korea [in Korean]. *Korean Journal of Counseling and Psychotherapy, 20,* 903–929.

Rogers, C. (1961). *On becoming a person.* Boston, MA: Houghton Mifflin.

Rogers, C. (1980). *A way of being.* Boston, MA: Houghton Mifflin.

Seo, Y. S., Kim, D. M., & Kim, D. I. (2007). Current status and prospects of Korean counseling psychology: Research, clinical training, and job placement. *Applied Psychology, 56,* 107–118.

Song, H., & Kang, Y. (2011). From a homogeneous culture to a heterogeneous society: Implications of multicultural school counseling for children and adolescents. *Journal of Asia Pacific Counseling, 1*(2), 139–150.

Yun, H. (2007). The Onmeum counseling. *Korean Journal of Counseling and Psychotherapy, 19,* 505–522.

• • •

Counseling in Taiwan

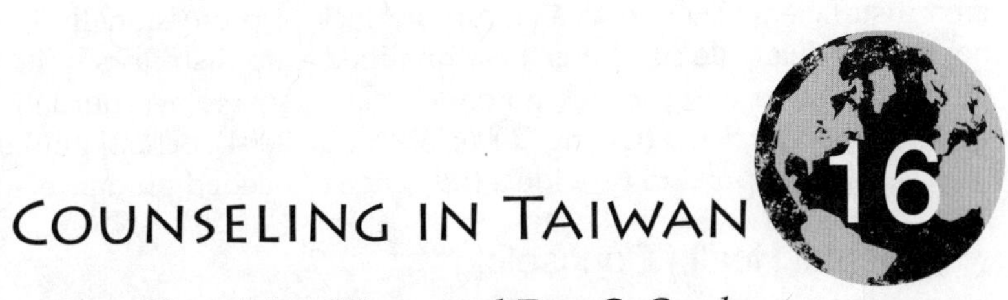

Yuh-Jen Guo, Shu-Ching Wang, and Don C. Combs

The professional practice of guidance and counseling was introduced in Taiwan from the United States in the middle of the 20th century (Wu, 1993). It originated as a result of a guidance project designed to support foreign students of Taiwanese or Chinese descent who lived alone while pursuing their education (Chang, 2006; Chen, 1999). The term *guidance* was adopted at this time to define and describe counseling practices used in educational systems and other organizations that were providing guidance and counseling-related services. Before *counseling* became the more commonly accepted term, both *counseling* and *guidance* were used interchangeably.

The Historical Development of Counseling

School Guidance

As a result of Western influences, Taiwan's Ministry of Education began implementing guidance practices in its public school systems in the 1950s (Chen, 1999). The Ministry of Education selected teachers and administrators to attend guidance and counseling educational programs in the United States. Graduates of these programs became crucial figures in the early development of school guidance in Taiwan. After public education was expanded from 6 to 9 years in 1968, the Ministry of Education began to incorporate guidance activities and career information into the middle school curricula (Chen, 1999). Teacher preparation programs in normal universities and teachers colleges quickly responded to this call for the implementation of a school guidance initiative in Taiwan. These institutions established guidance programs to train undergraduate teacher-counselors for certification (Wu, 1993).

Although school guidance programs in Taiwan's public schools became popular, the role of school guidance was still considered part of the disciplinary program (Chen, 1999). The Ministry of Education continuously demanded experimental projects and issued policy changes related to school guidance (Chang, 2006) that kept school guidance from becoming an independent and functional entity.

School guidance programs in Taiwan were rejuvenated in the early 1970s. Changes came from new legislation and policies. In 1972, the Ministry of Education approved the establishment of guidance centers in colleges, and in 1974, it extended these services to high schools (Chen, 1999). The Citizen's Education Law, passed in 1979, was a determining factor in the development of school guidance initiatives in the public school setting. In this legislation, school guidance became mandatory in elementary schools (Chang, 2006). In the 1980s, public universities officially established guidance centers, and high schools employed guidance teachers whose sole curricular responsibility was to provide guidance services (Chen, 1999).

The framework of school guidance was implemented through legislative mandates and regulations in the 1980s. However, the content of school guidance programs was considered insufficient. There was a significant lack of professionally trained guidance personnel to staff available positions. Less qualified administrators quite commonly headed the guidance offices, and certified guidance teachers were overburdened with the demands of the guidance curricula (Chang, 2006; W.-Y. Lin, 2004). School guidance programs were not sufficiently equipped to provide a full range of needed guidance and counseling services.

Mental Health Counseling

The concepts of mental health, counseling, and psychotherapy emerged in Taiwan during the late 20th century. The development of mental health counseling can be roughly divided into the pre- and postlicensure eras, with 2001 being the transition year when a licensure law was passed.

In the prelicensure era, counseling as a profession was not fully recognized in Taiwan. Psychiatrists were recognized by the "Psychiatric Law" as the primary professionals delivering psychiatric and mental health care (Department of Health, 1990). There were only two public psychiatric centers serving psychiatric patients before 1990 (Department of Health, 2011). Public mental health services were also available from the military, which began providing guidance to military members in the mid-20th century (Hu, Lee, Ting, Zhou, & Hong, 2009). The first author of this chapter, Yuh-Jen Guo, was an enlisted member of the Taiwanese military from 1988 to 1990. He became aware of a guidance program, commonly known as "Mailbox of Teacher Zhao," which was located in the division headquarters and accepted complaints and difficulties filed by soldiers. This program was an effort to combat the high suicide rate among enlisted soldiers. Taiwan's military began establishing mental health centers on bases and training guidance officers to meet soldiers' mental health needs in 1991 (Hu et al., 2009).

Two noteworthy nongovernmental organizations emerged in the prelicensure era. Teacher Chang and Lifeline were two creditable entities that began providing guidance and counseling services in community settings. Teacher Chang, founded in 1969, was well known for its services to youths and young adults (Teacher Chang Foundation, 2011; Wu, 1993). Lifeline was set up as a suicide prevention hotline in 1969 (Taiwan Lifeline International, 2011). However, these prelicensure efforts were reshaped after the passage in 2001 of the licensure law called the "Psychologist Law" (Chang, 2006).

The Current Status of Counseling

As stated previously, professional counseling entered a new era in 2001 with the passage of the national Psychologist Law, which regulated the scope of the practice of professional counseling and established criteria for professional licensure (Laws & Regulations Database of the Republic of China, 2001). This legislation established two types of mental health practitioner: clinical psychologists and counseling psychologists. The counseling psychologist license is for professional counselors and counseling psychologists. Licensure criteria require a master's degree in counseling or related studies, a 1-year postgraduate internship, and a passing score on the National Counseling Psychologist Exam.

This licensure law not only marked the legal birth of the counseling profession in Taiwan but added credibility by establishing counseling as a profession regulated by the government. This important change accelerated the development of the counseling profession in Taiwan, as a license is now mandatory for practitioners to provide counseling services. The licensure law also added visibility to the profession. However, regulation of the profession has been criticized by some who are concerned that the government now has legal authority, control, and power over the provision of counseling services (S. Wang, 2006).

Mental Health Counseling

Counselors in Taiwan have traditionally worked in school settings and are only now beginning to work in community-related mental health service settings (J. C. H. Lin, 2000). Under the new licensure law, licensed counselors are now highly qualified mental health care providers and are working diligently to build their professional identity as such (J. C. H. Lin, 2000). A new revision in the Psychiatric Law (Department of Health, 2007) also recognizes professional counseling as a treatment option for mental disorders.

A recent trend in mental health counseling, however, is the placement of counseling professionals (counselors, psychologists, and social workers) on school campuses to treat students' severe behavioral problems (J. C. H. Lin & Hung, 2002). This reflects the recognition by licensed counselors that counseling professionals must manage complicated mental health issues in schools as well as in their communities. In essence, counselors recognize that they must provide more than guidance services in the school setting. Accordingly, mental health counseling as well as guidance services are becoming more available in Taiwanese schools. As an example, a recent action in the Taiwanese congress passed a revision to the Citizen's Education Law to address the increase in school bullying. This revised legislation mandates that school systems employ professionally trained and licensed counselors in response to a shocking report that revealed that only 5% of current school counseling staff were qualified school counselors or guidance teachers (Qiu, 2011). It is hoped that this legislative action will result in the recruiting of an additional 2,221 licensed counselors and guidance teachers on school campuses by 2017 (Guan, Chan, Zhang, & Lin, 2011).

School Guidance and Counseling

School guidance and counseling programs face challenges from legislative changes (J. C. H. Lin & Hung, 2002; C.-H. Wang, 2006). The licensure law impacts the field of school counseling because it denies licensure to guidance teachers with only bachelor's degrees, which limits the ability of unlicensed guidance teachers to practice counseling on campus (C.-H. Wang, 2006). In keeping with the current trend to provide mental health services in the schools, unlicensed guidance teachers are under some pressure to pursue a graduate degree to meet professional licensure criteria.

Current educational policies and practices present additional challenges to school counseling. School counselors face curriculum burdens (Ministry of Education, 2003), high student:counselor ratios (a single counselor is responsible for 20 or more classes), and the use of regular classroom teachers in guidance offices (Ministry of Education, 2011). Since 1998, the Ministry of Education has pushed for educational reform and has imposed a new guidance system that integrates instruction, discipline, and guidance in school guidance and counseling programs (W.-Y. Lin, 2004). This 6-year guidance plan advocates a three-level prevention system. The first level places guidance responsibilities on all teachers and administrators (W.-Y. Lin, 2004). The second level involves school counseling, and the third level requires collaborations between school counseling and local community mental health resources (W.-Y. Lin, 2004). Opponents have voiced concerns that this approach may dilute the strength of school guidance and counseling when insufficiently trained classroom teachers and administrators are involved in significant school guidance and counseling tasks (C.-H. Wang, 2006). Defining the roles and functions of school guidance and counseling programs in this postlicensure era is fast becoming a major challenge.

Counselor Education

A unique structure exists for counselor training in Taiwan. Although the licensure law requires a minimum of a master's degree in counseling, counselor training actually starts at the bachelor's level and has evolved into a graduate system that is quite similar to the U.S. model, with master's and doctoral programs. Bachelor-level counselors who graduate from teacher preparation programs can be certified as guidance teachers. Graduate studies are also recommended for bachelor-level practitioners in order to meet the licensure requirements necessary to become counselors.

Counselor Preparation Programs

Counselor preparation programs in Taiwan are definitely influenced by the licensure law. As degree holders seek a license in counseling psychology, graduate programs attempt to provide specialized training and preparation course work that conforms to this license title. *Counseling* has been used as a department title in many universities; however, departments of counseling psychology have only been created in a few universities. Psychology departments also offer counseling psychology programs to train counselors.

One of the earliest counselor preparation programs in Taiwan began in 1971 at a normal university (Department of Guidance and Counseling, 2004). As of 2012, a total of 26 departments offer 16 bachelor's, 24 master's, and 8 doctoral degrees. Three rehabilitation counseling and two pastoral counseling programs offer five master's degrees, and one pastoral counseling program offers one doctoral degree. In addition, one marriage and family therapy program offers a master's degree. Of these 26 departments, 15 have "Counseling" in their titles, 4 "Psychology," 3 "Education," 2 "Counseling Psychology," 1 "Life and Death Studies," and 1 "Psychological and Social Work."

Bachelor's and master's degrees are often offered in guidance and counseling or in counseling; however, there is no indication that doctoral degrees are offered in counselor education. Instead, all doctoral degrees are offered in counseling psychology because of licensure requirements. Among the 26 universities, 11 are traditional teacher preparation universities (normal universities and universities evolved from traditional teachers colleges). These 11 teacher preparation universities offer 10 undergraduate, 11 master's, and 3 doctoral degrees. The two counseling programs emphasizing death studies are housed in a nursing college and a religious university. Such a wide variety of departmental names and majors depicts the diverse counselor training philosophies in Taiwan.

Counselor Education Curricula

As stated earlier, the counseling profession in Taiwan has been influenced by the United States; however, counselor training criteria do not necessarily follow the U.S. accreditation standards as set forth by the Council for Accreditation of Counseling and Related Educational Programs (CACREP). A review of the curricula of 14 undergraduate counseling programs in Taiwan reveals that mandatory courses in the CACREP domains are usually but not always required undergraduate counselor training programs in Taiwan. (a) Professional Orientation and Ethical Practice and (b) Assessment are required courses in all 14 programs. Research and Program Evaluation is required in 13 programs. Helping Relationships and Human Growth and Development are both required in 12 programs.

Ten programs offer Group Work, and six programs offer Career Development. Social and Cultural Diversity is not a required course in any of the 14 undergraduate counseling programs in Taiwan.

Master's counselor training programs in Taiwan require fewer CACREP-related courses than do undergraduate programs. This may be partially because those courses are required at the undergraduate level. The number of credit hours needed to graduate from a master's program ranges from 30 to 42 (without a thesis), which is different from CACREP's standard of 48. A review of available curriculum guides from 22 counseling programs reveals that many programs require core courses in psychology, such as Social Psychology and Personality Development. Many specialty courses are also offered as electives. These specialty courses include Mindfulness-Based Stress Reduction, Dream Work, Leisure Counseling, Online Counseling, Medical Counseling, and Social Therapy. Specific counseling formats or theoretical practices also appear in curriculum guides (e.g., psychodrama and music therapy).

The review of the 22 curriculum guides reveals that the only CACREP-related area required by all programs is research and program evaluation. Helping Relationships and Group Work are mandatory courses in 13 and 8 programs, respectively. Human Growth and Development and Career Development are mandatory in one program each. Social and Cultural Diversity is not a mandatory class in any of the 22 programs. One of the major factors influencing the curricula of Taiwanese counseling programs is the required domains for the licensure exam. There are six domains on the National Counseling Psychologist Exam, but these domains are not as extensive as those required by CACREP. The six domains are (a) Human Growth and Development, (b) Counseling Theories, (c) Helping Skills and Ethics, (d) Group Counseling, (e) Assessment, and (f) Mental Health and Abnormal Behaviors (Taiwan Guidance and Counseling Association, 2008). CACREP areas not required by Taiwan's national licensure exam are Social and Cultural Diversity; Career Development; and, most interesting, Research and Program Evaluation, the only course that is required by all master's programs in Taiwan. The exam requirements appear to direct most but not all curricula and course offerings in Taiwan's universities.

Diversity Issues

Taiwan is quick to embrace influences from numerous cultures around the globe. Diverse counseling specialties in Western cultures have migrated into the practice of professional counseling in Taiwan. The visibility of these specialties, such as psychodrama and art therapy, is enhanced through Taiwan's professional counseling associations. An online search results in a list of major counseling associations in Taiwan. This list illustrates the connection between the counseling profession in Taiwan and the global counseling movement:

- Association of Couple and Family Therapy in Taiwan
- Association for Taiwan Play Therapy
- Chinese Association of Group Psychotherapy
- Formosa Animal-Assisted Activity & Therapy Association
- Guidance Teacher Association
- Mental Health Association Taiwan
- Taiwan Adventure-Learning-Development Association *(adventure therapy)*
- Taiwan Art Therapy Association
- Taiwan Center for the Development of Psychoanalysis
- Taiwan Community Counseling Association
- Taiwan Counseling Psychology Association
- Taiwan Dance Therapy Association
- Taiwan Green Life Association *(horticultural therapy)*

- Taiwan Guidance and Counseling Association
- Taiwan Marriage and Family Counseling Association
- Taiwan Psychodrama Association
- Taiwanese Psychological Association
- Taiwanese Sandplay Therapy Association

This list shows that diverse forms of clinical practice in counseling have blossomed in Taiwan. The inclusion of different counseling techniques will surely enrich the quality of counseling services in Taiwan and provide a solid foundation for the further development of professional counseling in Taiwan.

Multicultural Counseling

As a multicultural and multiracial country, Taiwan has a rich and diverse cultural heritage. It is thus surprising that multicultural competency training is not mandated in either undergraduate or graduate counselor training programs in Taiwan. Liu (2006) studied counselor training curricula and publication records and concluded that counselor training in Taiwan does not emphasize multicultural counseling courses. In addition, there is a lack of scholarly publications in Taiwan devoted to multicultural issues. Given Taiwan's multicultural population, training in multicultural competency needs a significantly greater emphasis (Liu, 2006).

Taiwan's traditional cultures do influence the counseling profession. Counseling practitioners in Taiwan have explored the roles and functions of native cultures (e.g., philosophy and religion) in counseling practices (Huang, Kao, & Lia, 2008). Nonetheless, research and training efforts should provide a more global approach to the development of multicultural counseling competencies for professional counseling in Taiwan (Liu, 2006).

The Future

With the constant changes in Taiwanese society, there is a great demand for the expertise possessed by professional counselors. From 1976 to 2009, the suicide rate in Taiwan climbed as high as 19.30 per 100,000 persons (Tsai & Cho, 2011). New cultural phenomena, such as transnational marriage (Shu, Lung, & Chen, 2011), have raised complicated mental health issues for individuals, families, and schools. The recent revision of the Psychiatric Law (Department of Health, 2007) and a new mental health policy guide (Department of Health, 2010) clearly indicate the importance of professional counseling to treat and prevent mental disorders. It is obvious that professional counseling must play a new and more prominent role in Taiwan's future.

However, as an emerging profession in Taiwan, professional counseling is still in its infancy. With licensure legislation, Taiwanese counselors and counselor preparation programs now have the capability to solidify a professional identity and to define the perimeters of counseling practice. Mental health counselors are now credible service providers. School counselors continue to develop within the educational system but face potential threats of position cuts due to policy changes, budget shortages, and legislative revisions (W.-Y. Lin, 2004; C.-H. Wang, 2006). Both school and mental health counselors still have significant challenges to face in the future.

Given the increasingly complex mental health needs in schools and society, professional counseling must continue to grow in Taiwan. This will necessitate a continuing emphasis on mental health legislation to shape and guide counseling services to provide better mental health care to the Taiwanese people.

References

Chang, L.-F. (2006). 我國中小學輔導工作的回顧與前瞻 [The development of middle and elementary school guidance in Taiwan]. 現代教育論壇, *15*, 17–35.

Chen, P.-W. (1999). 邁向專業-台灣輔導界發展的回顧與前瞻 [Towards professionalism: The development of counseling in Taiwan]. *Asian Journal of Counselling*, *6*(2), 21–46.

Department of Guidance and Counseling. (2004). 本系簡介 [Introduction to the department]. Retrieved from http://gc.ncue.edu.tw/guide.html

Department of Health. (1990). 心理衛生法 [Psychiatric Law]. Retrieved from http://www.customs.org.tw/56.24.10.htm

Department of Health. (2007). 心理衛生法 [Psychiatric Law]. Retrieved from http://dohlaw.doh.gov.tw/Chi/FLAW/FLAWDAT10.asp

Department of Health. (2010). 精神醫療及心理衛生政策綱領 [Psychiatric treatment and mental health guiding policy]. Retrieved from http://dohlaw.doh.gov.tw/Chi/FLAW/FLAWDAT0202.asp

Department of Health. (2011). 行政院衛生署醫院管理委員會 組織架構圖 [Organizational chart of Hospital Management Committee, Department of Health, Executive Yuan]. Retrieved from http://www.cto.doh.gov.tw/hospital/

Guan, W.-Y., Chan, W.-S., Zhang, M.-S., & Lin, C.-C. (2011, January 13). 杜絕校園霸凌增聘2221位輔導人員 [Preventing bullying in schools: 2221 guidance counselors will be recruited]. *The China Times*. Retrieved from http://life.chinatimes.com/life/11051801/112011011300045.html

Hu, Z.-S., Lee, L.-W, Ting, H., Zhou, Z.-T., & Hong, W.-T. (2009). From mobilization to rehabilitation: A record of military mental health workers participate in "88 flood" rescue mission. 復興岡學報, *96*, 1–28.

Huang, F.-C., Kao, S.-R., & Lia, S.-Y. (2008). 一位諮商師在諮商與禪修中的自我成長經驗 [A counselor's self-growth process through counseling and Zazen]. 輔導與諮商學報, *30*(2), 37–62.

Laws & Regulations Database of the Republic of China. (2001). 心理師法 [Psychologist Law]. Retrieved from http://law.moj.gov.tw/LawClass/LawAll.aspx?PCode=L0020098

Lin, J. C. H. (2000). A comparative study on title preference, work settings, and direct services time of mental health professionals. *Bulletin of Educational Psychology*, *32*(1), 1–14.

Lin, J. C. H., & Hung, Y. C. (2002). Professional counselors as guidance service providers in junior high schools in Taiwan. *Bulletin of Educational Psychology*, *34*(1), 83–102.

Lin, W.-Y. (2004). 我國學校輔導團隊工作的建制 [The team work construction of Taiwan school guidance]. 現代教育論壇, *13*, 62–77.

Liu, A. (2006). 諮商師訓練的新挑戰-論多元文化諮商能力與訓練 [Multicultural counseling competencies and counselor training—New challenges for counselor training]. 弘光人文社會學報, *4*, 167–185.

Ministry of Education. (2003). 國民中小學九年一貫課程綱要綜合活動學習領域 [Elementary and junior high school nine year core curriculum standards in integrative activities]. Taipei City, Taiwan: Author.

Ministry of Education. (2011). 國民小學與國民中學班級編制及教職員員額編制準則 [Guidelines for classroom sizes and employee numbers in public elementary and middle schools]. Retrieved from http://edu.law.moe.gov.tw/LawContentDetails.aspx?id=FL008932&KeyWordHL=&StyleType=1

Qiu, Y.-L. (2011, January 12). 61班以上學校設專業輔導員 預計今三讀 [Third congressional vote today on "schools with more than 61 classes to add professional counselors"]. *The Liberty Times*. Retrieved from http://www.libertytimes.com.tw/2011/new/jan/12/today-life12.htm

Shu, B.-C., Lung, F.-W., & Chen, C.-H. (2011). Mental health of female foreign spouses in transnational marriages in southern Taiwan. *BMC Psychiatry*, *11*(4), 1–9. doi:10.1186/1471-224X-11-4

Taiwan Guidance and Counseling Association. (2008). 專門職業及技術人員高等考試 諮商心理師考試各應試科目命題大綱暨參考用書 [Counseling Psychologist National Exam: Content areas and study book lists]. Retrieved from http://www.guidance.org.tw/Counseling Psychologist/study_book.pdf

Taiwan Lifeline International. (2011). 本會簡介 [About Taiwan Lifeline International]. Retrieved from http://www.life1995.org.tw/content.asp?id=14

Teacher Chang Foundation. (2011). 認識張老師 [About Teacher Chang]. Retrieved from http://www.1980.org.tw/web3-20101110/about_us.html

Tsai, J.-F., & Cho, W. C. (2011). The secular trend of suicide rate and the socio-economic, media, and climatic factors in Taiwan, 1976-2009: A population-based study. *Journal of Affective Disorders, 129*, 270–274. doi:10.1016/j.jad.2010.08.008

Wang, C.-H. (2006). 從全國輔導教師協會的籌設談學校輔導工作的出路與挑戰 [From the preparation of Guidance Teacher Association to the discussion of the future and challenges of school guidance work]. 台灣心理諮商通訊電子報*, 182*. Retrieved from http://www.heart.net.tw/mainarticle/182-1.htm

Wang, S. (2006). From "support" to "resistance": On my changing positions regarding the licentiation of counseling psychologists. *Research in Applied Psychology, 30*, 21–36.

Wu, W.-T. (1993). Counselling and guidance in the twentieth century: The Taiwan experience. *Asian Journal of Counselling, 2*(1), 1–6.

• • •

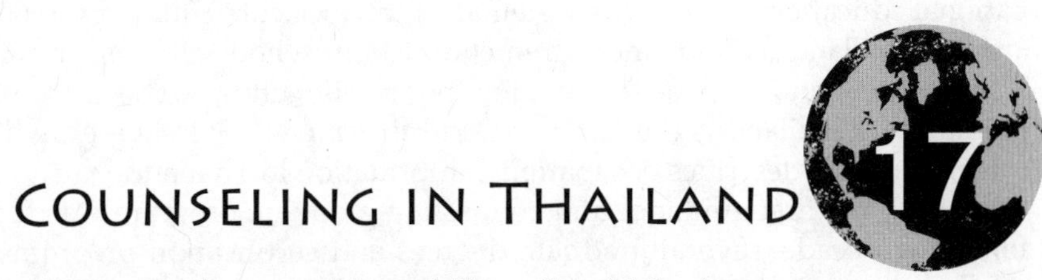

Counseling in Thailand

Varunee Faii Sangganjanavanich and Kannikar Nolrajsuwat

The Kingdom of Thailand, formerly known as Siam, is an independent country located in the center of Southeast Asia. Although Thailand's history spans more than 750 years, counseling is a relatively new profession. The purpose of this chapter is to describe historical perspectives, the current status, and future directions of the counseling profession in Thailand. The chapter also provides information regarding counselor education, counseling practice, and diversity issues in Thailand.

The Historical Development of Counseling

Thailand is a collectivist society where individuals value group and community engagement as well as family influence rather than a personal agenda. Families influence the major life decisions of individuals, including career development. Consequently, individuals either choose their careers based on the decisions of their families or parents or adopt traditional careers that have been in their families for generations. It is important for individuals to carry on family heritage and pride. Thus, the beginning of counseling in Thailand focused on career development rather than mental health issues.

In 1912, the Department of Education began to examine the career choices of young persons. The Department of Education suggested that school personnel encourage students to make career decisions based on their interests and abilities rather than choose careers based on family influence or follow in their parents' footsteps (Supmee, 1987). In 1948, the Department of Education made a concerted effort to collaborate with parents and families in order to provide guidance regarding the education and occupations of their children. However, individuals' career choices continued to be guided by their parents and families, according to societal norms. Several years later, the Department of Education increased its efforts to address career development issues among youth by creating the Educational and Vocational Guidance Subdivision to actively promote public understanding of education and to provide direct guidance to young individuals regarding college. Despite the ongoing and proactive effort to access young individuals directly through these initiatives, cultural expectations (e.g., that children pursue careers that are similar to their parents') continued to influence youth's career development, and young people continued to conform to their parents' guidance (Thipkrita, 2011). In addition, to address the career development needs of college students and graduates, the Division of Vocational Education established the Workforce Development Bureau in 1948. The purpose of the Workforce Development Bureau is (a) to provide educational and vocational guidance for the college student population through the use of vocational assessments and (b) to assist with job placement for college students and graduates.

In 1953, the first guidance program was created in public schools to assist middle and high school students in selecting careers based on their interests (Supmee, 1987). The Department of Education continued to develop multiple infrastructures to support an ongoing demand for guidance in school, such as training programs for guidance counselors, national education units, and a systematic guidance curriculum. By 1960, vocational guidance in Thailand had advanced tremendously in school settings, and the Department of Education expanded those services to other public settings. The cornerstone of vocational guidance in Thailand is the *National Occupational Outlook Handbook,* which systematically categorizes and describes occupational information in Thailand.

In 1961, the first guidance and counseling graduate program was founded, and in the following decade, several graduate degrees and certification programs in guidance and counseling were developed and expanded to cope with the increasing demand for guidance counselors in schools. However, several challenges came about as a result of this mass production. Guidance counselors who participated in brief certification programs (i.e., 3-month training) were not well trained in the counseling philosophy and process. Consequently, guidance counseling in school emphasized vocational concerns and academic advising rather than self-exploration and decision making. Toward the end of the 1980s, counseling services in schools began to expand, focusing on vocational and educational issues to address personal and social aspects of the students' lives. This expansion was not limited to the school setting but occurred in other settings such as colleges and hospitals as well.

A turning point in the development of the counseling profession in Thailand was the period of globalization in the late 1990s that highlighted the need for mental health services. Instant cultural changes as a result of economic and technological factors forced the Thai population to trade their simpler way of being for a faster and more competitive lifestyle. These changes produced social problems in Thailand, including chronic stress and addictions in adults and behavioral problems in children. As a result, educational institutions started to systematically produce counselors to serve the needs of the population.

The Current Status of Counseling

According to the Thai National Statistics Office (2011), 17.8% of the Thai population between the ages of 15 and 59 years old and 21.4% of the Thai population aged 60 or older report having mental disorders. A study conducted by the Thai Department of Mental Heath indicated that major sources of stress include financial difficulties, family relationships, employment, and politics (Ussavasodhi, 2011). Despite the increasing numbers of mental health concerns, there are no statistics of the number of mental health professionals in the country. In addition, the number of professional counselors in Thailand remains uncertain because of the continuing development of a counseling identity. It is important to note that the Thai government does not recognize the job title *counselor* (Scorzelli & Reinke-Scorzelli, 2001). The counseling profession operates from the interconnectedness among counselors and other related helping professionals, such as social workers and psychologists, who are more visible to the public. Although joining forces with other helping professionals gives counselors more opportunities for employment, they also face a difficult time differentiating themselves from other professionals. A majority of counselors in social agencies are trained in clinical psychology, counseling psychology, and social work. This has led to the undefined professional identity of counselors and underdeveloped professional counseling credentials, including training, certifications, and licensures. Currently there is no professional counseling association or standards to ensure the quality of counseling services.

Counseling in Various Settings

Definitions of counseling services vary from setting to setting. The main focus of school counselors is career exploration, academic concerns, and student behavioral issues. In the past, the majority of school counselors did not have a degree in school counseling and instead received only basic professional training related to student development and career guidance. However, newer generations of school counselors are required to have a postgraduate education that relates to counseling.

Various types of counseling are offered in social agencies, including addiction counseling, marriage and family counseling, and group counseling. Addiction counseling (i.e., counseling for substance abuse and dependence, pathological gambling) seems to be more systematic than counseling in other areas (i.e., career counseling, marriage and family counseling). In addiction counseling, counselors serve as part of a multidisciplinary team to help individuals who experience addictions (Tuicomepee & Romano, 2005). Inpatient and outpatient treatment and recovery centers exist throughout the country to treat many kinds of addictions.

Marriage and family counseling, including counseling children and adolescents, is reserved for psychiatrists and is generally conducted in hospital settings. It is important to note that the general population's knowledge about marriage and family counseling is limited. This may be influenced by Thai cultural belief. Because they believe that the family is a sacred unit, Thai individuals do not seek family counseling when they encounter family conflicts.

Group counseling is primarily utilized as a form of crisis intervention, for example helping women who are experiencing sexual abuse and unwanted pregnancy or relieving distress from natural disasters. In Thailand, group counseling is generally provided by counselors and social workers in public organizations (e.g., the Thai Red Cross) and private foundations (e.g., religious organizations). Recently, the Thai Ministry of Health expanded the reach of crisis counseling by implementing hotlines not only to support individuals with suicidal ideation but also to assist people facing psychological concerns.

Counselors in private practice settings generally serve as consultants to business organizations and schools. They provide education and trainings in areas such as team building, emotion management, and stress reduction. Because there are no guidelines or standards for practice and no licensing boards to govern counselors, individuals in private practice are viewed as educators or trainers rather than counselors.

Counseling's Relationship With Other Related Professions

Like in the United States, the fields of counseling, psychology, and social work share some similar characteristics and work settings. As a result, the roles of counselors, psychologists, and social workers in helping individuals are often difficult to differentiate. Social workers tend to have the most privilege in terms of employment opportunities and recognition from the public (Mongkolnchaiarunya, 2009). Social workers hold positions in such diverse settings such as hospitals and community agencies; a majority of these settings are nonprofit organizations such as the Thai Red Cross and public hospitals.

Currently the counseling profession is not well known to the Thai population, and the counselors remain somewhat invisible compared to other closely related professionals. For instance, it is rare that organizations call workers in these positions "counselors." Individuals who have counseling degrees are employed as social workers, case managers, and psychologists because these titles are better known to the public.

It is important to note that despite more than a decade of effort, the counseling, psychology, and social work professions have not yet established specific guidelines to govern licensure and credentialing. However, social work and psychology have established professional associations in Thailand, whereas there are no professional counseling organizations. Social workers have two main professional organizations: the National Council for Social Welfare of Thailand and the Social Workers Association of Thailand (Mongkolnchaiarunya, 2009). Psychologists have also developed a professional association, the Thai Psychological Association, which is listed in the American Psychological Association (2010) directory of national associations of psychology.

Best Counseling Practices

Similar to the general counseling process in the United States, the counseling process in Thailand begins by attending to the client's concerns and helping the client develop counseling goals and use microskills (i.e., listening, reflecting on content and feelings, summarizing) to facilitate his or her self-understanding and self-exploration. General assessments used by counselors include career and personality inventories and adjustment questionnaires that are available in the Thai language. Because there are no regulations and guidelines for practitioners in terms of administering and interpreting assessments, counselors trained in specific assessments can function independently without supervision from psychologists or psychiatrists.

Schools in Thailand do not tailor their programs to a particular theoretical orientation. Instead, counselor education programs focus on preparing counselors-in-training to be knowledgeable of all major approaches. Various theoretical approaches are used by individual counselors, including logotherapy, reality therapy, behavior therapy, cognitive therapy, and person-centered therapy. These approaches are adjusted to fit the Thai cultural context, which is greatly influenced by Buddhism. Scholars have speculated how different theoretical orientations align with the Thai culture. Scorzelli and Reinke-Scorzelli (2001) noted that cognitive approaches are suitable for use in the Thai culture because these approaches emphasize the importance of the here and now as well as suffering from one's own thought. Person-centered approaches are widely used by Thai practitioners because of their focus on humanism. Supmee (2011) believed that core conditions of growth, especially unconditional positive regard, fit well with the Thai cultural belief of accepting individuals as they are. This approach has been a central focus in counselor education in Thailand for decades.

The mindfulness-based approach also appears in the practice of many counselors in various settings and counselor training programs. Although there is no evidence indicating the reason for the popularity of this approach, it could be that the principles and practice of mindfulness align with Eastern and Buddhist philosophy, which is a powerful force in Thai society. Scholars have conducted research to examine the efficacy and effectiveness of Buddhist mindfulness interventions in counseling. For example, in a quasi-experimental study Disayavanish (2000) investigated the effect of insight meditation on personality and emotional quotient development. Extraversion–introversion, emotional stability, creativity, and strong-mindedness were examined before and after participants engaged in a 7-day intensive training on insight meditation. The findings indicated that after the training on insight meditation, participants scored higher in the domains of emotional stability and creativity ($p < .05$); however, levels of extraversion–introversion and strong-mindedness remained unchanged. A similar study conducted by Disayavanish (2001) indicated that mindfulness and clear comprehension derived from insight meditation practice helped reduce psychological complaints, such as somatic symptoms, anxiety, and insomnia. Disayavanish (2001) concluded that insight meditation training was an effective method for coping and promoting mental health.

Although expressive therapies such as art therapy and psychodrama have been introduced into the field of counseling in Thailand, the utility of these approaches is still limited. Like many Eastern societies, the Thai culture is nonexpressive in nature, and individuals refrain from being expressive with those they do not know well in order to remain polite and appropriate. In addition, training in these approaches is not available in Thailand, which challenges the advancement of these alternative methods in the field of professional counseling.

Diversity Issues

The population of Thailand is relatively homogenous in terms of ethnic and religious background. That is, 75% of the population is Thai, 14% has a Chinese background, and 11% of the population is made up of various tribes (Central Intelligence Agency, 2010). Some of these tribes have their roots in and are still well connected to nearby countries such as Burma, Cambodia, and Laos. Because these populations generally reside in remote areas, many social services, including counseling, are inaccessible to them. Although migrant individuals living in major cities have much more of an opportunity to access counseling services, they do not legally qualify for health care resources. As a result, tribal residents and immigrants continue to be underserved in Thailand.

Recent immigration issues have brought complexities to Thai society. Thai counselors are forced to attend to diversity issues and to acclimate to a multicultural counseling practice. Much of this attention is directed to religious groups in southern Thailand. Thailand is a Buddhist country: Approximately 94% of the Thai population is Buddhist; 5% is Muslim; and 1% identifies with other religious beliefs, including Christianity (Central Intelligence Agency, 2010). Although there are some variations in the Buddhism practiced in different regions in Thailand (i.e., northeastern versus central Thailand), the differences are minute. Other religious groups play less of a role in Thai society. Islamic groups demonstrate acculturation issues due to their different religious beliefs, dialects, and lifestyles. Kammayee and Nolrajsuwat (2010) found that college students who came from an Islamic culture encountered unique adjustment issues compared to students who were Buddhist. Islamic students found it difficult to adjust to a mainstream education system that did not integrate their religious belief into the curriculum and a college environment that did not facilitate expression of their religious and political beliefs.

Regardless of their religious beliefs, the majority of the Thai population practice various forms of indigenous healing (e.g., fortune telling, psychic readings, prayer, and magical spells) that have long been a part of Thai culture. Psychological difficulties are viewed as a life challenge that can be cured through integration of the mind, body, and spirit. A majority of individuals, particularly adults and older adults, rely on these indigenous methods rather than contemporary or Western mental health practices to relieve their psychological distress (Sakul-ariya & Nolrajsuwat, 2010). In addition, like many developing countries, Thailand has a wide social gap between privileged and socioeconomically disadvantaged individuals. People who have few resources to cope with psychological difficulties are forced to rely on traditional methods of healing because these are the only options available to them. This dynamic delays the development of the counseling profession among underserved populations in Thailand.

Counselor Education

As of 2012, a total of 23 institutions in Thailand offer degrees in psychology; of these, six offer graduate-level counseling programs, whereas only three provide doctoral-level training. These programs, which often represent a combination of counseling psychology and counseling, are training practitioners to respond to greater demand for counselors in Thailand.

The curricular requirements of Thai counselor training programs are comparable to standards utilized in the United States. There are eight core areas (i.e., professional orientation and ethical practice, social and cultural diversity, human growth and development, career development, helping relationships, group work, assessment, and research and program evaluation) as well as similar practicum and internship experiences to those identified by the Council for Accreditation of Counseling and Related Educational Programs. However, because counseling programs are generally housed in psychology departments, the professional identity of counselors remains unclear. In addition, no national standards or accrediting bodies govern the counselor education curriculum. To address this challenge, Thai counselor educators adopt Western standards of counselor training, because a majority of counselor educators are trained abroad (i.e., in the United States or United Kingdom). Consequently, the direction of counselor education and training continues to be questionable.

Despite the fact that institutions do not use the word *counselor* in their positions, the demand for counseling graduates is apparent, as evidenced by the increase in counselor education programs in Thailand since the beginning of the 21st century. Responding to this growth will require some counselor education programs to integrate technology to expand their programs, for example, by using satellite campuses to train counselors in remote areas of the country.

The Future

The increasing diversity in Thai society requires counselors to possess multicultural counseling competencies in order to effectively serve people from various cultural backgrounds. More integrative counseling approaches and interventions that incorporate both local (e.g., Eastern philosophy, indigenous healing) and global (e.g., standards of practice, quality assurance) wisdom need to be developed and examined. These innovative approaches may have a better fit with Thai culture. In addition, more research on evidence-based practice needs to be conducted. This initiative in turn may assist counselors in distinguishing themselves from other mental health professionals.

Overall, the mental health system in Thailand is still developing. There is a lack of infrastructure to ensure the professional standards of mental health practice (except psychiatry). Tantiphlachiva (2002) noted the importance of creating mental health laws in Thailand. Although current mental health practice is performed by qualified mental health professionals, there are no mental health laws to support some practices, such as involuntary admission and treatment, which puts mental health practitioners at risk for lawsuits and malpractice. Tantiphlachiva commented that advocacy for mental health laws at the legislative level is not likely to happen unless there is a sense of urgency among Thai mental health practitioners that remains lacking. Therefore, it is essential that counselors build a collaborative relationship with other mental health professionals in Thailand. Establishing alliances to collectively improve the infrastructure for mental health practice, including counseling, is a crucial task.

Although Thai professional counselors have made an effort to develop a clear professional identity for the profession, more efforts are needed among other related mental health professionals. Although psychologists and social workers are also developing credentialing systems and standards of practice, in some ways they are more advanced than counselors. For example, those professions have well-established professional associations and journals (e.g., the *Thai Psychological Association Journal*). Professional counselors need to actively promote the uniqueness of their services and differentiate themselves from other closely related professionals.

To advance the counseling profession, the professional identity of counselors needs to be strengthened. First, establishing a council of accreditation and national standards for counselor education programs is essential to fostering professional identity for counselors-in-training. The increase in the number of graduate training programs bodes well for the counseling profession. Although consistent counselor education standards and curricular experiences are needed, promoting these continues to be a challenge for counselor educators in Thailand. Second, professional licensures and certifications are critical to developing the credibility and accountability of the counseling profession. Introducing and reintroducing the counseling profession to consumers may promote understanding of counseling, and counselors may ultimately become accepted in Thai society. Lastly, counseling professional associations are important for establishing professional uniqueness, engaging in collective bargaining (e.g., lobbying and policy making), advocating for the profession, and delineating the roles and functions of Thai counselors.

References

American Psychological Association. (2010). *Directory of national associations of psychology.* Retrieved from http://www.apa.org/international/directories/national-orgs.aspx

Central Intelligence Agency. (2010). *The world factbook.* Retrieved from https://www.cia.gov/library/publications/the-world-factbook/geos/th.html

Disayavanish, P. (2000). The effect of insight meditation practice on personality and emotional quotient. *Journal of the Psychiatric Association of Thailand, 46,* 195–207.

Disayavanish, P. (2001). Mental health and the practice of insight meditation. *Journal of Clinical Psychology, 32,* 28–42.

Kammayee, R., & Nolrajsuwat, K. (2010, March). *Cultural adjustment of university students from three southern border provinces of Thailand.* Paper presented at the National Graduate Research Conference, Chiang Mai, Thailand.

Mongkolnchaiarunya, J. (2009, April). *Social work education and profession in Thailand: Sunrise or sunset.* Paper presented at the Seoul International Social Work Conference, Seoul, South Korea.

Sakul-ariya, R., & Nolrajsuwat, K. (2010, March). *Fortunetelling and psychological helping process.* Paper presented at the National Graduate Research Conference, Chiang Mai, Thailand.

Scorzelli, J. F., & Reinke-Scorzelli, M. (2001). Cultural sensitivity and cognitive therapy in Thailand. *Journal of Mental Health Counseling, 23,* 85–92.

Supmee, W. (1987). การแนะแนวในโรงเรียน [School counseling in Thailand (3rd ed.)]. Bangkok, Thailand: Thai Watana Panich Printing.

Supmee, W. (2011). ทฤษฎีให้บริการปรึกษา [Counseling theories (6th ed.)]. Bangkok, Thailand: Chulalongkorn University.

Tantiphlachiva, K. (2002). Mental health laws–Are they vital? Perspectives from Thailand. *Journal of the Psychiatric Association of Thailand, 47,* 281–286.

Thai National Statistics Office. (2011). *Mental health condition in Thailand.* Retrieved from http://web.nso.go.th/

Thipkrita, T. (2011). ครูแนะแนวภาคปฏิบัติ: ประสบการณ์จริงที่มากกว่าทฤษฎี [School counselors in practice: Experiences matter more than theories]. Bangkok, Thailand: Kid Dee Mee Dee Printing.

Tuicomepee, A., & Romano, J. L. (2005). Psychological well-being of Thai drug users. *International Journal for the Advancement of Counselling, 27,* 431–444.

Ussavasodhi, S. (2011, July 3). Stress level declining from recent years. *Siam Daily News.* Retrieved from http://siamdailynews.com/healthnews/2011/07/03/stress-level-declining-from-recent-years/

• • •

Counseling in European Countries

Counseling in The Czech Republic 18

Jack D. Simons and Alexandra Durcikova

The Czech Republic, a country about the size of South Carolina, is landlocked in central Europe. It is composed of two areas: Bohemia in the west and Moravia in the east. Its population of 10.2 million declined by 0.13% in 2011 (Central Intelligence Agency, 2010). The Czech people are considered independent, entrepreneurial, hardworking, and peaceful. They have found success in many ways. Former Czech president Vaclav Klaus was appointed head of the European Union (EU), and in 2011 Petra Kvitová became the Wimbledon women's tennis champion.

The Czech Republic was established on January 1, 1993, after a peaceful split from Slovakia, thus dissolving Czechoslovakia, which had been formed in 1918 (Hoskovec, 2004). In 1948, after World War II, Czechoslovakia became a communist country in the Eastern bloc, and later it was occupied by Russia from 1968 until 1989 (Willems, 2008). In November 1989, Czechoslovakia became a democracy through the Velvet Revolution, which coincided with the fall of the Berlin Wall. Czechoslovakia was a premier country in Europe and an economic and industry leader prior to World War II. However, communism completely stopped the advancement of industry. Since the fall of communism, the Czech Republic has become a stable developed country. This shows the resiliency of the Czechs.

Psychology has a long history in the Czech Republic. In fact, the first president of Czechoslovakia, Thomas Garrigue Masaryk, was a professor of psychology (Brožek & Hoskovec, 1995). However, the discipline was oppressed during the communist period. According to Plháková (2008), Gestalt psychology vanished during the 1950s because it interfered with Marxist ideology. It also conflicted with Pavlov's work, which had become the dominant theory in the Czech Republic. During this era, psychology and the Western influence were rejected. Nevertheless, the 50 years of oppression did not prevent the continued evolution of psychology and counseling.

Both marriage counseling and career counseling have existed for years in the Czech Republic (Brožek & Hoskovec, 1998; Kopp, 1938; Novak, 2006), and today academic counseling is common. Counselors working in all of these areas typically have master's degrees in psychology, unless they are former teachers who have taken additional courses to become school counselors. Sigmund Freud, the Father of Psychoanalysis, and Max Wertheimer, the

Father of Gestalt Therapy, were born in the Czech region, and books have been published about them and other Czech psychologists. There is potential for continued emergence of the counseling field in this country with strong psychological roots. Incidentally, counseling is the second largest division of the Czech Moravian Psychological Society. The present chapter is organized as follows. The first section focuses on the current status of counseling in the Czech Republic, whereas the second focuses on best counseling practices. The third addresses diversity. The fourth deals with counselor education and training, and the fifth discusses the future of counseling.

The Current Status of Counseling

The Ministry of Labor and Social Affairs (www.mpsv.cz) and the Ministry of Education, Youth, and Sports (www.msmt.cz) are government agencies that regulate counseling in the Czech Republic (Organisation for Economic Co-operation and Development, 2003). The role of counselors is explained in three governmental decrees that established the role of counseling in primary schools in 1962 and in secondary schools during the 1970s and 1980s (Majer, 2006). Decree No. 72/2005 specifies the role of counselors in school settings.

School Counseling

In 2004, Czech politicians enacted the Czech Education Act to keep the nation's educational system current with EU standards and move Czech education away from task achievement (e.g., rote memorization) toward creative and independent student interaction. The pedagogical model adopted during the communist period suggested that the teacher had all of the knowledge and would deposit it directly into the minds of the students. Student discussion and exploration of new ideas was downplayed. The new education act made radical changes by giving teachers more freedom to develop their own curricula so that students could use and apply the knowledge they acquired in school. What is surprising is that this new act encountered community resistance (Hraba, Mullick, Lorenz, Ve erník, & McCutcheon, 2002; Rosolová, 2009). Some believed that the new model was the result of a desire to keep up with American fads. The new approach to educating students in the Czech Republic appears revolutionary to some, although the same ideas had been proposed by Moravian pedagogical pioneer Jan Amos Komenský, the Teacher of Nations, 400 years before. To this day, Komenský's birthday (March 28) is celebrated as teacher's day. His work laid the foundation for the Czech Republic to develop some of the most respectable preschool programs in the world. Teachers use interactive learning techniques called *škola hrou,* which is learning through playing, a concept now being introduced to older students through the Czech Education Act. Because of this revitalization of Komenský's teachings for use beyond preschool, the Czech government is encouraging more school counseling services.

Decree No. 72/2005, which was passed in 2005, authorized more than 50 schools with more than 500 students each to hire counselors. There are now more than 200 school counselors providing services to students (Lazarová, 2008). This initiative progressed until the recent global economic crisis restricted the flow of money to education and has since slowed down. In addition, it has been challenging for principals to hire school psychologists because the only document that describes counseling services in schools, Decree No. 72/2005, does not address psychologists. No other decree or law discusses the job description of school psychologists (Zapletalová, 2002).

School Psychologists

An estimated 100 to 120 school psychologists are employed in Czech schools (Union of Psychologists Associations in the Czech Republic, 2011). An exact estimate is difficult to obtain because school principals employ psychologists under different classification titles and pay them differently (e.g., through EU grants). The absence of a concise legislative definition of the role of school psychologists worries principals. Principals run the risk of breaching legislation if they acknowledge employing school psychologists. The goal of school psychologists is to attend to the needs of students, faculty, and parents or guardians. They provide consultation, guidance and support for youth, and assistance in communicating with the school. Students present with personal problems (e.g., problems with learning or relationships), and psychologists may provide crisis intervention if needed. Moreover, they provide classroom guidance lessons.

School Counselors

School counselors work in primary, secondary, and technical schools. Unlike psychologists, school counselors are teachers with additional training. They fulfill their responsibilities as school counselors on top of their teaching responsibilities. School counselors provide career counseling, assist with educational problems (e.g., learning disabilities), and offer advice on developmental learning disorders. They are also responsible for developing and/or supporting substance abuse prevention programs and assisting students who present with pathology. Particular attention is given to students with disabilities, those who are gifted, and those who are socially disadvantaged (e.g., Romany [Gypsies]).

School Counseling Centers

According to Základni škola za Alejí (2011), school counseling centers have been established in accordance with Decree No. 72/2005. These centers offer assistance in managing and resolving educational, social, and learning difficulties. They employ various people, including school psychologists, school counselors, and prevention specialists (e.g., alcohol, drugs). Staff who work in these centers (a) assist students with special education needs, including those who are gifted; (b) advise and consult with students, parents, and teachers about mental health issues; (c) help ensure the academic success of all students; (d) develop prevention programs that will limit behavioral problems among students; (e) provide educational activities for faculty members and parents; (f) offer career counseling; and (g) consult with parents. Other services such as conflict mediation and stress management may also be provided (Linares, Díaz, del Carmen Pérez Fuentes, & Acién, 2009).

College Counseling

By 2003, there were 48 college counseling centers in the Czech Republic. Prior to that time it was not common to offer counseling services at universities (National Training Fund and the National Resource Centre for Vocational Guidance, 2003). Counselors working in college counseling centers began to consult with their counterparts in other EU countries. What resulted was the establishment of eight models of college counseling used in centers in the Czech Republic. According to Freibergova (2010), they are (a) the professional orientation model, which pertains to career development; (b) the personal services model, which pertains to personal issues; (c) the academic issues model, which pertains to advocacy; (d) the psychotherapeutic model, which pertains to mental health issues; (e) the training model, which pertains to counselor education; (f) the consultation model, which pertains to community-based outreach; (g) the research model, which pertains to counselor effectiveness; and (h) the guidance model, which pertains to integrating several of the models.

According to Freibergova (2010), the core counseling services offered at universities fall into four categories: (a) university applicants, especially those not admitted to state-funded institutions, are provided with information on scholarships and loans; (b) clients in all academic programs are provided with academic support, which may include referral; (c) clients receive career counseling services; and (d) clients receive additional support if they are unemployed. Those who provide career counseling in college counseling centers typically first assess the strengths, interests, and values of clients. Then they interpret the assessments and provide occupational information. Next they explain the benefits of favorable occupations. After clients are acquainted with companies, counselors assist them in developing a job search strategy (e.g., developing a résumé, preparing for interviews, and applying for jobs).

Career Counseling

After the Berlin Wall came down in 1989, comprehensive career counseling services once more began to be provided in the Czech Republic. Today the Czech Ministry of Labor and Social Affairs regulates these services, which are offered to graduating students or adults in a period of job transition (Organisation for Economic Co-operation and Development, 2003). Unemployment has been decreasing and was around 8.2% in 2011 (Ministry of Labor and Social Affairs, 2011). Of all of the EU countries, only Austria, The Netherlands, Luxemburg, Malta, and Germany have lower rates of unemployment. Career counseling services are offered in government-funded employment centers by career counselors who have bachelor's or master's degrees in social work (Sociální Revue, 2011). These counselors assist clients by providing education and training related to particular careers, sharing employment opportunities, and encouraging clients to participate in job clubs and/or counseling groups. "Services build on the knowledge in psychology and sociology, as well as law, economics, pedagogy, and medicine" (National Training Fund and the National Resource Centre for Vocational Guidance, 2004, p. 25).

Private Practice

According to Zdravnet (2011), master's-level psychologists or psychiatrists with specialized training in psychotherapy work in private practice. The services they provide in person or online (e.g., through Skype) include behavior therapy, gestalt therapy, Jungian analysis, psychoanalysis, hypnotherapy, and family therapy. In this area of practice, the field of psychology in the Czech Republic is similar to the field of counseling in the United States, which also requires a master's degree. Psychologists who practice independently have completed master's degrees in psychology plus at least 5 years of additional training. Requirements vary with regard to the expectations of training sites and the specialization areas of students (e.g., Jungian, Gestalt).

Professional Associations

Professional counseling associations provide support, services, and resources to school counselors and psychologists. The Association of Educational Guidance Counselors (www.asociacevp.cz) is a nonprofit organization established in 2005 with 92 active members, most of whom are employed by trade schools. Other members work in elementary, middle, and high schools; colleges; and state-run institutions (e.g., unemployment offices). The School Psychology Association of the Czech and Slovak Republics (www.lfhk.cuni.cz) was established in 1990 and has 220 members. About 80% of the members have training in psychology. The Czech Moravian Psychological Society (www.cmps.ecn.cz) is a member organization of the International Union of Psychological Science. In 2007, the organization had 970 members. The organization endorses positive psychology and the science practitioner model. Another organization that provides resources to counselors is Euroguidance (www.euroguidance.net). Euroguidance provides a range of services to guidance professionals who assist individuals seeking international jobs within the EU. The European Forum for Student Guidance, known as FEDORA (www.fedora.eu.org), was founded in Greece in 1988 and provides resources to advisers who support European students who wish to study and work across

Europe. Eighty-three EU universities are members of FEDORA. The National Training Fund (www.nvf.cz) was founded in 1994 by the Department of Work and Social Affairs with the support of the EU. It is a wonderful resource for career counselors who assist clients seeking education and employment. This website offers information on employment trends, education and employment policies, and more. The Union of Psychologists Associations in the Czech Republic (www.upacr.cz) came into existence in 1995. It is an umbrella organization that has unified the Czech Moravian Psychological Society and other professional organizations for psychologists in the country. The aim is to develop a credentialing body for the profession to improve communication among members, protect the public, and give psychology a voice in the legislature. This movement is especially helpful for psychologists who work in schools because no specific policy guides their role.

Cultural Considerations

Knowledge of Czech geography, language, politics, and characteristics is key to understanding Czech culture. This awareness sets the stage for providing Czechs with effective counseling services. In comparison to other EU countries, the Czech Republic is highly homogeneous, and several waves of Czechs have immigrated to the United States. Although Czechs tend to be individualistic, they are known for keeping personal distress to themselves. Counselors should be patient in their efforts to understand clients' presenting problems.

Krestan and Gazarik (2005) have made several useful suggestions for non-Czech counselors helping Czech clients. First, Czechs are proud of their cultural and intellectual traditions, and counselors should acknowledge this. This respect is important to creating a trusting relationship. There is a saying that every Czech is a musician; therefore, counselors can enter the emotional life of a Czech client through discussions about music, dance, and theatre. Second, counselors should not confuse Czechs with other Eastern Europeans. For example, Czechs perceive themselves as more cultured than Slovaks, and they are not to be confused with Russians, who occupied their country for 20 years. Third, given that Czechs have a history of fighting religious wars and that 59% of the Czech population is not affiliated with any religious group (Central Intelligence Agency, 2010), counselors should explore family beliefs. According to Krestan and Gazarik, the way to do this is to introduce controversial topics and allow time for discussion of them. Fourth, counselors should approach therapy seriously. Education is important to Czechs (in fact, the country's first university was formed 600 years ago). Assignments and discussions of readings can be highly successful. Fifth, counselors should assess for alcoholism in the family.

Alcohol Use

In the Czech Republic, drinking alcohol is socially acceptable, and Czechs are some of the top consumers of alcohol in the world. Persistent problems with alcohol use were even noted by the first president of Czechoslovakia, Thomas Masaryk (Butora, 1995). In the communist period, problems with alcohol were downplayed, although the aim was to wipe it out. Data on use and abuse were nonexistent, and the price of beer remained unchanged for decades. This likely contributed to problems (e.g., ongoing substance use and abuse, job loss, marital discord and divorce), and it is anticipated that in the coming years there will be a new population of alcoholics. These will include Romany (Gypsies), middle-class abusers, and overworked managers. Counselors can play a role here by doing research, writing, and supporting self-help programs.

Best Counseling Practices

Psychological counseling has a long tradition in the Czech Republic (Brožek & Hoskovec, 1995). Many books have been written about Czech psychologists, and the writings of

Freud, Jung, Adler, Kohut, and Frankl have been published in the Czech language (Hoskovec, 2004). There is more English- and Czech-language literature on psychology in the Czech Republic than on any other mental health field. The main psychology journals are *Czechoslovak Psychology, Psychology for Practice, Czech Moravian Psychological Society Quarterly, Psychology Today,* and *Psychology and Psychopathology of the Child* (Hoskovec, 2004).

Psychoanalysis and Jungian Analysis

In 1932, the first edition of the *Czech Yearbook of Psychoanalysis* was published (Hoskovcová et al., 2010). Shortly thereafter, a related professional organization, the Czech Psychoanalytic Society (www.psychoanalyza.cz), was founded. Today it is a small professional organization with just 22 members and 10 trainers. What is interesting is that most of the members are psychiatrists. The work of Freud's junior partner, Swiss psychiatrist Carl Jung, has also become an area of specialization for Czech psychologists (V. Šolc, personal communication, October 15, 2010). A Czech version of the Myers–Briggs Type Indicator is available for use with Czech speakers (Hoskovec, 2004).

Gestalt Psychology

Max Wertheimer is one of the three founders of Gestalt psychology (King & Wertheimer, 2005). He was born April 15, 1880, in Prague, and he wrote about Jewish mental health after World War I. Wertheimer foresaw the escalation of Nazi persecution when Hitler came to power. The Czech people praised him for this, but he eventually fled the country after the Nazis invaded. Thereafter, behaviorism was preferred because of the Nazi movement (Plháková, 2008). Wertheimer died in America at 53. Sadly, he was unable to discuss his life's work in America because he did not speak English.

Diversity Issues

The first president of the Czech Republic after the fall of communism, Vaclav Havel, championed a multicultural society by saying

> I am in favor of political system based on the citizen, and recognizing all his fundamental civil and human rights in their universal validity, and equality applied, that is, no member of a single race, a single nation, a single sex, or a single religion, may be endowed with basic rights that are any different from anyone else's. (Havel, 1991, p. 49)

Havel set the stage for equality among people, but this is easier said than done.

Ethnic Issues

Romany (Gypsies) emigrated from India around the 11th century. The estimated 150,000 to 300,000 Romany in the Czech Republic account for about 3% of the population (Open Society Institute, 2001). The Czech educational system fails to create equal opportunities for all, and this has resulted in Romany students being underserved (Rosolová, 2009). The EU has mandated that its member nations better serve Romany.

The Romany community has been associated with incest, crime, and a lack of intelligence. The values of the Romany and Czechs have differed. This has caused tension between the two groups, and rather than try to understand the Romany culture, the Communist regime simply tried to wipe their culture out (Helsinki Watch, 1991). At one point, this tension resulted in Czech and Slovak doctors being accused of the illegal sterilization of Romany women (Silverman, 1995; Thomas, 2006). Many Romany would have children (whom they would later give up for adoption) in order to collect welfare. Ongoing discrimination of Romany people has continued in the Czech Republic (Simons, Hutchison, & Baštecká, 2012).

The Czech nation is highly homogeneous; however, this is changing because of participation in the EU. Immigrants, mainly from Poland, Russia, Slovakia, Ukraine, and Vietnam, have been moving to the Czech Republic in greater numbers. They account for roughly 4% of the population (Euroguidance, 2007). Because the Czech Republic has a long history of mass emigration, it has not been prepared for mass immigration. Consequently, funding for managing and treating individuals coming into the country has been limited. Immigrants, including refugees and asylum seekers, have had to wait long periods of time to have their status reviewed by Czech officials.

Counselor Education

Most Czech counselors, regardless of their specialty (e.g., academic, career, marriage and family counseling), have a master's degree in psychology (Hoskovcová et al., 2010). Universities offer bachelor's, master's, and doctoral degrees in psychology. The master's degree allows a person to practice psychological counseling. Classes required in the master's psychology program at Masaryk University in Brno include Qualitative Research Methods in Psychology, Introduction to Cognitive Science, Case Writing Seminar and Counseling Psychology, Work of the Psychologist in a Crisis Center for Children and Adolescents, The Psychopathology of Everyday Life, Clinical Psychology, Psychotherapy Today, Gestalt Therapy, Family Therapy, Methodologies in Psychology, Forensic and Police Psychology, Cognitive-Behavior Therapy, and Psychology of Religion. A short 5-day internship is also required. Students select an area of specialization (i.e., health care, industrial organizational psychology, counseling children and adolescents, or marriage and family) and pick an internship site from a list provided by the school.

School counselor training is offered as a 2-year program beyond the master's degree in education. School counselor training for teachers involves pursuing an additional master's degree. The College of Education at Western Czech University in Plzen (www.zcu.cz) has a 2-year continuous program. Students are required to take (a) four semesters of School Counseling and Practice, (b) Special Education, (c) Problem Solving and Diagnosis in the School, (d) School Psychology, (e) two semesters of Psychological Counseling, (f) one semester of Legal and Ethical Issues in Counseling, and (g) Family Therapy. In addition, they have to participate in four semesters of an internship. During this time they develop skills and counseling programs for practical use in schools where they already work as teachers.

Social Work

The social work degree (bachelor's, master's, or doctorate) is offered at 14 colleges in the Czech Republic (Sociální Revue, 2011). At the bachelor's level students must designate social work as a secondary major. Courses taken are Introduction to Social Policy and Social Work, Social Work With Family, Introduction to Psychology, four semesters of an internship, Counseling Methods in Social Work, Law, Sociology, and Philosophy and Ethics in Social Work. At the master's level students take four semesters of Research Methods, one semester of Social Work and Virginia Satir, two semesters of Negotiation and Mediation, and two semesters of Thesis Work. Another semester class that master's-level students take is Approaches to Working With Clients and Organizational Culture. The bachelor's in social work is a unique program offered by Masaryk University in Brno. It appears to have been developed to address the tensions between Czechs and Romany. The curriculum consists of Roma Language, Human Rights, Social Pathology, Special Education Needs, Special Care for Children From Social Minority Groups, and Basics of Roma Culture. This program suggests that social work counseling in the Czech Republic is committed to responding to the needs of the citizens.

The Future

The Czech Republic has the potential to become a leader in providing counseling services to its citizens and to underprivileged groups seeking to make the Czech Republic home. As our review shows, the long and rich history of psychology in the Czech Republic, the persistence of the Czech people in overcoming hardship, and the diversity of educational programs are proof that the nation is ready to meet this challenge.

Yet legislation has to be passed to support movements that are happening now. Current movements in the field include placing more counselors and psychologists in schools, establishing more college counseling centers, paying greater attention to the needs of the Romany people and immigrants, and focusing on the negative effects of alcoholism. Yet only one decree governs counseling, and it does not distinguish among the roles of mental health professionals. This has confused employers, slowed down the growth of the counseling movement, and in some cases upset citizens. For example, the Education Act of 2004 has upset some people, especially teachers, as it requires them to develop and make use of new curriculum materials more reflective of their local community needs instead of using a one-size-fits-all nationwide curriculum. Diminishing EU funding for counseling initiatives is another concern. Current events show that the Czech people are moving away from the values engraved by communism (e.g., that everybody is the same) to support diversity and embrace other perspectives.

The future of counseling in the Czech Republic will depend on how quickly new laws about counseling services are passed. One association that can play a critical role in this process is the Union of Psychologists Associations in the Czech Republic, whose purpose is to unify psychologists in the Czech Republic and advocate for a national credentialing body. Other mental health providers (e.g., school counselors and social workers), their employers, and educational institutions should follow suit.

References

Brožek, J., & Hoskovec, J. (1995). Psychology in the Czech Republic. In A. Schorr & S. Saari (Eds.), *Psychology in Europe: Facts, figures, realities* (pp. 3–13). Ashland, OH: Hogrefe & Huber.

Brožek, J., & Hoskovec, J. (1998). Vocational guidance in Czechoslovakia: Its beginnings. *Studia Psychologica, 40,* 129–133.

Butora, M. (1995). Alcoholism in the Czech and Slovak Republics in the last 30 years. In R. K. Price, B. M. Shea, & H. N. Mookherjee (Eds.), *Social psychiatry across cultures* (pp. 39–50). New York, NY: Plenum Press.

Central Intelligence Agency. (2010). *The world factbook.* Retrieved from https://www.cia.gov/library/publications/the-world-factbook/geos/ez.html

Euroguidance. (2007). *Counseling and immigration services* (Publication No. 978-80-904005-1-1). Retrieved from http://www.naep.cz/download-variant.php?a=documents&generalile_variant_id=1897&

Freibergova, Z. (2010). National report from Czech Republic. In M. Katzensteiner, P. Ferrer-Sama, & G. Rott (Eds.), *Guidance and counselling in higher education in the European union* (pp. 47–59). Aarhus, Denmark: Counselling and Support Centre.

Havel, V. (1991). On home (P. Wilson, Trans.). *The New York Review of Books, 38*(20), 49.

Helsinki Watch. (1991). *Struggling for ethnic identity: Czechoslovakia's endangered gypsies.* New York, NY: Human Rights Watch.

Hoskovcová, S., Hoskovec, J., Plháková, A., Šebek, M., Švancara, J., & Vobo il, D. (2010). Historiography of Czech psychology. *History of Psychology, 13,* 309–334.

Hoskovec, J. (2004). Psychology in the Czech Republic—Changes since 1993. *Psychology Science, 46,* 22–29.

Hraba, J., Mullick, R., Lorenz, F., Ve erník, J., & McCutcheon, A. (2002). Education and support for the Czech reforms. *Sociology of Education, 75*, 147–168. doi:10.2307/3090289

King, D. B., & Wertheimer, M. (2005). *Max Wertheimer and Gestalt theory.* New Brunswick, NJ: Transaction.

Kopp, M. E. (1938). Marriage counselling in European countries; its present status and trends. *Journal of Heredity, 29*, 153–160.

Krestan, J., & Gazarik, R. M. (2005). Czech and Slovak families. In M. McGoldrick, J. Giordano, & N. Garcia-Preto (Eds.), *Ethnicity and family therapy* (pp. 724–740). New York, NY: Guilford Press.

Lazarová, B. (2008). Školní psychologie v České republice po roce 1989 [School psychology in the Czech Republic since 1989]. *Československá Psychologie, 52*, 480–492.

Linares, J., Díaz, A., del Carmen Pérez Fuentes, M., & Acién, F. (2009). Teachers' perception of school violence in a sample from three European countries. *European Journal of Psychology of Education, 24*, 49–59. doi:10.1007/BF03173474

Majer, P. (2006). *Výchovný poradcav školskom systéme pedagogicko-psychologického poradenstva* [The role of the school counselor in educational and psychological counseling]. Retrieved from http://www.spssza.sk/download/f4d9d66c2010-01-31.pdf

Ministry of Labor and Social Affairs. (2011). *Information on unemployment in the year 2011.* Retrieved from http://www.mpsv.cz/en/10282

National Training Fund and the National Resource Centre for Vocational Guidance. (2003). *Counseling services at Czech universities* (NTF-NRCVG Publication No. 80-86728-00-5). Retrieved from http://www.nvf.cz/publikace/pdf_publikace/euroguidance/eng/counselling_universities.pdf

National Training Fund and the National Resource Centre for Vocational Guidance. (2004). *Career guidance at labour offices in the Czech Republic* (NTF-NRCVG Publication No. 80-86728-20-x). Retrieved from http://www.nvf.cz/publikace/pdf_publikace/euroguidance/eng/guidance_labour_offices.pdf

Novak, T. (2006). *Manželské a rodinné poradenství* [Marriage and family therapy]. Prague, Czech Republic: Grada.

Open Society Institute. (2001). *Monitoring the European Union accession process: Minority protection.* Budapest, Hungary: Central European University Press.

Organisation for Economic Co-operation and Development. (2003). *Policies for information, guidance and counselling services.* Retrieved from http://www.oecd.org/dataoecd/53/34/2500586.pdf

Plháková, A. (2008). Reflections on the main schools of the world psychology in the Czech interwar psychology. *History of Psychology, 11*, 209–219.

Rosolová, K. (2009). *Language in search of practice: The progress of curriculum reform in the Czech Republic.* Unpublished doctoral dissertation, Michigan State University, East Lansing.

Silverman, C. (1995). Persecution and politicization: Roma (Gypsies) of Eastern Europe. *Cultural Survival Quarterly, 19*(2), 43–49.

Simons, J. D., Hutchison, B., & Baštecká, Z. (2012). Counseling in the Czech Republic: History, status, and future. *Journal of Counseling & Development, 90*, 233–237. doi:10.1111/j.1556-6676.2012.00029.x

Sociální Revue. (2011). *Studium sociální práce na vysokých školách* [The study of social work in post-secondary school]. Retrieved from http://socialnirevue.cz/item/studium-socialni-prace-na-vysokych-skolach

Thomas, J. (2006). *Coercive sterilization of romani women examined at hearing: New report focuses on Czech Republic and Slovakia.* Washington, DC: U.S. Department of State, Bureau of International Information Programs.

Union of Psychologists Associations in the Czech Republic. (2011). *The school psychologists association—Czech section.* Retrieved from http://www.upacr.cz/index.php?lng=en&kap=pedagogic

Willems, G. (2008). *The meaning of citizenship to young adults in the post-communist Czech Republic.* Unpublished doctoral dissertation, University of Minnesota, Minneapolis.

Základni škola za Alejí. (2011). *Školní poradenské pracoviště* [The school counseling center]. Retrieved from http://www.zszaaleji.cz/doc/210/

Zapletalová, J. (2002). *Co dělá školní psycholog?* [What is the role of school psychologists?]. Unpublished manuscript, Teaching College, J. A. Purkyne University, Usti nad Labem, Czech Republic. Retrieved from http://pf.ujep.cz/user_files/skolni%20psycholog.pdf

Zdravnet. (2011, August 12). *Private practice psychotherapy* [Career database information]. Retrieved from www.zdravnet.cz

• • •

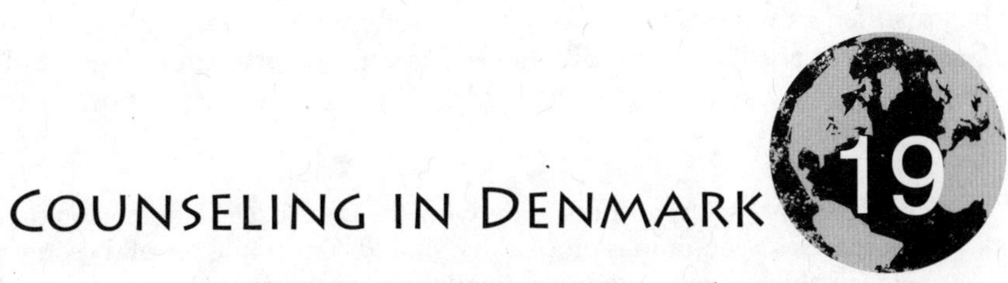

COUNSELING IN DENMARK

Rie Thomsen and Peter Plant

"There is a clear consensus in Europe that high quality guidance and counselling services play a key role in supporting lifelong learning, career management and achievement of personal goals" (European Center for Vocational Education, 2009, p. 1). This consensus includes Denmark. The policy link between lifelong learning and lifelong guidance has had a significant impact on policy making and practice in this area, as policy efforts and increased resources since the turn of the century have been focused on establishing a coherent system for the guidance and counseling of young people. *Counseling* is a broad term in Denmark: The field is broad and includes human resources in companies. This chapter focuses on career guidance. The Danish term for this, *vejledning* (leading someone on the way), covers personal counseling, school counseling, educational and vocational guidance and counseling, career guidance and development, and supervision of students during their college and university studies.

In addition to career counseling and career development services, a plethora of more generic counseling services are available in Denmark. Dixon and Hansen (2010) depicted a well-developed and widespread counseling profession based on various psychological theories and with a long tradition that shares its career counseling roots with psychometric testing in the 1880s. Since then, psychology, in the main, has moved away from career counseling into the area of general mental health. However, in schools, vocational training centers, colleges, and special psychological services for students in higher education, psychologists take care of individuals with such special needs.

Career guidance and counseling refers to

> a range of activities that enables citizens of any age and at any point in their lives to identify their capacities, competences and interests, to make educational, training and occupational decisions and to manage their individual life paths in learning, work and other settings in which these capacities and competences are learned and/or used. (p. 4)

This definition is from the 2004 European Union Resolution on Lifelong Guidance, which has been adopted by Denmark and all other member states (European Union, 2004). In this resolution, guidance activities include information and advice giving, counseling, competence assessment, mentoring, advocacy, teaching decision making, and career management skills. The term best suited to cover this broad array of activities is *guidance*, which is also the term widely adopted by many European countries and by trans-European coordinating bodies such as the European Lifelong Guidance Policy Network, of which Denmark is a highly active member. Thus, Danish educational, vocational, and career guidance has attracted increasing political attention over the past few years. Remarkable and controversial developments with consequences for social control have occurred as a result of this process. It is to these that we now turn.

The historical development of educational, vocational, and career guidance in Denmark dates back to the 1880s, when psychometric testing was seen as a modern approach. This has resulted in what is now viewed as a coherent guidance system with a focus on youth. Guidance for adults is more diverse and is somewhat scattered across different sectors and providers. The Danish Ministry of Education defines the purpose of the guidance system in these terms:

> In accordance with the ideas underlying the Danish legislation on guidance, guidance is regarded as a continuous process that should help young people become more conscious of their abilities, interests and possibilities, thus enabling them to make decisions regarding education and employment on a qualified basis. The youth guidance centres may be considered the first step in a lifelong guidance process. (Undervisningsministeriet [UVM], 2008)

Furthermore, a number of regional guidance centers provide guidance for young adults. Both types of centers are described in the next sections.

School and Youth Guidance: Comprehensive Reforms

A comprehensive reform of the educational and vocational guidance system for young people in Denmark, known as the Act on Guidance in Relation to Choice of Education, Training and Career, was passed in 2003 (UVM, 2003). This act removed school-based guidance from schools and placed these activities in municipal or regional centers that worked in conjunction with schools, other educational institutions, and other relevant partners.

The reform concerned the educational guidance of young people up to age 25; it established 48 public youth guidance centers and 7 regional public guidance centers that were in operation by 2004. Before 2004, guidance structures were seen as (too) diverse. A total of 27 types of officially recognized guidance services existed side by side in loosely coordinated networks (Organisation for Economic Co-operation and Development [OECD], 2002). Most of these services were situated within educational institutions and based on the model of the part-time teacher-counselor. This model was criticized as being too patchy, and the 2003 reform mirrored the findings and recommendations of the 2002 OECD guidance review country note on the Danish guidance system (OECD, 2002) in a remarkable synergy between national guidance policies and international OECD recommendations (Plant, 2009).

The 2003 reform focused on the notion that the educational guidance system should support a choice of education and career that should be of the greatest possible benefit to the individual *and* society. It also stressed that the individual's interests and personal qualifications, as well as the anticipated need for qualified labor and self-employment, should be taken into account in the guidance process. Furthermore, the establishment of a coherent guidance system was to target especially young people with a special need for guidance; contribute to a reduction of dropout rates; contribute to improving the individual's ability to seek and use information about choices of education and career; be independent of institution- and sector-specific interests; and lead to an improvement in the qualifications and competencies of guidance counselors (UVM, 2011b).

The delivery of youth guidance is divided between the municipalities and the Ministry of Education, each with different responsibilities and obligations. The centers are regulated by law and publicly financed. They are seen as independent, which reflects the aim to offer guidance that is independent of specific educational institutions and interests. The concept of independence refers back to an older ideal of neutrality (i.e., impartial guidance). The present centers, however, are far from being independent in the sense of nongovernmental organizations, and they are certainly not independent from the local policies of municipalities or the comprehensive monitoring and quality assurance (i.e., controlling) system of the Ministry of Education. The centralized and top-down quality assurance system is the hub of a centralized monitoring approach with a particular focus on the role of guidance in relation to dropout and retention rates and with a view to benchmarking the services' performance against each other. Fiscal and day-to-day responsibility lie with the municipality (youth guidance centers, or Ungdommens Uddannelsesvejledning [UU]) or the Ministry of Education (regional guidance centers, known as Studievalg) on a contractual basis. These contracts are highly specific in terms of targets, priorities, delivery modes, and economy.

Forty-Eight Youth Guidance Centers Covering 98 Municipalities

Youth guidance centers (UU) are responsible for guidance related to the transition from compulsory school to youth education. The main target groups for the youth guidance centers are pupils in lower secondary school (forms 6–10); youth younger than the age of 25 not in education, employment, or training (NEET); other young people younger than the age of 25 who seek guidance in relation to youth education programs or employment; and youth with a special need for guidance concerning choice of education, vocation, and career—a diverse group of young people with various problems related to the continuation or completion of an education program (Cirius, 2008).

One particular feature of these activities concerns the outreach nature of youth guidance. Guidance professionals visit the homes of young people who are not in education, training, or employment to make sure that they are "active" according to the law and thus in no danger of falling into the NEET category. This is social control in practice, and such outreach activities walk the thin line between guidance as an offer and guidance as an obligation.

Seven Regional Guidance Centers Covering the Whole Country

The regional guidance centers (Studievalg) are responsible for guidance in relation to the transition from youth education to higher education, and the main target groups are students in youth education programs; young people and adults outside of the education system who wish to enter a higher education program; and students in youth education programs with an extended need for guidance concerning choice of education, vocation, and career (Cirius, 2008).

Nonschool Guidance

However, guidance for young people in Denmark is not limited to the guidance centers. Other services are a part of the educational system. In educational institutions, guidance professionals work on a range of activities to increase completion rates. This is often done in cooperation with personal mentors and other types of personal support. These services operate under various legal rules regarding specific educational institutions such as upper secondary education, vocational training, and others. Educational institutions are obliged to offer guidance about the courses they offer and career guidance in relation to the transition from education to employment. Many of the guidance professionals working within the educational system are involved in competence assessment activities (Thomsen, 2007). These activities are publicly funded. The number of private providers is minimal but growing, as public guidance centers are increasingly obliged to serve those in need (i.e., NEETs). This potentially leaves room for other (private) providers to serve those who have more general guidance needs.

In addition to establishing the guidance centers, the 2003 act on guidance also mandated the Ministry of Education to disseminate information on education and training possibilities at all levels, on vocations and professions, on labor market conditions and statistics, and on study programs taught in English at Danish colleges and universities. This is done through a Web-based national guidance portal (www.ug.dk) that includes a national e-guidance platform that allows for personal guidance through e-channels. E-channels consist of a wide variety of virtual communication and guidance tools, such as phone, online chat, Web cam, text messaging, and e-mail. E-guidance is primarily aimed at resourceful youths and their parents, and the overall purpose is to relieve the counselors at the guidance centers. E-guidance is provided by professional guidance counselors in cooperation with the youth guidance centers, the regional guidance centers, and the national guidance portal in a decentralized structure.

Danish adult education associations engage in guidance activities with the individuals they encounter, and several trade unions also offer career guidance to their members. Job centers in the municipalities also offer some adult guidance. Beginning in 2010, a significant amount of vocational adult guidance has been offered by 13 regional adult and continuing education centers, known as *Voksen- og Efter Uddannelses Center,* based mainly on existing regional Labor Market Training Centers (*Arbejds Markeds Uddannelser*). These structures are networks of adult guidance and training/education providers. In short, adult guidance is provided by a patchwork of providers rather than a coherent system.

However, to ensure a coherent system and cross-sectional cooperation between the youth guidance centers, the regional guidance centers, and the educational system, Danish legislation obligates the youth guidance centers to cooperate closely with primary and lower secondary schools and youth education institutions in the local area, local businesses, and public employment services and job centers.

The regional guidance centers must cooperate with relevant partners in their region. Here, the relevant partners are youth education institutions, higher education institutions, social partners, industry, and commerce (Cirius, 2008). The 2003 act on guidance produces a multifaceted structure by emphasizing cooperation between different cross-sectional partners. This is one of the strengths of the Danish guidance system. It has a multifaceted structure and establishes structures for guidance both within the education system and in independent public centers for guidance. Still, developing a genuine life-long guidance approach is a challenge for the future.

In terms of cooperation on the national policy making level, the Ministry of Education has established a National Dialogue Forum for Guidance based on the 2003 Act on Guidance in Relation to Choice of Education, Training and Career. This forum does not function as a coordinating body, as one might expect, but is responsible for establishing dialogue between the ministry and relevant organizations such as educational institutions, the municipalities, national employers, employee organizations, trade unions, associations of guidance professionals, youth organizations, end users, and individuals holding leading positions in the field of guidance. The forum also aims to develop and enhance the level of quality in Danish guidance services (UVM, 2011b). In practice, it functions as a forum of debate rather than a policy-making body.

Over the past several decades, guidance in Denmark has become more professionalized. Since the 1960s, guidance professionals have been organized in various associations under the common umbrella of the Joint Council of Organizations in Guidance. In 2010, other professionals established a joint secretariat for the leaders of the 48 youth guidance centers known as the Center for Educational Guidance and Development. It distributes newsletters and press releases concerning youth guidance issues and aims to establish developmental projects in educational guidance, coordinate networks, and so on. Such developments are signs of the professionalization of guidance, as pointed out by the European Center for Vocational Education (2009) in discussing the move away from the part-time teacher-counselor model toward a new professional role:

> There are signs of change towards a more distinctive identity in a few countries. The new Ungdommens Uddannelsesvejledning (UU) youth career guidance centers in Denmark provide a distinctive location and staff identity for career guidance. Those who have chosen to meet the compulsory qualification requirements to work in the UU have abandoned any previous professional role and now typically identify themselves as career guidance practitioners. (p. 44)

Best Counseling Theories and Practices

North American and British theories on career counseling and career development have had an impact on Danish guidance counselors since World War II. Earlier than that the German psychometric influence was widespread. Since the turn of the 21st century, life-span theories; sociodynamic, constructivist, constructionist approaches; along with solution-focused, coaching, and career learning approaches to guidance and counseling have been adopted. An overview of some of these career guidance and career development theories is available in Danish (Højdal & Poulsen, 2007). General systems theory and philosophical counseling have also inspired Danish guidance counselors, along with rational decision making, solution-focused counseling, planned happenstance, and positive uncertainty approaches. In short, quite a range of approaches and concepts have been adopted. Løve (2005) noted that the Danish guidance profession has been inspired by three approaches: (a) a Rogerian person-centered approach, (b) eclectic step-by-step models, and (c) constructivist approaches. Thus, Danish guidance counselors do not work with a singular point of inspiration but eclectically, with several different ones (Plant, 2011).

The individual interview is the main guidance activity. Thus, the sheer number of individual interviews calls for creativity in terms of developing innovative methodologies, including the use of information and communications technology (ICT; Plant, 2007b). Many guidance counselors and their managers who seek inspiration on how to conduct group counseling and guidance in communities have been inspired by general systems theory, sociocultural approaches to learning, and coaching techniques. Thus, group methodologies and integrative approaches such as workplace-based guidance (Plant, 2007a) and guidance in communities (Thomsen, 2009) can be viewed as part of a collective turn in Danish career guidance to a search for a more efficient use of resources, a hunt for approaches that help avoid individualization, a search for new ways of targeting the demand for diverse guidance approaches, and a way of exploring other ways of organizing guidance.

Thomsen (2009) found that young people in transition from upper secondary education valued the fact that guidance resources were available in their immediate surroundings. Guidance was carried out in hallways, during lunch breaks, or on fieldtrips rather than in the office of the guidance counselor. The same reaction was found among adult workers in a downsizing factory. When guidance counselors in outreach work sat waiting in their offices, very few workers came to see them. They then started to move around in the production hall and in the lunchroom, talking to the workers there. Some of the workers then had questions for the guidance counselor, and others truly valued the opportunity to listen to one another's conversations with the guidance professional and, through listening, be inspired to form questions of their own.

Diversity Issues

Recent Danish legislation on educational and vocational counseling does not explicitly address diversity issues such as gender, ethnicity, or socioeconomic factors. However, many specific guidance projects, including some funded by the European Union, have addressed diversity, minority, or gender issues (cf. projects such as "Youth, Gender & Career" and "Gender, Ethnicity and Guidance"). Other types of research have been conducted on educational dropout and guidance and on vulnerable youth (Jensen, 2007; Pless, 2009).

On the whole, there is a plethora of guidance research, mostly of a qualitative nature (Plant, 2003). Evidence-based approaches, however, are of increasing interest, especially to policy makers. For example, a recent review of international research, mainly American studies, searched for evidence of how to effectively target the diversity of those in "real" need of guidance (Larsen, Christensen, Tiftiki, & Nordenbo, 2011).

Generally speaking, the policy focus since 2003 has been on what are called *youth with special guidance needs.* This term has been pivotal in policy development and professional practice discussions in recent years. It gives guidance a particular focus on the marginalized, the dropouts, the push-outs, and the NEETs. Other more general guidance needs tend to be neglected or referred to e-guidance. When the 2003 act on guidance was amended in 2008, the changes were based on a national evaluation of the 2003 act (Danish Evaluation Institute, 2007; Rolls & Cort, 2010). The evaluator, the Danish Evaluation Institute, pointed to the fact that the term *youth with special guidance needs* was used very inconsistently and that there were no common reference points among practitioners, either within or across the different guidance sectors. It was emphasized that the term *youth with special guidance needs* connoted education for young people with special needs (i.e., different physical or mental disabilities). On this basis, later amendments to the 2003 reform defined target groups in these terms: "The delivery of guidance should especially be targeted at young people who have or could have difficulties in choosing, taking up and completing an education or a vocation without an intensified guidance effort" (UVM, 2003, p. 4, our translation). This turned the focus from young people with special guidance needs to young people in need of intensified guidance efforts. This in turn spurred a discussion of whether an intensified guidance effort means more of the same (e.g., more individual interviews) or whether it means the development of new guidance activities that target young people in different ways and in ways that take diversity issues such as gender, socioeconomic factor, and ethnicity into account. This remains to be seen. But a number of guidance services now include mentoring, coaching, and group work as well as ICT-integrated approaches in a multifaceted response to the diversity of guidance needs. Diversity in guidance delivery modes, methods, and approaches is the key here.

Counselor Education

The 2003 act and later amendments set the standards for guidance counselor qualifications. Guidance counselors employed in guidance centers can obtain one of three qualifications: (a) a bachelor's degree in the field of public administration with a focus on educational and vocational guidance; (b) a diploma degree in educational, vocational, and career guidance; or (c) a master's degree in guidance. The bachelor's degree and the diploma degree, which aim to educate career guidance practitioners in all sectors, are obtained at University Colleges. The master's degree can be obtained at Danmarks Pædagogiske Universitetsskole, Faculty of Arts, Aarhus University, and focuses on research, leadership, development, evaluation, and teaching in guidance and counseling (Network for Adult Learning, 2009). Both the diploma degree and the master's degree are offered as part-time studies over 2 years (i.e., 60 points according to the European Credit Transfer System [ECTS]). The minimum entry requirements for both the diploma degree and master's degree are a completed short- or medium-cycle (2-year) higher education program and 2 years of relevant working experience, whereas the entry requirement for the bachelor's program is a high school certificate. The bachelor's degree in public administration includes a 90 ECTS specialization in career guidance, including a practicum of 20 ECTS.

The diploma degree is offered at six University Colleges under the same curriculum. The curriculum refers to the fields of sociology, economy, and trade (UVM, 2011a), but the specific course plans and literature reflect inspiration from pedagogies and psychology. The diploma degree is the main qualification route for 200–300 students per year on a national level. The course consists of four compulsory modules: Guidance and the Guidance Practitioner (10 ECTS), Guidance and the Individual (10 ECTS), Guidance and the Society (10 ECTS), and a master's thesis (15 ECTS). All modules include exams with external examiners from a national team of authorized censors. In addition, students choose three from among the following modules: Adult Guidance (5 ECTS), Career Choice and Choice Processes: Theories and Practice (10 ECTS), Guidance in Educational Institutions (10 ECTS), Special Needs for Guidance (10 ECTS), Innovation and Quality in Guidance Environments (10 ECTS), Transitional Guidance in Primary School (5 ECTS), Intercultural Guidance and Counseling (5 ECTS), Mentoring and Arrangements of Mentoring (5 ECTS), and the writing of a final thesis (15 ECTS). These modules have internal exams. Guidance counselors who have worked as such and who (through workplace learning or informal learning) have obtained competencies equal to the qualifications obtained through the diploma courses can apply for a competence assessment at the University Colleges.

The master's degree offers four modules: (a) Career Guidance and Career Development Theories; (b) Career Guidance, Society, and Guidance Policies; (c) Career Guidance Methods; and (d) a master's thesis. It is worth noting in relation to the psychology-oriented tradition of many other countries that Denmark follows a broader, more pedagogical/educational route in terms of its qualification routes. This tradition dates back to the 1960s and 1970s, when the combined roles of teacher-counselors were seen as the main model based on a person-centered approach, which in turn was a reaction against the then-prevailing rather mechanistic psychometric testing tradition of German origin.

The Future

In sum, Danish educational and vocational guidance is inspired by North American and British theories and approaches toward guidance. The overall activity is the individual interview based on dialogical methodologies, but new inspirations are emerging, such as a collective turn in educational and vocational guidance that includes career education in schools and adult learning. The 2003 Act on Guidance in Relation to Choice of Education, Training and Career aimed at professionalizing and deinstitutionalizing the formerly part-time Danish school counselors is based on the idea of impartiality and independence in terms of guidance structures. Institutional independence, however, is questionable and clearly policy driven. Most guidance counselors are now employed in full-time positions in municipal or regional guidance centers. Danish guidance counselors are inspired by a plethora of theories and approaches, mainly person-centered, constructivist, and lately sociocultural approaches.

The etymological root of the Danish word *vejledning* is "leading someone on the way," and the 2003 act on guidance established how guidance counselors should lead young people on the way to what is considered mainstream normality. Thus, from a social perspective, guidance can be viewed as one of the soft-steering mechanisms of society. Through guidance, people will make choices that will meet the interests of both themselves as individuals and society (i.e., the labor market). This leaves little room for alternative choices, and the social control aspect is evident. This became abundantly clear in a 2010 legislative initiative on youth education and employment known as the Youth Packages, which established an obligation to stay in education or work on the basis of both incentives and economic social welfare sanctions directed toward young people. This is a profound difference from other Nordic countries. Whereas Norway, Sweden, and Iceland have established young people's *right* to education (and guidance), the present government of Denmark has chosen to establish this as an *obligation*. Such issues are far from being matters of rhetoric, as there are fundamental differences between *having the right* to a service and *being obliged* to make specific choices at certain points in one's life. This places guidance in an intricate role of social control (Plant, 2010), policing the borders of societal normalization in a status quo perspective.

In short, the future of guidance lies embedded in the renewed policy focus on guidance in which one scenario is represented in the present center of attention on social control and economic sanctions. This is an impasse because it locks guidance into the role of preserving a societal status quo in which the opposite is badly needed in this present time of profound economic, social, and ecological change and challenge.

References

Cirius. (2008). *Guidance in education—The educational guidance system in Denmark.* Copenhagen, Denmark: Author.

Danish Evaluation Institute. (2007). *Vejledning om valg af uddannelse og erhverv* [Guidance on educational and vocational choice]. Copenhagen, Denmark: Danmarks Evalueringsinstitut.

Dixon, A. L., & Hansen, N. H. (2010). Fortid, nutid, fremtid (past, present, future): Professional counseling in Denmark. *Journal of Counseling & Development, 88,* 38–42.

European Center for Vocational Education. (2009). *Professionalising career guidance: Practitioner competences and qualification routes in Europe* (Vol. 164). Luxembourg: Publications Office of the European Union.

European Union. (2004). *Draft resolution of the council and of the representatives of the member states meeting within the council on strengthening policies, systems and practices in the field of guidance throughout life in Europe.* Retrieved from http://ec.europa.eu/education/policies/2010/doc/resolution2004_en.pdf

Højdal, L., & Poulsen, L. (2007). *Karrierevalg. Teorier om valg og valgprocesser* [Career choice: Theories on choice and processes of choice]. Fredensborg, Denmark: Studie og Erhverv.

Jensen, U. H. (2007). Youth with no formal education. In P. Plant (Ed.), *Ways—On career guidance* (pp. 17–29). Copenhagen, Denmark: Danish University of Education.

Larsen, M. S., Christensen, G., Tiftiki, N., & Nordenbo, S. E. (2011). *Forskning om effekt af uddannelses- og erhvervsvejledning. Et systematisk review* [Research on effects of educational and vocational guidance: A systematic review]. Copenhagen, Denmark: Danmarks Pædagogiske Universitetsskole, Århus universitet.

Løve, T. (2005). *Vejledning ansigt til ansigt.* Copenhagen, Denmark: Studie og Erhverv.

Network for Adult Learning. (2009). *Aspects on working life knowledge in Nordic adult counselling.* Helsinki, Finland: Author.

Organisation for Economic Co-operation and Development. (2002). *Review of career guidance policies—Denmark country note.* Paris, France: Author.

Plant, P. (2003). Research in educational and vocational guidance in the Nordic countries: Current trends. *International Journal for Educational and Vocational Guidance, 3*(2), 101–122.

Plant, P. (2007a). On the shop floor: Guidance in the workplace. In J. Athanasou & R. V. Esbroek (Eds.), *International handbook of career guidance* (pp. 307–328). London, England: Springer.

Plant, P. (Ed.). (2007b). *Ways—On career guidance.* Copenhagen, Denmark: Danish University of Education.

Plant, P. (2009). *Fæste. Dansk uddannelses- og erhvervsvejledning, 1886-2009* [Hold: Danish educational and vocational guidance, 1886-2009]. Fredensborg, Denmark: Studie og Erhverv.

Plant, P. (2010). Vejledningsret - vejledningspligt [Guidance right—guidance obligation]. *Vejlederforum Magasinet, 2011,* 1–3.

Plant, P. (2011). Zen - og kunsten at vejlede [Zen and the art of guidance]. *Vejlederforum Magasinet, 2011,* 1–4.

Pless, M. (2009). *Udsatte unge på vej i uddannelsessystemet* [Vulnerable youth in the educational system]. Unpublished doctoral dissertation, Aarhus University, Copenhagen, Denmark.

Rolls, S., & Cort, P. (2010). *A bridge to the future: European policy for vocational education and training 2002-10. National policy report—Denmark.* Thessaloniki, Greece: European Center for Vocational Education.

Thomsen, R. (2007, March). *Elements in the validation process.* Paper presented at the Network for Adult Learning conference "Recognition of Prior Learning: Nordic-Baltic Experiences and European Perspectives," Copenhagen, Denmark.

Thomsen, R. (2009). *Vejledning i fællesskaber - karrierevejledning fra et deltagerperspektiv* [Guidance in communities—Career guidance as seen from a participant perspective]. Unpublished doctoral dissertation, Danish University of Education, Copenhagen.

Undervisningsministeriet. (2003). *Lov om vejledning om valg af uddannelse og erhverv, Lov nr. 298 af 30. april 2003* [Act on guidance on educational and vocational choice]. Copenhagen, Denmark: Author.

Undervisningsministeriet. (2008). *Youth guidance centres.* Retrieved from http://www.eng.uvm.dk/Uddannelse/Educational%20and%20vocational%20guidance/The%20Danish%20guidance%20system/Youth%20Guidance%20Centres.aspx

Undervisningsministeriet. (2011a). *Curriculum for diploma degree in educational, vocational and career guidance.* Retrieved from http://www.ucl.dk/media(12659,1030)/Studieordning_DUEK%2C_2011.pdf

Undervisningsministeriet. (2011b). *Guidance.* Retrieved from http://www.eng.uvm.dk/~/media/Files/English/PDF/Fact%20sheets/101221_Guidance.ashx

• • •

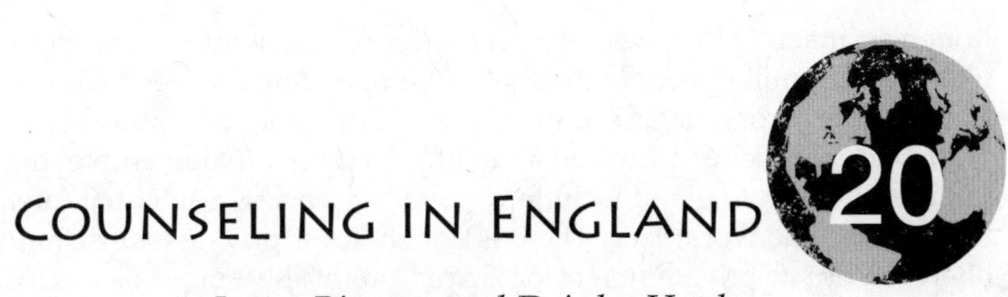

COUNSELING IN ENGLAND

Jenny Bimrose and Deirdre Hughes

Located on an island northwest of the continent of Europe, England is part of both Great Britain and the United Kingdom (UK). Great Britain comprises the two kingdoms of Scotland and England, together with the principality of Wales, and the UK also includes Northern Ireland. England, in 2011, had a population of approximately 53 million, which represents around 84% of the total population of the UK. It became a unified state in 927 and has had a significant cultural, economic, historical, social, and legal impact on the wider world. The hundreds of millions of people who speak the English language in many countries around the world are illustrative of this claim.

Distinct systems and traditions have grown up around counseling in the four home nations of the UK, so the scope of this chapter is limited to England. Because of the way counseling has developed in England, the particular focus is career counseling, though other types of counseling, such as school counseling, are also considered.

The Historical Development of Counseling

The development of counseling in the UK is more difficult to trace than that of psychoanalysis (Feltham, 2012). Regarded as subversive and radical, the introduction of psychoanalysis was initially strongly resisted. However, the extent and seriousness of the shell shock suffered by soldiers returning from the two world wars (1914–1918 and 1939–1945) stimulated demand for effective treatments, and the British Psychoanalytic Society was established in 1924, followed by the British Association of Psychotherapists in 1951. The historical roots of counseling originate in the vocational guidance movement of the United States, which "laid the foundations for counseling, and guidance for the young generally was a strong element" (p. 4). Counseling was influenced by guidance in other ways, as it was problem oriented as well as based in organizations rather than private practice (Feltham, 2012).

Despite the strong influence of career guidance on the development of counseling, the professional areas of counseling and psychotherapy are now regarded as being more closely aligned with each other than to career counseling. *Counseling and psychotherapy* is used in England as an umbrella term to cover a range of talk therapies. Career counseling (typically referred to as *career guidance* in England) is, in contrast, a much smaller professional community that bases its practices more broadly on multidisciplinary approaches, with the professional identities of members of the different professional associations generally less well developed. The primary purpose of career counseling is to support individual transitions related to the world of work throughout the life course. In contrast to many other countries, counseling for young people in schools in England is regarded as separate from career counseling, with a clear boundary (many would argue a boundary that is wholly unrealistic) drawn between the world of work and personal issues.

The Current Status of Counseling

Rough estimates of the size of the overall counseling workforce are pitched at around 70,000, with up to 5 million people thought to be operating in roles that require counseling skills (e.g., in social work, health care). Many of these roles are, however, voluntary or pastoral, with much counseling provided as an unpaid service. Other employment contexts for counseling services in England include voluntary agencies, residential care, the National Health Service, and the workplace. There is a significant private counseling sector, with services often run out of private homes or shared premises, though its exact size is hard to establish (Feltham, 2012). In addition, counseling takes place in the education sector, including schools, further education, and higher education. The existence of counseling services in schools dates back to the 1960s, with a recommendation for the appointment of school counselors contained in a government report (The Newson Report, 1963). Following this recommendation, there was some growth in school counseling, but by 1987, this initiative had stalled, with only 90 counselors in six local education authorities. This initiative has been described as "unco-ordinated and problematic" (Lang, 1999, p. 24), and its failure has been attributed to not embedding counseling in the culture of schools and neglecting to monitor it nationally (Robinson, 1996). By the 1990s, it seemed "that the movement was all but dead" (Baginsky, 2004, p. 2), with a decline in the number of specialist counselors in schools and a lack of training for teachers in counseling skills. The precise number of counselors in schools is currently unavailable because there is no official record of schools employing counselors.

The history of career counseling in England has some similarities with that of school counseling. One of the dominant themes of its history has been uncertain administrative frameworks (Peck, 2004). For those managing and delivering these services, the consequences have been extended periods of uncertainty and instability followed by reorganization and change (Bimrose, Hughes, & Colin, 2006), through which both organizations and individuals in the sector have been both expected and required to sustain delivery of high-quality, impartial career support services to clients. Career counseling became an established area of professional practice in schools after the passage of legislation in the early 1970s that gave local education authorities the legal responsibility to provide impartial careers advice to young people up to the age of 18. In the process of undergoing radical, structural change, career counseling is still currently available to all young people and generally available to adults who want it through a wide variety of sources, including schools, colleges, universities, local authorities, career companies, private companies, community-based organizations, and employers as well as national online and telephone helpline services.

Beginning in 1998, the so-called focusing agenda dominated the policy landscape for career support services, with its emphasis on addressing the needs of young people who were most at risk in their transition from full-time education (Organisation for Economic Co-operation and Development, 2003). In 2001, the new multidisciplinary service, Connexions, was introduced (Weinstock, 2001) for young people alongside a nationally funded program for adults seeking learning and work opportunities. These two strands of provision were intended to create a national network of partnerships across England (Ford, 2005) that were to work closely together, serving the needs of differing age groups. However, these policy developments exacerbated existing problems in the delivery of career counseling services, resulting in "tension and a lack of cohesion" (Mulvey, 2006, p. 14). The policy challenge of tackling welfare dependency through Getting Britain Back to Work (2011) and The Work Programme (2011) has resulted in even more blurring of the boundaries of job placement workers, career counseling professionals, and employment support staff. A new National Careers Service (Department for Business Innovation and Skills, 2010) launched in April 2012 has been designed as an all-age service to cater to the needs of anyone requiring career support.

Services for Adults

Counseling services for adults are many and varied. A range of services are provided by various private, public, charitable, and voluntary organizations, including marriage guidance, rape crisis interventions, HIV/AIDS counseling, drug or alcohol abuse counseling, and counseling for victims of torture. In the United Kingdom, the National Health Service provides a comprehensive range of health services, the vast majority of which are free at the point of delivery. It employs approximately 50% of all counselors, who work with patients with different needs, such as those recovering from accidents or those being treated for cancer or infertility.

Career support services for adults in England have developed in differing forms and in different settings, ranging from core services that are directly funded and have career information, advice, and guidance as their main activity to those embedded within and outside of formal learning and work arrangements (e.g., the workplace, the community, and penal institutions) that are supported by a variety of funding streams. Some examples include

- Jobcentre Plus, which offers a level of career counseling in which unemployed people can be referred for specialist services (e.g., a skills health check)
- A national telephone helpline and website that provides a free information, advice, and career counseling service to adults and young people
- Trade union learning representatives, who were established to provide career support to low-skilled and poorly qualified workers in the workplace

Services for Young People

Counseling services for young people are offered within educational institutions, such as colleges and universities. In these contexts, support is offered for a range of purposes, from exam stress to effective study, as well as for a range of personal issues, including relationships and sexual health. As previously mentioned, school counseling services are currently very limited in England and vary in terms of their scope and quality.

The delivery of career counseling services recently has been through Connexions services for young people in England (Department for Education and Skills, 2000). Radical changes to the structure, operation, and delivery of Connexions services were implemented in April 2008 (through the Education and Skills Bill, 2008). These changes provided the legal basis for raising the age for leaving education (now defined more broadly as education and training) and shifted the responsibility for delivering these services from central to local governments. Further legislation, the Education Act, 2011 (http://www.legislation.gov.uk/ukpga/2011/21/pdfs/ukpga_20110021_en.pdf), states that schools are under a legal duty to make sure their pupils have access to independent and impartial career counseling, with head teachers and governing bodies free to make their own preferred arrangements for career counseling.

Alongside these legal requirements, the government has made three commitments: first, to establish an all-age National Careers Service; second, to revitalize the professional status of career counseling; and third, to safeguard the partnership model between schools and external career counseling providers. The dominant political discourse asserts that school autonomy is at the heart of all highly performing education systems. As a consequence, many existing Connexions services for young people are being eroded or dismantled with the strong expectation that the demand for services will be filled by newly emerging social enterprises and/or private sector organizations operating within a free market. This has significant implications for how young people access career support services as the marketization of career counseling unfolds (Bimrose, Hughes, & Barnes, 2011). Given adverse economic conditions that have resulted in stringent budget cuts in the public sector, the professionalization of the workforce that is being stressed by the government is proving to be extremely challenging to implement (Hooley & Watts, 2011).

Professional Associations

The British Association for Counselling grew from the Standing Conference for the Advancement of Counselling. It was founded in 1977, when membership was extended from organizations to individuals. In September 2000, the Association changed its name to the British Association for Counselling and Psychotherapy (BACP). The name change was a formal acknowledgment that counselors and psychotherapists wished to belong to a united profession because they had common interests. Currently BACP is the largest professional association within the sector, with over 37,000 members in 2012 and well-established accountability and regulatory procedures. Through its work, it meets its remit for public protection while also developing and informing its members. The BACP website (www.bacp.co.uk/) indicates that services are delivered by trained practitioners who work with people over the short or long term to help them bring about effective change or enhance their well-being and explains how practices are based exclusively on psychological therapies. As far as credentialing goes, BACP has accredited nearly 10,000 counselor/psychotherapists. BACP counselor/psychotherapist accreditation is awarded to members who meet the standard for accreditation, and this standard is supported by the criteria for application. To become accredited, a practitioner must provide enough evidence to show that he or she can meet each criterion and meet the overall standard for the scheme.

There are also a number of career professional associations in the UK. These different professional associations have been operating in competition with one another for decades, but the six leading associations in the field (with approximately 6,000 members overall, though some practitioners are members of more than one association) came together in 2010 to develop new approaches to increase professionalism with and across the UK career sector. This group, the Careers Profession Alliance, which now comprises just five leading career professional associations, is "working to develop a coherent unified single voice of the careers profession for people working in careers education, information, advice, guidance and development in all its forms and various settings" (Careers Profession Alliance, 2012, p. 2). Determining the shape and form of the body that will represent all UK professional associations is a work in progress, and formal consultations are under way to help determine its structure and functions. It does seem likely, however, that career counseling professional associations in the UK will become unified in a more robust structure that will include a national register of career practitioners. This development will represent a revitalized professional body with a single voice for governments across the UK.

Best Counseling Practices

There is general agreement about the nature of problems that many young people face, with the characteristics of the school day and year meaning that the theoretical model used by counselors is often less important than the ability of the counseling intervention to accommodate these contextual constraints (Baginsky, 2004). Moreover, although the quality of the relationship between the counselor and client is crucial in any therapeutic alliance, it is particularly important for counseling young people. Best practices advocated for counseling this client group include being accepting and understanding, engaging in appropriate self-disclosure, being direct, using praise, giving advice, and using a proactive and creative approach (Geldard & Geldard, 2012).

Career counseling interventions are difficult to standardize, their impact is difficult to quantify (Bimrose, Barnes, Hughes, & Orton, 2004; Hughes & Gration, 2009), and those who are most in need are usually the least able to pay (Grubb, 2004). Although the matching approach (Parsons, 1909) is still central to policy and practice, there has been growing interest in meta-analytic investigations that examine the effectiveness of career interventions (Oliver & Spokane, 1988; Whiston, Sexton, & Lasoff, 1998) to help demonstrate how these can make a positive impact on individuals' lives. New constructivist approaches are being promoted that are linked to practitioners' making better use of client career narratives (e.g., Reid, 2005; Savickas, 2002; Young & Collin, 2004). These approaches are significantly different from the traditional approach that has dominated theory in this area, though the extent to which they are being implemented is uncertain. A fundamental tension also exists between constructivist approaches to the practice of career work and evidence-based theorists (Magnusson & Lalande, 2005; Mayston, 2002) because of differing philosophical ideologies and theoretical frameworks. There are early signs that a narrative approach (Cochran, 1997) is gaining traction with practical methods that support career exploration and decision making by engaging emotion and imagination. This offers possibilities for facilitating ways in which the career counselor can combine constructivist and evidence-based approaches.

Developments in information and communications technology, including social networking, are opening up new frontiers for capturing career behaviors and learning. Telephone helpline and Web-based services are on the increase. Their popularity is indicated by the 12 million website sessions, 100,000 e-mail enquiries, and 600,000 telephone calls made annually to the Careers Advice Service in England (UK Country Report, 2009). This is in addition to more than half a million face-to-face interventions delivered each year by the adult career service across England. The trend is for multimedia linkages and social networking developments to be extended. This presents new challenges for career counselors, with new policies that transform services and shift practice paradigms that are emerging from public spending cuts emphasizing the importance of continuing workforce development.

Diversity Issues

The principle of social equity is pivotal to effective counseling, as a key goal of the practice is to help all individuals realize their full potential irrespective of circumstances and constraints. Yet counseling continues to be criticized for focusing on the psychology of the individual and ignoring the impact of the social, economic, and cultural environments in which people live. Variables associated with social disadvantage (e.g., gender, race, age, disability, socioeconomic status, religion) have typically been treated separately in the counseling literature (Arredondo, Rosen, Rice, Perez, & Tovar-Gamero, 2005), with some theoretical approaches focusing on a specific variable for career counseling practice, such as gender (Bimrose, 2001, 2008). Similarly, approaches to diversity in counseling have largely been framed around single variables (e.g., youth and disability). However, this type of single focus limits a true understanding of the extent of disadvantage suffered. An understanding of intersectionality, or the impact of a number of factors associated with social disadvantage converging within a single individual (or group), is critical to an understanding of structural inequity (Begum, 1994). These factors include gender, race, socioeconomic status, and age (Bradley, 1996; Moore, 2009).

Migrants, for example, have multiple forms of identity, with fixed variables such as gender, disability, ethnicity, and age interacting with a variety of more fluid cultural, social, and other factors (e.g., unemployment and poverty). Given the potential intersection of such factors, a single individual will often suffer multiple forms of social disadvantage (e.g., an older female migrant is vulnerable to disadvantages associated with ethnicity and gender as well as age). The Office for National Statistics (2011) reported, "Final figures for 2010 show that annual net migration to the UK was 252,000, the highest calendar year figure on record." The increase in the number of migrant workers has resulted in an increased emphasis on community learning and development, though set within the context of diminishing resources for local organizations. The varied circumstances in which migrants navigate their way into and through labor markets indicate how different groups will require different levels and types of counseling support that take that context into account. There is, however, little evidence that these needs are being accommodated by either the career counseling or counseling professions (Bimrose & McNair, 2011). Examples of good practice do, however, exist that try to respond to some specialist needs. In England, for example, an online service with a dedicated language line was provided in at least nine languages other than English, and offered by trained career coaches to deliver these services.

Gender also represents a particular challenge for career counseling in England. The systemic disadvantage suffered by women in the labor market is well documented (Bimrose, 2001, 2008). The role of career counselors in promoting social mobility, increasing retention within education, and reducing dropout rates from education and employment is viewed by policy makers as crucial. However, in responding to the political agenda, career counselors may face an ethical dilemma in their practice, as they may risk exposing their clients to emotional and psychological damage by encouraging women to enter nontraditional occupational areas (Bimrose, 2004).

Counselor Education

The lack of reliable data on the training required for school counselors makes it difficult to make sense of the current situation. Although there appears to be a commitment to high-quality qualifications and training for counselors working in schools, it seems that this commitment does not yet match the reality (Baginsky, 2004). There are a number of options for prospective students and trainees of counseling, with both academic and work-based qualifications available. The BACP plays an important role in offering accreditation for different forms of training that meet their standards.

Training routes for career counselors are well documented. The Qualification in Careers Guidance for practitioners, with its emphasis on work-based learning and competency, was implemented nationally in the 2001–2002 academic year alongside the introduction of National Vocational Qualifications. Since then, a new work-based qualification framework has emerged, namely the Qualifications and Credit Framework. Two distinct routes into the profession currently exist: education based or work based. The education-based route involves either a 1-year full-time or 2-year part-time course in higher education. The workplace route requires practitioners to work toward occupational competence typically over a period of up to 2 years. Those who successfully complete a postgraduate Qualification in Careers Guidance are in some cases required to undertake further vocational training in their workplace before being deemed occupationally competent. In adult services, the work-based qualifying route is most common.

Because of the inconsistencies in types and levels of qualifications required across different parts of the sector, the government commissioned the Careers Profession Task Force in England in 2010 to review the qualification structure and make clear recommendations. These included the need to continue to offer both work-based and higher education routes into the profession and the recommendation that all practitioners have a specialist career qualification at Level 6 (equating to a final-year honors degree), with the ultimate goal of progressing to a postgraduate qualification. This made clear the parameters of what makes a qualified and competent career practitioner. The UK career practitioner register, when implemented, is likely to set out a new online career progression framework for new entrants into the profession.

The Future

After a slow start, counseling and psychotherapy have achieved a level of acceptance among the general public in England. The need for evidence-based practice is being heavily promoted so that the case for services can be argued with funding bodies. Critics of this approach warn against the difficulties inherent in the process of measuring the outcomes of practice because of the tendency to focus on short-term rather than longer term impact. Both counseling and career counseling in England are still heavily dependent on theoretical models exported from the United States, and limited progress has been made on the development of authentically multicultural frameworks. A major consequence of the global economic recession is the dramatic reduction in all publicly funded services in England that has been implemented as part of the austerity measures. It is predicted that the private sector will fill the gaps created by these cuts in public spending, though the extent and nature of this growth in services remains to be seen.

As a result of the changing economic and political landscapes, demand for counseling and career support from a broad spectrum of individuals is likely to increase, with the emergence of a plethora of new market players and cross-sector partnerships involving public, private, and third-sector organizations. These trends are not unique to England, as the Organisation for Economic Co-operation and Development (2010) reported that many governments are increasingly using private and nonprofit entities to provide goods and services to citizens. Counselors and career counselors will continue to experience considerable system change, and governments responsible for publicly funded career services face tough investment decisions. A multilayered landscape provides challenges and opportunities from which to learn, with the anticipated expansion of support services to citizens. The increased use of information and communications technology by a wide range of players operating in a counseling and career market will significantly impact the profession. Although the relationships among counselors, psychologists, career counselors, and other helping professionals remain fragmented, the political spotlight on the UK Careers Profession Alliance highlights the urgent need to work together effectively to safeguard citizens from rogue traders masquerading within a free market economy.

References

Arredondo, P., Rosen, D. C., Rice, T., Perez, P., & Tovar-Gamero, Z. G. (2005). Multicultural counseling: A 10-year content analysis of the *Journal of Counseling & Development. Journal of Counseling & Development, 83,* 155–161.

Baginsky, W. (2004). *School counselling in England, Wales and Northern Ireland: A review.* Retrieved from http://www.nspcc.org.uk/inform/resourcesforteachers/publications/schoolcounselling_wdf48931.pdf

Begum, N. (1994). Mirror, mirror on the wall. In N. Begum, M. Hill, & A. Stevens (Eds.), *Reflections: The views of Black disabled people on their lives and community care* (pp. 17–36). London, England: Central Council for Education and Training in Social Work.

Bimrose, J. (2001). Girls and women: Challenges for careers guidance practice. *British Journal of Guidance and Counselling, 29*(1), 79–94. doi:10.1080/03069880020019392

Bimrose, J. (2004). Sexual harassment in the workplace: An ethical dilemma for career guidance practice? *British Journal of Guidance and Counselling, 32*(1), 109–121.

Bimrose, J. (2008). Guidance with women. In J. A. Athanasou & R. V. Esbroeck (Eds.), *International handbook of career guidance* (1st ed., pp. 375–404). Dordrecht, The Netherlands: Springer.
Bimrose, J., Barnes, S.-A., Hughes, D., & Orton, M. (2004). *What is effective guidance? Evidence from longitudinal case studies in England.* Retrieved from http://www2.warwick.ac.uk/fac/soc/ier/publications/2004/egr2004.pdf
Bimrose, J., Hughes, D., & Barnes, S.-A. (2011). *Integrating new technologies into careers practice: Extending the knowledge base.* London, England: UK Commission for Employment and Skills.
Bimrose, J., Hughes, D., & Colin, A. (2006). *Quality assurance mechanisms for information, advice and guidance: A critical review.* Coventry, England: Warwick Institute for Employment Research.
Bimrose, J., & McNair, S. (2011). Career support for migrants: Transformation or adaptation? *Journal of Vocational Behavior, 78*(3), 325–334.
Bradley, H. (1996). *Fractured identities: The changing patterns of inequality.* Cambridge, England: Polity.
Careers Profession Alliance. (2012). *Blueprint for register of career development professionals and career progression framework (CPF).* Retrieved from http://www.icg-uk.org/hres/CPA%20Blueprint%20Final%20(V3).pdf
Cochran, L. (1997). *Career counselling: A narrative approach.* Thousand Oaks, CA: Sage.
Department for Business Innovation and Skills. (2010). *Quality assurance arrangements for the adult advancement and careers service.* Retrieved from http://www.bis.gov.uk/assets/biscore/further-education-skills/docs/q/09-1641-quality-assurance-adult-advancement-and-careers-service
Department for Education and Skills. (2000). *Connexions: The best start in life for every young person.* Nottingham, England: Author.
Feltham, C. (2012). What are counselling and psychotherapy? In C. Feltham & I. Horton (Eds.), *The Sage handbook of counselling and psychotherapy* (3rd ed., pp. 3–9). London, England: Sage.
Ford, G. (2005). *Am I still needed? Guidance and learning for older adults.* Retrieved from http://www.derby.ac.uk/files/icegs_am_i_still_needed_guidance_and_learning_for_older_adults2005.pdf
Geldard, K., & Geldard, D. (2012). Counselling young people. In C. Feltham & I. Horton (Eds.), *The Sage handbook of counselling and psychotherapy* (3rd ed., pp. 669–675). London, England: Sage.
Grubb, W. N. (2004). An occupation in harmony: The roles of markets and government in career information and guidance. *International Journal for Educational and Vocational Guidance, 4*(2–3), 123–139.
Hooley, T., & Watts, A. G. (2011). *Careers work with young people: Collapse or transition?* Retrieved from http://www.derby.ac.uk/files/careers_transition_paper.pdf
Hughes, D., & Gration, G. (2009). *Literature review of research on the impact offers and guidance-related interventions.* Retrieved from http://www.eep.ac.uk/DNN2/Portals/0/IAG/Literature%20Review.pdf
Lang, P. (1999). Counselling, counselling skills and encouraging pupils to talk: Clarifying and addressing confusion. *British Journal of Guidance and Counselling, 27*(1), 23–33.
Magnusson, K., & Lalande, V. (2005). *Canadian Research Working Group for Evidence Based Practice in Career Development (CRWG): The state of practice in Canada in measuring career service impact: A CRWG report.* Ottawa, Ontario, Canada: Canadian Career Development Foundation.
Mayston, D. (2002). *Assessing the benefits of guidance* (CeGS Occasional Paper). Derby, England: University of Derby, Centre for Guidance Studies.
Moore, S. (2009). "No matter what I did I would still end up in the same position": Age as a factor defining older women's experience of labour market participation. *Work Employment Society, 23,* 655–671. doi:10.1177/0950017009344871

Mulvey, M. R. (2006). Career guidance in England: Retrospect and prospect. *British Journal of Guidance & Counselling, 34*(1), 13–31.

The Newson Report. (1963). *Half our future.* Retrieved from http://www.educationengland.org.uk/documents/newsom/

Office for National Statistics. (2011). *Migration statistics quarterly report November 2011.* Retrieved from http://www.ons.gov.uk/ons/rel/migration1/migration-statistics-quarterly-report/november-2011/msqr.html

Oliver, L. W., & Spokane, A. R. (1988). Career intervention outcome: What contributes to client gain? *Journal of Counselling Psychology, 34,* 447–462.

Organisation for Economic Co-operation and Development. (2003). *OECD review of career guidance policies: United Kingdom country note.* Paris, France: Author.

Organisation for Economic Co-operation and Development. (2010). *Restoring fiscal stability and lessons for the public sector.* Paris, France: Author.

Parsons, F. (1909). *Choosing a vocation.* Boston, MA: Houghton Mifflin.

Peck, D. (2004). *Careers services: History, policy and practice in the United Kingdom.* London, England: Routledge.

Reid, H. (2005). Narrative and career guidance: Beyond small talk and towards useful dialogue for the 21st century. *International Journal for Educational and Vocational Guidance, 5*(2), 125–136. doi:10.1007/s10775-005-8790-5

Robinson, B. D. (1996). School counsellors in England and Wales, 1965-1995: A flawed innovation? *Pastoral Care in Education, 14*(3), 12–19.

Savickas, M. L. (2002). Career construction: A developmental theory of vocational behaviour. In D. Brown & Associates (Eds.), *Career choice and development* (4th ed., pp. 149–205). San Francisco, CA: Jossey-Bass.

UK Country Report. (2009). Fifth International Symposium on Career Development and Public Policy, Wellington, New Zealand. Retrieved from http://www.iccdpp.org/LinkClick.aspx?fileticket=QBJLJR10%2fQU%3d&tabid=249&mid=816

Weinstock, A. (2001). *Connexions and youth policy: A brighter future.* Retrieved from http://www.derby.ac.uk/files/icegs_connexions_and_youth_policy2001.pdf

Whiston, S. C., Sexton, T. L., & Lasoff, D. L. (1998). Career-intervention outcome: A replication and extension of Oliver and Spokane. *Journal of Counselling Psychology, 2,* 150–165.

Young, R. A., & Collin, A. (2004). Introduction: Constructivism and social constructionism in the career field. *Journal of Vocational Behavior, 64,* 373–388.

• • •

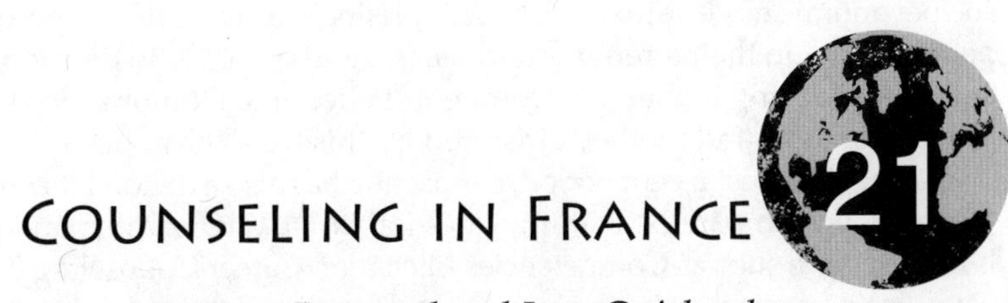

COUNSELING IN FRANCE 21

Jacques Pouyaud and Jean Guichard

This chapter presents a brief overview of counseling in France and underlines the major trends, outcomes, and challenges for this field, which is paradoxically both new and old in the context of French culture. Counseling is indeed a new paradigm in France, with the terms *counseling, counseling psychology,* and *counselors* referring to a wide and not yet clearly defined professional domain. This domain consists of multiple heterogeneous practices and practitioners (Cohen-Scali, Pouyaud, Baudouin, & Vignoli, in press). Consequently, definitions for these terms are neither very clear nor well known (Bernaud, Cohen-Scali, & Guichard, 2007). At the same time, this heterogeneous professional domain of counseling can also be described by historical facts, professional structures and associations, scientific models, and research that emerged in the beginning of the 20th century.

One of the great challenges facing this field in France is the structuring, clarifying, and perhaps building of a powerful, practical, political and scientific framework to help people cope in today's postmodern French society. The current situation in France is indeed marked by a very high demand for counseling among diverse social groups and individuals living with job insecurity. However, providing this counseling is not easy, and a major difficulty is a cultural question of vocabulary. As Blanchard (2000) pointed out, the French language does not have a clear translation of the English term or concept of *counseling*. The literal and closest translation is the verb *conseiller,* but it does not convey exactly the same meaning. The French meaning derives from the field of education and career guidance at the beginning of the 20th century. *Conseiller* means "to give advice" and suggests an exchange between an expert and layman. The major difference is that "for the French, counseling is far removed from the idea of therapy" (Tourette-Turgis, 1996, p. 25). In contrast to North America, counselors and psychotherapists are not considered to participate in a common occupational group. The term *counselor* is used by professionals who provide support for people who need help solving a social problem, a career problem, or a problem of integration in the job market, whereas *psychotherapist* is used when the work relates to clinical treatment.

The Historical Development of Counseling

The beginning of the counseling field in France was linked to questions of guidance and career development. The field was initially and mainly based on differential psychology and on the economic model of Taylorism. The central idea of matching person and workplace (the right man at the right place) led the counselor's work. With the help of standardized tests, particularly intelligence tests and skills assessments, the aim was to help students choose career paths that matched their skills and interests. In this initial period, assessment was at the heart of career counseling practices. The National Institute for Studies on Work and Vocational Guidance, which was founded by Pieron, has played an important role in the field since 1928 by establishing research; establishing assessment tools and new practices; publishing the only French scientific journal focused on career guidance and counseling issues, *L'Orientation Scolaire et Professionnelle* ("School and Vocational Guidance"); and training counselors to work in the educational system.

In the 1980s, a new conception of career counseling emerged following the introduction of career education aimed at adapting guidance practices to the new and more uncertain socioeconomic environment. Practices arising from this development aimed to help young people build on their strengths and weaknesses in order to develop the most efficient strategies for adapting to their environment (Pelletier & Dumora, 1984). Since the 1980s, a large number of tools and methods inspired by this trend have been developed and used.

During this most recent period, counseling has also extended its reach to include adults and organizations. In parallel with the question of lifelong learning and guidance, new practices have emerged, such as Competencies Elicitation Career Counseling (CECC). The past 20 years have also been marked by the increasing development of coaching within organizations.

The Current Status of Counseling

Like the populations of many other industrialized countries, the French population is growing consistently but is also aging. In 2011, France had 65 million inhabitants. The increase in population is attributed more to a high birth rate (2 children per woman, compared to the European average of 1.5) than to a high immigration rate (European Center for the Development of Vocational Training, 2008). From an economic point of view, the majority of jobs are in the service sector (76.4%), whereas employment in industry and agriculture has been declining since the 1980s. The unemployment rate is 9%. The unemployment rate among young people (age 16–25) remains one of the highest in Europe (25% compared to the European average of 20.5%) despite a significant decrease from 1995 to 2007. Unemployment affects mostly unqualified adults, seniors, and young people. Globalization and changes in living conditions since the 1990s have led to increasing social needs for counseling. Most counselors in France today work in the fields of education, social integration, health, and social work and within the private sector.

Although the act of counseling has been incorporated into many occupations (e.g., increasingly teachers in secondary or higher education, school librarians, in-company tutors, and mentor-managers are asked to support other people), the counseling profession is still not very formalized. However, within this heterogeneous field, a distinction can be made between professionals who work with young people and those who work with adults (school counselors vs. career counselors).

Counselors in the educational system and the world of work have various levels of training and social status. Members of the first group are familiar with the educational sciences and vocational psychology and are trained at the master's level in psychology. Members of the second group have more diverse educational backgrounds (from bachelor's to master's degrees in psychology but also degrees in economics, management, sociology, etc.) and are more familiar with the psychology of work and human resources. However, school and career-counseling psychologists, skills assessment counselors, and coaches all more or less think that their counseling practices can be described as a problem-solving procedure for anyone faced with a situation that has to be coped with (Tourette-Turgis, 1996).

This logic of reconciliation seems to prevail today. Since 2008, the French government has engaged in a reform of the public career service. While the private market of career counseling is expanding, public policy is trying to bring together school and vocational guidance in a great service of vocational counseling in which various professionals (e.g., school and career counseling psychologists, occupational integration counselors, and counselors who aim to help create business) are consolidated under one structure. The structure also includes documentation of employment and training. In order to describe these professionals more precisely, one can group different categories of counselors by field (Bernaud et al., 2007).

Education

The number of career counselors doubled between 1970 and 1980 as the school system became increasingly complex. Since 1981, those working with young people in schools have been called "school and career counseling psychologists" (*Conseillers d'Orientation-Psychologues*), and these professionals are employed by the state. There are approximately 4,000 school and career counseling psychologists in France. They conduct interviews and can use tests to help students and young adults choose their careers and find relevant information. They spend half of their time in junior or senior high schools and universities, where they either lead personal interviews with students or organize meetings or thematic workgroups in classrooms. The other half of their time is spent in a career counseling and information center, where they can help all populations (both young people and adults). In order to do this, they can use national documentation about occupational training courses provided by the National Office for Information on Education and Occupations (Office National d'Information Sur les Enseignements et les Professions).

The number of these psychologists has decreased since the beginning of the 21st century. During that time, psychologists had to face an increasing demand from students. They also had to work with people facing various difficulties in the labor market and the workplace (young people without qualifications, seniors, people with disabilities, foreign populations, and adults wishing to change jobs). These counselors use client-centered interviews as a central practice. They use fewer and fewer tests in their activities. Their need to develop quick support activities has resulted in the development of the short interview (Zarka, 1977, 2000) at the expense of long-term support.

Occupational Integration and Adult Careers

The number of career counselors for adults has been in a constant state of evolution since the 1970s. These counselors mainly help adults who have left school before graduating and adults who want to change careers. One category of counselors consists of those working for the *Pôle emploi* (employment center). The *Pôle emploi* is a new national agency service that addresses unemployment, training for adults, and unemployment benefits. Created in 2008 as a fusion of the National Employment Agency (Agence Nationale Pour l'Emploi) and the Association for Industrial and Commercial Employment (Association pour l'Emploi dans l'Industrie et le Commerce), the *Pôle emploi* aims to consolidate all unemployment services. In 2010, counselors who worked for the Association for Adult Vocational Training (Association pour la Formation Professionnelle des Adultes) were also integrated into the *Pôle emploi*.

These counselors specialize in the working job seeker. They use tools and methods often developed inside the public structure from an educational and developmental perspective model of career. Another category of counselors includes those who work with young people between 18 and 25 years of age who have left school before graduating. These counselors work as occupational integration counselors in local centers called *Missions locales* (local missions) or *Permanences d'Accueil d'Information et d'Orientation* (Job Information, Guidance, and Placement Centers). Their role is to guide and accompany young people with a personalized program as they develop the skills needed to enter the labor market.

The practices used to do this are very eclectic, as there is almost no national or local monitoring of counseling activities. The quality of these services is assessed based mainly on the number of young people helped.

Social Work

Faced with globalization, growing uncertainty in the world of work, and the need for mobility and employability, social workers experienced a crisis during the 1990s. These professionals (family social workers, youth workers, etc.) aim to help and advise individuals by taking into account the individuals' general life context. Their field has gradually become occupied by other professionals who specialize in specific situations (e.g., divorce, illness, poverty, domestic violence).

Health Care

In the health care field, counseling activities are always linked with support for individuals facing particular public health difficulties (e.g., drug use, alcoholism, nutrition deficiency, AIDS, posttraumatic stress, sexual abuse, accidents). Counseling is most often conducted by groups, associations, or clinics that specialize in assisting or defending victims. When counseling is conducted in health care settings (e.g., hospitals, clinics), professionals view themselves more as therapists, and the term *counseling* is used less frequently.

Organizations and Business

Like counseling in the noncommercial sectors just discussed, counseling in the private sector has increased rapidly since the 1990s. In many large companies, a counseling function has emerged within human resources division to support employees in managing their careers. This function is also linked to policies that try to avoid mass redundancy, support equality in the workplace, and support employment for young people or seniors. It also serves to support employees during the restructuring of organizations.

Another type of counselor has also emerged in companies over the same period. Such counselors can be grouped under the generic term *coaches.* Few studies on this new approach exist, although a professional association, the French Association of Coaching, was founded in 1996 to structure and promote the field. These professionals describe themselves as experts in a specific area of coaching. They are often involved with a company as independent contractors. They implement some individualized supports (e.g., for personal problems of management or leadership) and can also intervene at the group level (when it comes to issues related to work teams). There are also some coaches in the education field. These professionals help students address problems such as stress, anxiety, and a lack of confidence. Three fields of interventions can be identified: personal development, executive support, and psychopedagogical intervention. Practices are very heterogeneous and are often based on cognitive–behavioral approaches, but psychoanalytic, developmental, psychoeducational, and other approaches, including some nonscientific approaches, can also be found.

Best Counseling Practices

The most common counseling practice used in France is the interview, which is sometimes associated with standardized tests, such as interest inventories or tests of intellectual potential. The objective is always to help the person create a career path.

Different forms of interviews can be used, and these are often centered on the client. These interviews are associated with decision-making techniques based on cognitive and behavioral approaches. The interview technique used by French school and career counseling psychologists is a good example. The first phase is a needs analysis. The second phase involves a detailed evaluation of the client's situation, resources, limitations, beliefs, and values and the impact of all these factors on solving the career problem. Finally, the third phase involves setting up an action plan based on realistic and achievable solutions (Lecomte & Tremblay, 1987).

Some new forms of interviews can be used as well. Some of these are inspired by new theoretical perspectives, including constructivism and life design (Guichard, 2008; Savickas et al., 2009), whereas others are centered on new technology. The prevalence for online counseling is also rapidly growing. There are many Internet platforms on which young people can find information about careers and occupations. Using the Internet, young people have the opportunity to interact with professionals and counselors by asking questions via e-mail or posting on forums. These platforms are created by both private companies and public structures that are often associated with organizations that produce informative resources on jobs and training (e.g., the National Office for Information on Education and Occupations, newspapers and magazines that specialize in education).

More specific counseling methods also exist. Some of these methods have been adapted for counseling young people in schools and colleges, and others target workers who are retraining or unemployed, although there is considerable variation. Career counseling with young people is conducted in groups in the form of workshops that provide information about different jobs based on sources such as worker biographies (Guichard et al., 2008). Counselors also use group techniques, such as role-playing.

Two recent career counseling practices have been developed for adults going through a period of professional transition: CECC and validation of experiential learning. All adults who have participated in a professional activity have access to these two tools. CECC was introduced in 1991 and can take place at the request of the worker or his or her employer. It involves an assessment of the worker's professional skills, motivations, aptitudes, and interests with the goal of developing a career or training project. It is usually conducted in three phases (Aubret & Blanchard, 2010). The first phase involves establishing a working alliance based on an assessment of the client's needs. The second phase is devoted to exploring the client's interests, motivations, and skills and examining ways in which his or her career situation could develop. In the final phase, the counselor reveals the results of the tests and a summary of the elements collected over the course of the assessment, and future possibilities are discussed. The entire assessment takes approximately 20 hours spread out over several weeks and alternating between group activities, personal career exploration, information searches, and interviews. Vermersch's explanatory interview may be used for the interviews (Depraz, Varela, & Vermersch, 2003). The aim of this type of interview is to clarify what is being done and what has been done, focusing on putting actions into words after the event (Baudouin, Blanchard, & Soncarrieu, 2004).

Validation of experiential learning, introduced in 2002, provides any professional with the opportunity to obtain a diploma in recognition of his or her professional and/or personal experience. The validation process involves describing the professional skills and knowledge acquired and providing evidence that they were acquired during an experience that lasted a minimum of 5 years. A file is then created listing all of the elements in support of the equivalence of the relevant diploma. This file is then submitted to a jury that can confer all or part of the diploma. This diploma must correspond to the experiences of the individual. There is a counseling procedure in France to help applicants describe the activities and tasks related to the diploma.

The theoretical trends underlying current counseling practices are so diverse that it is difficult to draw a clear picture. However, counseling in France has been largely influenced by the work of Carl Rogers, which was translated into French in the 1960s (Rogers, 1962, 1968). The theoretical works of Holland and Super also represent a major contribution to practices used since the 1970s. Career counseling with adolescents and young adults is based on multiple approaches related to vocational development, mainly in English-language literature (e.g., Holland, Gottfredson, and Super) that has been translated and researched in France. Yet several French publications also have to be noted: the French Association of School and Career Counselors Bulletin (*Bulletin de l'Association des Conseillers d'Orientation-Psychologues*), the special edition on counseling of *L'Orientation Scolaire et Professionnelle* coordinated by Blanchard in 2000, and the handbook *Psychologie de l'Orientation* ("School and Career Development Counseling"; Guichard & Huteau, 2006). French researchers in career counseling are currently developing constructionist models to identify the manner in which young people establish their identities in relation to work (Baubion-Broye & Hajjar, 1998; Guichard, 2009).

Career counseling interventions with adults are mostly based on psychosociological models. For example, counseling practices with unemployed adults are largely inspired by work on self-esteem and self-efficacy. Their aim is to highlight the individual's strengths and resources. Bandura's self-efficacy theory thus provides the basis for a large number of counseling activities. However, the practices inspired by these approaches are not standardized and are used in different ways depending on the clients and counselors involved. The objective of most of these interventions is to help clients develop the way they see themselves. More specifically, the aim of counseling sessions may be to change a person's perception of work, jobs, and professions. Many counseling practices in professional development are based more or less explicitly on Moscovici's (1961) theory of social representations. Social representations are cognitive constructions (integrated sets of opinions, beliefs, attitudes, and knowledge) related to social reality that are socially constructed, are shared by members of a group, play a major role in communication, and guide ideas and actions. Career representations concern mainly jobs and the training required for them but also concern work, success, and unemployment. A large number of counseling procedures aim to help clients who are going through a period of professional change adjust their career representations. This generally involves helping them acquire new work or training experiences and then conducting one or more interviews to explore these experiences.

Diversity Issues

We have already discussed specific demographic issues in France. These characteristics have specific repercussions on counseling activities with particular groups of people. The first such repercussion concerns young people from immigrant families from southern Europe, the Maghreb, and sub-Saharan Africa. These young people are particularly affected by unemployment. More generally, some specific interventions exist for young people or others who have great difficulty integrating into the labor market. Castra (2003) proposed an intervention called the "Intervention on Supplies and Demands" (*Intervention sur les Offres et les Demandes*). This methodology is based on the theoretical approach of commitment (Joulé & Beauvois, 2002). It aims to develop social mechanisms for the recruitment and training of people with low skills for career integration. This methodology uses activity as the principal resource of development to drive the inclusion of these people. It aims to change social attitudes concerning exclusion. This method departs from traditional practices such as interviews (and the job interview). It allows the counsel to be viewed from another perspective: that of the building of a social action.

The second repercussion concerns the specific difficulties and needs of people in the second part or at the end of their career. France ranks 26th among the countries in the European Union in terms of employing people older than 50 (40% of men and 35% of women older than 50 are employed). However, the state aimed to reach 50% employment among people aged 55 to 64 by 2010 (European Center for the Development of Vocational Training, 2008). To achieve this, all companies with more than 50 employees will have to employ a larger number of people older than 50 years of age or incur a penalty. This obligation is likely to lead to an increased demand for counseling for these people. The CECC procedure and validation of experiential learning can be used by companies to respond to this employment policy, but the difficulty of convincing companies to work on these issues has to be noted. Since 2005, the French government has encouraged companies to establish strategic workforce planning, a structured approach to human resource management that aims to anticipate demographic and economic developments (e.g., trends related to retirement) and avoid brutal restructuring and layoffs.

Another characteristic of the French situation involves a general deterioration of working conditions in companies. France is facing a high increase in the rate of job-related suicides and ranked third in the world after Japan and Finland in 2005 (Du Roy, 2009). This situation has led the public authorities to consider passing a law requiring that large companies implement changes to prevent psychosociological risks. Improving working conditions and the well-being of employees should become a major aim for policy makers and human resources services in the coming years.

Counselor Education

Most counselors (psychologists or otherwise) have at least a bachelor's or master's degree in human and social sciences and notably in psychology, but only three master's programs exist in France in the fields of school and professional counseling and working with adults. These programs train practitioners to work in job centers and in skills assessment or human resources organizations. Most counselors then specialize in a particular counseling domain (e.g., vocational guidance, therapeutic counseling, integration counseling) through professional experience or additional training courses.

There is also a professional diploma program for school and career counseling psychologists. This 2-year program is open to people with a degree in psychology, and the diploma (a state diploma for school and career counseling psychologists) confers the right to the title of "psychologist and vocational counseling specialist." Such counselors work mainly in secondary schools and universities providing guidance related to educational choices and integration into the job market. This program, organized by the National Institute for Studies on Work and Vocational Guidance and three other centers, is the only professional program that recognizes the field of career counseling. These professionals are united by membership in the French association of school and career-counseling psychologists).

Given the growing demand for support in departments and companies, a number of degree-level diplomas focusing on short interventions (initial interview, information) are being established (e.g., there are six vocational degree specialties for occupational integration). In addition, private organizations offer an increasing number of short courses that are more or less related to counseling (e.g., interview preparation and coaching).

The Future

Currently there is a growing demand for counseling in all aspects of life (career, health, money, the family, the law, etc.). There is also political support for the development of the field of counseling at both the national and European levels, with a new law recognizing the right to vocational education and training and career information and counseling throughout life. Public services for employment, state unemployment insurance, and career services are being reorganized into a single service to cover the needs of individuals as a whole in a more structured way. This acknowledgment of counseling practices by French public policy authorities by itself is a strength. The main weaknesses of this social restructuring are based on the fact that the growing demand for professional training, guidance, and information has led to a sharp increase in the number of practitioners and their differences in terms of training, theoretical basis, and activity. Because of these differences, counseling remains an ill-defined field in which individual professionals do not see themselves as belonging to the same professional family.

In this situation, there is also a risk that this expanding sector will be perceived only in terms of a counseling market. The increase in the number of diverse training courses and services offered, for example in the area of coaching, is a striking example. The major risk is thus that the single term *counseling* will be used to describe, with little scientific basis, the wide variety of services offered, the priority of which is economic efficiency, which fails to centrally focus on the client. To overcome this problem, quality assurance must be assessed, practices must be differentiated, and clients must be protected and receive good service. Practitioners will consequently need to organize themselves in professional associations in order to maintain an ethical basis for their counseling practice. A major challenge for the future is to simultaneously select the most relevant, up-to-date practices while maintaining enough creativity for practitioners. This involves developing scientific networks for counseling with the aim of constituting a body of knowledge, research, and practices likely to lead to the formalization of counseling professions. It will entail scientists structuring a coherent field in which to continue developing research in a rapidly growing sector. Unfortunately, the lack of interest in this subject shown today by scientists serves to distance the human and social sciences as sources of innovation and organization for the counseling professions. Bringing research into this field within the scope of international scientific activity would help develop a body of knowledge. Becoming more involved in existing international bodies would enable researchers to compare international counseling issues with those developing in France.

As previously noted, a clear distinction is made in France between counseling, which is available to everyone, and psychotherapy, which is associated with the concept of treatment. Because of the heterogeneity and continuing increase in counseling activities, a real clarification of terminology and underlying theories is required, as is a legal structure for actions in the field of counseling. An evaluative, qualitative, and ethical approach to these practices also appears to be essential.

References

Aubret, J., & Blanchard, S. (2010). *Pratiques du bilan personnalisé* (2nd ed.) [Personalized career assessment practices]. Paris, France: Dunod.

Baubion-Broye, A., & Hajjar, V. (1998). *Evènements de vie, transition et construction de la personne* [Life events, transitions and the construction of the person]. Sainte-Agne, France: Eres.

Baudouin, N., Blanchard, S., & Soncarrieu, T. (2004). L'entretien de conseil en orientation: présentation de trois types d'entretien [Career counseling interviews: Presentation of three practices]. *Psychologie du travail et des organisations, 10,* 293–306.

Bernaud, J. L., Cohen-Scali, V., & Guichard, J. (2007). Counseling psychology in France: A paradoxical situation. *International Review of Applied Psychology, 1,* 131–151.

Blanchard, S. (2000). Le conseil en orientation: introduction [Career counseling: An introduction]. *L'Orientation Scolaire et Professionnelle, 29,* 3–26.

Castra, D. (2003). *L'insertion professionnelle des publics précaires* [The transition to work of precarious people]. Paris, France: PUF.

Cohen-Scali, V., Pouyaud, J., Baudouin, N., & Vignoli, E. (in press). Counseling in Europe: France. In R. Moodley, U. P. Gielen, & R. Wu (Eds.), *Handbook of counseling and psychotherapy in an international context.* New York, NY: Routledge.

Depraz, N., Varela, F., & Vermersch, P. (Eds.). (2003). *On becoming aware: A pragmatic of experiencing.* Amsterdam, The Netherlands: Benjamin.

Du Roy, I. (2009). *Orange Stressé* [Stressed orange]. Paris, France: La découverte.

European Center for the Development of Vocational Training. (2008). *Vocational education and training in France.* Retrieved from http://www.cedefop.europa.eu/EN/Files/5190_en.pdf

Guichard, J. (2008). Proposition d'un schéma d'entretien constructiviste de conseil en orientation pour les adolescents et jeunes adultes [Outline of a life designing counseling interview for adolescents and young adults]. *L'Orientation Scolaire et Professionnelle, 3,* 413–440.

Guichard, J. (2009). Self-constructing. *Journal of Vocational Behavior, 75*(3), 251–258.

Guichard, J., Abadie, N., Boy, T., Darré, S., Dernaucourt, C., Pouyaud, J., & Steinbruckner, M. L. (2008). *La Nouvelle Découverte des Activités Professionnelles et Projets Personnels* [The discovery of occupational activities and personal plans: An updated workshop method]. Paris, France: Ed Qui Plus Est.

Guichard, J., & Huteau, M. (2006). *Psychologie de l'orientation* (2nd ed.) [Vocational psychology]. Paris, France: Dunod.

Joulé, R. B., & Beauvois, J. B. (2002). *Petit traité de manipulation à l'usage des honnêtes gens* [Little treatise for manipulating honest people]. Grenoble, France: Presses Universitaires de Grenoble.

Lecomte, C., & Tremblay, L. (1987). *Entrevue d'évaluation en counseling d'emploi* [Assessment interview in employment counseling]. Montreal, Quebec, Canada: Institut de recherches psychologiques.

Moscovici, S. (1961). *La psychanalyse* [Psychoanalysis]. Paris, France: Presses Universitaires de France.

Pelletier, D., & Dumora, B. (1984). Fondements et postulats pour une conception éducative de l'orientation [Foundations and assumptions for an educational conception of career guidance and counseling]. In D. Pelletier & R. Bujold (Eds.), *Pour une approche éducative en orientation* (pp. 23–37). Chicoutimi, Québec, Canada: Gaëtan Morin.

Rogers, C. (1962). *Psychothérapie et relations humaines* [Psychotherapy and human relations]. Paris, France: Nauwelearts.

Rogers, C. (1968). *Le développement de la personne* [On becoming a person]. Paris, France: Dunod.

Savickas, M. L., Nota, L., Rossier, J., Dauwalder, J. P., Duarte, M. E., Guichard, J., … Van Vianen, A. E. M. (2009). Life designing: A paradigm for career construction in the 21st century. *Journal of Vocational Behavior, 75*(3), 239–250.

Tourette-Turgis, C. (1996). *Le counseling* [Counseling]. Paris, France: Presses Universitaires de France.

Zarka, J. (1977). Conseil psychologique et psychologie du conseil: quelques propositions [Psychological counseling and counseling psychology: Some proposals]. *L'Orientation Scolaire et Professionnelle, 6,* 21–51.

Zarka, J. (2000). Conseils et limites: limites du conseil, au-delà des limites. L'espace sans espace, l'espace des appels [Limits of counseling, beyond the limits. The area without space, the space of calls]. *L'Orientation Scolaire et Professionnelle, 29,* 141–169.

• • •

COUNSELING IN GERMANY 22

Josef Strasser

The beginnings of institutionalized counseling services in Germany can be traced back to the end of the 19th century. At that time the German state flourished, and progress in economic and scientific domains entailed advancement in social affairs. Different developments contributed to the institutionalization of counseling, such as the creation of youth welfare and special needs education, progress in medical and psychological research, as well as the development of psychodynamic approaches. The first institution that provided child guidance counseling was founded 1883 by a physician in Leipzig and was designed to support foster mothers of illegitimate children. This institution eventually became a counseling center for mothers in 1907. In 1903, Cimbal established a remedial pedagogic counseling center in Hamburg, and 3 years later a similar institution, the *medico-pädagogische Poliklinik für Kinderforschung, Erziehungsberatung und ärztliche erziehliche Behandlung* (medical pedagogical polyclinic for child research, child guidance, and medical educational treatment), followed in Berlin. Marriage problems were first specially targeted in a counseling center in Dresden in 1911 (Belardi, 1999).

A major impact on the development of child guidance centers stemmed from Alfred Adler's (1870–1937) individual psychology. In 1920, Adler initiated the first child guidance centers in Vienna, and 2 years later a child guidance center modeled on a community outreach program was established in Munich. These clinics were run by voluntary psychologists and physicians and were located in public schools to convey psychological ideas and knowledge to teachers and other laypersons. The success of these clinics led to the proliferation of similar institutions in the German Reich, and hence by the end of the 1920s, 42 child guidance clinics existed in Germany.

At this time, social and youth welfare received a legal foundation with the *Reichsjugendwohlfahrtsgesetz.* This development was promptly interrupted when the Nazis seized power in Germany, because the idea that families needed external advice and support did not match the ideology of the national socialist party (Abel, 1998). Counseling institutions that followed psychodynamic or social work approaches were shut down, handicapped, or converted, and psychiatric or clinically oriented institutions were fostered. After World War II, the social situation in Germany was determined by manifold states of emergency as cities were destroyed, families were shattered, and millions had to leave their homes. Hence, the need for external support and counseling services was enormous. When reestablishing counseling services, authorities relied on the traditions begun in the 1920s and also on U.S. traditions. With the idea of reeducating Germans, U.S. forces imported the concept of American child guidance clinics. The economic boom that began in the 1950s paved the way for different initiatives for social and educational reform in the 1960s and 1970s. The establishment of institutionalized counseling reached its climax at that time (Belardi, 1999).

The structure and quantitative dimension of counseling services did not change much, despite an ever faster growing need for professional support. This rising need led to a new counseling boom to implement new forms of services in different settings. It also led to new forms of cooperation between institutions and services, including cooperation among schools, child guidance centers, and youth welfare offices. These initiatives, however, remained at the level of pilot projects and depended on individual motivation (Strasser & Gruber, 2003). Because of financial shortages, states and communities have not invested more in counseling services since the late 1990s, and thus counseling institutions have not been expanded or strengthened (Schrödter, 2002). For example, despite growing numbers of students, the number of school counselors remained stable from 1975 to 2004 (Liermann, 2004).

The field of professional counseling was not strengthened to meet the increasing need for mental health services; instead, other forms of counseling were sought from nonprofessional counseling personnel such as teachers. Thus, the lack of a professional identity for counselors lingers on. A major characteristic of institutionalized counseling in Germany is the diversity of professions it involves. From the very beginning, people from all kinds of helping professions (physicians, psychiatrists, teachers, and later social workers) engaged in counseling activities. It was the expectation of some institutions, such as the child guidance clinics, that a multiprofessional team would cooperate to provide care. The multiprofessional profile offered some advantages, such as the existence of different perspectives that enable an adequate view of the problems of a diverse clientele, but it also hindered the emergence of a unique counseling profession and led to enormous variability concerning the conception and theoretical foundation of counseling as well as intervention strategies (Strasser, 2006). This makes it difficult to give a short and yet comprehensive overview of counseling in Germany. This chapter thus focuses on well-established counseling services that allow for rather general statements.

The Current Status of Counseling

School Counseling

The federal structure of Germany defines the educational sector and as a result makes school counseling quite diverse. The role of the school counselor depends almost entirely on the state (*Bundesland*) in which the position exists. In Bavaria, the largest of Germany's 16 federal states, there are multiple levels of school counseling: *Beratungslehrer* (counseling teachers) are primarily teachers with some additional training in counseling and work at schools, *school psychologists* work directly in certain state schools (e.g., in problem schools), and finally *school psychologists* that are employed in school advisory agencies at the district level and handle other state and all private schools (Schwarzer & Posse, 2008). School psychologists always have a double degree in psychology and pedagogy (teaching) or (rarely) a dedicated degree in school psychology.

School counseling in Germany became institutionalized and professionalized during the 1970s because of an increasing demand for counseling services. In 1973, the Standing Conference of the Ministers of Education and Cultural Affairs of the Länder in the Federal Republic of Germany decided to transfer the provision of school psychology services to counseling professionals outside of individual schools, whereas professionals housed in schools, called *Beratungslehrer* (counseling teachers), were to provide counseling to students and teachers.

To guarantee a sufficient supply of professionals, the following guidelines were developed: One school psychologist was to be available for a student population of 5,000, and every counseling teacher was to be responsible for no more than 500 students. School psychologists never reached these targets, and the actual ratio is 1 school psychologist per 12,000 students (Liermann, 2004). Only five states (Berlin, Hamburg, Bavaria, Saxony, and Thuringia) have met the original goal of 1 counseling teacher for every 500 students. In four states there are no counseling teachers at all. In 2010, around 15,000 teachers in Germany worked as counselors, and 1,143 school psychologists provided counseling services (Seifried, 2010).

The structural framework (Liermann, 2004) of school counseling is characterized by diversity; thus, there is great variability in the working conditions of school counselors and counseling teachers. Conditions may vary with the institutional placement of counselors (working within schools or outside of them, being integrated into faculty or not, belonging to governmental authorities or not); with the composition of teams (only school counselors or also social workers and child guidance experts); and the size of the team, which may vary from 1 to 20 counselors.

The professional tasks of school counselors (and school psychologists) cover three domains: individual casework, consultation with the school as an institution, and further education and training of teachers. The work of counseling teachers and school psychologists may differ and overlap due to the actual structural framework. Counseling teachers' tasks vary extensively and depend on the kind and size of the school. Work in small schools with less than 250 students differs considerably from counseling work within large school communities with up to 2,000 students (Grewe & Wichterich, 1999). Yet three main tasks can be distinguished: educational career counseling, individual casework, and consultation with schools and parents. *Educational career counseling* may involve giving general information about school careers to parents and students and may also involve providing individual career counseling based on standardized test results. *Individual casework* is indicated when learning and behavioral problems occur or when there are major discrepancies between a student's competence and his or her actual performance. *Consultation with schools and parents* may include providing information about school psychologists' work, disseminating information about innovative instructional approaches, and sharing knowledge of educational psychology.

Cooperating with other counseling service providers is another task of counseling teachers. The job functions of counseling teachers, school psychologists, and child guidance experts may overlap. Counseling teachers engage in less serious cases, when behavioral problems show up only in certain situations or when there are discrepancies between a child's intelligence and actual school performance. School psychologists are concerned with more difficult cases that sometimes involve chronic behavioral problems and disorders. But even in difficult cases, counseling teachers are often the first professionals contacted. Because long wait times are a major problem of school counseling and of child guidance centers as well, counseling teachers often remain the only contact person available (Liermann, 2004).

Because a wide range of potential roles and career paths lead to becoming a counseling teacher, the roles of these professionals remain rather unclear. Only a few studies give some insight into their actual roles and functions (Strasser & Gruber, 2008). The emphasis in counseling has gradually shifted from educational career counseling to individual casework. Since the late 1980s, most counseling teachers have spent around 60% of their time working with individual students and 30% providing educational career counseling. This emphasis on individual counseling has been observed in all school forms. On average, counseling teachers work with 48 students each year. According to their estimation, another 50 students are in need of counseling services, meaning they can only help half of the students in need of counseling (Grewe & Wichterich, 1999).

Nonschool Counseling

There is a multitude of different domains of institutional counseling, with the most established being in child and youth services (child guidance and family counseling, youth counseling, addiction counseling). Other areas of nonschool counseling in Germany include career counseling, marriage counseling, drug counseling, and social psychiatric counseling.

In general, there is an increasing need for counseling, which can be seen in, for example, the field of institutional youth counseling (especially child guidance). As the Federal Office of Statistics in Germany observed in a detailed documentation for 2006 (Statistisches Bundesamt, 2006b), 311,000 adolescents younger than the age of 27 sought educational or child guidance counseling because of individual or domestic problems. This number represents about 1,000 more consultations than in 2005 and 30% more than in 1996. Between 1991 and 2003 the number of cases of child guidance doubled (Körner & Hensen, 2008). In some areas of counseling juridical regulations exist, and in some of those areas, such as child guidance counseling, everybody has a right to counseling and consultation (Körner & Hensen, 2008). For this reason, the provision of some counseling services must be guaranteed in Germany.

Psychological counseling is mainly located within the scope of extended health care, social care, and educational systems. Traditionally it is free of charge or low cost for eligible clients. Moreover, psychological counseling services are integrated into different kinds of information centers, crisis centers, or social-psychiatric services at the local health authority. Counseling services that are provided by nonprofit institutions and youth welfare services are of minimal cost, and clients are asked for donations in return for consultation. Freelance psychological counseling and consultations that are provided online or over the phone are usually privately financed. In a few instances, reimbursement for expenses can be requested from private health insurance if the psychological counselor is an accredited *Heilpraktiker* (natural health professional) or *Heilpraktiker für Psychotherapie* (alternative practitioner for psychotherapy) and the counseling has a psychotherapeutic orientation.

Best Counseling Practices

In contrast to countries such as the United States and Great Britain, where counseling developed as a more autonomous discipline, in German-speaking countries counseling is seen as part of clinical, educational, or organizational psychology. Hence, counseling is neither theoretically, empirically, practically, nor professionally independent because its main concepts and models are derived from clinical-psychological perspectives. With the exception of Dietrich's (1983) outline of counseling psychology as an independent discipline, no thorough attempt has been made to develop a systematic and autonomous concept of counseling. Dietrich believed that counseling is located somewhere between psychotherapy and education. Despite the overlapping of these two disciplines and a lack of discriminatory power, he conceived of counseling as a definable scientific and practical domain with its own structure. Concerning the theoretical underpinning of counseling, Dietrich contended that there is an "inflation of theories" accompanied by a concurrent "theoretical deficit" (p. 20). This diagnosis is still valid, as it describes a situation in which counseling theorists and practitioners borrow from a multitude of theories from different domains and disciplines without developing conceptions that have a unique starting point in the specific demands and characteristics of the counseling process (Strasser & Gruber, 2003).

In Germany, psychotherapeutic approaches (be they of psychodynamic, behavioral, humanistic, or systemic origin) dominated counseling for a long time. Only recently has this clinical orientation been waning and the disorder-based model of clinical psychology been supplemented or replaced by different perspectives. Hence, psychosocial conceptions of counseling are developing that refer to counseling's roots in social work and that take into account network-related and ecological approaches. Two major tendencies can be observed in this respect: a shift from an individualist to a more context-related perspective and a progression from an emphasis on healing to a focus on developmental processes that acknowledge a person's existing resources. This emerging profile, which is context and resources oriented, conceives of counseling as the professional support of individuals in their everyday lives to help them cope with the challenges of their daily *Lebenswelt* (life world). The main disciplines on which counseling is based are social pedagogy, education, sociology, and psychology. This conceptual diversity corresponds to the diversity of intervention and action strategies. From its professional beginnings, counseling in Germany banked on such a methodical diversity regardless of the specific approach (psychotherapeutic, educational, or social work) that was emphasized. Hence, most practitioners follow an eclectic and integrative orientation that seeks to adapt methods and intervention strategies to the individual client's specific needs. Having such an adaptive strategy is preferred to rigidly clinging to fixed methods. Rogers's approach to counseling had a significant impact on the methodical orientation of counselors, as did psychodynamic approaches, namely Adler's individual psychology. Recently systemic and context-related forms of interventions have become increasingly important (Nestmann & Engel, 2002).

Practices in School Counseling

There is no regular counseling in German schools. If a problem occurs, contact is established first with the *Beratungslehrer* (counseling teacher), who can perform mediation in minor conflicts, organize tutoring in problem classes, and handle similar basic problems. If it is a more severe problem, either the counseling teacher or the student or parents contacts the school psychologist. It is rare that a school psychologist works at an individual school. Usually one school psychologist is responsible for several schools within a district-level agency (there are usually two to four psychologists in each district). The school psychologist will also be contacted if there is a conflict between a student and a faculty member (as the *Beratungslehrer* as a faculty member is automatically not considered neutral in such cases). The counseling teacher can hold meetings with classes regarding disciplinary problems or similar matters and can recommend a student for counseling with the school psychologist at the request of a teacher. If problems are not resolvable at this level, the school psychologist usually handles the diagnosis and then guides the client toward external support or counsels him or her until the problem is resolved. In addition, the school psychologist may

- organize and hold meetings for specific matters, such as drug prevention, antiviolence training, and so on
- advise in conferences regarding the social climate in school, violence problems, individual students, and so on
- advise the school administration in psychological matters
- provide psychological supervision and training for teachers of the school

There is also some variation in these roles based on the kind of school. For example, in *Förderschulen* (special needs schools) especially, practices may be different. In the district-level agencies, there is usually one specialized psychologist for every type of school who is paired with a supervisor for the *Beratungslehrer* of that type of school.

Talking with students is the main method counseling teachers use, because they are able to lead student-centered and cooperative conversations. Another professional requirement refers to their diagnostic competence, for they ought to be able to adequately assess individual cognitive, emotional, and social preconditions of learning. Hence, they are required to master an array of diagnostic procedures from systematic observation to the application of standardized tests (Grewe & Wichterich, 1999).

Differences in the practices of counseling teachers with different levels of experience were observed in a study by Lüttge, Grewe, and Höher (1985). This study showed that compared with counseling teachers with less experience, experienced counseling teachers combine individual and group approaches more often, address the whole class more often, and refer more students to external institutions. They are more often contacted by their teaching colleagues and cooperate more with colleagues within and outside their school. They have greater job satisfaction, are less affected by lack of acceptance, but experience more strain when confronted with difficult families.

Practices in Nonschool Counseling

Counseling in nonschool settings is usually practiced in counseling centers that are run by the state, the community, churches, or public or private charity organizations. In these centers teams of 3 to 10 counselors are employed. Only a few counselors work in private practices on their own. Unlike with psychotherapy, client expenses for counseling provided by health or social care providers are not reimbursed. The main setting for counseling is usually the individual counselor's office, although more informal contexts may also be used. Forms of involuntary counseling (scouting or visiting counseling) that challenge the traditional view that clients voluntarily have to "come" to counseling are becoming more popular in certain settings, such as in drug or youth counseling (Nestmann, Engel, & Sickendiek, 2004).

Diversity Issues

Responding to cultural and ethnic diversity is an increasing challenge for professionals working in Germany's educational, health, and social care systems. In 2010, 29.4% of all persons younger than 20 in Germany had migration backgrounds, and the number of second-generation immigrants was increasing (Herwartz-Emden, Schurt, & Waburg, 2010). Most people of foreign origin living in Germany were recruited as laborers during the economic boom of the 1960s and 1970s. The breakup of the Soviet Union led to waves of immigration from eastern Europe in the 1990s. Today the largest groups of immigrants have Turkish (14.2% of all immigrants), Russian (9.4%), Polish (6.9%), and Italian (4.2%) citizenship. As many immigrants get naturalized and are granted German citizenship, the actual cultural and ethnic backgrounds of people living in the country are quite difficult to assess. Immigration has the effect of greatly increasing diversity of many sorts, including ethnic, phenotypic, religious, and cultural diversity. Of the total population of Germany, 19% is of migrant background (Statistisches Bundesamt, 2006a). In several large cities citizens of foreign countries, naturalized citizens, and ethnic German immigrants together make up roughly one quarter or more of the entire population.

The diversity stemming from immigration creates many challenges. One of the most serious of these challenges is finding effective ways to educate minority children. Children who are themselves immigrants or who come from immigrant backgrounds typically perform markedly less well on standardized tests of academic knowledge and skills, are more likely to drop out of school or to be found in lower level schools, and are also less likely to complete higher education. The educational achievement gap between immigrants and others is larger in Germany than in most of the other countries in the Organisation for Economic Co-operation and Development (Strasser, 2011). Such educational disparities have obvious negative implications for immigrants and their families in terms of economic and social status. Given the range of migration experiences and the substantial variation in social context, it is difficult to generalize about the problems and difficulties immigrants have to struggle with. Migration is commonly associated with lower income, higher risk for unemployment, and problems with acculturation and social integration. Despite this, clients with migration backgrounds are underrepresented in regular counseling services (Pavkovic, 2004), and this disproportion is particularly evident for female clients. Although the number of minority clients seeking counseling services seems to have increased since 2000 (Friese, 2009), the situation is still not satisfactory. This may be because of the structural separation of migration-related services and specific counseling institutions. Theoretically speaking, migration services' tasks include performing general casework management, assisting minority clients in finding specific help, and referring clients to specialized health or social care institutions.

In practice, the cooperation between migration-related institutions and specific counseling services is deficient (Pavkovic, 2004). Because migration-related institutions are not able to meet their clients' specific psychosocial or educational needs, there is increasing discussion about how regular counseling institutions can improve minority clients' access to their services. One way to enhance the intercultural receptiveness of counseling services is to employ counselors who are proficient in minority clients' mother tongues or who also have migration backgrounds. Yet the existence of language skills is a sometimes necessary but not sufficient precondition for improved intercultural openness in counseling. Further requirements are the use of intercultural teams, the development of approaches that consider multiple perspectives, and the acquisition of multicultural counseling competencies by all counselors (Pavkovic, 2004). Hence, the professionalization of counseling is often seen as an answer to the problems and challenges that go along with cultural diversity. The professionalization of counseling in the educational system seems particularly necessary, because in Germany students, parents, and teachers are only minimally supported by counseling services. Hence, increasing access to educational counseling for persons with migration backgrounds has been formulated as an important goal in Germany's educational policy.

Unfortunately, little is known about counselors' professional competence when it comes to cultural matters. Although the international literature implies the need for multicultural counseling skills, such skills are not part of the curriculum in the training and education of school counselors in Germany. Hence, it is unclear whether and how counselors are able to deal with cultural diversity in their professional practice. Results of a recent interview study (Strasser & Rupprecht, 2012) implied that school counselors do not meet standards for professional multicultural counseling, as they reveal little awareness of their own cultural biases or of culturally appropriate intervention strategies. This may be attributed to deficits in their basic training and to difficulties in making use of professional experiences to develop adequate competencies. This study demonstrates the need for specific training programs to foster counselors' professional learning concerning multicultural competence. These conclusions may generalize to other areas of counseling as well.

Unfortunately, empirical research on matters of cultural and ethnic diversity in German counseling is very rare. The existing literature focuses primarily on conceptual considerations and produces rather general recommendations without taking into account the specific international literature on multicultural competencies. Hence, little is known about the specific counseling needs of different minority groups, about their perceptions of counseling services, and about what barriers hinder them from seeking professional assistance.

Counselor Education

Because counseling is not seen as an autonomous academic discipline by universities, there are no general, standardized training programs that beginning practitioners have to complete to become counselors in Germany. Such specific courses exist only for school psychologists and school counselors. Unlike *psychologist* and *psychotherapist* the term *coun-*

selor or *psychological counselor* is not legally protected. Although it is necessary to acquire a university degree in psychology to become psychologist, and although psychotherapists must complete postdegree training in one of the major therapeutic approaches, neither of these is required of counselors.

Hence, those working as counselors, sometimes only as a part-time job, may have considerable variability in their specific knowledge and skills. There are, however, specific training programs that are offered by professional associations, charitable further education providers, and private continuing education institutions. These programs usually equip participants with basic theoretical knowledge as well as practical skills. Often these programs are designed for counselors who are already employed, and they mainly consist of reading assignments and supervised case presentation sessions. As the content of such programs is not legally regulated and there is no obligation to complete them, it is up to the individual counselor to take responsibility to obtain adequate qualification and further education. Given the increasing professional requirements and the demands of an increasingly diverse clientele, further professionalization of counseling is being discussed (Nestmann et al., 2004). For instance, the Bundeskonferenz für Erziehungsberatung (Federal Conference for Child Guidance Counseling) recently developed basic professional requirements for counselors and offers corresponding training programs (Bundeskonferenz für Erziehungsberatung, 2011).

Those who employ counselors, such as agencies, clinics, or counseling centers, usually require a master's degree in psychology, social work, or education. Furthermore, it is often required that applicants document some basic training in therapeutic skills. Some institutions employ only applicants who have completed a comprehensive psychotherapy training program. Such programs are usually organized as postdegree training that participants pay for on their own. The question of whether completing a psychotherapy program with a particular clinical stance is adequate for counselors is increasingly subject to debate. Some child guidance counselors, for instance, emphasize the nonclinical aspects of their services (Strasser, 2006). Although such training is not mandatory, those who have it on their record find it easier to get employed and advance in their jobs.

In contrast to counseling outside schools, there are established standards for the education of school psychologists and counselors. School psychologists and school counselors differ from each other in their educational training and their specialization. School psychologists have studied teacher training psychology as an advanced subject or obtained a diploma in psychology in addition to their teacher training degree. In comparison, school counselors have less advanced training (Liermann, 2004).

Requirements concerning the amount and content of school counselor education differ from federal state to federal state. In Bavaria, for example, one may qualify as a school counselor by completing a specially designed teacher training program or a postdegree training for employed teachers. Because school counselors usually complete extra occupational education, they are faced with a special challenge. Acquiring the comprehensive foundations of the scientific discipline, of diagnostic competencies, and of counseling training in a highly compact form is time consuming. The counselors need to be willing to focus and to use their leisure time to write a qualifying thesis in addition to performing their full teaching obligation and preparing for written and oral exams (commonly during the summer holidays). During 2 years of further education at the Akademie für Lehrerbildung und Personalentwicklung Dillingen (academy for teacher training and human resource development in Dillingen), the soon-to-be school counselors complete nine 1-week courses. Three of the courses take place during the holidays. During the 9 weeks, the counselors are taught the scientific foundations of psychology, education, and sociology as well as practical knowledge and skills. The training content comprises personality psychology, educational-psychological diagnostics, counseling psychology, educational groundwork of counseling, learning difficulties, structural aspects of the educational system, relations between aspects of educational and occupational system, counseling institutions, and techniques. Although the curriculum comprises a wide variety of relevant themes, the relatively short duration of the training may entail only superficial learning (Grewe & Wichterich, 1999).

The Future

Taking the present situation as a starting point, one may project the future development of counseling in Germany. An examination of the current state of counseling reveals much ambivalence. On the one hand, counseling has become an established form of professional support that is highly institutionalized and that serves a multitude of different groups of people with all kinds of problems and difficulties. On the other hand, this highly specialized service reveals remarkable deficits in terms of professionalization. Although some see this fuzziness and the lack of professional regulations as constitutive of the domain and oppose further professionalization as regimentation and a form of patronizing (Schrödter, 2002), the need for developing the systematic and validated foundations of a contoured profession is increasingly being recognized. This need becomes evident when one looks at the needs that come with the increasing cultural diversity in Germany (Strasser & Rupprecht, 2012). The cultural adequacy of a counselor's approach and techniques is rarely questioned, and what is valid either across or within certain cultural communities is not yet determined to satisfaction. In addition, members of ethnic or cultural minorities sometimes remain excluded from counseling services (Nestmann & Engel, 2002). In all areas of counseling (health, social care, educational, vocational), a multicultural expansion will determine the future of German counseling. Opening up and adapting existing counseling services for minority clients as well as developing specific services are major challenges for practitioners. This holds true not only for cultural diversity but for diversity in terms of age and gender. The counseling needs of older adults are still widely neglected; few specific services exist for them, and those that do are often restricted to rather confined problem areas. The expansion of counseling for women will continue, as will the establishment of specific services for men.

Although traditional counseling in Germany has reacted to the diversity of clientele with a variety of approaches and services delivered by different types of professionals, it may be time to develop counseling as a more coherent and unique profession. This does not mean that the interdisciplinary approach has to be given up, but it must involve a greater effort to integrate different perspectives more consistently. To do this, more counseling-related research has to be conducted, because a well-developed knowledge base for the profession is still missing. This base is indispensable for the development of professional identity and having it will help to establish standards for training and accreditation as well. Different (but still occasional) initiatives that bring together counseling research and practice as well as the founding of new professional associations (Schrödter, 2002) indicate the direction of future trends.

References

Abel, A. H. (1998). Geschichte der Erziehungsberatung: Bedingungen, Zwecke, Kontinuitäten [History of child guidance counseling: Conditions, objectives and continuities]. In W. Körner & G. Hörmann (Eds.), *Handbuch der Erziehungsberatung, Bd. 1* (pp. 19–51). Göttingen, Germany: Hogrefe.

Belardi, N. (1999). *Beratung: Eine sozialpädagogische Einführung* [Counseling: A sociopedagogical introduction]. Weinheim, Germany: Beltz.

Bundeskonferenz für Erziehungsberatung. (2011). *Weiterbildung zum/zur Erziehungs- und Familienberater/in* [Further training for becoming a child guidance and family counselor]. Fürth, Germany: Author.

Dietrich, G. (1983). *Allgemeine Beratungspsychologie* [General counseling psychology]. Göttingen, Germany: Hogrefe.

Friese, P. (2009). Erziehungsberatung—Ein Regeldienst der Jugendhilfe versucht die interkulturelle Öffnung [Child guidance—A regular youth service tries to adapt to cultural diversity]. In R. Oetker-Funk & A. Maurer (Eds.), *Interkulturelle psychologische Beratung. Entwicklung und Praxis eines migrantensensiblen Konzeptes* (pp. 271–282). Norderstedt, Germany: Books on Demand.

Grewe, N., & Wichterich, H. (Eds.). (1999). *Beratungslehrer in der Praxis. Grundlagen, Aufgaben und Fallbeispiele* [School counselors in practice: Foundations, tasks and case examples]. Neuwied, Germany: Luchterhand.

Herwartz-Emden, L., Schurt, V., & Waburg, W. (2010). *Aufwachsen in heterogenen Sozialisationskontexten: Zur Bedeutung einer geschlechtergerechten interkulturellen Pädagogik* [Growing up in heterogenic socialization contexts: On the relevance of a gender- and culture-sensitive education]. Wiesbaden, Germany: VS Verlag für Sozialwissenschaften.

Körner, W., & Hensen, G. (2008). Erziehungsberatung: Strömungen, Entwicklungen und Standortbestimmung der institutionellen Beratung in der Jugendhilfe [Child guidance counseling: Movements, developments and the current position of institutionalized child and youth services]. In G. Hörmann & W. Körner (Eds.), *Einführung in die Erziehungsberatung* (pp. 10–26). Stuttgart, Germany: Kohlhammer.

Liermann, H. (2004). Schulpsychologische Beratung [School counseling]. In F. Nestmann, F. Engel, & U. Sickendiek (Eds.), *Das Handbuch der Beratung. Band 2: Ansätze, Methoden und Felder* (pp. 865–875). Tübingen, Germany: dgvt.

Lüttge, D., Grewe, N., & Höher, G. (1985). Beratungslehrer in Niedersachsen. Ergebnisse einer Befragung [School counselors in Lower Saxony: Results of a survey study]. *Schulverwaltungsblatt Niedersachsen, Heft 4,* 182–187.

Nestmann, F., & Engel, F. (2002). *Die Zukunft der Beratung* [The future of counseling]. Tübingen, Germany: dgvt.

Nestmann, F., Engel, F., & Sickendiek, U. (Eds.). (2004). *Das Handbuch der Beratung. Band 1: Disziplinen und Zugänge* [Handbook of counseling: Vol. 1. Disciplines and approaches]. Tübingen, Germany: dgvt.

Pavkovic, G. (2004). Beratung für Migranten [Counseling for migrants]. In F. Nestmann, F. Engel, & U. Sickendiek (Eds.), *Das Handbuch der Beratung. Band 1: Disziplinen und Zugänge* (pp. 305–311). Tübingen, Germany: dgvt.

Schrödter, W. (2002). Zwischen Visionen und Pragmatismus—Beratung und ihre neue Qualität [Between visions and pragmatism—Counseling and its new quality]. In F. Nestmann & F. Engel (Eds.), *Die Zukunft der Beratung* (pp. 79–94). Tübingen, Germany: dgvt.

Schwarzer, C., & Posse, N. (2008). Schulberatung [School counseling]. In W. Schneider & M. Hasselhorn (Eds.), *Handbuch der Pädagogischen Psychologie (Handbuch der Psychologie, Bd. 10,* pp. 441–451). Göttingen, Germany: Hogrefe-Verlag.

Seifried, K. (2010). *Versorgungszahlen Schulpsychologie* [Supply numbers school psychology]. Retrieved from http://www.bdp-schulpsychologie.de/backstage2/sps/documentpool/2010/2010_versorgungszahlen_schulpsychologie.pdf

Statistisches Bundesamt. (2006a). *Leben in Deutschland—Haushalte, Familien und Gesundheit. Ergebnisse des Mikrozensus 2005* [Living in Germany—Households, families and health. Results of the micro-census 2005]. Wiesbaden, Germany: Author.

Statistisches Bundesamt. (2006b). *Statistiken der Kinder- und Jugendhilfe* [Statistics of child and youth services]. Wiesbaden, Germany: Author.

Strasser, J. (2006). *Erfahrung und Wissen in der Beratung—Theoretische und empirische Analysen zur Entstehung und Entwicklung professionellen Wissens in der Erziehungsberatung* [Experience and knowledge in counseling—Theoretical and empirical analyses on the development of professional knowledge in child guidance counseling]. Göttingen, Germany: Cuvillier.

Strasser, J. (2011). Diversity as a challenge for teachers' professionalism—Outline of a research program. *Journal of Social Science Education, 10*(2), 14–28.

Strasser, J., & Gruber, H. (2003). Kompetenzerwerb in der Beratung—Eine kritische Analyse des Forschungsstands [Acquisition of competence in counseling: A critical review of the research literature]. *Psychologie in Erziehung und Unterricht, 50*, 381–399.

Strasser, J., & Gruber, H. (2008). Kompetenz von Beratungslehrern im Vergleich [Comparing school counselors' competencies]. In M. Gläser-Zikuda & J. Seifried (Eds.), *Lehrerexpertise—Analyse und Bedeutung unterrichtlichen Handelns* (pp. 239–260). Münster, Germany: Waxmann.

Strasser, J., & Rupprecht, M. (2012). *Cultural diversity: A challenge for the professional learning of school counselors in Germany.* Paper presented at the 18th European Conference on Educational Research, Cadiz, Spain.

• • •

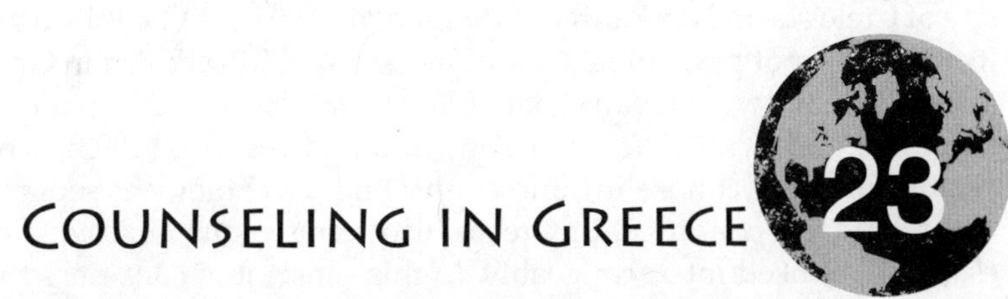

23 Counseling in Greece

Maria Malikiosi-Loizos and Theodoros Giovazolias

In Greece, the field of counseling as a distinct specialization is fairly new, as it has existed only in the past few decades. This can be attributed to the fact that Greek culture is traditionally regarded as a collectivist society in which family loyalty, adherence to group norms, and maintenance of harmony in relationships with group members are highly valued (Georgas, 1989). Collectivist societies maintain that the nuclear (and often the extended) family, rather than the individual, is the basic unit of society. In this context, counseling has traditionally been embedded within the support system of social relationships (Lampropoulos & Stalikas, 2009). Indeed, the importance of *the other* and the quality of *interdependence* are still emphasized in present-day Greece.

Although Greece is currently considered to be right in the middle of the individualist–collectivist spectrum (Mylonas, Gari, Giotsa, Pavlopoulos, & Panagiotopoulou, 2006), parents, siblings, as well as close friends are still a major source of social support for Greek people (Malikiosi-Loizos, Christodoulidi, & Gialamas, 2010). However, it is also true that there has been a shift in attitude toward other forms of support, such as counseling, as more people are willing to seek professional help not only in the large urban centers but also in rural areas (Papastylianou, Alexopoulou, Doulami, Tampouri, & Tsoli, 2009).

Counseling emerged in Greece in the 1950s, the period following World War II, when a noticeable external migration and internal urbanization took place, bringing rapid changes to the country's economy and the labor market. In an effort to address the problems emerging from these changes, and to support young people in their search for employment, the Ministries of Labor and Education introduced career guidance and counseling. The first course on career guidance was introduced in the Teachers' Academies curriculum in 1953 to help prepare future teachers in their role as supporters of their students' orientation process. However, it was not until 1976 that career guidance was introduced into the secondary education school curriculum. At the same time, the Ministry of Labor, through its Manpower Employment Organization, offered career guidance services, placing a particular emphasis on career counseling for young unemployed individuals (Malikiosi-Loizos & Ivey, 2012).

An educational reform act in 1997 brought important changes to school and career guidance. It became evident that vocational development was closely related to vocational psychology and psychological counseling. The National Center for Vocational Guidance was also established under this same educational reform act. Its main objectives are to ensure the coordination, support, and effective functioning of counseling and career guidance agents across Greece. Similarly, within the higher education system, specialization in career guidance was first introduced at the Higher Technological Educational Institute of Athens in 1998. A few years earlier, in 1993, a graduate program leading to a master's degree in career guidance and counseling had been initiated at the University of Athens (Malikiosi-Loizos & Ivey, 2012).

Until 1984, there was no distinct psychology department within Greek higher education institutions. Psychology as a discipline was part of the School of Philosophy at the Universities of Athens and Thessaloniki and was first established as a separate and autonomous department at the University of Crete in 1984. The psychology department of the University of Crete started operating in 1987, and in 1991 the Greek educational system graduated its first cohort of psychologists. Counseling was introduced in Greece in the 1990s with the appearance of two relevant textbooks, *Counseling and Counseling Psychology* (Dimitropoulos, 1992) and *Counseling Psychology* (Malikiosi-Loizos, 1993), which helped facilitate the establishment of counseling and counseling psychology as separate disciplines.

As in many countries, in Greece also terms *counselor, counseling psychologist,* and *psychologist* are used interchangeably. In this sense, it is considered very important that special efforts are being made to differentiate counseling from other forms of helping professions. Counseling psychologists normally have obtained a psychology degree from either a Greek university or abroad and are eligible for membership in the relevant professional societies. Counselors are primarily members of the Greek Counseling Association (www.hac.com.gr), which recognizes as counselors people who come from different backgrounds of study. In this chapter, we use the definition of counseling proposed by the British Association for Counselling (1991): *Counseling* is "the skilled and principled use of a relationship to facilitate self-knowledge, emotional acceptance and growth, and the optimal development of personal resources. The overall aim is to provide an opportunity to work towards living more satisfyingly and resourcefully" (p. 1).

The Current Status of Counseling

At present, there is increasing professional and research activity in counseling in Greece, and this is evidenced by a growing demand for specialized graduate education as well as counseling services. In the 2000s there was an increase in the publication of relevant textbooks, journals, newsletters, and articles as well as in the number of counseling and counseling psychology courses offered. Academic positions for counselors and counseling psychologists are regularly advertised, proving that the discipline is gradually acquiring acceptance and recognition among academics (Malikiosi-Loizos & Ivey, 2012).

In a similar vein, there has been an increase in parent counseling programs since the turn of the century organized mainly by the Institute of Ongoing Adult Education of the Ministry of Education. This is a free service for parents of children at any age. In parent counseling, participants have the opportunity to look at and share with other members their current parenting experiences and get practical feedback. The purpose is to improve communication, solve family problems, learn how to understand and handle special family situations (i.e., loss, serious physical or mental illness, child and adolescent issues), and create a better functioning home environment. About 20 individuals attend each group, and the process involves multiple counseling sessions that usually last at least 1 hour each and are conducted at regular intervals (e.g., on a weekly basis) for several months (approximately 12–25 sessions). The program started in 2002 with 40 groups taking place in the Athens area, and now there are more than 250 groups all over the country. The facilitators of these groups are counselors from different backgrounds (psychologists, social workers, educators) who undertake further training on specific issues of parent counseling.

Furthermore, since 1990 counseling professionals have also been recruited by private elementary and high schools. School counselors in Greece operate within the international goals and aims of school counseling. More specifically, they assist children in examining the problems they are experiencing and gaining insight into what factors maintain these difficulties; facilitate decision making; discuss difficulties in relationships and how to cope with them; identify useful coping strategies that the child already has and enhance these; and identify existing sources of support that may facilitate coping but are not being used, including peer, family, and other professional support. However, only a small number of private schools employ counselors on a full-time basis. Efforts are being made to provide this service in the public sector as well.

Counseling services are being developed across the country at the college and university levels as well. Psychological counseling in higher education has been recognized by the global psychology community as an essential factor not only for academic success but also for students' personal development and well-being (Rott, 2006). However, student counseling services in Greece have only been established in the past few years. So far, few universities have taken action to establish and sustain a foundation (center, office, or service) to provide counseling to their students, mainly because of limited financial recourses. The first student counseling center was founded at the University of Ioannina in 1989. A year later, a student counseling center was founded at the University of Athens. Other universities (i.e., the University of Piraeus, the University of Crete) have followed this initiative, but there is still much that can be done toward achieving the widespread provision of student counseling. One answer to the lack of funding and to increasing student needs has been the establishment of peer counseling centers in several departments of the University of Athens, a movement that started in 1995 and seems to be expanding.

On another level, there has been a growing awareness that the principles of counseling can prove to be very valuable in organizational structures that combine (or need to combine) efficiency with a facilitative climate. For example, since the 1990s there has been a noticeable increase in interest in counseling in work settings. This has led to the (albeit limited) direct employment of paid counselors or the employment of external counselors on a consultancy basis.

In sum, at present, psychological counseling in Greece is being practiced by psychologists, counselors, social workers, and other professionals both privately and in community mental health centers, higher education institutions, some private schools, and parental counseling groups run by the Ministry of Education and social service centers. Counseling focuses on issues of well-being, parental skills training and improvement, relationship improvement, conflict resolution, employment issues, problem solving, career development, and many others issues. These topics illustrate the wide range of counseling applications across different life situations (Malikiosi-Loizos & Ivey, 2012).

Counseling Associations

The first counseling professional association was the Greek Society of Counseling and Guidance, established in 1985. Since its inception, it has been actively involved in the expansion of career guidance and school counseling across the country. This is evident by its increasing membership (approximately 1,000 members) as well as its publication of a scientific journal called *Review of Counseling and Guidance.* Many professionals as well as academic counselors contribute their work to this publication.

Two more associations in counseling and guidance have also been established since 2000. Members of the Panhellenic Association of Counseling and Guidance (www.sylesyp.gr) are mainly secondary school educators who have completed a 1-year program of specialization in counseling and guidance offered at the School of Pedagogical and Technological Education (www.aspete.gr) and are qualified to work in school vocational guidance offices, centers for counseling and career guidance, and, also at the school level, in consulting offices of counseling and career guidance. They also qualify to work in staff agencies in close collaboration with the labor market. The Greek Society of Vocational Guidance Counselors (www.sesep.gr) is a professional society that aims to promote research and knowledge in counseling and vocational guidance as well as career management.

The Greek Association of Counseling (www.hac.com.gr) was established in 1994 and soon became a member of the European Association for Counselling. At present its 150 members (professional counselors) are involved both in private practice and teaching. The Hellenic Psychological Society (www.elpse.gr) was established in 1991 as the academic body of psychology in Greece aimed primarily at teaching and research. Full members of this society normally hold a PhD in psychology, but there is also the option for affiliate membership to PhD candidates. There are now more than 550 full members in the Hellenic Psychological Society, with the rate of new membership increasing rapidly. In 1999, the Society formed its first 10 divisions, among which is the Division of Counseling Psychology. The Division of Counseling Psychology (www.counselingpsychology.gr) numbers about 40 members and has been very active (through seminars, workshops, conferences, and publications) ever since the development of counseling psychology as a distinct field in Greece.

Credentialing Agencies

There is no official credentialing agency for counselors or counseling psychologists in Greece. Several private and public educational institutions offer counseling and psychotherapy programs that lead to a practitioner's certificate, but this certificate is not officially recognized by the state. Most of these credentialing agencies are affiliated and collaborate with Greek professional societies and other international societies and associations. They accept mainly graduates from humanist and health-related programs. However, several of them do not exclude candidates from other fields. Each educational setting organizes its own program, which lasts 3 to 4 years depending on the theoretical and therapeutic approach followed. All programs require several hours of practicum and supervision, and some of them also require personal therapy. The main theoretical and therapeutic approaches represented in Greek counseling psychotherapy training institutions include person-centered, Gestalt, cognitive–behavioral, family systems, psychoanalytic-psychodynamic, group analysis, Adlerian, Reich, and psychodrama approaches (Kalantzi-Azizi et al., 2003).

The Current Relationship Among Counseling, Psychology, and Social Work

The field of social work is well established in Greece, and studies in this field date back to the 1960s. The relevant courses started initially as 3-year programs of study but developed over time to 4-year university-level studies with a practicum. Social workers act more as supporters and consultants for clients' practical emotional issues and are employed in social service institutions and hospitals as members of a team along with psychologists, counselors, and other therapists.

As mentioned earlier, the boundaries between counseling and psychology are not clear cut. Psychologists become licensed as soon as they receive their bachelor's degree and can work privately or in hospitals and/or other institutions in the area of assessment and therapy. Counseling as such has developed more recently and does not have a clear identity yet. The roles of counselors and counseling psychologists are often confused. Both types of professional are considered to work therapeutically, but no legislation or any other type of recognition exists so far in this regard.

Best Counseling Practices

As noted earlier, the main theoretical and therapeutic approaches represented in Greek counseling psychotherapy training institutions stem from the person-centered, Gestalt, cognitive–behavioral, family systems, and psychoanalytic-psychodynamic paradigms. Thus, one can argue that these approaches are the most commonly used approaches in the practice of counseling. However, it is generally accepted that the majority of counselors use active listening and other client-centered skills, often in combination with psycho-educational interventions. Greeks often seek informal help and social support from family members in their efforts to overcome their distress. Greeks feel comfortable and open to sharing with family members their everyday difficulties with issues such as work stress, financial anxiety, sadness over a separation, and mourning the loss of a loved one (Lampropoulos & Stalikas, 2009). Hence, this traditional, family-oriented framework encourages the involvement of family members in the counseling process, which leads many counselors to use a more systemic therapeutic approach with their clients. Having said that, we should mention that in the past few years there has been noticeable growth in the use of more alternative modes of intervention, such as biodynamic counseling and psychotherapy, drama therapy, and art therapy, with both children and adults. Counseling in Greece is practiced much like in the rest of the Western world. Sessions are usually planned weekly, take place in the counselor's office (in either the public or private sector), last an hour, and follow the same ethical guidelines of confidentiality. Counselors are expected to abide by the ethical code of both the counseling association to which they belong to (i.e., the Greek Association of Counseling) and the specific institution for which they work (if they are not in private practice). The needs assessment as well as the action planning are determined by the particular setting within which the counselor is working as well as his or her theoretical background. Professional positions are usually advertised in local newspapers, through the Manpower Employment Organization, or online.

The evolution of computer technology has led to new forms of counseling and psychological therapies. Technological improvement is gradually resulting in altered ways of delivering counseling to help overcome problems associated with distance. Indeed, some interesting initiatives have been taking place in this context. For example, the Counseling Centre for Students at the University of Athens provides a computer-mediated Web consulting service. Communication is asynchronous, and the students are able to contact the service by using either an anonymous online form (the only requested data are the student's gender and age) or their personal e-mail account. The messages (questions) and answers from the anonymous online form are published on the website. Personal e-mails are posted only with the permission of the sender. Previous research (Efstathiou, 2006) has shown that the Web consulting service at the University of Athens enjoys high popularity among Greek students, and its current functioning is deemed satisfactory by both users and visitors. E-supervision has also been adopted by private colleges running counseling training programs.

This form of counseling is expanding into the private sector as well, resulting in many advertisements publicizing telecounseling by professionals. Similar to this, there are also specialized helplines for people with specific problems, such as a chronic illness (e.g., rheumatic disease, Alzheimer's disease), issues of drug or alcohol use or addiction, or various forms of abuse (e.g., domestic violence). Other helplines are of a more general scope and address issues of psychosocial and sexual health among adults, children, and adolescents.

Diversity Issues

The official language of Greece is Greek, and 98% of the population identify themselves as Greek Orthodox in their religious beliefs. Although Greek society is largely homogeneous in terms of ethnicity, language, and religion, since the 1990s a large number of economic immigrants (and political refugees) from the Balkans, Asia, and Africa have moved to Greece, creating a more diverse picture of contemporary Greece. It is estimated that about 7%–10% of the population in Greece is composed of people from other countries (Psalti, 2007). This fact has led to the realization of the need to consider multicultural concerns when counseling people from different cultural backgrounds. It is true that Greek counselors (and other mental health professionals) need to challenge the existing—mainly Western—theories of counseling and move toward the development of multicultural counseling competencies. This need has lately been a primary focus of Greek helping professionals. Everyone faces the challenge of identifying their current level of multicultural competence and learning how to work more effectively with culturally different clients.

As noted earlier, Greek society is thought to be at the midpoint in terms of a collectivist versus individualist orientation. The traditional extended and nuclear Greek family is patriarchal, with the father typically the provider and the mother a housewife. Nevertheless, with the support of gender equality legislation enacted during the past several decades and as a result of various socioeconomic changes, the position of women in Greek society has changed (Mylonas et al., 2006).

However, there are still some preconceived ideas regarding gender roles that are also related to attitudes toward counseling and help-seeking behaviors. For example, studies using Greek samples show that men hold more negative attitudes toward counseling and are more reluctant than women to seek professional help (Giovazolias, Leontopoulou, & Triliva, 2010).

These differences can be attributed to several factors. Frank (2000) offered a framework for understanding such differences. According to him, (a) women are less reticent about admitting their difficulties than men, (b) women in general have more psychological difficulties than men, and (c) women suffer more as a consequence of sexist practices. Although any of these explanations could be applicable in this case, the cultural context of Greece and more specifically the socialized views of masculinity (which encourage men to fix problems without help, deny psychological issues, and withhold the expression of emotion) are more conducive to the first point. In that sense, we can argue that the traditional male gender role—that men should be independent, controlled, and self-sufficient—may lead Greek males to significantly less self-admittance and, therefore, an underreporting of psychological (or other) concerns.

Related to this is that a fear of stigma has been found to act as a hindrance to attitudes toward counseling and help-seeking behaviors in general (Pederson & Vogel, 2007). The existence of a public stigma (i.e., negative views of a person by others) with regard to psychological difficulties is an indisputable fact for both men and women in Greece. Previous research has found that people tend to report more stigma in regard to people who are in counseling or who are seeking professional help (Angermeyer & Dietrich, 2006). It has been suggested that the internalization of these negative images (self-stigma) can lead to a self-perception of being weak or inadequate (lacking in self-efficacy) should one turn to a counselor for help. This function may be very relevant to the Greek context, in which the predominant sources of help for psychological concerns, as noted earlier, have long been the family or friends and counseling is still associated, albeit to a diminished level compared to the past, with severe problems and mental disturbances, negative images involving harmful behaviors, or people who have a complete lack of social support.

However, self-stigmatization may lead individuals with high levels of psychological distress to not recognize that their psychological condition is unusual, to not understand that there are relatively straightforward and effective ways of coping with the distress (e.g., through counseling), to not know how to obtain help in coping with the distress, or to avoid any help-seeking behaviors to limit the harmful consequences associated with being stigmatized.

Counselor Education

It was not until 2009 that the first two state university counseling master's programs started operating in Greece. However, European and American private colleges operating in

Greece offered master's programs in counseling and counseling psychology before this time. These colleges had started operating years earlier but are not yet officially recognized by the Greek state.

The two officially recognized graduate counseling programs offered by Greek universities have a similar curriculum leading to a master's degree. They comprise 10–12 theoretical courses, 2–3 labs in counseling skills and counseling processes, about 1,000 hours of supervised practicum, and about 40 hours of individual therapy. Both are 2-year, full-time programs that require a research-based master's thesis. Holders of the master's degree may continue to pursue their doctoral studies, which involves another 3 years of study and the writing of a doctoral thesis.

There are minor differences between the two officially recognized master's programs. The first program, a joint program of the University of Athens and the University of Thrace, offers a master's degree in either counseling psychology or counseling. Psychology graduates can apply for the counseling psychology program, and humanity graduates, teachers, and social workers can apply for the counseling program. The second program is offered by the University of Thessaly and leads to a master's degree in counseling.

There are also counselors and counseling psychologists in Greece who have either studied abroad (mainly in the United Kingdom, the United States, and Canada) or completed training programs offered by private, non–officially recognized colleges and organizations (called Colleges of Liberal Studies) in Greece. A clearer identity is attached to vocational counselors who have obtained their master's degree from the country's only graduate program in vocational guidance and counseling, offered at the University of Athens. Holders of this degree are usually education graduates who may be hired by private schools or work independently in private practice.

The Future

There is currently an increase in professional and research activity within the counseling field in Greece and a growing demand for focused graduate programs as well as effective counseling services. Counselors are actively involved in clinical, teaching, and research settings. However, in order to maintain accountability, counselors need to follow the scientist-practitioner model, supporting their practice with theory and research (evidence-based practice) and using their clinical experience to generate new research questions (Malikiosi-Loizos & Ivey, 2012). The maintenance of high educational and professional standards will ensure the effectiveness of the services offered and will make the profession even more accountable to the public. This is a crucial step that will also strengthen the professional position of counselors among other mental health professionals and enable them to provide counseling with the needed legal recognition.

Therefore, it is imperative to develop accredited graduate programs with systematically organized education in which trainees receive specialized training in theoretical, preventive, intervention, assessment, and ethical issues so that they are better prepared to face the new challenges of the ever-changing social reality. Any graduate program should be accompanied by a properly supervised practical experience as well as opportunities for personal development. All counseling psychologists and counselors currently working in Greece obtained their degrees abroad, mostly from European countries (i.e., the United Kingdom), the United States, and Canada. The first two graduate programs in counseling and counseling psychology were started in an effort to fill this gap and highlight the need for the advancement of the profession in Greece.

The efforts of the Division of Counseling Psychology of the Hellenic Psychological Society and the Greek Association of Counseling should be directed toward safeguarding the field by establishing credentials and instituting accreditation and licensure criteria.

The European Union has dictated a course of rigid austerity for Greece aimed at lowering the country's existing budget deficit from its current level of nearly 13% to less than

3%. In terms of wages and social standards, Greece in fact ranks among the worst paid countries in Europe. Furthermore, in terms of competitiveness, Greece has fallen to 83rd place on the World Economic Forum index (European Commission, 2011), below countries such as Botswana, Namibia, and Bulgaria. This situation has a number of implications for the everyday lives of the Greek people. More specifically, a growing number of people report a sense of frustration, uncertainty, disappointment, and ineffectiveness (often described as a sense of losing control) as well as a sense of inadequacy in family life due to a lack of time or money to maintain their former lifestyle. This in turn has created an increasing need for counseling interventions targeting these issues. Indeed, counseling can help people come to terms with these life events and give them more confidence to deal with the future. However, as the overall income of the Greek people has dropped dramatically, many face great difficulty paying for such services. One could argue that this situation calls for a reduction in counseling fees, which would result in a decrease in counseling psychologists' income.

In conclusion, despite the existing situation, one could argue that the future prospects of the counseling profession are favorable, as it is expected that the public will become increasingly more familiar with the concept of counseling and potential clients will be inclined to seek help from counselors rather than other, more medically oriented helping professionals (i.e., psychiatrists and clinical psychologists).

References

Angermeyer, M. C., & Dietrich, S. (2006). Public beliefs about and attitudes towards people with mental illness: A review of population studies. *Acta Psychiatrica Scandinavica, 113,* 163–179.

British Association for Counselling. (1991). *Code of ethics and practice for counselors.* Rugby, England: Author.

Dimitropoulos, E. (1992). *Counseling and counseling psychology.* Athens, Greece: Grigoris.

Efstathiou, G. (2006). *Diadiktyaki symvouleftiki foititon* [Students' psychological web consulting]. Unpublished doctoral dissertation, University of Athens, Greece.

European Commission. (2011). *Assessments of Greece's convergence programme.* Retrieved from http://ec.europa.eu/economy_finance/eu/countries/greece_en.htm

Frank, E. (2000). *Gender and its effects on psychopathology.* Washington, DC: American Psychiatric Press.

Georgas, J. (1989). Family values in Greece: From collectivist to individualist. *Journal of Cross-Cultural Psychology, 2,* 326–342.

Giovazolias, T., Leontopoulou, S., & Triliva, S. (2010). Assessment of Greek university students' counselling needs and attitudes: An exploratory study. *International Journal for the Advancement of Counselling, 32*(2), 101–116.

Kalantzi-Azizi, A., Stalikas, A., Malikiosi-Loizos, M., Roussi, P., Triliva, S., Pomini, V., … Arsenidou, E. (2003). *Katagrafi kai parousiasiton symperasmaton tis ypoepitropis gia ton kathorismotou ton kritirion tou ergou tou psychologou-psychotherapevti* [Assessment and presentation of findings of the subcommittee for the definition of the criteria for the practice of psychology-psychotherapy]. Unpublished manuscript.

Lampropoulos, G. K., & Stalikas, A. (2009). Psychology and counseling in Greece: Rapid contemporary development in the context of a glorious past. In L. H. Gerstein, P. P. Heppner, S. Ægisdóttir, S.-M. A. Leung, & K. L. Norsworthy (Eds.), *International handbook of cross-cultural counseling: Cultural assumptions and practices worldwide* (pp. 345–355). Thousand Oaks, CA: Sage.

Malikiosi-Loizos, M. (1993). *Counseling psychology.* Athens, Greece: Elinika Grammata.

Malikiosi-Loizos, M., Christodoulidi, F., & Gialamas, V. (2010). *Counseling in the Greek culture.* Manuscript in preparation.

Malikiosi-Loizos, M., & Ivey, A. E. (2012). Counseling in Greece. *Journal of Counseling & Development, 90,* 113–118.

Mylonas, K., Gari, A., Giotsa, A., Pavlopoulos, V., & Panagiotopoulou, P. (2006). Greece. In J. Georgas, J. W. Berry, J. R. Van de Vijver, C. Kagitçibasi, & Y. H. Poortinga (Eds.), *Families across cultures* (pp. 344–352). New York, NY: Cambridge University Press.

Papastylianou, A., Alexopoulou, G., Doulami S., Tampouri, S., & Tsoli, C. (2009). Typoisinaisthimatikis diapedagogikis apo ton patera kai stixia polipolitismikis simvouleftikis [Paternal types of emotional education and multicultural counseling]. In M. Malikiosi Loizos & A. Papastylianou (Eds.), *Counseling psychology in men* (pp. 159–192). Athens, Greece: Ellinika Grammata.

Pederson, E. L., & Vogel, D. L. (2007). Male gender role conflict and willingness to seek counseling: Testing a mediation model on college-aged men. *Journal of Counseling Psychology, 54,* 373–384.

Psalti, A. (2007). Training Greek teachers in cultural awareness. *School Psychology International, 28,* 148–162.

Rott, G. (2006). I pagkosmiopoiisi tis Anotatis Ekpaidevsis: Prokliseis kai efkairies gia tin askisi tis psychologikis symvouleftikis [The globalisation in the higher education: Challenges and opportunities for practising psychological counseling]. *Epitheorisi Symvoulevftikis kai Prosanatolismou, 76–77,* 118–129.

• • •

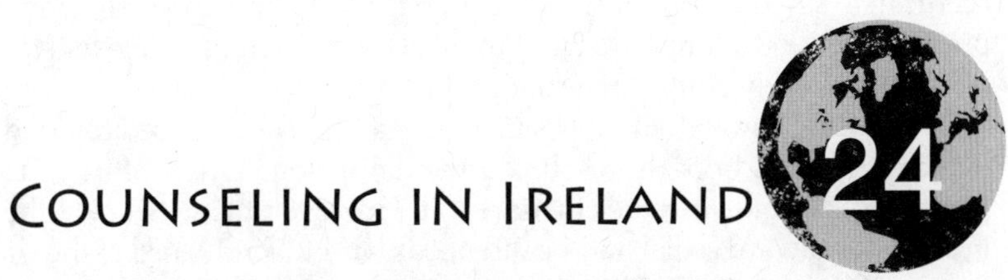

Counseling in Ireland

Padraig O'Morain, Garrett J. McAuliffe, Kayte Conroy, and Jennifer Johnson

The narrative of Irish life, as told for more than a century, has been largely a story of poverty and colonization with consequent fatalism and emotional repression. But relationships have mattered too and created a strong desire among the Irish to seek out a better future at home and abroad. More recently, the hand of modernism has resulted in massive changes in Irish attitudes toward sex, religion, emotional expression, and authority.

All of these themes, especially those of more recent origin, are important for counseling. The still unfolding story of Irish counseling is told in this chapter. Specifically, we present the history of the field in the Republic of Ireland, which has a population of 4.6 million people (Central Statistics Office Ireland, n.d.) and approximately the same square mileage as the U.S. state of West Virginia (Encyclopedia of the Nations, n.d.). This chapter contains a description of the development of counseling and its current status, including common practices, counselor training, and credentialing.

The island of Ireland is divided into two political entities. The Republic occupies most of the island, comprising 26 counties (some of which are subdivided into smaller administrative units, also called "counties"). The six counties of Northern Ireland form part of the United Kingdom. Both the Republic and the United Kingdom are members of the European Union. For convenience, we use the word *Ireland* to refer to the Republic of Ireland, as counseling in the Republic is the focus of this chapter.

A few clarifications on the Irish use of terms for helpers are in order. The services provided by counselors (or *counsellors,* as it is spelled in Ireland) and psychotherapists are seen as distinct from the services provided by psychologists. In regard to the distinction between counseling and psychotherapy, it seems fair to say that the public makes no distinction. The same body that accredits counselors accredits many psychotherapists. In this chapter, for the sake of convenience, the term *counseling* is used to refer both to counseling and to psychotherapy.

The Historical Development of Counseling

Ireland has experienced a particularly tumultuous history of invasion, rebellion, and assimilation. In the Irish narrative, independence was lost with the arrival of the Anglo-Normans in 1169 and regained in 1922 following the War of Independence. For the next 50 years, the Republic of Ireland was a largely isolated, Catholic, agricultural democracy characterized by poverty and emigration. This began to change in the 1960s, when a program of free trade and industrialization triggered the development of a modern industrial society (Ferriter, 2004). Also in that decade, television and other influences increased Ireland's connection with the outside world, particularly with the cultures of Britain and the United States. However, the conservative Catholic clergy and others greeted that modernization with chagrin.

Catholicism provided a complete guide to behavior and thinking for most of the Irish people until the 1960s. This is one explanation for why counseling had barely been heard of until the 1970s and 1980s. Moreover, the Irish Catholic Church was resistant to any intrusions into family life, especially in the area of sexuality (Barrington, 1987). It would not be accurate to say that the Catholic Church actively prevented the development of counseling prior to the 1960s. It had no need to do so because no space existed in which counseling as it is known today could take root and flourish.

Meanwhile, through the 1960s mental health services were provided in heavily stigmatized, overcrowded, and poorly resourced mental hospitals. The attitude toward mental illness in Ireland was to hide it rather than treat it. However, the 1960s saw the beginning of a change in attitudes toward social and health needs, and the influence of the Catholic Church began to wane (O'Morain, 2007). This change was accompanied by growth, slow at first, in the availability and popularity of counseling. Through a series of scandals, this growth accelerated in tandem with the decline of the Church as a source of counsel in the widest sense of that word.

Beginnings

In this context of emotional denial and repression, it is ironic that much of the impetus for the growth of counseling from the 1960s onward came from the Catholic Church and, though to a lesser extent, the Church of Ireland. Therefore, it is hardly surprising that when a counseling service emerged in the 1960s it was, for the most part, set firmly within a Catholic worldview and under the auspices of that Church. The Catholic Marriage Advisory Council, as the name implies, began to offer marriage counseling to Catholic couples in Ireland in 1962. Today this counseling agency, funded by state bodies and the Catholic bishops, is known as Accord (Accord, n.d.) and continues to flourish in a secular society. The same year, 1962, saw the establishment of a marriage counseling service for minority (Protestant) Church of Ireland couples. It later became a nondenominational service and, like Accord, continues to flourish under the name Relationships Ireland. Some of those trained for this marriage and family work later went on to become independent counselors and were involved in the establishment of the Irish Association for Counselling and Psychotherapy (IACP), which is the leading counseling organization in the country (Feldstein, 2011).

Another strand of counseling also commenced in the 1960s when career guidance counseling was introduced first to vocational training schools in Dublin and then to secondary schools. The Psychological Service of the Irish Department of Education supported this impulse. As part of this shift, University College Dublin introduced a course for career guidance teachers in the 1960s and put an emphasis on counseling as well as on career choice. Today the provision of guidance counseling is underpinned by legislation and provided as a program of the Department of Education and Skills.

Furthermore, the Institute of Guidance Counsellors was founded in 1968 to further promote professionalism within second-level schools (middle and high schools), third-level schools (colleges and universities), adult guidance services, private practice, and other settings (Institute of Guidance Counsellors, n.d.).

Despite these beginnings, the concept of counseling in Ireland had yet to take hold in the general population. Psychiatry and psychoanalysis were still the image of mental health intervention in the popular mind.

Emergence

The 1970s saw the beginnings of employee assistance programs, the establishment by a formerly Protestant adoption society of a nondenominational counseling service for single pregnant women, growth in school guidance counseling, and a counseling service for women who had been raped. Both the Catholic Church and the smaller Protestant Church of Ireland marriage counseling services were continually producing new counselors who went on, in some cases, to engage in general counseling. The scope of school counseling also began to increase.

The 1980s and the 1990s could be said to be the decades in which counseling became established in Ireland as an activity in its own right, no longer confined to specific areas or institutional control. The IACP was founded in 1981 out of a concern about unqualified people engaging in practice while calling themselves "counselors" (Feldstein, 2011). The 1990s also saw the deepening of the authority crisis in the Catholic Church. Child sexual abuse scandals contributed to the significant decline in the authority of the Church (Ferriter, 2004). It is probably not coincidental that the Irish Church scandals have been accompanied by a growth in the demand for counseling, as people turn away from the Church as a source of guidance. Unlike in the past, few today would think of going to the local priest for advice on personal dilemmas.

The Current Status of Counseling

Counseling in Ireland continues to grow in popularity among those seeking services as well as those seeking to join the profession. Although Irish counselors work in a variety of settings, such as community mental health agencies, private practice, and schools, in the absence of a statutory registration system it is impossible to say how many trained counselors are working in the country overall. Therefore, it is also not possible to provide a comprehensive breakdown of how many counselors work in many of the various sectors. However, it is known that private practice and school counseling are the largest areas in which counselors are found.

School Counseling

Approximately 1,200 practitioners work as guidance counselors, mostly in secondary schools. Until recently, about one fourth of schools (those with more than 500 pupils) were allowed to employ a full-time guidance counselor over and above their normal quota of teachers. However, this arrangement was terminated at the end of 2011 as the government reduced spending on public services (Murray, 2012). Schools may now re-deploy their school counselors to teach subjects for which there would otherwise be no teacher. The effect will be to reduce the presence of school counselors in the counseling role.

School counselors provide counseling for students experiencing a range of mental health issues, including depression, anger, bereavement, and bullying. Students may also come to their attention because of anxiety or continuous breaches of discipline. They may come to guidance counselors as a result of referral by concerned teachers or through self-referral. In addition, school counselors provide career guidance.

Counseling in Private Practice

Statistics on whether private practice counselors are working full time or part time are not available, but anecdotal evidence suggests that the overwhelming majority are working part time. Similarly, many of the agencies that use the services of counselors do so on a part-time or panel basis. Counselors in private practice usually work with clients on a one-to-one basis on a broad range of mental health and emotional issues. They may also work with couples or families. Clients are usually self-referred, although general practitioners (family doctors) also refer patients. In addition, some counselors in private practice see clients referred by employee counseling services.

Community Mental Health Counseling

The provision of community mental health counseling is somewhat patchy and underdeveloped in Ireland, possibly because counseling is a young profession in the country. Counseling in community settings is usually provided by nonprofit, nongovernmental organizations set up for that purpose or by training institutions that wish to provide counseling practice for their students. The nonprofit, nongovernmental organizations often rely on the free or almost-free services of counselors (Institute of Integrative Counselling and Psychotherapy, n.d.) who have obtained their counseling qualification but who need to accumulate a specified number of hours of practice before applying for accreditation with bodies such as the IACP.

Age Profile of Counselors

The average age of Irish counselors is relatively high. According to a recent IACP membership questionnaire, the average counselor is 45–55 years of age (IACP, 2009). The older age of Irish counselors may be attributable to the relatively recent development of counseling in Ireland, as explained previously, which makes the profession a second career for many individuals. This is because it is difficult to make a full-time living in private practice as a counselor in Ireland, primarily because of the lack of insurance reimbursement for services rendered.

Professional Associations and Credentialing

Today the IACP has approximately 3,500 members, suggesting a strong growth in interest in counseling since its foundation in 1981. The IACP is not oriented toward a particular counseling approach. Another accrediting body, the Irish Association of Humanistic and Integrative Psychotherapy (IAHIP), was formed in 1992 as an association specifically designed to represent humanistic and integrative psychotherapists. The IAHIP now has more than 700 accredited psychotherapists.

Although other bodies provide accreditation in certain specialty areas such as addiction counseling, the IACP and the IAHIP are currently the main accrediting bodies for counselors and psychotherapists. They recognize each other's supervisors, and dual membership in the IACP and the IAHIP is not uncommon. Despite the growth in IACP and IAHIP accreditation, any individual can continue to call himself or herself a "counselor" and set up a practice. As mentioned earlier, there is no mechanism in place to license counselors in Ireland. This is in contrast to the United States, which has the ability to license counselors in all 50 states.

Twelve helping professions have been listed for statutory registration by the Health and Social Care Professionals Council (CORU, n.d.-a.), which was appointed under 2005 legislation. (The name CORU is not an acronym but is derived from a Gaelic word meaning "fair," "just," and "proper.") Although the list includes psychologists and social workers, it does not include counselors. Social workers became the first professionals to be registered when the Social Workers Register opened on May 31, 2011. If counseling must wait until the other 11 professions on the list have been registered, then regulation may be quite some time away.

As noted previously, psychologists are not yet regulated or licensed in Ireland, although psychology is one of 12 professions that are due to be regulated by the state. However, psychologists have their own professional body, the Psychological Society of Ireland, which sets standards and provides an assurance to potential employers that the psychologist meets educational and other requirements. The status of the Psychological Society of

Ireland is recognized by CORU, the body that has the task of regulating the 12 professions (CORU, n.d.-b.). The Psychological Society of Ireland is the only body to which CORU provides a link from the psychologist section of its website.

Relationships With Other Helping Professions

Social workers do not provide counseling in the broad sense. However, counseling is seen as part of a range of skills. A large portion of social work is focused on working with vulnerable children and with families in need of support. Currently little can be found in the way of linkages between social workers and counselors in their day-to-day activities. An exception is the fact that the director of the bachelor in social studies (social work) degree at Trinity College Dublin, Ms. Gloria Kirwan, was until recently a member of the editorial board of *Éisteach*, the journal of the IACP, and has written for the journal.

Psychologists in Ireland include clinical, counseling, and educational psychologists. Counseling psychologists must complete an accredited honors undergraduate degree and an accredited postgraduate training program in counseling psychology. These are requirements of the Psychological Society of Ireland, which regulates psychologists. As mentioned earlier, psychology is among the professions listed for statutory registration.

Cost

The cost of counseling is a significant problem in Ireland. Although the government pays for counseling for some specific groups (such as people infected with hepatitis C caused by contaminated blood products), most counseling is private and must be fully paid for by the client. Health insurance companies do not reimburse for counseling. Therefore, recourse to counseling largely depends on income. Those with the lowest incomes cannot afford the fees.

Best Counseling Practices

Most Common Approaches

In the absence of statistics on counseling approaches in Ireland, views on the most common approaches are necessarily impressionistic and personal. With this caveat in mind, it seems fair to assert that the person-centered approach is the common thread running through much of the counseling in Ireland. For instance, in the directory of counselors on the website of the IACP many counselors describe their approach as person-centered, whereas many others use the term *humanistic* (IACP, n.d.-a.). Many of these same counselors describe themselves as "integrative," combining person-centered/humanistic approaches and cognitive behavior therapy as appropriate.

Among the most popular cognitive–behavioral approaches is choice theory/reality therapy. In 1985, the Institute of Guidance Counsellors began to regularly bring Dr. William Glasser to Ireland to teach choice theory and reality therapy (William Glasser Institute Ireland, n.d.). This initiative was highly successful, with large numbers of people studying this approach.

Addiction counseling is an important field of work in Ireland. The Irish Association of Alcohol and Addiction Counsellors (n.d.) accredits counselors in this area and has almost 1,000 members. Addiction counselors may work as team members in public, community, and private addiction services or individually as private counselors.

Client Rights and Ethical Standards

Regardless of the counseling approach being used, citizens of Ireland have personal rights under both the Constitution of Ireland and the European Convention on Human Rights Act. Specifically, the Mental Health Act of 2001 stipulates that treatment should be performed in the person's best interest; that any decision about care and treatment must respect the right to dignity, bodily integrity, and autonomy; and that the person receiving services must be able to express his or her views regarding their care. The Mental Health Commission (n.d.) provides information on client rights.

In addition to the statute-provided ethical codes, bodies such as the IACP and the IAHIP have adopted codes of ethics and practice that must be followed by members. These codes outline the fundamental values of counseling and general principles arising from these values, including but not limited to privacy, confidentiality, informed consent, and a complaint procedure.

Counselor Education

The bodies involved in the education and training of counselors in Ireland fall into two categories: those that provide both academic *and* practical training, and those that provide an academic education only.

Courses accredited by bodies such as the IACP tend to have certain components in common. Students study a variety of theories of counseling, participate in personal development through personal counseling, and provide counseling under supervision when they reach an advanced educational level. This practical experience is gained through placements with external bodies or through low-cost counseling services run by the institutions themselves (IACP, n.d.-b.).

In some cases, students work toward a diploma, which may take 2 to 3 years to obtain, or they may work toward a degree, which usually takes 4 to 5 years. The training body itself may award the degree if it is accredited by the state's Higher Education and Training Awards Council. Alternatively, a university may award the degree, either through a program being directly provided by the university itself or through a partnership with an autonomous school.

Following the completion of their studies for either a diploma or degree, the IACP requires students to complete 450 hours of client counseling before accreditation. Students graduating from courses that omit clinical placements and/or personal development are unlikely to be accredited by the leading accrediting bodies regardless of whether they have earned a diploma or a degree. The Higher Education and Training Awards Council is currently reviewing the whole area of standards and education in counseling and psychotherapy ("Editorial," 2011).

One training initiative stands out as an exemplar. This was the introduction by Maynooth University, near Dublin, of an extramural certificate in counseling skills course in 1984. Because it is an extramural (i.e., part-time, adult education, open to all) course, it introduced large numbers of people (more than 14,000 in the first 24 years) who had never attempted degree-level courses in the past to the possibility of a career in counseling (Maynooth University, n.d.). Many graduates of this academic course have gone on to complete diploma or degree courses leading to accreditation. For most of its history, Maynooth had been a university that trained young men to become Catholic priests. Thus, the Catholic Church contributed substantially to the development of counseling, even as its direct influence was dwindling.

Diversity Issues

A history of emigration meant that issues of multiculturalism and diversity were once largely absent from the development of counseling in Ireland. This began to change in the early 1990s, when a period of immigration began. However, at the time of this writing, immigration has declined and emigration has resumed because of the country's economic crisis.

Because of the years of immigration, there is a population of "new" Irish. They include persons from regions as diverse as Africa, South America, and Eastern Europe. Many of those who arrived as asylum seekers or who came for work live on relatively low incomes and may find it difficult to meet the cost of private counseling. However, low-cost counseling services are beginning to connect with immigrants.

Irish Travellers, of whom there are about 30,000 (Pavee Point, n.d.), make up another ethnic group in Ireland. The Travellers are a people who left the land centuries ago and proceeded to live a nomadic life, like the Romany do in Europe. Many live now in public housing. Travellers tend to form tight-knit groups and use their own language, *cant*, to talk to one another. This cohesion may very well discourage the sharing of family problems with "country people," as they describe the non-Traveller population. Although some counseling services are provided for Travellers, the vast majority of counselors have never met a Traveller in the counseling room.

All this said, many counselor training bodies, such as the Institute of Integrative Counselling and Psychotherapy, now include a core multicultural element in their training. As the immigrant population settles down and as their children grow up in a society in which counseling is a normal part of the landscape, the experience of diversity in counseling is expected to grow.

The Future

Despite credentialing issues and cost barriers, the counseling profession is growing rapidly in Ireland; however, change in the cost situation is not likely in the near future. There is no evidence to show that the government agenda will facilitate the direct provision of counseling services to those who cannot afford private counselors. And given the economic and fiscal challenges facing the country, no government in the medium-term future is likely to think about, let alone propose, the provision of counseling as part of the state's health care.

Under national health care, every Irish citizen is entitled to free hospital treatment, including inpatient mental health care (O'Morain, 2007). About half the population pays for private health insurance, which can often provide quicker access to inpatient care. Those private health care companies have not shown any enthusiasm for reimbursing the cost of outpatient counseling. In fact, little or no demand for such reimbursement has come from the bodies representing counselors. Licensure will probably need to precede even the possibility of such insurance reimbursement.

One interesting model for the provision of low-cost counseling has emerged, namely the provision of counseling in the community by training schools. In Tallaght, a large suburb of Dublin, for instance, the Institute of Integrative Counselling and Psychotherapy is training counseling students to degree level (i.e., its degree is officially recognized as equivalent to a university degree although the Institute itself is not a university) and has established a low-cost counseling service called the Village Counselling Service. Counseling is provided mainly by advanced students and graduates. The service is funded in two ways: through core funding from the state mental health service and through fees paid directly by clients. This model, if followed more generally in the country, could provide services for those who could not otherwise afford them.

As for the future of counselor training in Ireland, this whole area is being reviewed by the Higher Education and Training Awards Council. Moreover, training bodies and students hope to be in a position to flourish in a new regulatory environment (Psychological Therapies Forum, 2008), even though the shape and time of the arrival of that environment is unknown. These dynamics alone make it likely that counseling training will increasingly be done through courses leading to university degrees or equivalent degrees.

Conclusion

Counseling, which had hardly been heard of in Ireland in the 1960s, is now an accepted and familiar part of the landscape. However, it remains unaffordable for many and is unregulated on a statutory basis. Future developments are likely to see continuing moves toward regulation and toward greater access to counseling for people with low incomes. The speed with which these moves will take place, however, is entirely unpredictable.

References

Accord. (n.d.). *Catholic marriage care service.* Retrieved from http://www.accord.ie

Barrington, R. (1987). *Health, medicine and politics in Ireland 1900-1970.* Dublin, Ireland: Institute of Public Administration.

Central Statistics Office Ireland. (n.d.). *Population 1901-2006.* Retrieved from http://www.cso.ie/Quicktables/GetQuickTables.aspx?FileName=CNA13.asp&TableName=Population+1901+-+2006&StatisticalProduct=DB_CN

CORU. (n.d.-a.). *Professions to be regulated.* Retrieved from www.coru.ie

CORU. (n.d.-b.). *Psychologists.* Retrieved from http://www.coru.ie/regulated-professionals/professions-to-be-regulated/psychologists

Editorial. (2011, Autumn). *Éisteach, 11*(3).

Encyclopedia of the Nations. (n.d.). *Ireland.* Retrieved from http://www.nationsencyclopedia.com/economies/Europe/Ireland.html

Feldstein, S. (2011). *Celebrating 30 years.* Dublin, Ireland: Irish Association for Counselling and Psychotherapy.

Ferriter, D. (2004). *The transformation of Ireland 1900-2000.* London, England: Profile Books.

Institute of Guidance Counsellors. (n.d.). *As it was in the beginning—A brief history of the IGC.* Retrieved from www.igc.ie

Institute of Integrative Counselling and Psychotherapy. (n.d.). *Professional diploma in integrative counselling and psychotherapy.* Retrieved from http://www.iicp.ie/courseshow.php?id=12

Irish Association for Counselling and Psychotherapy. (2009). *Responses to IACP membership questionnaire—Supplement 1.* Dublin, Ireland: Author.

Irish Association for Counselling and Psychotherapy. (n.d.-a.). *Find a counsellor/psychotherapist.* Retrieved from http://www.irish-counselling.ie/index.php/find-a-counsellor-psychotherapist

Irish Association for Counselling and Psychotherapy. (n.d.-b.). *IACP register of recognised professional psychotherapy/counselling training courses.* Retrieved from http://www.irish-counselling.ie/index.php/recognised-training-courses

Irish Association of Alcohol and Addiction Counsellors. (n.d.). *About us.* Retrieved from http://www.iaaac.org/content/about.html

Maynooth University. (n.d.). *NUI certificate in counselling skills.* Retrieved from http://adulteducation.nuim.ie/courses/CounsellingSkills.shtml

Mental Health Commission. (n.d.). *Working together for quality mental health services.* Retrieved from http://www.mhcirl.ie

Murray, N. (2012, March 3). Loss of guidance service "will increase inequality." *The Irish Examiner.* Retrieved from http://www.examiner.ie/ireland/education/loss-of-guidance-service-will-increase-inequality-185875.html

O'Morain, P. (2007). *The health of the nation.* Dublin, Ireland: Gill & Macmillan.

Pavee Point. (n.d.). *Frequently asked questions.* Retrieved from http://www.paveepoint.ie/pav_faq_a.html

Psychological Therapies Forum. (2008). *Submission on the statutory registration of counsellors and psychotherapists in Ireland.* Retrieved from http://www.napcp.ie/zdocs/report-on-the-regulation-of-practitioners-1.pdf

William Glasser Institute Ireland. (n.d.). *History of WGII.* Retrieved from http://www.wgii.ie/index.php?option=com_content&view=article&id=59&Itemid=62

• • •

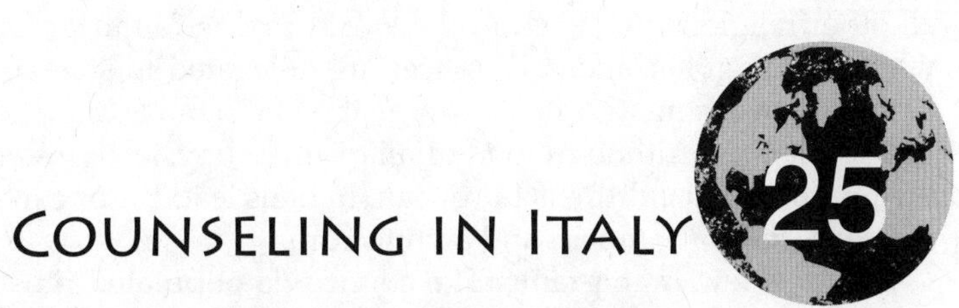

Counseling in Italy

Theodore P. Remley Jr., Davide Mariotti, and Tommaso Valleri

At the end of the Roman Empire the country of Italy was divided into regions with separate political entities. The country was not again united into a single governmental entity until 1870 (Duggan, 1994). Italy was the cultural center of the world from the 13th to the 16th centuries. More recently, the Italians fought on the same side as the United States during World War I but developed the Fascist Party and joined with Hitler during World War II (Duggan, 1994).

Italy is a peninsula located between Spain and Greece; the continent of Africa is less than 100 miles to its south, and it is bordered on the north by France, Switzerland, Austria, and Slovenia (Duggan, 1994). Because of its location among heavily populated countries and because it has access to the seas, Italy has both been a dominating force in Europe and been invaded by other countries throughout is existence. Its culture is envied throughout the world, and the country has enjoyed an economic success that has caused other powers to seek to conquer its land and resources. The development of the counseling profession in Italy has been profoundly influenced by the country's location, history, people, religious heritage, culture, politics, and living conditions.

Italy is surprisingly heavily populated. Italy has a population of just more than 61 million people (compared to 308 million in the United States) who live on about 116,000 square miles of land (roughly the size of Arizona, the sixth largest U.S. state). In Italy, there are about 500 people for each square mile of land, whereas in the United States there are only about 96 (WorldAtlas, 2011). This large number of people living in close proximity certainly has an impact on the issues and conflicts these people face on a regular basis and how they live their daily lives, which in turn has affected the development of the counseling profession in Italy.

The People of Italy

To understand the development of the counseling profession in Italy, it is helpful to have a perspective on the history of the country and a basic understanding of the people who live there. Despite having few immigrants, like most political entities in the world, Italy is not homogeneous. Instead the country is populated with groups of people who vary substantially in their values and way of life and how they deal with today's challenges. This is understandable in a country with deep historical, local roots that were fractured, often with great mutual animosity, for centuries. The land, culture, and people of Milan (located in the prosperous, industrial north) and Palermo (found on the poorer southern island of Sicily) are as different as in the land, culture, and people of two separate countries. Understandably, then, the counseling profession is developing along different lines in the various regions of the country.

The Italian language, the common Catholic religion, and a strong countrywide government are forces that unite Italians. Although it is possible to find German or Sardinian spoken in some northern pockets in the country, Italian is the official and universal language. More than 97% of Italians are Catholic (Adherents, 2011), even though almost all other religions practiced in the world can be found in Italy. Unlike the United States, where many governmental services are delegated to state and local political entities, the national government in Italy administers the schools, modes of transportation, and other public services. Although many Italians may physically resemble their Arabic neighbors, the predominant culture is European. Italians lead Europe in areas such as fashion design, culinary skills, art, music, and architecture.

Italy has few immigrants. The country is populated mostly by Italians, with only 2% of the population considered immigrants. Racial and cultural minorities are few and far between. As a result, diversity is not as valued in Italy as it is in some countries, and Italians are not as sensitive to the values, views, or rights of minority groups in their country. Although some counseling programs exist specifically to help immigrants, multicultural counseling is not a compelling topic among Italian counselors.

Cook and Furstenberg (2002) compared transitions from adolescence to adulthood in four countries (Italy, Sweden, Germany, and the United States). They concluded that Italian youth take longer to leave their parents' homes than young adults in other countries. Cook and Furstenberg said, "Italian tradition associates independence with three Ms to be achieved in the late teens or early twenties: *mestiere, matrimonio, e macchina* (a steady job, marriage, and a car)" (p. 265).

Cook and Furstenberg (2002) observed that Italians are more dependent on their families than are people in Sweden, Germany, and the United States because the government in Italy does not tax as heavily and thus does not provide as much for citizens as is provided in other European and Western countries. Cook and Furstenberg found that Italians leave their family of origin and start their own households later than in the other three countries. Between the ages of 18 and 30, Italians are earning college degrees at a higher rate than young people in other countries, and it takes longer to complete an undergraduate education in Italy (an average of 7 years). As a result, unemployment is very high among young adults. Young people in other countries appear to make up for underemployment and lower wages by cohabiting or living with other younger people, but neither of those options are prevalent in Italy, primarily because of cultural and religious traditions. Italian young adults usually stay in the homes of their parents until they get married. More than in other countries, Italian youth study in universities within commuting distance of their parental home, allowing them to live with their parents while they complete their college education. Middle-class children who live at home are more educated than their parents. As a result of the status education provides them, adult children living at home are given a great deal of autonomy, coming and going as they please. Italian families were originally hierarchical, with the father dictating some home activities and the mother dictating others, but now relationships between parents and adult children have become more egalitarian. Parents tolerate adult children's social and sexual activities, as the adult children tolerate patterns of living from their parents that they might consider outdated.

When they do leave their parents' home, Italians leave to marry more often than to live alone or cohabit. After they get married and have children, Italian women often stay home to raise children; however, Italian mothers are working outside the home at the same time they raise their children much more today than in years past (BBC News, 2006). There are fewer children per woman in Italy than in any of the other three countries studied by Cook and Furstenberg (2002). In fact, Italy has one of the lowest average numbers of children per woman in the world (Britannica, 2010).

The Current Status of Counseling

In Italy the counseling profession is rooted more in *assistenza sociale* (social care) than in psychology. Activities related to counseling can be found in the history of social assistance that began around the 1920s (Margarone, 1994). Social welfare initiatives were developed formally in Italy in 1929 by royal decree. Italian social welfare had a purely philanthropic and volunteer foundation. Also in the 1920s, the first all-female boarding schools were established to educate social workers, and in the 1950s these boarding schools were opened to males.

In Italy, a bachelor's degree in psychology entitles the bearer to be licensed by the Italian government as a psychologist. However, Italians make a sharp distinction between psychology and psychotherapy. To use the title "psychotherapist" or to practice psychotherapy in Italy, a licensed physician or licensed psychologist must attend and complete a 4- to 5-year psychotherapist training program after becoming licensed. The first degrees in psychology were established in Italian universities in the 1970s (Bosio, 2004). At that same time period, private schools of psychotherapy located outside of universities started to develop professional relationship-oriented instruction for students that was centered on the individual. However, these private schools of psychotherapy did not have a clear definition or offer specific expertise.

Counseling as it is known today was introduced in Italy only in recent times (Edelstein, 2007). As recently as the early 1990s Italians started to use the term *counseling* to refer to relational activities aimed at improving the quality of people's lives, primarily according to the person-centered theory of the American psychologist Carl R. Rogers.

From the 1990s to the present, counseling schools in Italy have tended to follow the European Association for Counselling standards. Italian counseling schools are private.

Currently the counseling profession is not regulated by the Italian government. As a result, no training criteria are required to enter the profession. In essence, in Italy today, anyone can claim to be a counselor and can offer counseling services (Fani & Valleri, 2009). The absence of standards has created substantial confusion and, in some cases, a real abuse of the term *counselor.* Some Italians translate the term *counseling* with the Italian word *consulenza,* which means "advice." Others use the word *counseling* to refer to the activities of a psychologist or to a psychological interview. Still others believe that *counseling* is more properly a set of helping skills (in communication, forming relationships, education, etc.) used by professionals, including counselors, psychologists, physicians, and social workers (Valleri, 2009).

In 2007, the Italian government issued *Decreto Legislativo 6 novembre 2007, n. 206, Attuazione della direttiva 2005/36/CE relativa al riconoscimento delle qualifiche professionali* (Legislative Decree of November 6, 2007, Number 206, Implementation of the Directive 2005/36/CE Relative to the Acknowledgment of Professional Qualifications). In Article 26, the law set forth for the first time some rules related to professional associations (Valleri, 2008). In essence, this new law follows European Union directives. Instead of the Italian government regulating new professions through passing laws and establishing registers, this law announced that the government intended in the future to regulate professional associations, which in turn would have the power to credential individual professionals (Valleri, 2008).

Some existing associations changed their procedures to meet the requirements of the decree. Associations that made the necessary changes included the Società Italiana di Counseling (SICo; the Italian Society of Counseling), the Associazione Italiana Counselling (AICo; the Italian Counseling Association), the Società Italiana Counselor ed Operatore Olistico (SICOOl; the Italian Society of Counselors and Holistic Professionals), and the Associazione Nazionale Counselor Relazionali (ANCoRe; the National Association of Relational Counselors).

AssoCounseling was formed in July 2009 (AssoCounseling, 2011). AssoCounseling was the first Italian association that created processes for protecting not only professional counselors but counseling clients as well. It is currently the most important Italian counseling association because of its work in the field of professional certification. AssoCounseling has some unique aspects that distinguish it from other organizations in the field of counseling in Italy. For example, AssoCounseling members are exclusively counselors. In addition, members of the AssoCounseling executive committee must be counselors and may not be members of other mental health professions.

Because there is no government register for counselors in Italy, AssoCounseling created the Registro Italiano dei Counselor (the Italian Register of Counselors). Professional counselors can enroll in this register after they have obtained the Certificato di Competenza Professionale in Counseling (CCPC; the Certificate of Professional Competence in Counseling). This certificate is a credential attesting to the possession of specific skills and knowledge related to specific areas of intervention within counseling.

Each candidate for the CCPC must demonstrate that he or she has obtained a diploma in counseling issued by a training school approved by AssoCounseling and has completed supervised experience as a counselor. Those counselors who meet these criteria may then take the professional assessment. After passing this examination, candidates become certified.

The CCPC is awarded to qualified members of AssoCounseling, and certificate holders have various levels of accreditation (professional counselor, counselor supervisor, or counselor trainer). In addition, certificates indicate counselors' areas of intervention (school, hospital, business, community, private counseling, etc.). Accreditation levels and areas of intervention are defined on the basis of work experience, training, and supervision.

AssoCounseling (2012) has defined the counseling profession in Italy as follows:

> Professional counseling is an activity whose goal is to improve the quality of life of clients, supporting their strengths and abilities for self-determination. Counseling provides a space for listening and reflection, in which clients may explore problems related to evolutionary processes, phase transitions, and states of crisis and strengthens the capacity of clients to choose or change. Counseling is an intervention that uses various methods borrowed from different theoretical orientations. It caters to individuals, families, groups, and institutions. Counseling can be provided in various settings such as private practice, education, health, business.

AssoCounseling, in agreement with other Italian associations and the European Association for Counselling, has adopted training standards and minimum requirements for various activities related to preparing counselors. According to the dictates of modern accrediting systems, the association will periodically review the requirements related to its members' lifelong learning, professional liability insurance, compliance with the code of ethics, and supervision.

Currently two main factors are hampering the recognition of the counseling profession by the Italian government. On the one hand, the country is experiencing a tremendous governmental institutional inertia that is hindering Italy from launching major reforms that are needed for all 2 million professionals in Italy. On the other hand, licensed psychologists are adamantly opposed to the Italian government recognizing counseling as a profession. Italian licensed psychologists argue that counseling is one of the skills practiced by psychologists and therefore that it is not a separate profession. Currently there are about 70,000 licensed psychologists in Italy and only 4,000 counselors. The 70,000 psychologists pay annual fees of around €10 million (equivalent to approximately $13.5 million U.S.) to the entity that licenses psychologists, which in turn gives Italian psychologists a great deal of leverage in influencing governmental officials and private institutions. Because of the strength of these psychologists, in July 2010 Italian counselors established a coalition of organizations to lobby for the recognition of counselors by the Italian government. That coalition is known as the Coordinamento Italiano delle Associazioni di Counseling (the Italian Committee for Associations of Counseling).

Counseling Practices in Italy

Counseling is not yet a widely used intervention in Italy because it is not a regulated profession. As a result of the lack of governmental regulation, both private and institutional clients have reasonable doubts about the effectiveness of counselors and counseling. A direct consequence of the lack of regulation of the counseling profession in Italy is that counseling occurs most often in private practice rather than in governmental agencies, nonprofit agencies, or businesses. Because there are no job categories for counselors in Italian governmental settings, they cannot find employment, and therefore their only alternative is counseling in private practice. In private practices in Italy, the counseling process is offered as an "experience of exploration, discovery of the resources and fragility of clients, not least of which is the recognition of the value of the uniqueness of clients as human beings" (Mariotti, 2010).

In Italy, approximately 97% of the population identify themselves as Roman Catholic (Adherents, 2011). The concept of the value of people and their unrepeatable uniqueness has deep roots in Italian culture as it is inevitably linked to the Christian religion and tradition of the Roman Catholic Church, which still has its center in the Vatican in Rome.

An Italian cannot call himself or herself a Christian (Croce, 1944). The concept of Italians proving to others their right to be viewed as Christians is evident in their endless charity work in schools, orphanages, hospitals, and so on. Over time, charity institutions have become voluntary and social and have represented the tissue of the Italian welfare system (Cipolla, Cipriani, Colasanto, & d'Alessandro, 2010).

In the context of this Christian Roman Catholic nation, the counseling profession has found fertile soil to develop interventions that have as their foundation the supporting of each unique person, especially in his or her moments of fatigue and weakness. The Italian belief that individuals are unique and have value without judgment rejects the medical model of mental health that emphasizes psychological problems and pathological personality profiles. As a result, counselors and the counseling process focus primarily on developments within life, such as taking evolutionary steps; facing a marriage crisis; finding a new job; dealing with a serious illness; and responding to dramatic events such as bereavement or natural disasters such as earthquakes, floods, and so on (AssoCounseling, 2011).

Italian clients approach counseling as an opportunity for growth and development, and entering counseling is not necessarily tied to critical events. Counseling occurs either through individual or group sessions primarily in private practice and also takes place through specific forms of group counseling, such as experiential seminars. In experiential seminars, clients participate in experiences that enable greater self-understanding with the aim of improving their quality of life or performance at work; their relationships; or their performance in other areas, such as sports.

Even though counseling is practiced primarily in private settings, in recent years counselors have begun to find positions in schools, social services agencies, health services, and other work settings (Istituto per lo Sviluppo della Formazione Professionale dei Lavoratori [ISFOL], 2006). According to Ascenzi and Corsi (2005), counselors are beginning to establish programs in schools to address the motivational problems of students, the regular developmental challenges young people face as they grow up, and family crises. Counselors have also begun to establish career counseling programs in both public and private settings (Di Fabio, 1998). This expansion of counseling into areas beyond private practice is occurring despite the fact that counselors are not recognized as professionals by the government.

Italian counselors have recently become particularly active in the area of health counseling services. They provide services to individuals and groups with the goal of providing emotional support to patients and preventing disease (Giusti & Masiello, 2003). Counselors are skilled at promoting well-being centered on increased self-care and better quality relationships. Greater visibility and legitimacy for counseling in the Italian public health sector was a consequence of the passage in 1990 of Law 135, which required that a diagnostic test related to the treatment and prevention of HIV/AIDS be preceded and followed by a counseling intervention.

The main counseling theoretical approaches used in Italy, in both private practices and other settings, were identified in a study issued by the Italian government in 2006. ISFOL (the Institute for the Development of the Professional Formation of Workers) is a public department in Italy concerned with scientific research on professional and vocational training. According to ISFOL (2006), the most popular theoretical models in Italy are behavioral and cognitive–behavioral approaches, the constructivist approach, the existential-humanistic approach, the psychodynamic approach, and the integrated approach. This ISFOL publication was the result of an analysis of the professional literature and a review of documents.

Many counselors also use art counseling, which includes the use of drawing, dance, music, and theater in counseling. A number of Italian counselors believe techniques such as these provide meaningful experiences that foster client self-understanding. Therapies that are known in the United States as alternative therapies are also popular with some Italian counselors. These therapies include reiki and qigong, which are related to Chinese medicine; meditation techniques; and other Eastern techniques used for self-understanding. Internet counseling is used infrequently in Italy. Although e-mail, cell phones, and the Internet are very popular with the Italian population, there is little evidence that counselors are utilizing electronic means of counseling in their practices.

Diversity Issues

Because Italy is an exceptionally homogeneous society in that 98% of Italians were born in Italy (WorldAtlas, 2011), and because few immigrants reside in Italy, diversity has not been seen as an important counseling issue in the past. However, immigration has increased in recent years, and the entire country is seeing the effects of different cultures being established within the almost exclusively Catholic, family-based culture Italians have known throughout their history.

The roles of women are changing as they begin to work more often after childbirth (BBC News, 2006; Britannica, 2010). Italians living in cities and regions where they never saw or interacted with people different from themselves are experiencing diversity for the first time. Lesbian and gay persons are becoming more open after living in the shadows, and Italians are expressing acceptance of homosexual lifestyles (Angus-Reid Public Opinion, 2007; Italy Magazine, 2007). Italians are aware that their insular world is becoming much more diverse. As a result, schools of counseling are addressing multicultural, diversity, and social justice issues as a new area of study. However, diversity is currently not a major topic in counselor preparation or continuing education.

Counselor Education

Counselors are educated in Italian private schools that operate outside the university structure. No universities in Italy offer either undergraduate or graduate degrees that approximate the counselor preparation offered at the master's level in U.S. universities. Most Italian schools of counseling are identified with a counseling specialization that is theoretically based. Many Italian private counseling schools offer both specialist training in psychotherapy that is available only to licensed physicians or licensed psychologists and training in counseling for individuals who are not licensed in those mental health professions. There are no educational prerequisites (such as a bachelor's degree) for individuals who wish to become trained as counselors. Consequently, a person with no more than the equivalent of an American high school diploma may attend a school of counseling and graduate as a counselor. If an Italian university were to establish a counseling training program, it most likely would be in psychotherapy only and thus would be reserved for psychologists and physicians (Di Fabio & Sirigatti, 2005). In the future, universities may develop advanced degrees in counseling, but if they do, the training will be only for physicians and psychologists, and the faculty who would teach the counseling courses most likely would be lacking in the basic training that is given to counselors.

In Italy today, there are no universally accepted standards for preparing counselors that might approach the influence of the standards of the Council for Accreditation of Counseling and Related Educational Programs (CACREP) in the United States. However, many Italian professional counselor preparation schools have adopted the counselor preparation standards that have been promulgated by AssoCounseling. This association is the most significant counseling professional association in Italy, and it has adopted the counselor preparation criteria of the European Association for Counselling. The counselor preparation standards recognize the major theoretical approaches in line with the Italian Ministero dell'Università e della Ricerca (Ministry of Universities and Research): systemic relational, transactional analysis, gestalt, existential-humanistic, and so on.

All counselor preparation schools in Italy may apply for AssoCounseling accreditation. Italian counselor preparation programs submit applications for accreditation to AssoCounseling and must demonstrate that they meet the AssoCounseling standards. Once a school has been accredited by AssoCounseling, the school must comply with the association's standards. The accreditation standards of AssoCounseling are as follows:

Duration. Each training course in counseling must have a minimum duration of 3 years to allow students a reasonable period of time to explore and resolve their personal issues and to learn the theories and techniques of counseling. The minimum number of hours of didactic instruction is 450 hours. In addition, students must complete 150 hours of supervised practical counseling experience.

Content. Students preparing to be counselors are required to be educated for a minimum of 450 hours in five distinct areas: general knowledge (112 hours), skills and techniques (48 hours), the theoretical model of the school (120 hours), self-exploration (100 hours), and supervised practice (220 hours: 150 hours of practice and 70 hours of supervision). In the United States, a 3-credit course usually includes about 45 clock hours of instruction. Therefore, the Italian counselor preparation program of 450 clock hours in private schools is roughly equivalent to a 30-credit master's program in the United States. However, it is important to consider that the program must include no less than 3 years of study, which is longer than the 2-year counselor preparation programs accredited by CACREP in the United States.

General knowledge. Categories of general knowledge, which are generally equivalent to the core areas in CACREP, include nonspecific or preparatory materials such as general psychology, social psychology, group psychology, developmental psychology, theory and techniques of communication, and the history of counseling.

Skills and techniques. AssoCounseling's skills and techniques requirement is similar to the skills courses, ethics courses, and practicum and internship courses required by CACREP. The skills and techniques preparation includes instruction in counseling techniques, ethics and professional conduct, simulated role play, and counseling practice with actual clients under the supervision of a counselor educator.

Self-exploration. The self-exploration requirement for Italian counselors in training is very different from the CACREP requirements in the United States. Whereas CACREP encourages counseling students to explore their own personal issues through a counseling experience while preparing to become a counselor, the AssoCounseling standards *require* students to become involved in counseling sessions (either individually or in a group) for a minimum of 100 hours. Specifics of the personal counseling experience regarding where and under what circumstances students are to receive their personal counseling are not mandated. However, personal counseling must be a part of a school's curriculum in order for the school to be accredited by AssoCounseling.

Internship. The supervised internship is a minimum of 150 hours. Italian schools generally establish agreements with public or private agencies to provide a supervised experience in counseling for their students. However, students have the option of establishing a private practice in counseling or starting a counseling-related business to meet the requirements of their internship.

Teachers. AssoCounseling has no specific standards related to who may teach students of counseling in accredited schools. Teachers generally include professional counselors who are graduates of counselor preparation program, psychologists, and psychotherapists. In Italy, postdegree training is required by the government for psychologists to become psychotherapists.

The Future

The people of Italy are receptive to counseling, and the culture is one that supports the concept of maximizing human potential. Italian counselors are well prepared with a curriculum that parallels counselor education programs in the United States and is in line with counselor preparation standards throughout Europe. Standards that have been developed in Italy by AssoCounseling for counselor preparation, counselor certification, and recognition of counseling schools that prepare counselors suggest that the nation is moving toward standardization of the counseling profession.

The major hurdle that must be overcome for the counseling profession to become more fully established is achieving recognition by the Italian government as a profession separate and distinct from other similar professions. Counselors with a proper education and credentials cannot find employment in government agencies, schools, colleges, or nonprofit agencies until they can become licensed by the government as professionals. With strong opposition from licensed psychologists, who outnumber counselors approximately 70,000 to 4,000, convincing Italian legislators to recognize counseling as a profession will be very difficult. However, by establishing the hallmarks of a profession, including counselor preparation standards, certification of counselors, and accreditation of schools that prepare them, Italian counselors are moving forward with their goal of achieving governmental and societal recognition as a profession.

References

Adherents. (2011). *The largest Catholic communities.* Retrieved from www.adherents.com

Angus-Reid Public Opinion. (2007, February 21). *Italians divided over civil partnership law.* Retrieved from http://www.angus-reid.com

Ascenzi, A., & Corsi, M. (2005). *Professione educatori/formatori. Nuovi bisogni educativi e nuove professionalità pedagogiche* [Professional educators/trainers: New educational needs and new pedagogical skills]. Rome, Italy: Vita e Pensiero Editore.

AssoCounseling. (2011). *2° Convegno Nazionale: Counseling: Quale futuro?* [Second national congress: Counseling: What is the future?] Retrieved from http://www.assocounseling.it/convegno_2011/video.asp

AssoCounseling. (2012). *Definition of counseling.* Retrieved from http://www.assocounseling.it/associazione/definizione-counseling.asp

BBC News. (2006, March 27). *Italian women shun "mamma" role.* Retrieved from http://news.bbc.co.uk

Bosio, A. (2004). *Professioni psicologiche e professionalizzazione dell psicologia* [The psychological professions and the professionalization of psychology]. Milan, Italy: FrancoAngeli.

Britannica. (2010). *Italy.* Retrieved from http://www.britannica.com/EBchecked/topic/297474/Italy

Cipolla, C., Cipriani, R., Colasanto, M., & d'Alessandro, L. (2010). *Achille Ardigo e la sociologia* [Achille Ardigo and sociology]. Milan, Italy: FrancoAngeli.

Cook, T. D., & Furstenberg, F. F. (2002). Explaining aspects of the transition to adulthood in Italy, Sweden, Germany, and the United States: A cross-disciplinary, case synthesis approach. *Annals of the American Academy of Political and Social Science, 580,* 257–287.

Croce, B. (1944). *Perchè non possiamo non dirci "cristiani"* [Why don't we say "Christians"?]. Naples, Italy: G. Laterza & Figli Ristampa.

Di Fabio, A. (1998). *Psicologia dell'orientamento. Problemi, metodi e strumenti* [Psychology of careers: Problems, methods, and tools]. Rome, Italy: Giunti Editore.

Di Fabio, A., & Sirigatti, S. (2005). *Counseling: Prospettive e applicazioni* [Counseling: Perspectives and applications]. Milan, Italy: Ponte alle Grazie.

Duggan, C. (1994). *A concise history of Italy.* Cambridge, England: Cambridge University Press.

Edelstein, C. (2007). *Il counseling sistemico-pluralista* [Systemic and pluralistic counseling]. Trento, Italy: Centro Studi Erickson.

Fani, L., & Valleri, T. (2009). *Counseling professionale e dintorni* [Professional counseling and its surroundings]. Milan, Italy: AssoCounseling. Retrieved from http://www.assocounseling.it/approfondimenti/articolo.asp?cod=89

Giusti, E., & Masiello L. (2003). *Il counseling sanitario. Manuale introduttivo per gli operatori della salute* [Health counseling: Introductory manual for health workers]. Rome, Italy: Carocci Faber.

Istituto per lo Sviluppo della Formazione Professionale dei Lavoratori. (2006). *Consulenza alla persona e Counseling: Ambiti di intervento, approcci, ruolo e competenze del Counselor* [Personal counseling and counseling: Intervention approaches, the counselor's roles and responsibilities]. Rome, Italy: Author.

Italy Magazine. (2007, March 7). *Gay is natural for most Italians, poll says.* Retrieved from http://www.italymag.co.uk/italy/gay-natural-most-italians-poll-says

Margarone, A. (1994). *Apprendere sperimentando* [Learn by experimenting]. Rome, Italy: Carocci.

Mariotti, D. (2010, May). *Un piccolo aiuto a essere persona: Metodologia dell'intervento di counseling* [A little help to be a person: Counseling intervention methods]. Paper presented at "La pratica del Counseling in Italia e negli USA: Etica, metodologie di lavoro e formazione alla professione a confront" ["The Practice of Counseling in Italy and the USA: A Comparison of the Ethics, Methodology, and Training for the Counseling Profession"], a bilateral conference of Komidè, Studio e Scuola di Counseling, Italy, and Old Dominion University, United States, Pesaro, Italy. Retrieved from http://www.komide.net

Valleri, T. (2008). Decreto Legislativo *Qualifiche*: Al via il riconoscimento delle associazioni professionali [Qualifications: The recognition of the professional associations]. *Simposio, Rivista di Psicologi e Psicoterapeuti, 4*(1), 9.

Valleri, T. (2009). *Counseling=consulenza psicologica?* Milan, Italy: AssoCounseling. Retrieved from http://www.assocounseling.it/approfondimenti/articolo.asp?cod=108

WorldAtlas. (2011). *Explore your world.* Retrieved from http://www.worldatlas.com

• • •

Counseling in Romania

Andreea Szilagyi and Cristina Nedelcu

In this chapter, Romanian professionals who perform counseling-like activities are referred to as *counselors* regardless of their work setting and their contextually defined title. Although the profession is not recognized in Romania per se, the title is not protected, and counseling-related positions are frequently linked to other occupational titles. For example, the website of the Ministry of Labor, Family and Social Protection of the Classification of Occupations uses the term *counselor* to describe 79 occupations that cover such fields as diplomacy, geology, engineering, and education, and so on (Ministry of Labor, Family and Social Protection of the Classification of Occupations, 1995). Terms such as *psychotherapy, school counseling, career counseling,* and *psychological counseling* are not clearly delimited even among professionals in Romania. In addition, counselors experience professional identity issues and role confusion in relationship with some other helping professionals (psychologists, social workers), with clients in schools, and in the labor market.

The Historical Development of Counseling

The term *school counselor* was introduced in 2010 through an order issued by the Ministry of Labor, Family and Social Protection (http://www.mmuncii.ro/pub/imagemanager/images/file/COR/COR_08/050312Grupa%20Majora%202.pdf, occupational code 235903). Though from an administrative point of view the position is stronger than when such specialists were considered teachers, the counselor's status remains contextual (Szilagyi, 2005). For example, if a counselor leaves his or her particular school, the professional title is automatically lost.

During the communist regime, the profiles and number of career specializations were regulated by a governmental plan outlining the need for and availability of job opportunities. An individual's career was rarely a matter of personal choice. As a result, vocational guidance activities were mainly used to serve the state's interests. Romanian career counseling has experienced a rich developmental journey through a 90-year evolution from the initial vocational guidance movement to contemporary career development models (Whitmarsh & Ritter, 2007).

With the fall of communism in 1989, average Romanian citizens experienced immediate changes. Skills such as entrepreneurship, independent thinking, and consumer decision making became critical. Counselors were now employed in schools, nongovernmental organizations (NGOs), foundations, and in the labor market.

The official recognition of counseling began in 1995, when school counselors were recognized under the Education Law. In the most recent Education Law (issued in 2011), counseling activities remain as they were described in the 1995 law. The implementation methodologies may include changes, but these remain to be seen.

There is a very clear distinction in the international literature between guidance, counseling, and therapy. In Romania, parts of the public consider *counseling* to be an imported word that replaces the older term *guidance;* others perceive counseling and guidance as tasks that any psychologist could perform with or without proper training and experience.

If a profession is defined as having a specific body of knowledge, accredited training programs, a professional organization, credentialing of practitioners, a code of ethics, and legal recognition (Myers & Sweeny, 2001), it is clear that the counseling profession in Romania is in the beginning stages. As we show here, there are training programs in Romania, certification, a professional association, progress in the field of ethics, and some legal recognition.

The Current Status of Counseling

Following the 1989 revolution, the Romanian education system was reorganized to more closely align with those of Western Europe. In addition, the national curriculum and the grade promotion system were redrafted to help students better develop the skills necessary for competition in the free market (Bethell & Mihail, 2005; Velea & Botnariuc, 2002). As a direct consequence, school counseling emerged and developed in Romania in the mid-1990s as an intensive process of psychopedagogical assistance for pupils and other persons involved in the secondary school process (teachers, parents, other school authorities). The Institute for Sciences of Education (ISE), a government think tank that was granted the authority to develop school counseling recommendations, developed a code of ethics and quality standards for career counseling.

Included in these education reforms were various policies that highlighted the need for counseling to replace the state's job assignment mechanism. The Ministry of Education, Research, Youth, and Sport orders and other central government policies provided a base for the development of psychopedagogical assistance and interschool psychopedagogical assistance centers in 1995. These centers provided services consistent with what counselors in the United States recognize as school counseling. The first step in the process was the development of the theoretical level in universities through the inclusion of special counseling courses in the Departments of Education. The trend started in public universities but was adopted by private universities as well. The 1995 education law created the legal framework for the process of counseling to be developed in schools (the secondary system). One result was the introduction, in 1998, of the area called "counseling and career guidance" within the secondary school curriculum. The activities of this curricular area are covered within headmasters' classes, which are mandatory. The providers of these services are mainly psychopedagogues (in the schools that have the necessary teaching staff with this specialty) or are social sciences teachers or teachers of another specialty appointed by the school board.

Great progress in counseling was achieved in 1998 when a ministry order established the District Centers for Psychopedagogical Assistance. In addition, the order established the role of school offices in providing psychopedagogical assistance. Such centers were founded in each district and also in Bucharest. The District Centers for Psychopedagogical Assistance have the following goals:

- counseling students, parents, and teachers on issues related to teacher–student communication, students' adjustment to school requirements, and the adjustment of school activities to students' needs
- improving relationships between students, teachers, parents, the school, and the local community
- preventing and reducing factors that may lead to dysfunctional student behavior
- preventing and reducing school dropout
- preventing and reducing psychological discomfort
- preventing and reducing dysfunctional behavior among students
- counseling and guiding students in choosing their careers
- evaluating students at the request of parents, school staff, or the school inspectorate
- providing the materials necessary for career counseling and guidance
- cooperating with the local community in order to reach educational goals
- offering support for teacher training activities (Ordinul Ministerul Educatiei, 2005)

The function of the District Centers of Resources and Educational Assistance and of the Bucharest District Centre is to coordinate the educational services in the territory. These centers include several departments: counseling and psychological assistance, school guidance and counseling, social assistance projects and educational programs, training and professional development, counseling and prevention of juvenile delinquency, and the secretariat. The main objectives of the district centers are

- including in the mandatory educational system all children regardless of their individual and social background
- providing supplementary support to maximize the quality of the educational process according to the biopsychosocial potential of each child
- supporting teaching staff with educational activities
- ensuring the conditions necessary for students to develop their personalities and adjust to their school, social, and professional lives
- involving parents in specific school activities in order to establish effective relationships between school, family, and community for the better social integration of the students

Other services provided are school counseling and guidance; services for students with disabilities; mediation services; and information and counseling services for teachers, parents, children, and other members of the community (Tomsa, 2010, p. 73).

The 1995 Education Law specified that schools with more than 800 pupils must have a full-time counselor. Small salaries and insufficient professional recognition (counselors are considered less important than teachers) make professionals avoid these jobs. According to the Ministry of Education, Research, Youth, and Sport, there are 1,985 school counselors (S. Tibu, personal communication, July 31, 2012).

A school counseling study conducted in 2010 revealed serious inconsistencies between the framework objectives, the contents, the level of the target population (pupils), and the methods used by school counselors. The results demonstrated the lack of common standards for counseling educational programs and pointed out the confusion experienced by teachers in relation to counseling programs and their own tasks in school (Masari, 2010). In our view, as professional accreditation and a national certification do not exist yet, confusion is only natural at this point.

Outside of school counseling, only one other area in the field has a rather well-defined status. This is career counseling, which developed mainly as a result of economic conditions. There is fairly well-organized career counseling programming in several university centers, but there is still not yet a college counseling and student affairs specialty. Most universities have centers for information and career counseling (or centers for counseling and career guidance) that generally deliver career counseling services to students and are also involved in promoting the university's programs, organizing volunteering activities, and so on.

Generally speaking, such centers exist in all major universities, public and private. From an administrative point of view, they report to the university's president. ISE, through its counseling department, informally supervises their activity and organizes annual meetings under the umbrella of Euroguidance (http://euroguidance-en.ise.ro/index.html), which facilitates cooperation among counseling professionals from Romania and other European countries. However, attendance at the annual meetings is not mandatory, and as a result the network is far from fully functional.

Career counseling is strongly related to the Global Career Development Facilitator (GCDF) training program. This is the only career counseling certification program that exists in Romania (and southeastern Europe). The GCDF training program in Romania is currently embedded within university master's programs or is provided to individuals who are already involved or interested in career development. The training follows a national curriculum developed by a Romanian team of experts to meet local and European labor market needs (Szilagyi, 2008). At the moment, more than 280 GCDF specialists are certified in Romania. Most of them work as school counselors, college counselors, and human resources specialists in business, NGOs, and governmental agencies.

School counseling is administrated by the Ministry of Education, according to the Education Laws, but career counseling enjoys a less restrictive environment. Career counselors are encouraged to open private offices, but because of economic downsizing not many have the courage or the resources to do it. Career counseling services are also provided through the network of the Ministry of Labor and managed by the National Employment Agency through its county offices. There are around 100 specialists providing career counseling services within 41 county and 6 municipal offices (www.anofm.ro/site-uri-agentii-judetene). The other specialties recognized in the United States by the Council for Accreditation of Counseling and Related Educational Programs (clinical mental health, marriage and family, addiction) are traditionally under the umbrella of psychotherapy in Romania.

Besides universities, the future of counseling in Romania is being shaped by entities such as ISE, National Board for Certified Counselors (NBCC) Romania, and the Association of Romanian Counselors (the national professional association). These organizations are focused on school and career counseling. The Department for Counseling within ISE is mainly concerned with research and publication and with creating networks for counselors by organizing conferences and workshops. NBCC Romania was established in 2007 as a consultative and educational body that supports the counseling profession in the country. NBCC Romania works with academic institutions, professional organizations, government agencies, NGOs, and other private enterprises interested in developing the counseling profession.

Although there were a few attempts to organize professional organizations, none of them could get approved nationally. The Association of Romanian Counselors, which was founded in 2008 and has around 200 registered members, aims to represent and support all Romanian counselors.

Best Counseling Practices

Currently Romania seems to be facing a state of confusion and lack of consistency regarding the models and theories promoted through educational programs. The main reason for this is that, as mentioned before, Romania has no clear set of accepted national standards, no national certification system, and no professional accreditation scheme. Each counseling program promotes whatever resources it might have. Because there are very few genuine counselor educators, educators from other professions are stepping in and trying to learn about counseling (through conferences and workshops, short courses, graduate classes, postdoctoral studies, donated books and magazines, etc.) and then passing this knowledge and skills on to their students. Currently not a single counselor educator in Romania holds a PhD in counseling.

Another outcome of this situation is that non–counselor educators lack practical experience, supervision experience, and supervision of supervision interaction. As a result, quality is not always assured; however, we are optimistic that the administrative details (e.g., the number of specialists, instruments used, trainings implemented) are becoming more and more regulated. Several master's programs in counseling are accredited by the state. Now it is necessary to adopt quality standards.

As mentioned before, school counselors come from several sources within the social sciences; therefore, scholars do not always share a common point of view. Professors who teach counseling can be psychologists, psychotherapists, education specialists, or even management experts. There are also cases of very committed but self-taught counseling professors coming from the fields of business administration or social work.

The emphasis for the initial counseling programs was more on theories and models and less on techniques, skills training, and supervision. It is impossible to talk about consistency with regard to the models and theories promoted through the educational programs. Each educator comes with his or her own vision. Graduates of the first generation of master's programs in school counseling, for example, had no access to practica, internships, or even enough skill exercises during regular classes.

The most common models perpetuated by counselor training programs are the cognitive and cognitive–behavioral models. These models, together with the trait and factor approach, are specific to schools whose counselor educators come from a non-psychotherapy background. At first glance, these models seem to be considered by Romanian counselors (and counselor educators) as being the easiest to apply.

In these cases, students do not have the chance to work under supervision. Although some internship activities are organized, the supervisors have little or no training in counseling supervision. Thus, most of the time supervision is purely administrative, and some advice is provided to the students.

It has been observed that career counseling in Romanian schools focuses on work-related problems and is viewed as a process of informing and psychometric testing. Counselors involved in school counseling try to achieve maximum compatibility between students' resources, aspirations, and interests on the one hand and the real offerings of the educational system and labor market on the other (Tomsa, 2010).

One can immediately see the difference in universities whose counselor educators have backgrounds in psychology and psychotherapy. These students have more substantial access to practical experience and to testing (psychologists by law are allowed to use formal testing). In addition, students are exposed to more sophisticated models and techniques of counseling, including person-centered theories, gestalt and reality therapies, rational emotive behavior therapy, transactional analysis, and solution-focused brief therapy. Students usually also have access to good-quality supervision. Some schools of psychology have developed their own system of therapy. For example, the University of Bucharest promotes a model called "unification therapy," which echoes elements of psychodynamics, gestalt, group, neurolinguistic programming, and transpersonal therapies; meditation; and other approaches (Mitrofan, 2002).

School counselors who come from other specializations (e.g., social work, sociology, special education) have even more diverse training. Usually counselor educators serving in these programs come from education departments, and not many practicum hours are required of their students.

The use of the Internet is highly promoted within counseling programs. Students are trained to look for resources online and to encourage their clients to become more proactive when it comes to using technology. However, some of the information that ministries provide online is not always reliable. In 2004, ISE and the Ministry of Labor organized training for distance counseling (mostly telephone counseling) that targeted counseling centers within universities.

Common standards of practice for school counselors are sorely needed to achieve some uniformity in training. School counselors have a great need for training in play therapy and rational emotive behavior therapy. Universities and other counseling organizations in Romania acknowledge this need for training by organizing and conducting workshops by foreign experts each year.

Diversity Issues

Europe is shaped by diversity of almost every kind: linguistic (there are altogether 77 autochthonic languages and 17 dialects spoken in Europe), ethnic, and cultural (Launikari & Puukari, 2005). Yet outside of the capital city of Bucharest and the country's other large cities, the Romanian people have had relatively little direct exposure to other cultures, races, religions, and lifestyles. Following are a few areas specific to Romanian culture that counselors should consider when dealing with diversity in Romania:

- *Gender roles.* Stereotypes concerning behavior toward women that exist in southeastern European cultures can be applied to Romanians as well. Because of the *machismo* in Romanian culture, women are expected to do housework (and keep a job, as a trademark of the communist regime). Men are expected to act mannerly toward women but also to make decisions without consulting their wives. Yet because of women's increasing social and professional visibility, perceptions of gender roles in marriage have been changing toward a more Western way of thinking, at least in larger cities.
- *Race.* There are relatively few people of color in Romania. Most of them are African students and few immigrants who live in Bucharest and a few other large cities. Someone may utter an offensive term in English because he or she is not aware of the acceptable term, not because the person really means to be offensive. Latin-origin people may encounter preferential treatment from some Romanians, many of whom are very proud of, and even defensive about, their Latin origins.
- *Sexual orientation.* Laws that once discriminated against sexual minorities have recently been changed, but Romania still has a rather homophobic culture. The younger generation in large cities tends to be more accepting, having been exposed to Western culture. The gay scene has recently grown, but it is still small, underground, and confined mostly to the largest cities.
- *Religion.* More than 85% of the Romanian population is Eastern (Romanian) Orthodox, with less than 5% Roman Catholic, 4% Protestant, 0.3% Muslim, and 0.2% Jewish. The Romanian Orthodox Church is hierarchical, dogmatic, and fairly well to do. New churches are being built even in poor villages to accommodate the growing membership. Clients' lifestyles and decision making may be influenced by religion (Institutul National de Statistica, 2002).
- *Disability.* Some people hold prejudicial attitudes toward people with disabilities, who were traditionally often institutionalized or kept out of public view in Romania. In addition, there is very little infrastructure in place to accommodate people with disabilities, although all institutions are legally required to be handicap accessible.
- *Ethnicity.* Eighteen ethnic minorities are represented in the Romanian Parliament. Among them, the Roma minority seems to be the most exposed to discrimination, especially in recent years. There are an estimated 619,000 Romany in Romania, about 3.2% of the country's 19.043 million people (Comisia Centrala Pentru Recensamântului Populatiei si al Locuintelor, 2011). With few resources and little education, Romany have rarely been able to compete for jobs or start their own businesses and are often victims of harassment in the workplace.

One of the biggest challenges for clients and counselors in Romania is learning tolerance and acceptance. Romanians tend to be very tolerant and accepting, wonderful hosts to their foreign guests. Romanians also tend not to discriminate against strangers. Counselors interact every day with people who share different values, experiences, and attitudes and beliefs, whether these people re women, children, at-risk youth, ex-convicts, retired persons, religious or ethnic minorities. Still, all specialists who offer counseling and mental health services in Romanian communities would benefit from education that emphasizes multicultural competencies (Szilagyi, 2006).

Counselor Education

Increasing demand for counseling services has led to more counselor education programs. As a general rule, counselors trained in Romanian universities are graduates of programs mainly developed within the Faculty of Psychology and Education Sciences. To work in the labor market, career counselors are allowed to have a bachelor's degree in any field, but a master's degree in career counseling is required. However, in reality career counselors usually have completed a graduate program in some other field (sometimes with only one class in career counseling). In 2003, the University Politehnica of Bucharest started the first career counseling master's program in Romania (four semesters) in cooperation with the National Board for Certified Counselors. That program offered a counseling-related certification training program (GCDF) for the first time in Romania.

The University of Bucharest offers a four-semester master's program in school counseling and career development that is managed by the Department of Education's Faculty of Psychology and Education Sciences. The same university provides a four-semester master's program in school counseling through its Distance Learning Department (www.unibuc.ro). In Bucharest, students can also attend a master's program developed by the University Politehnica, which is focused mainly on career counseling and career management in professional and technical fields. The program is managed by the university's Center for Guidance and Career Counseling and by the Department of Training for Teaching Personnel (www.upb.ro).

Spiru Haret University provides a master's program in psychological and school counseling through one of its centers in Brasov (www.spiruharet.ro), whereas Titu Maiorescu University in Bucharest provides a master's program in school psychology and school counseling under the umbrella of the Faculty of Psychology (www.utm.ro). Babes Bolyai University has developed a master's program called "School Counseling: Development and Mental Health" that is managed by the Faculty of Psychology. However, school counseling is also offered at the graduate level in a program developed by the Department of Education (www.ubbcluj.ro).

In Iasi, school counselors graduate from a master's program called "School Counseling and Interventions in School and Vocational Guidance" developed by Petre Andrei University through the Faculty of Psychology and Education Sciences (www.upa.ro). Within the public Alexandru Ioan Cuza University, the Faculty of Psychology has developed a master's program in school psychology and counseling (www.uaic.ro).

The Petroleum-Gas University of Ploiesti provides a master's program in school counseling and career development managed by the Faculty of Philology and Sciences through the Education Sciences Department (www.upg.ro).

Counselor training is mainly based on theories and techniques developed in the United States and Western Europe. Scholars notable for the adaptation of existing resources and the development of new ones for Romanian counselors include Mihai Jigau, Gheorghe Tomsa, and George Vaideanu.

Educational programs usually do not have a strong component of practicum, internship, or supervision. The focus is generally on theory and experiential activities organized in classes in which the skills are practiced with peers and professors. The first steps toward a Romanian certification in counseling supervision were taken in 2007 when NBCC International organized a pilot supervision certificate training program in Bucharest. NBCC Romania implemented a certification program for supervision in counseling at a basic level in 2012 (http://www.europeanbcc.eu/supervision/).

It is important to mention that when we talk about accreditation in relationship with the universities that offer counseling programs, we mean only academic accreditation. Romania does not have a professional accreditation system for counseling, and this is considered perfectly normal because counseling is not a recognized profession.

The Future

The counseling community in Romania is definitely on its way to finding a professional identity and is in the process of creating its own counseling standards. This is a response to some internal social and educational needs as well as to external pressures. Romania is also in the midst of a learning process. Some valuable counseling books from countries with strong counseling traditions are now being translated. Foreign theories are adapted to the country's specific requirements. Educational programs are offered, foreign specialists are invited to lecture, and Romanian students go to universities abroad to gain new specializations.

It is likely that the majority of problems the counseling community is facing could be resolved by introducing a national certification in counseling, which is expected to happen in the next 5 years. A strong and clear educational program incorporating experience, assessment and supervision, a code of ethics, and continuing education could help integrate counselor education programs in various universities. This recognition would help counselors establish a professional identity and would better regulate the use of the title "counselors" regardless of the professional setting. Another aspect of note is testing. We expect the profession to become strong enough to be able to achieve the necessary legal status to use formal testing, which is now available only to psychologists.

We believe that the Romanian public is ready to accept mental health services from counselors, not just from psychologists or psychiatrists. NBCC Romania is preparing to launch a short training program in mental health facilitation that would complement career and school counseling trainings.

Our personal goal is to create a PhD program in counselor education in one of the universities that already has experience with graduate programs in counseling. For the short term, we envision better services within college counseling centers, supervision centers within universities, more publications, stronger networks, and unified efforts for lobbying for the profession.

Even though the need for counseling in Romania is great, some institutions that should be leading in this area are reluctant to do so in an environment marked by economic transition from a communist regime to a postcommunist/Western type of society. Political difficulties, recession, and unemployment are priorities in government programs, which is completely understandable. However, we believe that a smart investment in national career and school counseling programs could solve some of those issues in the long run.

References

Bethell, G., & Mihail, R. (2005). Assessment and examinations in Romania. *Assessment in Education, 12,* 77–96.

Comisia Centrala Pentru Recensamântului Populatiei si al Locuintelor (2011). Comunicat de presa privind rezuitatele provizovorii ale recensamântului [Press release on prosisional results of population and housing census] Romania: Author.

Institutul National de Statistica. (2002). *Romania in cifre. Vol IV* [Romania in figures. Vol. IV]. Retrieved from www.insse.ro/cms/files/RPL2002INS/vol4/tabele

Launikari, M., & Puukari, S. (Eds.). (2005). *Multicultural guidance and counseling: Theoretical foundations and best practices in Europe.* Jyväskylä, Finland: Centre for International Mobility and Institute for Educational Research.

Masari, G. A. (2010). Romanian experiences of primary school teachers on school counseling. *Procedia-Social and Behavioral Sciences, 2,* 694–697.

Ministry of Labor, Family and Social Protection of the Classification of Occupations. (1995). *Clasificare Ocupatiilor din Romania* [The classification of occupations in Romania]. Retrieved from http://www.dsclex.ro/ocupatii/cor1.htm

Mitrofan, I. (Ed.). (2002). *Orientarea experientiala in psihoterapie* [The experiential orientation in psychotherapy]. Bucharest, Romania: Romanian Society for Experiential Psychotherapy.

Myers, J. E., & Sweeny, T. J. (2001). Specialties in counseling. In D. C. Locke, J. E. Myers, & E. L. Herr (Eds.), *The handbook of counseling* (pp. 43–54). Thousand Oaks, CA: Sage.

Ordinul Ministerul Educatiei. (2005). *The Ministry of Education (MoE) Order No. 5418/08.11.2005.* Retrieved from http://www.cmbrae.ro/legi/omedc_5418.pdf

Szilagyi, A. A. (2005). The status of counseling profession in Romania. In T. W. Clawson, T. Collins, A. A. Szilagyi, & G. Boarescu (Eds.), *Career counseling and the global labor market* (pp. 25–28). Tg. Mures, Romania: Petru Maior University.

Szilagyi, A. A. (2006). Multicultural counseling. In M. Cozarescu (Ed.), *Theoretical issues and Romanian implications: Intercultural education in the context of Romania's integration in European Union* (pp. 117–120). Bucharest, Romania: Academia de Studii Economice.

Szilagyi, A. A. (2008). The GCDF certification around the world—Review of counseling and guidance. *Official Journal of the Hellenic Society of Counselling and Guidance, 86–87,* 153–157.

Tomsa, G. (2010). School counseling in Romania: Realities and further prospects. *Buletinul Universitatii Petrol-Gaze din Ploiesti, 1C,* 68–75.

Velea, S., & Botnariuc, P. (2002). *Education reform in Romania during the last 12 years* (Working paper for the Summer University). Budapest, Hungary: Central European University.

Whitmarsh, L., & Ritter, R. (2007). The influence of communism on career development and education in Romania. *The Career Development Quarterly, 56,* 85–94.

• • •

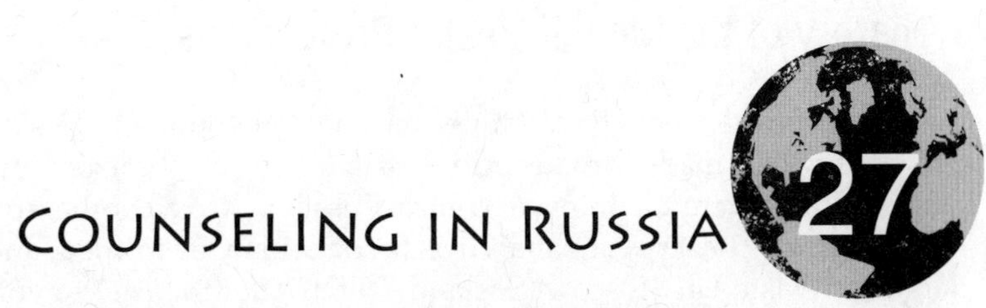

Counseling in Russia

Christine L. Currie, Marina V. Kuzmina,
Ruslan I. Nadyuk, and Sergei V. Yevdoschenko

The Russian Federation, a vast nation that spans 11 time zones across the continents of Europe and Asia, has a 1,000-year intellectual and spiritual tradition. The Russian nation has weathered the cataclysms of its history and today finds itself facing an array of political, economic, and social challenges that call for the development of adequate mental health services. The counseling profession is one of the more recent innovations. In order to understand the position of counseling among the present trends in the mental health professions in Russia, it is helpful to understand the country's current situation as well as the forces that shape its counseling environment.

Political and Religious History

From Genghis Khan to Napoleon to Hitler's army during World War II, Russians have endured hardship, suffered sieges, and pushed back foreign invaders through strong leadership, overpowering force, and spiritual unity. In particular, the first half of the 20th century brought Russia unremitting political violence and economic upheaval. Millions perished in World War I, and the bloodshed continued as Lenin's Bolsheviks seized control during the 1917 Revolution and forcefully subdued all opposition. When Lenin died 2 years after founding the Soviet Union in 1922, Stalin ascended to lead a vindictive totalitarian regime that annihilated somewhere between 3 million and 60 million people in the 1930s through political policies and a purge known as the Great Terror. He deported nearly 3.3 million ethnic minorities to Siberia or the Central Asian Republics, 43% of whom perished from disease or malnutrition. He also forced agricultural collectivization, which resulted in the starvation of millions of people in what is sometimes called "the Ukrainian Genocide." Stalin's terror campaign against religion was brutal: In 1917, there were 54,000 Russian Orthodox churches in Russia; by 1939, only hundreds remained. Countless thousands of religious clergy were executed (Gascoigne, 2001).

By no means did those events mark the end of Russian suffering, as Russia was subsequently drawn into World War II. To put Russia's losses in perspective, consider this: The United States mourned the loss of more than 500,000 combatants and the destruction of Pearl Harbor. The Soviet state endured 2 years of occupation and the razing of much of the land ranging from its western borders almost a thousand miles to the Volga River. Estimates of the unprecedented slaughter suffered by its citizens begin at 20 million, more than any other country in the war.

After the war, Stalin set up communist governments in many Eastern European countries, hanging the Iron Curtain and ushering in the Cold War era. The last leader of the Soviet Union, Mikhail Gorbachev, attempted to reform the communist system through perestroika (restructuring) and glasnost (openness). When the attempted reforms failed, Gorbachev resigned as president in 1991. The Soviet Union collapsed days later (Gascoigne, 2001).

History of the Mental Health Professions

Russian political events have influenced the development of its mental health professions. Psychology had made inroads into Russia during the time of Sigmund Freud (1856–1939), whose works were all translated into Russian. A psychotherapy journal was published from 1910 to 1914, a psychoanalytical association was formed, and a psychoanalytical kindergarten existed in Moscow (Sosland, 1997). After the 1917 Revolution, however, psychology and psychiatry became tools in the hands of the totalitarian government. In the Soviet Union the subject of psychology was usually housed in the philosophy department and was at the service of the Communist party and the Soviet system so that the government could control it. Only Communist party members could teach or study psychology. Psychological concepts incompatible with Marx's and Lenin's ideologies were banned. Any citizen whose ideas posed a threat to the existing authority could be given a psychiatric diagnosis and confined to a psychiatric hospital. This psychiatric confinement would be documented in the person's work history and government paperwork, thereby seriously limiting job opportunities. Psychology became a repressive power, a dangerous tool. The totalitarian government contributed to a Russian mindset that to be open and candid with anyone outside of close family and friends is dangerous. Conversations about personal concerns took place with drinking friends or face to face, in the kitchen. A continuing distrust of psychology had its roots during this time.

Starting in 1962, psychology became a separate department in some of the major universities located in key cities such as Moscow and St. Petersburg. However, it was not until perestroika (1989–1993) that psychology was organized into a separate university department across the country. At that time the study of psychology became open to the general public. In addition, the social work profession was instituted by the Russian government in 1991 in response to the needs of a society in turmoil after the collapse of the Soviet Union.

The Current Status of Counseling

> In a nation that keeps its suffering to itself, and where neither antidepressant medication nor psychotherapy has yet taken root, vodka is widely regarded as *the* remedy for a range of physical and emotional problems. (Althausen, 1996, p. 683, emphasis in the original)

In 1991, Boris Yeltsin became the first president of the newly formed Russian Federation, and the social and economic changes that took place during this time influenced the growth of the mental health professions. The communist infrastructure had disintegrated, but the new government did not yet have the financial means or organization to meet the social needs of its citizens. Therefore, in 1991, the social work profession was born in Russia. In addition, because Russians had been closed off from the West for 70 years, there was a hunger for new knowledge, including Western psychology. Countless educational institutions sprang up, including psychology programs from various orientations.

Today, 20 years after the overthrow of communism in 1991, Russia's economic and political legacy is still unfolding. Stripped of the Eastern bloc and the 14 now-independent former Soviet Republics, the Russian Federation is looking to deeper historical roots to rediscover its identity. For a millennium, the Russian Orthodox Church has considered itself responsible for the *soul care* of its people. As it becomes apparent that the current social needs in Russia are too great for the government to adequately meet, many think that the Russian Orthodox Church and other religious organizations must take the initiative to meet these needs. But the needs are proving too great for the church alone. The mental health professions, including the newly formed counseling profession, may play an increasingly important role in Russia.

Social Work Influence and Social Psychological Help

The Russian counseling profession is beginning to emerge as a branch of social work. Separate university departments for the purpose of counselor training do not currently exist, although most Russian universities house a psychology department. Professional associations are just starting to be formed, and there is no credentialing or licensing process. The counseling profession is emerging from a directive by the Ministry of Education and Science of the Russian Federation (2009), which has added a specialization called "social psychological help" under the social work umbrella. Social psychological help will be roughly the equivalent of counseling as it is currently understood in the United States, with its emphasis on counseling skills and its strengths-based approach. This branch will be specifically designated *help* and not counseling, so as not to be confused with the field of psychology, which is often called "psychological counseling." This specialization will be offered at the bachelor's level.

Career Counseling

The career counseling profession follows a different path from that of the United States, where vocational guidance developed partly as a result of the population migration to large urban areas in the early 1900s during the Industrial Revolution (Aubrey, 1977; Neukrug, 2007). In Russia, however, schools and factories were closely linked, and the world of work was taught in the schools starting in the primary grades. Vocational guidance began in the former Soviet Union in 1924; however, individuals were placed in professions not only based on aptitude and preference but also according to government needs (Brewer, 1942). Because psychology had come to Russia before the 1917 Revolution, vocational guidance in schools became the domain of school psychologists, who often coordinated with teachers (Popova, 2003).

The nature of career counseling changed with the fall of communism, perestroika, and the ensuing search for economic and political stability. In order for career counseling to be meaningful, it must occur in the context of political stability, clarity concerning the manner in which the society is organized and operates, and perspective concerning the future job market. From 1985 to 2000, Russia possessed none of these necessary components. The emphasis of President Vladimir Putin's first term, which began in 2000, was saving Russia from economic and political collapse. During his second term he began to use publicly, repeatedly, and emphatically the terms *stability, clarity,* and *long-range planning.* These ongoing emphases may provide the environment in which career counseling can once again become a meaningful component of counseling practice.

Twenty years after the fall of communism, career counseling in Russia is not a separate specialty. It is performed by psychologists in schools and universities as well as by professional counselors in counseling centers. Some career counseling may also be done by state social workers and psychologists working in municipal centers for marriage, family, and children designed to help the most difficult family situations and crises. Currently there is a deficit of both professional counselors and counseling centers. For example, in the city of Krasnodar there are approximately 100 professional counselors working in a city of 1 million people.

Who seeks career counseling services? The majority of career counseling clients are high school students and first- and second-year university students. In the first decade of the 21st century, nearly all of the job opportunities advertised were for individuals ages 23 to 38. Jobs open to those older than 40 years old tend to be low-paying sales or service work. Age discrimination did not exist in the Soviet Union but is apparent in the wild capitalism of contemporary Russia.

School Counseling

Counseling also takes place in schools. Each school usually has only one school psychologist because of inadequate government funding. School psychologists handle similar problems as school counselors in the United States: bullying, excessive absences, low grades, family problems, running away, and problem behaviors in class, among others.

Counseling Orphans

The need for trained counselors is evident, as Russia is beset by a myriad of social problems due to the economic and political upheaval connected with the fall of the communist infrastructure in 1991. A few statistics will demonstrate that the situation is ripe for the introduction of a new mental health profession. In 2010, there were approximately 700,000 orphans in Russia, more even than after World War II. Approximately two thirds of these children are *social orphans,* taken from their families because of abuse or alcoholism or abandoned by their parents for various reasons (Achmatova, 2010). At the age of 18, orphans are customarily released from orphanages without further support, and statistics paint a dismal picture of their prospects without appropriate interventions. Approximately 40% end up in prison, 40% become alcoholics or drug addicts, and 10% commit suicide. Only 1% complete higher education, and only 10% go on to hold steady jobs, raise families, and live relatively stable lives (Solidarity Fund, 2011).

The mental health professions are utilizing numerous venues to address the compelling needs apparent in the orphan population. The Russian-American Institute in Moscow has founded the Child Welfare System Education and Training department within the School of Social Work and Counseling. This new department will have a threefold thrust of providing training for orphanage workers, training and support for Russian adoptive parents, and training in life skills for orphans. In addition, the Russia Without Orphans conference in April 2012 provided training for workers, adoptive parents, and counselors as well as addressed public policy issues that impact orphans. Trained counselors are needed to work with these children inside as well as outside orphanages, when as adults they must adjust to living and working in society.

Substance Abuse Counseling

In its State Anti-Narcotic Policy, the Russian government recognized the pressing need for trained substance abuse counselors by issuing a directive that calls for the training of specialists by the year 2020. Between 1990 and 2003, vodka sales in Russia increased by 68%, such that Russian hard liquor consumption is now estimated to be the highest in the world (Nemtsov, as cited in Shlapentokh, 2005). One study indicated that one third of all deaths, three fourths of all murders, and almost half of all external causes of death (such as industrial accidents and car accidents) are alcohol related (Nemtsov, as cited in Shlapentokh, 2005). Both expert and public opinion in Russia blame the high alcoholism rate for the short life expectancy of 59.5 years for Russian men, compared to 73.17 years for women. In contrast, life expectancy in the United States averages 78.24 years: 75.78 for men and 80.81 years for women (Central Intelligence Agency, 2011). In addition to alcohol, the use of opiates such as heroin is also on the increase. It is estimated that there are 2 million opiate users in Russia. This estimate represents 2% of the Russian adult population, a figure much higher than the approximate 0.4% world adult population of opiate users (Bobrova et al., 2008).

The State Anti-Narcotic Policy opens the door for the field of addiction counseling to burgeon in Russia, with the potential for counselors to work alongside the psychology and medical professionals who have traditionally handled substance abuse problems in narcology hospitals. During the communist era, alcoholism was viewed as strictly a medical problem and was therefore treated by physicians through medical means. When Russia opened to the West, some programs began to integrate counseling into their traditionally medical treatment. The new Russian directive that calls for the training of substance abuse counselors allows both public and private institutions to oversee substance abuse treatment. Approximately 1,500 to 2,000 substance abuse treatment centers were operating in Russia in 2012, but more are needed and standards of quality must be defined. Many substance abuse treatment centers struggle because they are self-supported and not able to send workers to Moscow or other large cities for training. Therefore, in addition to centers of professional competence in key cities, more regional training in counseling is needed to improve the quality of services. New government standards have opened the door for a specialty in addiction counseling, and this may prove to be the fastest growing specialty for the Russian counseling profession (M. Kitmanov, personal communication, January 24, 2011).

Other Counseling Needs

Other statistics indicate the need for counselors in Russia. Of the 99 countries for which the World Health Organization tracks suicide statistics, Russia ranks highest, with 70.6 male and 11.9 female suicides per 100,000 people. This contrasts with the United States, which has 17.6 male and 4.1 female suicides per 100,000 people (World Health Organization, 2003). The reported adult prevalence of HIV/AIDS in Russia stands at 1.1% compared to 0.6% in the United States (Central Intelligence Agency, 2011). There is a need for more educational programs on HIV prevention and care, as well as counseling for individuals and families affected. The incidence of domestic violence in Russia is estimated to be 4 to 5 times greater than in other developed countries, with approximately 14,000 Russian women killed by male partners each year (Horne, 1999). Although social service organizations have begun to provide aid for victims and families, more counseling services, shelters, and other support services are needed. In addition, Russia has been cited as a source, transit stop, and destination point for the trafficking of men, women, and children for the purposes of sexual exploitation and forced labor (Central Intelligence Agency, 2011). With their social justice emphasis, counselors can be involved with individuals and the social systems that impact them.

Where Counselors Work in Russia

The need for well-trained counselors in Russia is compelling. Counseling as a distinct professional field is just beginning to emerge as a branch of the social work profession. The word *counselor* in Russia is used generally to describe all those employed in the mental health professions. Counselors work in psychiatric hospitals and psychiatric clinics, often under the supervision of medical doctors. They may also work in orphanages. They serve as state social workers engaged with poor families, individuals with disabilities, and the elderly population. They serve in rehabilitation centers with people recovering from addictions. School counselors are often teachers who complete some psychology training so that they can offer counseling services in addition to performing their teaching responsibilities. A few counselors also work in private practice, although the concept of paying for psychological services in a private practice setting has not been widely accepted in Russia.

Because the ranks of practicing counselors in Russia include all of these types of service providers, it is difficult to determine how many are employed. In Krasnodar, a region with a population of approximately 5 million people, we estimate that there are approximately 200 counselors, more if all regional state social workers are considered. Almost all possess some level of qualification or certification.

Professional Associations

Throughout Russia, counselors (including psychologists, psychiatrists, and social workers) support and organize themselves. For example, professionals in Krasnodar have two separate centers organized around the regional and city psychiatric hospitals, respectively. Each center supports continuing education and training and opens its facility auditoriums and halls for training and conferences. In conjunction with its School of Social Work and Counseling, the Russian-American Institute in Moscow has formed an association of counselors as a vehicle for ongoing training in the form of seminars and conferences. In the fall of 2011 the School launched the Center for Counseling and Soul Care in order to provide counseling services to the public as well as to operate as a potential training site for its students. Similar centers exist in St. Petersburg and elsewhere.

Best Counseling Practices

From the time of Genghis Khan to Napoleon to the Germans during World War II, Russia has had a long history of defending itself against foreign invasions in order to guard its political and cultural independence. Neither entirely Western nor entirely Eastern in mindset and culture, Russians guard their national pride and identity as a Slavic nation with different roots and values than those of the often pragmatic and materialistic West. This nationalistic rivalry between Western and Slavic people remains a prominent dynamic in current Russian social and political views and will affect the development of counseling practices as well. Western methods and approaches to therapy will need to be adapted and adjusted to fit Russian culture and society.

Several counseling techniques may prove to be particularly effective in Russian culture. In a country with a 99.4% literacy rate, and where education is highly valued, psychoeducational programs tend to be appealing. Because Russians are generally hesitant to trust those outside their close circle of family and friends, psychoeducational programs have the additional advantage, in contrast to individual therapy, of offering helpful information without requiring significant self-disclosure. Psychoeducational programs on various topics may be successfully developed in venues such as schools, universities, medical clinics, and churches.

Russians are accustomed to strong leadership and central authority; therefore, techniques that are directive rather than nondirective in nature may prove to be more culturally congruent. In addition, suffering is viewed differently in Russia than in the United States. Long, cold winters with limited sunlight, along with difficult living conditions and deprivations, have produced an acceptance of suffering in many Russians. Techniques that overemphasize optimism and limitless possibilities are not likely to be as well accepted in Russia as in the United States. Another aspect of Russian culture that impacts counseling techniques is its strong nuclear family system, which gives the culture a more communal rather than individualist quality. Effective counseling techniques in Russia must take this communal aspect into account.

The difference between psychological diagnosis and counseling therapy is still not always clear among professionals or the general public. This difference requires emphasis in the educational curriculum and national standards. Schools such as the Russian-American Institute in Moscow are intent on developing a curriculum and standards that will lead to the recognition of counseling as a therapeutic approach to mental health distinct from either psychological or psychiatric diagnosis and the systemic evaluation and correction of social work.

Professionals with a therapeutic counseling approach, in addition to those who emphasize psychological diagnosis or systemic injustice or economic inequities, will increasingly find their way into universities, institutes, clinics, hospitals, counseling centers, schools, and the armed forces. In the long run, there will potentially be increased cooperation between these mental health professions. But in the near term, therapeutic counseling will continue to distinguish itself from its professional cousins as counselors find new positions and develop new ways of bringing their healing arts to Russian society. As practitioners move toward therapeutic models, the clientele of counseling may change as well. Under communism, psychology and psychiatry were associated with the certifiably insane or with the ploys of political propaganda. Understanding of what counseling is, who counselors are, and how counseling can help is becoming more enlightened. The concept that counseling, whether delivered in the form of psychoeducational programs or on an individual basis, can help relatively well-functioning people to function even better is beginning to take root in Russia. Perhaps an analogy can be drawn between the popular growth of counseling in the West since the end of World War II. The popularity of counseling in Russia appears to be on a similar trajectory since the fall of the Soviet Union in 1991.

Diversity Issues

Russia is home to 160 different ethnic groups and indigenous people living in a land that borders 14 different countries. The delivery of counseling services to such a wide variety of people spread over such a large land mass presents obvious challenges. However, an important unifying aspect of this diverse nation of cities is its common language. Although its 141.9 million people speak more than 140 different languages and dialects, *almost all of them also speak Russian.*

In addition, Russia is a nation of urban centers. The largest country in the world, Russia's land mass is almost twice that of the United States, even though its population is only half as large—141.9 million compared to 308.7 million (Central Intelligence Agency, 2011; U.S. Department of State, 2010). However, statistics on population density—22 people per square mile in Russia versus 76 per square mile in the United States—are entirely misleading. Russia has 13 cities of more than a million people compared to 9 such cities in the United States (Russian Census, 2002; U.S. Census Bureau, 2009). Moreover, almost 20% of Russia's entire population lives in these massive urban centers compared to 8% of the U.S. population who live in its own nine largest cities. By this key measure, Russia is more urban than the United States, and this urbanization has a significant impact on its social problems, the delivery of its social services, and the type of training programs that may prove effective in meeting its social needs. Counseling training programs strategically planted in these large urban areas may prove to be an effective means of training counselors to reach the more remote and sparsely populated areas of the country.

Up to 80% of Russian counseling clients are women, teenagers, and children. Russian males will usually not go to see a counselor on their own but may join if a wife or children bring them into the process. Russian society in general holds traditional roles for men and women as well as traditional views on sexual orientation. Homosexuality is a matter of personal secrecy. Individuals with disabilities rarely come for counseling because of issues with both finances and physical accessibility. Disability pensions tend to be inadequate for the provision of food, so counseling services are an unaffordable luxury. In addition, although there are approximately 10 million people with disabilities in Russia, they are rarely seen in public, partly because buildings and public transportation are not handicap accessible. This inaccessibility limits the ability of individuals with disabilities to physically get to the places where counseling services are located.

Although immigration has brought many different ethnic groups to Russia, this diversity has not yet been addressed by the counseling profession. For example, the city of Krasnodar has more than 100 different ethnic groups and nationalities, and yet there is almost no training in diversity issues. At the present time diversity training is perceived as something dangerous that may split a society that has been continually shaken since the fall of communism. For the most part, the perception is that Russia needs unity at this time, not a discussion of issues that may potentially divide its population. Since the second term of President Putin, the emphasis has been on building a stable political climate; building a growing economy; and improving living standards, including developing quality health care, a modern educational system, affordable housing loans, and realistic retirement plans. When these basic needs are met, the culture may be more open to the discussion of diversity issues.

Counselor Education

Despite Russia's ethnic diversity and massive size, the Russian educational system has achieved a 99.4% literacy rate, higher than that of the United States. Approximately 7 million students attend the country's 1,090 higher education institutions, almost all of which are state supported (Central Intelligence Agency, 2011; U.S. Department of State, 2010). Russia places a high value on education, and directives from the Russian government form the basis of curriculum development.

In order to meet the needs of a rapidly changing society following the fall of the communist regime in 1991, the field of social work emerged in Russia in 1991. As noted previously, the counseling profession is now officially established as a branch within the social work field as a result of a government directive that went into effect in 2011 (Ministry of Education and Science of the Russian Federation, 2009). Another government policy calls for the creation of an addiction counseling specialty, which will enable counselors to work alongside psychologists and medical doctors to treat addictions.

Also under consideration by the Ministry of Education is the addition of actual practice in the skills of the profession, what American counseling programs term *practicum* and *internship* experiences. These work experiences in real-world settings would supplement the purely theoretical curriculum traditionally offered in the past. Although it is as yet unclear how skills in the profession will be tested, these regulations are an important step in distinguishing the Russian counseling profession as separate from that of psychology.

In Russia, by definition, individuals can call themselves counselors if they meet one of the following criteria: (a) they have a university (college) degree in psychology or social work, (b) they are a medical doctor or psychiatrist with 1 year of training in counseling from their medical university, or (c) they have a baccalaureate (bachelor's) degree plus an additional certification from a counseling organization. Counseling certifications in Freudian theory, Jungian theory, psychodrama, and other theories are offered by European organizations through their affiliates in Moscow and St. Petersburg. For example, the Eastern European Gestalt Association offers professional certification in gestalt therapy through its office in St. Petersburg, and the International Association of Analytical Psychology has also certified Russian therapists. These programs typically offer continuing education that first certifies the student as a therapist and then qualifies the therapist as a junior or senior trainer of other therapists. Programs in positive therapy, art therapy, and various rehabilitation methodologies also exist. These programs tend to be transplanted from the West to Moscow or St. Petersburg and then emanate throughout Russia from those locations.

Most counselors are trained in the psychology or social departments of a Russian university or institute of higher education (Высшее Учебное Заведен). In American English, *institute* translates as "college," but Russians also use a word that sounds like "college" to indicate a vocational trade school. The word *institute* in the Russian context is what an American would call a "college." Russian institutes are smaller and more limited in their academic offerings than Russian universities. In Russian academia, counseling per se does not exist as a separately recognizable faculty governed by national academic criteria. Faculty and government criteria exist for psychology and social work, and the counseling field is just beginning to emerge as a branch of the social work profession for training purposes.

The Future

The counseling profession in Russia could grow quickly in the first half of the 21st century for several reasons. The Russian government has recognized the need for skills-based training and a strengths-based approach by establishing counseling (social psychological help) as a new branch of the social work field. International certification programs are being established in Russia and are likely to continue growing. In addition, many counseling centers are opening in major cities throughout Russia, moving beyond the academic and economic centers of St. Petersburg and Moscow. The public's suspicion of psychology as a forensic and political weapon is evolving as people learn that counseling can provide effective help in a variety of areas through a strengths-based approach.

Moreover, the need for counseling in Russian society is evident. Marriage and family counseling will likely grow beyond the traditional pastoral function of Russian churches and synagogues. Child counseling can potentially broaden to include play therapy, art therapy, and other methods as practitioners and the populace become more familiar with them. The need for youth and teenage counseling and guidance increases as the communist Pioneer Clubs and Komsomol become part of the previous generation's history. Addiction and rehabilitation counseling may hold the most potential for growth in the next 5 to 10 years because of the increasing problem among youth. As Russia prepares to host the Winter Olympics in 2014 and the World Cup in soccer in 2018, there is also renewed and increasing interest in sports counseling and psychology. In the business world there is an increased need for professional coaching and mentoring.

Although the potential for growth in the counseling profession in Russia is evident, its expansion is linked not only to the needs of the people but also to Russia's economic recovery. Currently the salaries of mental health professionals are low; therefore, although many students complete mental health degrees, relatively few continue to work in the field because they cannot survive financially. The mental health professions in general must become more financially attractive in order to thrive, and much of that success has to do with the health of the Russian economy.

As Russia participates as a global partner with the rest of the world, a new Russian society continues to emerge. The social and mental health needs of the new Russia are compelling, and the need for counselors in a wide range of fields is evident.

References

Achmatova, N. (2010, June 4). Russia facing an orphanage and adoption crisis. *Asia News*. Retrieved from http://www.asianews.it/news-en/Russia-facing-an-orphanage-and-adoption-crisis-18587.html

Althausen, L. (1996). Russian families. In M. McGoldrick, J. Giordano, & J. K. Pearce (Eds.), *Ethnicity and family therapy* (2nd ed., pp. 680–687). New York, NY: Guilford Press.

Aubrey, R. F. (1977, February). Historical development of guidance and counseling and implications for the future. *The Personnel and Guidance Journal, 55,* 288–295.

Bobrova, N., Rughnikov, U., Neifeld, E., Rhodes, T., Alcorn, R., Kirichenko, S., & Power, R. (2008). Challenges in providing drug user treatment services in Russia: Providers' views. *Substance Use & Misuse, 43,* 1770–1784. doi:10.1080/10826080802289291

Brewer, J. M. (1942). Beginnings in other countries. In *History of vocational guidance: Origins and early development* (pp. 219–236). New York, NY: Harper & Brothers.

Central Intelligence Agency. (2011, January 13). *The world factbook: Central Asia: Russia.* Retrieved from http://www.cia.gov/library/publications/the-world-factbook/geos/countrytemplate_rs.html

Gascoigne, B. (2001). *History of Russia.* Retrieved from http://www.historyworld.net/wrldhis/PlainTextHistories.asp?historyid=ac14

Horne, S. (1999). Domestic violence in Russia. *American Psychologist, 54*(1), 55–61. doi:10.1037/0003-066X.54.1.55

Ministry of Education and Science of the Russian Federation. (2009, December 8). *Federal Educational Standard for Higher Professional Education* (Order 709). Retrieved from http://www.edu.ru/db/cgi-bin/portal/spe/spe_new_list.plx?substr=%F1%EE%F6%E8%E0%EB%FC%ED%E0%FF+%F0%E0%E1%EE%F2%E0&st=2009

Neukrug, E. (2007). *The world of the counselor: An introduction to the counseling profession* (3rd ed.). Belmont, CA: Thomson Higher Education.

Popova, A. (2003). Cultural and historical influences on the concepts of guidance in late 20th century Russia. *British Journal of Guidance and Counseling, 31,* 325–342. doi:10.1080/0306988031000147910

Russian Census. (2002). *List of cities and towns in Russia by population.* Retrieved from http://en.wikipedia.org/wiki/List_of_cities_and_towns_in_Russia_by_population

Shlapentokh, V. (2005). Russia's demographic decline and the public reaction. *Europe-Asia Studies, 57,* 951–968. doi:10.1080/09668130500301337

Solidarity Fund. (2011). *Kraski Deistva: Blagatvoritelni Fund Solidarnast* [The colors of childhood: Charitable fund solidarity]. Retrieved from http://www.kraskidetstva.ru/topmenu/chtodelaem/proforientacionnyy_proekt/

Sosland, A. (1997). The state of psychotherapy in Moscow. *International Journal of Psychotherapy, 2,* 229–233.

U.S. Census Bureau. (2009, July). *List of United States cities by population.* Retrieved from http://en.wikipedia.org/wiki/List_of_United_States_cities_by_population

U.S. Department of State, Bureau of European and Eurasian Affairs. (2010, June 14). *Background note: Russia.* Retrieved from http://www.state.gov/r/pa/ei/bgn/3183.htm

World Health Organization. (2003). *Suicide rates: Suicide rates (per 100,000) by country, year, and gender.* Retrieved from http://www.who.int/mental_health/prevention/suicide/suiciderates/en/

• • •

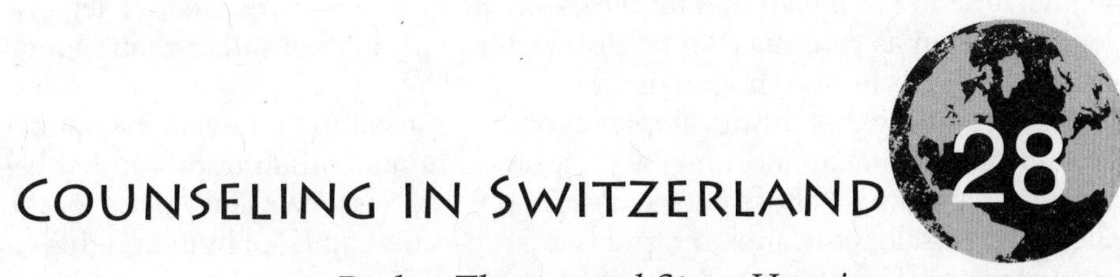

Counseling in Switzerland

Roslyn Thomas and Stacy Henning

In 1952, the American Personnel and Guidance Association was formed in the United States to strengthen the various counseling professions. This association later evolved into the American Association of Counseling and Development and then into the current American Counseling Association (ACA) as its ranks grew. Today, with an identity of its own, counseling is a well-respected profession in the United States and is considered distinct from psychology, social work, and psychiatry. Much like in the initial days of professional counseling in the United States, Swiss counseling programs confront challenges associated with pioneering a new profession by connecting with counseling colleagues from around the world and contextualizing the profession within the cultural and historical traditions of the home country (Thomas & Henning, 2012).

Switzerland came into being in 1848 when the country became a federal state. With a population of 7 million inhabitants, this small landlocked country located in the heart of Western Europe shares much of its history with its neighbors, Austria, Italy, France, and Germany. The federal constitution defines Switzerland as a state composed of 26 culturally diverse cantons (states) with far-reaching autonomy and an internal rivalry that from a foreign perspective begs the question: Why are they part of the same country? (Luck, 1985). But the closer one looks at how the cantons exist, the more one can observe why the country has become enormously successful. It is as if each canton acknowledges that, although they do not necessarily need one another, they understand the power of being together.

The Swiss health care system is fragmented into 26 cantonal authorities that differ in terms of policy, legislation, and structure (Luck, 1985). Health insurance is compulsory, although contributions vary between cantons. A feature of this system is that cantons are thoroughly integrated into the sociocultural context of the country, and there is collaboration between universities and psychiatric services (Thomas & Henning, 2012).

Swiss cantons are remarkably similar to U.S. states. Both countries have a federal system in which states and cantons have powers that the federal government does not. The unique Swiss form of government (decentralized power) has elaborate mechanisms designed to find a compromise to every issue. This seems to make Swiss cantons more autonomous than U.S. states. Switzerland is characterized by a system of direct democracy in which citizens vote on issues of importance and individuals have a high degree of participation in law making. Citizens who hold diverse views have a voice, and a high level of political awareness is ensured for all.

Because of the quadrilingual nature of Switzerland (there are four national languages: German [64%], French [20%], Italian [7%], and Romansch [0.5%]), counselor education, training, and professional practice are divided among regional and linguistic interests. The practice of counseling in the different regions of Switzerland is enriched and at the same time complicated by approaches practiced in neighboring France, Germany, and Italy. The result is indistinct relationships between accrediting organizations with regard to the management and validation of the counseling profession. The dearth of literature and the limited collaboration between the various counseling associations and credentialing agencies in Switzerland has meant that until recently peoples' moral, existential, legal, and psychological dilemmas continued to be dealt with in a cantonal rather than federal manner, a factor that lends itself to fragmentation.

It seems fitting that the development of the counseling profession in continental Europe should find a home in a country with a proud humanitarian tradition that has long been a place of asylum for those persecuted for political reasons. Geneva, the location of one of the first counselor education programs, is seen as the capital of human rights supported by a belief in social justice and advocacy (Wright, 2005). As a meeting place where world leaders come together to negotiate treaties and agreements, the city is home to the International Committee of the Red Cross and more than 200 international, United Nations, governmental, and nongovernmental organizations. This workforce is one group that frequently uses counseling services.

The Current Status of Counseling

Like in many other European countries, counseling in Switzerland evolved largely from the work of the clergy, social workers, nurses, and Christian associations that offered pastoral care to the communities they served. Some set up early psychotherapy training. There are several examples of internationally renowned Swiss contributors to the mental health field, including psychoanalyst Alexander Müller, transactional analyst Leonhard Schlegel, and psychologist Carl Jung. Their rich legacy provides a foundation that Swiss counselor training programs still draw on.

Like in many other countries, counseling in Switzerland exists within the framework of psychiatry and psychology (Sabbadini, 2010). Clinical counseling must compete with psychology, psychiatry, and other helping professions for its place. As counseling becomes a more sought-after form of intervention, Swiss counselors meet the challenges inherent in making sense of their work in a profession that is new to this part of the world. Reflection on questions of definition, training, and accreditation are ongoing. These reflections serve to counter the dominant conceptual framework of confusion and protectionism present in the counseling profession and build a strong voice for the future.

Since the beginning of the 21st century, skilled Swiss counseling professionals trained in a range of therapeutic approaches have broadened and enriched the field (Sabbadini, 2010). Among practicing counselors are psychiatrists, psychologists, and psychoanalysts, some with formal training in professional counseling. Sabbadini (2010) argued that there is still little homogeneity between counseling programs with respect to compulsory standards, training, consistent terminology, legislation, and diplomas awarded. Professional counseling has much self-growth and realization yet to undergo in Switzerland.

Counseling in Switzerland takes many different forms and is carried out by a diverse group of people—professional and laypeople alike—with varying degrees of preparation and training. Counselors provide mental health support to the population through individual, couples, and family counseling and group work, yet the majority offer individual therapy. At present, there are no official data on the number of counselors practicing in Switzerland. Some are registered members of the two main national associations: the Swiss Association for Counselling (SGfB) and the Swiss National Association for Counselling (ANSCo). However, there are many nonaffiliated individuals as well. Professional educators and social workers with counseling training may work in public jobs in which they introduce a counseling approach to the workplace. Counselors increasingly work in medical settings, institutions, schools, and companies in interdisciplinary teams composed of other professionals, such as psychologists and psychiatrists, to develop and implement treatment plans.

One of the oldest forms of counseling in the United States is school guidance and counseling. However, school counseling does not formally exist in Switzerland. Services in the school setting are provided by child psychologists. There is no educational degree needed to train school guidance counselors in Switzerland or any immediate plan to require such a degree.

Examples of counselor education programs in Zurich, Geneva, and Ticino are illustrative of the growth of counselor training in Switzerland since the start of the 21st century. These include the establishment of private training institutes among the Swiss German community and the formation of the Centro al Dragonato in Bellinzona, Ticino, in 1989 (Rezzonico & Meier, 2003). The latter evolved from collaboration among several colleges (the University of Milan, the University of Italian Switzerland, and the University of Applied Sciences of Southern Switzerland) as part of a research project to promote counselor training and strengthen the theoretical models in rehabilitation, counseling, and social intervention (Rezzonico & Meier, 2010). Professional counseling and counselor education continue to evolve and grow in Switzerland.

Switzerland is host to the first counselor education professional degree program to be taught in English in continental Europe. Students may arrive from different countries to pursue a program that prepares graduates to be licensed in the United States or to remain in Switzerland if they qualify for residency. Those who remain mostly serve the international community, which equals 40% of the Geneva population.

In 1991, the European Association for Counselling (EAC) was founded to support the development of counseling across Europe (EAC, n.d.). In 2005, ANSCo (largely Italian) was started. ANSCo was a member of the EAC and served as a reference association for counseling and as a platform for counselors or clients looking for support in Switzerland (ANSCo, n.d.-a). In May 2006, SGfB (largely Swiss German) was founded (SGfB, n.d.-a). This organization emerged as a network of 11 counseling-related associations and institutions (many private) offering different theoretical approaches to counselor training. The Swiss German associations defined counseling and developed their statutes, ethical principles, and guidelines (SGfB, n.d.-b). In 2011, there were a total of 18 affiliated organizations and more than 150 members (SGfB, n.d.-c).

The essential difference between SGfB and ANSCo was philosophical. SGfB emphasized vocational training and apprenticeship; ANSCo emphasized an academic route through the university graduate system to a counseling qualification. Extensive, well-regulated, state-controlled apprenticeship programs unique to Switzerland exist as a genuine alternative for nonuniversity graduates. These include almost any of 200 professions or trades. Apprenticeships last 3–4 years, and graduates receive a coveted state diploma on completion. Individuals are trained at a company or organization and attend school once or twice per week. After completing an apprenticeship, young people start work or can begin an academic career through further education in a technical college or university. Some of the member organizations of SGfB are also those that provide coaching training. As such they are part of a largely unregulated profession of coaching in Switzerland and face their own accreditation and regulatory challenges.

In an effort to ensure quality control and a professional identity for counseling, ANSCo and Webster University in Geneva registered the term *ANSCo Counsellor* with the Federal Institute of

Intellectual Property in 2009. This trademarked term equated Swiss national standards for the counseling profession with ANSCo standards. To receive individual ANSCo accreditation, graduates required a master's-level degree in counseling; after obtaining such a degree, they could use the title "ANSCo Accredited Professional Counsellor" after their name (ANSCo, n.d.-a).

Until June 2012, the two professional bodies ANSCo and SGfB were separate. In June 2011 they collaborated in an effort to seek out common ground in the interest of crafting a strong national counseling association. In June 2012 ANSCo dissolved, and these members now have the opportunity to transfer their membership to the SGfB.

SGfB requires a proposed examination at the federal level under the auspices of the responsible federal body, the Federal Office for Professional Education and Technology (OPET; SGfB, 2012). This examination will lead to an advanced federal diploma. It will comprise a written and oral exam and an audio- and videotaped review. At a final colloquium, candidates will explain their concept of counseling and practice. The federal exam is subject to review by OPET (SGfB, 2012). Once the examination is accepted by the federal office, OPET will decide on the acceptance of international diplomas and certifications. The counseling profession will have a federal title if SGfB is successful. The final title will recognize counselors and distinguish them from social workers, psychologists, and psychotherapists (Thomas & Henning, 2012).

The SGfB examination is expected to result in the title "counsellor with advanced federal diploma of professional education and training" (*Höhere Fachprüfung für Beratung im psychosozialen Bereich*). To be admitted to this examination, one must have a tertiary education (*Tertiärabschluss*). A lower examination resulting in the title "supporter/adviser with competency certificate" (*Begleiter/Begleiterin von Entwicklungs- und Veränderungsprozessen mit eidg. Fachausweis*) will fall under the auspices of the Swiss Coaching Association and the Schweizer Kader Organisation (SGfB, 2012).

Within SGfB are many nurses, clergy, and individuals who have completed an apprenticeship; most are trained in nonuniversity programs. SGfB requires a minimum of 600 lessons and a 40- to 60-page paper, self-development, 30 hours of supervision, and at least 1 year of practice at 50% employment. Candidates need 5 years of counseling experience, personal therapy, intervision (peer supervision), and endorsement from a supervisor to sit for the examination.

Professional organizations and groups in Switzerland have the advantage of learning from such groups in North America, Canada, and Australia, all of which practice the traditional Western version of clinical counseling (Hohenshil, 2010). They are in a position to assess the current practice of counseling in the Western world and of psychology in Europe and combine and adapt the two to fit the culture of the local Swiss communities. In this way Switzerland may look to the already established counseling profession in the United States and the United Kingdom and the related established professional guilds (American Counseling Association [ACA], National Board for Certified Counselors [NBCC}, Council for Accreditation of Counseling and Related Educational Programs [CACREP], British Association for Counselling and Psychotherapy [BACP]) to develop local professional practice.

ACA developed to provide members with assistance with "leadership training, publications, continuing education opportunities, and advocacy services" and to help "counseling professionals develop their skills and expand their knowledge base" (ACA, 2011). One of the most critical services ACA provides its members and the general public is the *ACA Code of Ethics* (ACA, 2005). The *ACA Code of Ethics* may be used as a basis for other nations developing the counseling profession. It provides boundaries and principles for counseling practice for its constituents and guides members in ethical decision making (Wheeler & Bertram, 2012). Furthermore, the ACA Ethics Committee serves members by processing ethical complaints and providing consultation on ethical issues. As professional counseling develops in Switzerland, constituents have adopted a professional code of ethics (ANSCo, n.d.-b; SGfB, n.d.-b). The *ACA Code of Ethics* (ACA, 2005) and the *Ethical Framework for Good Practice in Counselling and Psychotherapy* (BACP, 2010) have been foundational documents in the development of ethical counseling codes in Switzerland.

Several other professional organizations in the United States could share their history and, if suitable, provide culturally appropriate mentoring to other countries. ACA has organized divisions, professional committees, and listservs to respond to the variety of member interests. These groups are based in subspecialties of counseling and are a rich source of information for current and developing counseling curricula, pedagogy, practice, research, legislative efforts, and accreditation. They may be considered one potential starting point for developing professions of counseling worldwide.

Best Counseling Practices

In contrast to the traditional professions of psychiatry, psychoanalysis, and psychology, the central philosophy of counseling in Switzerland is that individuals have adequate resources to manage their lives but that in a given situation these resources may be unavailable. In contrast to approaches based on the more traditional pathogenic paradigm, counseling has adapted to make a different philosophical assertion and respond to societal changes. It aims to mediate between events and the individual, enabling the client to seek his or her growth potential and understand the symbolic meaning of life (Sabbadini, 2010). Counselors apply cognitive, affective, behavioral, constructivist, and/or systemic strategies to address issues of wellness and personal growth and sometimes pathology as well. All the while counselors pay attention to generating interest in multiculturalism, social justice, and advocacy within a country that has been multicultural in its own way for centuries (Thomas & Henning, 2012).

In their work, counselors are trained to use a framework that deals with understanding the inner life of the client as a biopsychosocial and spiritual subject. Although the counseling profession in Switzerland consults the *Diagnostic and Statistical Manual of Mental Disorders* (American Psychiatric Association, 2000) and the International Classification of Diseases–10 (World Health Organization, 2007), counselors are hesitant to routinely apply diagnostic labels. This is to be attentive to the social construction of a disease category mindset and points to a health-driven rather than a pathology-driven orientation.

The positive use of psychiatric diagnostic codes is appreciated in Swiss counseling. The value of the codes can be seen in the construction of treatment plans and in the provision of consistent structure and vocabulary for clinicians and for use by organizations such as the World Health Organization and insurance companies. However, there is little agreement among local professionals regarding the meaning of many terms. Diagnoses may be more political than scientific. A counseling perspective includes a broader notion of relative well-being, hardiness (Kobasa, 1979), perceived self-efficacy or optimistic self-beliefs (Bandura, 1997), positive psychology (Seligman, 2011), cognitive appraisal (Lazarus & Folkman, 1991), and learned resourcefulness (Rosenbaum, 1990). It is noted in the emerging literature that many clients have been poorly served by a clinical framework of people's experience that assumes vulnerability at the expense of strength, resilience, community bonds, and an ability to cope (Almedon & Summerfield, 2004). Counseling graduates in Switzerland are trained to recognize that not all individuals have the same mental health experiences (Rezzonico & Meier, 2010).

Counseling's contribution is to apply mental health and psychological and human development principles in the context of communities, hospitals, schools, universities, corporations, religious organizations, and private practice. In this way it aims to assist the individual to overcome the psychological and existential or emotional discomfort that prevents full and creative expression and to be a facilitating element in the dialogue between the organization and the person. The client is helped to develop an awareness of resources, to facilitate the emergence of new narratives, and to open up new scenarios and possibilities. The counselor resists the temptation to give advice but asks appropriate questions; the counselor does not take responsibility for the client's choices but rather provides information and orientation (Thomas & Henning, 2012).

As in Western countries, counseling in Switzerland is especially useful in times of crisis or change—after a serious accident, with trauma, with grief, with disability, with a terminal illness, after the loss of a job or of a family member, with marital problems, or with the breakdown of a meaningful relationship, all events that can upset a normal pattern of life. As a largely nondirective approach it is also useful for individuals, couples, families, or groups, whether in the community, at work, or at home. Other groups with specific counseling needs include young adults in transition from school to work, the socially disadvantaged, humanitarian workers, people with antisocial or offender behaviors, substance abusers, and older adults.

As the counseling profession forges its way in Switzerland, many counselors start full- or part-time private practices. This is in contrast to social workers, who work more closely within state organizations. Until recently the profession of social work was poorly developed, lacking a university chair and a scientific association. Between 2006 and 2012 the beginning of several master's programs ensured that the status of social work was commensurate with that of professions such as teaching and psychology.

Although online counseling is increasingly being offered, there is little empirical evidence of the benefits and drawbacks of Internet therapy as part of counseling practice in Switzerland. Throughout much of the world, including Switzerland, the Samaritans offer the public a voluntary, anonymous, private crisis line through a protected chat room via a secure Internet site. The aim is to provide understanding and empathetic and impartial listening while maintaining anonymity and confidentiality. This service is not seen as a substitute for therapy. ACA and BACP have produced booklets and guidelines for telephone and online counseling, supervision, training, contracting, and associated ethical concerns that can be drawn on as resources as these services develop (Milne, 2010).

Diversity Issues

The underlying constitutional structure and principles of Swiss federalism recognize the need to accommodate linguistic, cultural, and social diversity peacefully. The principles of inclusive consensus rather than simple majority rule help safeguard diversity and cantonal autonomy and recognize compromise as a strength and not a weakness. Citizen participation in political decision making is maximized through direct democracy, respect for constitutional norms and the rule of law, and a prevailing spirit of tolerance and compromise in which diversity is cherished (Luck, 1985).

Today Switzerland shares much in common with its European neighbors despite the country's traditional isolation from the European Union. The *Swiss Social Report* (Suter et al., 2008) documents the country as one of the wealthiest in the world, in which the richest 20% of the population own 80% of the total private assets. Upward or downward social mobility is easy, and class structure is not particularly visible. The middle class is large, and the Swiss are relatively well protected from social problems by the state.

Although it was true until recently, this picture is no longer wholly accurate. New socioeconomic tensions mean that the broader underpinnings of prosperity and success are under pressure. Switzerland's present position is characterized by contradictions and new domestic trends (Suter et al., 2008). For example, when shareholders make large profit demands from banks and multinational corporations at the same time as they report mass layoffs, individuals with little education or a diminished ability to work must now be supported by the state. As more people avail themselves of state support, withdrawal of state funding impacts pension and social welfare benefits (especially disability insurance and welfare). The outcome is a reduced ability to counteract social problems and an increasing gap between low- and high-income households, between the different social classes, and between the sexes. An example relates to women's participation in the workplace. This has consistently increased so that in 2010 Switzerland was about average for Europe (i.e., women made up 45% of the workforce and only 11% of executives; Bachelet, 2011). Despite this, many women with the same education as men still earn less (Suter et al., 2008). In addition, a sizable minority of secondary school graduates cannot find an apprenticeship or continue their studies.

Although foreign labor has been a key factor in Switzerland's prosperity, the 18% national average presence of foreigners across the country leads to resentment and blame for everything from the housing shortage to overcrowded nurseries and schools. High-risk groups are low-income families, youth, the long-term unemployed, victims of the economic crisis, individuals with a reduced capacity to work (i.e., persons who are ill or who have disabilities), women from foreign cultures with insufficient vocational training or low levels of education, and divorced individuals with three or more children (Suter et al., 2008). Similar tensions exist on issues such as ageism, sexual identity, and nontraditional relationships. With their emphasis on the facilitation of human relationships rather than on diagnosis, treatment, and medication, counselors seem well placed to work sensitively with those from many different cultural, economic, and social backgrounds as they adjust to geopolitical and socioeconomic changes.

Counselor Education

Counselor training standards vary widely in Switzerland. For example, the SGfB mandate is primarily to support and train counselors with a practical emphasis and a drive for clinical practice within the community as opposed to a traditional university-based, academic focus. With respect to university training, typical psychology training involves a 4-year bachelor's degree followed by a 2-year master's degree in either psychology or counseling. Counselor education at the master's level is now more highly valued. When students are enrolled full time, the practitioner training program can be completed within 2 years. This allows for candidates to combine work and study if they choose. The Swiss master's program in counseling requires the completion of 16 courses, including a 3-course practicum/internship. Programs may adopt an interdisciplinary view based on a wide range of disciplines such as philosophy, psychology, and sociology. They also attend to psychotherapy outcome research as well as to the experience of practitioners by offering an integrative course design.

The core theoretical model in counselor education may include a range of perspectives, such as integrative, psychodynamic, client-centered, cognitive–behavioral, systemic, gestalt, mind/body psychotherapies, constructivist, existential, and transactional analysis. An integrative approach identifies a core theoretical model but suggests that no single psychotherapy or counseling approach is significantly more effective than any other approach and that all have something to offer the clinician. Rather than focus solely on a particular approach, this integrative approach affirms the inherent value of each individual.

Integrative programs may encourage students to consider the nature of the problem, the personality of the client, and the setting of the therapy when drawing up a treatment plan for their work with a client. In such a program, students are helped to progressively understand and respond appropriately to the person at the affective, behavioral, cognitive, spiritual, cultural, systemic, and physiological levels of functioning.

Counseling clinicians are increasingly required to be flexible and responsive to the specific requirements of the context in which they work and to tailor the delivery of counseling to the needs of each client within the particular context (Asay & Lambert, 2004). In particular, research shows that the quality of the therapeutic relationship is a key determinant of the success of the therapy (Hubble, Duncan, & Miller, 1999; Rogers, 1951; Yalom, 2002). Training therefore focuses on a therapeutic relationship that is flexible and responsive to client needs, with learning outcomes developed from professional standards established in the professional field of counseling (ANSCo, n.d.-a).

The Future

Swiss counseling programs will evolve and expand as the profession seeks to meet the demands of individuals seeking mental health services, as training opportunities develop, as the quantity and quality of research grows, and as awareness of the profession spreads. Switzerland may also draw on the established profession of psychotherapy and counseling in the United States and the United Kingdom and the related established professional guilds (ACA, NBCC, Council for Accreditation of Counseling and Related Educational Programs, BACP) to develop the many facets of the practice of counseling locally.

Although the counseling profession in Switzerland has begun to develop its own professional guilds and codes of ethics, it still experiences a struggle for recognition in Switzerland and Europe. Frustration has been fueled by the acknowledgment that when translated, the word *counseling* has different meanings. For instance, in French and German it means "adviser," a role counseling in Switzerland does not ascribe to as a central methodology in clinical mental health work.

As of June 2012 there is now one strong national Swiss Association for Counselling (SGfB) covering regional and linguistic interests (*Sprachreregionen;* SGfB, n.d.-a). This association is committed to developing and ensuring the quality of psychosocial counseling in the country. With the validation of the federal examination, counseling may be fully legitimized as a separate profession within the mental health community. If local counselors continue to develop the profession at home and maintain best practices adopted from counseling professionals around the world, they will be equipped to support individuals and groups undergoing life, developmental, and/or spatial transitions in Switzerland.

References

Almedon, A. M., & Summerfield, D. (2004). Mental well-being in settings of "complex emergency": An overview. *Journal of Biosocial Science, 36,* 381–388.

American Counseling Association. (2005). *ACA code of ethics.* Alexandria, VA: Author.

American Counseling Association. (2011). *About us.* Retrieved from http://www.counseling.org/AboutUs/Default.aspx

American Psychiatric Association. (2000). *Diagnostic and statistical manual of mental disorders* (4th ed., text rev.). Washington, DC: Author.

Asay, T. P., & Lambert, M. J. (2004). The empirical case for the common factors in therapy: Quantitative findings. In M. Hubble, B. Duncan, & S. Miller (Eds.), *The heart and soul of change: What works in therapy* (pp. 23–55). Washington, DC: American Psychological Association.

Bachelet, M. (2011, March 24). *Executive director Michelle Bachelet addresses European Parliament.* Retrieved from http://www.unwomen.org/2011/03/executive-director-michelle-bachelet-addresses-european-parliament/

Bandura, A. (1997). *Self-efficacy: The exercise of control.* New York, NY: Freeman.

British Association for Counselling and Psychotherapy. (2010). *Ethical framework for good practice in counselling and psychotherapy.* Retrieved from http://www.bacp.co.uk/admin/structure/files/pdf/566_ethical_framework_feb2010.pdf

European Association for Counselling. (n.d.). *EAC news.* Retrieved from http://eacnews.net/european-association-for-counsellors

Hohenshil, T. H. (2010). International counseling: Introduction. *Journal of Counseling & Development, 88,* 3.

Hubble, M., Duncan, B., & Miller, S. (1999). Directing attention to what works. In M. Hubble, B. Duncan, & S. Miller (Eds.), *The heart and soul of change: What works in therapy* (pp. 407–448). Washington, DC: American Psychological Association.

Kobasa, S. C. (1979). Stressful life events, personality and health: An inquiry into hardiness. *Journal of Personality and Social Psychology, 37,* 1–11.

Lazarus, R., & Folkman, S. (1991). The concept of coping. In A. Monat & R. Lazarus (Eds.), *Stress and coping: An anthology* (3rd ed., pp. 189–206). New York, NY: Columbia University Press.

Luck, J. M. (1985). *A history of Switzerland—The first 100,000 years: Before the beginnings to the days of the present.* Palo Alto, CA: Society for the Promotion of Science and Scholarship.

Milne, A. (2010). *Understand counselling.* London, England: Hodder Education.

Rezzonico, G., & Meier, C. (2003). *Le Narrative del Centro al Dragonato* [The narrative of the centre of Dragonato]. Bellinzona, Switzerland: Guigno.

Rezzonico, G., & Meier, C. (Eds.). (2010). *Il counselling cognitivo relazionale* [Cognitive relational counseling]. Milan, Italy: FrancoAngeli.

Rogers, C. R. (1951). *Client centered therapy.* Boston, MA: Houghton Mifflin.

Rosenbaum, M. (Ed.). (1990). *Learned resourcefulness: On coping skills, self-control, and adaptive behavior.* New York, NY: Springer.

Sabbadini, S. A. (2010). Counselling come filosofia e come professione [Counseling as a philosophy and as a profession]. In G. Rezzonico & C. Meier (Eds.), *Il counselling cognitivo relazionale* (pp. 67–74). Milan, Italy: FrancoAngeli.

Seligman, M. (2011). *Flourish: A visionary new understanding of happiness and well-being.* New York, NY: Free Press.

Suter, C., Perrenoud, S., Levy, R., Kuhn, U., Gazareth, P., & Joye, J. (2008). *Swiss Social Report 2008.* Retrieved from http://sozialbericht.ch/Rapport_social/en/index.html

Swiss Association for Counselling. (2012, March 19). *6. ordentliche Generalversammlung der Schweizerischen Gesellschaft für Beratung/Counselling SGfB* [Summary of the 6th annual general meeting of the Swiss Association for Counselling]. Zürich, Switzerland: Author.

Swiss Association for Counselling. (n.d.-a). *Accueil. Association Suisse de Conseil SGfB* [Home. Swiss Association Counselling SGfB]. Retrieved from http://www.sgfb.ch/index.php?option=com_frontpage&Itemid=1&lang=francais

Swiss Association for Counselling. (n.d.-b). *Code éthique* [Code of ethics]. Retrieved from http://www.sgfb.ch/index.php?option=com_content&task=view&id=3&Itemid=5

Swiss Association for Counselling. (n.d.-c). *Portrait* [Portrait]. Retrieved from http://www.sgfb.ch/index.php?option=com_content&task=view&id=20&Itemid=2

Swiss National Association for Counselling. (n.d.-a). *Counselling.* Retrieved from http://ansco.ch/index.php?option=com_content&view=article&id=48&Itemid=2&lang=en

Swiss National Association for Counselling. (n.d.-b). *Ethics and professional conduct code.* Retrieved from http://ansco.ch/index.php?option=com_content&view=article&id=52&Itemid=57&lang=en

Thomas, R., & Henning, A. (2012). Counseling in Switzerland: Past, present, and future. *Journal of Counseling & Development, 90,* 505–509.

Wheeler, A. N., & Bertram, B. (2012). *The counselor and the law: A guide to legal and ethical practice* (6th ed.). Alexandria, VA: American Counseling Association.

World Health Organization. (2007). *International statistical classification of diseases and related health problems, 10th revision.* Retrieved from http://apps.who.int/classifications/apps/icd/icd10online/

Wright, T. (2005, July 1). *Swiss put human rights at center of UN reform.* Retrieved from http://www.nytimes.com/2005/06/30/world/europe/30iht-rights.html

Yalom, I. D. (2002). *The gift of therapy: Reflections on being a therapist.* London, England: Judy Piatkus Publishers.

• • •

Counseling in Middle Eastern Countries

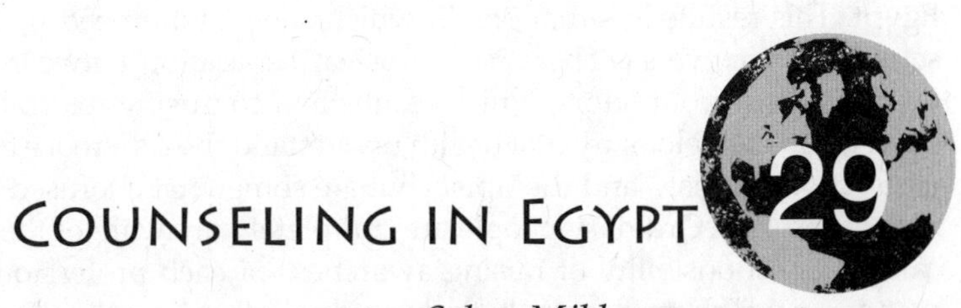

Counseling in Egypt 29

Sehar Mikhemar

This chapter starts with a historical review of counseling in Egypt before proceeding to a discussion of the current status of the field. It then considers the best practices for Egyptian society given its unique habits and belief system. This is supplemented with an elaboration of diversity issues inside the Egyptian community. The chapter also presents data about counselor education and training in Egyptian institutes and presents the prospects for counseling in the near future.

The counseling profession in Egypt is not independent from psychological services. There is confusion, even among some professionals, about the definition and role of the counselor and how counseling services differ from other psychological services. People commonly consider counseling a light form of therapy and have little understanding of the limits and separation between psychotherapy and counseling. One possible reason for this misconception is the minimal contact between Egyptian institutions that train therapists and the international community.

The first psychological clinic in Egypt was established by Dr. Abdel-Aziz El-Kossey in 1934. Dr. El-Kossey was the head of the Mental Health Department at the Faculty of Education, Ain Shams University (Eid, 2005). Within a short period of time, most mental health departments in faculties of education and faculties of arts established clinics that offered psychological services without separation of therapy and counseling services. Scholarships to Europe and the United States in the 1960s and 1970s had a significant impact on the development of psychological studies and practices in Egypt. Beneficiaries of those scholarships were trained primarily in therapy and secondarily in counseling techniques. This leading generation was responsible for training thousands of students and founding the basis of therapy and counseling in Egypt. Some of the more significant names of the generation include El Qabani, Abdel-Aziz H. El-Kossy, Mostafa Zewar, Mostafa Soueif, Salah Mikhemar, Hoda Barda, Yousef Mourad, Hamed Zahran, Samia El-Kattan, Farag Ahmed Farag, Farag Taha, and Abd-El Rakeb El Behery.

Unfortunately, scholarships sponsored by the Egyptian government dropped off significantly after the early 1970s, and most fellowships awarded by private institutions, ostensibly to make up for this decrease, focus on science and engineering. The result has been a widening gap in the abilities of counseling students trained in Egypt and those trained in Western countries. Counseling education and training in Egypt needs to be updated to help students learn and practice more modern techniques. The language was another barrier that affected the development of counseling in Egypt. Gielen (2006) noted that English has become the language of communication among international psychologists, and this has limited the ability of some Egyptian professionals to publish their ideas and research results. There also has been some miscommunication between Arabic researchers and those at the international level, and this has limited the exchange of research ideas, methods, and results. This barrier works both ways, preventing ideas in the international community from proliferating quickly in Egypt and putting a ceiling on the reach of very valuable work done locally.

As in education, there is no separation between counseling and therapeutic practice in Egypt. This results in situations in which clients who need therapists are treated by counselors and vice versa. There is an unclear separation between the duties of psychiatrists, therapists, and counselors, which results in a confusing referral process. Most workers and students in the field of mental health understand the difference between the tasks of psychiatrists, psychologists, and therapists but are somewhat confused about the roles of therapists and counselors. Ordinary people are completely unaware of these differences. Professionals carry the responsibility of raising awareness of each profession's duties and clarifying the manner in which they can help and serve people. More attention should be given to the limits of and differences among these professions and when a referral process should be done.

The Current Status of Counseling

Accurate data on the total number of counselors in Egypt are nonexistent. There is no specific organization concerned with gathering statistics on counselors as a separate group. Counselors are employed by a wide variety of institutions, including mental health hospitals, counseling centers, private clinics, social organizations, and schools. Counseling services are mainly offered by private agencies as opposed to government-run agencies. Many believe that psychological services are mainly for patients with special needs. Thus, most counseling agencies offer counseling and psychological services for populations with special needs, but it is not clear whether this is the cause or the result of this common belief.

Egypt has many psychological associations; the two most important are the Egyptian Association for Psychological Studies (established in 1948), which is academically oriented, and the Egyptian Psychologists Association (established in 1881), which concentrates on helping practitioners (Ahmed, 2004). The existence of these associations has helped in developing awareness, raising the number of publications, and building connections between practitioners. There is no independent association for counseling; however, the Arabic Association of Counseling is currently under development.

There is a distinction between the kinds of services offered by private counseling centers and those offered by the few public centers. Public counseling centers are mostly university centers like those in Cairo and Ain Shams Universities. In theory these centers offer counseling services as well as training. But because they are well known among professionals and nearly unknown among ordinary people, their main role is offering training courses for professionals and students in the fields of psychology and mental health. Private counseling centers focus on counseling practice. Counseling services in private agencies are rarely provided by fully specialized centers; instead, counseling is usually offered through agencies that offer a variety of psychological services.

School Counselors

There are sharp differences between counseling in universities and in grade schools. Universities traditionally do not have counselors. According to the guide for the accreditation of higher education institutes (2009), providing academic counseling for helping students became a condition for the accreditation of universities by the Ministry of Higher Education, but adoption has been slow, and there are no conditions on the qualifications of counselors. In contrast, according to the guidelines of the Ministry of Education, every school should have a school counselor called a "psychological professional." Moreover, use of the term *psychological professional* is sometimes inconsistent in both common use and research. The problem becomes more complex when one is translating terms between English and Arabic. For example, in a study of the efficacy of school counselors, Abd-Elgawad (2006) translated the term *psychological professional* into English as *school psychologist* and defined him or her as the person who offers counseling and guidance services to students.

Many public schools do not have a counselor on staff. According to the Ministry of Education, the total number of school counselors in middle and high schools in Egypt in 2011 was 9,082. The demand for school counselors in that same year was 31,736. This means that there was a shortfall in 2011 of 22,654 counselors. Comparing this with figures for 2007 yields a very interesting result. The number of school counselors in middle and high schools in 2007 was 6,180, and the demand was 28,285, yielding a shortfall of 22,105 school counselors. So although the number of school counselors rose significantly between 2007 and 2011, the shortage remained more or less the same. There are three main reasons for the lack of sufficient school counselors in schools. First, the availability of limited financial resources means that the government both underhires and underpays public school counselors, which pushes counselors to seek employment in private schools. Second, the lack of awareness about the roles and responsibilities of school counselors leads to an underestimation of what counselors can do inside the school. Many schools assign their school counselors office work and rarely give them the opportunity to help students psychologically or academically. Third, there are insufficient numbers of qualified school counselors. International schools hire mostly expatriate counselors.

Psychology and Counseling

Among the general population the terms *psychology* and *counseling* are used interchangeably. People use the word *psychology* to refer to psychiatry, psychological assessment, therapy, and counseling services. This leads to confusion over the roles and specifics of each field and can lead people to seek help from the wrong specialist. Organizations, both private or governmental, usually hire counselors or psychologists with any background in psychology. The term *social work* is usually used to describe social efforts such as volunteer work, community development, and charity work. Social workers usually work in areas distinct from counseling or psychological services. Social workers concentrate on issues of national priority, such as birth control, literacy, and improved health services. Social Service Institutes specialize in training social workers, who are usually called "social professionals."

The Egyptian code of ethics, created by the Egyptian Psychologists Association in 1995 and updated in 1997, was an important first step toward making the psychological professions ethical, culturally sensitive, and organized. The current Egyptian code of ethics explains how the psychologists should behave in response to specific issues, not how the counseling service should be handled. This code was created by a group that included psychiatrists but not psychotherapists or counselors, and as a result it often fails to focus on critical issues for psychological practice and the counseling profession. The current Egyptian code of ethics is not widely followed by counselors or therapists; in fact, many professionals are not even aware it exists.

Best Counseling Practices

The preferred therapy technique in Egypt has historically been psychoanalysis. In the 2000s, however, behavior theory has become the leading therapy technique in counseling practice. Some other techniques are also used by counselors, such as rational emotive behavior therapy. This technique works well in Egyptian society, in which some unhealthy beliefs and practices are very common. These beliefs include the use of corporal punishment to encourage politeness and superstitious beliefs in the evil eye. The rational emotive behavior therapy is very effective because it helps many clients take responsibility for their actions and believe that they can create change if they alter their thoughts and behaviors.

Spiritual or religious therapy is used by most practitioners. Most Egyptians are fairly religious, and many would seek advice from Muslim or Christian clerics before seeking counseling or therapy services. Some believe that their disorders originate from the devil, black magic, or other supernatural sources. These beliefs are decreasing among the more educated Egyptians. Because religion is so ingrained in the culture, counselors often use religious terminology; whether this is meant literally or allegorically depends on the counselor and the client. For instance, some counselors might tell a client, "Try to pray and think about it again. Otherwise the devil is standing between you and your parent [or spouse or friend]. So pray and listen to the Koran/Bible."

Play therapy and art therapy techniques are used with children in some clinics, but these techniques need to be used more, and the counselors who use them need more thorough training. Egyptian counselors still know little about specific types of counseling, such as group counseling, couples counseling, and career counseling. The available training courses are usually theoretical, with a minimal focus on practical training.

The Family in Counseling

Family ties in Egypt are very strong, and thus significant others have a tremendous effect on the counseling process and are usually involved, either directly or indirectly. The problem that motivates the client to seek counseling services is the primary variable that decides which significant others will be involved and how much.

Many clients seek confidentiality, especially if the issue involves a type of behavior that is socially unacceptable or unwelcome, even if this behavior is not a disorder or even a problem. Clients ask for confidentiality, insist on it, and worry about it. Some psychological disorders may cause embarrassment or ostracism, as many people in Egyptian society still see psychological disorders as shameful. There are also concerns about sexual and marital relationships. Sex is a sensitive and complicated issue, and people approach it in a very cautious manner—this is especially true of women. Parents may have reservations speaking about sexual issues. For instance, in a program held by Family Health International to meet adolescents' reproductive health needs through the use of friendly clinics, the parents of nonregular attendees did not allow their kids to visit the program's clinics for fear that they might speak about socially and religiously unacceptable topics (Family Health International, 2009). One of the topics that stimulated religious reservations was female circumcision. Other clients with more common or less embarrassing types of problems often come to a counselor with a family member or a friend who knows about the problem. This type of social support is very common in Egypt; even when seeking physical health care it is very rare for people to go alone. Relationship and family conflicts are common because of the expectations and pressures produced by the social and emotional nature of Egypt's tightly knit society. Some other common problems Egyptian counselors treat include anxiety, fear of failure, fear of the unknown, shyness, career planning, stress, and fear of confrontation.

The Use of the Internet in Counseling

Information technology and the Internet have been invaluable to counseling professionals, helping them obtain information about new practices and/or read about specific counseling theories and techniques. However, online counseling services are nonexistent in Egypt, likely an issue of supply more than demand. Phone lines that offer counseling services through cell phones and landlines are common. Some websites in the Arabic language offer psychological help without stating that it is therapy or counseling; many of these websites were developed by psychiatrists and focus on psychiatric practices. Other websites have been established by people who are not professionals in therapy or in counseling. Some professional sites even allow authors, journalists, and religious clerics to offer psychological services.

Listservs are a new method that counselors and graduate students can use to communicate with each other. The Internet can be very useful for practitioners as they become more aware of the availability of online courses and training. The course criteria and training subjects available in Egypt are outdated, and the Internet is proving essential as part of the updating process.

Diversity Issues

Clients' views on gender in the counseling process depend on their social status and level of education; many people from low social or educational backgrounds may refuse to allow a female family member to speak to a male counselor in a room by herself. Also, some males of lower socioeconomic status may discount the qualifications of or feel too shy to speak to a female counselor. This attitude is more common in rural areas and is diminishing in larger urban centers. The majority of students in psychological and counseling studies are female.

Most immigration in Egypt is within-country immigration. That is to say that immigration happens from the countryside to big cities such as Cairo and Alexandria. The reasons behind this in-country immigration include the abundant choices for continued education in reputable institutes or the perception that it is easier to find better jobs with higher salaries. Egypt has a limited number of immigrants from other countries, and immigrants to Egypt usually either are absorbed into the native culture very quickly or do not stay in the country for very long.

Socioeconomic Status and Counseling Services

Socioeconomic status can play a huge role in the counseling process. People from middle and higher socioeconomic classes understand and appreciate the value of psychological services. Many people from lower socioeconomic classes may consider counseling to be a luxury given their challenging financial situation. According to the World Population Data Sheet, 19% of the Egyptian population lives on less than $2 U.S. per day (Population Reference Bureau, 2011). Priority always goes to the essentials. Even if they consider health care essential, many people in the lower socioeconomic classes are not aware that, like physical problems, psychological problems are serious health problems that need to be handled by professionals.

Age can be an important factor in the counseling process. Older counselors traditionally gain more respect and trust and gain it faster than younger people, even if the younger counselors are more qualified. The Egyptian community is hierarchal, so older people have more authority and gain trust because of their age and perceived experience.

In developing countries, the extended family performs some functions that in developed countries are performed by counseling personnel (Knox & Farmer, 1977). Generally every family has an older male who is considered the head of the family, and he is the one family members consult before making big decisions and/or to receive help solving a problem. In Egypt this is still the case in rural areas, but in the larger cities there is more flexibility in decision making, as most people make decisions as individuals with input only from the immediate family.

Counselor Education

Many Egyptian universities and institutes offer psychological studies through three major departments. First, psychology departments offer undergraduate and graduate studies concentrating on cognitive psychology and measurement processes. Graduates work as psychology teachers, psychologists, and school counselors or regular counselors. Second, mental health departments offer graduate studies for students who want to focus on counseling and therapy research and practice. Third, special needs departments offer undergraduate and graduate studies for students who want to serve the population with special needs. Currently the majority of graduate students are joining departments of special needs because there are many special needs organizations with thousands of job vacancies.

Even though graduate studies in Egypt included clinical psychology diplomas by the mid-1950s and applied psychology diplomas by the late 1950s, and despite the recent availability of graduate diplomas in educational psychology and mental health, the only specific graduate study offered in counseling is a graduate diploma in counseling offered by faculties of education. The length of the program is 1 year (approximately 22 hours; 18 hours theoretical and 4 hours practical), and the courses include subjects such as counseling theory, mental health counseling, counseling programs, counseling clients with special needs, psychopathology counseling, career and educational counseling, problems of children and adolescents, tests and measurements in counseling, research, and practical training. As in other arts and education studies in Egypt, the teaching method involves lecturing, and the course material is usually developed by the course professor.

The diploma courses cover a wide variety of counseling information and skills. The theoretical part of the program requires some updating, but most of the change that is needed is in terms of practical training. Establishing supervised internship courses would be helpful, and there is also a need for some training on ethics. The diploma has not proven to be a great asset in terms of finding work, and thus the number of students enrolled in the program is decreasing.

There are many training courses available within the psychology field in general and a few in counseling specifically. The courses are offered through counseling centers in universities, institutes, associations, and private psychological centers. Some examples of available training courses are behavior modification, diagnosis of children's behavioral problems, counseling, addiction therapy, counseling children with autism, treating children with special needs, use of cognitive behavior therapy for depression, and marriage counseling. The training courses are primarily academic in nature. There is a shortage of practical workshops that focus on specific counseling techniques.

Currently there is no licensing exam for counseling. To open a therapy clinic one must have a license along with a PhD and a minimum of 2 years of experience.

The Future

After the Egyptian revolution of 2011, there are new plans for developing the country in every field, especially in terms of removing barriers to research and new practices. It is expected that the counseling field will develop rapidly by 2020. With the passage of time, more attention and appreciation will be given to psychological services, especially in larger cities. Egyptian society has many problems that could benefit from counseling services. The majority of people do not know much about counseling, and many come across counseling services by chance. The effects of counseling on those who manage to find it are almost always significant and immediate. This leads to good client retention and excellent word of mouth for the profession.

The following are some suggestions for supporting the development of counseling in Egypt:

- First, raise awareness of counseling concepts and services by highlighting the positive effects they have on people's quality of life. This is a challenging task for counselors but an essential step for improving the counseling profession in Egypt. Substantial effort will be needed to explain counseling services, the counselor's role, and counseling ethics.

- Second, establish an independent association for counseling. This should be supplemented with a plan to establish associations for branches of counseling such as school and career counseling. These future associations need to develop guidelines for practicing counseling and determine the details of the profession, counselors' competencies, the norms and licensing requirements for qualified counselors, and applicable codes of ethics.
- Third, develop and update counseling knowledge by providing high-quality education and practical training and workshops for counseling students and new practitioners.
- Fourth, fund research and evaluation studies in counseling. Egyptian associations and libraries have many studies about counseling programs and counseling studies that offer effective solutions for problems specific to the Egyptian community. Help should be given to counseling researchers to publish in English and develop connections with the international counseling community. It is also essential to review the use and definitions of technical terms to come up with a single definition for each term and to review the Arabic translations of terms that often give rise to confusion.

The wide use of the Internet among youth in Egypt may motivate counselors to offer online counseling services in the near future. The consistent increase in the country's population may lead to an increased use of group counseling because of its ability to serve more clients. Counseling techniques will improve in the future and move away from the old, repetitive techniques to more expressive, fun, and brief techniques such as play and art therapy. The use of cognitive behavior therapy may be one of the most successful ways to treat many Egyptian clients in the future because of the nature of their problems.

References

Abd-Elgawad, A. (2006). *Counseling self efficacy of school psychologists and its relation with other variables in school climate.* Unpublished master's thesis, Fayoum University, Fayoum, Egypt.

Ahmed, R. A. (2004). Psychology in Egypt. In M. S. Stevens & D. Wedding (Eds.), *Handbook of international psychology* (pp. 378–403). New York, NY: Routledge.

Eid, I. (2005). *Introduction to counseling.* Cairo, Egypt: Al Angelo Almasryia Library.

Family Health International. (2009). *Meeting adolescents' reproductive health needs in Egypt.* Retrieved from http://www.fhi360.org/NR/rdonlyres/ekxjlrmpykt7whyjkstxdc6v2ehylvibatwnhvex4afpszrpffmhqosoyp3gtssk6rrday5ervrpnj/MeetingAdolescentsRHNeedsEgyptRH.pdf

Gielen, U. P. (2006, December). *Arab psychology and the emerging global psychology movement: A modest proposal.* Paper submitted to "Third International Conference: Social Sciences and Interdisciplinary Studies: An Integrated Perspective," Kuwait University, Kuwait City, Kuwait.

Knox, A. B., & Farmer, H. S. (1977). Counseling and information services for adult learners. *International Review of Education, 23,* 467–470.

Population Reference Bureau. (2011). *World population data sheet.* Retrieved from http://www.prb.org/pdf11/2011population-data-sheet_eng.pdf

• • •

Counseling in Israel

Moshe Israelashvili

The nickname for an Israeli-born person is *sabra,* the name of a prickly pear cactus that is prickly on the outside but tender and sweet on the inside. This metaphor represents the well-established image of the Israelis as a people with a rough and tough exterior but a warm and friendly interior. The present chapter outlines some of the circumstances that have shaped—and are still shaping—both the life and image of the Israelis as well as the status and role of counseling within Israeli society.

The Historical Development of Counseling

The life expectancy of the Israeli population is one of the highest in the world. This means that the level of medical care in Israel is also high. However, it is well known that longevity has to do with more than medical care alone, such as an individual's family history (Friedman et al., 1995), living conditions, and so on. In light of this, one would expect Israel to be a calm and peaceful place where people have few reasons to worry about daily hassles. Yet having been exposed to media reports, many people think of Israel and think of wars, political tension, and security issues—that is, they think of a place that deserves that travel warning that has been issued by the U.S. Foreign Affairs Ministry over the years. However, many travelers who visit Israel experience a kind of culture shock when they confront the reality of daily living there. Far from its image as an armed society, travelers generally find Israel to be a mixture of modern and ancient places, with snow in the north and desert in the south and endless shopping centers and merchant stands almost everywhere. It has crowded streets in which people of all colors and ethnicities sit side by side in coffee shops or along the Mediterranean Sea beach. It is a country in which one meets soldiers carrying guns and security guards at the entrance to every mall and yet feels completely safe walking in most places and feels bad for tourists who may complain about not feeling safe in their place of residence. Such positive experiences justify Lonely Planet's (2010) nomination of Tel Aviv as one of the top 10 cities for 2011 for being "a modern Sin City on the sea . . . a truly diverse 21st-century Mediterranean hub" as well as TripAdvisor's (2011) nomination of Jerusalem as one of 2011's top 25 destinations in the world (based on travelers' choice) for its "profound cultural and historical significance."

The truth about Israel is that both images are accurate, depending on the circumstances. Established in 1948 with less than 1 million Jewish people, Israel has become a vibrant, well-developed, and modern home for 7.5 million. During the 64 years of its existence Israel has been involved in more than a dozen major armed conflicts with the Arab nations that surround it as well as experienced endless security problems on a daily basis. Moreover, Israel has no natural resources and is also very short on water. However, in spite of—and maybe because of—its endless stream of problems with political security and natural resources, Israel has become a well-developed and modern state, very Westernized, with an advanced academic and industrial life that truly justifies its label as "a start-up nation" (Senor & Singer, 2009). Israel has the highest birth rate in the Western world; however, Israel is essentially an immigrant society, as many immigrated and still immigrate to Israel because of their connection to Judaism. However, Israeli society includes people of all ethnicities, religions, and values. Generally speaking, Israel can be divided into three major groups: Jews (75%), Arabs (20%), and others (5%). Yet within each of these groups are several subgroups. For example, orthodox Jews can be further differentiated as national-religious and ultra-orthodox; and individuals can be differentiated as Soviet born (15% of the Israeli population) and other. The Arab population can be differentiated as Muslim-Arab (81% of the Arab population), which can be further divided into the Falach (land owners) and Bedouin (originally the wondering tribes); Christian-Arab (10%); and other (9%; i.e., Druze, Adyghe-Sharkas, Bahá'í). Taking into account the various birthplaces of Jewish people who immigrated to Israel in order to feel safe after the Holocaust, it is evident that this society represents a kaleidoscope of ethnic and social groups (Israelashvili & Benjamin, 2009).

Thus, various significant social questions about Israeli society emerge: How do various existential problems influence Israeli society? Why are people willing to stay in Israel? Why is life expectancy so high in Israel? How do the various ethnic groups live together? All of these questions and more are very important for reaching a better understanding of the role of counseling within Israeli society. Although this is not the place to address all of them, three prominent answers are presented here.

A Meaningful Life

Living in Israel forces its inhabitants to think about the meaning of life as well as their own goals and values in life. For example, all Jewish 18-year-old high school graduates, both male and female, and some of the non-Jewish population are required to serve in the Israel Defense Forces, males for 3 years and females for 2 years. As soon as they give birth, women are aware—and many speak about it during pregnancy—that they will have to experience the relatively dangerous military service of their beloved offspring, not to mention the reserve military service their husband has to undergo on an annual basis up to the age of 45. Thus, Israeli inhabitants experience not just a potential internal discussion within themselves about their attitudes toward their nation, family, and so on but rather a daily encounter with personal reminders of the need to find the meaning of their own place in such an abnormal corner of the world (Israelashvili, 2005). Like the parent who must enlist his or her child, or the Arab Israeli citizen whose Arab village is under missile attack because of attacks directed from Lebanon on surrounding Jewish villages, people living in Israel do not have the privilege of not addressing these questions; those who do not have good answers are willing to emigrate abroad.

Social Support

It is well established in the Jewish religion, and hence in Jewish history, that Jews must take care of other Jews; Judaism is a collectivist religion, not just a religion that focuses on the individual's relationship with God. For Arab people living in Israel, the traditional collectivist nature of their lives still connects them strongly to their family and tribe. Moreover, the ongoing community crisis that all segments of Israeli society have undergone since the establishment of the country has made people aware of the crucial importance of mutual help in times of war and trauma. For this reason and others, both Jewish and non-Jewish people in Israel intensively interact with each other as well as with strangers. Many Israelis have no limitations on their interventions in others' lives along with little hesitation about exposing their own lives (and their salary, intimate relationships, and political orientation) to other people. The positive aspect of this is a general feeling of connectedness and social support, mainly from family members, but also from neighbors, colleagues, or simply someone who shares the same crisis. Thus, Israeli society is not the best place to live one's *own* life; one is part of one's family, community, and state.

Everything Is Personal

Within this context (i.e., finding meaning in life and social support) stands one of the outstanding qualities of Israeli society: the feeling that *everything is personal.* Someone who criticizes Israel for any reason (e.g., for its care for Palestinians' human rights) might somehow be perceived as criticizing an Israeli personally (i.e., because of his or her relatedness to this state and/or his or her ethnicity), which sometimes is true (Cohen, Jussim, Harber, & Bhasin, 2009). In addition, criticizing the Israeli government cannot be ignored because citizens also give their share to the existence of the state and have the right to make decisions about its political life. The distance between people is very short and sometimes does not exist at all (e.g., "Isn't your son serving in the same military unit that my husband was serving in [well, about 15 years ago, it's true, but still]? I know exactly what you are feeling").

The Current Status of Counseling

Genetic counseling, counseling in psychiatric hospitals, organizational counseling, vocational and career counseling, and counseling in military service are only a few of the contexts in which counseling is practiced in Israel. Nevertheless, there is a significant gap between the widespread informal practice of counseling and its limited formal status (Israelashvili & Wegman-Rozi, 2011). Because of historical reasons, from the legal and public perspectives, social work and psychology are the dominant professions that are authorized to deal with issues related to mental health and well-being. Yet there are two exceptional circumstances in which counseling is predominant, and these are within schools (school counseling) and within other organizations (organizational counseling).

Organizational Counseling

Currently the use of organizational counseling is very popular, such as in the banking system, in high-tech companies, and among organizations that have customer service departments. Yet most organizational counseling is supplied by private companies. Hence, these counselors are not related to any union, nor do they have annual conventions or discussions. Two counseling societies that do exist are the Vocational Counseling Association and the Family Counseling Association. Unfortunately these associations are not prominent and are hardly acknowledged as professional networks for those who wish to be updated and/or represented in various contexts.

School Counseling

The only subprofession within counseling that is well known to the public, that has some legal position in Israel, and that has its own active and relatively significant association is school counseling. Of the several historical and practical explanations for this (Israelashvili & Benjamin, 2009), two are mentioned here. First, the importance of education in the Jewish tradition is well known. Hence, even before the establishment of the State of Israel, the energy, resources, and attention that were devoted to supplying better education, including school counseling, were significant. Second, the role of the school in the development of Israeli children is even greater than the role of the school in other nations. In the early days of Israeli society (1900–1960), when kibbutzim (i.e., equal rights/equal duties agricultural communities) were established, the role of schools was not only to free the parents to do their work but also to convey the socialist message to their offspring. In addition, since the establishment of the State of Israel the school has played a major role in times of war and trauma. It should not be surprising that following a review of the literature on mental health and war trauma among children in Israeli schools, Abel and Friedman (2009) acknowledged the school as a major source of social support and a facilitator of recovery in addition to the children's parents. Moreover, when cities in Israel have been attacked by missiles, it is the role of the school staff to debrief the children, enable them to interact with one another in order to feel social support, and sometimes even to guide them in how to support their parents. School counselors in Israel are in charge of helping children who are in need of individual help in times of personal and/or community crisis as well as guiding their school team about how to manage resourcefully in times of difficulty. Hence, unlike some other states in the world, the role of the school counselor in Israel is not limited to addressing academic problems alone but, to a great extent, addressing the students' well-being as well. Practically speaking this means that the emerging school mental health movement (e.g., Goldenson, 2011) has a long history within the Israeli school system.

In light of its importance, a special counseling wing exists in the Israel Ministry of Education called the Psychological-Counseling Department. This wing has several subunits. The *Psychological Unit* supervises the educational psychologists who work on a municipal basis mainly conducting educational and psychological diagnoses, short-term psychological interventions, school team consultations, and crisis interventions. The *School Counseling Unit* is responsible for developing and applying counseling policies in all Israeli educational institutions. Among the issues that the School Counseling Unit deals with are guiding developmental and prevention programs, establishing guidelines for the promotion of a positive school climate, promoting interventions for stressful situations, and organizing professional development for school counselors. Another unit is the *Prevention and Development Programs Unit.* This unit is responsible for developing programs related to health and wellness, with special attention to cultural issues (e.g., Jews vs. Muslims). The list of programs includes developing life skills, preventing substance abuse and sexual vulnerability, and preventing aggression and maladjustment. Another unit is the *Learning Disabilities Unit,* which is responsible for promoting an optimal educational environment for children with learning disabilities. Lastly, the *Emergency Counseling and Psychological Services Section* is responsible for preparing the educational system for stressful situations and emergencies, such as missile attacks, wars, evacuations, and suicidal behavior.

School counselors are expected to address four major issues in their work: the child as an individual, the educational environment, the learning process, and the family and community. Erhard and Harel (2005) identified three distinct profiles of Israeli school counselors in terms of their role behavior: The traditional profile (40% of Erhard and Harel's sample), in which individual counseling for students was prominent; the prevention profile (20% of the sample), in which a guidance curriculum with an emphasis on prevention programs was prevalent; and the balanced profile (40% of the sample), in which the time devoted to the main counseling responsibilities was allocated in relatively equal proportions.

Currently there are about 4,300 school counselors working in Israeli schools, both Jewish and non-Jewish, and even in kindergartens. As mentioned previously, in addition to school counselors there are educational psychologists who are employees of the county but are professionally guided by the Psychological-Counseling Department. There are about 2,100 educational psychologists in Israel. Both on a daily basis but especially in times of crisis, school counselors and school psychologists are supposed to collaborate and support the whole school population (i.e., students, families, and school staff; Klingman & Cohen, 2004). In terms of an international comparison, the ratios of both school counselors and school psychologists per student are the highest in the world (Jimerson, Stewart, Skokut, Cardenas, & Malone, 2009). Nevertheless, the need for more school counselors is evident, especially in schools with high rates of immigrant children and Arab adolescents (Mansbach-Kleinfeld et al., 2010).

Best Counseling Practices

The Israel Psychoanalytic Institute was established in Jerusalem by Freud's colleagues and students who left Europe because of the rise of the Nazi movement and immigrated to Palestine (the name given by the British Empire to the area between the Jordan River and the Mediterranean Sea). Since then, the psychodynamic approach has been the prominent approach for healing people with mental health problems used by psychologists, psychiatrists, and social workers. The gradual shift in the professional orientation of many mental health practitioners, especially toward a cognitive–behavioral approach, is at the core of the major conflict that is currently taking place within the Israel Psychological Association and related institutions.

The history of counseling in Israel can also be traced back to the period of Palestine, when the Hadassah Vocational Institute was established in 1946. This institute, which exists to this day, was meant to help Jewish Holocaust survivors as well as Jewish veterans of World War II find jobs in their new homeland. Given the major cultural differences that existed for the hundreds of thousands of refugees who immigrated to Israel from 1946 to 1955 in search of a safer place to live, the Hadassah Institute team had to initiate studies on various aspects of emerging Israeli society. This was done in collaboration with the Department of Psychology in the Hebrew University of Jerusalem and the psychology branch of the new Israel Defense Forces. However, unlike the fields of psychology and psychopathology, counseling in Israel was open to all schools of thought, and counselors' training paid homage to various theoretical approaches. Yet of the various theoretical orientations, two approaches were most prominent: the humanistic approach and the rational emotive approach. Although the humanistic approach is still the leading theoretical framework for counseling in practice, in recent years a growing number of counselors have been exposed to and have practiced other theoretical orientations, including cognitive behavior therapy, gestalt therapy, reality/choice therapy, and solution-focused brief therapy.

Group Counseling

The unique characteristics of the Israeli population (i.e., living in a semi-Western multicultural and multireligious society, living under continuous threats to their existence, being highly developed technologically and academically, and having relatively intensive personal [informal] consideration for everything around themselves) highlight the relevance of two counseling orientations. The first is group counseling, which is supported by the social connectedness of Israeli society, as is evident, for example, in adolescents' high degree of social self (Tatar & Myers, 2010). This notion has been deliberately promoted by Shechtman (2007). In her explorations of adults and youth of all religions and socioeconomic levels, Shechtman demonstrated the power of group work among the Israeli population in terms of reducing aggression (Shechtman & Ifargan, 2009), promoting interpersonal acceptance and understanding (Shechtman, Wade, & Khoury, 2009), as well as reducing mental health problems (Shechtman & Leichtentritt, 2010) and war-related traumas (Shechtman & Mor, 2010). The second orientation is toward spiritual counseling.

Spiritual Counseling

Living in the Middle East in general and in Israel in particular means that one is exposed to death on almost a daily basis. Most people know somebody who was killed in war or terrorist attacks. Moreover, even young children (aged 1–2 years) are indirectly exposed to death, as when terrorist events occur, the TV repeatedly shows pictures of Israeli citizens who have been killed or wounded (Slone & Shoshani, 2008). In such an atmosphere, people address their spiritual values (Beit-Hallahmi, 2011), and for many, religion becomes a major factor in their survival.

Actually, religiosity has always been a major power for people who live or visit the Middle East. It is both the power that attracts people to visit and/or live in Israel as well as the reason that some people break down, as is evident in the case of *Jerusalem syndrome* (i.e., a psychological phenomenon that can appear in people of all religions and backgrounds and that involves the presence of religiously themed ideas, delusions, or other psychotic-like experiences that are triggered by a visit to the city of Jerusalem; Kalian, Catinari, Heresco-Levi, & Witztum, 2008). However, the spiritual lives of people living in Israel might also be a major barrier in their seeking help (Abu Raiya & Pargament, 2010). Special training for counselors working with ultra-religious Jews, along with special methods of intervention targeted for this population, have already been developed and practiced effectively (Erhard & Erhard-Weiss, 2007).

Diversity Issues

Many would assume that the rich diversity of the Israeli community should be consolidated into two major sectors: the Jewish population, which speaks Hebrew; and the Arab population, which speaks Arabic. A more profound look at both the Arab community and the Jewish community quickly raises two additional considerations: (a) the large diversity among subgroups within Israeli society; and (b) the gradual change in the direction of growing proximity between the various subgroups, such as the Jews and the Arabs (Israelashvili & Kakunda-Mualem, 2011), because of daily mutual exposure to each other as well as processes of modernization within each subgroup, such as the ultra-orthodox Jews. Nonetheless, cultural differences cannot and should not be ignored. For example, the locus of Israeli Arabs' stress is identified primarily in the sphere of family issues, whereas Jews are likely to complain more about personal and mental health issues (Azaiza, 2005). Differences also exist in help-seeking behaviors, with Arab youth being more reluctant to seek help but preferring, when confronted with a major problem, to get help from formal help systems (e.g., school counselors), whereas Jewish youth are more likely to turn to informal sources for help (e.g., parents and friends; Sherer & Karnieli-Miller, 2007). Hence, many counselors find themselves advocating the need for multicultural counseling as well as exploring best practices for working with people of different cultural backgrounds (e.g., Dwairy, 2009).

Counselor Education

School counseling, organizational counseling, vocational counseling, and genetic counseling are being taught in Israeli universities, mainly as graduate programs. However, usually the completion of a related undergraduate program is required as a prerequisite for application to a graduate counseling program. All university graduate programs are research oriented and hence provide PhDs to those who complete the entire program. However, until recently most graduate students applied for work positions (e.g., in school settings) already during their MA studies and were later recruited into daily practice as counselors, not continuing on to doctoral studies. Yet since the beginning of the 21st century, and especially following the Ministry of Education's nomination of an MA degree as a prerequisite for receiving a counseling position, counselors who strive to be promoted in their occupational track (e.g., to become a counselor inspector) are applying later for PhD studies, with many more applications than university instructors in Israeli universities.

All counseling programs that are taught in Israeli universities are also taught in Israeli colleges. However, family counseling and marriage counseling are taught only in colleges, not in universities. College counseling programs are practice oriented. This orientation attracts many candidates, and many of them feel more prepared for counseling practice on the transition to work (Kulik & Israelashvili, 2012). However, later on college graduates tend to encounter difficulties when applying for PhD studies because in order to be accepted to a PhD program, they must first prove their research skills, including the completion of a (sometimes additional) MA thesis.

Among the various counselor training programs, the ones dealing with school counseling are the most developed. This is because of the large number of positions offered to school counselors nationwide. School counselors are required in all educational settings, in all societal segments, from as early as kindergarten (i.e., in university, students can specialize in counseling kindergarten teachers, parents, and children who are related to various organizational settings, such as community centers, family health centers, and kindergartens of all levels). In accordance with their well-established position within the Israeli educational system, the training of school counselors is not complete when they graduate from university or college. Rather, continuing studies and long-term training are offered to novice school counselors under the supervision of their municipal counselor inspector. Continuing studies for other counselors (e.g., vocational counselors) exist but only on a sporadic basis.

The Future

Several recent advancements in the field of helping professions in Israel provide an opportunity for a positive prospective assessment of the place that counseling will have in the future society. One such advancement is the possibility that the definition of *treatment* will officially include various kinds of techniques, such as cognitive behavior therapy, rather than classical dynamic psychological treatment. Such a change would significantly promote individual counseling for people who wish to reach a greater sense of well-being. Another one is the increasing modernization of various groups and subgroups within Israeli society, which is exposing many of these groups to the efficacy of counseling.

However, such a positive prospective assessment regarding the future of counseling in Israel does not mean that the field's theoretical orientation or practice will appear as it does today. Rather, it seems that e-counseling will have a greater role and impact on the development of counseling in Israel. There are two interrelated reasons for this. The first concerns the intensive involvement of many Israeli companies and people in the high-tech industry. Although exposure to the cyber world is not unique to Israel, the prominent role of the cyber industry in the Israeli labor market, and especially the fact that most leading cyber companies in the world have at least one research and development center in Israel, indicate that its exposure to cyber issues will be even greater than it is currently and than in other places in the world. The second concerns recent theoretical and applied developments made by leading Israeli counseling researchers regarding use of the Internet in counseling practice. One line of development is Barak and colleagues' clarifications regarding the nature of Internet-supported therapeutic interventions (Barak, Klein, & Proudfoot, 2009), exploration of the utility of online support groups (Barak & Sadovsky, 2008), and application of accumulating knowledge in e-counseling interventions such as the SAHAR ("Helping and Listening in the Web") suicide prevention e-program (www.sahar.org.il). Another channel of development in e-counseling is Gati and colleagues' integration of the Internet in identifying career-related difficulties in decision making (Gadassi & Gati, 2009; Gati, Kleiman, Saka, & Zakai, 2003).

In sum, following the Holocaust, the State of Israel was established as a homeland for all Jewish people around the world. However, living in Israel was, and to some degree still is, hard for many people, especially in terms of the constant threat to life. An exploration of the mechanisms that support Israelis in overcoming repeated stressful encounters will likely promote the power of motivation, faith, and social support over stress, risk, and crisis. Nevertheless, sometimes people need someone who will guide them on how to overcome a given situation, and counseling—rather than psychotherapy—would be helpful in supporting *all* (Jewish and non-Jewish) Israeli citizens' efforts toward pursuing well-being and tranquility.

References

Abel, R. M., & Friedman, H. A. (2009). Israeli school and community response to war trauma: A review of selected literature. *School Psychology International, 30,* 265–281. doi:10.1177/0143034309106493

Abu Raiya, H., & Pargament, K. I. (2010). Religiously integrated psychotherapy with Muslim clients: From research to practice. *Professional Psychology: Research and Practice, 41,* 181–188. doi:10.1037/a0017988

Azaiza, F. (2005). Parent-child relationships as perceived by Arab adolescents living in Israel. *International Journal of Social Welfare, 14,* 297–304. doi:10.1111/j.1369-6866.2005.00372.x

Barak, A., Klein, B., & Proudfoot, J. G. (2009). Defining Internet-supported therapeutic interventions. *Annals of Behavioral Medicine, 38,* 4–17. doi:10.1007/s12160-009-9130-7

Barak, A., & Sadovsky, Y. (2008). Internet use and personal empowerment of hearing-impaired adolescents. *Computers in Human Behavior, 24,* 1802–1815. doi:10.1016/j.chb.2008.02.007

Beit-Hallahmi, B. (2011). Ambivalent teaching and painful learning: Mastering the facts of life (?). In V. Talwar, P. L. Harris, & M. Schleifer (Eds.), *Children's understanding of death: From biological to religious conceptions* (pp. 41–60). New York, NY: Cambridge University Press. doi:10.1017/CBO9780511852077.004

Cohen, F., Jussim, L., Harber, K. D., & Bhasin, G. (2009). Modern anti-Semitism and anti-Israeli attitudes. *Journal of Personality and Social Psychology, 97,* 290–306. doi:10.1037/a0015338

Dwairy, M. (2009). Culture analysis and metaphor psychotherapy with Arab-Muslim clients. *Journal of Clinical Psychology, 65,* 199–209. doi:10.1002/jclp.20568

Erhard, R., & Erhard-Weiss, D. (2007). The emergence of counseling in traditional cultures: Ultra-orthodox Jewish and Arab communities in Israel. *International Journal for the Advancement of Counselling, 29,* 149–158. doi:10.1007/s10447-007-9035-8

Erhard, R., & Harel, Y. (2005). Role behavior profiles of Israeli school counselors. *International Journal for the Advancement of Counselling, 27,* 87–101.

Friedman, H. S., Tucker, J. S., Schwartz, J. E., Tomlinson-Keasey, C., Martin, L. R., Wingard, D. L., & Criqui, M. H. (1995). Psychosocial and behavioral predictors of longevity: The aging and death of the "termites." *American Psychologist, 50,* 69–78. doi:10.1037/0003-066X.50.2.69

Gadassi, R., & Gati, I. (2009). The effect of gender stereotypes on explicit and implicit career preferences. *The Counseling Psychologist, 37,* 902–922. doi:10.1177/0011000009334093

Gati, I., Kleiman, T., Saka, N., & Zakai, A. (2003). Perceived benefits of using an Internet-based interactive career planning system. *Journal of Vocational Behavior, 62,* 272–286. doi:10.1016/S0001-8791(02)00049-0

Goldenson, J. (2011). When there is no blueprint: The provision of mental health services in alternative school programs for suspended and expelled youth. *Child & Youth Services, 32,* 108–123. doi:10.1080/0145935X.2011.581958

Israelashvili, M. (2005). Staying normal in an abnormal world: Reflections on mental health counseling from an Israeli point of view. *Journal of Mental Health Counseling, 27,* 238–247.

Israelashvili, M., & Benjamin, B. A. (2009). Context and diversity in the provision of counseling services in Israel. In L. H. Gerstein, P. P. Heppner, S. Ægisdóttir, S.-M. A. Leung, & K. L. Norsworthy (Eds.), *International handbook of cross-cultural counseling: Cultural assumptions and practices worldwide* (pp. 449–464). Thousand Oaks, CA: Sage.

Israelashvili, M., & Kakunda-Mualem, H. (2011, July). *Life perceptions and personal (mal) adjustment among adolescents and emerging adults who are living in a mixed-cultural community.* Paper presented at the Asia Pacific Rim International Counselling Conference, Hong Kong.

Israelashvili, M., & Wegman-Rozi, O. (2011). Formal and applied counseling in Israel. *Journal of Counseling & Development, 90,* 227–232.

Jimerson, S. R., Stewart, K., Skokut, M., Cardenas, S., & Malone, H. (2009). How many school psychologists are there in each country of the world? International estimates of school psychologists and school psychologist-to-student ratios. *School Psychology International, 30,* 555–567. doi:10.1177/0143034309107077

Kalian, M., Catinari, S., Heresco-Levi, U., & Witztum, E. (2008). Spiritual starvation in a holy space—A form of Jerusalem syndrome. *Mental Health, Religion & Culture, 11,* 161–172. doi:10.1080/13674670600970527

Klingman, A., & Cohen, E. (2004). *School-based multisystemic interventions for mass trauma.* New York, NY: Kluwer Academic/Plenum.

Kulik, S., & Israelashvili, M. (2012). *The Israeli novice school counselor: Hassles, adjustment, and retrospective implications.* Unpublished research report, Tel Aviv University, Tel Aviv, Israel.

Lonely Planet. (2010). *Lonely Planet's top 10 cities for 2011.* Retrieved from http://www.lonelyplanet.com/usa/new-york-city/travel-tips-and-articles/76165

Mansbach-Kleinfeld, I., Farbstein, I., Levinson, D., Apter, A., Erhard, R., Palti, H.,. . .Levav, I. (2010). Service use for mental disorders and unmet need: Results from the Israel Survey on Mental Health Among Adolescents. *Psychiatric Services, 61,* 241–249. doi:10.1176/appi.ps.61.3.241

Senor, D., & Singer, S. (2009). *Start-up nation: The story of Israel's economic miracle.* New York, NY: Twelve.

Shechtman, Z. (2007). *Group counseling and psychotherapy with children and adolescents: Theory, research and practice.* Mahwah, NJ: Erlbaum.

Shechtman, Z., & Ifargan, M. (2009). School-based integrated and segregated interventions to reduce aggression. *Aggressive Behavior, 35,* 342–356. doi:10.1002/ab.20311

Shechtman, Z., & Leichtentritt, J. (2010). The association of process with outcomes in child group therapy. *Psychotherapy Research, 20,* 8–21. doi:10.1080/10503300902926562

Shechtman, Z., & Mor, M. (2010). Groups for children and adolescents with trauma-related symptoms: Outcomes and processes. *International Journal of Group Psychotherapy, 60,* 221–244. doi:10.1521/ijgp.2010.60.2.221

Shechtman, Z., Wade, N., & Khoury, A. (2009). Effectiveness of a forgiveness program for Arab Israeli adolescents in Israel: An empirical trial. *Peace and Conflict: Journal of Peace Psychology, 15,* 415–438. doi:10.1080/10781910903221194

Sherer, M., & Karnieli-Miller, O. (2007). Intentions for advice and help seeking among Jewish and Arab youth in Israel. *Youth & Society, 39,* 33–53. doi:10.1177/0044118X06296690

Slone, M., & Shoshani, A. (2008). Indirect victimization from terrorism: A proposed post-exposure intervention. *Journal of Mental Health Counseling, 30,* 255–266.

Tatar, M., & Myers, J. E. (2010). Wellness of children in Israel and the United States: A preliminary examination of culture and well-being. *Counselling Psychology Quarterly, 23,* 17–33. doi:10.1080/09515071003718384

TripAdvisor. (2011). *Top 25 destinations in the world 2011.* Retrieved from http://www.skyscrapercity.com/showthread.php?t=1385480

• • •

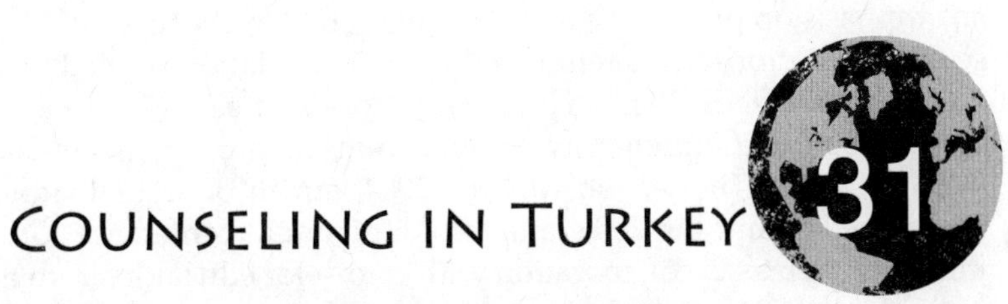

Counseling in Turkey

Fidan Korkut Owen and Oya Yerin Güneri

Having emerged in the 1950s, counseling in Turkey can be regarded as a relatively new field (Doğan, 2000), especially compared to other branches of the social sciences, such as psychology, which dates back to 1915, the Ottoman period (Kağıtçıbaşı, 1994). However, considering that the secular modern Turkish Republic was established in 1923, counseling has existed for 60 years of the 88-year-old republic. It is from this historical perspective that we reflect on the major developments and issues within Turkish counseling and then reflect on the future of the field.

The Historical Development of Counseling

Since the 1950s, there has been a strong American impact on counseling in Turkey. This American influence started with visits by American educators and the return of Turkish scholars who were sent to the United States to receive graduate education in counseling (Aydın & Hatipoğlu Sümer, 2001). In the initial years the term *guidance* was used. Guidance was intended as a service provided by teachers. In those years scientific institutions such as the Test and Research Bureau and the Guidance and Research Center for children with intellectual disabilities were established. In the 1960s, the role of counseling in the overall well-being of students was emphasized by makers of education policy. The increased role of guidance and counseling in education required trained counselors to work in the schools. Consequently, the first graduate program in educational psychology and guidance opened in 1965 at Ankara University (Doğan, 2000). In the 1970s, guidance services started in 23 schools. Because there were insufficient numbers of counselors, graduates of other departments such as sociology, philosophy, and education—who were not trained as counselors—were appointed as guidance teachers (Stockton & Yerin Güneri, 2011). This decision negatively impacted the development of the profession and created conflict between counseling graduates and graduates of other programs working in the schools as

Author Note. We would like to thank Dr. Lynette Bikos and Dr. Dean W. Owen for their feedback on this chapter.

school counselors. The Turkish Council of Higher Education established and opened undergraduate guidance and psychological counseling programs beginning in 1981. Related developments included the establishment of the Turkish Psychological Counseling and Guidance Association (TPCGA) in 1989 and increases in the number of graduates from guidance and counseling programs. Together, these events contributed positively to the identity of the profession. In the 1990s, major steps toward the scientific and professional development of the field included the publication of the *Journal of Psychological Counseling and Guidance* in 1990 and the *Psychological Counseling and Guidance Bulletin* by the TPCGA in 1997. The first Psychological Counseling and Guidance Congress was held in 1991. In 1996, counselors were appointed to elementary schools for the first time (Doğan, 2000).

The period between 2000 to 2010 also included significant developments. The first was an emphasis on preventive and developmental approaches to be adopted by school counselors. This priority was reinforced in 2001 regulations issued by the Ministry of National Education (MONE, 2001). These regulatory decrees were followed by the development of increasingly comprehensive school counseling programs in 2006 by a group of experts (MONE, 2006). The second was the 2004 launch of annual student conferences devoted to counseling and the 2006 launch of a biannual conference for applied counseling. The third was increased collaboration with counselor educators from the United States through individual efforts of Turkish counselor educators and the TPCGA. These collaborations included the invitation and participation of well-known American counselor educators, theorists, researchers in the National Psychological Counseling and Guidance Congress. In addition, manuscripts from American authors were included in TPCGA journals and books. The fourth development was an increase in the number of publications, and the fifth was an increase in the number of undergraduate and graduate programs. Finally, this decade witnessed crucial efforts by the counseling profession for increased recognition of the field. The Commission of Professional Unity also made several visits to the Turkish Grand National Assembly during this period.

In summary, during the 60-year history of the counseling profession in Turkey, visible progress has been made in advancing the field in terms of research and publication, training, professionalism, and recognition. Our review echoes the findings of others (e.g., Çınarbaş, Korkut Owen, & Çiftçi, 2009): Strong ties between counseling and the field of education have formed the identity of the profession. Thus, the history of counseling in Turkey to a large extent reflects the history of school counseling.

The Current Status of Counseling

The majority of counselors are employed by MONE and work in public elementary and secondary schools. The Ministry reported that as of October 2011 more than 18,000 counselors were employed in public education (TPCGA, 2011). These counselors provide two types of services: direct school-based services and services through regional guidance and research centers. These guidance and research centers, which number more than 200, have three main functions: to deliver diagnostic services for students with special needs, to deliver individual and group guidance services in schools that do not have a guidance counselor on staff, and to offer general support to guidance services within schools.

Counselors are increasingly becoming an integrated component of higher education in Turkey, with dedicated counseling centers now required on all university campuses. The Higher Education Law, passed in 1984, mandated the establishment of a counseling and guidance center on each university campus to service the individual, educational, and career counseling needs of university students. Currently virtually all Turkish universities provide counseling services through a variety of organizational structures. These services are typically provided by a variety of professionals, including psychologists, counselors, psychiatrists, and social workers (Yerin Güneri, 2006). These university services are typically divided into two general areas of service: mental health services associated with student health centers, and educational/career planning and personal social counseling services offered by counseling and guidance centers. The exact numbers of counselors working in these settings is still the subject of ongoing research and documentation.

Counselors in Turkey serve in a variety of governmental agencies, including the Turkish Employment Organization (TEO), the Ministry of Justice, and the Ministry of Health. In addition counselors serve in the military forces and in special education and rehabilitation centers. Counselors may not legally engage in private practice and conduct psychotherapy in Turkey without the collaboration or supervision of psychiatrists. Recently researchers noted that 92% of employed counselors ($N = 392$) work in the educational system (school, special education institutions, etc.), 3% in the health care system, 3% in the justice system (Family and Child Court), and 2% in other work settings (e.g., social services and military, human resources; Korkut Owen, Acar, Haskan, & Kızıldağ, 2010).

Within the Turkish educational system expectations for counselors are broadly defined by MONE. Essentially counselors are (a) to provide guidance and psychological counseling, (b) in a systematic manner, (c) to groups or individuals, (d) in order to ensure that students' needs are met and problems are solved. Counselors usually conduct guidance programs and psychoeducational programs in groups of 10 or more. They rarely provide individual counseling. If individual counseling is required, it is typically limited to two or three sessions (Çınarbaş et al., 2009). School counselors provide mostly individual counseling, seminars, crisis intervention, consultation, and career counseling services (Yerin Güneri, Büyükgöze Kavas, & Koydemir, 2007). Yerin Güneri (2006) found that universities offered the following counseling services: individual counseling or psychotherapy, emergency services, consultation, outreach programs for students, and group counseling or psychotherapy.

Another employment area in Turkey is career counseling. Unlike in the public schools, in which career education and guidance services are provided by school counselors, services for adults are provided by a wide variety of individuals with varying degrees of training and specialization. Dedicated centers for career development in colleges and universities are only now being widely established, and such services for adults outside of educational institutions are rare and in their infancy. Perhaps one of the most widely utilized services in Turkey is that of TEO (Owen, Korkut Owen, & Kurter, 2011). Even though there is no specialized career counseling program, psychologists and counselors are employed by TEO as career counselors.

Because the majority of counseling positions are government jobs, they fall under the Turkish Civil Service System and therefore require that applicants take the Civil Service Personnel Selection Exam (Kamu Personel Seçme Sınavı), a nationally administered and highly centralized exam. Candidates who successfully complete this exam are deemed qualified to work as school counselors, although *guidance teacher* (*rehber öğretmen*) is the term used by MONE. Successful candidates may be assigned to vacant counseling positions throughout the country, or they may apply to a private school or tutoring institution.

The counseling profession in Turkey is represented by the TPCGA, which is headquartered in Ankara and represented by 11 regional offices. As of October 2011, membership exceeded 2,600 (TPCGA, 2011). There are no formal requirements to become certified as a professional counselor, nor are there procedures for or official accreditation of undergraduate and graduate training programs, or an agreed-on specialty title and definition for counseling (Doğan, 2000). Under the current structure, only the TPCGA and the Turkish Council of Higher Education are involved in standardization and accreditation activities within Turkey. Turkey is currently a candidate for membership in the European Union, and this has prompted a number of changes to its higher education system in an effort to conform to similar systems in other European Union states. As a result of these efforts, Turkey joined the Bologna Declaration in 2001. One of the general principles of the Declaration is quality enhancement and assurance in higher education. Regarding the establishment of a national quality assurance system, the Turkish Council of Higher Education appointed an academic evaluation and quality assurance council. Within the requirements of the evaluation process subjected by the council, counseling programs have begun creating strategic plans (Korkut & Mızıkacı, 2008).

Counselor education program chairs (or their representatives) met for the first time in 2000 and began focusing attention on the restructuring of counselor education programs in an attempt to seek a common training philosophy and standardization of the curriculum and programs. Since 2003, these meetings have become annual affairs and have done much to promote progress in the field of counselor education. In the absence of nationwide standardization, the formation of an accrediting body is essential to improving and standardizing professional training in the field (Stockton & Yerin Güneri, 2011). Similarly, YÖRET, the Foundation for the Advancement and Training of the Higher Education Counselors, was established in 1972 to advocate for and promote the advancement of counseling (YÖRET, 2011).

In Turkey, the relationships among counseling, psychology, and social work are becoming more collaborative. As is the case in other countries, the various professions are continuing their work toward an evolving and mutually acceptable position that seeks to recognize the unique contribution of each of the helping professions. There are some differences in the roles and functions of psychology and counseling in Turkey. For instance, counselors are located mostly in the school systems as school counselors. Some school counselors graduated from psychology training programs. Psychology in Turkey is still perceived primarily as clinical psychology, and psychologists work in a broad range of public and private settings that provide health, educational, and social services for children, adults, and elderly persons (Bolak Boratav, 2004). The overlap between the practice of counselors and the practice of clinical psychologists has recently become more evident, particularly in nonpsychiatric settings (Aydın & Hatipoğlu Sümer, 2001). That is, although it is difficult to draw a clear line between the professions, the normality–abnormality distinction may help to find a consensus point in resolving the conflict between counselors and clinical psychologists. School counselors conducted psychosocial projects to help schoolchildren, teachers, and parents in areas affected by the 1999 earthquakes. During this period, counselors, psychologists, psychiatrists, and social workers worked together in teams to implement the Psychosocial School Project of UNICEF and MONE. According to MONE law, child protection laws, and so forth, all of these professions are mandated to collaborate.

Best Counseling Practices

In Turkey, the counseling process is predominantly taught from the American literature. In 2001, MONE implemented developmental and preventive regulations into counseling programs. Since then, the number of group guidance and psychoeducational group studies has increased. During the psychological counseling and guidance process, school counselors use mostly group guidance work (e.g., Güner, 2007) and psychoeducational groups (e.g., Çelik, 2004). No counseling model has been developed according to the Turkish culture, but counselors are familiar with established (e.g., existential counseling and therapy) and emerging counseling approaches and models (e.g., developmental counseling and therapy). Although person-centered counseling seems to be the preferred approach among school counselors, Turkish clients prefer directive, action-oriented counseling approaches such as cognitive behavior therapy (Mocan Aydın, 2000). Vassaf (1983) concluded that directive behavioral approaches and preventive mental health interventions are more effective with clients of a rural background. Clients from metropolitan areas, in contrast, may be more receptive to therapy approaches that focus on emotions, insight, and self-exploration. Cognitive–behavioral approaches to therapy are receiving increased recognition in the field (e.g., Şahan & Duy, 2011). Demir and Aydın (1996) reported that although behavioral procedures are frequently utilized, humanistic and existential orientations are also used, largely for establishing a good rapport before the implementation of relevant behavioral techniques.

There is no detailed research on the counseling process in Turkey. One study tested the proposition that similarity in nationality between counselors and American expatriate clients living in Turkey would result in improved counseling outcomes (Bikos & Çiftçi Uruk, 2005). Results indicated no differences as a function of counselor nationality in (a) clients' and counselors' ratings of the working alliance, (b) progress on goals, or (c) clients' ratings of utilization intent.

Significant others (spouses, parents, etc.) are frequently involved in the counseling process. Many people in Turkey still rely on strong family relationships, friendship networks, and indigenous healers for social support and treatment (Bolak Boratav, 2004). Some of school counselors' roles and responsibilities, as articulated by MONE (2006), are to cooperate with parents and inform parents about the curriculum. During the provision of guidance services, cooperation with parents is expected. Even though there are no family counseling graduate programs yet, the existence of certificate programs has meant that working as a family and marriage counselor is on the rise.

Counselors use the Internet and other forms of computer technology for counseling purposes. Locations such as the Mersin University counseling and guidance center provide online counseling to students (Mersin University, 2011). Recently some websites have started to provide online psychological services (e.g., www.sanalpsikolog.gen.tr). These services are provided by psychiatrists, psychologists, and counselors as part of their private practice. The Internet and other forms of computer technology are mostly used for career counseling in Turkey. A recent national initiative resulted in the adoption of an online assessment and career planning platform for all students in public and private elementary and secondary schools. This National Vocational Information System, which became available on April, 1, 2010, through MONE, provides a fully interactive website that offers online assessment, instant profile information, and multiple links to education and career information. This system was the result of a cooperative effort among many institutions, including TEO, the Turkish Council of Higher Education, the Turkish Statistical Institute, the State Planning Organization, the Turkish Confederation of Employers Associations, the Confederation of Turkish Trade Unions, and others. Although labor market research has intensified in recent years, Turkey still lacks a thorough labor market information system at the national and local levels. Developing such a labor market information system requires a coherent approach to labor market analysis for the purpose of human resources development. Recently, MONE and TEO cooperated on the *Handbook on Labour Market Information* (Bjerre & Yardımcı, 2007). TEO is represented across Turkey by 60 major Vocational Information Centers. Vocational Information Centers have become repositories for a wide range of career information as well as sources for assisting individuals in linking careers with educational and training programs across the country. Recent advances in the integration of technology have made this information available digitally in the form of CDs and online sources. In addition to the Vocational Information Centers there are nearly 300 Special Employment Offices located throughout the country whose function is primarily placement. In this way, TEO, which functions as the Turkish national employment service, is able to provide current national, regional, and local information and services oriented primarily toward assisting individuals in seeking employment (Owen et al., 2011).

During the counseling process, counselors integrate other techniques such as art, play, psychodrama, and metaphors. Turkish counselors quite commonly integrate Western techniques into their practice. There are many research studies on psychodrama (e.g., Karataş, 2009); art therapy activities such as writing, poetry, and drawing (e.g., Gizir, 2006); and metaphor (e.g., Karaırmak & Güloğlu, 2011).

Diversity Issues

Turkey has a population of 73,722,988 (Turkish Statistical Institute, 2010) from diverse ethnic backgrounds, with various attitudes and lifestyles (traditional and modern), living in different parts of the country (Mocan Aydın, 2000). Turkey shares characteristics of other developing countries, such as continuing urbanization, a high fertility rate, and unmet demands for education and work opportunities due to a large population of young people (Sümer, 1998). The Turkish Statistical Institute (2011) indicated that 18.8% of the population lives in poverty. Among those who live in poverty, migrants from rural to urban areas, people who live in rural areas, and seasonal agricultural workers and their children require special attention.

One of the issues that influences the counseling process in the country is increased internal migration due to industrialization, the increase in the population, and security concerns in the eastern and southeastern regions of the country (Koşar Altınyelken, 2009). Because of the migration from rural to urban areas and the high unemployment rate among migrants, children work the streets collecting recyclables, selling small items, and begging. Not surprisingly, this leaves these children vulnerable to many risks. One study conducted with female students indicated that migrant students from rural areas also experience difficulties with discrimination, language, and bullying and that their self-esteem was at risk (Koşar Altınyelken, 2009).

Another issue relates to gender bias. Within the country is a highly educated group of women who pursue careers in a variety of fields. Consequently, their family roles rival those of their husbands. For example, in the past 80 years, Turkey has been successful in moving from having virtually no female participation in engineering to having greater proportions of women in the field than the United States and Europe (Smith & Dengiz, 2010). However, poor women in the cities or in rural areas continue to achieve low levels of education, hold diminished positions in the extended family, have low levels of employment, depend on their husbands, and experience domestic violence. These gender issues require intervention from counselors and other mental health professionals.

Counselors in Turkey work in schools in various regions of the country with diverse groups who have different needs and issues. Especially for students who live in poverty, school plays a crucial role in social, academic, and career development, and school counselors take an active part in being the agent and advocate for change in the system for the benefit of students. School counselors also play a role in educating parents and collaborating with other support groups in the community. Educational achievement and continuing education are perceived as the keys to a better future. Therefore, school counselors emphasize providing academic support to students and improving student academic achievement.

Unfortunately, the research on issues of poverty and diversity is lacking. For example, a meta-analysis of 30 issues of a TPCGA journal published since 1990 indicated that the majority of the studies reported in the journal were conducted with university students (Güven, Kısaç, Ercan, & Yalçın, 2009). Although this overreliance on convenience samples is understandable, it results in research gaps related to underserved and underrepresented groups. Marriage counseling and career guidance are the most frequently studied topics. Another issue in counseling diverse groups is the counselor education curriculum itself. Currently only two counseling training programs in Turkey include a multicultural counseling course as an elective in their curricula (Kağnıcı, 2011). However, with the rise of postmodernism in the Western world, counselor educators in Turkey have started discussing the validity of the Western view of counseling for the Turkish culture (e.g., Mocan Aydın, 2000; Poyrazli, 2003). Thus, it is expected that this movement may lead to (a) improvements in counselor education training in response to cultural needs, (b) the provision of counseling services to diverse groups, and (c) increased research in response to local and cultural needs.

Counselor Education

In the 1960s and 1970s, a number of undergraduate and graduate programs in guidance and counseling were opened. In 1983, six undergraduate guidance and counseling programs opened to train school counselors (Doğan, 2000). This decision garnered much opposition from counselors who defended the view that counseling programs must be offered at the graduate level (Aydın & Hatipoğlu Sümer, 2001). The graduates of these programs received the title of "guidance teacher." The content of the courses, the name of the program, and the title given to graduates emphasized guidance.

Since 2006 there has been an increase in the number of undergraduate and graduate counseling programs because of the increase in the number of public and private universities in Turkey (Güney & Güney, 2011). Currently there are 165 universities (103 public, 62 private) in various parts of the country. In 41 of these universities (35 public, 6 private) there are 90 counseling programs (55 undergraduate, 21 master's, and 14 doctoral; Turkish Council of Higher Education, 2011). These programs are housed in colleges of education and departments of educational sciences. Entry into the university is possible only through a nationwide entrance exam. For example, in 2010 approximately 1.6 million students took the entrance exam. Only one fourth of the students passed and were admitted to 4-year institutions of higher education (Turkish Council of Higher Education Student Selection and Placement Center, 2011). Undergraduate counseling programs are popular. Undergraduate counselor education curricula include courses such as introduction to education, introduction to philosophy, introduction to psychology, introduction to sociology, school counseling, developmental psychology, measurement and evaluation, statistics, research methods, abnormal psychology, exceptional children, theories of counseling, counseling skills, group counseling, ethics, individual counseling practicum, group counseling practicum, and school observation. In some programs career counseling and crisis counseling courses are also offered. In 2007, a national counseling program and curriculum was adopted and distributed to universities for implementation by the Turkish Council of Higher Education. Unfortunately, this document was developed with extremely limited input from counselor educators. This nationalization of the training curriculum demonstrates the powerful influence of the centralized higher education system.

In graduate-level programs courses from various areas of counseling are offered. In general, graduate students at the master's level are expected to complete their program in a minimum of 2 years, doctoral students in 4 years. Students enrolled in master's and PhD programs write dissertations. In all programs both research and practice are emphasized. There is increasingly more emphasis on science and research, especially quantitative research methods. As Korkut (2007) concluded, clinical practice courses are limited in scope and number. In general there are no specializations in graduate programs; however, only two graduate-level programs in two universities (Ankara University and Istanbul University) currently provide such specialized training in career counseling. One of these programs is housed in the business department and the other in the human resources department (Owen et al., 2011). Many faculty members in counseling departments received training in the United States. In graduate programs, courses and textbooks resemble those used in counselor education programs in the United States.

The Future

Counseling in Turkey has witnessed significant improvements since the 1950s. Major issues for the next 5 to 10 years are expected to include defining professional identity, establishing accreditation of counselor training programs, standardizing credentials, ensuring sufficient resources for undergraduate counselor training programs, appointing noncounseling professionals (e.g., teachers and graduates of other programs) to school counselor positions, and negotiating the role of MONE in these issues. It is also predicted that Turkey's application process to the European Union will positively impact the accreditation of programs and licensure and that the TPCGA and researchers in the field will increase their national and international efforts to resolve issues regarding professionalism (Çınarbaş et al., 2009).

In addition, the field of counseling in Turkey must respond in the near future to issues created by the educational system as well as social and economic change. For example, the education system, which is currently based on national exams, will continue into the future. Because this exam places so much pressure on students and their parents, school counselors who work in schools and in private tutoring institutions will continue to emphasize success on this exam.

Yeşilyaprak (2009) predicted that changes in the population and economic conditions will continue to influence the future of counseling in Turkey. Yeşilyaprak listed some of the changes that are occurring in the 21st century and that will impact the field of counseling. These changes include a decrease in the fertility rate, an increase in life expectancy, an increase in unemployment, an increase in school enrollment, an increase in the number of nuclear families, increased consumption, and changes in the job market. Yeşilyaprak concluded that changes in society and the economy will lead to increased demand for counseling. Expected changes in the field of counseling include the use of short-term counseling; the rise of multicultural counseling; the use of technology in counseling; increases in collaboration with other helping professions; the provision of counseling in settings such as the military, health care, and business; and the development of indigenous treatment approaches.

Researchers in the future should evaluate how to provide counseling services to people living in poverty and what the impact of migration is on families and children. The counseling needs of people in rural areas will also be an area of research interest. Practitioners working in the field will need continuing education to refresh their knowledge and skills and to become more effective at helping diverse groups of clients.

In conclusion, even though counseling has existed for the past 60 years, the field has witnessed rapid advancement in terms of research, practice, and professional identity. Today, the counseling field is flourishing with the rich national literature, the many published books in Turkish, books on various fields of counseling translated from English, international collaborations with researchers from the United States and Europe, increased research published in international journals, international conferences, national conferences with international participants, and measures developed for the culture. Thus, this field, which has seen many successes, both nationally and internationally, will likely witness many more advances in the future and become a more active contributor to the international counseling field.

References

Aydın, G., & Hatipoğlu Sümer, Z. (2001). Who does psychotherapy? A historical look at the controversy among mental health professionals. *Bogaziçi University Journal of Education, 18,* 69–76.

Bikos, L. H., & Çiftçi Uruk, A. (2005). Counseling outcome as a function of counselor nationality for American expatriate clients. *International Journal for the Advancement of Counseling, 27,* 523–539.

Bjerre, M., & Yardımcı, Y. (2007). *Handbook on labour market information: Handbook on enterprise-based surveys of short and medium term qualification demands on the labour market.* Retrieved from http://svet.meb.gov.tr/svet/general/Labour/LabourMarketHandbookTurkeyMarch07.pdf

Bolak Boratav, H. (2004). Psychology at the cross-roads: The view from Turkey. In M. J. Stevens & D. Wedding (Eds.), *Handbook of international psychology* (Vol. 19, pp. 311–330). New York, NY: Bruner-Routledge.

Çelik, Ş. (2004). *The effects of an attachment oriented psycho educational-group-training on improving the preoccupied attachment styles of university students.* Unpublished doctoral dissertation, Middle East Technical University, Ankara, Turkey.

Çınarbaş, D. C., Korkut Owen, F., & Çiftçi, A. (2009). Counseling in Turkey: A blend of Western science and Eastern tradition. In L. H. Gerstein, P. P. Heppner, S. Ægisdóttir, S.-M. A. Leung, & K. L. Norsworthy (Eds.), *International handbook of cross-cultural counseling: Cultural assumptions and practices worldwide* (pp. 475–488). Thousand Oaks, CA: Sage.

Demir, A., & Aydın, G. (1996). Student counselling in Turkish universities. *International Journal for the Advancement of Counselling, 18,* 287–301.

Doğan, S. (2000). The historical development of counselling in Turkey. *International Journal for the Advancement of Counselling, 22,* 57–67.

Gizir, C. A. (2006). Bir kayıp sonrasında sorun yaşayan üniversite öğrencilerine yönelik yas danışmanlığı modeli [A grief counseling model for university students experiencing difficulties after a loss]. *Mersin University Journal of the Faculty of Education, 2,* 195–213.

Güner, İ. (2007). *Çatışma çözme becerilerini geliştirmeye yönelik grup rehberliğinin lise öğrencilerinin saldırganlık ve problem çözme becerileri üzerine etkisi* [The effect of conflict resolution group guidance program on aggression and problem solving]. Unpublished doctoral dissertation, İnonu University, Malatya, Turkey.

Güney, D., & Güney, A. (2011). 1933'den günümüze Türk yükseköğretiminde niceliksel gelişmeler [Quantitative developments in Turkish higher education since 1933]. *Journal of Higher Education and Science, 1*(1), 1–22.

Güven, M., Kısaç, İ., Ercan, L., & Yalçın, İ. (2009). Türk Psikolojik Danışma ve Rehberlik Dergisi'nde yayınlanan makalelerin çeşitli özellikler açısından incelenmesi [An investigation of publications in *Turkish Psychological Counseling and Guidance Journal*]. *Turkish Psychological Counseling and Guidance Journal, 4*(31), 80–87.

Kağıtçıbaşı, Ç. (1994). Psychology in Turkey. *International Journal of Psychology, 29,* 729–738.

Kağnıcı, D. Y. (2011). Teaching multicultural counseling: An example from a Turkish counseling undergraduate program. *Eurasian Journal of Educational Research, 44,* 111–128.

Karaırmak, Ö., & Güloğlu, B. (2011, October). *Bireyle psikolojik danışma uygulamasında süreç yönelimli metaphor kullanımı* [Process-based metaphor usage during individual counseling]. Paper presented at the 11th National Turkish Psychological Counseling and Guidance Congress, Selçuk/İzmir, Turkey.

Karataş, Z. (2009). Psikodrama ile yapılan grup çalışmasının ergenlerin sürekli kaygı düzeylerine etkisi [The effect of group psychodrama on adolescents' state anxiety level]. *Çağdaş Eğitim Dergisi, 34*(360), 31–37.

Korkut, F. (2007). Counselor education, program accreditation and counselor credentialing in Turkey. *International Journal for the Advancement of Counselling, 29,* 11–20.

Korkut, F., & Mızıkacı, F. (2008). Avrupa Birliği, Bologna süreci ve Türkiye'de psikolojik danışman eğitimi [European Union, Bologna process, and counselor education in Turkey]. *Educational Administration: Theory and Practice, 53,* 99–122.

Korkut Owen, F., Acar, T., Haskan, Ö., & Kızıldağ, S. (2010, May). *PDR mezunları üzerine bir izleme çalışması* [A follow-up study with counseling program graduates]. Paper presented at Hacettepe University and Azerbaijan State Pedagogy University, International Teacher Training Policies and Problems Congress, Ankara, Turkey.

Koşar Altınyelken, H. (2009). Migration and self-esteem: A qualitative study among internal migrant girls in Turkey. *Adolescence, 44*(173), 149–163.

Mersin University Psychological Counseling and Guidance Center. (2011). *Online Psikolojik Danışma* [Online counseling]. Retrieved from http://www.mersin.edu.tr/meui/psikolojik-danisma-ve-rehberlik-merkezi/online-psikolojik-danisma

Ministry of National Education. (2001, April 17). Rehberlik ve psikolojik danışma hizmetleri yönetmeliği [Counseling and guidance services regulation]. *T.C. Resmi Gazete,* 24376.

Ministry of National Education. (2006). *İlköğretim ve orta öğretim kurumları sınıf rehberlik Programı* [Elementary and secondary school classroom guidance program]. Retrieved from www.orgm.meb.gov.tr

Mocan Aydın, G. (2000). Western models of counseling and psychotherapy within Turkey: Crossing cultural boundaries. *Counseling Psychologist, 28,* 281–298.

Owen, D. W., Korkut Owen, F., & Kurter, M. F. (2011). Career development and counseling in Turkey: An evolving profession. *Career Planning and Adult Development Journal, 27*(1), 39–52.

Poyrazli, S. (2003). Validity of Rogerian therapy in Turkish culture: A cross-cultural perspective. *Journal of Humanistic Counseling, Education and Development, 42,* 107–115.

Şahan, B., & Duy, B. (2011, October). *Bilişsel-Davranışçı yaklaşıma dayalı psikoeğitim programının kız öğrencilerinin benlik saygısı, kontrol odağı ve akılcı olmayan inançları üzerine etkisi* [The effect of a cognitive behavioral psycho-education program on female students' self-respect, locus of control, and illogical beliefs]. Paper presented at the 11th National Turkish Counseling and Guidance Congress, Selçuk/İzmir, Turkey.

Smith, A. E., & Dengiz, B. (2010). Women in engineering in Turkey—A large scale quantitative and qualitative examination. *European Journal of Engineering Education, 35*(1), 45–57.

Stockton, R., & Yerin Güneri, O. (2011). Counseling in Turkey: An evolving field. *Journal of Counseling & Development, 89,* 98–104.

Sümer, S. (1998). Incongruent modernities: A comparative study of higher educated women from urban Turkey and Norway. *Acta Sociologica, 41,* 115–129.

Turkish Council of Higher Education. (2011). *Üniversiteler* [Universities]. Retrieved from http://www.yok.gov.tr/en/content/view/527/222/

Turkish Council of Higher Education Student Selection and Placement Center. (2011). *Selection and placement of students in higher education institutions in Turkey.* Retrieved from http://osym.gov.tr/belge/1-12654/2010-2011-ogretim-yili-yuksekogretim-istatistikleri.html

Turkish Psychological Counseling and Guidance Association. (2011). *Psikolojik danışman sayıları* [The number of counselors]. Retrieved from https://www.pdr.org.tr/HaberDetay.aspx?id=188

Turkish Statistical Institute. (2010). *Haber bülteni: Adrese dayalı nüfus sistemi 2010 sonuçları* [News bulletin: The results of the address-based consensus for 2010]. Retrieved from http://www.tuik.gov.tr/PreHaberBultenleri.do?id=8428

Turkish Statistical Institute. (2011). *Haber bülteni: Yoksulluk araştırması sonuçları* [News bulletin: Results of poverty study]. Retrieved from http://www.tuik.gov.tr/PreTablo.do?tb_id=23&ust_id=7

Vassaf, G. (1983). Conflict and counseling: Psychological counseling with university students in the emerging nations—Turkey. *School Psychology International, 4,* 31–36.

Yerin Güneri, O. (2006). Counseling services in Turkish universities. *International Journal of Mental Health, 35*(1), 26–38.

Yerin Güneri, O., Büyükgöze Kavas, A., & Koydemir, S. (2007). Okul psikolojik danışmanlarının profesyonel gelişimi: Acemilikten olgunlaşmaya giden zorlu yol [Professional development of Turkish school counselors: The tough road from novice to expert]. In D. W. Owen, F. Korkut Owen, & R. Özyürek (Eds.), *Gelişen psikolojik danışma ve rehberlik: Mesleklesme sürecindeki ilerlemeler* (pp. 139–162). Ankara, Turkey: Nobel.

Yeşilyaprak, B. (2009). Türkiye'de psikolojik danışma ve rehberlik alanının geleceği: Yeni açılımlar ve öngörüler [The development of the field of psychological counseling and guidance in Turkey: Recent advances and future prospects]. *Ankara University, Journal of Faculty of Educational Sciences, 42*(1), 193–213.

YÖRET. (2011). *YÖRET Vakfı Hakkında* [About YÖRET Foundation]. Retrieved from http://www.yoret.org.tr/tarihce.html

• • •

Counseling in North American Countries

32 Counseling in Canada

Roberta A. Neault, Blythe C. Shepard, Krista E. Benes, and Sareena Hopkins

The development of the Canadian counseling profession has been significantly shaped by the context in which counseling is delivered. Consisting of 10 provinces and three territories, Canada is the second largest country in the world in total area but has a relatively small population (approximately 34 million people). Canada's diverse landscape includes freshwater glaciers in the Rocky Mountains, rolling flat plains in the prairies, and the world's longest stretch of coastline. Canada's cultural history is as rich as its geography and has been profoundly influenced by the social, economic, and spiritual norms of its many Aboriginal peoples, including First Nations, Métis, and Inuit. Today Canada continues to embrace an increasingly diverse population, holding one of the highest per capita immigration rates and serving as home to more than 34 ethnic groups. It is a bilingual country, with both English and French as official languages at the federal level. Canada's political structure is a democratic one that divides responsibilities between the federal government and the provinces and territories. Although discussion on education policy and counseling service occurs at the pan-Canadian level, federal responsibilities for these areas have been largely transferred to the provinces and territories. This presents unique challenges for the counseling field, as there is no single authority governing policy planning, service delivery, or funding. As a result, it is virtually impossible to paint one cohesive national picture of counseling in Canada. Rather, we have a mosaic with 13 provincial and territorial contributors.

The counseling profession in Canada has a long history and developed from the mental health and vocational guidance movements. The Canadian National Committee for Mental Hygiene was formed in 1918 to diagnose and treat mental illness and to undertake psychiatric assessment of the military for shell shock. In the early 1920s, testing, advising, and provision of vocational information was offered in junior and senior high schools. The 1930s saw an increased focus on psychological testing to aid in the selection and classification of military personnel and the formation of guidance clinics to meet the needs of school-age children. By the 1940s, guidance counseling had become a formal part of the education system, and several provincial guidance associations had been formed. After World War II, postsecondary counseling was funded by the federal government, and war veterans were encouraged to seek out vocational guidance.

With the advent of various counseling theories in the 1940s and 1950s, Canada saw a decrease in the role of school counselors as guidance counselors and an increase in client-centered, individualized approaches to counseling. School counselors and teachers who had specialized training in counseling were now hired. In 1965, the Canadian Guidance and Counselling Association was formed to serve the needs of counselors who worked in the area of guidance and counseling, with school counselors making up the majority of members. By 1969, there were 14 master's-level counseling programs in Canada housed within faculties of education.

Over the next decade there was an increase in specialization and integration across professions and an increase in the number of counseling-related associations. By the 1980s school-based counseling programs in all provinces were taking a preventive approach focused on self-esteem, decision making, career exploration, and planning. Since the early 1990s, professional associations related to counseling have grown in number and in strength. The field of counseling is dynamic, and Canada is in many ways moving toward a coming of age as it strives to provide coherent and comprehensive policies and services to meet the distinct realities and needs of Canadians.

The Current Status of Counseling

A research project conducted in 2010 by the Canadian Counselling and Psychotherapy Association (CCPA; formerly the Canadian Guidance and Counselling Association) identified 140 professional associations related to counseling in Canada. The largest of these is the CCPA, with more than 4,000 members. It is difficult to accurately estimate the number of counselors currently practicing in Canada. Based on projections from those provinces that produce data, a rough estimate is that there are approximately 40,000 persons across Canada providing counseling related to mental health and/or personal growth. The challenge in determining a firm number is partly due to the lack of common nomenclature across the profession. In a survey conducted in the fall of 2010, respondents identified more than 70 different preferred professional titles in addition to the 12 titles that have been identified provincially through regulatory processes: counselling therapist, psychotherapist, mental health therapist, conseiller/*conseillère d'orientation,* marriage and family therapist, career counselor, *orienteur, orienteur professionnel, psychoeducateur,* registered clinical counselor, counsellor, and vocational guidance counsellor (CCPA, 2011a). Canada's National Occupational Classification system identifies more than 40 job titles that include the term *counselor.*

Survey participants also identified more than 60 unique areas of practice. The most common were general mental health, marriage and family, addiction, career, school-based, and postsecondary counseling. Less common were areas of play, somatic, creative arts, sexuality, pastoral, trauma, and Aboriginal wisdom. From this list it is clear that some Canadian counselors define their practice by client group (e.g., mental health, family, addiction, Aboriginals) and others define their practice by counseling approach or modality (e.g., career, play, creative arts, pastoral). Since the 1980s there has also been tremendous growth in the number of environments in which counselors work, including hospitals, mental health clinics, university counseling centers, crisis centers, employee assistance programs, employment centers, addiction clinics, courts, and correctional institutions. In addition, many counselors now work in private practice either full or part time. It is not surprising that to support such diverse types of practice, Canadian counselors draw from a wide range of theories and models, from client centered to behavioral and constructivist to test based.

In 2005, the CCPA cohosted with the British Columbia Association of Clinical Counsellors the first of a series of national symposia aimed at strengthening professional identity, promoting mobility, and increasing cohesion with respect to the regulation of the profession. At that symposium, entry to practice competencies aimed at the prevention of public harm were presented and agreement was obtained to validate these foundational competencies nationally. The second national symposium, which was federally funded by Human Resources and Social Development Canada, was held in 2008. This symposium updated key stakeholders on the current status of mobility and regulation in each jurisdiction in Canada. In addition, stewards of the profession were invited to collaborate on national standards that would be used to address impediments to occupational mobility. During the next year, the Project Working Group on Labour Mobility researched a variety of titles, definitions, and scopes of practice to determine typical attributes or features. In addition, a variety of codes of ethics and standards were compared. These research findings were shared at the federally funded 2009 national symposium attended by provincial counseling-related associations that represented a variety of counseling modalities. The intent was to share areas of professional consistency and common purpose in order to inform each jurisdiction's planning, increase the cohesion of professional standards, and advance the mobility of the counseling profession.

In an effort to determine areas of alignment with respect to professional title, the definition of counseling and psychotherapy, and scope of practice as a foundation for an overarching national framework to enhance labor mobility, the Project Working Group developed a bilingual national survey in 2010 that was circulated to all counseling and counseling-related organizations in the nation. In total, 46 organizations and 1,416 individuals responded to the survey, which presented research-based titles, a definition, and a scope of practice statement and asked respondents to rate the degree to which each of the three items reflected their professional identity and core beliefs.

At the 2011 National Symposium on Counselor Mobility held in Ottawa, the findings of the survey were presented and confirmed by members of the profession. In both the definition and the scope of practice sections of the survey responses consistently showed more than 93% agreement and always less than 4% disagreement. The following definition was accepted at the 2011 symposium based on the strong survey results:

> Counselling is a relational process based upon the ethical use of specific professional competencies to facilitate human change. Counselling addresses wellness, relationships, personal growth, career development, mental health, and psychological illness or distress. The counselling process is characterized by the application of recognized cognitive, affective, expressive, somatic, spiritual, developmental, behavioural, learning, and systemic principles. (CCPA, 2011a, p. 14)

The broad scope of practice validated through the survey was as follows:

> The counselling profession is attentive to and responds to diversity and inclusiveness; works in the best interest of individuals, couples, families, groups, organizations, communities, and the public-at-large; works in the domains of cognition, emotion, expression, somatics, human development, behaviour, learning, and interactive systems; promotes mental health by developing and enhancing: (a) personal, relational, sexual, career, and spiritual growth and well-being, (b) personal awareness and resources, and (c) decision-making and problem solving; remediates or provides treatment for disorders in cognitive, behavioural, interpersonal, and emotional functioning; applies specific and recognized evaluation and assessment methods; and may also include supervision, education, training, consultation, research, diagnosis. (CCPA, 2011a, pp. 14–15)

These definitions serve as a crucial anchor for the profession in Canada.

Although the regulation of counselors remains inconsistent across the country, these efforts are promoting greater cohesion. Canada has a national nonstatutory, regulatory regime that has all of the elements of those professions that are regulated under legislative statutes, including a code of ethics, standards of practice for counselors, procedures for complaints and disciplinary action, a Council on Accreditation of Counsellor Education Programs (CACEP), and a program for counselor certification (the Canadian Certified Counsellor).

Only five provinces have an umbrella health professions governance statute that could be used as a framework for regulating counseling: Alberta, British Columbia, Manitoba, Ontario, and Quebec. In the other provinces, it would appear that a dedicated and separate counseling regulation statute would have to be approved by the legislature. Currently some national associations (e.g., the CCPA and the Canadian Association for Music Therapy) provide a basis for regulating members of their provincial bodies by way of occupational titles granted under the federal Trade-Mark Act. However, this is a limited form of title protection that still relies on member cooperation and goodwill. At present the situation in Canada is one of variable regulation and is likely to remain this way for some time. Of Canada's 10 provinces and three territories, Quebec (1969), Nova Scotia (2011), and Ontario (2009) have legislation related to the regulation of the profession of counseling. Quebec has recently added the activity of psychotherapy and the title psychotherapist (2012) to its array of regulated activities and titles. Nova Scotia has regulated the title of counseling therapist. The Transitional Council of the College of Regulated Psychotherapists and Regulated Mental Health Therapists of Ontario will begin registering candidates in 2013. Regulation of the profession is currently being pursued in British Columbia, New Brunswick, and Prince Edward Island.

As a result, many practitioners who provide counseling services may be registrants of an existing health, social service, or education profession (e.g., psychologists, registered or psychiatric nurses, clinical social workers, or school counselors). In some provinces, only a few persons who advertise that they provide counseling services are not regulated through an existing college; in other provinces, there are many persons who provide counseling but are not regulated, except possibly through voluntary self-regulation.

For many Canadians, access to counseling is impacted by government funding priorities and insurance regulations. Through the Canadian health care system, basic medical plans cover access to medical doctors and psychiatrists but not counselors or psychologists. Some extended health care plans cover services provided by professionals from regulated professions (e.g., psychologists and social workers), but in most jurisdictions in Canada services provided by counselors are not covered because counseling is not yet a regulated profession. In many communities, the government funds organizations to offer specific mental health, family, wellness, or career and employment services; however, waitlists for counseling can be very long. Although many agencies offer fee-for-service counseling with sliding scales to make services more accessible to clients, it is not uncommon for people to discontinue their counseling treatment because of high costs.

Best Counseling Practices

A report on career development best practices in Canada acknowledged that a variety of terms and definitions are used for best practices but identified "five key criteria [for best practices] . . . including: supported, evidence-based, sustainable, replicable, and relevant" (Goss Gilroy, 2009, p. 8). In this section we focus on counseling practices within Canada that fit these criteria.

Canadians have made significant contributions to the literature on the working alliance (Bedi, Davis, & Arvay, 2005; Horvath & Bedi, 2002). Although it may be referred to slightly differently (e.g., therapeutic alliance, counseling relationship), most Canadian counselors accept the working alliance as foundational to any successful work with their clients. This may in part explain the apparent inconsistency in terms of theoretical influences or preferred modalities—counselors see many possible routes to achieve counseling success as long as an effective working alliance is in place.

Another possible explanation for the variety of approaches in Canadian counseling is the diversity within the clients that counselors serve. Although specific diversity issues are discussed in more depth later in this chapter, in general most Canadian counselors consider it important to attend to matters of culture. Significant contributions in this area have been made by Peavy (1997). In his sociodynamic counseling, a constructivist perspective, culture is considered foundational to working with any client. Peavy emphasized the importance of building a strong cooperative relationship, facilitating the client's ability to help himself or herself, coconstructing meaning, and developing and implementing relevant and realistic plans. Canadian counselors also recognize the important contributions to counseling from non-Western cultures, and many integrate practices from beyond their borders (Oulanova, Stein, Rai, Hammer, & Poulin, 2009). There have been important contributions to guide counseling with Aboriginal populations (i.e., First Nations, Métis, and Inuit), particularly in terms of incorporating family and community input and taking a holistic approach that acknowledges the significance of spirituality (Oulanova et al., 2009).

As Canadian counselors have become more culturally competent and have learned how to work more effectively with members of diverse cultural groups, many have also begun to rethink more traditional counseling conventions. Amundson's (2009) *Active Engagement* textbook asks important questions about where and how counseling is conducted, encouraging counselors to move their counseling practice out of the office, use experiential approaches, and engage significant others in the therapeutic process. Similarly, Canadian Richard Young is a codeveloper of contextual action theory, an approach that integrates context into counseling techniques (Young, Valach, & Domene, 2005).

Assessment is another construct interpreted differently by Canadian counselors. Some use the term interchangeably with *test*, but most counselors view assessment as a comprehensive and ongoing *process* that may or may not include the use of formal or standardized assessment tools. Although there is little consistency in the use of assessment across Canada, there is general agreement that a holistic approach that blends the use of standardized and nonstandardized approaches and integrates information from a variety of sources is effective (Mackey, 2010).

Innovative contributions to the field of counseling have been developed throughout Canada. Hope is viewed as an essential foundation by many (e.g., Jevne, 2009; Niles, Amundson, & Neault, 2011). Peruniak's (2008) work has focused on quality of life. Several Francophone authors have also made significant contributions, including Limoges's (2003) work on maintenance/balance and Riverin-Simard and Simard's (2009) work on the lifelong learning intelligence model. Two different groups of Canadian counselor educators and researchers have produced innovative approaches to trauma therapy: observed and experiential integration (Bradshaw, Cook, & McDonald, 2011) and therapeutic enactment (Westwood, Keats, & Wilensky, 2003).

As approaches to counseling continue to change to respond to the needs of Canadians, so too do the methods by which they are delivered. There is increasing use of technology (e.g., telephone counseling, e-counseling) to support outreach to clients; however, this is not universally embraced by Canadian counselors. In a recent survey of 107 practicing counselors, only 23% indicated that their practice used e-counseling, and 50% indicated that their practice used telephone counseling. However, some government funders are now requiring telephone or e-counseling as part of their services. A legal brief commissioned by the CCPA (2011b) highlighted several ethical and professional liability concerns associated with e-counseling, including the laws that will apply if a counselor and client are in different geographical regions, the counselor certifications that are necessary (e.g., if the client is in a region where counselors are regulated but the counselor is in a region where regulation is not in place), and limits to applicable insurance. It is interesting that due to the geographic realities of the Canadian population, the largest counselor training programs are making significant use of e-learning for most of their courses, but the graduates of these programs still primarily work in person with their clients.

Although most Canadian counselors and counseling psychologists have been trained in a scientist-practitioner model, the bulk of counseling research is generated through universities rather than private practice or community-based agencies. However, agencies and counselors are often willing partners in research projects (e.g., providing access to clients and implementing research protocols). Within career counseling, for example, there have been significant advances in in situ research by the Canadian Research Working Group on Evidence Based Practice in Career Development (Lalande & Magnusson, 2007). Counselors working in areas of career and educational guidance are well supported in Canada by labor market information, including the National Occupational Classification system, Job Futures (www.jobfutures.org), a national job bank (www.jobbank.gc.ca), and industry-specific information produced by sector councils.

Diversity Issues

Within Canada, it is challenging to consider diversity issues separately from best practices or promising practices. Canadians generally embrace diversity; as a country they have adopted a mosaic rather than a melting pot approach, in which cultural differences are preserved and celebrated. This, not surprisingly, has implications for counselors.

Several Canadian researchers and theorists have made significant contributions to research and counseling practice related to diversity. Arthur and Collins (2010) introduced culture-infused counseling in recognition that all people are influenced by their cultures; editors Oulanova et al. (2009) compiled a collection of articles that introduce alternative healing methods, including Aboriginal and holistic mind–body practices.

Several specific diversity issues are uniquely Canadian, or Canadians approach these issues slightly differently than professionals in other countries. For example, McCormick (1991) emphasized the interconnectedness of First Nations people and helped counselors to understand the importance of embracing interdependence. This approach also has implications for working with clients from other collectivist cultures. Many communities have supports for immigrants and newcomers to Canada; however, the needs of international workers or global careerists are less understood, and services targeted to these populations are limited.

Services to French-speaking Canadians are not uniformly available across the country. In federally funded programs there is typically a requirement to offer services in both official languages. However, in some communities with smaller Francophone populations, the services may simply be a translation of English services rather than drawn from the rich body of work produced by Francophone counselors and researchers.

The Canadian Charter of Rights and Freedoms (Section 15) declares that every person is to be considered equal regardless of age, color, ethnicity, physical or mental ability, race, religion, or sex. In 1996, the Canadian Human Rights Act was amended to specifically prohibit discrimination based on sexual orientation, and in most Canadian provinces and territories there is similar legislation. The Employment Equity Act (1986) further identified women, visible minorities, persons with disabilities, and Aboriginal peoples as being underrepresented in the workforce and therefore requiring special attention. Throughout Canada there are counseling programs specifically designed to support members of these targeted groups. However, this approach is not without controversy; in light of the Canadian commitment not to discriminate against any individuals, members of nontargeted groups periodically challenge such policies, claiming that they are being discriminated against (Tuo, 2010).

Of specific importance to counselors are rules related to confidentiality, the protection of privacy, freedom of information, and the age of consent. Although some of these rules are Canada-wide, many vary by province or territory. Therefore, it is crucial for counselors to understand the rules specific to their geographic location.

Counselor Education

Across Canada, most counseling psychology training programs are housed within faculties of education that have a focus on the K–12 school system; however, most graduates from counseling programs tend to work in community settings with adult populations

(Young & Nicol, 2007). Some of the challenges these programs present include the need for small class sizes, a larger number of courses than most graduate programs in education due to attention to both research and practice, and the intense supervision requirements.

The most common entry standard for being registered as a counselor (regulated or non-regulated) is a master's degree in counseling or a related field. Currently there are about 48 graduate-level programs in Association of Universities and Colleges of Canada institutions (www.ccpa-accp.ca). All provinces have at least one graduate counseling program, with the exception of Prince Edward Island.

Master's-level counseling programs can voluntarily submit to a self-study that is reviewed by the CACEP under the auspices of the CCPA. In order to become accredited, a counselor education program must fulfill certain requirements or standards with regard to institutional settings, program mission and objectives, program content, practicum experiences, student selection and advising, faculty qualifications and workload, program governance, instructional support, and self-evaluation. Currently three programs are accredited at the master's level in Canada; at the doctoral level, four counseling psychology programs are presently accredited by the Canadian Psychological Association.

Course areas typically offered at the master's level are counseling theories, skills and interventions, consultation, assessment and testing, multicultural counseling (diversity), professional ethics, learning and human development, research and evaluation, career-life development, group counseling, and counseling in specialized settings. Supervised practice is a requirement of all programs recognized by the Association of Universities and Colleges of Canada. The number of direct client contact hours required varies from 75 to 500. The CCPA requires 120 hours of direct work with clients (in individual, family, and/or group counseling) under the supervision of a qualified professional (to be increased to 150 hours in 2013) with a strong recommendation that applicants obtain 20 hours of group counseling. It is expected that supervisors have expertise in the area of counseling, including conceptual knowledge and practical experience as well as a master's degree or higher in the area of counseling or a closely related field. The CCPA requires that supervisors have a minimum of 4 years of successful practice in the field and belong to a recognized counseling association or a provincial or territorial regulatory college.

The diffuse identity of the counseling profession is evident in the different requirements across the provinces. For example, in British Columbia counselors must have 100 hours of clinical supervision in order to become a Registered Clinical Counsellor, whereas in Alberta, unlike most provinces, graduates with a master's degree in counseling psychology normally seek registration with the College of Alberta Psychologists. In addition, there are differences in emphasis among various regulatory bodies. For example, some jurisdictions acknowledge counseling psychologists' work with clinical populations through the use of such terms as *maladjustment, disability,* and *treatment.* In other jurisdictions, the definition emphasizes nonclinical populations ("the work of counselling psychology is generally with reasonably well adjusted people" and "counselling psychology is the fostering or improving of normal human functioning"; Bedi et al., 2011, p. 130).

The Future

During a recent international meeting at a counseling conference the counseling profession in North America was described as being in its adolescence. The metaphor was used to illustrate that, although it has moved beyond infancy, it is not yet fully independent. Human development models describe the adolescent stage as a time of exploring and experimenting and of trying on new roles and identities. This seems to fit well for the current state of counseling in Canada as it enters the second decade of the 21st century.

During their "teenage" years, Canadian counselors have been trying to establish their uniqueness. This is being manifested in numerous apparently disconnected ways that together speak to some of the angst of growing up. The Career Development Chapter of the

CCPA, for example, recently proposed a revision to the Career Counselling specialization of the Canadian Standards and Guidelines for Career Development Practitioners, identifying career counselors as fully counselors as well as fully career practitioners. Although efforts to build cohesion have advanced the field, regulation, nomenclature, and standards remain inconsistent. In some provinces, counselors have established their professional identity as psychologists, but in many parts of the country psychologists require doctoral-level education and extended internships, making many counselors with master's-level educations ineligible for registration as psychologists. Some associations of psychologists have invited counselors in but as younger siblings without the full scope of practice psychologists have.

Many of the current trends in Canadian counseling seem likely to continue. Canada is a multicultural nation and in the future will rely even more on immigration and international workers to meet its needs for skilled labor (Galloway, 2011; Government of Canada, 2011). Although in the past not all counselors saw themselves as requiring cultural competency, in current training and future practice the importance of a culture-infused approach is increasingly accepted. Similarly, the move to more holistic approaches is likely to continue. Canadian counselors are increasingly recognizing that their clients' lives are not compartmentalized—career counseling *is* personal counseling, and physical health is closely connected to mental well-being.

As the regulation of counselors across Canada continues to occur, there will be a growing need for applicants to obtain clinical supervision in order to meet the criteria for more direct face-to-face client contact hours than was required in their programs. Although psychologists at the doctoral level receive course work in clinical supervision, most graduates of counseling programs do not receive training in supervision. Supervision training programs for those professionals with advanced skills and experience will be increasingly necessary.

Similarly, there will be more pressure on programs to become accredited by CACEP in order to meet the demands of students who want to be assured of the quality of their academic program. Accredited programs will advance the profession in Canada by creating and strengthening standards that meet the needs of Canadian society, that encourage the use of a variety of theoretical approaches, and that support the ongoing evaluation and review of programs.

When asked what they expect to see over the next decade, Canadian leaders in the counseling field gave the following responses:

- Over the next 10 years, I expect our profession will become more inclusive, more international in scope, and more relevant to the life experiences of our clients. (David Paterson, Simon Fraser University)
- The major issue faced by the counseling profession in Canada over the next 10 years will be forging a national professional identity from the disparate parts that currently exist. (Ron Lehr, Acadia University)
- In many settings, the view of "self as professional" is moving towards an intertwining of the provision of counseling services and the indicators of client change: counseling process and client outcome are being viewed as equal components of the counseling enterprise. In order for counseling to continue to develop, this needs to become an even more prevalent facet of counselor practice and a more central part of counselor preparation programs. (Bryan Hiebert, University of Victoria)
- I see counseling as a human encounter in which client and counselor are equally engaged in a mutual process: basically the search for meaning. This calls for counselors to develop advanced knowledge, skills, and resources. (Armelle Spain, Université Laval)
- In the coming decade, I foresee counseling breaking away from time/stage models to become more spatio-horizontal. Current models will be put aside as they require high language competency and are therefore not adequately inclusive. (Jacques Limoges, Université de Sherbrooke)

- Health care in Canada is moving toward a more collaborative team/patient-centric model of care. It will be critical for counselors to articulate their role within these health care teams. (Barbara MacCallum, CCPA)

These perspectives point to continued growth for the profession. If Canada is currently in its adolescence, the next decade will no doubt see its coming of age.

References

Amundson, N. E. (2009). *Active engagement: The being and doing of career counselling* (3rd ed.). Richmond, British Columbia, Canada: Ergon Communications.

Arthur, N., & Collins, S. (2010). *Culture-infused counselling* (2nd ed.). Calgary, Alberta, CA: Counselling Concepts.

Bedi, R. P., Davis, M. D., & Arvay, M. J. (2005). The client's perspective on forming a counselling alliance and implications for research on counsellor training. *Canadian Journal of Counselling, 39,* 71–85.

Bedi, R. P., Haverkamp, B. E., Beatch, R., Cave, D., Domene, J. F., Harris, G. E., & Mikhail, A. (2011). Counelling psychology in a Canadian context: Definition and description. *Canadian Psychology, 52*(2), 128–138.

Bradshaw, R. A., Cook, A., & McDonald, M. J. (2011). Observed and experiential integration (OEI): Discovery and development of a new set of trauma therapy techniques. *Journal of Psychotherapy Integration, 21*(2), 104–171.

Canadian Counselling and Psychotherapy Association. (2011a, April 7–8). *"As it was said" report: 2011 National Symposium on Inter-Provincial/Territorial Mobility Within the Counselling Profession.* Retrieved from http://www.ccpa-accp.ca/_documents/Symposium/AsitwassaidReportApril7-82011.pdf

Canadian Counselling and Psychotherapy Association. (2011b). *Did you know? Possible pitfalls when offering e-counselling services.* Ottawa, Ontario, Canada: Author.

Galloway, G. (2011, July 6). Ottawa moves to avert "skills crisis." *Globe and Mail Update.* Retrieved from http://www.theglobeandmail.com/news/politics/ottawa-notebook/ottawa-moves-to-avert-skills-crisis/article2088674/

Goss Gilroy. (2009). *Development of an approach to assess, identify and share career development services best practices.* St. John's, Newfoundland, Canada: Forum of Labour Market Ministers – Career Development Services Working Group. Available at http://www.flmm-cds.ca/CMFiles/Best%20Practices%20Final%20Report%20-20%20Feb%202009.doc

Government of Canada. (2011). *Working in Canada.* Retrieved from http://www.workingincanada.gc.ca/

Horvath, A. O., & Bedi, R. P. (2002). The alliance. In J. Norcross (Ed.), *Psychotherapy relationships that work: Therapist contributions and responsiveness to patients* (pp. 37–70). New York, NY: Oxford University Press.

Jevne, R. F. (2009). *Tea for inner me: Blending tea with reflection.* Millet, Canada: Elske Consulting Associates.

Lalande, V., & Magnusson, K. (2007). Measuring the impact of career development services in Canada: Current and preferred practices. *Canadian Journal of Counselling, 41,* 146–157.

Limoges, J. (2003). *A balanced work life: A matter of maintenance.* Ottawa, Ontario, Canada: Canadian Career Development Foundation.

Mackey, J. (2010). Best practices in assessment interpretation. *The Bulletin, 14*(3). Retrieved from http://www.contactpoint.ca/PDFs/ContactPointBulletin_v14n3.pdf

McCormick, R. M. (1991). Healing through interdependence: The role of connecting in First Nations healing practices. *Canadian Journal of Counselling Psychology, 31*(3), 172–184.

Niles, S. G., Amundson, N. E., & Neault, R. A. (2011). *Career flow: A hope-centered approach to career development.* Upper Saddle River, NJ: Prentice Hall.

Oulanova, O., Stein, I., Rai, A., Hammer, M., & Poulin, P. A. (Eds.). (2009). *Within and beyond borders: Critical multicultural counselling in practice.* Toronto, Ontario, Canada: Centre for Diversity in Counselling and Psychotherapy. Retrieved from http://www.oise.utoronto.ca/cdcp/UserFiles/File/Publications/within_and_beyond_borders.pdf

Peavy, R. V. (1997). *Sociodynamic counselling: A constructivist perspective.* Victoria, British Columbia, Canada: Trafford Publishers.

Peruniak, G. (2008). *A quality of life approach to career development.* Toronto, Ontario, Canada: University of Toronto Press.

Riverin-Simard, D., & Simard, Y. (2009). *The organizational competencies of the reception, referral, counseling and support services: Toward a lifelong learning intelligence model.* Quebec City, Quebec, Canada: Ministère de l'Éducation, du Sport et du Loisir.

Tuo, L. (2010, July 31). *Canada to face multiculturalism backlash on "equal opportunity."* Retrieved from http://news.xinhuanet.com/english2010/world/2010-07/31/c_13423456.htm

Westwood, M. J., Keats, P. A., & Wilensky, P. (2003). Therapeutic enactment: Integrating individual and group counselling models for change. *Journal for Specialists in Group Work, 28*(2), 122–138.

Young, R. A., & Nicol, J. J. (2007). Counselling psychology in Canada: Advancing psychology for all. *Applied Psychology, 56*(1), 20–32.

Young, R. A., Valach, L., & Domene, J. F. (2005). The action-project method in counseling psychology. *Journal of Counseling Psychology, 52,* 215–223.

• • •

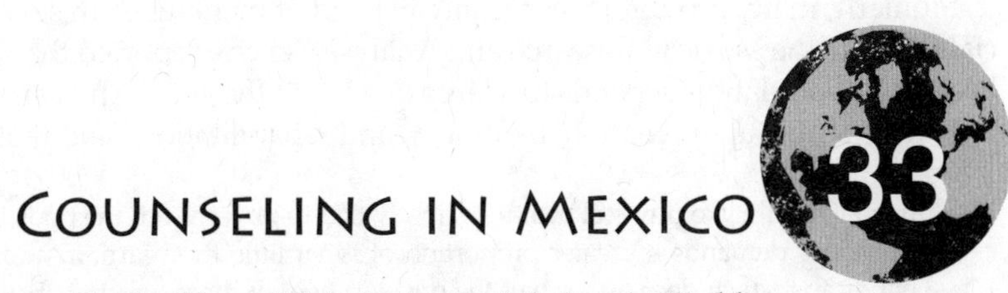

Counseling in Mexico

Antonio Tena Suck, Eitan Kleinberg, and J. Scott Hinkle

Like many societies, Mexico has tried to explain the human condition for decades. Examples of this can be found throughout the Mexican colonial period, from the creation of asylums to house the insane, to academic reflections on psychological metaphysics, to the search for treatments for mental health pathology (Portal, Suck, & Hinkle, 2010). Today Mexico has a national mental health policy as well as a countrywide mental health program. However, like many countries, it does not have wide access to community mental health care despite this national policy. The approximate mental health budget is about 1% of the total health budget. Despite this lack of resources, treatment facilities for severe mental illness exist in Mexico, as does training in primary care for the treatment for mental health anomalies. There are approximately 2.7 psychiatrists, 0.1 psychiatric nurses, and 0.2 social workers per 100,000 in the population (World Health Organization, 2005). But there is no credible information about the actual numbers of counselors and psychologists in Mexico.

The Historical Development of Counseling

Defining *Counseling* and *Counselor* in Mexico

Portal et al. (2010) indicated that in Mexico, mental health and human development problems have been resolved through a variety of disciplines. These include psychiatry, psychoanalysis, and psychology, and it has now become necessary to define the identity of the counseling psychologist or counselor. The terms *counseling* and *counselor,* although unknown to most Mexican people, elicit different meanings in certain sectors of society. A counselor can be defined as an adviser, consultant, therapist, psychologist, or lawyer. These definitions give rise to a variety of applications of the term *counselor* and can result in confusion regarding the role and field of the professional counselor. Counseling has been referred to more specifically as psychological support and psychological help; however, this definition is vague and confusing. The confusion is compounded by the fact that a large portion of the Mexican population seek support and advice from nonprofessionals or from those in other fields, including traditional healers, priests, ministers, and physicians. Thus, the term *counselor* combined with *psychologist* has led Mexican helping professionals to the term *psychological counseling.* However, defining the identity of the psychological counselor remains a challenge. It is necessary for Mexican psychological counselors to strengthen their professional identity as well as respond to trends in the areas of mental health and quality counseling services, particularly for the poor.

Among the major trends that arise from social, educational, and health-related problems are those regarding special education, work with vulnerable groups such as older and indigenous people, and services for migrants and immigrants. In addition, today's Mexican counselor serves people with addictions and eating disorders. For example, according to a national public health institute, the prevalence of childhood obesity in Mexico is 20% (Instituto Nacional de Salud Pública, 2006). This places Mexico as the country with the highest prevalence of childhood obesity in the world. Fortunately, counseling for related health and wellness concerns among Mexican children is currently receiving more focus.

Similarly, many groups are especially in need of mental health services. The Division of Social Policy of the Mexican Research and Analysis Service reported that "maintaining the mental health of a population depends to a large degree on the successful carrying out of public health initiatives aimed at prevention, treatment, and rehabilitation" and that

> mental health, like physical health, is closely tied to poverty. For the poor, the incidence of these sufferings demands a greater proportion of what little they earn, in addition to the resulting handicaps which decrease or halt the development of those affected. (Sandoval de Escurdia & Muñoz, 2006, p. 15)

Poverty

An Economic Commission for Latin America report, *Social Panorama of Latin America 2008*, indicated that there are 68 million indigent people in Mexico (Comisión Económica para América Latina, 2008). A national social development policy report noted that based on the results of the National Household Income and Expenditure Survey, the percentage of people living in "food poverty" (those with a per capita monthly income less than $949 pesos in urban areas and less than $707 pesos in rural areas) increased from 13.8% to 18.2% between 2006 and 2008 (Consejo Nacional de Evaluación de la Politica de Desarrollo Social, 2009). This same report also indicated that those living in "poverty of capabilities" (without resources for health and education) increased from 24.7% to 25.1% (from 21.6 to 26.7 million people). Moreover, those living in "poverty of wealth" (without resources to meet their needs for housing, clothing, and transportation) rose from 42.6% to 47.4% (from 44.7 to 50.6 million people) during this same time.

The risk for mental health problems associated with poverty has increased largely because of the need for all Mexican family members, including mothers and children, to join the labor force. This puts Mexican children at a disadvantage, as they often cannot attend school and are exposed to various types of exploitation. As a result, traditional family roles are changing, resulting in difficulties with family communication and child supervision that add to family stress (Medina-Mora & Villatoro, 2005; Portal et al., 2010). Similarly, changes are occurring in the structure of the traditional Mexican family. In 1990, traditional families (father, mother, and children) made up 70% of the population, but by 2005 they had fallen to 67%; the percentage of single-person households increased from 6.3% in 2000 to 7.5% in 2005 (Alcántara, 2009). Furthermore, approximately 15 million children and adults in Mexico suffer from mental disorders, but only 3,000 health professionals are available to provide services.

Poor families in Mexico have more depression and anxiety symptoms, and their children have greater exposure to medical illness, family stress, inadequate social support, and parental depression, than families that are not poor. Poverty is also associated with chaotic family and community environments, increased psychological stress, illiteracy, unemployment, and street begging (Portal et al., 2010).

Drug Use

Just as poverty accentuates the need for counseling services, drug use contributes to a major public health problem. It has spread to almost all social groups and is linked to criminal behavior. Moreover, living in the streets is a major risk factor leading to drug use. Another significant issue is the many factors that contribute to teen pregnancy, such as the lack of sexual and reproductive education, increased drug use, dysfunctional family dynamics, and changes in cultural patterns (Portal et al., 2010).

People With Disabilities

In Mexican society the most vulnerable groups include people with disabilities, individuals who have special educational needs, indigenous people, and emigrants. In 2000, 1.8% of the Mexican population suffered some type of disability (Compañia de Jesús, 2005). Of people with disabilities, 75% attended school at some time, but only 0.7% of that population completed formal education. Limited mobility is the most prevalent (45.3% of individuals with disabilities), followed by visual disability (26%), mental disability (16.1%), hearing disability (15.7%), and finally language disability (5%; Instituto Nacional de Estadística, Geografía e Informática, 2005). To address children's disabilities, 46,000 teachers were trained in special education in 2004 (Compañia de Jesús, 2005). On the other end of the age spectrum, significant losses gradually affect older adults, including loss of employment, loved ones, and mental health capacity, thus contributing to isolation and depressed mood. These can all be helped by counseling services.

Indigenous Groups

Although poverty, youth, and old age are associated with mental health issues, Mexican indigenous communities are identified as one of the least healthy groups in the country. Of Mexico's total population, 8.5% is indigenous; these individuals have the lowest levels of education, employment, and housing. They also do not have the community infrastructure necessary to attend to their health problems (including their mental health problems). Members of the 63 recognized indigenous groups in Mexico live on the average about 5 years less than members of the general population, and their children are highly vulnerable to malnutrition, which results in developmental delays. Moreover, indigenous children's mental health is affected by racism and discrimination, and their death rate is 58% higher than the death rate of Mexico's non-indigenous children (Instituto Nacional de Estadística, Geografía e Informática, 2005; Portal et al., 2010). Obviously, this creates a great need for counseling services.

Emigration

Mexicans emigrate in search of better options for survival and by so doing expose themselves to several stressors, such as multiple changes in residence, adaptation to a new culture and language, and discrimination. Mexican emigrants also face financial uncertainty, identity loss, fears of persecution, and unfamiliarity with local laws. Moreover, anxieties among emigrants as well as migrant workers can result in problems with drugs and an increase in risky sexual behaviors and mental health problems (Portal et al., 2010).

Mental Health Epidemiology in Mexico

The prevalence of mental disorders such as schizophrenia, depression, and dementia have increased in recent decades. Thus, Mexico has seen an increase in the number of young people who have few educational and employment opportunities because they have psychiatric disorders. The current economic crisis and significant social changes have contributed to the mental health of today's Mexicans. Results from the National Survey of Psychiatric Epidemiology indicated that 28.6% of the Mexican population had suffered from a mental disorder at some time in their lives and that only 10% received specialized mental health care (Medina-Mora et al., 2003). Moreover, 12.1% of these people presented with a severe mental disorder

(Instituto Nacional de Estadística, Geografía e Informática, 2005). Overall, the prevalence of mental disorders at any given time in Mexico is estimated to be between 10.5% and 13.8% (World Health Organization World Mental Health Survey Consortium, 2004).

Affective disorders are found in 9% of the population of Mexico City between 18 and 65 years of age (2.5 times more often among women), with 7.8% of these people experiencing severe depressive episodes. The prevalence of anxiety disorders is estimated to be less than that of depression, affecting 8.3% of the population. The most common anxiety-related diagnoses include agoraphobia without panic (3.8%) and social phobia (2.2%; Medina-Mora et al., 2003; Medina-Mora & Villatoro, 2005).

Mental health service utilization in Mexico is approximately 24% because people may wait a long time before seeking help, and it is estimated that approximately 15% will resort to self-medication. Although 25% to 30% of Mexican people are considered to need specialized care, only about 13% request services. The most common disorders in descending order are anxiety disorders, alcohol abuse, and depression. It is estimated that among children and adolescents ages 4 to 16 living in Mexico City, approximately 16% have a mental disorder and 50% have psychiatric symptoms (Compañia de Jesús, 2005).

The National Human Rights Commission in Mexico reported that 40% of students in primary and middle schools are victims of bullying. Therefore, the Secretary for Public Education designed a program on gender equality and violence prevention that aims to raise awareness among children about ill treatment inside and outside of school (Sosa, 2010).

Another relevant fact that highlights the need for adequate training of mental health professionals pertains to violence against women (National [Mexico] Institute of Statistics and Geography, 2011). This phenomenon affects 67% of women in Mexico and is manifested as partner violence among 47% of married or coupled women (World Health Organization, 2001).

Thus, Mexico needs counselors with multicultural and systemic counseling skills rather than traditional strategies that focus on the individual. Mexican counselors need to maintain a healthy openness in order to recognize their own prejudices and stereotypes as well as acquire particular understanding of the social group with which they are working (Portal et al., 2010). As counseling matures in Mexico, counselors will need to continually revise and reformulate applicable mental health theories and practices with the goal of promoting the use of integrative services with a vast and multicultural population. At the same time, this will require Mexican counselors to be scientist-practitioners who are capable of submitting their research to professional journals as well sharing their findings at professional meetings.

Finally, it is nearly impossible to understand a Mexican client without taking into account the role of religion or spirituality in his or her life. Integrating spiritual aspects into the counseling process is important for many. Including spirituality is essential for promoting the therapeutic process, as spiritual beliefs have historically been a great source of strength for many Mexicans (see Portal et al., 2010).

A Brief History of the Mental Health Field in Mexico

Although the development of counseling in Mexico is a recent phenomenon, it was preceded by a host of historical events. For instance, in 1557, Brother Alonso de la Veracruz reported observations of the effects of changes in the environmental climate on human mental activity in *Physica Speculatio.* The first mental hospital in the Americas was founded by Bernardino Álvarez in 1567, and this Hospital of San Hipólito in Mexico City treated and protected the insane (Robles, 1942, 1950).

Benito Díaz de Gamarra published *Elementa Recentioris Philosophiae* in 1774 about the treatment of mental disorders. Just more than 100 years later, *Optical Psychiatry* was published in 1884 by Rafael Serrano on the etiology of psychosis, and Ezequiel Chávez introduced the first high school–level psychology course in the late 1800s. In the late 1900s, reeducative therapy (a precursor to behavior modification) was formulated. In 1916, the first psychology laboratory in Mexico was founded by Enrique Aragon (Robles, 1942, 1950).

In the 1930s and 1940s, the first psychology degree program and psychology department in Mexico were founded. In the early 1960s, psychology grew from a philosophical to a more experimental position with an emphasis on behavior modification. Graduates from these programs began to pursue graduate degrees in other countries, culminating in real advances in the field of mental health Mexico. At this time in the United States, the predominant mental health professions were psychiatry, psychiatric nursing, psychology, social work, and psychological counseling (Portal et al., 2010).

Mexico is in the process of a transformation aimed at improving standards of living, which has resulted in the need to train professionals, including counselors, to respond to the challenges of resolving mental health–related problems. This process must adopt the necessary resources and strategies to accomplish comprehensive national health goals. The tasks of counselors in Mexico have been defined by today's global and national issues, including exposure to social inequality, violence, corruption, economic crises, environmental destruction, and migration. In addition, the influence of foreign cultures, the growth in the media, and the impact of technology have contributed to numerous social concerns. The World Health Organization (2005) has established mental health guidelines that focus not only on diagnosis and treatment but also on the prevention of mental health problems in the individual as well as the collective society (Compañia de Jesús, 2005). The counseling profession in Mexico is assiduously working toward meeting these World Health Organization guidelines.

The need for mental health services in Mexico has prompted the promotion of professional counseling services and will necessitate the responsible development of the profession. NBCC Mexico's goal is to enhance the development of counseling as a well-respected profession via counselor education and a certification process (Portal et al., 2010). Mexican national policies have historically placed little emphasis on counseling. Although laws related to mental health professions are rare, an exception is the Mental Health Law of the Federal District, enacted in 2011, which includes regulations regarding the practice of psychology. Outside of this specific law, the vast majority of national regulations usually refer only to the practice of psychiatry. In fact, many professionals now working for the development of counseling in Mexico have a background in psychotherapy, as training and educational programs for counselors have been limited.

Best Counseling Practices

The historical events just described led to what is known today as psychological counseling in Mexico. This practice includes psychoanalysis, behaviorism, and humanistic-existential therapy. Currently counseling also embraces Gestalt approaches, psychodynamic therapy, cognitive behavior therapy, systems therapy, reality therapy, and narrative therapy, among many others. Portal et al. (2010) indicated that Mexico is known for its sharp contrasts in economic, political, and social development, and for this reason psychological counselors have taken on the fundamental role of assisting with strategies to resolve problems related to health, education, career-related productivity, and poverty.

Counselor Education

The Universidad Iberoamericana (UI), in collaboration with the University of Scranton in Pennsylvania, developed a master's program in counseling psychology (community counseling) in 2004. The master's in counseling psychology is a postgraduate professional program that trains professionals dedicated to counseling in the areas of prevention, evaluation, diagnosis, and intervention (World Health Organization, 2001). Counselor training at UI teaches developing practitioners innovative strategies that enable them to respond to ongoing changes in Mexico.

The partnership with the University of Scranton offered a unique advantage for both programs. UI faculty members, assistant academics, and students traveled to the United States to complete part of their training. Alternatively, faculty from the University of Scranton taught courses at UI. It is important to note that UI's is the only program outside the United States and Canada that is accredited by the Council for Accreditation of Counseling and Related Educational Programs.

As a postgraduate program designed to train master's-level professionals to perform counseling services for the Mexican society, the program requires its students to demonstrate skills in prevention, diagnosis, and intervention. In addition, the identification of cultural groups, services at different life stages, and professional ethics are emphasized. During their 700-hour internship, counseling students learn to intervene at the societal level and to promote prevention while controlling risk factors for relapse.

The counseling program at UI attempts to provide a viable answer to the great need for psychosocial development in Mexico by focusing on services that promote economic, social, and psychological functioning for minority groups suffering exclusion, poverty, and inequality. Students develop a clear identity as community counselors involved with social justice. Specific needs to which the services of the graduates are directed include the development of health and welfare, family and couples development, domestic violence, addictive and compulsive behaviors, and mental dysfunctions. Counselors at UI are taught to promote long-term solutions for individuals, groups, and communities in collaboration with professionals in other specialties.

Stemming from a partnership among the National Board for Certified Counselors (NBCC), UI, and the University of Scranton, a bilingual counseling journal, *Selected Topics in Counseling Psychology,* was established in 2005. This journal has published six issues, facilitating the popularization of the counseling profession with the public and specialized audiences. Similarly, counselors have published in other professional journals, such as *Psicología Iberoamericana.*

The development of counseling in Mexico has been supported by NBCC, the mental health facilitators program, and the Mexican Association of Psychological Counseling and Psychotherapy (AMOPP). AMOPP is also the certification partner of NBCC Mexico and coordinates the national certification of Mexican counselors.

Counselor Professional Association

AMOPP was established in 2008 by UI students, alumni, and academics. It is the only association that currently represents Mexican counselors. Because few professionals identify themselves fully as counselors, the association decided to include psychotherapists and clinical psychologists as well, who until then had no national representative association. The association was created with the aim of promoting professional identity, interdisciplinary activities, and labor union protection among mental health professionals. To date, it has organized various training workshops, organized three international conferences, written a code of ethics, and established services for people who would otherwise have no access to counseling. In addition, AMOPP has worked for several years in conjunction with NBCC to create a national professional counselor certification. This certification, when completed, will distinguish trained mental health professionals and professional standards, along with an ethical code.

National Counselor Certification and Mental Health Facilitators

There are significant gaps in the ideal standards required to be a health professional in Mexico. Similarly, there is a serious problem with people claiming to be counselors (without having adequate skills and credentials), which results in unsuccessful counseling treatment and in some cases the client suffering significant harm. Currently national certification has clear standards of preparation, an ethical code, an examination, and supervised clinical practice to certify Mexican counselors. The certifying process began in late 2011.

The Mental Health Facilitator (MHF) program (Hinkle & Henderson, 2007), although not a training designed for professional counselors, has proved to be very attractive, with about half of the more than 100 MHFs in Mexico functioning as professional counselors. Many Mexican counselors have completed MHF training with the clear intention of becoming trainers of future generations of MHFs. This will clearly benefit segments of the Mexican population that have historically had no access to mental health services. For further information about the global MHF program, go to www.nbccinternational.org/mhf.

Conclusion

People are the real wealth of any nation; thus, positive human development expands the choices for people in Mexico, leading to more meaningful lives. Human development encompasses the creation of an environment in which people can develop their full potential and lead productive, creative lives in accordance with their needs and interests.

Fundamental to creating choices is building human capacity in Mexico, defined as leading long and healthy lives, having access to learning, and having the social services and resources needed to achieve a decent standard of living. Without these, many opportunities in life are inaccessible. Counseling in Mexico can help facilitate such human development and capacity building.

However, for this to become a reality, current issues and concerns need to be addressed, including

- human security and safety from the chronic threats to everyday life, such as hunger, unemployment, and social conflict
- social progress, including access to education, health and nutrition services, economic growth, and reducing inequalities
- efficiency of resources, as measured by growth and productivity directly benefiting the poor, women, and other marginalized groups
- participation in freedom, including human empowerment; democratic governance; gender equality; and civil and political rights and cultural freedom, particularly for socially excluded groups as defined by urban/rural location, gender, age, religion, ethnicity, or physical or mental parameters
- sustainability for future generations in social, economic, and ecological terms

These issues reveal the relevance of, importance of, and demand for counselors in Mexican society. The role of the professional counselor is growing, and clearly these individuals will be called on to be a force for positive change in contemporary Mexico. To have a successful impact, counselors will need to integrate various counseling approaches and techniques as well as stay up to date on clinical research that will inform counselor education and practice (Demichelis, 2005). With the support of organizations such as the University of Scranton and NBCC, the continued efforts to organize inter-American counseling conferences in Mexico, recent developments toward a national certification system, and the establishment of AMOPP, the advancement of counseling is steadily moving forward. Although the counseling profession is in the embryonic stage in Mexico, it appears to have a solid and promising future. Mexico will continue to promote professional counseling as well as the accreditation of more postgraduate counselor education programs.

References

Alcántara, L. (2009, January 13). Familia al estilo mexicano [Mexican-style family]. *El Universal.* Retrieved from http://www.eluniversal.com.mx/primera/32323.html

Comisión Económica para América Latina. (2008). *Panorama social de América Latina 2008* [2008 Social panorama of Latin America]. Santiago de Chile, Chile: Author.

Compañia de Jesús, Conferencia de Proviciales Jesuitas en América Latina. (2005, April). *Proyecto Educativo Común de la Compañía de Jesús en América Latina* [Common Educational Project of the Society of Jesus in Latin America] (Issue brief). Retrieved from http://cpalsj.org/publique/media/PEC.pdf

Consejo Nacional de Evaluación de la Politica de Desarrollo Social. (2009). *Informe de evaluación de la política de desarrollo social (2009) e informe sobre desarrollo humano (2008) gasto Público y desarrollo humano* [Assessment report of the Social Development Policy (2009) and Human Development Report (2008) public expense and human development]. Mexico City, Mexico: Author.

Demichelis, V. (2005). Integrative movement in psychological counseling: Select themes in psychological counseling. *Mexico, 2,* 15–26.

Hinkle, J. S., & Henderson, D. (2007). *The mental health facilitator.* Greensboro, NC: National Board for Certified Counselors.

Instituto Nacional de Estadística, Geografía e Informática. (2005). *Cuéntame. Población. Migración* [Tell me. Population migration]. Retrieved from http://cuentame.inegi.org.mx/poblacion/migracion.aspx?tema=P

Instituto Nacional de Estadística y Geografía. (2010). *Población de México: Migración* [Mexican population: Migration]. Retrieved from http://cuentame.inegi.org.mx/poblacion/migracion.aspx?tema=P

Instituto Nacional de Estadística y Geografía. (2011). Encuesta Nacional Sobre la Dinámica de las Relaciones en los Hogares [National Survey on the Dynamics of household relationships] ENDIREH (2006). In R. Castro & I. Casique (Coords.). (2008), *Violencia de género en las parejas mexicanas, Análisis de la ENDIREH México en mujeres.* Retrieved from http://www.inegi.org.mx/est/contenidos/Proyectos/Encuestas/Hogares/especiales/endireh/endireh2006/default.aspx

Instituto Nacional de Salud Pública. (2006). *Encuesta nacional de salud y nutrición 2006* [2006 Health and nutrition national survey]. Mexico City, Mexico: Author.

Medina-Mora, M. E., Borges, G., Lara, C., Benjet, C., Blanco, J., Fleiz-Bautista, C., ... Aguilar-Gaxiola, S. (2003). Prevalencia de Trastornos Mentales y Uso de Servicios: Resultados de la Encuesta Nacional de Epidemiología Psiquiátrica en México [Prevalence of mental disorders and use of services: Psychiatric epidemiology national survey results in Mexico]. *Salud Mental, 26*(4), 1–16.

Medina-Mora, M., & Villatoro, J. (2005). *The epidemiology of mental health in Mexico. Special report on mental health. Work summary: Mental health in Mexico: Perspectives and Challenges.* Mexico City, Mexico: Instituto National de Psiquiatría.

Portal, E. L., Suck, A. T., & Hinkle, J. S. (2010). Counseling in Mexico: History, current identity, and future trends. *Journal of Counseling & Development, 88,* 33–37.

Robles, O. (1942). *Natural philosophical research. The books of the spirits. Brother Alonso de la Veracruz.* Mexico City, Mexico: Imprenta Universitaria.

Robles, O. (1950). *Mexican philosophers of the 16th century. Contribution to the history of philosophy in Mexico.* Mexico City, Mexico: Editorial Manuel Porrúa.

Sandoval de Escurdia, J., & Muñoz, R. (2006). *La Salud Mental en México* [Mental health in Mexico]. Retrieved from http://www.salud.gob.mx/unidades/cdi/documentos/SaludMentalMexico.pdf

Sosa, M. A. (2010, September 8). CNDH: 40% de estudiantes sufre bullying [CNDH: 40% of students suffer bullying]. *Periódico El Universal.* Retrieved from http://www.eluniversal.com.mx/notas/707516.html

World Health Organization. (2001). *Informe sobre la Salud en el mundo 2001: Salud Mental, nuevos conocimientos, nuevas esperanzas* [2001 world health report: Mental health, new knowledge, new hopes]. Geneva, Switzerland: Author.

World Health Organization. (2005). *Mental health atlas* (Rev. ed.). Geneva, Switzerland: Author.

World Health Organization World Mental Health Survey Consortium. (2004). Prevalence, severity and unmet need for treatment of mental disorders in the World Health Organization World Mental Health Surveys. *Journal of the American Medical Association, 291,* 2581–2590.

• • •

Counseling in the United States 34

Marcheta Evans, Thelma Duffey,
Bradley T. Erford, and Samuel T. Gladding

The counseling profession in the United States has evolved through the years from a discipline of guidance and vocational counseling to one that emphasizes the importance of wellness, context, and culture. It shares a seat at the table with other mental health disciplines, providing support, direction, guidance, and advocacy to clients and students in diverse settings and practices. Counseling practice considers the needs of the whole person within their cultural and systemic context. Following is an abbreviated account of significant milestones and developments in counseling delineated by decade.

The Historical Development of Counseling

Counseling developed in the late 1890s and early 1900s out of a humanitarian concern to improve the lives of individuals and families adversely affected by the Industrial Revolution. The social welfare reform movement (now known as social justice), the spread of public education, and various changes in population makeup (e.g., the enormous influx of immigrants) also influenced the growth of this budding profession.

The National Vocational Guidance Association was established in 1913 to serve as the professional organization for counselors. This association, which was later renamed the National Career Development Association, was one of four organizations central to the merger and development of the American Personnel and Guidance Association (APGA). Four persons emerged as leaders in the development of counseling during the 1900s: Frank Parsons, Jesse B. Davis, Eli Weaver, and Clifford Beers. Each was instrumental in laying the profession's foundation in distinct ways (Gladding & Newsome, 2010; Herr & Erford, 2011).

In the 1930s, E. G. Williamson generated the first counseling theory. A counselor-centered theory, it argued that the task of the counselor was to ascertain a deficiency in the client and then to prescribe a procedure to rectify the problem. This was akin to the medical model, which supports the role of practitioner as expert. Also in the 1930s, the government established the U.S. Employment Service, which published the first edition of the *Dictionary of Occupational Titles,* a major source of career information for counseling practitioners.

One decade later, Carl Rogers published *Counseling and Psychotherapy,* which challenged Williamson's counselor-centered approach as well as major tenets of Freudian psychoanalysis. Rogers emphasized the importance of the client in the healing process by developing a client-centered approach to counseling. This influence remains today.

The 1940s and 1950s brought two important legislative acts. The George-Barden Act of 1946 granted stipends and paid internships for counseling students. Later, the National Defense Education Act of 1958 provided funding to train school counselors. The goal of the National Defense Education Act was to identify high school students with math and science capabilities and encourage these students to attend universities and major in the hard sciences. Also, this legislation launched the school counseling profession into prominence in American education (Tang & Erford, 2010).

During the 1950s, APGA was formed out of the Council of Guidance and Personnel Associations. The Council of Guidance and Personnel Associations was a loose confederation of organizations primarily concerned with educational and vocational guidance. Also during this decade, new theories of helping emerged, including rational emotive behavior therapy, transactional analysis, and cognitive therapy.

The Vietnam War, the civil rights movement, and the women's movement influenced counseling in the 1960s. Each stirred passions and highlighted mental health needs within society. Many counselors attempted to address the needs that evolved from these societal events. This focus brought on the advent of humanistic counseling theories and the phenomenal growth of the group movement. Furthermore, community mental health centers were born as a result of legislation such as the 1963 Community Mental Health Centers Act. Finally, as counseling as a profession developed, APGA published a code of ethics for counselors in 1961 and the Education Resources Information Center Clearinghouse on Counseling and Personnel Services was founded in 1966.

The 1970s saw the emergence of new initiatives related to diversity, such as working with women, minorities, and people with disabilities. These initiatives were in part the result of Title IX, affirmative action, and legislation for persons with disabilities. As counseling as a profession continued to develop, the Association of Counselor Educators and Supervisors (ACES), a division of APGA, outlined the original standards for a master's degree in counseling in 1973. Also, the 1960s and 1970s saw a booming growth in the number of school counselors, to the point that every state department of education had some regulation endorsing or requiring that school counselors be included in a multidisciplinary services team.

The diversification of counseling set the stage for specialized training as a curriculum in counselor education programs. It also prompted the development of new counseling concepts, such as the idea of the *community counselor*—a counselor who could function in multidimensional roles regardless of employment setting. This decade also saw the development of helping skills programs that concentrated on relationship and communication skills and saw the passage of the first state counseling licensure law in Virginia in 1976. In 1977, ACES approved guidelines for doctoral preparation in counseling. During the 1970s, APGA membership increased to almost 40,000.

The 1980s witnessed expansive growth in counseling as a profession. In 1981, the Council for Accreditation of Counseling and Related Educational Programs (CACREP) was formed as an affiliate organization of APGA and refined the standards first proposed by ACES. Complementary to the work of CACREP, the National Board for Certified Counselors (NBCC), formed in 1982, began to certify counselors nationally. To address the changing demographics of its membership, APGA was renamed the American Association for Counseling and Development (AACD). An international counseling honor society, Chi Sigma Iota, was also formed during this time. In addition, liability insurance policies, new counseling specialty publications, legal defense funds, legislative initiatives, and a variety of other membership services became available to AACD members. A significant milestone of the 1980s involved developing the American Association of State Counseling Boards. This association was formed to be legally responsible for the registration, certification, and licensing of counselors within its jurisdictions in the United States. Also, school counselors were being called on to provide mental health services in schools to address the emotional impact accompanying societal and cultural transitions. As a result, the 1980s saw a rise in the number of comprehensive developmental school counseling programs to address student needs for preventive, developmental, and intervention services (Tang & Erford, 2010).

A salient development exemplifying the diversity within counseling in the 1980s was the evolution of AACD division membership. The focus of these divisions includes group work, counselor education, humanistic education, human growth and development, measurement and development, religious and value issues, employment and career development, rehabilitation, multicultural concerns, addiction and offender work, and military personnel (Gladding & Newsome, 2010).

The new decade of the 1990s brought with it significant changes that broadened the landscape of counseling. First was the renaming of the AACD to the American Counseling Association (ACA) in 1992. As the profession matured and evolved, the new name better reflected the membership and mission of the organization. Also in 1992, counseling as a primary mental health profession was included for the first time in the health care human resource statistics compiled by the Center for Mental Health Services and the National Institute of Mental Health. In 1997, the Association for Lesbian, Gay, Bisexual and Transgender Issues in Counseling was formed to focus on the needs of sexual minorities. By the beginning of the 21st century, there were approximately 100,000 counselors in the United States.

One of the significant markers of the 1990s was Sue, Arredondo, and McDavis's (1992) writing of the multicultural counseling competencies and standards. Although these competencies primarily applied to counseling with people of color, they set the stage for a larger debate regarding the nature of multicultural counseling. The 1990s also brought with it a focus on health care and an increase in the number and influence of managed health care organizations. Conglomerates emerged, many counselors became providers, and a new emphasis on legislation connected with these organizations forced counselors to become increasingly informed and active as legislative proponents (Barstow, 1998). In addition, there was a renewed focus within the decade on counseling issues related to the whole person. Counselors became more aware of social factors important to the development and maintenance of mental disorders and health.

In 1997, the American School Counselor Association (ASCA) developed the National Standards for School Counseling Programs (Campbell & Dahir, 1997). These standards served as the basis for comprehensive developmental curricular programming across the country but lacked a framework for implementation. ASCA addressed this need in 2003 by constructing the ASCA National Model (ASCA, 2003, 2005), which provided structure for planning, developing, implementing, and evaluating a comprehensive school counseling program.

The 2000s were an equally compelling decade for the profession. Counseling formally celebrated its 50th anniversary as a profession under the umbrella of the ACA in 2002. Along with this celebration came a realization that topics, issues, and concerns of the early 21st century would most likely change with the needs of clients and society. A new ACA division, the Association for Creativity in Counseling, was established in 2004 to bring greater focus to the innovation and resourcefulness of the counselor and the role of creativity, diversity, and relational development within the counseling profession (T. Duffey, 2007).

The 2000s revealed a heightened focus on the changing roles of men and women, innovations in media and technology, poverty, homelessness, trauma, loneliness, and aging, among other topics, and captured counseling's attention as the new century began. Among the most pressing topics as counseling celebrates its 60th anniversary in 2012 are matters of violence, trauma, and crisis; managed care; wellness; social justice; technology; leadership; and identity.

The Current Status of Counseling

More than 665,500 jobs were held by counselors in 2008, and there is a projection of 782,200 jobs in the counseling field by 2018, suggesting an 18% increase. Counseling specializations include school/vocational (275,800), rehabilitation (129,000), mental health (113,300), substance abuse and behavior disorder (86,100), marriage and family therapy (27,300), and work in other counseling settings (33,400; Bureau of Labor Statistics, 2011).

Following are the median annual salaries of counselors in 2008: educational, vocational and school counselors, $51,050; substance and behavior disorder counselors, $37,030; mental health counselors, $36,810; rehabilitation counselors, $30,930; marriage and family therapists, $44,590. Counselors well established in private practice usually earn the highest rate of pay, which can range from $50 to $150 an hour (Bureau of Labor Statistics, 2011).

Counselor Education

The minimum academic requirement for becoming a professional counselor is a master's degree. Currently the master's degree can range from 36 to 60 semester hours of training, with most accredited programs requiring a 48 semester hour minimum.

Accreditation

CACREP is the primary accrediting body for counseling programs. In 2009, CACREP revised its accrediting standards. Accreditation can be attained in the following programs: addiction counseling; career counseling; clinical mental health counseling; marriage, couple, and family counseling; school counseling; and student affairs and college counseling. In addition, CACREP accredits doctoral programs in counselor education and supervision.

Accredited master's programs range from a minimum of 48 semester (or 72 quarter) hours of study to 60 semester (or 90 quarter) hours. A doctoral program typically requires a master's degree culminating in a minimum of 96 semester hours or 144 quarter hours of graduate-level course work (CACREP, 2009).

Master's counseling students must demonstrate proficiency in eight common core curricular experiences and knowledge areas for competency. These are professional orientation and ethical practice, social and cultural diversity, human growth and development, career development, helping relationships, group work, assessment, and research and evaluation. In addition, each student is required to complete a practicum and internship that encompass a minimum of 700 clock hours of clinical experience.

In addition, the Council on Rehabilitation Education accredits academic counseling graduate programs. These programs enroll students who work with individuals with disabilities in a variety of settings and positions. Council on Rehabilitation Education master's-level programs require a minimum of 48 semester hours or 72 quarter hours.

Certification and Licensure

NBCC is the primary certifying organization for professional counselors. This organization grants a general practice credential, National Certified Counselor, and offers other specialty credentials in mental health, school, and addiction counseling.

Licensure requirements vary greatly from state to state. Every state in the United States has a licensure process that typically requires a written examination and the completion of clinical hours under the supervision of an approved supervisor.

Cultural and Diversity Issues

The demographics of the United States are changing dramatically, and the United States is considered one of the most diverse nations in the world. In 2010, the U.S. Census Bureau noted a 9.7% increase in the population, which totaled 308.7 million people. Also, this report highlighted the fact that more than half of this growth was due to increases in the Hispanic population. In addition, more women than ever before participate in the workforce (Bureau of Labor Statistics, 2011). The life expectancy of people living in the United States is also on the rise. It should not be surprising that Sue and Sue (2008) reported three major cultural trends affecting counselors in their work: the graying of the workforce, the feminization of the workforce, and the changing complexion of the workforce. Each of these cultural factors must be considered when offering services and training new counselors. In addition, the United States has moved toward a more affirming counseling philosophy and practice in work with sexual minority clients (Dworkin & Pope, 2012). There is a proliferation of scholarly research focusing specifically on the needs of this diverse segment of the U.S. population, resulting in more individuals from the lesbian, gay, bisexual, and transgender community seeking counseling services (Page, 2007). Furthermore, CACREP (2009) requires that the training of future counselors incorporate a specific emphasis on working with diverse sexual populations. Finally, the *ACA Code of Ethics* stresses the ethical importance of counselors being culturally competent when working with diverse populations (ACA, 2005).

Visible racial/ethnic minority groups have historically been hesitant to seek counseling, in part because of stigma and discriminatory practices within mental health professions (Sue & Sue, 2008). However, this stigma seems to be decreasing with the inclusion of multicultural training, which is now focused on counselor cultural awareness, knowledge, and skill development. More people of diverse ages, sexual orientations, and backgrounds are seeking counseling services.

Unfortunately, for most of their history in the United States, counseling theory, application, and techniques have ignored cultural differences or treated diversity as unimportant. Today important cultural differentiations are being embedded into theories applied to every environment, diversity is celebrated in all settings (especially the classroom), and the counseling profession no longer embraces culturally biased deficit models. Today multicultural counseling competence is a key training component in counselor education. Behaviors and attitudes are shaped by racial and ethnic traditions, resulting in important cultural distinctions in decision making and learning. In fact, multicultural counseling is now known as the Fourth Wave of Counseling.

This is salient given that individuals in the United States continue to experience discrimination, prejudice, economic hardship, and social stigmatization. Environmental stressors, such as the economy, homelessness, job loss, terrorism, war, and natural disaster, create havoc in the lives of many people. In these cases and others, counselors in the United States are becoming ready resources. It is fitting then that counselors consider the unique societal norms and practices that may influence their work. Dominant among these is society's reluctance to accept and capacity to endure painful emotions. According to Greenspan (2003), a significant U.S. cultural norm involves the societal avoidance of painful feelings. In fact, Greenspan described the United States as an emotion-phobic society. Many people are socialized to rationalize painful feelings, project them onto others, practice blame rather than genuinely self-reflect, and in some cases assume the mantra that "you fake it 'til you make it." These responses often lead to addictions, which are prevalent cultural concerns (T. Duffey, 2005).

Individuals also suffer from privilege. Christopher Lasch (1978) described the plight of many Americans in his seminal book *The Culture of Narcissism*. He spoke to the consequences of living in an increasingly self-absorbed society, one influenced by power, consumerism, and individualism. Harold Kushner (1986) wrote in his bestseller *When All You've Ever Wanted Isn't Enough: The Search for a Life That Matters* that oppressed and disenfranchised people are not alone in their suffering. People who may appear to be the epitome of success are also at risk.

Young people are particularly vulnerable to this attitude of excess and materialism. M. Duffey and Duffey (2005) wrote how members of Generation Y are keenly influenced by the media's fascination with the daily lives and celebrated status of young people enjoying unearned gains. Young people may become desensitized to the realities of hard work and feel entitled to privileges they may never hold. Regardless of the many advantages that are available to them, young people who seek to emulate this lifestyle of excess and unearned fame risk feeling restless, unfulfilled, and isolated (M. Duffey & Duffey, 2005).

Certainly a culture's advantages can at times be its greatest challenges. Counselors can assist people to navigate their concerns, determine what is meaningful in their lives, and develop a genuine capacity for understanding their own experiences and the experiences of others. Various counseling theories can support this work. This is particularly salient because with advances in health care, people are living longer. Many older adults question their place in the world and struggle to maintain an identity of worth in a culture that often idealizes youth. Members of the sandwich generation, also known as baby boomers, care concurrently for aging parents and growing children. Many question how to balance self-care with the growing demands on their time and finances. Divorce also creates challenges for families. In addition, increasing numbers of baby boomers are moving into postretirement life stages. Many experience losses that come with this transition. These include loss of vocation, of contact with historically significant colleagues, of physical strength, and of mental acuteness.

Best Counseling Practices

Several counseling theories are effectively used within the U.S. culture. Psychodynamic theories focus on insight, whereas cognitive theories challenge clients to reconsider faulty beliefs. Behavioral theories focus on patterns of reinforcement, whereas existential theories consider issues of meaning making and encourage clients to make sense of their experiences. Family systems theories are also popular within U.S. culture. In addition, multicultural theory and relational-cultural theory specifically address the developmental and contextual frameworks promoted within the counseling profession. These last two theories directly account for the important dynamics of context, culture, gender, power, and privilege, variables directly related to U.S. cultural experiences.

School counselors use evidence-based practices to ensure that interventions with students have demonstrated empirical support. Unfortunately, until recently, little cogent empirical evidence existed that substantially supported school counseling services. However, a recent meta-analysis on school counseling outcome research (Whiston, Tai, Rahardja, & Eder, 2010) and qualitative synthesis by Whiston and Quinby (2010) integrated about 50 years of research and indicated that school counseling interventions generally yield small (d = .20) to medium (d = .50) effect sizes. Although this may not sound particularly impressive, because these effects are applied across millions of school-age children annually, the implications are actually quite profound and there is much cause for optimism.

Whiston, Sexton, and Lasoff (1998) analyzed school-based career and educational planning interventions and found similar support for the academic and career interventions that school counselors provide. Likewise, the positive effects of fully implemented, comprehensive school counseling programs (e.g., group guidance, small-group counseling, consultation, advocacy, individual planning, individual counseling) on academic achievement, career, and personal and social development are well documented in the school counseling literature (Brigman & Campbell, 2003; Carrell & Carrell, 2006; Lapan, Gysbers, & Kayson, 2007; Lapan, Gysbers, & Petroski, 2001; Lapan, Gysbers, & Sun, 1997; McGannon, Carey, & Dimmitt, 2005; Nelson, Gardner, & Fox, 1998; Sink, 2005; Sink & Stroh, 2003; Whiston & Wachter, 2008).

Finally, rigorous curricular planning and the preparation of all students to access college or advanced technology training have been strongly advocated by the Education Trust (2011) and College Board (2011). Although few outcome studies have been conducted to determine the effectiveness of this philosophical shift, it is clear that an increasing number of minority students are applying to and being accepted to begin postsecondary study at 2-year and 4-year colleges. Indeed, African Americans are gaining acceptance to postsecondary educational opportunities at higher than per capita rates; however, (6-year) graduation rates from 4-year colleges and universities for minorities are only about 40% compared to greater than 60% for nonminority students.

Counseling Contexts

Although individual counseling is a popular option for clients, family members and loved ones also participate in counseling sessions. The decision to involve family members depends on the counselor's theoretical orientation, the needs of the client, and the counseling goals. Counselors using a family systems perspective encourage multiclient participation, which offers a unique context that one person alone cannot provide.

The use of technology and social media in counseling practice is also becoming increasingly popular (Haberstroh, 2009). This is a constantly evolving process, and the ACA established a cyberspace task force in 2010 to initiate discussions on the ethical use of technology in counseling. This concern is also to be addressed in revisions to the *ACA Code of Ethics.* Message boards are gaining popularity and assist clients in connecting with people undergoing similar situations. Local labor market information is available on the Internet, and career counselors provide consumers with valuable career and workplace information.

Counseling Settings and Interventions

Counselors in the United States work in various settings, including agencies, hospitals, hospice, schools, private practice settings, homes, and natural surroundings. Regardless of where they work, counselors everywhere engage their clients through talk and other innovative means. Art, drama, metaphors, dance, music, and poetry are just a few of the resources available. Textbooks relating to creativity in counseling serve as guides for counseling professionals interested in using innovative media in their work (T. Duffey, 2005; Gladding, 2011; Jacobs, 1994; Rubin, 2008). Counselors are called to consider the contextual, multicultural, and relational factors that affect their clients' experiences. Indeed, focusing on these issues is a fundamental identifying quality of professional counselors.

The Future

In 2005, the presidential team of the American Association of State Counseling Boards approached the presidential team of the ACA to collaborate on issues of portability for licensure. At that point, the requirements, standards, and titles for each state licensing board varied. This variance was perceived as hindering the goal of portability and further fragmenting the profession. When the groups met, members discussed broadening their scope beyond the portability issue. A workgroup was established to address specific professional issues and identify a core professional definition. The task force, identified as 20/20: A Vision for the Future of Counseling, had grown from the original 29 organizations to 31 organizational participants as of 2011. The goal of the committee's work is to collectively define who counselors are as a profession and provide structure for how they present themselves as a unified voice. Representatives from all ACA divisions and regions, CACREP, Chi Sigma Iota, NBCC, the Commission on Rehabilitation Counselor Certification, and the Council on Rehabilitation Education participate in this work.

20/20 targeted seven professional consensus areas: (a) strengthening identity, (b) presenting counselors as one profession, (c) improving public perception and recognition and advocating for professional issues, (d) creating licensing portability, (e) expanding and promoting the research base of professional counseling, (f) focusing on students and prospective students, and (g) promoting client welfare and advocacy. The work of 20/20 resulted in a consensus definition of counseling in 2009: "Counseling is a professional relationship that empowers diverse individuals, families, and groups to accomplish mental health, wellness, education, and career goals" (20/20: A Vision for the Future of Counseling Committee, 2012). The 20/20 task force's next goal involves addressing the issue of licensure portability among states. However, each identified area continues to be a critical element of the development of counseling as a profession in the United States.

Additional areas affecting the future of counseling in the United States include the ACA's focus on working with immigrants and refugees, the need to engage in evidence-based practices and to provide evidence of effectiveness and accountability, the evolution of technology and social media and their impact on the counseling relationship, student-to-counselor ratios, the development of competing accrediting and certification organizations, crisis response planning, international collaborations and development, the need of school counselors to focus on college access and career transitions for students, and the globalization of the profession.

References

American Counseling Association. (2005). *ACA code of ethics.* Alexandria, VA: Author.

American School Counselor Association. (2003). *The ASCA national model: A framework for school counseling programs* (1st ed.). Alexandria, VA: Author.

American School Counselor Association. (2005). *The ASCA national model: A framework for school counseling programs* (2nd ed.). Alexandria, VA: Author.

Barstow, S. (1998, June). Managed care debate heats up in Congress. *Counseling Today, 1,* 26.

Brigman, G., & Campbell, C. (2003). Helping students improve academic achievement and school success behavior. *Professional School Counseling, 7,* 91–99.

Bureau of Labor Statistics. (2011). *Occupational outlook handbook, 2010-2011 edition.* Retrieved from http://stats.bls.gov/oco/ocos067.htm

Campbell, C. A., & Dahir, C. A. (1997). *The ASCA national standards for school counseling programs.* Alexandria, VA: American School Counselor Association.

Carrell, S. E., & Carrell, S. A. (2006). Do lower student to counselor ratios reduce school disciplinary problems? *Contributions to Economic Analysis & Policy, 5*(1), 1–24.

College Board. (2011). *About us: The College Board.* Retrieved from http://www.collegeboard.com/about/index.html

Council for Accreditation of Counseling and Related Educational Programs. (2009). *2009 CACREP accreditation manual.* Alexandria, VA: Author.

Duffey, M., & Duffey, T. (2005). The American reincarnation of the superfluous experience: Finding meaning in Generation Y. In T. Duffey (Ed.), *Creative interventions in grief and loss therapy: When the music stops, a dream dies* (pp. 225–235). New York, NY: Haworth Press.

Duffey, T. (2005). When the music stops: Releasing the dream. In T. Duffey (Ed.), *Creative interventions in grief and loss therapy: When the music stops, a dream dies* (pp. 1–24). New York, NY: Haworth Press.

Duffey, T. (2007). Promoting relational competencies in counselor education through creativity and relational-cultural theory. *Journal of Creativity in Mental Health, 2*(1), 47–59. doi:10.1300/J456v02n01_05

Dworkin, S. H., & Pope, M. (2012). *Casebook for counseling lesbian, gay, bisexual, and transgender persons and their families.* Alexandria, VA: American Counseling Association.

Education Trust. (2011). *About the Education Trust.* Retrieved from http://www.edtrust.org/dc/about

Gladding, S. T. (2011). *The creative arts in counseling* (4th ed.). Alexandria, VA: American Counseling Association.

Gladding, S. T., & Newsome, D. R. (2010). *Clinical mental health counseling in community and agency settings* (3rd ed.). Upper Saddle River, NJ: Pearson.

Greenspan, M. (2003). *Healing through the dark emotions: The wisdom of grief, fear, and despair.* Boston, MA: Shambala.

Haberstroh, S. (2009). Strategies and resources for the practice of online counseling. *Journal of Professional Counseling: Practice, Theory, and Research, 37*(2), 1–20.

Herr, E. L., & Erford, B. T. (2011). Historical roots and future issues. In B. T. Erford (Ed.), *Transforming the school counseling profession* (3rd ed., pp. 19–43). Columbus, OH: Pearson Merrill.

Jacobs, E. E. (1994). *Impact therapy.* Odessa, FL: Psychological Assessment Resources.

Kushner, H. (1986). *When all you've ever wanted isn't enough: The search for a life that matters.* New York, NY: Fireside.

Lapan, R. T., Gysbers, N. C., & Kayson, K. (2007). *How implementing comprehensive guidance programs improves academic achievement for all Missouri students.* Jefferson City: Missouri Department of Elementary and Secondary Education, Division of Career Education.

Lapan, R. T., Gysbers, N. C., & Petroski, G. (2001). Helping 7th graders be safe and academically successful: A statewide study of the impact of comprehensive guidance programs. *Journal of Counseling & Development, 79,* 320–330.

Lapan, R. T., Gysbers, N. C., & Sun, Y. (1997). The impact of more fully implemented guidance programs on the school experiences of high school students: A statewide evaluation study. *Journal of Counseling & Development, 75,* 292–302.

Lasch, C. (1978). *The culture of narcissism.* New York, NY: Norton.

McGannon, W., Carey, J., & Dimmitt, C. (2005). *The current status of school counseling outcome research.* Amherst: University of Massachusetts, Amherst, Center for School Counseling Outcome Research.

Nelson, D. E., Gardner, J. L., & Fox, D. G. (1998). *An evaluation of the comprehensive guidance program in Utah public schools.* Salt Lake City: Utah State Office of Education.

Page, E. (2007). Bisexual women's and men's experiences of psychotherapy. In B. A. Firenstein (Ed.), *Becoming visible: Counseling bisexuals across the lifespan* (pp. 52–71). New York, NY: Columbia University Press.

Rubin, L. (2008). *Popular culture in counseling, psychotherapy, and play-based interventions.* Jefferson, NC: McFarland.

Sink, C. A. (2005). Comprehensive school counseling programs and academic achievement—A rejoinder to Brown and Trusty. *Professional School Counseling, 9,* 9–12.

Sink, C. A., & Stroh, H. R. (2003). Raising achievement test scores of early elementary school students through comprehensive school counseling programs. *Professional School Counseling, 6,* 350–364.

Sue, D. W., Arredondo, P., & McDavis, R. J. (1992). Multicultural counseling competencies and standards: A call to the profession. *Journal of Counseling & Development, 70,* 477–486.

Sue, D. W., & Sue, D. (2008). *Counseling the culturally diverse: Theory and practice* (5th ed.). Hoboken, NJ: Wiley.

Tang, M., & Erford, B. T. (2010). The history of school counseling. In B. T. Erford (Ed.), *Professional school counseling: A handbook of theories, programs, and practices* (2nd ed., pp. 9–22). Austin, TX: PRO-ED.

20/20: A Vision for the Future of Counseling Committee. (2012). *Consensus definition of counseling.* Retrieved from http://www.counseling.org/20-20/definition.aspx

U.S. Census Bureau. (2010). *Population change: 2000 to 2010.* Retrieved from http://2010.census.gov/2010census/data/

Whiston, S. C., & Quinby, R. F. (2010). Outcomes research on school counseling interventions and programs. In B. T. Erford (Ed.), *Transforming the school counseling profession* (3rd ed., pp. 58–69). Columbus, OH: Pearson Merrill.

Whiston, S. C., Sexton, T. L., & Lasoff, D. L. (1998). Career intervention outcome: A replication and extension. *Journal of Counseling Psychology, 45,* 150–165.

Whiston, S. C., Tai, W. L., Rahardja, D., & Eder, K. (2010). School counseling outcome: A meta-analytic examination of interventions. *Journal of Counseling & Development, 89,* 37–55.

Whiston, S. C., & Wachter, C. (2008). *School counseling, student achievement, and dropout rates: Student outcome research in the state of Indiana.* Indianapolis: Indiana State Department of Education.

• • •

Counseling in Oceania Countries

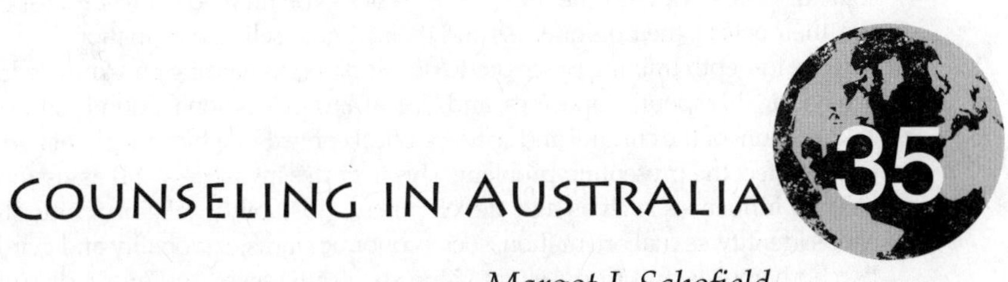

Counseling in Australia

Margot J. Schofield

The development of community-based counseling in Australia began formally with the establishment of the National Marriage Guidance Council in 1948 to address an increased awareness of marriage and relationship issues following World War II. This led to the subsequent development of a professional association for marriage guidance counselors in the 1960s that evolved into the Australian Association of Relationship Counsellors. The development of other more specialized forms of counseling followed a similar pattern of development, largely over the second half of the 20th century. For instance, although the early beginnings of school psychology go back to the early 20th century, the professional development of school counseling and psychology occurred post-1945.

There was a rapid expansion in the number of diverse professional bodies across the spectrum of counseling and psychotherapy in the 1970s and 1980s. State-based general counseling associations emerged from 1972 onward, and by 2008 there were counseling associations in all states and territories of Australia with the exception of the Northern Territory (Schofield, 2008a, 2008b). Associations were also established for specific areas of counseling, such as rehabilitation counseling and loss and grief counseling in 1976, family therapy in 1979, guidance and counseling in 1985, Christian counseling in 1986, career counseling in 1989, and transpersonal counseling in 1993; a national association of generalist counselors was established in 1998 (Schofield, 2008b).

As a result of the proliferation of professional bodies for both counseling and psychotherapy in Australia, and because of concerns about a lack of agreed-on standards, there was a clearly identified need to develop a more unified voice for the field in the 1990s. A key feature of the profession at this time was a widespread desire to combine counseling and psychotherapy within one overarching professional structure. This led to the formation of a federation of professional associations, the Psychotherapy and Counselling Federation of Australia (PACFA), in 1998. This occurred after 3 years of intensive consultation and consensus building among more than 40 professional associations and a large number of counseling and psychotherapy training bodies (Schofield, Grant, Holmes, & Barletta, 2006). PACFA was established as an inclusive, consensus-based, and widely representative peak body that sought to develop and advance psychotherapy and counseling through education, research, and self-regulation of the profession. It aimed to act as a peak body, establish and monitor standards, maintain a register of practitioners, support development and cohesion in the profession, and work with member associations to protect and serve the public.

Although counseling and psychotherapy have maintained more separate identities in many parts of the world, particularly for regulatory purposes, in Australia the drive to hold the two groups together was supported by an examination of definitions that revealed a broad overlap between activities. A broad consensus-gaining process in Australia defined the combined area of professional practice as represented by PACFA in the following way:

> Professional psychotherapy/counselling:
>
> - Utilise counselling, psychotherapeutic, and psychological theories, and a set of advanced interpersonal skills which emphasise facilitating clients' change processes in the therapeutic context. This work with client processes is based on an ethos of respect for clients, their values, their beliefs, their uniqueness and their right to self-determination.
> - Require in-depth training processes to develop understanding and knowledge about human behaviour, therapeutic capacities, and ethical and professional boundaries.
> - Take account of the cultural and socio-political context in which the client lives and how these factors affect the presenting problem. This includes awareness and assessment of social and cultural influences such as age, development, (dis)ability, religion, cultural identity, Indigenous identity, sexual orientation, socioeconomic status, nationality and gender. Professional Psychotherapists and Counsellors value such differences and avoid discrimination on the basis of these aspects of identity.
> - May involve intervening with current problems, immediate crises, or long-term difficulties. The work may be short-term or long-term, depending on the nature of the difficulties, and may involve working with individuals, couples, families or groups.
> - Counselling and Psychotherapy occur in a variety of contexts in the public and private sectors.
> - Regard ongoing clinical supervision, professional development, self-awareness, self-development, self-monitoring and self-examination as central to effective and ethical practice. Such practices lead to enhanced capacity to utilise the self of the practitioner effectively in the therapeutic relationship.
>
> Although Counselling and Psychotherapy overlap considerably, there are also recognised differences. While the work of Counsellors and Psychotherapists with clients may be of considerable depth, the focus of Counselling is more likely to be on specific problems, changes in life adjustments and fostering clients' wellbeing. Psychotherapy is more concerned with the restructuring of the personality or self and the development of insight. At advanced levels of training, Counselling has a greater overlap with Psychotherapy than at foundation levels. (PACFA, 2012a)

Following its founding in 1998, PACFA's membership reached 43 member associations comprising more than 3,000 members by 2005. By 2012, however, through both amalgamation and attrition, there were 31 member associations of counseling and psychotherapy (PACFA, 2012b). The member associations represent a variety of counseling and psychotherapy approaches that are organized into nine theoretically oriented sections on the PACFA Register, as shown in Table 35.1.

There are currently five large professional counseling associations that are not affiliated with PACFA: the Australian Counselling Association, the Australian Guidance and Counselling Association (AGCA), the Australian Society of Rehabilitation Counsellors, the College of Counselling Psychologists of the Australian Psychological Society, and the Rehabilitation Counselling Association of Australia. Large psychotherapy associations that are not members of PACFA include the Australian and New Zealand Art Therapy Association, the Australian Association for Cognitive and Behaviour Therapy, the Australian Psychoanalytic Society, and the Psychoanalytic Psychotherapy Association of Australasia.

The Current Status of Counseling

A key task in the process of professionalization is to document the profile of the workforce. This is particularly challenging for unregulated professions such as counseling, as there is

TABLE 35.1
Psychotherapy and Counselling Federation of Australia Member Associations

Theoretical Section and Associations
General counselling and psychotherapy
Australian Association of Transactional Analysis
Association of Personal Counsellors, Inc.
Association of Solution Oriented Counsellors and Hypnotherapists of Australia
Australian Association of Buddhist Counsellors and Psychotherapists
Australian Hypnotherapists Association
Christian Counsellors Association of Australia, Inc.
Clinical Counsellors Association, Inc.
Counselling and Psychotherapy Association Canberra and Region
Counselling Association of South Australia, Inc.
Counsellors and Psychotherapists Association of New South Wales, Inc.
Counsellors and Psychotherapists Association of Victoria, Inc.
Professional Counselling Association of Tasmania
Psychotherapists and Counsellors Association of Western Australia
Queensland Counsellors Association, Inc.
Body-oriented psychotherapy
Australian Radix Body Centered Psychotherapy Association
Australian Somatic Psychotherapy Association
Counselling and psychotherapy educators
Australian Association of Buddhist Counsellors and Psychotherapists
Society of Counselling and Psychotherapy Educators
Experiential therapy
Association of Transpersonal and Emotional Release Counsellors
Association of Soul Centered Psychotherapists, Inc.
Australian and New Zealand Psychodrama Association, Inc.
Australian Radix Body Centered Psychotherapy Association
Gestalt Australia New Zealand
Melbourne Institute for Experiential and Creative Arts Therapy
Music and Imagery Association of Australia
Expressive arts therapies
Dance Therapy Association of Australia
Melbourne Institute for Experiential and Creative Arts Therapy
Family/relationship therapy
Australian Association of Family Therapy
Australian Association of Relationship Counsellors
Queensland Association for Family Therapy
Hypnotherapy
Association of Solution Oriented Counsellors and Hypnotherapists of Australia
Australian Hypnotherapists Association
Integrative psychodynamic psychotherapy
Australian and New Zealand Association of Psychotherapy (New South Wales)
Australian Somatic Psychotherapy Association
Melbourne College of Contemporary Psychotherapy
Psychoanalysis/psychoanalytic psychotherapy
Australian and New Zealand Society of Jungian Analysts
Australian Centre for Psychoanalysis

no complete counselor database. Such information can inform future workforce planning, service provision, and professional development. Although there have been no comprehensive workforce studies of counselors in Australia, data from a number of sources provide part of the picture required for more comprehensive planning.

Types and Demographic Characteristics of Counselors

National occupational data collected in the Australian Census, based on Australian and New Zealand Standard Classification of Occupations categories, report a total of 14,848 counselors and psychotherapists across the health and community services sectors in 2006 (Australian Institute of Health and Welfare, 2009). In the health services sector, there were 1,681 general counselors, 1,380 drug and alcohol counselors, and 1,378 psychotherapists (n = 4,439). In the community services sector, there were 4,088 counselors, 2,923 student counselors, 1,298 family and marriage counselors, and 2,110 rehabilitation counselors (n = 10,419). These figures likely underestimate the actual number of counselors because some people who work primarily as counselors may identify in the census under another professional identity, such as psychologist, social worker, nurse, or teacher. For instance, the 2006 census recorded 12,066 psychologists and 12,437 social workers. By 2010, the Psychology Board of Australia had registered nearly 29,000 psychologists, highlighting that the census data reflected a considerable underestimate (Psychology Board of Australia, 2010).

Another source of counselor employment data is the Australian Government Department of Education Employment and Workplace Relations (DEEWR), which estimated the number of employed counselors at 16,900, with a median age of 47 years, and 78% being female (DEEWR, 2011). DEEWR also noted that counselors were less likely than the total job market to be in full-time employment, with only 63.5% working full time compared with 70.5% in the total job market. Earnings for counselors are comparable with those for social workers but considerably below those for psychologists, who tend to have more postgraduate qualifications (DEEWR, 2011).

A number of recent studies of the counseling profession in Australia have provided more detailed profiles of segments of the profession. Pelling (2005) profiled the membership of one of the national counseling bodies, the Australian Counselling Association. The sample of 241 counselors was largely female (76%), with a median age of 50, and the majority lived in urban areas (69%). In another survey, a sample of 317 Australian counselors who advertised in the Australian Yellow Pages as personal, marriage, or family counselors were 70% female, with an average age of 50, and 86% were Caucasian (Pelling, Brear, & Lau, 2006).

Among 316 therapists in a 2004 workforce study of professional associations affiliated with the peak body PACFA, participants reported a mean age of 53, and 74% were female (Schofield, 2008a). Their primary employment titles were counselor (42%), psychotherapist (33%), other health professional (11%), professional in a nonhealth sector (5%), and other (9%). Around 40% were also members of other professional groups: 11% were social workers, 10% psychologists, 9% nurses, and 7% allied or complementary health professionals. The average length of practice was 13 years.

The most comprehensive workforce study to date was an online survey of 1,004 counselors and psychotherapists drawn from all known professional bodies (Schofield & Roedel, 2012). Respondents had a mean age of 53, and 77% were female. The primary employment title was counselor (61%), psychologist (17%), social worker (5%), nurse (3%), medical practitioner (2%), and other (12%; Orlinsky, Schofield, Schroder, & Kazantzis, 2011).

Qualifications

Qualifications and level of counseling experience vary across different studies and data sources. DEEWR (2011) reported that 21% of counselors have a postgraduate qualification, 39% a bachelor's degree, 13% an advanced diploma or diploma (1–2 years postschooling), 10% a certificate, and 11% no postschool qualification. A 2008 national survey found that 64% had a postgraduate qualification, 26% a graduate degree, and 7% a diploma (Schofield & Roedel, 2012) and that the average length of practice was 14 years (Orlinsky et al., 2011).

Work Settings

Counseling was historically undertaken primarily in community-based counseling agencies, often set up by mainstream Christian churches or bodies such as the Marriage Guidance Councils of Australia. Those agencies have evolved considerably over time along with changing social norms, expectations, and needs. Some of the current leading nongovernmental agencies that provide counseling services include Anglicare, Centacare Catholic Family Services, CatholicCare, Interrelate Family Centres, LifeWorks Relationship Counselling and Education Services, Relationships Australia, and Unifam Counselling and Mediation. At the same time, counseling services were incorporated into certain high-need areas, such as schools and other educational institutions, rehabilitation facilities, and drug and alcohol treatment facilities. Nongovernmental agencies are increasingly attracting government block funding to offer counseling to a large range of high-risk groups presenting with child protection issues, family violence and sexual assault, substance abuse, parenting issues, veterans issues, relationship problems, and family mediation issues.

Apart from some of the larger and better known counseling services, information about work settings is relatively sparse. Some information can be gleaned from a number of surveys of counselors that sought information about their work settings. For instance, in a 2004 PACFA survey, private practice was by far the most frequently cited work setting (51%), with 43% of therapists reporting that their primary place of employment was solo private practice, 7% reporting that they were employed in a group private practice, and 1% reporting that they were employed in a private practice setting (Schofield, 2008a). A further 19% reported that their primary place of employment was a nongovernmental organization or community agency, whereas 12% were employed in the health sector, 10% were employed in education, and 3% performed primarily unpaid voluntary counseling. The majority (52%) worked in more than one employment setting ($M = 1.7$).

Of those in private practice, the largest number worked from their own homes (38%; Schofield, 2008a). A further 28% worked from rented professional rooms; 12% were located with other health professionals; 9% worked from rooms that they owned separate from their residence; 9% were located within a medical practice or center; and 5% undertook some private practice within the setting of their main employment, such as a health, education, or counseling setting (Schofield, 2008a).

The Schofield (2008a) study found that there were considerable differences in primary work settings by employment title: 83% of psychotherapists compared with 41% of counselors worked primarily in private practice. Conversely, 32% of counselors worked primarily in nongovernmental organizations and community agencies compared with 8% of psychotherapists. The relatively unregulated nature of counseling and psychotherapy in Australia restricts opportunities for employment in the main health sector and probably results in a high proportion in private practice, followed by nongovernmental and community-based agencies.

School Counseling

Nearly 3,000 student counselors were identified in the 2006 Australia Census. The AGCA (2008) reported that titles, qualifications, and staff:student ratios vary considerably across Australia's six states and two territories. The three major titles are school psychologist, school counselor, and guidance officer (a role that requires both psychology and teaching qualifications). Registration as a psychologist is required to perform school counseling in government schools in the Australian Capital Territory, South Australia, Tasmania, and Victoria. Several states allow qualifications in either psychology, counseling, or guidance and counseling.

An international study of school psychology estimated that there were approximately 2,000 school psychologists in Australia, with about 60% of these being members of the AGCA (Jimerson, Stewart, Skokut, Cardenas, & Malone, 2009). Estimated staff:student ratios in government schools range from 1:850 in the Australian Capital Territory to 1:3779 in South Australia. The estimated national counselor:student ratio in Australia was 1:1587, making it fairly comparable with the United States (1:1506), placing these two countries in 11th and 10th places, respectively, among the 48 countries studied (Jimerson et al., 2009).

Best Counseling Practices

Theoretical Orientation

The development of counseling in Australia drew from major theoretical trends in both the United Kingdom and the United States. Counseling training programs have historically been strongly influenced by humanistic, person-centered, and experiential approaches, and these remain the strongest and most enduring influences. Cognitive-behavioral, relationship, family, and systems approaches have gained prominence as secondary influences. Since the 1980s, solution-focused and narrative approaches gained considerable influence, and more recently contemporary integrative approaches such as mindfulness-based therapies, creative art-based approaches, and transpersonal approaches have gained in popularity.

A study of 1,004 counselors and psychotherapists asked about the salience of a range of theoretical orientations in their practice (Orlinsky et al., 2011). Salient or highly salient influences on respondents' practice were cited as follows: humanistic/person-centered theory (65% of respondents), family/systems theory (33%), psychoanalytic/psychodynamic theory (32%), cognitive-behavioral theory (23%), and cognitive theory (6%). The mean number of salient orientations was 1.78, supporting the trend toward eclectic/integrative approaches. This contrasts with an earlier survey of Australian counseling psychologists (Poznanski & McLennan, 1998) that identified the main theoretical orientations as cognitive-behavioral (30%), psychodynamic (17%), family/systems (11%), behavioral (8%), and eclectic (7%). It appears that there is a clear trend toward more eclectic/integrative or pluralistic approaches as well as expected differences in orientation between counselors and psychologists.

Psychotherapy training programs initially developed within psychoanalytic and psychodynamic traditions. Family and relationship therapies and experiential approaches such as gestalt therapy, psychodrama, and body-oriented approaches have subsequently exerted strong influences. A number of unique theoretical approaches have been developed by Australian therapists and have been influential in Australian counseling practice. Some of these include narrative therapy, the conversational model, no bullshit therapy, and a range of Indigenous healing practices.

Narrative Therapy

One of the better known Australian approaches is narrative therapy, developed at the Dulwich Centre in Adelaide (White & Epston, 1990). Narrative therapy is situated within the postmodern collaborative therapy tradition and is based on a number of key principles, as outlined by Morgan (2000):

- Narrative therapy seeks to be a respectful, non-blaming approach to counselling and community work, which centres people as the experts in their own lives.
- It views problems as separate from people and assumes people have many skills, competencies, beliefs, values, commitments and abilities that will assist them to change their relationship with problems in their lives.
- Curiosity and a willingness to ask searching questions are important principles of this work.
- There are many possible directions that any conversation can take (no single correct direction).
- The person consulting the therapist plays a significant part in mapping the direction of the journey.

Narrative therapy provides an accessible and respectful approach for engaging populations typically considered difficult to engage, such as Indigenous Australians; young people; prisoners; male perpetrators of violence; and people suffering from schizophrenia, anorexia/bulimia, or trauma. Some key therapeutic ideas developed by White include externalizing the problem ("the person is not the problem, the problem is the problem"), reauthoring the dominant stories of people's lives, and double-listening to accounts of trauma (i.e., listening to the accounts of trauma itself and how people have responded to trauma; White, 2007; White & Epston, 1990). This approach has had a significant influence in shaping the development of counseling in Australia as well as internationally.

The Conversational Model

The conversational model (Hobson, 1985; Meares, 2004) is a psychodynamic-interpersonal psychotherapy based on a psychology of the self derived from developmental observations. It was developed initially in the United Kingdom by Robert Hobson but developed further in the Australian context by Russell Meares at Westmead Hospital in Sydney. A key focus is on the minute particulars of the therapeutic conversation. A central concept in the conversational model is the importance of providing a deeply empathic experience of the therapeutic relationship and conversation in which the client feels understood. This involves exploring concepts of self, boundary formation, the empathic mode of listening, subjective experience, the development of affect, and use of language in the development of the self. Some key bodies of literature informing the contemporary approach include attachment theory, infant development research, trauma, affect, memory, consciousness, intersubjectivity, and relational psychoanalytic theory (Meares, 2004).

No Bullshit Therapy

No bullshit therapy was devised by Jeffrey Young of the Bouverie Centre at La Trobe University, Melbourne, to provide a more culturally appropriate and effective approach for negotiating the counseling relationship mutually with people who hold "strong anti-therapy stances toward counselling (i.e. people who hate being psychologised, see therapists as warm and fuzzy and not trustworthy, feel confounded by jargon, or are disempowered by specialist knowledge" (Young, 2012, p. 1). Young suggested that the very term *no bullshit therapy* can open doors to people and groups who are suspicious of counseling. In this approach, the counselor seeks to negotiate honesty and directness in the relationship with the client. Depending on the language of the client, the counselor may initiate a discussion early in the first session about the preference to practice no bullshit therapy—"where I don't bullshit you and you don't bullshit me." This approach can disarm people who are very suspicious of therapy and "can create a context for productive straight talking—especially if combined with warmth and care and an acknowledgment of constraints" (Young, 2012, p. 1). Young argued that the therapy is "provocative, even cheeky, but it leads to a real sense of authenticity. And it has a particular resonance with Aussie culture" (Dredge, 2008, p. 13). The approach has been used productively in the development of drought counseling in rural Victoria, as farming and rural communities were viewed as difficult to engage in traditional approaches to therapy (Young, 2011).

Diversity Issues

Three aspects of Australian society impact on the development and practice of counseling. The first is the geographic character of Australia, whose population is concentrated in a small number of metropolitan areas and then spread out along the eastern coastal strip. Very large portions of the continent are sparsely populated, with poor access to and choice of services. The availability of counselors decreases with increasing remoteness, resulting in large inequities in access to counseling services. This differentially affects regions with potentially high needs and has resulted in a search for other models of delivering counseling to geographically isolated individuals and groups. These include a growing focus on the provision of telephone and Web-based counseling services.

Lifeline (www.lifeline.org.au), established in 1963 as a 24-hour crisis telephone support line, is now the largest and best known crisis support service in Australia. It has grown to be a national organization of around 1,000 staff with 11,000 volunteers in more than 60 locations nationwide. Counseling services are now offered through phone, face-to-face, and online mediums. More recently developed phone and online services include AnxietyOnline, Crisis Support Services (Mensline, SuicideLine, Suicide Call Back Service), Kids Helpline, and ParentLine.

The second characteristic that affects the practice of counseling in Australia is the high number of immigrants and the diverse ethnic mix of the population. About 1 in 4 Australians was born overseas. The major source countries in order of importance are the United Kingdom, New Zealand, China, India, and Italy. However, trends suggest that the number of migrants from Europe is declining and the number from Asia is increasing (Department of Immigration and Citizenship, 2012). Increasing numbers of new immigrants come as refugees and asylum seekers from war-torn countries and have high rates of exposure to trauma and abuse. This changing profile has brought dramatic differences in the client population and in the skills required of counselors. There has therefore been a growing focus on developing effective ways of working with complex trauma. The development of such approaches has been facilitated by new treatment and support settings, such as asylum seeker and refugee support and treatment settings, and specialist centers in trauma treatment.

The third aspect of Australian society that affects counseling is the complex and difficult history of its Indigenous population, who have suffered serious cultural disintegration as a result of European settlement, loss of country and land (which is so important culturally), and successive government policies (including the White Australia policy, which resulted in large numbers of Indigenous children being removed from their families and brought up either in missions or by White families). This has resulted in what are now referred to as the Stolen Generations, generations of Indigenous people who were separated from their families, their communities, and their land and who therefore suffered extreme loss of identity and emotional well-being. In addition, many were abused and came to feel that they did not belong to either White or Indigenous society.

There is a strong need for Indigenous counseling and healing models to address issues associated with the complex intercultural history and the traditional holistic and community-based values of Indigenous Australians. Milroy (2008) highlighted the importance of the restoration of harmony and balance in the lives of Indigenous people. An Aboriginal and Torres Strait Islander Healing report (2011), described four priority themes related to healing for Indigenous people. These were: (a) building connection to culture, (b) using land and country as a source of healing, (c) helping leaders be strong, and (d) creating well-being through strengthening cultural identity. Indigenous spirituality and culture is widely thought to be at the heart of healing.

There are a number of award-winning approaches to counseling Indigenous Australians. These include the Marumali program (www.marumalihealth.com.au), which comprises a range of workshops for Aboriginal survivors of removal policies and their families (the Circle of Healing Program). Marumali also provides training programs for Aboriginal and non-Aboriginal counselors and health workers aimed at developing skills to meet the specific support needs of members of the Stolen Generations. Devised by a member of the Stolen Generations, the workshops offer insight into removal policies and their effects on individuals, families, and communities; silence and the transgenerational effects of oppression; the spiritual dimensions of healing; and the importance of identity and belonging. Other Indigenous social and emotional well-being programs include the Family Wellbeing Program (McEwan, Tsey, & the Empowerment Research Team, 2009) and the Yorgum Aboriginal Family Counselling Service (Lawrence, 2010).

Caruana (2010) described the core characteristics of Indigenous healing models as involving

- Indigenous ownership, design, and evaluation of services
- a holistic and multidisciplinary approach that addresses mental, physical, emotional, and spiritual needs, with a focus on familial and community interconnectedness as well as connections to the environment and the spiritual realm
- centrality of culture and spirituality (i.e., cultural renewal is seen by some as an essential precursor to healing)
- a focus on the historical source of the trauma rather than individual pathology
- a positive, strengths-based approach to promote the resilience of Indigenous people
- preventive and therapeutic strategies rather than reactive responses
- a commitment to healing as a process that takes considerable time, rather than as an event
- a commitment to adaptability, flexibility, and innovation (i.e., programs must be inclusive to ensure that they reach people who may not have strong cultural ties)
- the utilization of particular approaches best suited to the Indigenous context, such as narrative therapy, group processes, a combination of Western and traditional practices, and the use of traditional healers

Counselor Education

Counselor training programs initially developed in the nongovernmental sector and were set up in the post–World War II period by the newly established Marriage Guidance Councils of Australia and a number of church-based counseling services. The Marriage Guidance Councils set professional standards for counselors and provided training, accreditation, and counseling services to the public. These early initiatives evolved over the latter half of the 20th century, and the training programs offered by these agencies evolved with them.

As the demand for well-trained counselors increased and concerns emerged about the adequacy of training in the private sector, the development of counselor training programs within Australian universities began in the 1980s. Initially, counseling skills training mostly occurred within other professional training programs, such as education, psychology, or social work. The establishment of focused counselor training programs in the university sector occurred mostly at the postgraduate level. However, since 2000 there has been a shift to offering 3-year bachelor's degrees in counseling. Following deregulation of the higher education sector, both bachelor and master-level degrees are now also provided by accredited private providers.

Counselor Education Providers

A 2005 study identified 143 different counseling and psychotherapy training providers offering courses at the bachelor's, master's, and doctoral levels as well as graduate diplomas and graduate certificates (Schofield, 2008b). These course providers included universities, private providers, and professional associations. A wide range of terminology was used to describe the focus of the courses, ranging from *counseling* to more specialized areas such as *grief and palliative care counseling, gestalt therapy, systemic therapy/family therapy, human services/relationship therapy, school counseling and guidance, marriage and family counseling, arts counseling,* and *ministry.*

The Department of Industry, Innovation, Science, Research and Tertiary Education listed 36 higher education bodies providing counseling undergraduate and postgraduate courses in Australia in 2012, offering a total of 146 courses (Australian Government MyUniversity, 2012). These providers are accredited within the national higher education sector that governs universities and other accredited degree-granting bodies. Many other training providers are not accredited under the Higher Education Act. These include many that are registered under vocational training authorities and some that have no official status.

Counselor Education Standards

There are no government-regulated standards for counselor training in Australia. Rather, standards have been set by different professional associations as membership criteria and thus can vary widely across associations. Also, because counseling is not regulated, anyone can claim the title of counselor regardless of his or her level of training (in some cases, none at all). There is therefore a widespread perception that counselors are inadequately trained and supervised. This has been a major barrier to increasing the number of employment positions for counselors and gaining recognition as a mature profession.

Surveys of practitioners provide evidence of the wide disparity in training standards. A survey of PACFA-affiliated therapists found that 59% held postgraduate qualifications (Schofield, 2008a) compared with only 23% of members responding to an Australian Counselling Association survey (Pelling, 2005). This difference probably reflects different membership requirements at the time. Both associations have since changed their training standard requirements. The Australian Counselling Association now recognizes four levels of membership, requiring a 1-year diploma without any stated supervised experience at Level 1 and a minimum of a 3-year bachelor's degree with 6 years of postqualification experience and 1,000 hours of client contact at Level 4.

PACFA has further differentiated training requirements for undergraduate and postgraduate pathways, making it clear that a tertiary-level qualification or equivalent is a minimum requirement for gaining full membership in a PACFA member association (2012c). Since 2009, counseling or psychotherapy training courses at the undergraduate level have required a minimum of 3 years of training and a higher number of direct teaching contact hours (minimum 350 hours). Postgraduate courses require at least 2 years of training with 200 hours of person-to-person psychotherapy and/or counseling training and 50 hours of supervision relating to 200 hours of client contact. A minimum of 10 hours of supervision relating to 40 client contact hours must have been taken place within the training program. Both pathways require 750 hours of supervised work experience posttraining before the counselor is eligible for registration with PACFA.

The AGCA requires teacher training (a minimum of 4 years) and relevant postgraduate qualification in a counseling or guidance field. Rehabilitation counselors require a bachelor's or postgraduate degree in rehabilitation counseling as well as 1 year of full-time equivalent experience under supervision in rehabilitation counseling.

Course Accreditation

A rigorous course accreditation scheme is a core component of a mature profession once training standards have been agreed on. It provides a quality assurance function that underpins the standards of training and practice and provides opportunities for strengthening courses toward meeting those standards. At the start of the 21st century, it became clear that there was a strong perceived need for a national course accreditation scheme in Australia to map and strengthen the education and training of counselors and psychotherapists (Schofield, 2008b). PACFA, through its Education Program Accreditation Committee, has developed course accreditation standards and implemented the course accreditation scheme. Areas addressed by the accreditation standards include assessing characteristics of the institution offering the program, the program objectives and course work, the nature and extent of practical experience (skills development), the staff profile, the organization and administration of the program, and program evaluation processes and outcomes. Implementation of this relatively new scheme is a developmental process, and as of July 2012 courses from 9 universities and 14 nonuniversity providers had been accredited by PACFA (PACFA, 2012d).

Continuing Professional Development

No professional preparation program is ever complete, and advances in knowledge, skills, and technology within the profession require lifelong continuing education for counselors and psychotherapists as well as monitoring and review of professional standards. All professional associations identified here require ongoing professional development of their members.

The Future

Counseling is at an exciting crossroads in its development as a profession in Australia. There is strong growth in demand for training programs, growing demand for services, and development of some promising initiatives to target unique aspects of the Australian context. Australia is also unique, along with New Zealand, in being a bridge between the East and the West. There is growing evidence of the influence of Eastern models such as Buddhist-informed models and models that appreciate the importance of the communities and families in which people live.

Australia is also positioned in a part of the world that is particularly vulnerable to climate change effects. This has led to growing interest in the development of innovative approaches to responding to community disasters such as drought, fire, and flood. Community development and group-based activities are seen as an integral part of offering counseling services in this context (Young, 2011).

Rates of mental distress are rising, and a current challenge for the profession is to ensure that counselors are adequately trained to assess and deal appropriately with mental health problems or have appropriate referral options in place. Although mental health counseling has traditionally been seen as the domain of psychologists and psychiatrists, it is clear that the size of the problem and consumer preferences require a wider range of options. Counselors are able to provide services in areas that find it difficult to attract psychologists or psychiatrists and are seen by the public as more approachable. For counselors to achieve better recognition and involvement, there need to be pathways for them to demonstrate that they meet the National Mental Health Worker Standards and to go through an accreditation process. The profession is currently advocating for recognition to provide services funded by the government under the expanded mental health policies implemented in 2006 known as the Better Access Initiative.

Part of the approach to addressing access issues has been the development and evaluation of counseling technologies, such as phone and Internet approaches. Such approaches also include interactive Web-based programs designed to assist clients with a particular type of problem, mostly based on cognitive-behavioral principles. For instance, MoodGYM is an interactive Web program designed to prevent depression. It has five modules: an interactive game, anxiety and depression assessments, downloadable relaxation audio, a workbook, and feedback assessment ("MoodGYM Training Program," 2012). The program has been evaluated and has shown promise as an alternative counseling delivery model. The future of counseling promises to bring more innovation, yet the client–therapist relationship will inevitably remain at the heart of professional practice.

References

Aboriginal and Torres Strait Islander Healing Foundation. (2011). *Our healing, our solutions*, Vol. 2, July–December 2011. Retrieved from http://www.healingfoundation.org.au/wp-content/uploads/2012/03/Our-Healing-Our-Solutions-Jul-Dec-2011.pdf

Australian Government MyUniversity. (2012). *My university course search—Counselling*. Retrieved from http://www.myuniversity.gov.au/CourseSearch

Australian Guidance and Counselling Association. (2008). *An Australia wide comparison of school counselor/psychologist guidance services 2008*. Retrieved from http://www.agca.com.au/article.php?id=22

Australian Institute of Health and Welfare. (2009). *Health and community services labour force 2006* (Cat. No. HWL 43). Canberra, Australia: Author.

Caruana, C. (2010). *Healing services for Aboriginal and Torres Strait Islander children and families.* Retrieved from www.aifs.gov.au/conferences/aifs11/docs/caruana.pdf

Department of Education Employment and Workplace Relations. (2011). *Job outlook: An Australian government initiative.* Retrieved from http://joboutlook.gov.au/Documents/2721.pdf

Department of Immigration and Citizenship. (2012). *Population flows 2010-2011 at a glance.* Retrieved from http://www.immi.gov.au/media/publications/statistics/popflows2010-11/pop-flows-at-a-glance.pdf

Dredge, R. (2008, March/April). "No bull therapy" helps farmers through drought. *La Trobe University Bulletin,* p. 13.

Hobson, R. F. (1985). *Forms of feeling: The heart of psychotherapy.* London, England: Tavistock.

Jimerson, S. R., Stewart, K., Skokut, M., Cardenas, S., & Malone, H. (2009). How many school psychologists are there in each country of the world? *School Psychology International, 30,* 555–567.

Lawrence, M. (2010). *Yorgum Aboriginal Family Counselling Service.* Retrieved from http://www.aifs.gov.au/afrc/pubs/newsletter/frq017/frq017-6.html

McEwan, A., Tsey, K., & the Empowerment Research Team. (2009). *The role of spirituality in social and emotional wellbeing initiatives: The Family Wellbeing Program at Yarrabah* (Discussion Paper No. 7). Darwin, Australia: Cooperative Research Centre for Aboriginal Health.

Meares, R. (2004). The conversational model: An outline. *American Journal of Psychotherapy, 58,* 51–66.

Milroy, H. (2008). Children are our future: Understanding the needs of Aboriginal children and their families. In A. S. Williams & V. Cowling (Eds.), *Infants of parents with mental illness* (pp. 121–140). Bowen Hills, Queensland, Australia: Australian Academic Press.

MoodGYM training program. (2012). Retrieved from http://www.moodgym.anu.edu.au

Morgan, A. (2000). *What is narrative therapy?* Retrieved from http://dulwichcentre.com.au/what-is-narrative-therapy.html

Orlinsky, D., Schofield, M., Schroder, T., & Kazantzis, N. (2011). Utilization of personal therapy by psychotherapists: A practice-friendly review and a new study. *Journal of Clinical Psychology, 67,* 828–842. doi:10.1002/jclp.20821

Pelling, N. (2005). Counsellors in Australia: Profiling the membership of the Australian Counselling Association. *Counselling, Psychotherapy, and Health, 1,* 1–18. Retrieved from http://www.cphjournal.com/archive_journals/V1_I1_Pelling_1-18_7_05.pdf

Pelling, N., Brear, P., & Lau, M. (2006). A survey of advertised Australian counsellors. *International Journal of Psychology, 41*(3), 204–215.

Poznanski, J. J., & McLennan, J. (1998). Theoretical orientations of Australian counselling psychologists. *International Journal for the Advancement of Counselling, 20,* 253–261.

Psychology Board of Australia. (2010, December 21). *Australia's psychology workforce profiled.* Retrieved from www.psychologyboard.gov.au/News/Media-Releases.aspx

Psychotherapy and Counselling Federation of Australia. (2012a). *Definition of counselling and psychotherapy.* Retrieved from http://www.pacfa.org.au/resources/cid/41/parent/0/t/resources/l/layout

Psychotherapy and Counselling Federation of Australia. (2012b). *Member associations list.* Retrieved from http://www.pacfa.org.au/memberassoc

Psychotherapy and Counselling Federation of Australia. (2012c). *PACFA professional training standards.* Retrieved from http://www.pacfa.org.au/resources

Psychotherapy and Counselling Federation of Australia. (2012d). *PACFA Education Program Accreditation: EPAC.* Retrieved from http://www.pacfa.org.au/resources/cid/4/parent/0/t/resources/l/layout

Schofield, M. J. (2008a). Australian counsellors and psychotherapists: A profile of the profession. *Counselling and Psychotherapy Research, 8*(1), 4–11.

Schofield, M. J. (2008b, June). *Best practice self-regulatory model for psychotherapy and counselling in Australia: Final report.* Melbourne, Australia: Department of Human Services. Available at http://www.health.vic.gov.au/pracreg/hp-review/psychotherapy

Schofield, M. J., Grant, J. A., Holmes, S., & Barletta, J. (2006). The Psychotherapy and Counselling Federation of Australia: How the federation model contributes to the field. *International Journal of Psychology, 41*(3), 163–169.

Schofield, M. J., & Roedel, G. (2012). *Australian psychotherapists and counsellors: A study of therapists, therapeutic work, and professional development.* Melbourne, Australia: La Trobe University.

White, M. (2007). *Maps of narrative practice.* New York, NY: Norton.

White, M., & Epston, D. (1990). *Narrative means to therapeutic ends.* New York, NY: Norton.

Young, J. W. (2011). *A "no bullshit" approach to counselling in drought-affected rural communities.* Unpublished doctoral dissertation, La Trobe University, Melbourne, Australia.

Young, J. W. (2012). *No bullshit therapy.* Retrieved from http://www.bouverie.org.au/programs/community-services-team/drought-project/no-bullshit-therapy

• • •

Counseling in New Zealand

Judi H. Miller and Dale S. Furbish

New Zealand is an island nation of 4 million people situated in the South Pacific with a land area two thirds that of California. The country is also called Aotearoa, the indigenous Māori name meaning "Land of the Long White Cloud," and is frequently referred to as Aotearoa New Zealand. Two main islands, the North Island and the South Island, make up the land. One of the last land masses in the world to be settled, its first peoples were the Polynesian Māori, who are thought to have first reached the land in the mid-1200s. The first European contact was in 1642 when the Dutch explorer Abel Tasman sailed around the coastal regions. New Zealand became a British possession in 1840 with the signing of the Treaty of Waitangi by some of the Māori leaders and representatives of the British Crown. The Treaty of Waitangi is the founding document of New Zealand and continues to define essential relationships between Māori and the government. The country became a Commonwealth Realm in 1947, whereby it is recognized as a sovereign nation within the British Commonwealth. Today it is a constitutional monarchy organized along democratic lines with a unicameral parliament. New Zealand has a multicultural population that is 78% European, 14.6% Māori, 9.2% Asian, and 6.9% Pacific peoples (Pasifika; Statistics New Zealand, 2006).

The Historical Development of Counseling

Geographic isolation, a relatively small population, and British colonial heritage have melded to shape the distinctive nature of counseling in New Zealand. Over the years, the country's counseling field has been heavily influenced by theory and practices originating overseas, especially those from the United States and Great Britain. Yet the New Zealand context has resulted in a locally influenced application of counseling. As in other former British colonies such as Australia, counseling has developed from a number of professional origins, such as psychology, social work, and education (Patton, 2009). More recently, however, the divisions among these disciplines have become more pronounced.

Central to the development of counseling in New Zealand has been the role of the government. During their relatively short history, guidance and counseling services have helped the government address educational and vocational guidance and public concern about adolescent delinquency, violence, sexual abuse, moral decline, and increased unemployment (Miller, 2004). Guidance and counseling services originated in the early 1900s in the form of vocational guidance services operated by the YWCA and YMCA to attend to the vocational and educational needs of youth, predominantly boys, who were leaving school early, often without jobs (Winterbourn, 1974). In 1935, the election of the first Labour Government heralded in a range of welfare policies to expand government-supported social services and address the needs created by economic depression and growing numbers of unemployed people.

As part of this initiative, free guidance counseling was made available for school pupils in targeted schools and the Vocational Guidance Service was brought under the control of the Department of Education. However, specific training for those who delivered guidance counseling was not comprehensive. Typically teachers who were interested in assisting students to find employment or enter further education or vocational training were given the task of providing guidance. In the 1940s, the Psychological Service and a Visiting Teacher Scheme (the equivalent of social workers in primary and intermediate schools) were added to the government's Department of Education service. Their focus was on an apparent rise in unemployment and adolescent delinquency. Their function was remedial. Prior to this, psychologists had mostly worked in medical settings. Educational psychologists, however, continued to work outside the schools, which left the way clear for teachers working in secondary schools to move into counseling roles when the government became interested in establishing them.

In the late 1950s, the government established the Special Committee on Moral Delinquency in Child and Adolescents and distributed its report to all New Zealand households. An outcome of this report was a cautious interest by the government in establishing school guidance counselor positions. With the urbanization of Māori, Māori youth became prominent as at-risk secondary school pupils. In 1960, therefore, the first two secondary school guidance counselors were appointed at schools with large Māori enrollment. Their success resulted in the government approving the appointment of guidance counselors in all secondary schools within a decade. This widespread deployment of guidance and counseling services encouraged a shift in focus from remedial to educational. Training for these counselors began as a 12-week induction course run by the Department of Education. However, by 1973 specific training for guidance counselors became available at a number of universities. Vocational guidance officers also gained their training in these programs despite the shift in their focus from education to employment when unemployment figures rose.

Therapeutic counseling for a broader age range of people was conducted in fully subsidized government or quasi-government environments such as hospitals and community health agencies. The telephone service Lifeline, established by churches in the early 1960s, later became community based. The government also employed or financially supported social workers and a diverse group of lay helpers, such as marriage guidance counselors, Samaritan telephone counselors, and church-based welfare workers. This situation continued until the 1980s, when a new government introduced rapid political change in New Zealand. This shift from government-provided services to individual responsibility has been reflected in terms such as *user pays* and *market principles*. Examples of the impact of these changes included the introduction of fees for service in marriage guidance counseling and the search for Lotteries Board funding by some church-based social service agencies and other agencies supporting counseling for gamblers, men's violence programs, and other addiction programs.

By the late 1980s, other social issues that were gaining prominence were mirrored in changes to the curriculum of counselor education. First, a redressing of past injustices to Māori encouraged the introduction of biculturalism into programs. Second, the once private concerns of family violence and sexual abuse became public issues and ones that required governmental response (Miller, 2004). The government was prepared to subsidize the cost of counseling victims of violence and sexual abuse by approved counselors. The counselor training curriculum in both universities and polytechnics changed accordingly with the introduction of brief counseling models and courses on family violence and sexual abuse.

In 1988, as a result of the user-pays ethos, the Vocational Guidance Service was restructured in a way that reduced its counseling function. By 1990 the service was split into an employment service (ACCESS) and the renamed Career Development and Transition Service (Quest *rapuara*). Vocational guidance counselors were no longer eligible for study awards to attend university-based training. Career and vocational counseling was migrated to Quest *rapuara* external to schools. In the schools themselves, a teacher was usually appointed as a career adviser and provided with limited time to perform this role along with teaching responsibilities.

The Current Status of Counseling

Counselors and Psychologists

An informative strategy for providing a coherent picture of the current status of counseling in Aotearoa New Zealand is to describe the structural arrangements of counseling-related professional associations. This is particularly pertinent because with the government playing such an integral role in the development of New Zealand counseling, the normal professionalization process whereby professions seek and gain registration has been interrupted. Unlike many counselors and therapists in the United Kingdom and United States, the great majority of New Zealand counselors are not registered psychologists and do not have psychology credentials.

Although some counselors are employed in social agencies and private practice, many are still employed in the education sector. The development of different professional associations (rather than different divisions within one association) essentially limited the jurisdictions of counselors and has produced a fractionalized professional identity for New Zealand counselors. The New Zealand Association of Psychotherapists was founded in 1947 to promote fellowship and support among psychotherapists who mostly worked in medicine, psychiatry, psychology, and social work. Although membership criteria were inclusive and the term *psychotherapist* was not protected, school counselors, whose qualifications were in education rather than in psychology, were not eligible to join. In 1969, the New Zealand Psychological Society became independent of the British Psychological Society. Its members pursued registration of psychologists, and in 1981 the Psychologists Act 1981 was passed. Registration was not, however, compulsory, so in 1989 the New Zealand College of Clinical Psychologists was founded to enforce strict membership criteria and protect the term *clinical psychologist.*

In 2003 the Health Practitioners Competence Assurance Act was passed and members of these three professional associations successfully applied for registration of their members under appropriate scopes of practice. In that same year, the Social Workers Registration Act 2003 was passed and a social workers registration board established the criteria for their registration. These acts resulted in claims of professional jurisdiction in which only psychologists, clinical psychologists, and psychotherapists (i.e., those registered under the Health Practitioners Competence Assurance Act) could be employed by the Ministry of Justice and Ministry of Health. Their work is focused on the assessment and treatment of individuals and families who may be referred by school or medical personnel.

Because counselors had not sought registration, they looked to their professional association, the New Zealand Association of Counsellors Te Ropu Kaiwhiriwhiri o Aotearoa

(NZAC), to apply for registration under the Health Practitioners Competence Assurance Act (2003). This exemplifies interrupted professionalization, whereby a professional association rather than a government agency takes on an accrediting role. This action, however, was not embraced by the membership and has resulted in heated debate and division within the association (Miller, 2011). Many members perceived a threat to the NZAC's original (1974) aim to promote fellowship and support among school guidance counselors, and others were concerned that registration would exclude members who had experience but limited formal qualifications. Original membership in the association remained small (fewer than 400 mostly school and some vocational guidance counselors) until 1992, when a government policy encouraged counselors and therapists to join professional associations in order to gain access to funding for specific counseling services that they provided.

Third-Party Funding

Third-party funding is available to subsidize counseling for people living on a disabilities benefit and for people using employee assistance services. This funding is different from that of managed care in the United States in that it is provided by quasi-government agencies. In the Family Courts, which were established in 1980 to deal constructively and sensitively with family matters, couples seeking divorce were able to attend up to four fully subsidized counseling sessions with an approved counselor. Although most counselors are accredited to access the disabilities subsidy, only registered counselors are eligible for subsidies through the Family Court. Another source of third-party funding has, however, had a major influence on the practice, professionalization, and provision of counseling in New Zealand. This was introduced by a government policy in 1992 to subsidize funding for the counseling of survivors of sexual abuse under a unique "no fault or blame" legislation of the Accident Compensation Act (1992; Miller, 2004). The accreditation criteria established by the government for counselor eligibility for this funding stipulated that the counselor has undergone approved counseling training, has experience working with people who have experienced sexual abuse, and is a member of a professional association. Because the membership criteria for the NZAC were less stringent than those for any other association, this policy resulted in a dramatic increase in membership from 500 in 1991 to 950 in 1993 to 2,400 in 2002 and a shift in the proportion of members who were counselors in private practice (the group most eligible for accident compensation funding) from 24% in 1990 to 51% in 1993.

At the time, Miller (1996) argued that the accreditation requirements of the Accident Compensation and Insurance Corporation were having undue influence on policies of the NZAC. Changes were instituted in the code of ethics, criteria used for membership, subscription fees, and requirements for maintaining membership. In a recent review of association documents, Miller (2011) noted that members of the NZAC continue to be concerned about the influence the Accident Compensation and Insurance Corporation has on its policies.

School Counselors

The 1989 Education Act required principals to ensure that students have access to quality guidance and counseling (Section 77). However, this does not guarantee that all schools will employ the suggested ratio of 1 counselor for every 200 pupils. The professional union of school counselors is the Post Primary Teachers' Association, but around 60% of school counselors are also members of the NZAC. In 2012, the membership of the NZAC was 2,034, with 939 counselors in private practice and 309 school counselor members. In a survey of these members, Manthei (1999) identified the most serious problems dealt with by school counselors as family problems, depression, suicide attempts, sexual abuse, drug abuse, and bullying. The most frequent problems encountered were career decisions, family problems, educational problems, peer conflict, and disruptive behavior. In a recent review of NZAC documents, Miller (2011) noted that school guidance counselors are feeling sidelined both in their places of work and in their association. They are being required by the Teachers Council to increase their classroom teaching role and are concerned that the NZAC focus on registration deflects attention from school counselor issues.

Career Counseling

In 1994, a small group of career counselors, most of whom were members of the NZAC, formed their own Career Practitioners' Association–Auckland. Within a year they were seeking support to establish a national careers practitioners association. As a result, in 1997 the Career Practitioners Association of New Zealand (CPANZ) was formed. CPANZ brought together individuals who provided career services in a number of settings. The association intended to be inclusive, and therefore membership criteria were not robust. Applicants who had experience in career issues were offered membership regardless of formal credentials or training in career theory and practices. Indeed, the chosen name for the organization was intentionally ambiguous in its use of the term *career practitioner.* A career practitioner is a person who provides career services. There was particularly adamant sentiment that the term *career counselor* not be used. CPANZ membership therefore comprises largely secondary school and tertiary institution career advisers, employees of government agencies such as The Careers New Zealand (the successor to Quest *rapuara*), and those who provide vocational services to Accident Compensation Commission clients.

At this time in New Zealand, there were no university-level qualifications in career topics. However, in 1997, Auckland Institute of Technology began offering a specific qualification to train those in the career industry. As the number of graduates from Auckland Institute of Technology increased, and with the commencement of career qualifications at other postsecondary institutions in New Zealand, CPANZ modified its professional-level membership requirement in 2008 to include a formal qualification in career development (yet the level of qualification was set at diploma, which is less than a bachelor's degree). This action significantly increased the credibility and professional status of the career industry. At the same time, the association changed its name to the Career Development Association of New Zealand to better reflect its mission and to mirror the names of professional career associations in other countries.

The Ministry of Education (2009) has developed guidelines for career education and guidance in New Zealand secondary schools. The guidelines reflect a whole-school philosophy to career programs and are built around developing lifelong career management competencies. Schools are to assist students in developing self-awareness, competencies to explore options, and flexible and adaptable decision making. Yet the guidelines are vague about the qualifications and skills of those who are required to implement the services and thus are a concern. Furbish (2011) found that school advisers do not regard career theory as highly relevant and that career advisers tend not to believe that they can apply career theory in their work. More specific guidance has been provided by the recently developed Career Education Benchmarks (CareersNZ, 2011). The benchmarks provide goals for career education and guidance programs in secondary schools and indicate that school career advisers should possess a graduate diploma in careers in order for the benchmarks to be fully implemented. However, the benchmarks are only suggestive and are nonbinding on schools.

Diversity Issues

Although counseling practices were originally imported from the United States and United Kingdom, a number of well-respected practices have antipodean roots and adaptations. The impetus for developing practices that are less focused on Western psychological theory and more culturally and socially appropriate comes from a number of sources. The most important is the resurgence of partnership obligations within the founding New Zealand constitutional document, the Treaty of Waitangi. The history of the treaty is beyond the scope of this chapter; however, its implications for counseling practice in New Zealand are significant. By the turn of the 21st century, the treaty had evolved into a document that served to highlight not only a series of broken promises, particularly with respect to land, but also unmet expectations for Māori and governance (Kingi, 2007). However, persistence by Māori and changing government policies created opportunities for a number of grievances to be addressed within the Treaty of Waitangi Act (1975).

Why is this pertinent to counseling practice in New Zealand? Māori currently make up 14.6% of the total New Zealand population (Statistics New Zealand, 2006) but on average have fewer assets than the rest of the population and are at greater risk for many negative economic and social outcomes. Māori have higher unemployment rates than other cultures and make up almost 50% of the prison population (Department of Corrections, 2007). Furthermore, Māori suffer more health problems, including higher levels of alcohol and drug abuse and smoking, and Māori women and children are more likely than any other ethnic group to experience domestic violence (Mana Māori, 2009). Since the 1990s, therefore, health care services in Aotearoa New Zealand have attempted to develop contemporary Māori models of health and well-being for use by and guidance of district health boards and health training institutions. The most well-known model is Mason Durie's Whare Tapa Whā (four-walled house) model, which describes four dimensions of balanced well-being: *te taha wairua* (spiritual health), *te taha hinengaro* (emotional and psychological health), *te taha Tinana* (physical health), and *te taha whānau* (a healthy social environment; Durie, 2007).

Counseling and psychology have likewise attempted to incorporate Māori models into their training and practice. Counseling agencies that have a focus on families, for example Relationship Services, acknowledge the importance of *whānau,* or family group identity, for Māori and adopt group and family wellness models. The impediment is that most counseling credentials are still essentially based on an understanding of Western models. The use of Māori models by counselors is therefore mainly the domain of Māori counselors. Although Māori make up a significant proportion of the counseling client base, high numbers of Pasifika peoples and people from Malaysia, Japan, Korea, Taiwan, and China also access counseling services. Some multicultural counseling approaches from the United States have helped inform the practice of counselors working with these populations.

Best Counseling Practices

Counselors in New Zealand tend to continue using their original model of training in their practice. Miller (2009) surveyed students who had been university trained in the solution-focused model of counseling and found that 79% of graduates recorded their main framework as still solution focused. These graduates work in schools, in community agencies, in private practice, and some in careers work. This postmodern, social constructionist approach, along with narrative therapy, which originated in Australia and New Zealand (White & Epston, 1990), has been adopted by New Zealand counselors as a socially and culturally appropriate model. School and community counselors have embraced these models that focus on social justice, respect for the client, and an acknowledgment of the importance of context and interaction. They also commonly adopt integrative and person-centered approaches because these too have been taught in university counselor training programs. Although talk therapies dominate the field of counseling, there is scope in any private practice to incorporate other techniques, such as art, play, and drama. Furthermore, telephone counseling and online counseling are gaining acceptance.

As in many parts of the world, trait factor models of career counseling have historically influenced New Zealand practitioners in career counseling. Yet the trait factor assessment tools that are commonly used in the United States and United Kingdom have not been as generally accepted in New Zealand. Perhaps one influence has been the iconic New Zealand attitude of free spirit that conflicts with the perception of categorization by trait factor approaches. More practical, however, is the influence of the small market in New Zealand for assessment tools. Paper-and-pencil assessments typically require significant investments to standardize and validate for a potential client group. The small New Zealand population equates to a limited market for assessments, thereby restricting the appeal to authors and publishers to invest in the New Zealand market.

Similar to personal counseling, postmodern models of career counseling have become popular in New Zealand. Among the most widely used has been systems theory (Patton & McMahon, 1999), developed in Australia and therefore viewed by many career counselors as regionally relevant. Moreover, systems theory can accommodate multiple career influences at the microsystem, mesosystem, exosystem, and macrosystem levels. Thus, a host of variables such as culture, geography, and family are considered along with individual characteristics. This theory has been adopted by the Ministry of Education to conceptualize a career model for use in schools.

New Zealand has been an innovator in the use of the Internet to provide career information. Careers New Zealand's website (www.careers.govt.nz) has received international recognition for the quality of its occupational information. Careers New Zealand has also embraced the use of telephone and Internet chat approaches for providing career assistance. These technologies have been especially useful for providing services to New Zealand's residents, many of whom live in rural and small towns that do not have career services offices.

Counselor Education

The training of counselors in Aotearoa New Zealand universities developed from mostly U.S.-derived curricula. There were regional differences across universities: The University of Canterbury emphasized behavioral technology, career development, research methods, and consulting skills; the University of Waikato emphasized casework, intensive field experience, and enhancement of the guidance functions of the teacher; Massey University emphasized field-based community counseling; and the University of Auckland focused on psychological and community counseling. These regional differences later reflected a desire to adopt models that acknowledge the local social, cultural, and education environment. At the University of Canterbury a microskills approach focus changed to a problem-solving approach and now a solution-focused approach. At Waikato University the initial model of social influence was replaced by the narrative approach. At Massey University the human resource model was replaced by an eclectic and then an integrative model.

In the 1990s counselor training programs developed in polytechnics, colleges of education, counseling agencies, and specialist institutes (e.g., the Gestalt Institute, the Neurolinguistic Programming Training Institute), leading to a variety of new qualifications (Hermansson & Webb, 1993). This increase in credential offerings encouraged many universities to upgrade their counseling qualifications from diploma to master's degrees. The recent worldwide emphasis on outcome studies and the value of evidence-based practice has encouraged counselor trainers to teach quantitative research methodologies.

Graduate counselor training and education programs are now available in about 20 institutions, including universities, polytechnics, and private training enterprises. Undergraduate programs in polytechnics and private training enterprises provide entry into the profession for a number of people whose academic backgrounds would not allow them entry into university programs.

In the career counseling field, opportunities to gain a tertiary-level career-specific qualification have only recently become available. In 1996, Auckland Institute of Technology (now Auckland University of Technology) introduced the first career-specific qualification to train career counselors, the graduate certificate in career development. A graduate certificate does not have an equivalent in the United States but is an upper university–level qualification for students who usually possess an undergraduate degree. The graduate certificate therefore provides specialized theory and practice to students who have an academic background in another discipline. The graduate certificate was expanded to a graduate diploma in 2000 at Auckland University of Technology, and in 2005 that university began offering the only postgraduate qualification in career counseling in New Zealand, the master of career development. Two other tertiary-level qualifications have become available in New Zealand: a diploma at Nelson Marlbourgh Institute of Technology and a career counseling specialization in the applied social sciences degree at Otago Polytechnic.

Counseling psychology has not been well developed in New Zealand. The only postgraduate qualification in counseling psychology was introduced in 2005 at Auckland University of Technology. The limited training opportunities in counseling psychology reflect the limited acceptance of the specialization by professional psychology, which is dominated by clinical and industrial psychology.

The Future

Major influences on counseling in Aotearoa New Zealand are expected to come more from the social, cultural, and economic environments than from the profession itself. The percentage of Māori in the population is expected to rise, as is the number of immigrants. There is current concern in the community about rising incidents of family violence, the escalation of drug-related crime, and increases in the number of children living below the country's poverty threshold. School counselors are expected to combat bullying and cyberbullying among students, and New Zealand statistics for youth suicide are among the highest in the world. It is expected that attempts to address these social issues will lead counselor trainers, counselors, and government agencies to collaborate in efforts to find the most effective models. Adaptation of Māori models of well-being could provide some guidance.

The credentialing of counselors in New Zealand is likely to be an ongoing issue. At the professional level, it is very likely that some form or registration will need to be adopted. Currently the NZAC is considering a form of self-regulation as an alternative to registration under the Health Practitioners Competence Assurance Act (2003). Registration will inevitably affect changes in counselor training.

Criteria for professional-level membership in the Career Development Association of New Zealand are also likely to be an issue. Current requirements are for only a diploma (subdegree) qualification, which does not support the field's aspirations for professional status. A model has been provided by the Career Industry Council of Australia that requires professional members of any of their affiliated professional associations to possess an advanced qualification from a program endorsed by the council. Requirements for higher academic-level qualifications for career counselors and endorsement of training programs by the Career Development Association of New Zealand are needed to promote the credibility of career counseling in New Zealand.

A final word about the future of counseling in New Zealand acknowledges the demographics of the country. New Zealand is a small country with a relatively small population compared to the United States and the United Kingdom. Although we have discussed the growing need for counseling services, it is possible that in the future the number of counselors will reach a saturation point as more providers of counselor training establish programs. The other side of the equation is the influence of government policies that either support counseling services or reduce them. Much counseling is funded by public funds, with very little private sector resources. Changes of government and changes in government policies can produce dramatic shifts in counseling activities. Advocacy and representation by professional associations in the past have not been highly influential on public-funded support for counseling. This results in an uncertain future for the profession.

References

CareersNZ. (2011). *Career education benchmarks.* Retrieved from http://www2.careers.govt.nz/educators-practitioners/planning/benchmarks/#c32770

Department of Corrections. (2007). *Over-representation of Māori in the criminal justice system.* Wellington, New Zealand: New Zealand Government Press.

Durie, M. (2007). Counselling Mäori: Marae encounters as a basis for understanding and building relationships. *New Zealand Journal of Counselling, 27*(1), 1–8.

Furbish, D. (2011). The influence of professional standards on New Zealand career development practice. *Australian Journal of Career Development, 20*(3), 10–17.

Hermansson, G., & Webb, S. (1993). Guidance and counseling in New Zealand: Weathering a decade of transformation. *International Journal for the Advancement of Counseling, 16*(3), 213–229.

Kingi, T. R. (2007). The Treaty of Waitangi: A framework for Māori health development. *New Zealand Journal of Occupational Therapy, 54*(1), 4–10.

Mana Māori. (2009). *Community action to prevent family violence toolkit.* Wellington, New Zealand: New Zealand Government Press.

Manthei, R. (1999). School counseling in New Zealand. Part II: Student problems and counsellors' use of outside agencies. *New Zealand Journal of Counselling, 20*(1), 38–46.

Miller, J. H. (1996). From unity to diversity: An account of the growth, development and change in the New Zealand Association of Counsellors as identified through Association newsletters. *New Zealand Journal of Counselling, 18*(2), 36–49.

Miller, J. H. (2004). Third-party funding and counseling in New Zealand: Implications for counseling services and professional autonomy. *International Journal for the Advancement of Counseling, 26*(3), 285–299.

Miller, J. H. (2009). Does teaching a solution-focused model of counselling work? A follow-up of graduates. *Counselling and Psychotherapy Research, 9*, 1–8.

Miller, J. H. (2011). More than a decade of considerable change: An interpretation of the New Zealand Association of Counsellors newsletters 1997–2009. *New Zealand Journal of Counseling, 32*(1), 1–16.

Ministry of Education. (2009). *Career education and guidance in New Zealand schools.* Retrieved from http://nzcurriculum.tki.org.nz/Curriculum-resources/Learning-and-teaching-resources/Career-education

Patton, W. (2009). At the crossroads: Counseling psychology in Australia. In L. H. Gerstein, P. P. Heppner, S. Ægisdóttir, S.-M. A. Leung, & K. L. Norsworthy (Eds.), *International handbook of cross-cultural counseling: Cultural assumptions and practices worldwide* (pp. 489–502). Thousand Oaks, CA: Sage.

Patton, W., & McMahon, M. (1999). *Career development and systems theory.* Pacific Grove, CA: Brooks/Cole.

Statistics New Zealand. (2006). *Quick stats.* Retrieved from http://www.stats.govt.nz/Census/2006CensusHomePage/QuickStats/quickstats-about-a-subject/culture-and-identity/ethnic-groups-in-new-zealand.aspx

White, M., & Epston, D. (1990). *Narrative means to therapeutic ends.* New York, NY: Norton.

Winterbourn, R. (1974). *Guidance services in New Zealand education.* Wellington, New Zealand: New Zealand Council for Educational Research.

• • •

Counseling in South and Central American Countries

Counseling in Argentina 37

Andres Sánchez Bodas, Mercedes Ballbé ter Maat, and Lucrecia Sánchez Berneman

Argentina, a country of 42 million situated in the southern part of South America, is bordered by Chile, Uruguay, Brazil, Paraguay, and Bolivia. The language is Castellano, a dialect of Spanish brought to the Americas by colonizers originating from the Castilla la Vieja region in Spain. Prior to colonization, this region of the Americas was populated by aborigines with diverse customs and languages who were systematically exterminated by Spanish colonizers and their local conspirators (Bayer, 2009). Currently small groups of the descendents of Native Americans of South America live in small tribes in the northern part of the country in provinces near the borders of Bolivia and Paraguay and in the south in the Patagonia (Instituto Nacional de Estadísticas y Censos de la República Argentina [INDEC], 2009).

Argentina is predominantly of southern European descent, with nearly 80% of its population having ancestors from Italy and Spain. Other immigrant groups, in minor percentages, are from Germany, England, Russia, Poland, and Armenia. Immigrants from the Middle East are not numerous enough to warrant counting (INDEC, 2009).

It is said that Argentines share the customs and cultural worldviews of Italians but speak Spanish. Together with Uruguay and Chile, Argentina is vastly different from the rest of South America, where pre-Hispanic Native American cultures are still flourishing. Argentina abolished slavery and the African slave trade on its independence from Spain in 1816. As a result, African culture is almost nonexistent (INDEC, 2009).

Argentina enjoys a wealth of natural resources and climates. Its vast territory includes jungles in the northeast; thousands of miles of Atlantic Ocean coastline to the east; the majestic Andes mountain range to the West; and the Pampas, the domain of the gauchos, at its heart. With hot climates in the north, intermediate temperatures in the center, and extreme dry and cold weather in the south, Argentina culminates in the Tierra del Fuego (Land of Fire) across the Argentine Sea from Antarctica and the Islas Malvinas, islands claimed by the United Kingdom.

Argentina has a democracy seated in the capital of Buenos Aries, and citizens elect their president every 4 years. A total of 70% of Argentines are followers of the Roman Catholic faith, and the rest are Protestants or Jews (INDEC, 2009). The country's middle class is tied to agricultural

Author Note. We extend special appreciation to Adriana Petrini of the National Board for Certified Counselors, who assisted with the translation of this chapter.

crops and cattle production. Argentina is famous for its meats and wine, along with industry and tourism. Unfortunately, the country has struggled throughout with governmental instability, corruption, and social unrest for many years, making it very difficult for the population to prosper.

The Historical Development of Counseling

Counseling as a distinct profession in Argentina was launched with the creation of the first educational program in Buenos Aires in 1986. Its graduating class of approximately 20 students paved the way in 1989 for the creation of Holos, the Argentine Center for Humanistic Psychology and Counseling in Buenos Aires. Founded by Sánchez Berneman, Holos fostered growth in the counseling field and provided a unique identity for the profession.

Privately owned in the early 1990s, Holos offered the first courses toward a degree in counseling while applying in 1991 for official institutional and degree recognition (registration) by the Argentine Department of Higher Education. Soon thereafter, the Argentine Association of Counselors was created to operate as a regulatory entity for the counseling profession. The Board of Directors and its members generate and coordinate activities to improve the counseling profession, including the teaching of degree courses, supervision for field experiences, and the provision of a code of ethics.

In addition to the Argentine Association of Counselors, National Board for Certified Counelors (NBCC) Argentina was created to develop and regulate a certification credential for those who met its educational and training standards. NBCC Argentina, working under the guidance of NBCC International (a nonprofit organization based in the United States dedicated to providing standards for the certification of counselors), also provides guidelines for continuing education.

The official application for a counseling degree was approved in 1992 by ministerial decree (Ministerio de Educación de la Nación Argentina, 1992), but it was not until 1998 that counseling was recognized by the government as an official educational degree. Additional recognition was noted by the publication of *¿Crear salud o curar enfermedad?* (*Creating Health or Curing Illness?*; Sánchez Bodas et al., 1993), the first book about counseling written and edited by Argentinean professionals. Since then, the number of university degree programs in counseling has grown exponentially. More than 25 institutions teach counseling in the capital city of Buenos Aires and in the provinces of Buenos Aires, Misiones, Santa Fe, and Salta. Other programs are being started in other cities in the interior of the country and are adding different approaches and tracks, such as the systemic family model.

Current Trends

Growth and International Recognition

It is estimated that there are nearly 5,000 graduates of counseling programs and more than 2,000 others enrolled in postgraduate work in counseling in Argentina. This has made counseling one of the fastest growing professions (in terms of average enrollment) in Argentina in the first decade of the 21st century (Argentine Association of Counselors, personal communication, August 30, 2011). According to an internal survey of 500 Holos graduates, 60% of graduates practice in settings such as organizational boards, educational institutions, labor and nongovernmental organizations, health-related fields, community centers, and religious settings, each with a different counseling focus (Holos, 2009).

The growth of the profession has been recognized internationally. At the 35th International Counseling Conference in Paris in 1998, a delegation of 36 Argentinean counselors proposed a plan of studies for counseling programs that was recognized as best practice for training counselors. Argentina became a member of the International Association for Counselling and held the 37th International Counseling Conference in 2004 in Buenos Aires, which involved an audience of delegations from around the world.

In 2007, Holos organized the Third Inter-American Congress on Counseling (also known as the Counseling Congress of the Americas) in which participants, including representatives from the United States, Venezuela, Mexico, and Cuba, met to share best practices. Counselors from Argentina presented research at the Fourth Inter-American Congress on Counseling held in Nicaragua in 2008 and organized the Fifth Latin American Congress on Counseling in Buenos Aires in 2009. Finally, professionals from Argentina collaborated with the Universidad Iberoamericana in 2010 to organize the Sixth Latin American Congress in Mexico City, Mexico.

It is important to note that all Latin American events were cosponsored by the international division of the NBCC. These partnerships proved fruitful in 2011, when, after a 4-year endeavor to adapt educational and practice standards similar to those of the NBCC, counselors in Argentina became eligible to obtain the National Certified Counselor–Argentina Certification designation.

Growth of the Knowledge Base

Parallel to the growth of counseling in Argentina and through international recognition, a number of publications emerged. This fulfilled several needs of Argentine counselors. First and foremost, there seemed to be a search by individuals and groups for a counseling identity. The book *¿Que es counseling?* (*What Is Counseling?;* Sánchez Bodas, 2008) illustrates this point. Second, there was a demand for information on counseling theories and practices developed in Argentina based solely on the local experience. Examples of scholarly publications that made a mark in the way counselors are trained today include books such as *Practica del counseling en Argentina* (*Counseling Practice in Argentina*) by Grinblat et al. (2008), *Psicología general del counseling* (*General Psychology of Counseling*) by Dietrich (1986), and *Counseling humanístico* (*Humanistic Counseling*) by Sánchez Bodas et al. (1999).

Lastly, evidence-based research studies emerged that corroborated work conducted throughout the profession's 80-year existence and validated the effectiveness of the profession in Argentina. A landmark study was conducted in 2007 and published as a 2008 chapter in Sánchez Bodas (2008). This study reported the positive effects of counseling based on the results of a survey of 376 counselees on their perceptions of the efficacy of the counseling process (40 of whom were randomly selected to participate in interviews).

School Counseling

Although counseling programs offer course work and a postgraduate specialization in school counseling, this field as a distinct discipline has not been fully developed. The growth of school counseling in Argentina has been slow in comparison to the growth of counseling in mental health institutions, organizational settings, and community organizations.

The reasons for this are varied. Counseling is a relatively new profession, and most graduates tend to seek employment in places in which counseling has long been accepted. This cannot be said about educational settings where the employment of school counselors is relatively new. School counselors as professionals are not regulated by the Ministry of Education. They are not mandated as essential to the education setting and compete with school psychologists (*psicopedagogos*), who have been in schools since the late 1990s. School psychologists provide student testing and assessment as well as therapy, providing a barrier to the employment of school counselors.

Since 2007 there has been a trend in a handful of privately run high schools to hire school counselors to facilitate prevention workshops on drug addiction, sexuality, domestic violence, and bullying. This is clearly an area of enormous untapped potential, and counselors are working to identify the demand for counseling services in schools and to develop appropriate programs.

Psychology and Social Work

There seems to be an understanding among clinicians in the work setting that professionals in the fields of counseling, psychology, and social work have a common goal—maximizing the welfare of their clients. For the most part, professionals work side by side and in teams without conflict, understanding the unique contributions that each discipline offers for clients. Yet the Colegio de Psicólogos de la República Argentina (College of Psychologists of Argentina) does not appear to accept counselors as legitimate mental health professionals and argues against the multidisciplinary treatment team and multiple treatment modalities used in many mental health settings. Moreover, the College does not acknowledge counseling as a profession, choosing to treat it as a competitive field despite the growing number of psychologists who understand the strengths and differences of both professions and appreciate the benefits of working alongside counselors in interdisciplinary practice.

Best Counseling Practices

Theoretical Approaches

Argentine counselors are well known for integrating therapeutic modalities that enrich their practice. Most counselors, however, work from humanistic and existential theories because those are the philosophies taught in the majority of counseling training programs in Argentina. Using Carl Rogers's (1966, 1972) model as a foundation, counselors integrate diverse resources from gestalt therapy, psychodrama, and assisted equine therapy and incorporate tasks that involve, for instance, daydreaming, focusing, corporal movements, and artistic creations. An approach known as *counseling filosófico* or *terapia filosófica* is also widely practiced based on theories found in Lou Marinoff's book *Mas Platón menos prosac* (*More Plato Less Prozac;* Marinoff, 2000). This philosophy is grounded in increasing the prevalence of counseling as a treatment option and reducing the number of psychotropic medications used in mental health practice.

Although counseling is based primarily on talk therapy, the body, the felt experience, imagination, metaphor, play, and the arts are regularly integrated into the profession. This approach is characteristic of counseling training programs that emphasize a holistic approach centered on the person. A lesser taught and practiced philosophy derives from Virginia Satir's family-oriented systemic theory with transpersonal and psychoanalytic orientation perspectives; cognitive behavioral theory is not taught in counseling programs and therefore not known to be practiced.

Where Counselors Work

The recognition of counseling as a profession and the availability of work opportunities in public and private settings are increasing. In the first 10 years of the profession, counseling was limited to private offices and institutions that had agreements with university programs to place practicum and internship students-in-training. These included community agencies and churches of varied denominations. Since then, counseling has expanded into mental health hospitals and clinics as well as a handful of private secondary schools. For instance, the Hospital School of Doctors Jose de San Martin in Buenos Aires has incorporated a group of counselors working in the field of palliative care with terminally ill patients since 2000. This has been a pivotal move in increasing the recognition of counselors as integral members of the health care team. Training programs have also paved the way in the substance abuse and addiction arena, in which an abundance of counselors are currently working.

Government offices, especially in Buenos Aires and its neighboring municipality of San Isidro, have hired counselor teams to conduct employee workshops on addiction, family violence, gender issues, and peer mediation. Prominent insurance companies have followed suit, as have several large businesses, which now hire counselors as part of their human resources departments. It is estimated that approximately 3,000 counselors are working throughout the country in different settings practicing unique specialties (Argentine Association of Counselors, personal communication, August 30, 2011).

How Counselors Work

Given that the foundation of counseling training programs in Argentina is primarily based on a holistic approach grounded in Carl Rogers's person-centered, humanistic theory, counseling is delivered in a variety of formats and settings depending on where the client is counseled. If the client is at a private or public mental health clinic, a series of agency protocols (e.g., intake interviews and psychosocial assessment) must be followed that assist in determining the best course of treatment with the most appropriate clinician. Typically the client is interviewed two or three times, and the client and counselor together enter into a process by which both agree on the goals and plans for counseling. Diagnosis and a prescribed treatment protocol based on psychopathology are not the focus of counseling, and therefore great emphasis is placed on the collaborative approach among the client and counselor, the couple and counselor, and the family or group and counselor. Counselors in private practice also follow this approach; it is rare to find counseling services being provided in informal settings and not following a process for acknowledging client-driven goals. Technology, such as the use of the Internet to assist in counseling, is scarce and not readily used in agencies, although a few private practitioners are exploring technology as an option for providing services.

The *Diagnostic and Statistical Manual of Mental Disorders* (American Psychiatric Association, 2000) is not used in a systematic fashion by counselors in Argentina, although it is consulted when and if the intake interview yields possible client symptoms indicative of a psychiatric disorder. Counselors in Argentina are not allowed to treat clients with severe pathology and are trained to refer such clients to psychotherapists, psychologists, or medical doctors. A research study conducted in 2007 illustrated this point by concluding that more than 60% of the counseling sessions offered in 2007 successfully treated relational conflicts brought to counseling by couples and families (Sánchez Bodas, 2008). It is worth noting that counselors working in private and public settings alike respect and do not violate this professional boundary. Novice counselors obtain ongoing supervision for the first few years of practice to ensure quality practice in this regard.

Diversity Issues

In order to understand issues of economic and cultural diversity among those living in Argentina, one needs to understand the country's history and the political and economic volatility that exists in that region of the world. As mentioned previously, colonization annihilated the majority of the native populations and brought an influx of Italians and Spaniards to Argentina, making these two cultures the dominant groups today (45% and 31% of the population, respectively; INDEC, 2009). In the extreme north and south of the country live approximately 30 Native American tribes that continue to fight for territorial rights. Some reside in large metropolitan areas but in humble, poverty-stricken homes, having little or no resources and little access to counseling through community service centers.

There are several large communities of diverse European origin: Poles (the third largest minority), Brits (the fourth largest), Russians, Armenians, and Germans (INDEC, 2009). Since the late 1980s, Bolivians, Paraguayans, and Peruvians of Native American descent have slowly migrated to large cities in Argentina because of economic hardship in their own countries (INDEC, 2009). Add to this the small numbers of Chinese, Korean, and

Japanese immigrants, and one can see that Argentina has grown to become a true mixing bowl of racial integration. In sum, Argentines are predominantly of southern, White-European descent in tradition, religion, and culture, congregating primarily in middle-class and wealthy neighborhoods of provincial capitals and in Buenos Aires, where counseling is most highly developed.

It is our opinion that because of the substantial linguistic and cultural homogeneity among Argentines, ethnic and racial discrimination do not influence the practice of counseling. Sexual orientation also does not seem to be an issue that affects the practice of counseling. The capital of Buenos Aires is recognized by the world's gay community as a space where homosexuals can transit, visit, and live without experiencing a great deal of discrimination. This is evidenced by the wealth of references in newspapers and magazines to this topic and by the growing number of hotels and bars for homosexuals. Argentina legalized homosexual marriage in 2010.

Classism, socioeconomics, and social injustice are stronger determinants of the discrimination seen between the upper and middle classes who may be able to afford private practice counseling and the relatively large low-income individuals and families who seek counseling at community centers. This divide, however, is not seen in the type of issues for which counseling is sought.

Counselors in community centers and private practice both work with groups of ex-prisoners transitioning back to society and begging, homeless street children and their families. These two groups account for a great deal of diversity in the client population because of conflicts related to a shrinking middle class, social injustice, and social discrimination. Most problems addressed in counseling are related to a noticeable deficit in the education of adults and their children, conflict in families and couples, addictions, sexuality, the lack of a father figure, the need to manage a large number of children, and difficulty setting boundaries with children. The role of the counselor appears to be defined by intense preventive work, containment of the problem, and counseling with the goal of facilitating the resolution of cognitive and emotional pain.

School counselors who work in educational institutions observe a difference between free public education and the education offered in private schools. Private schools offer multiple services and opportunities not seen in public schools, including foreign languages, computers, honors and advanced courses, and sports. This inequality perpetuates classism, prejudice and inequality, and discrimination. As indicated by Maslow's (1999) hierarchy of needs, the majority of children in public education settings remain longer at the base of the pyramid; attending to basic needs is the primary focus of school counselors. In private schools, however, counseling barely focuses on basic needs, which are typically provided for by the family unit.

Despite the great diversity of the clientele in Argentina, the counseling profession has not yet advanced to the point of integrating issues of cultural and socioeconomic diversity into practice. Counselors appear to be aware of the unique characteristics and circumstances of the individual, the family, and the group but not within the cultural context in which they live and work. It is not well understood why these issues are not at the core of counseling given the striking divide between the wealthy (typically White) and the poor (typically darker skinned, of native descent). This is an untapped area that deserves further attention and research.

Counselor Education

Counselor education programs in Argentina emerged from model programs already established in the United States and England. To meet the needs of Argentine society, the counseling profession and the educational programs that followed were developed by a group of pioneers who believed in teachings that focused on working within the normalcy of the individual, whereas the specific scope of counseling lies in the crises of persons or groups who do not suffer psychiatric pathologies. The result yielded counseling objectives and a curriculum founded on an adapted definition by Dietrich (1986) that describes the counselor as a professional who aims to focus on the client's potential for active learning, the client's capacity for self-help, and the development of self-esteem and self-direction.

In 2012, nearly 25 universities and private institutions in Argentina offer counseling degrees, and more are expected as professional counseling becomes better known.

An updated resolution by the Ministry of Culture and Education states the following:

> A degree in Psychological Counseling and/or Specialized Psychological Counseling qualifies a person to establish a relationship of psychological assistance, preventive in nature in which the counselor, making use of verbal communication and based on resources taken from humanistic psychology, tries in a relatively short period of time to promote, in a person or in normal groups who are disoriented, unduly stressed, confused, or undergoing a crisis, active learning processes, their capacity of self-determination, their operative ability, and the development of their capabilities. Such a role may be performed either independently or under an employment relationship. (Dirección General de Cultura y Educación, 2010, p. 3)

Time has proven not only the virtues of this definition but also its drawbacks: Its limited scope and the difficulty of finding an identity separate from that of psychology are challenges for the practice of counseling in this country.

Counselor Student Competencies

Educational programs developed a core set of student competencies under the assumption that counselors are consulted by individuals or groups of individuals who need guidance in their decision making, in solving a particular problem, or in resolving a particular conflict. Thus, counseling students learn to (a) provide emotional assistance to clients, (b) provide preventive advice, (c) promote actions that will improve the client's quality of life, (d) assist clients in making favorable decisions given changing times and processes, and (e) facilitate the transformation and deployment of human potential.

Students learn counseling skills to listen unconditionally and empathically rooted in authenticity in which technical responses (e.g., verbal, imaginary, philosophical, creative, corporal) will enable clients to recover their lost integrity and to choose more favorable ways of behaving and being in the world. In this professional development path, the interest of counselor training programs lies in creating relational conditions that favor client psychospiritual well-being at the individual, interpersonal, and community levels.

Curriculum

As a result of a 2011 resolution by the Ministry of Culture and Education, the original curriculum developed in 1987 was strengthened by a team of educators led by one of the authors of this chapter, Andres Sánchez Bodas. The outcome, a degree in Superior Technician in Psychological Consultation—Counseling, encompasses a 4-year education with 1,616 clock hours of classroom instruction (equivalent to approximately 35 semester-long courses or 105 credit hours in the U.S. university system). This makes Argentine training programs competitive with similar programs around the world.

The Future

Counseling in Argentina is an established profession with title protection and an educational degree that shares the aforementioned new vision and plan for the future. The profession has suffered and unfortunately will continue to suffer opposition from the College of Psychologists of Argentina, an organization that does not appear to understand the potential contribution of counseling and instead views it as competition.

The Superior Technician in Psychological Consultation—Counseling degree gives counseling an important place among the helping professions by increasing the number of credit hours of education, increasing the number of hours in direct client work, and adding research courses to the curriculum. At the same time it opens up the profession to the incorporation of new professional projections. Society continues to demand more counseling professionals; this is a trend that we see in different regions of the country and across socioeconomic barriers. This makes possible the integration of counselors with other professionals in inter- and cross-disciplinary teams as well as their incorporation in nontraditional work settings such as business, education, health centers, geriatric centers, and addiction and other specialized centers.

Argentinean counselors have been associated with educational institutions around the world, organizing international congresses and events, and obtaining certifications based on degrees and programs developed in other countries. This has contributed to great professional growth. We believe that Argentinean counselors' current commitment to best practices, education, supervision, and ethics provide the basis necessary for further development of the profession. We look forward to counselors continuing to gain greater acceptance among psychologists, other helping professionals, and the population at large. We anticipate the successful expansion of the profession as Argentinean counselors continue to demonstrate their value to society.

References

American Psychiatric Association. (2000). *Diagnostic and statistical manual of mental disorders* (4th ed., text rev.). Washington, DC: Author.

Bayer, O. (2009). *Obras completas* [Complete works]. Buenos Aires, Argentina: Editorial Página 12.

Dietrich, G. (1986). *Psicología general del counseling* [General psychology of counseling]. Barcelona, Spain: Editorial Herder.

Dirección General de Cultura y Educación. (2010). *Tecnicatura superior en consultoría psicológica* [Superior technician in psychological consultation—Counseling]. Buenos Aires, Argentina: Author.

Grinblat, A., Allocatti, M., Alonso, C., Amendola, V., Apellaniz, L., Arlenghi, A., . . . Vitale, M. (2008). *Practica del counseling en Argentina* [Counseling practice in Argentina]. Buenos Aires, Argentina: Editorial Zanun.

Holos. (2009). *Encuesta sobre inserción del counseling en Argentina* [Survey on the insertion of counseling in Argentina]. Unpublished survey, San Isidro, Buenos Aires.

Instituto Nacional de Estadísticas y Censos de la República Argentina. (2009). *Estadísticas de inmigración y de habitantes* [Population and immigration statistics]. Buenos Aires, Argentina: Author.

Marinoff, L. (2000). *Mas Platón Menos prosac* [More Plato less Prozac]. Madrid, Spain: Editorial Rustica.

Maslow, A. H. (1999). *Toward a psychology of being*. New York, NY: Wiley.

Ministerio de Educación de la Nación Argentina. (1992). *Resolución Ministerial N° 212/92* [Argentina Department of Education Resolution No. 212/92]. Buenos Aires, Argentina: Author.

Rogers, C. (1966). *Psicoterapia centrada en el cliente* [Client-centered therapy]. Buenos Aires, Argentina: Editorial Paidos.

Rogers, C. (1972). *El proceso de convertirse en persona* [On becoming a person]. Buenos Aires, Argentina: Editorial Paidos.

Sánchez Bodas, A. (2008). *¿Que es counseling?* [What is counseling?]. Buenos Aires, Argentina: Editorial LEA.

Sánchez Bodas, A., Astiz, A., Beltran Costa, R., Cortese, A., Frezza, E., Gallino, O., . . . Van Rafelghem, M. (1993). *¿Crear salud o curar enfermedad?* [Creating health or curing illness?]. Buenos Aires, Argentina: Editorial Holos.

Sánchez Bodas, A., Rodriguez, E., Poliak, J., Van Rafelghem, M., Horvath, J., Grosz, L., . . . Lombardini, J. (1999). *Counseling humanístico* [Humanistic counseling]. Buenos Aires, Argentina: Editorial Holos.

• • •

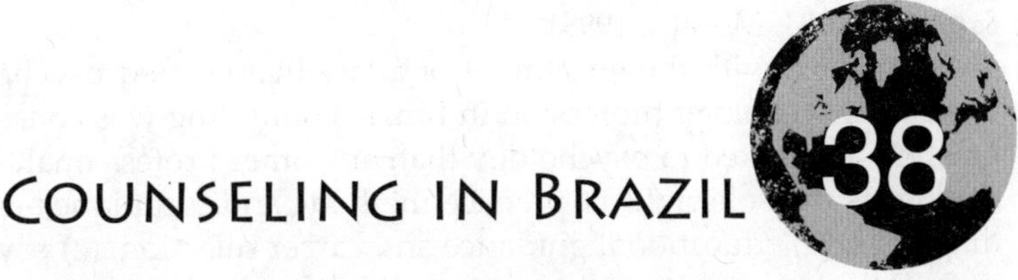

Counseling in Brazil

Aida Hutz-Midgett, Marco Antônio Pereira Teixeira, and Claudio Simon Hutz

Brazil is the largest and most populous country in Latin America. It is a country of contrasts, for there are vast cultural, geographical, social, and economic differences among regions. In large urban areas, the most economically privileged layers of the population have access to state-of-the art education, health services, and quality leisure. The less privileged, however, live in poverty. Although Brazil has shown sustained economic growth and improved income distribution since 2000, social inequality is still significant and a major problem the country has not overcome. Nevertheless, employment rates have increased and more students have enrolled in higher education, suggesting increased potential for personal and social development. In this chapter, we discuss career-related counseling services offered within the landscape of this vibrant and unique developing country.

The Historical Development of Counseling

Counseling in Brazil emerged to help people with vocational and educational choices in the 1920s, both within schools and in the general population (Grinspun, 2011). The first educational and career guidance activity was attributed to Swiss engineer Roberto Mange, who in 1924 created a career guidance course for mechanics students in São Paulo. In this early period (i.e., the 1920s and 1930s), counseling was linked to applied psychology, which was developing in the areas of medicine, education, and work organization (Sparta, 2003). In 1931, the first agency to provide vocational guidance was established in Sao Paulo; it operated out of the Institute of Education at the University of São Paulo and was later discontinued in 1935. At the same time, other schools also initiated career and vocational guidance services (Grinspun, 2011).

In 1942, a reform in the Brazilian secondary education system mandated the creation of vocational technical schools that included educational guidance services in their curricula. This led to the establishment of the role of the educational adviser, whose job was to help students adapt to the school context and discern career choices (Grinspun, 2011; Sparta, 2003). However, specialized training for those conducting this activity was nonexistent.

With the creation of the Getulio Vargas Foundation, a major educational and research institution in Brazil, in 1944, the career counseling movement started to gain momentum (C. S. Hutz,

Gauer, & Gomes, 2011). In 1945 and 1946, the Foundation offered courses for professionals in the areas of career selection, educational guidance, and vocational rehabilitation (Sparta, 2003). In 1947, the Institute of Career Guidance was established within the Getulio Vargas Foundation and went on to become a productive research center and a training provider.

During this period, counseling was mainly related to helping clients select a career, although career counselors working in the schools also dealt with other issues related to student adaptation. The predominant theoretical model for the counseling profession was the trait-and-factor approach combined with the use of psychometric instruments, which sought to identify clients' skills and link them with career opportunities (Sparta, 2003). In the 1940s, with the arrival of Carl Rogers's humanistic ideas to Brazil, the concept of counseling began to expand, and the term *psychological counseling* was used to describe a specific client–counselor relationship that was considered therapeutic in nature (Gomes, Holanda, & Gauer, 2004; Morato, 1999).

From 1962, with the enactment of a law that created psychology programs and regulated the psychology profession in Brazil, counseling was considered an activity that was most closely linked to psychology than any other professional field. The law granted psychologists the sole right to practice methods and techniques related to (a) psychological diagnosis, (b) educational guidance and career selection, (c) psychoeducational guidance, and (d) the treatment of adjustment problems. According to this legislation, all psychology programs were required to provide a *counseling-related curriculum,* although no theoretical approach was recommended as the best practice.

Over time, however, training in psychology in Brazil acquired a strong clinical basis focused on psychotherapy and theoretical diversity. As a result, counseling lost its scope of practice and became linked solely to interventions focused on career issues (i.e., career counseling) and those based on a person-centered approach (i.e., psychological counseling). Today training in counseling is provided through undergraduate psychology programs that last for 5 years but is not standardized or mandatory in all programs.

It is important to note that counseling in Brazil is not an independent professional field. In the 1960s, when psychology became a regulated profession, psychology programs were receptive to counseling approaches accepted in North American academic fields. As a result, counseling was embedded within the larger umbrella of professional psychology. Moreover, the title "professional counselor" is seldom used in Brazil. Most psychologists who perform activities characterized as counseling identify their practice as either clinical, school, or organizational psychology. This is partly due to the fact that the Portuguese equivalent translation of the word *counseling* is "advice giving." This expression has restricted meaning, conveying an activity with little professional consistency and without a scientific basis for practice.

Because the clinical practice of counseling in Brazil has become confounded with the actual practice of psychology, this chapter covers only the field of career counseling, which has a clearly established identity in the country and an active national association. However, career counseling in Brazil is not practiced just by psychologists, except with regard to the use of psychological instruments. Other professionals, such as those in the field of education, can also practice career counseling, especially in school contexts.

The Current Status of Counseling

Since the 1980s, the career counseling movement in Brazil has been expanding and gaining more visibility. This is partly due to the resumption of research productivity, which was stagnant in the 1970s. The first doctoral dissertations and master's theses in career counseling were completed in the late 1970s and early 1980s (Abade, 2005). This encouraged the consolidation of existing services in some universities and created new research centers interested in learning more about career and educational guidance.

In the 1990s, the Brazilian Association of Professional Advisors, currently the Brazilian Association of Vocational Guidance (ABOP), focused on (a) bringing together career counselors in the country, (b) strengthening professional identity, (c) stimulating development, and (d) promoting the skills career counselors offer the general population. To advance its goals, ABOP has conducted symposiums, supported training programs and events, published a newsletter, actively engaged with other international associations in the area of career counseling, and published a peer-reviewed journal (Melo-Silva, 2007).

The most recognized scholarly events specific to career counseling in Brazil are the symposiums held by ABOP that take place every other year. These events bring together professionals, researchers, and students. From 1995 to 2009, eight symposiums were held, and the last two were held simultaneously with the First and Second Latin American Conferences on Vocational Guidance of ABOP, which attracted participants from Brazil, Mexico, Argentina, Venezuela, Colombia, Uruguay, Portugal, Spain, and France (Melo-Silva, 2007; Melo-Silva & Lassance, 2008). The internationalization of these professional conferences reflects ABOP's commitment to stay current with cutting-edge global practices of career and vocational counseling; disseminate Brazilian ideas and practices; and promote an international exchange of ideas, research, and joint collaboration. On a similar note, ABOP is also affiliated with other international associations such as the Red Latinoamericana de Orientación Professional (Latin American Network of Professional Guidance) and the International Association for Educational and Vocational Guidance.

In addition to engaging in international collaborations, ABOP disseminates knowledge by publishing the *Brazilian Journal of Vocational Guidance,* a peer-reviewed journal released since 2003 (from 1998 to 1999 the journal was named *Journal of ABOP;* http://pepsic.bvsalud.org/scielo.php?script=sci_serial&pid=1679-3390&lng=en&nrm=iso). The journal is open access, which facilitates the dissemination of knowledge to the academic community and practitioners. In recent years, the journal has been receiving increased international contributions, especially from Latin America and Europe.

Who Practices Counseling

Despite ABOP's attempts, it is difficult to estimate the actual number of professionals working in career counseling in Brazil. Because certification is not required for the practice of career counseling, there are no records of how many qualified professionals are working in the area. In 2012, ABOP had about 400 members (A. Hutz & Hutz, 2012), but the number of professionals who conduct activities related to career counseling is certainly much greater. In addition, career counseling is seldom the only or the main activity carried out by professionals, especially psychologists. For example, many clinical psychologists who practice psychotherapy in private practice also work at times with clients on career-related issues. Although these professionals are practicing career counseling, they often do not identify as career counselors and are not affiliated with ABOP.

The lack of systematic records also makes it difficult to accurately describe where career counselors work and the types of interventions they conduct; however, some information is available. According to a national survey (n = 84) conducted at an ABOP professional meeting, career counseling is practiced mainly by psychologists and secondarily by educators (Melo-Silva, Bonfim, Esbrogeo, & Soares, 2003). Most professionals work in schools, universities, or private practice or at a career counseling nucleus or group (the latter is often linked to psychology programs in universities). In addition, some institutions, both public and private, are active in the field of advising, consulting, offering job placement services, and providing career-related counseling (Melo-Silva, Lassance, & Soares, 2004).

School Counseling

It is important to emphasize that the main demand for career counseling in Brazil comes from students who are completing high school, as most of them are expected to continue on to higher education (Melo-Silva et al., 2004; Sparta & Gomes, 2005). Consequently, services often target this population and are aimed to help students select their major area of study, which has to be decided prior to taking the *vestibular* (i.e., entry exams that are developed by each university). However, this is starting to change, as many universities are adopting a national exam. Other types of interventions are also utilized, such as career planning, preparation for job searches, preparation for careers in preschools, preparation for retirement, and career counseling for adults experiencing distress related to a career transition.

Career Counseling

Currently the practice of career counseling in Brazil varies in terms of theoretical approach. Although trait-and-factor was the main model until the 1960s, criticisms about relying solely on testing in the 1970s and 1980s created room for other theories and ways of approaching career counseling and vocational guidance in Brazil. Currently several theoretical approaches are influential.

In particular, career counseling was strongly influenced by the psychodynamic theory of Bohoslavsky (1971), who arrived in the country in the 1980s. Bohoslavsky, an Argentine psychologist, criticized counseling that was based strictly on test results, suggesting that from this perspective the client was treated as a passive subject in the face of making career choices. Personal characteristics were taken as innate and combined with occupational possibilities, removing the client's sense of autonomy and personal responsibility. In contrast, Bohoslavsky proposed the clinical approach, which aimed to help clients make their own choices while the counselor assisted in addressing the conflicts that hindered the decision-making process. The psychoanalytic underpinning of this approach, which valued the subjective and potentially conflicting aspects involved in choosing a career, was well received among Brazilian psychologists. This was consistent with the strong emphasis placed on psychoanalysis by psychology training programs in Brazil.

Another popular theoretical approach is called the sociohistorical approach (Bock, 2002). This approach, which is based on Marxist theory, seeks to emphasize the dialectical relationship that the individuals have with the sociocultural environment to which they belong. One of the goals of counseling from this perspective is to help clients become aware of these sociohistorical determinations as they relate to their educational and occupational path so that clients can elect to engage in conscious actions to transcend their sociohistorical realities.

In addition to Bohoslavsky's clinical approach and the sociohistorical perspective, other theoretical models have influenced career counseling in Brazil. Among the internationally recognized career theories, the developmental model of Donald Super (Super, Savickas, & Super, 1996) and the cognitive model of Pelletier, Noiseux, and Bujold (1977) provide the basis for various interventions. In recent years, the constructivist ideas of Savickas (2005) have also been incorporated into some counseling nuclei. Holland's (1997) theory has gained visibility because of Brazil's recent translation and adaptation of the Self-Directed Search inventory. Career counseling in Brazil is also influenced by other approaches that are not specific to the area of career and vocational guidance but that primarily impact the delivery of interventions—for example, the Pichon-Rivière group dynamics perspective, psychodrama, and psychoeducational models (Melo-Silva et al., 2004).

In short, the theoretical frameworks that underlie the practice of career counseling in the country are varied. However, all interventions have at least two common basic goals: greater knowledge of the self and greater knowledge of educational and/or occupational opportunities. In addition, some approaches may also include discussions about career choice and its determinants as well as about the contemporary world of work (Melo-Silva et al., 2004).

Interventions are carried out mainly through individual sessions or small groups. One reason for using groups is to optimize resources—several clients are served at the same time. In addition, group work enables the exchange of experiences among participants, which often helps to reduce anxiety and promote mutual support. In general, clients meet with a counselor for eight sessions, but the total number of intervention hours varies, with an average of 15 (Melo-Silva et al., 2004). The sessions are usually conducted in individual offices, rooms appropriately sized for groups, or a classroom when counseling is conducted in schools or universities.

The techniques used in career counseling vary widely and are selected according to the characteristics and needs of the clients. Counseling activities may include group work (e.g., games, art work, psychodrama, and experiential exercises); individual sessions; the completion of career inventories and/or surveys to promote reflection; and the sharing of professional information and other resources such as texts, magazines, videos, and computer programs (Melo-Silva et al., 2003). Career counselors also use the Internet, mainly to research and share information with clients; some university career centers have their own websites for this purpose. However, generally in Brazil no career counseling interventions are offered solely through the Internet, although some national research findings suggest that online interventions could be effective (Melo-Silva et al., 2004; Spaccaquerche, 2005). In addition to online career interventions, another area that could benefit from further development is the availability of more specific information regarding the current labor market.

Furthermore, the use of interest inventories and/or psychological tests in career counseling is not always considered necessary in Brazil. By legal determination, psychological tests can only be used by psychologists, which means that educators, for example, cannot use these tools. In addition, among psychologists the use of tests depends on the theoretical approach or model of intervention. For example, professionals practicing career and vocational counseling who rely on qualitative interventions aimed to promote self-knowledge do not have a need for a standardized assessment, as this approach does not require it. Recently, however, with the upgrading and development of new instruments (Nunes, Okino, Noce, & Jardim-Maran, 2008), support for psychological evaluation has been gaining momentum, and assessment has been reestablishing itself as an important element in career counseling.

Diversity Issues

Issues related to diversity are not yet mainstream in career and vocational counseling in Brazil. This is partly due to the fact that counseling services are sought mainly by high school students who want to pursue higher education—these students are usually late adolescents, White, and middle or upper class. Thus, to many Brazilians who are practicing counseling, issues of diversity are not apparent. At the same time, there is no specific training in psychology or other helping professions dedicated to issues of diversity and multicultural awareness (A. Hutz & Hutz, 2012). Therefore, with a few exceptions, systemic issues are not yet understood or addressed. However, the practice of career counseling in public schools, which are usually attended by students of low socioeconomic status who are often visibly diverse, has brought unique challenges to the field.

Young people in public education often find themselves in a disadvantageous position when it comes to choosing a profession because the quality of education in these schools is much lower than that in private schools. Thus, students who attend public schools tend to perform worse on the entrance examinations of the public universities, which are free of charge and of the highest quality. As a result, they cannot attend these universities (Bastos, 2005). At the same time, the socioeconomic state of the country does not allow for the majority of youth to attend private universities, where access is less competitive but expensive. Therefore, career counselors must be prepared to explore educational and occupational alternatives with clients, often helping them build their lives based on expectations that are viable yet consistent with their interests and aspirations.

The implementation of affirmative action programs in public universities has contributed to making more salient issues related to socioeconomic status, race, ethnicity, and culture. The goal of affirmative action in Brazil is to expand educational access and career opportunities to people living in poverty as well as to people who identify as Black and/or Brazilian Indian (A. Hutz & Hutz, 2012). In order to retain students of diverse backgrounds, universities have relied on counseling services to facilitate integration and adaptation to the academic environment as well as to provide interventions aimed at helping students transition from school life to work in order to maximize their chances of obtaining a job.

The expansion of international exchange programs in Brazil has also brought to light issues related to multiculturalism and cross-cultural awareness. Brazil has increasingly been receiving international students who experience unique barriers to their adaptation process and who could benefit from counseling (Bardagi, Andrade, & Teixeira, 2010). Many international students come to Brazil without well-defined personal and professional goals, and as a result they often end up in classes that are not best suited for their interests. Thus, career counseling interventions could contribute significantly to better accommodating these students in the university context. Despite the obvious need for interventions aimed at this population, research studies in this area are scarce, as are professionals who are qualified to address this type of demand (Bardagi et al., 2010).

Counselor Education

As previously mentioned, in Brazil professionals who engage in career counseling activities are usually psychologists or educators with degrees from institutions of higher education. However, there is no specific training in career counseling or even a system for obtaining certification, which is common to other similar specialized areas. Training often comes from psychology programs that offer classes and internships in career and educational guidance (Melo-Silva et al., 2004). However, the available training is often insufficient to enable a practitioner to work effectively with the depth of issues that emerge in career counseling.

In addition to certain psychology programs, training in career counseling is also offered through a single postdegree specialization course or cluster of courses. These courses are offered by universities or other institutions. In general, these courses provide greater depth of knowledge than the ones offered through psychology programs, and many provide opportunities for supervised practice (Soares, 1999). However, there is no standardization in terms of content, which has contributed to the heterogeneity of theoretical approaches and techniques observed among professionals working in the area.

The lack of a standardized curriculum for a unified field of career counseling has been of concern to ABOP since the 1990s. In 1999, a special issue of the *Journal of ABOP* sought to locate and describe the various training programs for career counseling in the country. Over time, discussions held among association members culminated in a draft of national guidelines for training in career counseling (Lassance, Melo-Silva, Bardagi, & Paradiso, 2007). This proposal established a set of skills, abilities, and a knowledge base that would be required for the training of career counselors organized into three areas: (a) theoretical content, (b) practical training, and (c) personal and ethical development. This proposal was not backed by a legal mandate, but it served as a guideline for those in academia who were currently dedicated to training career counselors.

The Future

Career counseling has been growing and consolidating over the years. Although it is still mainly utilized for counseling high school students who wish to attended universities, efforts are being made to expand the field. Therefore, one can expect the development of interventions aimed at client populations who have not received enough attention, such as high school students of low socioeconomic status, college students, persons who are unemployed, people with disabilities and chronic diseases, individuals diagnosed with mental illness, and people in transition to retirement.

Research and scholarly activities in the area are also expected to expand and gain momentum. Studies show an increase in research productivity in Brazil both in the number of theses and dissertations (Noronha et al., 2006) and in the publication of peer-reviewed articles (Noronha & Ambiel, 2006). However, productivity is still relatively low (A. Hutz & Hutz, 2012). Currently most publications come from the southeastern and southern regions of Brazil, and collaboration between researchers from different institutions is still rare (Teixeira, Lassance, Silva, & Bardagi, 2007). Thus, efforts will be needed in the academic community to promote greater collaboration among researchers across more regions of the country, placing emphasis on socioracial and ethnic diversity. For example, very little is known about the lived experiences and career development needs of indigenous peoples, coastal individuals, and rural people, to name just a few. Another diversity issue that needs further research is the relationship between sexual orientation and career development, a subject that is often neglected in the national career counseling literature.

Strengthening the field of career counseling in Brazil requires the development of more effective communication and lobbying on the part of ABOP with government sectors that create and implement public policies. Also, as it relates to education, career counseling is not offered in a standardized way in schools. Therefore, it would be beneficial for ABOP to increase its political voice with the Ministries of Labor and Education with the aim of learning more about how issues related to career counseling can be implemented by the two ministries. In fact, an official collaboration with the Ministry of Labor has already been established for this purpose (International Centre for Career Development and Public Policy, 2010). As a result of these efforts to expand the scope of practice, it is likely that issues of curriculum and training effectiveness will be the focus of heated debate in the future.

Conclusion

As a result of a mandate, counseling in Brazil emerged to meet the career and vocational needs of clients. Counseling was embedded under the larger umbrella of psychology in the 1960s when psychology was established as a field of study. Therefore, professionals who engage in counseling activities generally identify as clinical, school, or organizational psychologists; however, some also come from the field of education. Currently most career counseling activity in the country consists of counseling White middle- or upper class high school students who are preparing to take the *vestibular* (university entrance exam) in order to attend a university. However, there is growing awareness of other less mainstream populations who are beginning to receive services and benefit from the holistic work of career counselors.

In order for the profession to continue to grow, there is a need for more research through academic collaborations that include regions of the country that have been less active and that bring to light issues related to socioracial and ethnic diversity. Finally, it is crucial for ABOP to strengthen its public policy and lobbying efforts to standardize training and expand counseling's scope of practice.

References

Abade, F. L. (2005). Orientação profissional no Brasil: Uma revisão histórica da produção científica [Professional guidance in Brazil: A historical revision of the scientific production]. *Revista Brasileira de Orientação Profissional, 6*(1), 15–24.

Bardagi, M. P., Andrade, A. M., & Teixeira, M. A. (2010). Apoio institucional a estudantes estrangeiros e minoritários no Brasil: Algumas considerações [Institutional support to foreign and minority students in Brazil: Some considerations]. In C. S. Hutz (Ed.), *Avanços em Psicologia Comunitária e intervenções psicossociais* (pp. 297–325). São Paulo, Brazil: Casa do Psicólogo.

Bastos, J. C. (2005). Efetivação de escolhas profissionais de jovens oriundos do ensino público: Um olhar sobre suas trajetórias [The making of professional choices by youngsters from public schools: An overview of their trajectories]. *Revista Brasileira de Orientação Profissional, 6*(2), 31–43.

Bock, S. D. (2002). *Orientação profissional: a abordagem sócio-histórica* [Vocational guidance: Sociohistorical approach]. São Paulo, Brazil: Cortez.

Bohoslavsky, R. (1971). *Orientación vocacional: La estrategia clínica* [Vocational guidance: The clinical strategy]. Buenos Aires, Argentina: Galerna.

Gomes, W. B., Holanda, A. F., & Gauer, G. (2004). História das abordagens humanistas em psicologia no Brasil [History of the humanistic approaches in Brazil]. In M. Massimi (Ed.), *História da Psicologia no Brasil do Século XX* (pp. 105–130). São Paulo, Brazil: Editora Pedagógica Universitária.

Grinspun, M. P. S. Z. (2011). *A orientação educacional: Conflitos de paradigmas e alternativas para a escola* (5th ed.) [Educational guidance: Paradigm conflict and alternatives for the school]. São Paulo, Brazil: Cortez.

Holland, J. (1997). *Making vocational choices: A theory of vocational personalities and work environments.* Odessa, FL: Psychological Assessment Resources.

Hutz, A., & Hutz, C. S. (2012). Counseling in Brazil: Past, present, and future. *Journal of Counseling & Development, 90,* 238–242.

Hutz, C. S., Gauer, G., & Gomes, W. B. (2011). Brazil. In D. B. Baker (Ed.), *The Oxford handbook of the history of psychology: Global perspectives* (pp. 581–597). New York, NY: Oxford University Press.

International Centre for Career Development and Public Policy. (2010, December). South America: Brazil. *Policy Points, 10,* p. 8. Retrieved from http://www.iccdpp.org/Portals/1/Documents/PolicyPoints/POLICY.POINTS.10.pdf

Lassance, M. P., Melo-Silva, L. L., Bardagi, M. P., & Paradiso, A. C. (2007). Competências do orientador profissional: Uma proposta brasileira com vistas à formação e certificação [Competencies of the professional counselor: A Brazilian proposal regarding certification]. *Revista Brasileira de Orientação Profissional, 8*(1), 87–93.

Melo-Silva, L. L. (2007). Histórico da Associação Brasileira de Orientação Profissional e da *Revista Brasileira de Orientação Profissional* [The history of the Brazilian Association of Professional Orientation and of the *Brazilian Journal of Professional Orientation*]. *Revista Brasileira de Orientação Profissional, 8*(2), 1–9.

Melo-Silva, L. L., Bonfim, T. A., Esbrogeo, M. C., & Soares, D. H. P. (2003). Um estudo preliminar sobre práticas em orientação profissional [A preliminary study about the practices in professional orientation]. *Revista Brasileira de Orientação Profissional, 4*(1/2), 21–34.

Melo-Silva, L. L., & Lassance, M. C. P. (2008). Revbop: Relatório de gestão dos períodos 1997-1999 e 2003-2007 [Revbop: Report of the 1997-1999 and the 2003-2007 periods]. *Revista Brasileira de Orientação Profissional, 9,* 1–12.

Melo-Silva, L. L., Lassance, M. C. P., & Soares, D. H. P. (2004). A orientação profissional no contexto da educação e trabalho [Professional orientation in the context of education and work]. *Revista Brasileira de Orientação Profissional, 5*(2), 31–52.

Morato, H. T. P. (1999). *Aconselhamento psicológico centrado na pessoa: Novos desafios* [Person-centered psychological counseling: New challenges]. São Paulo, Brazil: Casa do Psicólogo.

Noronha, A. P. P., & Ambiel, R. A. M. (2006). Orientação profissional e vocacional: Análise da produção científica [Professional and vocational guidance: An analysis of the scientific publications]. *Psico-USF, 11*(1), 75–84.

Noronha, A. P. P., Andrade, R. G., Miguel, F. K., Nascimento, M. M., Nunes, M. F. O., Pacanaro, S. V., ... Cozza, H. F. P. (2006). Análise de teses e dissertações em orientação profissional [Analysis of theses and dissertations in professional orientation]. *Revista Brasileira de Orientação Profissional, 7,* 1–10.

Nunes, M. F. O., Okino, E. T. K., Noce, M. A., & Jardim-Maran, M. L. C. (2008). Interesses profissionais: Perspectivas teóricas e instrumentos de avaliação [Professional interests: Theoretical perspectives and assessment instruments]. *Avaliação Psicológica, 7,* 403–414.

Pelletier, D., Noiseux, G., & Bujold, C. (1977). *Desenvolvimento vocacional e crescimento pessoal*: Enfoque operatório [Vocational development and personal growth: Operative approach]. Petrópolis, Brazil: Vozes.

Savickas, M. L. (2005). The theory and practice of career construction. In S. Brown & R. Lent (Eds.), *Career development and counseling: Putting theory and research to work* (pp. 42–70). Hoboken, NJ: Wiley.

Soares, D. H. P. (1999). A formação do orientador profissional: o estado da arte no Brasil [The formation of a professional adviser: The state of the art in Brazil]. *Revista da ABOP, 3,* 7–21.

Spaccaquerche, M. E. (2005). Orientação profissional online: uma experiência em processo [Professional guidance online: An experience in process]. *Revista Brasileira de Orientação Profissional, 6,* 63–74.

Sparta, M. (2003). O desenvolvimento da Orientação Profissional no Brasil [The development of vocational guidance in Brazil]. *Revista Brasileira de Orientação Profissional, 4,* 1–11.

Sparta, M., & Gomes, W. B. (2005). Importância atribuída ao ingresso na educação superior por alunos do ensino médio [Attributed importance of higher education for medical students]. *Revista Brasileira de Orientação Profissional, 6,* 45–53.

Super, D. E., Savickas, M. L., & Super, C. M. (1996). The life-span, life-space approach to careers. In D. Brown, L. Brooks, & Associates (Eds.), *Career choice and development* (3rd ed., pp. 121–178). San Francisco, CA: Jossey-Bass.

Teixeira, M. A. P., Lassance, M. C. P., Silva, B. M. B., & Bardagi, M. P. (2007). Produção científica em orientação profissional: Uma análise da *Revista Brasileira de Orientação Profissional* [An analysis of the *Brazilian Journal of Vocational Guidance*]. *Revista Brasileira de Orientação Profissional, 8,* 25–40.

• • •

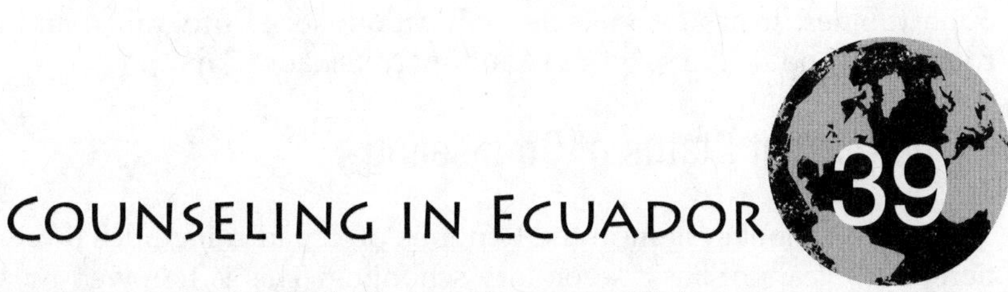

39 Counseling in Ecuador

Robert L. Smith and Maria Alexandra Valarezo

The Republic of Ecuador is located in South America between Peru and Columbia. It is about the size of Nevada and was named Ecuador because it is on the equator. A wide range of cultures and governments have influenced what is now Ecuador. The main language spoken is Spanish, and the nationality is Ecuadorian. The estimated population is 14,790,608 ("Republic of Ecuador," 2011). This review emphasizes the history that has shaped Ecuador's current educational system, the current status of counseling, and the future of counseling and counselor training.

The pre-Inca indigenous history of Ecuador, rich in culture and politics, lasted about 50 years, beginning in 1480 and ending with the Spanish conquest led by Francisco Pizarro and Diego Almagro. This was the beginning of the Spanish language in Ecuador. The Spanish settled in the major city of Quito and began establishing Pacific ports. In the northwest rainforest region known as Esmeraldas, Africans began to settle and established the Zambo Republic (*Zambo* refers to an intermixture of African and Native peoples). After several conflicts, the Spanish made alliances with representatives of the Zambo Republic. This arrangement produced 300 years of revolts, conflict, and revolutions that denied nationality for the Indio and Africans.

In 1822, Ecuador broke from Spain and joined the Confederation of Gran Colombia, which included present-day Colombia and Venezuela. In 1830, Ecuador became an independent republic. However, what followed were continuous ethnic disturbances and domination by a White European sector. Civil wars were common occurrences, including assassinations that slowed economic, social, and educational development. There was a brief calm period during World War I, followed by violence and dictatorship.

Since 1979, three elected presidents of Ecuador have been removed from office. The number of people living in poverty increased drastically over this time, and the size of the upper class White elite also increased. The "dollarization" of Ecuador's national currency occurred in 2000. Ecuador is currently considered a constitutional democracy consisting of a number of political parties and military and police forces that are very powerful.

The economic situation in Ecuador has affected the advancement and utilization of mental health specialists, including counselors. Only the wealthy can afford professional mental health services. The economy is supported by the Andean valleys and coastal farms, in which vegetables and fruits—including bananas, plantains, taro, potatoes, corn, barley, quinoa, wheat, coffee, sugar, cacao, and coconuts—are the economic base. Meats are also produced from hogs, cattle, and sheep. Most Ecuadorians produce their own food ("Culture of Ecuador," n.d.).

Ecuador's exports include petroleum, bananas, shrimp and other seafood, timber and wood products, fruits, and flowers. Petroleum processing is the major industry, with oil coming from the Amazonian region. Even though there are a variety of natural resources in the Republic of Ecuador, the economy is characterized by high unemployment and considerable underemployment. This situation has produced an increase in the number of migrations from Ecuador to other countries, including the United States, to search for job opportunities. It has also affected education, social programs, and the establishment of counseling and health services ("Culture of Ecuador," n.d.).

The Current Status of Counseling

The public school system in the Republic of Ecuador includes 6 years of primary education and 3 years of basic secondary schooling. This is followed by a diversified secondary program, with students opting for 2 or 3 years of study in the humanities, science, or technology. A 2-year vocational program is also offered. Education in the public schools is compulsory from ages 6 to 15. The academic year runs from October to July, and the primary language of instruction is Spanish.

Public school counselors are employed in Ecuador under the umbrella of guidance or vocational counselors. Counseling in the high school setting is often referred to as *orientation,* in which counselors provide testing, career counseling, and academic advising. Several tests, such as the Wechsler Intelligence Scale for Children, Spanish version, are the same as those used in the United States. The student:counselor ratio is high despite attempts to adopt a regulation suggesting a counselor:student ratio of 1:300. One of the larger public high schools in Guayaquil has a guidance counselor:student ratio of 1:1500 (S. Whitman, personal communication, August 8, 2011).

Guidance counselors work closely with ninth-grade students who are required to make decisions concerning their future educational paths. The current educational policy in Ecuador allows for the placement of students in one of three educational areas: (a) the medical science field, in which students enroll in courses such as biology and chemistry; (b) an engineering track, in which students enroll in a sequence of math courses; or (c) a teaching track, in which students enroll in social sciences course work. This system requires careful planning, counseling, and testing of students because decisions at this age affect subsequent educational experiences. Guidance counselors, school administrators, parents, and students themselves have questioned the public school system's policy because of the high stakes and stress related to early career decision making. Questions raised have caught the attention of the President of Ecuador, who is reconsidering the policy of requiring students to decide on a program of study before they are ready to make a choice (L. Cavallero, personal communication, August 3, 2011). Private schools offer another choice to school-age children. These are children whose parents can afford the educational costs associated with private education.

Guidance counselors in Ecuador's public schools who work with academic and career planning issues are also faced with addressing many of the same problems faced by children and adolescents from other Latin American countries. Problems in school and society include bullying, school phobia, child nutrition, medical care, language barriers, gaming addictions, the use of firearms, home-related issues, poverty, and children working at an early age. Early-age working is a major problem in Ecuador and represents a challenge for guidance counselors within and outside of the school setting. Some school-age children start working at age 4 or 5 and work full or part time until age 18. These children, specifically those in Quito, generally work as vendors selling small gifts, vegetables, fruits, gum, and candies. Older children work as laborers, as entertainers on the streets or in markets, and at other menial jobs. Young children begin working by the age of 4 or 5 because of the need and poverty experienced by their families. Current and long-term economic and social factors have exacerbated this problem. These children are from poor, rural families and have come to the cities looking for work. As a result of working on the street, they are vulnerable to health problems, sexual and physical abuse, stealing, prostitution, and drug abuse. Children who live with their family and work on the street are often physically, emotionally, and/or sexually abused by family members and neighbors.

Most working children are not seen by school guidance counselors because they do not enter the public school system, as school is not completely free. Many parents in Ecuador cannot afford the fee required by the public schools. The cost of school supplies and uniforms is beyond the reach of many who want to educate their children.

Counseling and mental health volunteer nonprofit agencies provide most of the counseling services for working children. One example of such an agency is El Centro de la Niña Trabajadora (The Center for the Working Girl), founded in 1991 by the Sisters of the Good Shepherd, a Catholic order. This center evolved in response to the prevalence of child labor due to urban migration and poverty. This nongovernmental, nonprofit organization is devoted to helping working children, especially girls, and their families overcome poverty and improve their quality of life ("What Are Working Children?" 2008). Funding is difficult to come by, but El Centro de la Niña Trabajadora has been able to utilize psychologists and social workers in conjunction with volunteers to provide counseling services to working children so that they can eventually be integrated into public school programs. Once these children are in the public school system, school counselors are able to work with them.

Counselors in the schools provide personal, career, and testing services despite the fact that the term *consejero* (counselor) has not been clearly defined in Ecuador. Therefore, the term *counselor* is not used by mental health professionals in schools, private practice, hospitals, or clinics.

Guidance counselors are trained in vocational counseling or mental health at one of the three major universities in Ecuador or in some cases in the United States. The training in Ecuadorian universities is not equivalent to that in U.S. counselor education programs. The term *counselor* is not used to describe university graduates who complete a mental health degree in Ecuador. It is currently not part of the psychology vernacular (Cruza-Guet, Spokane, Leon-Andrade, & Borja, 2009). This is true despite the fact that mental health professionals perform many of the same functions as counselors in the United States. Like in many developing countries, American schools in Ecuador have more counselors that have been trained in the United States. University-level psychologists provide academic and personal counseling, testing, and support for students in selecting and completing a program of study.

Counseling organizations such as the American Counseling Association have not yet been established in Ecuador. Graduates of psychology programs join regional or national psychology professional associations such as the Asociacion Ecuatoriana de Psicologia, Federacion Eduatoriana de Psicologia Clinica, or Colegios de Psicologos (Cruza-Guet et al., 2009). There has been minimal activity involving the credentialing of counselors in the Republic of Ecuador, particularly because of the lack of graduate programs that prepare them. Once counselors are recognized and graduate programs are in place that adhere to standards set forth by the Council for Accreditation of Counseling and Related Educational Programs, organizations such as the National Board for Certified Counselors can perhaps facilitate the credentialing of counselors in the Republic of Ecuador.

Best Counseling Practices

Counseling practices in Ecuador range from the use of indigenous healing activities to the more recent infusion of humanistic and constructive approaches. Practicing mental health workers, mainly psychologists, often follow their training in psychoanalysis or behaviorism. Jungian and Freudian approaches, along with hypnosis regression, eye-movement desensitization and reprocessing, family constellation, and movement/art therapy are being used. Like in several of the Latin America countries there also seems to be an acceptance of solution-focused approaches and narrative practices (L. Cavallero, personal communication, August 3, 2011; Smith & Montilla, 2006). However, there does not seem to be a predominant counseling approach used in Ecuador. Perhaps this is reflective of the few and widely diverse university programs that currently prepare mental health professionals in the country. Discussions with parents frequently take place in the school setting, and couples often attend counseling sessions in private agencies. There does not seem to be extensive use of technology by mental health field practitioners or by those training mental health workers. Labor market data are insignificant considering the state of the economy and the high unemployment rate in Ecuador.

Mental and physical health healing has historically been performed by the *currandero,* or shaman. *Curranderos* are seen as talented healers whose services often benefit patients experiencing either mental or physical pain. These professional folk healers are widely patronized in the lower income rural areas of Ecuador. Their backgrounds vary, as do their reasons for entering the practice of folk healing. In many instances the work and secrets of folk healing are passed on by master healers over several generations. In some cases, individuals who themselves were healed by a *currandero* after trying traditional medical practices take on the role of a folk healer (Mull & Mull, 1983). There is a concern among established folk healers that the methods and practices of folk healing are not being passed on to younger generations and that these secrets may eventually be lost. The healing practices used by *curranderos* are broad in scope and could include several of the following: cleansing the spirit through the use of wands, integrating religious practices, prescribing special drinks and food, using herbals, using body massages with oils, using breathing exercises, and using body movement. *Curranderos* work with problems identified as *espanto* (soul loss) and *susto* (fright illness). Other identified problems presented to *curranderos* and researched by Cavender and Albán (2009) include *mal projimo* (evil or bad neighbor), *duende* (caused by encounter[s] with bad spirits), and *brujeria* (caused by witches projecting negative energy).

Curranderos in the Ecuador highlands make extensive use of magical plants to treat supernatural folk illnesses such as *susto* (fright sickness), *mal viento* (ill wind), *mal projimo* (bad neighbor), and *mal aire* (bad air, usually infused with the spirits of the dead). These *curranderos* are known as *limpiadores* (cleaners; Cavender & Albán, 2009). The magical plants are used to cleanse individuals or homes from *mal pollution* (bad air). Investigations of the use of magical plants have revealed that only one, *guanto rojo* (*Datura sanguine*), is classified as a hallucinogenic.

Diversity Issues

The culture and lifestyles of Ecuadorians are as diverse as the country's geography. Ecuador is a multicultural, multiethnic nation that could be considered multinational ("Culture of Ecuador," n.d.). It has a wide range of indigenous cultures and two Afro-Ecuadorian cultures. There is a large number of Spanish colonists in Ecuador, as well as German, Italian, Lebanese, and Asian immigrants. Although Spanish is the national language, 13 indigenous languages are spoken ("Culture of Ecuador," n.d.).

In all walks of life, people identify as *ecuatorianos* or *ecuatorianas* (Ecuadorians). An Ecuadorian national identity emerged historically in several sectors. The elites and the upper class, along with ideologues in the military and the press, have used the concept of *blanco–mestizo* to both identify with the masses (through the concept *mestizo*) and affirm their distance from them (through the concept *blanco*). The elites also have the concept of *gente de bién* or *gente bién* (good people, people of good or proper background). They are complemented by the new elite that sometimes is known as the *gente de bienes* (rich people). The concept of *sociedad* (society) refers to the old elite both internally and among the new rich ("Culture of Ecuador," n.d.).

Among the elite and the newer wealthy, identity as Ecuadorian is paralleled by identity as good, righteous, Catholic, civilized White people who share a European and U.S. orientation. Colonial wealth is important, as is the maintenance of high status allowing for great power and substantial influence. Among the middle classes, the elite focus on Whiteness is conjoined with the elitist ambivalent stigma of *mestizaje* (a mix of the Native Indian and European races). The middle class tends to identify with their families, jobs, and a general sense of the republic without worrying about their ethnicity ("Culture of Ecuador," n.d.).

Poverty is widespread in Ecuador and affects more than half of the population. Indigenous people who are at the forefront of movements of self-affirmation favor socialist reforms. Africans in Ecuador are caught between the dominant elite, the prejudices of the middle and upper classes, and a tenuous relationship with the indigenous population.

Historically the African population and other indigenous people have identified with similar cultural groups nationally. Language has been a common denominator to identify with others across country borders, such as Colombia, Peru, Bolivia, and Argentina ("Culture of Ecuador," n.d.). Being identified as indigenous has also served as a unifying factor. Recently an emphasis has been placed on a Black ethnic identity despite minimal political or financial support ("Culture of Ecuador," n.d.).

Africans in Ecuador identify more tenuously with those who would seem to be phenotypically similar, and the processes of identity are stronger within their own regions than they are internationally. In the past decade, movements for a Black ethnic unity have taken place. However, the Black ethnic unity drive suffered from a lack of funding, while at the same time the indigenous leaders have possessed considerable resources for international ethnic nationalist movements of self-affirmation ("Culture of Ecuador," n.d.).

Social programs, including social security, have been established but with inadequate funding because of economic problems. Indigenous organizations, national unions, and the poorer sectors of society have pushed for social and educational change. One demonstration of this activity is the development of several organizations: Fundación Natura (ecological preservation), the Confederation of Indigenous People of Ecuador, Ecuador's Indigenous Awakening, the Shuar Federation, the Confederation of Indigenous People of Amazonian Ecuador, and the Association of Ecuadorian Blacks ("Culture of Ecuador," n.d.).

As in many Latin American countries a common thread of beliefs and cultural values seems to unite Ecuadorians. *Familism,* or the importance of strong interdependent ties with nuclear and extended family members, is prevalent throughout Ecuador (Zubieta, Fernandez, Vergara, Martinez, & Candia, as cited in Cruza-Guet et al., 2009). The culture can be viewed as collectivist (Smith & Montilla, 2006) with an emphasis on harmony with nature, natural forces, and relationships with one another. Yet others have observed that Ecuadorians maintain a sense of "individual character" (Tousignant & Maldonado, as cited in Cruza-Guet et al., 2009). Within the family structure the man is seen as the breadwinner and the head of the household, whereas the wife often stays and works at home.

Outside invaders have attempted to infuse their beliefs, values, and rituals into Ecuadorian culture while Ecuadorians have sought to maintain their own traditional beliefs, values, and rituals. Beliefs retained over time include thoughts and ideas related to causes of mental and physical problems as well as to methods used to cure these ailments. Today two forces are in existence: (a) attempts to modernize and use science to solve medical and other problems and (b) traditional beliefs and attitudes that focus on folk healing practices to solve physical and mental ailments. Folk healing, traditional cultural customs, and spiritual beliefs are particularly strong in rural areas, where either the priest or the *currandero* (healer) is frequently sought out to resolve mental health difficulties and heal physical ailments.

Counselor Education

Master's-level counselor education programs do not exist in Ecuador. Programs conferring a PhD in counselor education or a PhD in psychology are also unavailable. Mental health educational programs at universities admit students immediately after high school (Cruza-Guet et al., 2009). These are 5-year programs consisting of 3 years of study in psychology, 2 years of practice (considered to be an internship), and a thesis (L. Cavallero, personal communication, August 3, 2011; Sierra & Bermudez, as cited in Cruza-Guet et al., 2009). Graduates of programs accredited by the Ecuadorian Ministry of Education are eligible for a certificate to practice with individuals, groups, and families. Graduates use the title of *psicologo* (psychologist) or state that they are *licenciado en psicologia* (have a degree in psychology) and are often referred to as *psicoterapeutas* (psychotherapists; Cruza-Guet et al., 2009).

The Future

Perhaps after reading this chapter one might think that the future of counseling in Ecuador is bleak or that the field is at best slow to gain recognition. We however are optimistic and can see a possible bright future for counseling in the Republic of Ecuador. After reviewing the history of counseling in the United States and several other countries, one realizes the impact of circumstance, context, and timing on the evolution of the profession. Ecuador has made progress in recognizing that mental health issues extend across the globe. The training of mental health professionals exists at several universities, and guidance counselors already have a place in the public school system.

When considering the high rate of unemployment, the increasing number of teen suicides, depression, stress-related problems, domestic violence, gender issues, drug use, and drug trafficking, one immediately recognizes the need for counseling in the Republic of Ecuador. It is these needs and future leadership in Ecuador that hold promise for counseling and counselor preparation programs. It is foreseeable that graduates of these programs will eventually define counseling and the counselor's role. We believe that by understanding the culture of Ecuador and the mental health needs of its citizens, and by respecting its healing practice traditions, counselors will increase the availability of quality counseling services in future decades.

An international task force has suggested specific strategies to facilitate counseling and counselor training in Ecuador and other Latin American countries (Gonzalez & Ledezma, 2009). The recommendations include the following:

1. Consider the creation of guidance commissions at the national, state, and local levels.
2. Include the role of guidance and supervision in draft laws on education.
3. Consider an entry, continuation, and exit system for higher education instead of just a university education entry system.
4. Facilitate the creation of undergraduate studies in guidance and counseling.
5. Include mandatory guidance and counseling modules in teacher training programs.
6. Restructure guidance policies; this should be established jointly by the Ministry of People's Power for Higher Education, Ministry of People's Power for Education, and National Guidance and Counseling, which in turn should redefine the vision, mission, and goals of Guidance and Counseling programs (Gonzalez & Ledezma, 2009).
7. Integrate guidance and counseling curricular activities into all levels or subsystems of education that define the functions of guidance counselors.
8. Bring about the adoption of the Professional Practice of Guidance and Counseling Law introduced by the Venezuelan Associations of Guidance Counselors Federation in the National Assembly.
9. Create guidance and counseling departments in each college or university.

10. Propose the concept of *guidance for self-determination* or *self-development* instead of the term *vocational guidance.*
11. Make guidance and counseling the linking organ between the ministries responsible for education, higher education, and labor.
12. Develop the idea of vocational guidance.
13. Create a technology network for vocational exploration.
14. Allocate more resources for guidance practitioner training.
15. Highlight jobs and study offers in nontraditional areas.
16. Highlight a stronger link between university and work.
17. Consider generic and specific competencies at the beginning of higher education.
18. Develop the idea of professional courses for people who do not have a degree in guidance careers but want to join the field. These professional courses would be considered as a measure to cover the immediate shortfall of guidance counselors.
19. Reconsider the functions of guidance counselors.
20. Develop a profile of students.
21. Conduct a census to determine the number of guidance practitioners in each country.
22. Promote the creation of university career choices.
23. Establish learning modules that allow students to explore vocational interests starting at the elementary level (Gonzalez & Ledezma, 2009).

These recommendations could bode well for the future of counseling and counselor education in Latin America, including the Republic of Ecuador.

References

Cavender, A. P., & Albán, M. (2009). The use of magical plants by curranderos in the Ecuador highlands. *Journal of Ethnobiology and Ethnomedicine, 5*(3). Retrieved from http://www.ethnobiomed.com/content/5/1/3/

Cruza-Guet, M., Spokane, A., Leon-Andrade, C., & Borja, T. (2009). Diversity, hegemony, poverty, and the emergence of counseling psychology in Ecuador. In L. H. Gerstein, P. P. Heppner, S. Ægisdóttir, S.-M. A. Leung, & K. L. Norsworthy (Eds.), *International handbook of cross-cultural counseling: Cultural assumptions and practices worldwide* (pp. 393–400). Thousand Oaks, CA: Sage.

Culture of Ecuador. (n.d.). Retrieved from www.everyculture.com/Cr-Ga/Ecuador.html

Gonzalez, J., & Ledezma, M. A. (2009). Guidance and counseling in Latin America: General considerations about the criteria of coherence, cooperation and quality. *Orientacion y Sociedad, 9,* 1–10.

Mull, J. D., & Mull, D. S. (1983). A visit with a currandero. *Western Journal of Medicine, 139,* 730–736.

Republic of Ecuador. (2011). Retrieved from http://thegpe.org/ecuador

Smith, R. L., & Montilla, R. E. (2006). *Counseling and family therapy with Latino populations: Strategies that work.* New York, NY: Routledge.

What are working children? (2008). Retrieved from http://www.cenitecuador.org/en/about/working-children

• • •

COUNSELING IN GUATEMALA 40

María del Pilar Grazioso, Jennifer Keller, Roberto Swazo, and Andrés J. Consoli

Guatemala is one of the seven countries in Central America that straddle the thin strip of land between the Pacific Ocean and the Caribbean Sea that connects North and South America. It is bordered to the north and west by Mexico and to the east by Belize, Honduras, and El Salvador. Its population of 14.3 million lives in an area less than 43,000 square miles, or 109,000 square kilometers. It is a multiethnic, multicultural, and multilingual country where 24 languages are spoken—21 indigenous Mayan languages, Spanish, Xinca, and Garífuna.

According to 2003 data from the National Institute of Statistics, the ethnic composition of Guatemala's population is as follows: *ladino*, 60%; indigenous, 39.5%; and Garífuna 0.5%. In Guatemala, *ladino* refers to anyone who is not indigenous or who claims both indigenous and European ancestry and speaks Spanish as his or her primary language (Luján, 2002). The vast majority of the indigenous population is Mayan.

When the Spanish conquered the region in the 16th century they put in motion a process of cultural blending that in many ways continues today. During 300 years of Spanish colonial rule (1524–1821), Christianity was imposed and economic and political power was held by European-born *peninsulares* (from the Iberian Peninsula) and Creoles. Mayan religion, traditions, and languages were deliberately suppressed. After gaining independence from Spain in 1821, *ladinos* continued to hold economic and political power. In 1841, a republic was founded that was ruled for 30 years by conservative governments. This period was followed by a liberal era (1871–1944) that saw a series of civil and political reforms as well as dictatorships. In 1944, a revolution that ended a dictator's rule led to the 1954 counterrevolution that triggered the beginning of the guerilla movement in Guatemala (Luján, 2002). In 1960, a civil war erupted that lasted 36 years and claimed hundreds of thousands of lives before the Peace Accords were signed in 1996. The majority of the victims of this armed conflict were from indigenous groups. In the 21st century, Guatemala has continued its journey toward democracy.

Among Guatemala's assets are its rich history and traditions, geographical location, climate, cultural diversity, and potential for development in various sectors. In spite of these strengths, however, its population is affected by violence, poverty, migration, limited access to education and health services, high illiteracy rates, addictions, endemic diseases such as HIV/AIDS, demographic challenges, environmental threats, and natural disasters. Most significant for the counseling profession is the fact that the country is currently living out one of the most violent periods of its history (Matute, 2007).

According to the World Bank's (2011) country brief for Guatemala, although approximately 15% of Guatemala's population lives in extreme poverty, "inequality and poverty—especially in rural and indigenous areas—are among the highest in the region. Stark disparities are embedded in access to health, basic education, social services, and opportunities" (General Overview, para. 3). Reports from the United Nations Development Program (2010) state that the groups most affected by this inequality are women, children (especially those younger than age 3), school-age girls, indigenous communities, sick people, and people living with disabilities (particularly in rural areas). Migration has had a significant impact on the country's population in recent years. The International Organization for Migration estimates that approximately 1 million Guatemalans live in the United States and that between 6,000 and 12,000 new Guatemalan migrants arrive each year (Smith, 2006).

Data indicate that 95% of the population have access to elementary school education, whereas only 20% to 37% have access to secondary school (United Nations Development Program, 2010). Since 2005, literacy rates have improved yearly, with slightly higher rates reported for men than for women in 2009—82.6% versus 78.6%, respectively (United Nations Development Program, 2010). Although the Peace Accords stipulate that 5% of the country's gross domestic product must be assigned to education, currently less than 2% actually is (Secretaría de la Paz de la Presidencia de la República de Guatemala, 2009).

According to the 2009 National Mental Health Survey, 25% of the Guatemalan population between the ages of 18 and 65 reported a mental illness, including depression, posttraumatic stress disorder, bipolar disorder, or substance abuse (mostly alcohol abuse). In addition, 5% of those surveyed reported suicidal thoughts (with 56% of this group reporting that they had attempted suicide). Despite this documented need, only 2.3% of respondents reported that they had sought help from a mental health professional (López, 2009).

Diversity Issues

One of the key features of Guatemala is its ethnolinguistic diversity and complexity: It has the largest indigenous population of any Central American country. Many indigenous individuals who no longer adhere to a traditional indigenous lifestyle describe themselves as *ladinos*. This may create a statistical or demographic challenge because they base their ethnic self-selection on language and traditions, not physical traits. Therefore, the concept of ethnic identity in Guatemala may not be the same as in other countries in Latin America or the United States.

The Garífuna is a distinct ethnic group made up of African-descent mulattoes, and Amerindians (i.e., Carib and Arawak) mixed with Africans (i.e., West Africans originally from Nigeria). There are Garífuna populations in Guatemala, Honduras, Belize, and Nicaragua (Anderson, 2007).

There are vast differences between urban and rural life in Guatemala. Residents of rural communities and urban centers often barely recognize one another as belonging to the same country. The majority of the indigenous population lives in poor, rural communities with limited access to human services, education and training, and jobs and with inadequate infrastructure that does not facilitate sustained development. Guatemala City is the nation's capital and home to approximately 3.1 million people, mostly *ladinos* (Instituto Nacional de Estadística, 2003).

Religion

The Guatemalan constitution guarantees religious freedom; however, there appears to be little tolerance across faiths. Roman Catholicism has historically been the predominant religion. Many indigenous people combine their Mayan religious rites with other Christian traditions. Although the Catholic Church has had more historical and traditional influence in the country, fundamentalist Protestant churches have expanded their affiliations as well as their influence in urban and rural communities since the 1980s. Minority groups and religions with small communities include Jews, Muslims, and followers of some Indian sects. In the 1980s, during the civil war, the government allied itself with conservative Protestant groups and accused the Catholic Church of helping leftist guerillas. The 1995 Agreement on the Identity and Rights of Indigenous Peoples was approved to provide freedom of practice and to promote respect for the forms of spirituality practiced by the Maya, Garífuna, and Xinca.

Bilingual Education

Because of the country's linguistic diversity, a counselor would benefit from being multilingual. Efforts to implement bilingual education in rural areas have been difficult but successful (Patrinos & Vélez, 2009). The rationale behind these programs is to facilitate the learning process among students whose primary language is not Spanish while promoting and maintaining their culture through language. The concept of bilingual education in Guatemala City carries a different connotation than it does in rural areas: It implies that students acquire a second language, usually English, German, French, or Italian. The middle class and well-off are typically able to afford this type of education for their children. In rural areas bilingualism usually refers to speaking a Mayan language and Spanish.

Gender and Age Issues

Guatemala is considered a young country because 4 out of every 10 inhabitants (44% of the population) are younger than 15 years old. Its population is also growing rapidly and has a life expectancy of 66 years (Grazioso, 2007). Therefore, most services are designed to meet the needs of a young emerging population. As a result, older adults (especially those in rural communities) are typically neglected because of the lack of social services and limited jobs. This situation results in deteriorating health and isolation (Population Reference Bureau, 2009). Being an elderly woman complicates matters because society is dominated by males (Equipo de Estudios Comunitarios y Acción Psicosocial, 2009; Erazo, 2008).

The 1985 Constitution of Guatemala does not include specific provisions about gender equality, but Article 4 upholds the principle of equality for all individuals. In 2002, the penal code was amended to criminalize discrimination. Gender-related legislation, however, is enforced in too few cases, and strong patriarchal traditions persist in the judiciary. For instance, nearly one third of households are headed by women, who earn a lower average wage than their male counterparts (Green, 1994; Rousseau & Foxen, 2010). However, unlike men, women face discrimination and isolation and suffer from the stigma of being single mothers or not having a mate. These issues are compounded by their lower earning capacity and limited access to services (Moran, 2010). After the civil war many women, particularly those in rural communities, found themselves in the unfamiliar role of head of household (Bastos, 2007).

The Current Status of Counseling

Because of Guatemala's cultural and socioeconomic diversity and the vast differences between urban and rural life, the counseling services that are available throughout the country vary greatly. There are two very different approaches to counseling today. One is carried out by indigenous shamans, religious leaders, midwives, and community leaders (Valle, 2002), and the other resembles the Western conceptualization of counseling and involves education and formal training. Although the majority of the population might have more access to the former, the latter is the one we address in this chapter.

Although it developed out of clinical and psychological disciplines, counseling is gradually evolving and becoming recognized as its own profession, pulling away from its medical and humanistic roots. A review of the literature reveals that today counseling in Guatemala addresses family planning, HIV/AIDS, posttraumatic stress disorder related to either natural disasters or violence, addictions, and intrafamily violence (Toro-Alfonso, 2009). However, counselors in Guatemala also work with a number of issues that have not been widely reported in the literature, such as prevention; crisis intervention; and school, vocational, and child and family counseling.

Counseling activities in Guatemala may be divided into two categories depending on whether they are practiced in urban or rural areas. For the most part, counseling and psychological services in urban areas are performed in a private practice setting by a psychologist or a professional counselor with formal education and training. These professionals serve both adults and children from diverse socioeconomic groups and are paid in local currency according to the length and duration of sessions. Typically the *Diagnostic and Statistical Manual of Mental Disorders, Fourth Edition, Text Revision,* and the International Classification of Diseases–10 are used. Trust and rapport are developed naturally as the counseling sessions evolve.

No distinction is made between school counselors and school psychologists. Both complete assessments and psychological evaluations; conduct career and vocational counseling; and work with parents, teachers, and students. Among pastoral counselors, there are marked differences among Christian denominations (e.g., Catholics and Protestant groups). Pastoral counselors are trained in churches or religious organizations and offer specific services for church members. Family counselors receive formal training through logotherapy or systemic, cognitive, or integrative approaches.

In rural areas, people seeking counseling services are generally underprivileged and living in poverty. Counseling in rural areas is performed informally by an elder/leader of a village or town. He or she is paid in the form of a donation or through the exchange of goods or services. Trust and rapport are already present because the elder/leader is well known in the community. An outsider who wishes to provide counseling services must earn this trust. Counselors from outside the community are advised to consult with community leaders before making any type of diagnosis. There are limited numbers of professionally trained private practitioners in rural areas. The few there are provide services pro bono or through rural community agencies. School counselors or psychologists are essentially nonexistent.

In terms of spirituality, rural areas often experience a convergence of indigenous Mayan religious beliefs and Christian principles. We are unaware of any family counselors working in rural areas.

Licensing and Accreditation

In Guatemala, professionals in any field may practice after graduating with a licentiate degree, a 5- to 6-year undergraduate university degree. Today there is no undergraduate counseling degree per se, but two licentiate degree programs—one in family sciences and the other in psychology—include counselor training. School and mental health counseling is not accredited in Guatemala. The Association of School Counselors (Asociación de Orientadores Escolares) was founded in 1997. Today it has 100 members—most of whom are educational or school psychologists, clinical psychologists, or pedagogues—and a listserv of more than 800. The association organizes seminars, conferences, and continuing education courses.

Previously, in order for psychologists to practice, they had to be registered in the professional College of Humanities, which was founded in 1952. It was not until 2008 that psychology obtained formal licensure when the College of Psychology was established. Today steps are being taken toward licensure requirements for professional counselors (i.e., the field is moving toward the creation of a professional counseling association) and the creation of a code of ethics and a certification process. This evolving process is likely to enhance the development of a professional identity (Hanna & Bemak, 1997; Maples & Altekruse, 1993; Pistole & Roberts, 2002).

Best Counseling Practices

Given the diversity that prevails in Guatemala, best counseling practices are likely to be those that spring from social-contextual and cultural paradigms (Sommers-Flanagan & Sommers-Flanagan, 2004) yet follow an integrative model. Nonetheless, despite their training and the level of development of the profession, counselors are practicing either as psychotherapists, as clinical psychologists, or as school psychologists without much emphasis on prevention, psychoeducational interventions, or developmental orientation. Today the counseling process generally follows a psychotherapeutic or consultation approach, with case conceptualization and action planning performed according to the theoretical framework in which the counselor was trained. Some professionals conduct assessments and diagnosis, and others refer to other clinical psychologists to do this. Although there is a psychoanalytic emphasis in training, currently there is a recognized move toward cognitive, systemic, existential, and integrative approaches. There is no research, however, that can attest to this.

A movement toward a professional practice and training that follows ethical principles (American Counseling Association [ACA], 2005; Lemus, 2011) is guiding the profession and prompting actions to prevent dual relationships in the 2010s. Every counselor must take into account his or her own cultural realities and recognize and respect potential differences. For example, an urban *ladino* counselor may have certain expectations relative to time and productivity. However, time as a social and personal construct is far more fluid and less important for indigenous people because the conceptualization of "getting something done" might be very different. People from rural communities seeking counseling may choose to meet with a counselor to discuss their situation in a backyard, on the street, or in a field. Thus, counseling is not performed solely in offices and clinics. This alone is a departure from what is commonly considered best practices in the *ACA Code of Ethics*. Because spirituality is so intertwined with daily life in indigenous rural communities, the idea of examining or disclosing problems to a stranger (e.g., a counselor) could be a radically different, if not foreign, approach. Many individuals from rural areas and indigenous communities traditionally prefer to share their concerns with a god rather than with another person. As counselors attend to community needs they are using innovative techniques such as art, play, drama, crafts, narratives, and role play. And as access to technology improves, the use of the Internet for supervision and counseling is beginning to be considered in areas where there are no or very few counselors.

In training programs, counselors are encouraged to develop multicultural competencies (Arredondo, 1999), advocacy skills, and social justice skills (Toporek, Gerstein, Fouad, Roysicar-Sodowsky, & Irsrael, 2005) and to foster transformative action that enhances and promotes wellness and participation (Montero, 2006).

Counselor Education

In Guatemala, the counseling profession is still seen as a fairly new discipline, and it is not fully recognized as a bona fide occupation compared to social work and psychology. Two terms, *orientación* and *consejería,* are used indiscriminately to refer to counseling. (In this chapter we include the terms as they are used in Guatemala.) This lack of definition has contributed to the struggle to establish a unified professional identity as well as the credibility enjoyed in other countries (Hanna & Bemak, 1997; Pistole & Roberts, 2002).

Counseling as it is practiced today in Guatemala has its roots in psychiatry's medical model; psychology, which for many years was considered a discipline within the humanities; and pedagogy, particularly in terms of vocational counseling (*orientación vocacional*) and school counseling (*consejería escolar;* Quevedo, 2003).

In Guatemala, like in most of Latin America, a licentiate degree, or *licenciatura,* requires at least 5 years of study following high school. It is an intermediate degree between a bachelor's and a master's and is accepted as a terminal degree for the practice of psychology.

The profession of psychology emerged in 1946 in Guatemala with the development of university psychology training programs. Eventually these undergraduate programs would include clinical, educational, school, organizational/industrial, and forensic psychology.

To obtain a professional degree, counselors receive training in the following undergraduate and graduate academic university programs: (a) a six-semester technical degree in vocational and labor counseling, known as *orientación vocacional y laboral;* (b) a licentiate degree in psychology; (c) a licentiate degree in educational psychology; (d) a licentiate degree in family sciences, counseling, and family psychotherapy, with an emphasis on logotherapy; (e) a licentiate degree in psychology and social counseling; (f) a master's degree in clinical counseling, mental health, and psychosocial intervention; and (g) a master's degree in counseling psychology and mental health.

School counselors, known as *orientadores,* began to be trained in 3-year technical degree programs in the 1960s. Today there are no longer any school counselor training programs per se; the professionals working in school counseling have degrees in educational psychology, school psychology, or clinical psychology.

In 2002, Universidad del Valle began an innovative pilot program that offered continuing education courses in mental health counseling. In 2005, this program began to operate as a master's program within the psychology department. Students in this program have diverse educational backgrounds, although the majority have psychology degrees. Almost all of the students come from urban areas.

Universidad del Valle adopted a curricular model that closely follows the structure of mental health programs in the United States. The program was set up utilizing a model in which intensive courses were taught in English over 3.5 days by counselor educators from the United States. Because of the pedagogical difficulties of translating lectures, the program eventually began to hire bilingual (Spanish–English) counselor educators, counseling psychologists, and psychotherapists from the United States, Puerto Rico, and Argentina. This change proved to be a pedagogical asset because aside from the linguistic advantages of using Spanish as the program's lingua franca, it integrated the Latin and North American worldviews and cultural dynamics faced by Guatemalan counselors-in-training. Furthermore, it made the program accessible to more students. The program also emphasizes training graduates to teach later cohorts.

Currently the 60-credit master's program at Universidad del Valle offers a generic mental health track that incorporates a community internship and clinical, school, and family counseling. Some of the unique features of the program are (a) 3.5 days of classroom sessions combined with Internet student platforms, (b) a curricular model styled on the Council for Accreditation of Counseling and Related Educational Programs model, (c) the involvement of experienced counselor educators from the United States and South America, and (d) coteaching opportunities to train local talent. Some of the challenges facing the program include (a) the lack of a certification body to license graduates; (b) the lack of local and international accreditation, in part due to the lack of full-time, on-campus doctoral faculty; and (c) high tuition costs, which make the program less accessible to many prospective students.

The Future

In a rapidly changing society that is coping with the aftermath of an armed conflict that lasted almost 40 years, Guatemalans are attempting to find ways to establish a healthy society. The counseling profession faces a myriad of challenges in different areas that must be addressed in a systematic way. The disproportionate balance between the mental health needs of Guatemalans and the growth of the counseling profession constitutes a challenge to counselor educators in the country and their international collaborators. In a country challenged by sizable socioeconomic and ethnic differences, and by the distress caused by crime, every citizen is affected in one way or another. Indigenous groups are among the most vulnerable populations with respect to mental health needs because they must cope with isolation, a conflict between traditional and modern beliefs, and a lack of resources and educational opportunities (Rousseau & Foxen, 2010). The counseling profession in Guatemala is facing many challenges that will shape its future development. The following are some of the concerns that must be addressed in the next decade.

Accessibility

Expanding counselor education programs and making them available to students of all sectors of society is critical. Effective marketing strategies should be used to attract the attention and interest of undergraduate students pursuing degrees in psychology, education, and sociology among others. Educating the college population about the role of counselors in schools and the community should start early and must be done systematically by providing informative sessions in different programs and colleges that will spark awareness and interest. These recruiting strategies will ensure a steady flow of applicants to counselor training programs.

Mental Health Awareness and Prevention Campaigns

One of the key ways to debunk the myth of mental health issues in a society is to alert, educate, and increase social awareness. In order to reach the masses with educational campaigns and augment the level of awareness and normalization, counselor education programs (faculty and counselors-in-training) and professional counselors in the community must engage the media to reach as many citizens as possible. For instance, announcements in newspapers, articles, short radio and TV interviews, and flyers as well as new social media should be part of systematic information campaigns. Providing information about symptoms of mental health, warnings, and resources available in the community is essential to empowering citizens. Another strategy to broaden the scope of counseling is to create consortia, coalitions, and alliances with other human services professions in order to reach as many people as possible.

Promoting Healthy Behaviors to Decrease Violence

Counselor education programs and practitioners should strategize with schools in order to disseminate the basic principles to promoting healthy behaviors that lead to a decrease in violence. Helping people to identify their stressors and ways to channel their anger and frustration in a civil manner should be part of a concerted operation from preschool through university. Consulting with community leaders and including them in these campaigns creates inclusion and prevents professional isolation. Including laypersons not associated with the counseling profession helps to mitigate elitism and favoritism toward certain populations.

Wellness Model and Professional Identity

A wellness and developmental model must be the pillar of counselor education programs that purposefully distance themselves from the strict model of psychopathology and abnormal behavior. Counselor education programs must instill the principle that people are a source of potential and have the ability to change, grow, and develop. Current counselor educators have the responsibility to form a clear counseling professional identity in a country where human behavior is still seen through the filters of traditional psychology. The development of chapters, associations, a code of ethics, and specialized licensing must occur in order for counseling to gain respect and a position within the human services professions. Initial steps in this direction include the translation into Spanish of the *ACA Code of Ethics*, which is being used as an operational foundation for those currently working in the field.

Advocacy and Social Justice

Counselors in Guatemala must advocate for those who have traditionally been oppressed and marginalized even though advocacy at the individual, group, family, and societal levels may not be one of the guiding paradigms for practicing the profession. Counselors in Guatemala must also recognize that providing services on a volunteer or pro bono basis is an integral part of responsible practice.

References

American Counseling Association. (2005). *ACA code of ethics.* Retrieved from http://www.counseling.org/Resources/CodeOfEthics/TP/Home/CT2.aspx

Anderson, M. (2007). When afro becomes (like) indigenous: Garifuna and Afro-Indigenous politics in Honduras. *Journal of Latin American and Caribbean Anthropology, 12,* 384–413.

Arredondo, P. (1999). Multicultural counseling competencies as tools to address oppression and racism. *Journal of Counseling & Development, 77,* 102–108.

Bastos, A. S. (2007). Familia, género y cultura. Algunas propuestas para la comprensión de la dinámica de poder en los hogares populares [Family, gender, and culture: Some proposals for understanding the power dynamic in poor homes]. In D. Robichaux (Ed.), *Familia y diversidad en América Latina: Estudio de Casos* (pp. 103–132). Buenos Aires, Argentina: Consejo Latinoamericano de Ciencias Sociales.

Equipo de Estudios Comunitarios y Acción Psicosocial. (2009). *Tejidos que lleva el alma: Memorias de las mujeres mayas sobrevivientes de violación sexual durante el conflicto armado* [Weavings worn by soul: Memories of Maya women survivors of rape during the civil war]. Guatemala City, Guatemala: F & G Editores.

Erazo, J. (2008). *La dinámica psicosocial del autoritarismo en Guatemala* [Psychosocial dynamic of authoritarianism in Guatemala]. Guatemala City, Guatemala: F & G Editores.

Grazioso, M. P. (2007). Sobre la enseñanza de la consejería en Guatemala [Teaching counseling in Guatemala]. In J. Toro Alfonso (Ed.), *Reflexiones en torno a la sexualidad y género* (pp. 335–359). Guatemala City, Guatemala: Universidad del Valle de Guatemala.

Green, L. (1994). Fear as a way of life. *Cultural Anthropology, 9*(2), 227–256.

Hanna, F. J., & Bemak, F. (1997). The quest for identity in the counseling profession. *Counselor Education and Supervision, 36,* 194–206.

Instituto Nacional de Estadística. (2003). *Censos Nacionales XI de Población y VI de Habitación* [XI National Population Census and VI National Housing Census]. Retrieved from http://www.ine.gob.gt/Nesstar/Censo2002/survey0/index.html

Lemus, M. (2011). *Principios éticos de la consejería en Guatemala. Una visión desde el ejercicio profesional* [Ethical principles of counseling in Guatemala: A view from professional practice]. Unpublished manuscript, Universidad del Valle de Guatemala, Guatemala City.

López, V. (2009). *Encuesta Nacional de Salud Mental Guatemala 2009* [National Mental Health Survey]. Retrieved from http://www.libertopolis.com/wp-content/uploads/2009/09/encuesta-nacional-salud-200911.pdf

Luján, M. L. (2002). *Breve historia contemporánea de Guatemala* [A brief contemporary history of Guatemala]. Mexico City, Mexico: Fondo de Cultura Económica.

Maples, M. F., & Altekruse, M. D. (1993). Counselor education 2000: Extinction or distinction? *Counselor Education and Supervision, 33,* 47–52.

Matute, A. (2007). *Informe estadístico de la violencia en Guatemala* [Statistical report on violence in Guatemala]. Retrieved from http://www.pnud.org.gt/data/publicacion/Informe%20Estad%C3%ADstico%20de%20la%20Violencia%20en%20Guatemala%20final.pdf

Montero, M. (2006). *Hacer para transformar: El método en la psicología comunitaria* [Doing to transform: Community psychology method]. Mexico City, Mexico: Paidós.

Moran, P. (2010). Women, neglect and abuse, and the consequences. In D. Kohen (Ed.), *Oxford textbook of women and mental health* (pp. 278–288). New York, NY: Oxford University Press.

Patrinos, H. A., & Vélez, E. (2009). Costs and benefits of bilingual education in Guatemala: A partial analysis. *International Journal of Educational Development, 29,* 594–598.

Pistole, C. M., & Roberts, A. (2002). Mental health counseling: Toward resolving identity confusions. *Journal of Mental Health Counseling, 24,* 1–19.

Population Reference Bureau. (2009). *Population Reference Bureau Annual Report 2009.* Retrieved from http://www.prb.org/pdf10/annualreport2009.pdf

Quevedo, M. (2003). *El servicio de orientación académica y el counseling en la educación superior y su importancia en el desarrollo profesional* [Academic guidance and counseling in higher education and its relevance in professional development]. Unpublished master's thesis, Universidad de San Carlos de Guatemala, Guatemala City.

Rousseau, C., & Foxen, P. (2010). "Look me in the eye": Empathy and the transmission of trauma in the refugee determination process. *Transcultural Psychology, 47*(1), 70–92.

Secretaría de la Paz de la Presidencia de la República de Guatemala. (2009). *Informe 2009 Avances sobre el Cumplimiento de los Acuerdos de Paz* [Report on progress made in complying with the Peace Accords]. Guatemala City, Guatemala: Author.

Smith, J. (2006). *Guatemala: Economic migrants replace political refugees.* Retrieved from http://www.migrationinformation.org/feature/display.cfm?ID=392

Sommers-Flanagan, J., & Sommers-Flanagan, R. (2004). *Counseling and psychotherapy theories in context and practice: Skills, strategies, and techniques.* Hoboken, NJ: Wiley.

Toporek, R., Gerstein, L., Fouad, N., Roysicar-Sodowsky, G., & Irsrael, T. (2005). *Handbook for social justice in counseling psychology: Leadership, vision, and action.* Thousand Oaks, CA: Sage.

Toro-Alfonso, J. (2009). *Perspectivas sobre género y sexualidad en Guatemala: Hacia una sociedad respetuosa de la diversidad* [Perspectives on gender and sexuality in Guatemala: Towards a society that is respectful of diversity]. Guatemala City, Guatemala: GTZ.

United Nations Development Program. (2010). *Guatemala: Hacia un estado para el desarrollo humano: Informe Nacional de Desarrollo Humano 2009/2010* [Guatemala: Towards a state for human development: National report on human development 2009/2010]. Guatemala City, Guatemala: Author.

Valle, A. (2002). *Estudio exploratorio para la implementación de una maestría en consejería* [Exploratory study on the implementation of a master's program in counseling]. Unpublished manuscript, Universidad del Valle de Guatemala, Guatemala, Guatemala City.

World Bank. (2011). *Guatemala country brief.* Retrieved from http://web.worldbank.org/WBSITE/EXTERNAL/COUNTRIES/LACEXT/GUATEMALAEXTN/0,,contentMDK:22254443~pagePK:1497618~piPK:217854~theSitePK:328117,00.html

• • •

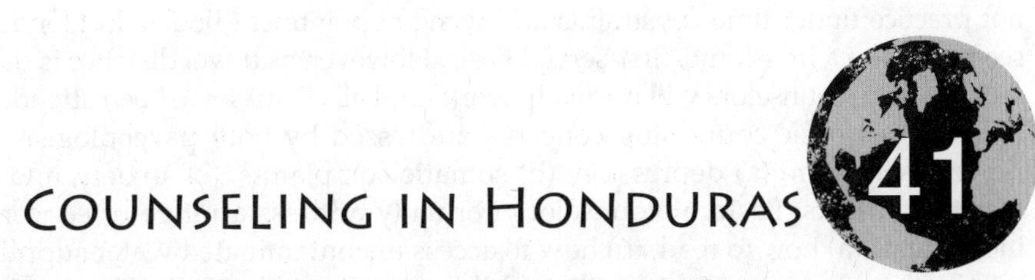

Counseling in Honduras 41

Antoinette Ginés-Rivera and Georgina Panting-Sierra

Honduras, the Central American republic whose name means "depth" for its deep waters off the coast, is rated as one of the poorest countries in the Western Hemisphere. With just more than 8.1 million inhabitants, it has approximately the same size and population density as the state of Virginia (Central Intelligence Agency, 2011). According to the U.S. Department of State (2010), Honduras has one of the highest unemployment rates among Central American countries, with an average yearly income of $1,829 per capita gross domestic product (unless specified, all dollar amounts are in U.S. dollars). The general Honduran population endures significant economic deprivation, low education, and deficient social structures rooted in the effects of depression, domestic violence, and poor health due to limited health services (Alarcón, 2003; Brown, Nesse, Vinokur, & Smith, 2003; Sells et al., 2007; Sladcova, 2007). Yet even while experiencing such distress, Latin American people do not readily seek outside counseling, as it is traditionally identified only for the psychotic (*los locos;* Acosta, Groh, Hernandez, & Rathbone, 1990). In fact, when one seeks outside counseling or a person is described as "complicated and problematic," this is frowned on as *"shameful"* (Acosta et al., 1990, p. 39, emphasis added).

Overall, the dominant belief in the Honduran culture is that mental illness within the family is related to dishonor and results in guilt and shame (Alarcón, 2003; Ginés-Rivera, 2010). Consequently, this mindset hinders efforts to treat clients in Honduras, as seeking professional mental health services is perceived as virtually unthinkable. However, the alternative approach, and one that is woven into the fabric of this culture, is to seek out and understand religious and folk beliefs for the causes and treatment of mental illness (Alarcón, 2003; Ginés-Rivera, 2010; Sells et al., 2007). This is generally achieved through a member of the local clergy, who is considered and respected as the chief community leader trustworthy enough to serve the mental health needs of the Honduran people.

There exists a general deficit in the literature on indigenous mental health practices in Latin America, particularly in the country of Honduras (Ginés-Rivera, 2010; Sells et al., 2007; Sladcova, 2007). To date few studies have explored counseling practices specific to the Honduran population (Ginés-Rivera, 2010). According to Sells et al. (2007), "Counseling and psychology do not exist as professions in Honduras in the same way that the professions exist in the United States" (p. 434). In fact, the concept of professional counseling is unfamiliar to most Hondurans, as only the wealthy can afford professional psychological care (Ginés-Rivera, 2010; Sells et al., 2007). Thus, for the purpose of this chapter, clergy, namely lay pastors and Catholic priests, are identified as "counselors" to differentiate them from professional psychologists. Each of these roles is discussed throughout this chapter.

There are significant differences in counseling practices in Honduras and the United States, and poverty is the central factor contributing to these disparities. For example, counseling practices as recognized in Honduras are not implemented from a for-profit business perspective but from a benevolent, ministerial, and community empowerment standpoint, in which lay pastoral counselors are creating their own identity within the Honduran culture (Ginés-Rivera, 2010; Sells et al., 2007). One other difference is that Honduran counselors generally do not practice under time constraints and using appointment books. In Honduras, counselors see people on a first-come, first-served basis. However, as travel distance is usually a factor in seeking help, counselors will normally work until all clients have been attended to.

The most basic counseling concerns addressed by both psychologists and lay pastoral counselors are (a) depression, (b) somatic complaints, (c) anxiety, and (d) family and marital conflicts. Pastoral counselors normally address a range of concerns by teaching individuals (a) how to read, (b) how to access uncontaminated water supplies, and (c) why vaccinations are important for their children (Sells et al., 2007). There exists a "profound intrinsic spirituality and commitment to religious values for most counselors" that helps counselors understand their efforts as "doing important things" for the community at large by implementing "a spiritual/religious perspective as the motivation for their work" that is "less likely to be a paid position" (p. 435). Even as efforts are currently being made to promote mental health care in Honduras, resources continue to be scarce, and counselor training is implemented with limited to nonexistent teaching staff, trainers, textbooks, manuals, assessment materials, and equipment (Alarcón, 2003; Ginés-Rivera, 2010). Here we hope to describe current issues and trends in counseling and psychological practice in Honduras so that readers will appreciate the importance of respecting, developing, and gaining an accurate perspective of the people of Honduras.

The Current Status of Counseling

In Honduras, mental health professionals may function in most capacities with merely a 5-year undergraduate degree. There are two reasons for this. The first is the great disparity between the number of professional mental health workers and the overwhelming need for mental health services. The second is the scarcity of counselor education training programs, opportunities, and resources, which is addressed later in the chapter.

According to the World Health Organization (2008), in Honduras

> the number of human resources working in the health system is 6.12 per 100,000 people. The breakdown according to professions is as follows: 0.82 psychiatrists, 0.67 medical doctors, 2.58 nurses, 0.78 psychologists, 0.29 social workers, 0.22 occupational therapists and 0.76 other professionals. (p. 15)

These numbers do not take into account school counselors. In Honduras, school counseling is practiced by a different group of professionals trained mostly by the Universidad Pedagógica Nacional Francisco Morazán (Francisco Morazán Pedagogy University) as guidance counselors. The relationship between school counselors, social workers, and mental health professionals is essentially nonexistent.

The Colegio de Psicólogos de Honduras (COPSIH) is the governing body of the Honduran psychology profession. This association was founded in 1982 when the Honduran National Congress approved its regulations and code of ethics (Donaire, 2001). COPSIH estimates that there are 5,000 psychologists in Honduras, with only 28% registered as members of COPSIH (N. Padilla, personal communication, March 21, 2011). The two requirements to become a COPSIH member are having an undergraduate degree in psychology and paying a one-time enrollment fee of $60 and a monthly fee of $10 (L1,126.13; L188.61 Honduran Lempira). There are currently no laws or regulations that mandate practicing professionals to become members of COPSIH. COPSIH houses the Tribunal de Honor (Jury of Honor) responsible for investigating charges against its members and protecting consumers. COPSIH provides continuing education opportunities by organizing workshops and conferences each year to enhance professional development.

Psychologists choose a specialization, usually focusing on one of three major areas: forensic, organizational, or clinical psychology.

- *Forensic psychology.* This is the newest arena of practice for psychologists. With the establishment of oral trials in the Honduran judicial system, psychologists have been hired by the Ministerio Publico (Secretary of Justice) to conduct psychological evaluations to determine whether a person is competent to stand trial. An interdisciplinary mental health team composed of psychologists, social workers, and psychiatrists collaborate during the defendant's due process as one component of the final verdict.
- *Organizational psychology.* With the significant growth in the number of industrial parks being built by international companies seeking inexpensive manual labor, there is now a need for psychologists who specialize in the selection, orientation, and training of employees. Many psychologists seek out these types of jobs because international companies pay higher salaries than Honduran employers. Psychologists working for these companies normally earn approximately $7,200–$9,000 a year compared to the country's average yearly salary of $1,829 (N. Padilla, personal communication, March 21, 2011). Responsibilities include heading up the company's human resources department as well as collaborating with the Honduran Ministry of Labor on behalf of the company and its employees.
- *Clinical psychology.* These professionals conduct psychological evaluations and provide counseling services in various settings, including governmental agencies, faith-based organizations, hospitals, and private practice or *consultorios.*

The Instituto Hondureño de la Niñez y la Familia (Honduras Children and Family Institute) is a governmental organization that hires psychologists to work on issues concerning child abandonment, homeless minors, adoptions, juvenile criminology, teen pregnancy, and the prevention of violence against women and families. Because of the overwhelming number of children in need of shelter, food, and services, the Instituto Hondureño de la Niñez y la Familia has joined forces with various faith-based organizations in an effort to reach as many children as possible in the urban cities. One particular organization, Orphan Helpers, Inc., from the United States, assigns paid staff *coordinadores* to various governmental institutions, where children, adolescents, and young adults are mentored and encouraged throughout their institutionalized placement (R. Yeargain, personal communication, July 30, 2011). These Honduran staff workers are paid from donations and funds from the United States and are not professional mental health workers. However, the organization has been making great strides in planning for North American mental health professionals to conduct counseling training for their staff. In addition, several substance abuse treatment facilities offer counseling services related to treating addictions. One example of such a center is Proyecto Victoria (Victory Project), a faith-based organization that has been operating as a substance addiction rehabilitation program since 1977.

There are two psychiatric hospitals in the entire country of Honduras servicing approximately 8 million people. The Mario Mendoza and Santa Rosita psychiatric hospitals are both located in the capital city of Tegucigalpa. Although the staff work diligently to provide proper services to their patients, conditions would be considered unacceptable in developed countries. For example, the U.S. Bureau of Citizenship and Immigration Services (2002) reported that Santa Rosita "was filled beyond capacity with 100 male and 70 female permanent in-patients, 80 to 90 percent of whom had been abandoned by their families" (p. 3). Psychiatric hospitals "deal simultaneously with people suffering from mental retardation, people diagnosed with an assortment of mental illnesses, particularly schizophrenia, as well as a handful of violence-prone common criminals ordered into psychiatric care by the country's judiciary" (p. 3). San Felipe hospital is another location where psychologists work with clients managing terminal illnesses such as HIV/AIDS and cancer. Professionals working in this setting earn an average of $500 a month.

Anderson (2000) stated that the World Bank has channeled financial support to primary health care in Honduras; nevertheless, mental health care has been neglected:

> As a consequence, illness and injury due to family abuse, alcoholism, and major mental illness were virtually ignored and patients were forced to rely on the few understaffed and poorly funded tertiary hospitals that exist in the country. In addition, mental health hospitals receive no additional funding and are currently operating at pre 1993 budget levels. This leaves patients in substandard conditions, attended by poorly staffed and in some cases poorly trained clinical support. (p. 107)

This reality precludes Hondurans from receiving the mental health care they desperately need and discourages trained professionals from seeking job opportunities under such frightening circumstances.

Clinical psychologists in private practice (*consultorios*) earn between $35 and $45 per therapy session and between $50 and $250 per psychological evaluation compared to psychologists in the United States, who earn approximately $125 to $175 per session and $800 to $1,500 per evaluation. Among the salient presenting problems, clinical psychologists commonly treat mood disorders, substance abuse, and marital conflict, including issues of infidelity and domestic violence (N. Padilla, personal communication, March 21, 2011). Posttraumatic stress disorder is also prevalent among Hondurans, as a study on psychopathological reactions estimated that "over 492,000 adults may have developed [posttraumatic stress disorder] from Hurricane Mitch alone" (Kohn, Levav, Donaire, Machuca, & Tamashiro, 2005, p. 293). Native clinical psychologists recognize that stress levels and anxiety run high in the general population because of the high prevalence of crime, issues related to abandonment, sexual abuse, gang activity, and sociopolitical conditions. Many relational and emotional problems are connected to poverty and to the unstable Honduran democracy. As stated by Sells et al. (2007),

> For individuals in this culture, the face of professional human care giving is different. It is an extended relationship more than it is a business. The population is without disposable wealth to afford the "luxury" of professional counseling, and the population is without health insurance to fund or supplement the cost. (p. 434)

Regardless of the setting in which they work or the population they serve, lay counselors and psychologists consistently meet daily challenges when trying to alleviate intrapsychic issues and promote social justice in a context of poverty and social chaos.

Best Counseling Practices

The average counseling experience in Honduras is approached and implemented as an expression of charity, ministry, and friendship. Thus, the usual standard of counseling services is provided by a community's lay clergy. Pastoral counselors may choose to obtain a certificate in seminary or Bible institute training to enhance their mental health care skills and responsibilities; however, because of the economic stress on the country, the average pastoral counselor cannot afford such opportunities (A. Fearon, personal communication, August, 15, 2009). For the clergy who have this privilege, a number of seminaries throughout the country offer programs to facilitate the development of pastoral counseling skills. These include Escuela de Teológica VIDA in the city of La Ceiba and Seminario Teológico Pentecostal de Honduras in the city of Siquatepeque (J. C. Andino Zavala, personal communication, August, 2, 2011). In some instances in which the counseling issues concern marriage or family life, counseling may be implemented by a married pastoral couple who offer emotional and spiritual assistance. Lay counselors are more apt to work from a church office, making home visits when necessary (A. Fearon, personal communication, August 10, 2009).

According to one Honduran psychologist, no predominant theory is practiced in the country. Psychology training programs teach fundamentals of general counseling theories such as cognitive behavior therapy, family systems, psychoanalytical approaches, social learning, and humanistic psychology. Psychologists may opt to study abroad and return with the particular theories they were trained in (N. Padilla, personal communication, March 21, 2011). However, most usually choose to practice family systems, psychodynamic, or cognitive behavior therapy modalities.

Psychologists normally use the following tests to conduct assessments: the House-Tree-Person test, the Bender Visual–Motor Gestalt Test, the Minnesota Multiphasic Personality Inventory, the Wechsler Intelligence Scales, and career counseling tools. However, because of the high cost of assessments and the lack of distributors of such tools in the country, professionals must often resort to using photocopies and outdated versions of the tests. The norms for these assessment tools are usually not standardized on the Honduran population; therefore, norms for other countries, such as Mexico and Spain, are used.

Because trust is a core factor within the family, most referrals to clinical psychologists are made by family members or close friends, and counseling sessions may involve key family relatives depending on their concern and the relevance of their input to the process. Professional psychologists are identified as experts expected to give advice, direction, and concrete recommendations rather than to facilitate a collaborative clinical relationship as is practiced in the United States. Most professionals use an intake form to collect the client's basic demographic information. However, whether to develop a formal treatment plan or maintain written records is the personal decision of each professional, for no entity enforces record keeping (N. Padilla, personal communication, March 21, 2011).

Although use of the Internet and technology is widespread in Honduras, this technology is chiefly utilized in the metropolitan areas. It is not currently used in counseling services, as poverty has greatly contributed to making technology inaccessible to the general population. This also impedes the marketing strategies of mental health providers.

Diversity Issues

Honduras, which has an estimated area of 43,300 square miles, is located in Middle America, bordering the Caribbean Sea between Guatemala and Nicaragua and the North Pacific Ocean between El Salvador and Nicaragua. It is estimated that 97% of Hondurans are Catholic and 3% are Protestant (Central Intelligence Agency, 2011). The native language is Spanish, and spoken dialects such as Amerindian, a combination of Spanish and Mayan, continue to exist today. *Amerindian* is an indigenous term given to the ancestors of the native populations to distinguish them from postimmigrants (Europeans, Africans, etc.) and from all other ethnic groups. The two major tribes in Honduras are the Miskito and the Garifuna Indians.

Miskito Indians

The Caribbean Mosquito Coast (or Miskito Coast) historically comprised an area along the eastern coast of present-day Nicaragua and Honduras, and part of the Western Caribbean Zone was named after the local Miskito Indians. Making up more than 50% of the indigenous population in Honduras, the Miskito Indians are the largest indigenous and Afro-indigenous group in Honduras. Most speak the Miskito language and English because of the influence of British settlers. Miskito men usually travel away from home for seasonal work as wandering workers or agricultural laborers. Because of their coastal location, fishing is also a major means of employment. Miskito Indians are the poorest group in Honduran society. Whereas other Indians have integrated into urban cities, the Miskitos have remained on the coast and in the rural areas off the coast. The main concerns of the Miskito tribe are land rights, the development of social programs, health care, and education.

Garifunas Indians

The Garifunas reside on the Caribbean coast. They came to Honduras because the British expelled them from the island of St. Vincent. In April 2011, the approximately 250,000 Garifunas in the area celebrated 214 years in Honduras (Griffin, 2004). The Garifunas are a mixed race, generally referred to as the "Black Caribs" because of their African heritage. Living as they do in the coastal areas, the Garifunas rely heavily on the fishing industry. The Garifunas' old Caribbean language and culture continue to survive today. Yet this Honduran population endures racism, prejudices, and stereotypical stigmas that continue to reflect the fact that they are not accepted in the country (Pine, 2009).

Honduran mental health professionals normally do not practice in the rural areas where these groups live and thus can provide no mental or emotional relief for these indigenous peoples. However, various missionary brigades from around the world travel to these parts to teach and to address the spiritual and human needs of these indigenous populations.

Socioeconomics

Honduras is one of the poorest countries in the Western hemisphere, with an extraordinarily unequal distribution of income and massive unemployment. The World Bank (2011) estimated a per capita gross national income of $1,600 in 2007 with an increase of $1,829 per capita, according to the U.S. Department of State (2010). Nearly two thirds of Hondurans (63.3%) live in poverty (defined as living on less than $2 a day). Traumatic experiences such as vulnerability, hunger, and lack of even the most basic human needs can have a deep impact on people's psyches.

Immigration

People with no socioeconomic power in the country often hope to migrate to the United States to find a better life for themselves and their families. Poverty and inequality increase the likelihood that people will decide to leave the country to seek opportunities elsewhere. This adds to family disintegration and to children being left behind by their parents. Frequently these children are sent to live with extended family; they may experience deprivation of love, deprivation of attention, and discipline, which makes them vulnerable to gang involvement and delinquency (Panting-Sierra, 2005) and increases the risks of mental stress and illness.

Gender

Honduran women live under the oppression of gender-related violence. A culture centered in *machismo* (men's superiority and power) and *marianismo* (women as passive and self-sacrificial) is the catalyst for violence directed toward women. According to Leslie (2001), gender-related violence "acts to disempower women by terrorizing them into submission and by instilling in them the impossibility of struggling for social change" (p. 51). An extreme manifestation of this situation is *femicide,* "a legal and political term to refer to the murder of women killed because *they are women"* (Prieto-Carron, Thomson, & Macdonald, 2007, p. 25, emphasis in the original). *Honduras Weekly* reported that "there have been approximately

2,278 femicide deaths registered in the country during the past decade, including a total of 351 in 2010, compared to 407 in 2009 and 252 in 2008, according to Honduras's National Institute for Women" ("Femicide Deaths in Honduras Grow to 34," 2011, para. 2). The United Nations High Commission for Refugees determined that victims of gender-related violence trauma may experience psychosomatic symptoms such as headaches, sore backs, gastrointestinal disturbances, dissociation, and posttraumatic stress disorder (Leslie, 2001).

Counselor Education

The World Bank (2011) estimated that the literacy rate in Honduras was 84% in 2007. Honduras has one of the lowest literacy levels in Latin America and the Caribbean, with an average of 6.5 years of schooling for adults (United Nations Development Program, 2011). The Consejo de Educación Superior (Higher Education Council), a branch of the Universidad Nacional Autónoma de Honduras (Autonomous National University of Honduras), is in charge of approving and supervising psychology training programs. For a baccalaureate degree in psychology, the council requires no less than 57 credits and a practicum experience as standard requisites.

According to a study conducted by Salgado (2000), there are eight higher education institutions in the country; however, most people are cannot afford to complete a college degree because they must join the workforce at a very young age. Those who do have the opportunity to become psychologists choose to pursue either (a) a baccalaureate degree in psychology from the Universidad Nacional Autónoma de Honduras, (b) a baccalaureate degree in psychology from the Universidad Católica de Honduras (Honduran Catholic University), or (c) a baccalaureate degree in organizational psychology from the Universidad Tecnológica Centroamericana (Central American Technological University).

The Universidad Nacional Autónoma de Honduras is equivalent to a state university in the United States and is the most reasonably priced university in the country. The cost is $14 per semester, and students are allowed to take as many as six classes per term. The university offers a 4-year, 57-credit baccalaureate degree (*licenciatura*) in psychology that requires 800 hours of practicum experience and 40 hours of community service.

The Universidad Católica de Honduras is a private institution that offers both a baccalaureate and a master's degree in psychology. In order to enroll in the bachelor's program, candidates must pass an admissions test and pay $10. Once enrolled, students complete a 4-year, 60-credit program, paying $146 every trimester. Universidad Católica de Honduras is the only institution that currently offers a postgraduate degree in the field of psychology. It offers a 2-year, 22-course cohort master's degree program in four different cities around the country. Students must complete a core curriculum of 18 classes, and on completing these core courses, they then select five elective courses in a specific area of interest: forensic psychology, organizational psychology, social psychology, or family therapy. The cost of this program is $3,828. Candidates may pay in monthly installments of $160 over 2 years.

The Universidad Tecnológica Centroamericana offers a 4-year, 57-credit bachelor's degree in organizational psychology. The cost for students is $360 per term (four courses).

As distance learning is now a component of psychology and counseling training programs worldwide, many students are attempting to pursue online postgraduate training abroad. However, this trend is in its seminal stages, and we were not able to locate statistics for enrollment in online programs.

The Future

Martín-Baró (1994) stated that the role of psychology in Central America is to "produce an answer to the great problems of structural injustice, of war and national alienation that overwhelm our peoples" (p. 41). In order to achieve such an ambitious objective, several affairs need to be addressed simultaneously in the coming decade. Affordable postgraduate programs and continuing education opportunities for those in the trenches are essential. As reported in Ginés-Rivera's (2010) study on the needs of pastoral counselors in Honduras, this training process should emphasize techniques and models that are pertinent to people living in extreme poverty and enduring issues of social justice warranted to be intentionally addressed by mental health professionals from within the country. The proper authorities need to implement and enforce mechanisms so that 100%—not 28%—of practicing professionals are accountable to COPSIH, the Honduran Psychological Association.

Another recommendation is to conduct research exploring the implications of the differences and/or similarities in counseling dynamics among Hondurans residing around the world and those residing in Honduras. For instance, it may be that Hondurans who migrate to the United States experience different stressors related to acclimating to a new country and culture. Insofar as expectations for life in the United States and its alluring promises for a "better life" are concerned, research shows that although "people are aware of the difficulties" (Sladcova, 2007, p. 195), the hardships involved in deportation and discrimination will undoubtedly exacerbate new stressors. Research in this area would be beneficial in terms of counseling Central American migrants.

In conclusion, the counseling profession in Honduras continues to be a subject of significant concern, examination, and development. Since 2009, pastors from Honduras have joined forces with U.S.-based Regent University's Honduras Project to develop a professional Spanish counseling curriculum as well as partnered with the Universidad Tecnológica Centroamericana to develop an online counseling certificate program (J. Sells, personal communication, October 26, 2011).

The results from Ginés-Rivera's (2010) study confirm a significant need to expand an indigenous counseling model specific to the Honduran cultural context and fundamental to the local counselor in enhancing and implementing effectual counseling practices. The intent of the Honduras Project is for Honduran pastors and Regent University scholars to work collectively to enhance the counseling responsibilities *currently* in place and to facilitate best practices in implementing indigenous counseling methodologies. We, the authors, are committed to working with and supporting the Honduras Project in their efforts to improve the mental health needs of Hondurans.

References

Acosta, S., Groh, L. S., Hernandez, G., & Rathbone, B. (1990). Counseling Hispanics in the United States. *Journal of Pastoral Care, 44,* 33–41.

Alarcón, R. D. (2003). Mental health and mental health care in Latin America. *World Psychiatry, 2,* 54–56.

Anderson, A. J. (2000). Sectorization and sub-sectorization of mental health services in developing countries. *International Journal of Psychosocial Rehabilitation, 4,* 107–109.

Brown, S. L., Nesse, R. M., Vinokur, A. D., & Smith, D. M. (2003). Providing social support may be more beneficial than receiving it: Results from a prospective study of mortality. *Psychological Science, 14*(4), 320–327.

Central Intelligence Agency. (2011). *The world factbook.* Retrieved from https://www.cia.gov/library/publications/the-world-factbook/geos/ho.html

Donaire, V. (2001). *Historia de la psicología en Honduras* [History of psychology in Honduras]. Tegucigalpa, Honduras: Ingraco.

Femicide deaths in Honduras grow to 34. (2011, February). *Honduras Weekly.* Retrieved from http://hondurasweekly.com/femicide-deaths-in-honduras-grow-to-34-201102163405/

Ginés-Rivera, A. (2010). *A needs assessment of pastoral counselors in Honduras: A delphi study* (Doctoral dissertation). Available from ProQuest Dissertations and Theses database. (UMI No. 3405789)

Griffin, W. (2004). *Garifuna NGO recognized for protecting the environment.* Retrieved from http://www.garinet.com/cgi-bin/gksitecontent_ssi.cgi?ACTION=VIEW_ONE_CONTENT&ITEM=10&CATEGORY=57&CONTENT_ID=286&COLOR1=CCCC99&COLOR2=FFFFCC

Kohn, R., Levav, I., Donaire, I., Machuca, M., & Tamashiro, R. (2005). Psychological and psychopathological reactions in Honduras following Hurricane Mitch: Implications for service planning. *Revista Panamericana de Salud Publica, 18*(4/5), 287–295.

Leslie, H. (2001). Healing the psychological wounds of gender-related violence in Latin America: A model for gender-sensitive work in post-conflict contexts. *Gender and Development, 9*(3), 50–59.

Martín-Baró, I. (1994). *Writings for a liberation psychology* (A. Aron & S. Corne, Eds.). Cambridge, MA: Harvard University Press.

Panting-Sierra, G. (2005). *Relationship between resiliency attitudes and selected risk factors of gang involvement in adult Honduran males.* Unpublished doctoral dissertation, Northern Illinois University, Dekalb.

Pine, A. (2009, October). *Threat to and systematic destruction of Garifuna peoples.* Retrieved from http://www.quotha.net/node/435

Prieto-Carron, M., Thomson, M., & Macdonald, M. (2007). No more killings! Women respond to femicides in Central America. *Gender and Development, 15*(1), 25–40.

Salgado, R. (2000). *La educación superior en Honduras* [College- and graduate-level education in Honduras]. Retrieved from www.ufg.edu.sv/ufg/theorethikos/art7.doc

Sells, J. N., Giordano, F. G., Bokar, L., Klein, J., Panting-Sierra, G., & Thume, B. (2007). The effects of Honduran counseling practices in the North American counseling profession: The power of poverty. *Journal of Counseling & Development, 85*, 431–439.

Sladcova, J. (2007). Expectations and motivations of Hondurans migrating to the United States. *Journal of Community & Applied Social Psychology, 17*, 187–202.

United Nations Development Program. (2011, June). *Honduras: Country profile: Human development indicators.* Retrieved from http://hdrstats.undp.org/en/countries/profiles/HND.html

U.S. Bureau of Citizenship and Immigration Services. (2002). *Honduras: Information on mental health care.* Retrieved from http://www.unhcr.org/refworld/docid/3f51f8386.html

U.S. Department of State. (2010). *Honduras.* Retrieved from http://www.state.gov/outofdate/bgn/honduras/172098.htm

World Bank. (2011). *Honduras.* Retrieved from http://data.worldbank.org/country/honduras

World Health Organization. (2008). *Mental health system in Honduras: Report of the assessment of mental health systems in Honduras using the WHO Assessment Instrument for Mental Health Systems (WHO-AIMS).* Geneva, Switzerland: Panamerican Health Organization

• • •

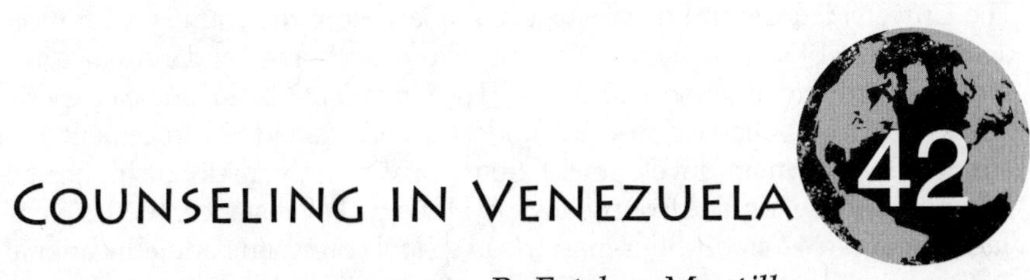

Counseling in Venezuela

R. Esteban Montilla

The Bolivarian Republic of Venezuela is a country situated at the northern end of South America with a population of approximately 27.7 million people. The inhabitants of this country constitute a culturally highly diverse group: close to 65% are mestizo, or persons with European, African, and Amerindian ethnic features; about 20% are White, of Spanish, Portuguese, Italian, or German phenotype; about 10% are Black, of African descent; nearly 2% are Native Amerindian; and increasing percentages are from Asia and the Middle East, including China, India, Syria, Lebanon, Palestine, and Saudi Arabia.

Venezuela is a federal republic, a democratic and developing country with 23 states, a Capital District, and a group of offshore islands. The country is blessed with a variety of natural resources, such as petroleum, natural gas, gold, diamonds, bauxite, and other minerals, which together with the agricultural and manufacturing industries give the country a promising economy. Yet the nationalization of many private institutions, the rise of many public business enterprises, governmental managerial strategies, along with many other social factors have largely failed to render the expected results, leading to a shortage of basic goods, currency devaluation, asphyxiating inflation, an increasing budget deficit, and worrisome macroeconomic imbalances.

The current president, Hugo Rafael Chávez, is a socialist political leader who has been in power since 1999 and is trying to implement a social and populist revolution to achieve a better distribution of the wealth in the country. He is highly concerned with the rampant poverty, widespread corruption, massive foreign debt, tattered federal health system, and energy shortages. His fiscal and economic policies are undergoing serious evaluation and reform. Specifically, he is trying to secure high-quality physical and mental health access for all people.

Venezuelans face all of these challenges with hope and optimism as they put their trust in their collective resilience and group efficacy. On his cultural dimension scale, Hofstede (2003) ranked Venezuela as a strong collectivist society in which resilient relationships are fostered and mutual solidarity is expected from each member of the community. This cultural characteristic needs to be considered in order to understand Venezuelans' personality, human development, learning styles, relational patterns, cognitive constructions, worldviews, and approaches to wellness.

The Current Status of Counseling

Counselor Education

From its official beginnings in the 1940s until 1990, counseling in Venezuela was exclusively offered at education institutions in the form of school counseling (*orientación*). Several public universities offer undergraduate and graduate degrees in school and career counseling. The Universidad del Zulia, one of the oldest institutions of higher education in the country, founded in 1891, offers a BEd with a major in school counseling and two 40-credit-hour master's in school counseling and career counseling. The Universidad de Carabobo offers a BEd with a major in school counseling and an MEd with an emphasis in school guidance and counseling. The Universidad Central de Venezuela, the largest in the country with more than 60,000 students, offers a BPsy with a major in counseling psychology and guidance as well as a specialty (EdS) and an MEd in school counseling. The Universidad Pedagógica Experimental Libertador offers an MEd in school counseling, and The Universidad Centroccidental Lisandro Alvarado offers a BA in human development. Some private universities also offer graduate programs in school counseling and counseling psychology. For instance, the Universidad Católica del Tachira offers a 42-credit-hour master's in school counseling and educational psychology.

Even though school counseling (*orientación*) is still the predominant program, several private and public institutions promote counseling beyond the schools. For instance, the Colegio Universitario Padre Isaías Ojeda offers two associate of arts degrees: one in prevention counseling and social action and the other in psychosocial therapy. These degrees prepare counselors to provide treatment to children, adults, and older adults affected by drug abuse and sexual exploitation as well as physical and psychological abuse. The emphasis of these programs is also on wellness, as these counselors function as holistic health promoters, social justice advocates, family therapists, and community educators. The associate of arts degree in psychosocial therapy is also offered by the School of Public Health and Social Development at the Universidad de Carabobo.

Other counseling training efforts beyond school counseling include the tenacious work of Dr. Fernando José Bianco, a Venezuelan psychiatrist and graduate of the School of Medicine of the Universidad Central de Venezuela and Temple University. Bianco is a past-president of the Venezuelan Medical Association and of the World Association for Sexual Health. In 1975 he founded the Center for Psychological, Psychiatric, and Sexual Research Studies of Venezuela, and in 1991 this institution of higher education was recognized by the Consejo Nacional de Universidades, the office of the Venezuelan Department of Education that authorizes undergraduate and graduate programs. This center offers four programs related to counseling: an MA in sexuality counseling, an MA in behavioral counseling, an MA in parenting counseling, and a specialty (EdS) in counseling children.

In the early 2000s, Drs. R. Esteban Montilla and Robert L. Smith started offering a 2-year specialty in family and professional counseling to train religious leaders and clergy to provide counseling services. This program was sponsored by the Universidad Nacional Experimental Rafael María Baralt of Cabimas, Zulia. Through the Universidad Evangélica Nicaragüense Martin Luther King, Jr., of Managua, Nicaragua, they also offer an MA with emphases in theology and professional counseling. More than 70 religious leaders have graduated from the program and are currently serving as pastoral counselors, professional counselors, and family therapists throughout the 10 regions of Venezuela. The Centro Clínico de Atención Integral a la Familia, under the auspices of the Universidad Nacional Experimental de Guayana, offers a 2-year specialty in family counseling to professionals from disciplines such as nursing, sociology, education, medicine, theology, psychology, and law.

There is also a coordinated effort between NBCC International and the Federación de Asociaciones Venezolana de Orientadores (Venezuelan Federation of School Counselors) to expand the scope of school counseling. Currently the Venezuelan government is proposing the Sistema Nacional de Orientación, which understands school counseling as a social and liberating praxis that promotes the development of human potential at the personal, family, and community levels. Although the emphasis of this governmental project is still within the school and university setting, it has the potential to open the door for counseling practice to clinical, industrial, and health care settings.

It is important to understand that counseling in Venezuela is a profession highly connected to the fields of psychology, education, and theology. Therefore, the majority of professional counselors are educators with training in school counseling and psychologists who have graduated from programs in counseling psychology. In any case, only an undergraduate degree is required to function as a professional counselor in the country. For instance, a psychologist in Venezuela has completed a BA in psychology. Also, there are professional counselors with undergraduate degrees in disciplines such as education, social work, theology, and communication who later pursued a master's degree in behavioral counseling, sexuality counseling, school counseling, career counseling, family counseling, or pastoral counseling. In addition, since 2000 a number of new associate-level programs in counseling have been created, to the point that historically large institutions such as the Universidad de Carabobo now have AA programs in psychosocial counseling.

Counselor Regulation

Professional counseling is not recognized in Venezuela as an autonomous profession, and thus the legal regulation to practice it is connected to other disciplines. For instance, school counseling (*orientación*) is seen as part of education; therefore, it follows the guidelines delineated by the Ley Orgánica de Educación 2009 (Organic Law of Education, 2009) and other rules pertaining to the teaching profession in the country. Counseling and clinical psychology are governed by the Ley del Ejercicio de la Psicologia de Venezuela 1978 (Regulations for the Practice of Psychology, 1978). Pastoral counseling, family counseling, and substance abuse counseling are practiced under the auspices of religious institutions that are regulated by the Dirección General de Justicia y Cultos of the Secretary of Interior and Justice of Venezuela.

Professional Associations

Several professional associations provide certification for professional counselors. Certification is a voluntary procedure on the part of a professional who chooses to be held accountable to an organization by willingly going through a peer review that evaluates his or her education, skills, and attitudes. For example, the Federación de Asociaciones Venezolana de Orientadores, in cooperation with NBCC International, offers certification for school counselors who have a BEd in school counseling. The Venezuelan chapter of the Sociedad Interamericana de Counseling (Interamerican Counseling Society) offers certification to professional counselors. This certification is offered to people with an undergraduate degree in counseling psychology, clinical psychology, human development, or school counseling as well as to prospects who have earned a master's or doctoral degree in counseling or family therapy. This professional association also grants certification as associate professional counselors to people with a 2- or 3-year college degree (AA) in substance abuse counseling, psychosocial counseling, or pastoral counseling as well as to indigenous healers and midwives who demonstrate they have the required competencies to practice counseling.

Best Counseling Practices

Definition of Counseling

Professional counseling involves the movement from individuality to community as a person, couple, family, or group come to the conclusion that it is not possible to continue moving forward with only their own coping resources. Consequently, they seek the assistance of a professional counselor to explore, address, and discern new ways of moving toward wholeness. This definition goes along with the etymology of the word *counseling,* which is related to *consilium,* or the coming together to dialogue and deliberate with a purpose, and *consulere,* which implies meeting to seek consultation about a particular issue or concern. The understanding of counseling as an attempt to seek counsel and guidance from a wise member of the community appears to be a continuation of a long healing tradition among collectivist societies.

Lessire and Gonzalez (2007) defined *counseling* as an intervention to help people assess their needs, appraise their potentials, and evaluate their possibilities to implement life-affirming projects within their historical and cultural context. Vilera (2008) understood counseling as a process of empowering people to embrace their limitations and strengths as they relate to others and to social institutions with a clear purpose of life, unwavering determination, self-respect, and a profound sense of existential responsibility. Casado (2000) and Calonge (2004), referring to school counseling, suggested that most theoretical foundations influencing this profession are individualist, centered on human deficiencies and obsessed with inner processes to the point of ignoring all social cultural forces that affect human behavior. Therefore, they proposed that counseling is a social enterprise of personal, family, and community transformation and thus needs to be studied and practiced from a collectivist psychosocial perspective.

The Counseling Process

The counseling process in this collectivist and multicultural society needs to recognize the relational and ecological dimensions of the human being. The person as an indivisible and holistic being exists and moves within an all-encompassing set of contexts such as biology, culture, life span, and axiology that mutually influence each of the existential dimensions: cognitive, affective, behavioral, social, and spiritual.

The first larger context to consider is biology, which regulates all human activities, including thoughts, emotions, behaviors, social connections, and transcendence. This control is mediated by the genetic makeup of the person, the endocrine system, chemical and physical metabolic impulses, neurological processes, evolutionary memories, and all other physiological interactions. The second context is culture, which refers to the environment, language, ethnicity, sociological and political atmosphere, and art and technology of a particular group or community. These cultural factors have tremendous impact on each dimension of the human existence that cannot be ignored in the assessment and intervention of any counseling experience.

The third all-inclusive context to recognize is the life-span moment of each person. Life-span perspectives or life course paradigms suggest that human development encompasses the events of an entire life and that these events occur within a sociocultural context and historical reality (Baltes, 1987). The salient features of the life span include the following:

1. Development is a lifelong process characterized by both continuous and discontinuous factors.
2. There is considerable diversity in the directionality of changes that varies depending on the category of behavior.
3. Human development involves growth and decline. It is not a movement toward greater efficacy; rather, throughout life, development is marked by gain and loss.
4. Plasticity, or performance variability, within an individual refers to the capacity that human beings possess for change in unique ways. People's capacities and abilities are not fixed or predetermined. On the contrary, they can be modified at any time of the life course if the right conditions exist.
5. Significant historical life events and social embeddedness, such as education, health care, and working conditions, play a key role in human development.

The fourth all-embracing context to consider is the axiological reality of human beings, who have inalienable rights and inherent dignity that need to be respected in any form of counseling. The worth of a person is not connected with social, economic, political, or religious stands but solely the fact that the person is human. The values and principles held by a person, when not in violation of the universal declaration of human rights, are to be respected and encouraged by mental health professionals. This context speaks of an ethical practice committed to excellence, respect for human freedom, and equal justice for all.

Professional counselors in Venezuela use a plethora of counseling intervention techniques that range from the most traditional European and North American approaches to deeply held indigenous models. In 1936, when school counseling programs started to be offered in the country, psychodynamic and Adlerian models were embraced by pioneers (Lessire & Gonzalez, 2007). After 1964, when institutions of higher education such as the Universidad de Carabobo started forming professional school counselor training programs, other approaches, including the cognitive–behavioral model promoted by Albert Ellis, Aaron Beck, and Burrhus Frederic Skinner as well as the person-centered approach of Carl Rogers, were added to the intervention toolbox. Since 1990, other theoretical frameworks, such as postmodern approaches, family systems models, and community-oriented methods, have been welcomed to the practice of counseling in the country (Lessire & Gonzalez, 2007).

An emerging indigenous theoretical framework is gaining momentum among counseling practitioners in the country. This collectivist approach proposes that the first movement in counseling is *movement toward community,* in which a person, couple, family, or group joins efforts with a professional counselor to talk about issues and to explore new ways of being. This professional collaborative work begins with steps to increase the level of trust, which is understood as the ability humans have to predict the behavior of another person. It is expected that as a client comes to the counseling office he or she will have a level of distrust because the counselor is not a member of their group. This distrust could decrease as the counselor demonstrates through a compassionate posture that he or she genuinely cares for the well-being of the person, group, and community. This emphatic listening to the client's verbal and nonverbal communication while showing an affirming respect of cultural and social values might prepare the way for a powerful life-giving therapeutic experience. Once the client is treated with dignity, he or she could begin to trust the counselor and disclose his or her dreams and concerns. People from collectivist societies consider loyalty to be one of the most important factors in trusting another person. The counselor demonstrates loyalty by keeping confidentiality, of course within the legal boundaries, and remains committed to the client's personal growth and development.

The availability and empathic hospitality of the professional counselor contributes to diminishing the level of distrust as well as encouraging the full participation of the individual, couple, family, or group in the therapeutic process. The level of trust falls along a continuum and increases or decreases based on the words, behaviors, and actions of both the counselor and client. The patience and perseverance of both parties prepares the way for a strong healing relationship. A sense of mutuality could lead to a gradual acceptance of the counselor as a member of the client's group.

The second movement is toward *the in-depth exploration of the cognitive, affective, behavioral, social, and spiritual dimensions.* This takes place as the counselor is welcomed into the group and begins to recognize the thoughts, ideas, beliefs, imagination, and perceptions that inform and give life to the client. An attentive counselor who is willing to embark on the exploration of this cognitive dimension needs to keep in mind the sacredness of this task as people open the doors of their inner being. Initial reflection on the different factors of this dimension needs to be free of judgment, critical disputing, and shameful remarks. A curious and respectful posture conveys to the client the genuine interest the counselor has in the person's story.

This kind of reflective presence and experience of togetherness invites the client to freely communicate his or her emotions and feelings to the professional counselor. At this level, the client realizes that he or she is important to the mental health professional and begins to share whatever makes him or her happy, sad, afraid, angry, guilty, peaceful, or anxious. This exploration of the affective dimension with a sense of acceptance leads to a better understanding of the person's needs. As mutual affection grows and love becomes the foundation of the therapeutic relationship, the counselor and client enter into a kind of communion that facilitates mutual healing and fosters holistic development.

The exploration of behavior and conduct follows as the client starts to speak liberally about his or her concerns with specific action patterns and lifestyles that trouble him or her. The availability of the counselor and neighboring spirit secure the way for exploring the depth of the relationships and social networks available to the client for psychological support and mental tranquility. Also, identifying family members, friends, peers, and community agencies that might be sources of distress for the client can assist the therapeutic relationship in moving the person toward a more liberating way of being in the world. The consideration of aspects such as transcendence, sense of purpose, faith, and legacy, besides leading to hope, can help in ascertaining motivational forces for change. The spiritual dimension, in which matters of the soul are recognized, might assist clients and counselors in the process of learning to deal with the mysteries of life.

The third movement of the counseling process entails *the profound organization, analysis, and conscientization of the cognitive, emotional, behavioral, social, and spiritual issues that arise throughout the exploration.* This deep examination of each of these dimensions is a collaborative effort between the counselor and client, who together identify the different issues that might be keeping the client from thriving. This process of diagnosing or breaking all of these dimensions into small pieces to make sense of the client's life might lead to the establishment of clear treatment goals.

The fourth movement makes reference to *the treatment intervention and follow-up plan agreed to by counselor and client.* In this movement the issues that have been identified by both parties are addressed in order of importance for the client. The counseling techniques used correspond to the particular dimension being addressed.

Diversity Issues

The people of Venezuela are very heterogeneous in terms of ethnicity, identity, customs, language, and socioeconomic status. This multiculturalism requires professional counselors to approach their clients with a profound sense of humility, as most cultural assumptions might be illusionary in nature (Montilla & Medina, 2006). However, the collectivist worldview appears to be a cohesive and common factor among the members of this South American society. Collectivism is a social pattern consisting of closely connected people who see themselves as part of one or more groups (Triandis, 1995). Collectivism refers to a way of being in the world in which connection to a group or community constitutes the most prevalent feature. This multifaceted cultural construct influences people in many different ways, including through identity formation, cognition, motivation, the expression of emotions, communication, self-perception, well-being, and social connections (Hofstede, 1980; Triandis, 1995). People who ascribe to this existential paradigm believe that keeping and nurturing healthy relationships is the main duty of human beings. Also, according to this worldview success and excellence are weighed by the quality of the relationships people maintain. Relationships, as the core of human existence, are meant to be respected and nurtured throughout the life span (Kim, 1994). Principles such as respect, solidarity, mutuality, freedom, harmony, benevolence, communication, and familism serve as the guarantors of the person (Schwartz, 1992; Schwartz & Bilsky, 1990).

In collectivist societies, people's identities are connected, influenced, and shaped by members of the family, group, and cultural context as well as by the social rules and norms established by the collective (Greenfield, 1994; Triandis, 1994). Thus, a person's way of thinking, expressing emotions, behaving, and relating can be fully understood in the context of the whole collective.

The collective worldview starts from the premise that human beings cannot survive and flourish disconnected from others, nature, and the universe. These webs of relationships are so important that living in isolation from the group implies infirmity, shame, and anxiety (Triandis, 1995). The group serves as the source of support, social status, protection, and opportunity. This commitment and loyalty to the ingroup is reciprocal, as the care is mutually provided and exercised. The dignity and worth of the person are inalienable; however, they are also strongly connected to the reputation of the group (Triandis, McCusker, & Hui, 1990). This could explain the many social constraints concerning thoughts, behaviors, styles of relating, and affective demonstrations when interacting with people of authority and outgroups.

A failure to understand the collectivist dimension of the people of Venezuela could negatively affect the outcome of the counseling process. Another sociocultural challenge for this multicultural and interdimensional society is the increasing political tension between government supporters and members of opposition parties. Professional counselors occupy an important role in serving as mediators of peace and harmony. They have the training to successfully help move from debate to dialogue as people and organizations manage their conflicts. The heart of the counseling intervention centers on keeping and fostering relationships.

As social beings, people need relationships to survive, grow, and flourish. Social connections represent the center of life for people and groups. Each dimension of the human existence revolves around connections and relatedness. Relationship implies empowerment and mutuality, which Jordan (2000) understood as openness to mutual influence, emotional availability, and a cognitive commitment marked by loyalty. Miller (1984) proposed that relationships give people five main existential gains: (a) a space to increase vitality, aliveness, and energy; (b) a place to be empowered; (c) an ideal atmosphere in which to grow in knowledge about self and others; (d) an inviting and accepting world conducive to reaffirming a sense of worth; and (e) a place for fuller connections and enriching interchanges in which collaboration, cooperation, trust, and respect reign.

Collective societies are committed to making these relational gains a reality, and toward that end they establish norms and rules with the intention of creating a healthy social environment in which people can survive and thrive (Morris & Peng, 1994). The breaking of these agreed-on regulations could imply discipline and reprimands. In rare cases of the extreme abuse of the sacredness of relationship, people could be cast out from the group and be considered outsiders and traitors.

In collectivist societies, very few things in life can be considered personal and private. For instance, even choosing a spouse, having children, or deciding on a career is more than a personal matter. The person or couple has the responsibility for making the decision, but the ingroup members have valid input to contribute as well. In fact, counsel from the family or group is often sought and is highly valued in such matters (Hui, 1988; Triandis, 1995).

The Future

The future of counseling in Venezuela is very promising, as today more and more institutions of higher education are offering counseling degrees. In addition, the government is promoting the reestablishment of a school counseling system that plans to place school counselors in most public elementary schools, secondary schools, high schools, colleges, and universities (Ministerio del Poder Popular para la Educación Universitaria, 2009). Even though this effort is centered on school counseling, it opens the door to counseling practice beyond educational settings because it proposes that a person's holistic development cannot take place in isolation from the community. Also, many counseling centers in the private sector are offering counseling of various types.

There are several mental health professional associations in Venezuela, including the Federación de Asociaciones Venezolana de Orientadores, which represents most school counselors in the country; the Asociación Venezolana de Psicoterapia (Venezuelan Association of Psychotherapy), which brings together a diverse coalition of mental health professionals; the Venezuelan chapter of the Sociedad Interamericana de Counseling, which is composed of professional counselors, family counselors, and pastoral counselors; and the Federación de Psicólogos de Venezuela (Venezuelan Federation of Psychologists), which represents the psychologists of the country. They all join efforts to provide much-needed mental health services to members of the society. This is not an easy task because it requires these helping professionals to suspend their personal needs, to set aside any trace of superiority, and to put rivalry on hold in order to concentrate on providing high-quality mental health care for millions of people who urgently need these services.

Making counseling services available to as many people as possible is an act of justice. The concept of justice among collectivist societies transcends distributive justice to include a kind of solidarity that takes sides with the oppressed and marginalized. Justice is understood and applied in the context of other principles such as equality, liberty, solidarity, compassion, loyalty, respect, and community; because justice is a relational phenomenon, it is always seen as social. Therefore, to speak of social justice is redundant. Collectivists tend to allocate resources to their group members in proportion to their needs, not according to their production or merit (Leung & Bond, 1982).

The future of professional counseling has to include avoiding the professional trap of thinking that a particular theoretical framework or discipline of the helping professions is superior to others. Professional identity needs to be focused on the mission rather than on the body of knowledge, because all of these professions drink water from the same well. The mission of promoting total well-being as well as addressing structures that impede the growth and development of people has to be the link that connects the different disciplines. This mission can be accomplished when educators serving as school and career counselors, psychologists trained in counseling or clinical psychology, religious leaders equipped as pastoral and family counselors, and professional psychotherapists from the rest of disciplines work hand in hand with traditional healers and technical clinicians in the process of creating a better world in which justice, peace, and love reign.

References

Baltes, P. B. (1987). Theoretical propositions of life-span developmental psychology: On the dynamics between growth and decline. *Developmental Psychology, 23*, 611–626.

Calonge, S. C. (2004). Fundamentos contextuales de la orientación educativa [Contextual foundations for school counseling]. *Investigación y Postgrado, 19*(1), 145–170.

Casado, E. (2000, December). *Una visión psicosocial alternativa para la orientación* [An alternative psychosocial vision for school counseling]. Presentation at the III Jornadas Nacionales de Investigación. Maracaibo, Venezuela.

Greenfield, P. M. (1994). Independence and interdependence as developmental scripts: Implications for theory, research and practice. In P. M. Greenfield & R. R. Cocking (Eds.), *Cross-cultural roots of minority child development* (pp. 1–37). Hillsdale, NJ: Erlbaum.

Hofstede, G. (1980). *Cultural consequences: International differences in work related values.* Beverly Hills, CA: Sage.

Hofstede, G. (2003). *Culture's consequences: Comparing values, behaviors, institutions, and organizations across nations* (2nd ed.). Newbury Park, CA: Sage.

Hui, C. H. (1988). Measurement of individualism–collectivism. *Journal of Research in Personality, 22*(1), 17–36.

Jordan, J. V. (2000). A model of connection for a disconnected world. In J. Shay & J. Wheelis, (Eds.), *Odysseys in psychotherapy* (pp. 147–165). New York, NY: Ardent Media.

Kim, M. S. (1994). Cross-cultural comparisons of the perceived importance of conversational constraints. *Human Communication Research, 21,* 128–151.

Lessire, O., & Gonzalez, J. (2007). Fundamentos conceptuales que han caracterizado la evolución del proceso de la orientación en Venezuela [Conceptual foundations that characterized the evolution process of school counseling in Venezuela]. *Paradigma, 28*(2), 211–223.

Leung, K., & Bond, M. H. (1982). How Chinese and Americans reward talk-related contributions: A preliminary study. *Psychologia, 25,* 32–39.

Ley del Ejercicio de la Psicologia de Venezuela. (1978, September 11). *Gaceta Oficial de la Republica de Venezuela* [Regulations for the practice of psychology]. N° 2.306 Extraordinario. Caracas.

Ley Orgánica de Educación. (2009, August 15). *Gaceta Oficial de la República Bolivariana de Venezuela* [Organic law of education]. N° 5.929. Extraordinario. Caracas.

Miller, J. G. (1984). *Toward a new psychology of women.* Boston, MA: Beacon Press.

Ministerio del Poder Popular para la Educación Universitaria. (2009). *Sistema Nacional de Orientación* [National System of Orientation]. Caracas, Venezuela: Author.

Montilla, R. E., & Medina, F. (2006). *Pastoral care and counseling with Latino/as.* Minneapolis, MN: Fortress Press.

Morris, M. W., & Peng, K. (1994). Culture and cause: American and Chinese attributions for social and physical events. *Journal of Personality and Social Psychology, 67,* 949–971.

Schwartz, S. H. (1992). Universals in the content and structure of values: Theory and empirical tests in 20 countries. In M. Zanna (Ed.), *Advances in experimental social psychology* (Vol. 25, pp. 1–65). New York: Academic Press.

Schwartz, S. H., & Bilsky, W. (1990). Toward a theory of the universal content and structure of values: Extensions and cross-cultural replications. *Journal of Personality and Social Psychology, 58,* 878–891.

Triandis, H. C. (1994). Theoretical and methodological approaches to the study of collectivism and individualism. In U. Kim, H. C. Triandis, Ç. Kâgitçibasi, S. Choi, & G. Yoon (Eds.), *Individualism and collectivism* (pp. 41–51). Thousand Oaks, CA: Sage.

Triandis, H. C. (1995). *Individualism and collectivism.* Boulder, CO: Westview Press.

Triandis, H., McCusker, C., & Hui, C. (1990). Multimethod probes of individualism and collectivism. *Journal of Personality and Social Psychology, 59,* 1006–1020.

Vilera, A. G. (2008). Desarrollo humano y sentido de existencia: Abordajes [Approaches to human development and purposive existence]. *Revista de Teoría y Didáctica de las Ciencias Sociales, 13,* 29–52.

• • •

Analysis, Synthesis, and Future

Overview and Analysis of Global Counseling

43

Norman E. Amundson, Spencer G. Niles, and Thomas H. Hohenshil

This book has been an ambitious undertaking, and it is no small task to identify some of the patterns that flow among the many chapters that have been written. It is clear that there is considerable diversity between and within countries. The complexity that has been described reflects many historical, economic, social, cultural, and religious differences. Nevertheless, some themes do emerge, and we would like to highlight some of them using a developmental and general transition framework.

Establishing the Need for Counseling Services

As a starting point it is important to recognize that counseling has not developed in a vacuum. Many countries have had a rich and well-established tradition of helping others through support from families, community elders, religious support workers, and indigenous healers. In bringing the discipline of counseling forward it is important to ensure that it is embedded alongside these other forms of helping. The field of counseling makes its unique contribution through its emphasis on development, preventive action, a holistic perspective, freedom of choice, and empowerment.

The need for counseling can be understood by examining many of the forces that have challenged countries throughout the world. Of major importance has been the shift from an agricultural to an industrial—and then in many cases—to a knowledge-based economy. This has created tremendous social and economic pressure. Migration from the countryside to the cities has led to higher levels of poverty, higher levels of crime, racial tension, unreliable social structures, new types of illnesses, and greater injustices. In some situations the resulting turmoil has resulted in wars, and this in turn has created more stress and forced further migration of people. Of course, we would be remiss in just focusing on the problems. People have also gained many new freedoms through this transition process. Traditional roles have been challenged, creativity has been supported, and new possibilities for growth and development have flourished. Counseling has played a key role in these developments and also has proven to be an important advocate for equality and the rights of women, people of different ethnic backgrounds, individuals with disabilities, those with different sexual orientations, and so on.

The forces impacting people have become global in nature, and lives have changed dramatically through technological and informational advances. It is not uncommon in the most isolated villages to see people using cell phones and tuning in to world events through the World Wide Web. The impact of social media has changed the way in which people interact with one another and in some countries has even served as a means of challenging existing social and political structures.

Widespread health concerns such as HIV/AIDS have ravaged many countries, creating unprecedented family disruption. Countless children have been orphaned and grandparents have been thrust into the role of parents. On top of this, the cost of health delivery has skyrocketed and placed basic health services out of reach for many people. National and global conflict has also played a significant role in wasting precious resources through the widespread destruction of people and property. For those not directly involved there are also issues of migrating refugees and economic uncertainty. Even the physical environment has been dramatically impacted. Fish stocks have been depleted, weather patterns have changed, ultraviolet rays are of increasing concern, and the list goes on and on. People are having to come to terms with a rapidly deteriorating ecosystem.

Change has occurred at an unprecedented rate, and this has set the stage for a wide range of personal and social issues, including anxiety, depression, suicide, unemployment, underemployment, marital problems, family dysfunction, gambling, substance abuse, mental health concerns, chronic illness, and so on. The complexity and unpredictability of these changes do not lend themselves to simple and linear solutions. Within this context it is not difficult to document the need for counseling services.

Introducing Counseling Services

Although it may not be difficult to see the need for some form of counseling service, in many countries searching for the right language to express what is meant by "counseling" is challenging. There are typically words for advice giving and therapy but sometimes nothing that adequately expresses the special focus of counseling. Thus, the challenge is one of not only introducing a service but also educating people about the special qualities of that service. For many people there is also a strong stigma associated with seeking help with personal problems. People may see counseling as just another form of therapy. Similarly, if they are expecting advice giving they may be frustrated if they are not given direct answers to their questions.

This situation is further complicated by the range of people involved in offering different forms of counseling service. These include psychologists, psychotherapists, psychiatrists, pastors, teachers, and social workers. For many people these services are not clearly differentiated, and thus there are questions about where and how counseling fits with the services that are already established.

Counseling as a discipline can run into some cultural problems because of its focus on the democratic ideals of individualism and self-expression. Although these may fit within a Western culture, in many other cultures with a more collectivist stance restraint and obedience to authority are highly valued. Also, within a more collectivist culture there can be significant barriers to sharing one's problems with people (strangers) from outside the family or the community. Diversity issues can also play an important role in counseling. The credibility of counselors can be impacted by age, gender, sexual orientation, and so on. In the minds of many, being qualified to engage in counseling depends on much more than simply having a certificate on the wall.

A further significant issue is the way in which spiritual issues are addressed within the counseling process. For many people counseling and spirituality are inseparable and an important part of the exploration and healing process. Within this context counselors must operate from a holistic perspective that includes spiritual as well as cognitive and emotional well-being.

Despite these many challenges, counseling in many countries seems to be finding its way and providing an important service within the general helping paradigm. In the initial stages many people have turned for help to counselor training programs in Western countries, notably the United States, Britain, Canada, Australia, and France. For many, this has meant going abroad for counselor training and then returning to their country of origin with a mission to implement counseling services. This process has been further advanced through the efforts of various counseling and nonprofit associations. Also, groups such as the National Board for Certified Counselors, Chi Sigma Iota, and the American Counseling Association have played an active role in reaching out and providing support to counselors in a number of different countries.

It would be misleading, however, to assume that the development of counseling has reached a similar plateau in all countries. There are vast differences between some developing countries and the general experience in the Western world. Counseling is frequently only available to a limited group of people—often the more affluent members of the society in both developing and developed countries. Also, there is a major difference between counseling services in urban and rural areas, although significant advances in communication technology (e.g., cell phones, Internet) are beginning to bridge this gap.

The specific pathway toward the development of counseling has varied depending on the circumstances of the country. For some the initial focus has been on industrial development, and this has placed vocational counseling in a primary role. Others have gained their impetus through the educational system, and thus school counseling has become paramount. In some situations the push toward counseling has come through spirituality and various religious groups. And last but certainly not least is the impact of disease (e.g., HIV/AIDS), natural disasters, and armed conflict on the development of counseling services.

The Global Consolidation of the Profession

As counselors at a global level have become trained they have begun to consolidate their position and are setting in place the necessary structures for their profession. Myers and Sweeny (2001) indicated that by definition a profession includes a specific body of knowledge, a professional organization, accredited training programs, credentialing of practitioners, a code of ethics, and legal recognition. These indexes have been met, or are in the process of being met, in many countries.

It is interesting to note the extent to which the work of Carl Rogers has played a significant role in establishing a model for the counseling relationship throughout the world. This special counseling relationship often challenges some cultural conventions, but at the same time it is widely recognized as providing a new way of offering help to others. Many other methods are also frequently mentioned in the various chapters of this book. Some of these include the humanistic, existential, systemic, cognitive–behavioral, transpersonal, psychoanalytic, transactional analysis, sociohistorical, narrative, solution-focused, constructivist, and constructionist counseling methods. It is interesting to note that often the favored counseling method depends heavily on which methods were introduced into the country by local counseling professionals or by others who served as external consultants.

The move toward professionalism has been hindered by much of the confusion over definitional issues regarding the specific roles and functions of counselors. In most cases there is also a lack of information about how many people are actually working in the field and what their level of training is. This confusion can be exacerbated by turf wars between various groups. This applies to different counseling groups, although the major issues usually arise between psychological and counseling associations. It should also be mentioned that there are some good examples of how different counseling groups within a single country are coming together and trying to develop integrated professional counseling associations.

In some countries covered in the book there have been problems between traditional mental health practices (e.g., traditional healers, faith healers) and modern counseling practices. There also are examples of collaboration and more integrated service delivery among these groups. Some of the problems are particularly marked in rural settings, where the focus often leans more heavily toward indigenous healing practices.

Professional credentialing and the development of codes of ethics are done in many different ways. In some countries government agencies play a key role, in other situations leadership is provided by professional counseling associations, and in some nations NBCC International is playing a central role in developing professional credentialing and codes of ethics. The move toward more culturally appropriate counseling methods has particular relevance for the development of ethical codes of practice. Resolving ethical dilemmas as they relate to dual relationships, boundaries, and confidentiality is of particular concern. This often comes back to differences between cultures with respect to an individualist or more collectivist orientation.

There has been significant growth in local counselor training. This usually happens within universities, generally at the undergraduate level. Although the counseling curriculum generally follows a Western model, some schools are working toward the inclusion of methods more closely attuned to their own cultural settings. One of the shortcomings of many local counselor training programs is the lack of practicum experiences. Students often receive good theoretical training but lack the opportunity to engage in supervised practice.

The development of counseling as a profession usually requires governmental support. Although there have been many efforts to recognize counseling as a profession there still are gaps when it comes to receiving financial support. As in many Western countries, psychiatry and psychology have placed themselves at the forefront when it comes to receiving funding for mental health services.

Growth and Development Needs

As counseling has grown in countries around the world it is apparent that there is a need to move beyond a strictly Western approach and consider models in which indigenous practices are more fully integrated into counseling theory and practice. This can take many forms, and there is a need to broaden the focus to more fully incorporate methods that focus on the family and the broader community. There is also a need to consider more carefully how relationships are formed in different societies, how spirituality needs to be part of the counseling discussion, and how one can better understand the relationship between the natural and spiritual worlds.

Developing a more integrated multicultural counseling approach can often be achieved by creating more positive relationships with indigenous healers and with others working in related fields. Although traditional professionalism is important, there is also a need to learn from people who work from different frameworks. Although it is desirable to foster better working relationships within a culture, there is also a need for counselors to stand firm when it comes to some diversity issues. It is essential that counselors advocate for those most in need. In some situations it is necessary to advocate and educate people about the rights of women, individuals with disabilities, and those with different sexual orientations.

Another area for growth and development concerns the need for counseling in rural areas. As was mentioned earlier, most of the development of counseling has occurred in urban centers. Perhaps the telephone and social media might offer some possibilities for an expansion of counseling services into areas that are underserved. It would seem that in many situations this is already under way, particularly with respect to the use of cell phones.

There is a need for government support and additional resources in many countries. In working toward this end it might be helpful for counselors to conduct evaluations and do research that would support an evidence-based approach to theory and practice. A professional counseling service must have a research basis for the development of new ideas and also must support ongoing evaluation efforts. Such research can be helpful in terms of acquiring financial and other types of support from governmental agencies and other groups for the development of counseling services in various countries.

Currently many countries are simply relying on translations of Western-based assessment instruments. Although this might have some utility, there is a definite need to develop more culturally appropriate instruments. Standardized assessment can be used effectively in counseling, but its effectiveness depends on the development of tools that fit with specific cultural characteristics.

Many countries have expressed a desire to have more regular and supportive contacts with counselors from other countries. There is a real hunger for global connections, particularly among those counselors who are trying to build a professional service within their countries. The work of NBCC International is particularly notable in this regard. There is a need to reach out to the broader international counseling community and share information and resources.

There is a strong need to more effectively regulate the quality of counseling practices at national and international levels. In most situations there is little regulation, and the title of "counselor" is used in many different contexts. This leaves the public vulnerable in articulating the credibility and the differences among various credentials. The professionalism of counseling depends on the creation of more effective regulatory bodies with policy and financial support from government and from their members.

Global Challenges for the Future

In conclusion, we highlight here four challenges for the future. Many of these points have been made already, but nevertheless it seems worthwhile to pull them together.

1. *Strengthening the professional identity of counseling.* Defining who we are as a profession and creating strong associations that reflect that identity are continuing challenges for most of the 40 countries reviewed in this book.
2. *Improving the training of counselors.* Here we would make use of the Council for Accreditation of Counseling and Related Educational Programs core areas of counselor development as a common ground for counseling programs. Particular attention should be paid to the need for adequate practical training, including supervised internships. In providing training, one needs to ensure sufficient cross-cultural sensitivity, including a recognition of the importance of religion and spirituality as part of a more holistic approach to service delivery.
3. *Advocating for better client services.* There is a need to reduce the counselor-to-client and counselor-to-student ratios in school counseling and to increase the number of community-based counselors. As counselors we also need to explore ways of working more effectively with technology and social media. Our services must attend to those most in need, and this includes reducing the discrepancies between rural and urban areas.
4. *Advocating for the profession.* Efforts must be made to educate governments and policy leaders on counseling-related issues, including the importance of diversity, justice, and human rights. To help make the case for a professional service we as counselors must expand and develop research, conduct appropriate evaluation, and encourage accountability. We must also look beyond our borders and focus on building a more globalized profession with opportunities for ongoing collaboration and support. Within this more global counseling community, greater licensing portability also needs to be supported. By doing this, we should all become more globally literate.

References

Myers, J. E., & Sweeny, T. J. (2001). Specialties in counseling. In D. C. Locke, J. E. Myers, & E. L. Herr (Eds.), *The handbook of counseling* (pp. 43–54). Thousand Oaks, CA: Sage.

• • •

Appendix International Counseling Resources

International Counseling Journals (English Language)

Asia Pacific Journal of Counselling and Psychotherapy
http://www.tandf.co.uk/journals/RAPC
Asian Journal of Counselling
http://www.fed.cuhk.edu.hk/en/ajc/index.htm
Australian Journal of Career Development
http://www.acer.edu.au/press/ajcd
Australian Journal of Counselling Psychology
http://www.groups.psychology.org.au/GroupContent.aspx?ID=4407
Australian Journal of Guidance and Counselling
http://www.agca.com.au/article.php?id=5
British Journal of Guidance & Counselling
http://www.tandf.co.uk/journals/titles/03069885.asp
Canadian Journal of Career Development
http://www.ceric.ca/cjcd/
Canadian Journal of Counselling and Psychotherapy
http://www.ccacc.ca/en/resources/canadianjournalofcounselling/
Career Development International
http://www.emeraldinsight.com/products/journals/journals.htm?id=cdi
The Career Development Quarterly
http://onlinelibrary.wiley.com/journal/10.1002/(ISSN)2161-0045
Chinese Mental Health Journal
http://en.cnki.com.cn/Journal_en/E-E059-ZXWS-2011-04.htm
Counselling Australia
http://www.theaca.net.au/journals_and_articles.php
Counselling Psychology Quarterly
http://www.tandf.co.uk/journals/titles/09515070.asp

Eisteach (Irish Association for Counselling and Psychotherapy)
http://www.iacp.ie
European Journal of Counselling Psychology
http://www.counselling-psychology.eu/journal.htm
Exemplar (Chi Sigma Iota)
http://www.csi-net.org/displaycommon.cfm?an=1&subarticlenbr=36
Hellenic Journal of Psychology
http://www.pseve.org/journal.asp
Inside Out (Irish Association of Humanistic and Integrative Psychotherapy)
http://iahip.org/journal
International Journal for Educational and Vocational Guidance
http://www.springer.com/education+%26+language/journal/10775
International Journal for the Advancement of Counselling
http://www.springer.com/psychology/psychotherapy+%26+counseling/journal/10447
International Journal of Behavioral Consultation and Therapy
http://baojournal.com/IJBCT/IJBCT-index.html
International Journal of Evidence Based Coaching and Mentoring
http://www.business.brookes.ac.uk/research/areas/coachingandmentoring/
International Journal of Lifelong Education
http://www.tandf.co.uk/journals/tf/02601370.html
International Journal of Mental Health Promotion
http://www.ijmhp.co.uk/
International Journal of Mental Health Systems
http://www.ijmhs.com/
International Journal of Psychology and Counselling
http://www.academicjournals.org/ijpc/Terms.htm
International Perspectives in Psychology: Research, Practice, Consultation
http://www.apa.org/pubs/journals/ipp/index.aspx
International Social Science Journal
http://www.unesco.org/new/en/social-and-human-sciences/resources/periodicals/issj-social-science/
Journal for International Counselor Education
http://digitalcommons.library.unlv.edu/jice/about.html
Journal of Counseling & Development (International Section)
http://onlinelibrary.wiley.com/journal/10.1002/(ISSN)1556-6678
Journal of Multicultural Counseling and Development
http://onlinelibrary.wiley.com/journal/10.1002/(ISSN)2161-1912
Journal of Psychology in Chinese Societies
http://www.chineseupress.com/asp/JournalList_en.asp?CatID=1&Lang=E&JournalID=6
Journal of Vocational Behavior
http://www.journals.elsevier.com/journal-of-vocational-behavior/
Lifelong Learning in Europe
http://www.lline.fi/
New Zealand Journal of Counselling
http://www.nzac.org.nz/new_zealand_journal_of_counselling.cfm
Nigerian Journal of Guidance and Counselling
http://ajol.info/index.php/njgc
School Psychology International
http://spi.sagepub.com/content/current
South African Journal of Psychology
http://www.psyssa.com/Mypsyssa/myjournal.asp
Therapy Today (British Association for Counselling and Psychotherapy)
http://www.therapytoday.net/

International Counseling Articles (English Language)

Chi Sigma Iota Bibliography of International Counseling Articles
http://www.csi-net.org/displaycommon.cfm?an=1&subarticlenbr=843
Internet Counseling and Psychology
http://construct.haifa.ac.il/~azy/refindx.htm
United Nations Educational, Scientific and Cultural Organization (UNESCO; Search for "Guidance & Counseling")
http://www.unesco.org/new/en/
World Health Organization (Search for "Guidance & Counseling")
http://www.who.int/mental_health/en/

International and Regional Counseling Associations

Association for Multicultural Counseling and Development
http://www.multiculturalcounseling.org/
Chi Sigma Iota Counseling Academic and Professional Honor Society International
http://www.csi-net.org/index.cfm
European Association for Counselling
http://www.eacnet.org/
European Board for Certified Counselors
http://www.europeanbcc.eu
Inter American Counseling
http://counselingamericas.org/sic_quien.php
International Association for Counselling
http://iac-irtac.org/
International Association for Educational and Vocational Guidance
http://www.iaevg.org/iaevg/index.cfm?lang=2
International Coach Federation (Life and Career)
http://www.coachfederation.org/
International Society for Mental Health Online
https://www.ismho.org/home.asp
National Board for Certified Counselors (NBCC) International
http://www.nbccinternational.org/home
World Federation for Mental Health
http://www.wfmh.org/index.html

Counseling Associations for Individual Countries

Canadian Counselling and Psychotherapy Association List of Associations by Country (Click on "Other countries")
http://www.ccacc.ca/en/aboutus/associations/
Chi Sigma Iota List of Counseling Associations by Continent
http://www.csi-net.org/displaycommon.cfm?an=1&subarticlenbr=843

• • •

INDEX

A

D

E

(Continued)

F

G

H

I

J

K

N

O

P

Q

R

S

(Continued)

U

V

W

X

Y

Z